B. Brindle - Dec 2012

Heinemann
Higher
Mathematics

David Clarke   John Dalton   Carole Ford
Douglas Goodall   Jim Pennel   Tom Sanaghan

D1186799

1
2
3
4
5
6
7
8
9
10
11
12
13
14
15
16

Heinemann Educational Publishers,
a division of Heinemann Publishers (Oxford) Ltd,
Halley Court, Jordan Hill, Oxford, OX2 8EJ

OXFORD   BLANTYRE   MELBOURNE   AUCKLAND   IBADAN
NAIROBI   GABORONE   PORTSMOUTH NH (USA)   CHICAGO

© Scottish Secondary Mathematics Group 1998

All rights reserved. No part of this publication may be reproduced, stored in a
retrieval system, or transmitted in any form or by any means, electronic,
mechanical, photocopying, recording, or otherwise without either the prior written
permission of the publishers or a licence permitting restricted copying in the United
Kingdom issued by the Copyright Licensing Agency Ltd, 90 Tottenham Court
Road, London Q1P 9HE.

First published 1998

99   00   10   9   8   7   6

ISBN 0 435 51613 2

Original design by Wendi Watson

Original cover design by Aricot Vert
Cover photograph: Science Photo Library

Typeset and illustrated by TechSet, Gateshead, Tyne and Wear

Printed in Great Britain by The Bath Press, Bath

Acknowledgements:
The publisher's and authors' thanks are due to the Scottish Examination Board
(SEB) for permission to reproduce questions from past Higher Grade Mathematics
Examination papers. These are marked [Higher].
   The answers have been provided by the authors and are not the responsibility of
the examining board.
   Specimen assessments are based on all information currently available.
Become a registered user to obtain updates from our website at
www.heinemann.co.uk/Higher_Mathematics
   With many thanks to Maureen McKenna and Jim McAnally for their positive
and constructive feedback on the proofs.

Photo acknowledgements:
p. 69 Peter Gould; p 300 Science Photo Library

The authors of this book:

Thomas J. Sanaghan	Beeslack Community High School
John B. Dalton	Earnock High School
Carole L. Ford	Kilmarnock Academy
James K. Pennel	Lasswade High School Centre
Douglas H. Goodall	St Thomas of Aquin's High School
David Clarke	University of Strathclyde

Publishing team:

Editorial
Philip Ellaway
Sarah Caton
Lesley Montford

Design
Phil Richards
Colette Jacquelin

Production
David Cooke

Cover picture: **vectors in space**

High above the Earth a space shuttle orbits. The diagram shows its velocity
resolved into two components – one at a tangent to the orbit, the other
towards the centre of the Earth.

There is more about components of vectors in Chapter 13.

About this book

This book is designed to provide you with the best preparation possible for your Higher Mathematics examinations.

Finding your way around

To help you find your way around when you are studying and revising use the:

- **edge marks** (shown on the front page) – these help you to get to the right chapter quickly;
- **contents list** – this lists key syllabus ideas covered in the book so you can turn straight to them;
- **index** - if you need to find a topic the bold number shows where to find the main entry on a topic;
- this symbol shows where we recommend the use of a graphics calculator or computer.

Remembering key ideas

We have provided clear explanations of the key ideas and techniques you need throughout the book, with worked examples and carefully graded exercises that take you from the basics right up to exam standard. Where appropriate, formal proofs and brief investigative exercises are included.

Key ideas you need to remember are listed in a summary of key points at the end of each chapter and are marked like this in the chapters:

> If $f(x) = a^x$, then $f^{-1}(x) = \log_a x$.
>
> If $f(x) = \log_a x$, then $f^{-1}(x) = a^x$.

Exercises and exam questions

In this book questions are carefully graded so they increase in difficulty and gradually bring you up to exam standard.

- **past exam questions** are marked [Higher]
- **revision exercises** on pages 120, 224 and 315 are of two types:
  A exercises are questions at unit assessment level
  B exercises are questions at course assessment level
- **specimen assessments** for Units 1(H), 2(H) and 3(H) and a specimen course assessment are included to help you prepare for your exams.
- **answers** are included at the end of the book – use them to check your work.
- **Essential skills** from Standard Grade are covered in a separate unit for you to refer to if you need them (see p. 320).

Contents

4 Trigonometry: graphs and equations

5 Recurrence relations

6 Differentiation

Unit 2

11 Addition formulae

12 The circle

Unit 3

13 Vectors

14 Further calculus

15 Exponential and logarithmic functions

16 The wave function

Essential skills

1 The straight line

This chapter shows you how to use algebra to describe straight lines.

Gradients

The slope of a line is described by its gradient. The gradient of the straight line joining $A(x_1, y_1)$ and $B(x_2, y_2)$ is denoted by m_{AB} where

The gradient of $AB = m_{AB} = \dfrac{\text{Change in } y}{\text{Change in } x}$

$= \dfrac{y_2 - y_1}{x_2 - x_1}$

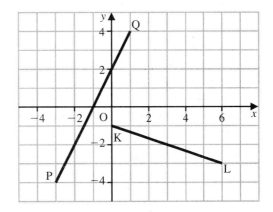

Example 1

Find the gradient of the lines
(a) PQ   (b) KL

(a) $m_{PQ} = \dfrac{4 - (-4)}{1 - (-3)} = \dfrac{8}{4} = 2$

(b) $m_{KL} = \dfrac{(-3) - (-1)}{6 - 0} = \dfrac{-2}{6} = -\dfrac{1}{3}$

Exercise 1A

1 Find the gradient of each line in this diagram:
(i)   AB   (v)   PQ
(ii)   CD   (vi)   RS
(iii) EF   (vii) TU
(iv) GH   (viii) VW

2 Make a conjecture* about the gradients of lines that
  (a) slope upwards from left to right.
  (b) slope downwards from left to right.

3 Find the gradients of the lines joining
  (a) L(1, 5) and M(−2, 4).
  (b) T(−5, −3) and U(8, −6).
  (c) H(0, −7) and I(−3, 4).
  (d) P(−6, 0) and Q(4, −1).

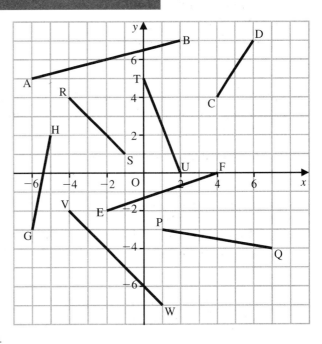

---

*A **conjecture** is a conclusion based on incomplete evidence.

4 (a) Find the gradients of lines IJ
and KL in the diagram opposite.
  (b) Make a conjecture about the
gradients of lines parallel to the *x*-axis.
  (c) Write equations to represent the lines,
IJ and KL.

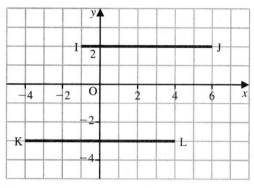

5 Write the equation of the line parallel to the *x*-axis and passing
through T(5, −2).

6 (a) Using $m = \dfrac{y_2 - y_1}{x_2 - x_1}$ write
expressions for the gradients
of the lines AB and CD in the
diagram opposite.
  (b) Write equations to represent
AB and CD.
  (c) Gradients of lines parallel to the
y-axis are said to be **undefined**.
State the equation of the line with
gradient undefined that passes
through F(3, −2).

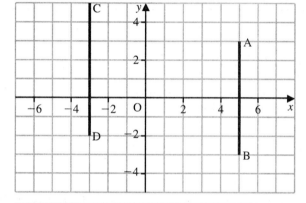

7 (a) In the diagram opposite find
the gradients of the lines
    (i) AB   (ii) PQ   (iii) ST
  (b) What do you notice about the
gradient of each line?
  (c) What else do you notice about
the lines?
  (d) Make a conjecture about lines
with the same gradient.

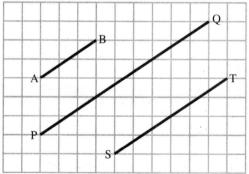

8 K is the point (−3, 4), L is (5, 6), M is (8, 1) and N is (0, −1).
Find the gradient of each side of KLMN and prove that it is a
parallelogram.

9 The line BA is produced to cut OX at C.
  (a) Angle BAE $= \theta°$.
Which other angle equals $\theta°$?
  (b) Write an expression for m_{AB}.
  (c) Write an expression for $\tan \theta°$.
  (d) Make a conjecture about the gradient of a line and the
tangent of the angle it makes with the positive direction of
the *x*-axis.

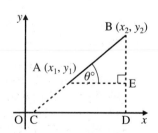

10 Find the angle that the line joining K(2, 3) and L(4, 7) makes
with the positive direction of the *x*-axis.

From the above questions we can state the following:

> **(a)** lines that slope
> - upwards from left to right have a positive gradient
> - downwards from left to right have a negative gradient
>
> **(b)** lines parallel to the
> - x-axis have gradient zero and equations of the form $y = a$
> - y-axis have gradient undefined and equations of the form $x = b$
>
> **(c)** parallel lines have equal gradients
> **(d)** the gradient of a line is the tangent of the angle it makes with the positive direction of the x-axis.

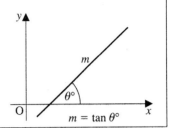

$m = \tan \theta°$

Collinearity

Two lines in a plane can either be:

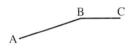

at an angle

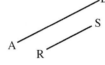

parallel and distinct

parallel and form a straight line

Points that lie on the same straight line are said to be **collinear**.

Example 2

Prove that the points P(-6 -5), Q($0, -3$) and R($12, 1$) are collinear.

$$m_{PQ} = \frac{-3 - (-5)}{0 - (-6)} = \frac{2}{6} = \frac{1}{3} \qquad m_{QR} = \frac{1 - (-3)}{12 - 0} = \frac{4}{12} = \frac{1}{3}$$

As the gradients of PQ and QR are equal and Q is common to both PQ and QR, the points P, Q and R are collinear.

Exercise 1B

1 Prove that the points A($-2, 1$), B($-1, 0$) and C($7, -8$) are collinear.

2 Which sets of points are collinear?
   (a) A($-5, -3$), B($-1, 0$) and C($7, 6$)
   (b) P($2, -6$), Q($-1, 3$) and R($-3, 8$)
   (c) S($-5, -6$), T($2, -2$) and U($10, 2$)
   (d) E($6, -4$), O($0, 0$) and F($-9, 6$).

3 (a) Find the gradient of the line joining U($-5, -5$) and V($10, 1$).
   (b) Which point, S($5, -1$) or W($7, 0$), lies on the line UV?

4 Calculate the gradient and describe the slope of the line joining each pair of points:

(a) A(0, 10), B(4, 2)   (b) D(1, 7), E(7, 10)
(c) G(−10, 5), H(2, −7)   (d) J(−9, −9), K(7, −7)
(e) L(−5, 3), P(8, −2)   (f) C(2, 8), N(2, 0)
(g) Q(−1, 10), R(2, −6)   (h) S(−1, 5), T(7, 5)
(i) M(−5, 9), U(−5, −3)   (j) N(−5, 0), C(0, 3)

5 A(2, 1), B(8, 3), C(9, 9) and D(3, 7) are the vertices of a quadrilateral.
(a) Calculate the gradient of each side.
(b) Explain why ABCD is a parallelogram.

6 Find the angle that the line joining each pair of points makes with the x-axis:

(a) (1, 0), (7, 6)   (b) (2, −3), (4, 9)   (c) (0, 0), (1, $\sqrt{3}$)
(d) (−8, 8), (5, −5)   (e) (−8, 3), (4, −2)   (f) (3, 9), (3, −2)

7 The tangent of the angle that a straight line makes with the x-axis is 2. If the point (5, 4) lies on this line find where the line crosses the x-axis and the y-axis.

8 OPQR is a rhombus with O the origin, P(−3, 5) and Q(−6, 0). Find the gradients of OR and QR.

9 A plane has crashed in the desert at the point P(−15, 12).
A search party sets out by Land Rover from Q_1 passing in a straight line through Q_2.
A helicopter sets out from R_1 and flies in a straight line over R_2.
If the search parties continue in these directions will either of them encounter the crashed plane?

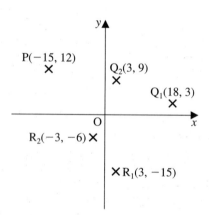

10 K(−2, 7), L(8, 7), M(14, −1) and N(4, −1) are the vertices of a quadrilateral.
(a) Find the gradient of each side of the quadrilateral.
(b) Calculate the angle that the lines LN and KM make with the x-axis.
(c) Explain why KLMN is a rhombus.

Investigating perpendicular lines

In the diagram triangle OBA has been rotated through 90° about O to form triangle OCD.
OB is **perpendicular** to OC.

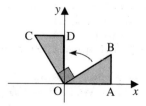

Exercise 1C

1 (a)

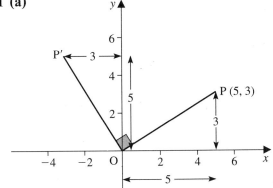

(b)

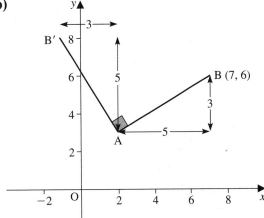

OP is rotated through 90°
about O to OP′.
  (i) Find the coordinates of P′
 (ii) Calculate m_{OP} and $m_{OP'}$
(iii) Calculate $m_{OP} \times m_{OP'}$

AB is rotated through 90°
about A to AB′.
  (i) Find the coordinates of B′
 (ii) Calculate m_{AB} and $m_{AB'}$
(iii) Calculate $m_{AB} \times m_{AB'}$

2 For each point Q(7, 2) and T(8, −3):
  (i) plot the point
 (ii) draw the line joining the point to the origin
(iii) rotate the line through an angle of 90° about O
(iv) find the gradients of these two perpendicular lines
 (v) multiply the gradients of the original line and the
      perpendicular line.

3 For each pair of points **(a)** E(−1, 1), F(−2, 5) and
(b) G(−2, −3), H(−1, −7):
  (i) plot the points and join them with a straight line
 (ii) rotate this line through 90° about the first point
(iii) find the gradients of the two perpendicular lines
(iv) multiply the gradients of the original line and the
      perpendicular line.

4 Make a conjecture about the product of the gradients of
perpendicular lines.

Gradients of perpendicular lines

> If two lines with gradients m_1 and m_2 are perpendicular then
> $m_1 \times m_2 = -1$

Proof
Under a rotation of 90° about O: A(a, b) → B($-b$, a)

$$m_{OA} = \frac{b-0}{a-0} = \frac{b}{a} \quad \text{and} \quad m_{OB} = \frac{a-0}{-b-0} = -\frac{a}{b}$$

$$m_{OA} \times m_{OB} = \frac{b}{a} \times \frac{a}{-b} = -1$$

If OA is perpendicular to OB, then
$m_{OA} \times m_{OB} = -1$.

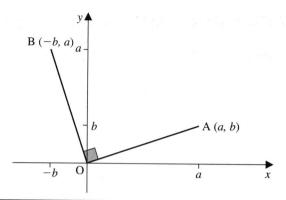

Conversely, if $m_1 \times m_2 = -1$ then the lines with gradients m_1 and m_2 are perpendicular.

Example 3

If P is the point $(2, -3)$ and Q is the point $(-1, 6)$, find the gradient of a line perpendicular to PQ.

$$m_{PQ} = \frac{6 - (-3)}{-1 - 2} = \frac{9}{-3} = -3$$

Since $\frac{1}{3} \times -3 = -1$, the gradient of a line perpendicular to PQ is $\frac{1}{3}$.

Example 4

Triangle RST has coordinates R(1, 2), S(3, 7) and T(6, 0). Show that the triangle is right-angled at R.

$$m_{RS} = \frac{7 - 2}{3 - 1} = \frac{5}{2} \qquad m_{RT} = \frac{0 - 2}{6 - 1} = -\frac{2}{5}$$

$$m_{RS} \times m_{RT} = -\frac{2}{5} \times \frac{5}{2} = -1.$$

Since $m_{RS} \times m_{RT} = -1$, RS is perpendicular to RT.

Exercise 1D

1 The gradients of lines are given below. Which of the following lines are perpendicular to each other?

$m_{AB} = -2 \qquad m_{PQ} = \frac{1}{4} \qquad m_{LM} = 3 \qquad m_{RS} = 2 \qquad m_{CD} = \frac{1}{2}$

$m_{EF} = -3 \qquad m_{JK} = -\frac{1}{3} \qquad m_{GH} = -\frac{1}{2} \qquad m_{TU} = -\frac{1}{4} \qquad m_{VW} = -4$

2 Write the gradient of the line perpendicular to the line with gradient:

(a) 1   **(b)** $-\frac{1}{7}$ **(c)** 5   **(d)** $\frac{2}{3}$

(e) $-\frac{5}{2}$ **(f)** $-\frac{3}{7}$ **(g)** undefined

3 A is the point $(-1, -2)$ and B is $(8, 1)$.
Find the gradient of a line perpendicular to AB.

4 P is the point with coordinates $(3, -3)$ and O is the origin.
OQ is perpendicular to OP. Find the gradient of OQ.

5 A$(-2, 2)$ and C$(3, -1)$ are opposite vertices of kite ABCD.
Find the gradient of diagonal BD.

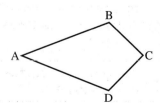

6 Given that K, L and M are the points
(−5, 0), (−2, 3) and (3, −2) respectively,
prove that triangle KLM is right-angled.

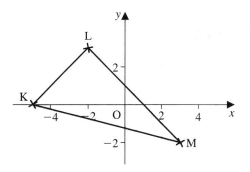

7 LM makes an angle of 76° with the positive direction of the
x-axis. KN is perpendicular to LM. Find the gradient of
KN.

8 If AB and CD are produced (extended)
will they meet at right angles?

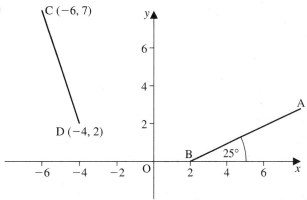

9 The points A(−3, 8), B(8, 6), C(3, −4) and D(−8, −3) are
vertices of a quadrilateral ABCD.
   (a) Calculate m_{AC} and m_{BD}.
   (b) Could ABCD be a rhombus? Explain.
   (c) Could ABCD be a square? Explain.

10 P(−6, 3), Q(1, 4) and R(−5, −4) are vertices of triangle PQR.
M(−2, 0) is the mid-point of RQ.
   (a) Calculate m_{RQ} and m_{PM}.
   (b) Explain why triangle PQR is isosceles.

Equation of a straight line: $y = mx + c$

The equation of a straight line is a formula that describes the
relationship between the x- and y-coordinates of all the points that
form the line.

> The equation of a straight line with gradient m and y-intercept
> c is $y = mx + c$.

Proof

P(x, y) is any point on the line except A.

For every position of P the gradient of AP is $\dfrac{y - c}{x - 0}$

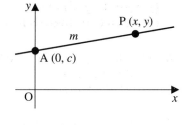

so: $m = \dfrac{y - c}{x}$

$y - c = mx$

$y = mx + c$

As $y = c$ when $x = 0$, the point A(0, c) also lies on the line with equation $y = mx + c$.

Example 5

What is the equation of the line with gradient 2 passing through (0, -5)?

$m = 2$ and $c = -5$

So the equation of the line is $y = 2x - 5$.

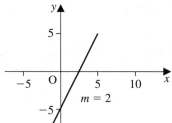

Example 6

Find the gradient and the y-intercept of the line $4x + 3y = 2$.

$4x + 3y = 2$

$3y = -4x + 2$

$y = -\tfrac{4}{3}x + \tfrac{2}{3}$

The gradient is $-\tfrac{4}{3}$ and the y-intercept is $\tfrac{2}{3}$.

Example 7

Show that the point (2, 7) lies on the line $y = 4x - 1$.

$y = 4x - 1$

When $x = 2$, $y = 4 \times 2 - 1$

$y = 7$

Because the coordinates (2, 7) satisfy the equation $y = 4x - 1$, this point must lie on the line.

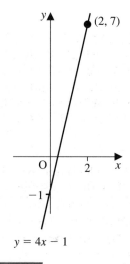

$y = 4x - 1$

Exercise 1E

1 Write the equation of the line with gradient 3 that passes through the point:
   (a) (0, 2)   (b) (0, 5)   (c) (0, 0)   (d) (0, -1)

2 Sketch and label the lines from question 1. Your sketch should show a **family** of parallel lines whose equations all have the general form $y = 3x + c$.

3 Write the equation of the line with gradient -2 that passes through the point:

    (a) $(0, 3)$ **(b)** $(0, 1)$ **(c)** $(0, -1)$ **(d)** $(0, -5)$

4 (a) Sketch and label the lines from question 3 on the same diagram.

   (b) Write a general equation for this family of lines.

5 Sketch three members of the family $y = x + c$.

6 (a) Write the equations of the lines through $(0, -1)$ with gradients

    (i) 2   (ii) -2 (iii) 3

   (b) Sketch and label these lines on the same diagram.

   (c) Write a general equation for this family of lines.

7 For each line write the gradient and the coordinates of the point where it cuts the y-axis:

    (a) $y = 5x + 2$ **(b)** $y = \frac{1}{2}x - 4$ **(c)** $y = -3x - 1$

    (d) $4y = x + 12$ **(e)** $2y = 6x - 4$ **(f)** $x + y = 7$

    (g) $2x + 3y = 9$ **(h)** $3x + 2y + 1 = 0$ **(i)** $9x + 3y = 0$

8 State whether or not each point lies on the given line.

    (a) $y = 3x + 5$, $(2, 1)$ **(b)** $y = 4x - 6$, $(-3, -18)$

    (c) $y = -2x + 3$, $(1, 5)$ **(d)** $y = \frac{1}{4}x + 8$, $(-12, 5)$

    (e) $y = -\frac{1}{2}x - 4$, $(6, -1)$ **(f)** $y = 0.1x + 2$, $(13, 0.7)$

Equation of a straight line: $Ax + By + C = 0$

It can also be shown that any equation of the form $Ax + By + C = 0$, where A and B are not both zero, is a **linear** equation, i.e. it is the equation of a straight line. This equation may be used as an alternative to the form $y = mx + c$.

> ▶ $Ax + By + C = 0$ is the **general equation** of a straight line.

Example 8

Rearrange the equation of each line into the form $Ax + By + C = 0$ and identify the values of A, B and C.

(a) $y = 2x + 5$ **(b)** $y = -\dfrac{4x}{3}$ **(c)** $x = 7$

(a) $y = 2x + 5$
     $2x - y + 5 = 0$
$A = 2, B = -1, C = 5$

(b) $y = -\dfrac{4x}{3}$
     $3y = -4x$
     $4x + 3y = 0$
$A = 4, B = 3, C = 0$

(c) $x = 7$
     $x - 7 = 0$
$A = 1, B = 0, C = -7$

Exercise 1F

1 Rearrange these equations in the form $Ax + By + C = 0$:

(a) $y = \frac{1}{4}x - \frac{1}{2}$ **(b)** $\frac{2}{3}y = x - 5$ **(c)** $y = \frac{3}{4}x$

2 Find the equation, in the form $Ax + By + C = 0$, for the line:
(a) through $(0, 3)$ with gradient -5
(b) through the points $(0, -4)$ and $(6, 8)$
(c) through $(0, -1)$ with gradient 4
(d) through $(0, 2)$ at an angle of $135°$ with the positive direction of the x-axis
(e) formed by the set of points with equal x- and y-coordinates
(f) that is vertical and passes through the point $(1, 6)$
(g) that is horizontal and passes through the point $(2, -5)$.

3 Which of the following are equations of straight lines?

(a) $3x = 5$ **(b)** $y = x^2$ **(c)** $5y = -2x$

(d) $x + 2y + 3 = 0$ **(e)** $x^2 + y^2 = 16$ **(f)** $\frac{1}{2}x = \frac{1}{4}y$

(g) $xy = 1$ **(h)** $7x + y = 0$ **(i)** $x = 4y + 9$

(j) $8 = -x + 2y$ **(k)** $x = y^2 - 1$ **(l)** $y = x^3 + 5$

(m) $x = 7$ **(n)** $y = \dfrac{x}{5}$ **(o)** $4 = y$

The equation of a straight line: $y - b = m(x - a)$

The equation of a line may be found if its gradient and the coordinates of **any** point that it passes through are known.

> The equation of a straight line with gradient m and passing through (a, b) is $y - b = m(x - a)$

Proof
$P(x, y)$ is any point on the line except A.

For every position of P the gradient of AP is $\dfrac{y - b}{x - a}$

$$m = \frac{y - b}{x - a}$$

$$y - b = m(x - a)$$

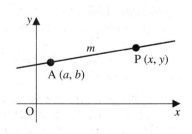

As $y = b$ when $x = a$, the point $A(a, b)$ must also lie on the line with equation $y - b = m(x - a)$.

Example 9
Find the equation of the line with gradient $\frac{1}{2}$ passing through $(5, -2)$.

Using $y - b = m(x - a)$, where $m = \frac{1}{2}$, $a = 5$, $b = -2$:
$$y - (-2) = \tfrac{1}{2}(x - 5)$$
$$y + 2 = \tfrac{1}{2}(x - 5)$$
$$2y + 4 = x - 5$$
$$2y = x - 9 \quad \text{or} \quad x - 2y - 9 = 0$$

The equation of the line is $x - 2y - 9 = 0$.

Example 10
Find the equation of the line passing through $P(-2, 0)$ and $Q(1, 6)$.

$$m_{AB} = \frac{6 - 0}{1 - (-2)} = \frac{6}{3} = 2$$

Using $y - b = m(x - a)$, where $m = 2$, $a = -2$, $b = 0$:
$$y - 0 = 2(x - (-2))$$
$$y = 2x + 4$$

Note: $a = 1$, $b = 6$ from point Q could have been used as an alternative.

Exercise 1G

1 Find the equation of the line through the given point and with the given gradient:
   (a) $(3, 2)$, 5 **(b)** $(-5, -4)$, 2 **(c)** $(1, 5)$, -4
   (d) $(0, -3)$, $\frac{1}{4}$ **(e)** $(4, 3)$, $-\frac{1}{2}$ **(f)** $(0, c)$, m

2 Find the equation of the line through each pair of points:
   (a) $(4, 5), (2, 3)$ **(b)** $(1, 0), (-2, -6)$
   (c) $(-3, -5), (2, 5)$ **(d)** $(0, 0), (4, -2)$
   (e) $(1, -4), (3, -6)$ **(f)** $(4, 2), (-2, 4)$

3 Find the equation of the line:
   (a) through $(3, 1)$ and parallel to $y = 3x - 4$
   (b) through $(1, -2)$ and perpendicular to $y = \frac{1}{2}x + 5$
   (c) parallel to $y = 5x$ and passing through $(-2, 3)$
   (d) parallel to $y = -3x + 9$ and passing through the origin
   (e) through $(7, -5)$ and perpendicular to the x-axis
   (f) parallel to the x-axis and passing through $(3, -2)$
   (g) through $(4, 5)$ and parallel to the line joining $(-1, -3)$ and $(3, -1)$
   (h) that passes through $A(6, 1)$ at right angles to the line joining A to $B(7, -1)$.

4 PQRS is a rectangular field of barley. A farm road runs in a straight line from the farm at O along one side of the field. Relative to the x- and y-axes shown, P is the point with coordinates $(3, 8)$ and OQR has equation $y = 2x$.

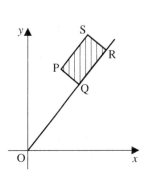

Find the equation of
   (a) PS   **(b)** PQ

5 Part of the motorway system near Glasgow is shown in diagrammatic form opposite. The Maryville interchange is taken as the origin with coordinate axes running east/west and north/south.
The M73 goes towards Cumbernauld on a bearing of 014°.
The M8 and M80 meet at $(-7.5, 6)$.
Junction 4 on the M74 is at $(5, -6)$.
The M8 meets the M73 at right angles.
  (a) Find linear equations for
      (i) the M74   (ii) the M73   (iii) the M8
  (b) Find coordinates for the junction of the M8 and the M73.

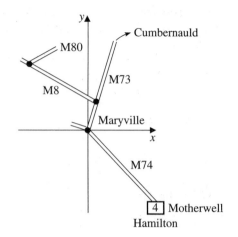

Geometrical constructions

Over 2000 years ago the Greek mathemaician Euclid wrote his textbook the *Elements* showing many different **geometrical constructions** – ways of drawing geometrical shapes. The next three sections show you some constructions and the algebra that relates to them.

Perpendicular bisectors

Here is the construction to find the **perpendicular bisector** of a line AB – a line at right angles to AB passing through its mid-point:

Set compasses to more than half the length of AB. With the point at A, draw arcs on both sides of AB.

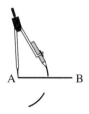

Keep the compass setting. With the point at B, draw arcs above and below AB to intersect those already drawn at C and D.

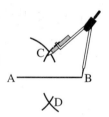

Draw the line CD. This line is the **perpendicular bisector** of AB.

Exercise 1H

1 (a) Draw the perpendicular bisector of a line AB as described above. What shape is ACBD?
  (b) Why is CD the perpendicular bisector of AB?

2 (a) Draw a triangle PQR. Draw the perpendicular bisectors of each side.
  (b) What do you notice about the three perpendicular bisectors?
  (c) Test your conjecture by drawing another triangle and its perpendicular bisectors.

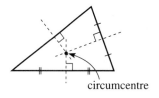

The **perpendicular bisectors** of the sides of any triangle are said to be **concurrent**. Their point of intersection is called the **circumcentre** of the triangle.

You need to be able to find the equation of a perpendicular bisector. This example shows you how.

circumcentre

Example 11

A is the point $(1, 3)$ and B is the point $(5, -7)$. Find the equation of the perpendicular bisector of AB.

Let E be the mid-point of AB.

The coordinates of E are $\left(\dfrac{1+5}{2}, \dfrac{3+(-7)}{2}\right) = (3, -2)$

The gradient of AB is $m_{AB} = \dfrac{3-(-7)}{1-5} = -\dfrac{5}{2}$

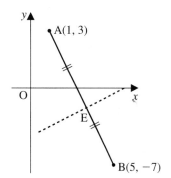

The gradient of the perpendicular bisector $= \frac{2}{5}$, since $m_1 \times m_2 = -1$.

The perpendicular bisector of AB has gradient $\frac{2}{5}$ and passes through $(3, -2)$.

Using $y - b = m(x - a)$:
$$y - (-2) = \tfrac{2}{5}(x - 3)$$
$$5y + 10 = 2x - 6$$
$$5y - 2x + 16 = 0$$

The equation of the line is $5y - 2x + 16 = 0$.

Exercise 1I

1 Find the equation of the perpendicular bisector of the line joining each pair of points.
  (a) A(2, 8) and B(4, 6)　　　(b) P(9, 5) and Q(−1, 3)
  (c) L(−4, 6) and M(−2, −2)　(d) Q(0, 3) and D(5, 4)
  (e) C(−2, 0) and E(8, 1)　　(f) A(5, −7) and J(6, 4)

2 Find the equation of the perpendicular bisector of each side of the triangle with vertices:
  (a) P(1, 3), R(0, 4) and Q(5, 2)
  (b) D(−4, 2), A(9, 2) and V(7, 1)
  (c) L(−2, −8), C(0, 5) and M(1, 2)
  (d) Q(−3, 1), R(−4, −2) and S(7, 0).

3 In each of the triangles that you drew in question 2 in Exercise 1H, check that the point of intersection of the perpendicular bisectors is the centre of a circle that passes through all the vertices of the triangle.

This circle is called the **circumcircle** of a triangle and its centre is the **circumcentre**.

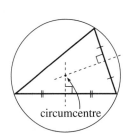

circumcentre

Altitudes of a triangle

An **altitude** of a triangle is a line from a vertex perpendicular
to the opposite side. A triangle has three altitudes.

This is how to draw an altitude of a triangle:

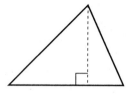

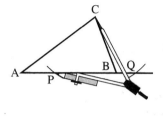

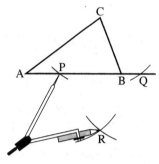

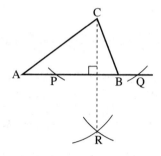

With centre C draw an arc
to cut AB at P and Q
(produce AB if necessary).

Keep the compass setting.
With centres at P and Q
draw two arcs meeting at R.

CR is the required altitude.

Exercise 1J

1 (a) What shape is CPRQ above?
   (b) Why is CR perpendicular to AB?

2 (a) Draw a triangle. Draw all its altitudes.
   (b) What do you notice about these altitudes?
   (c) Test your conjecture by drawing another triangle and its
         altitudes.

Question 2 above shows you that the three altitudes of a
triangle are **concurrent**. Their point of intersection is
called the **orthocentre** of the triangle.

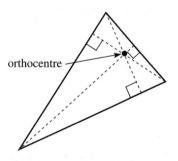

You need to be able to find the equation of an altitude. This
example shows you how.

Example 12
A is the point (2, −4), B is (3, 1) and C is (−5, 0).
Find the equation of the altitude from A.

The gradient of BC $= m_{BC} = \dfrac{1 - 0}{3 - (-5)} = \dfrac{1}{8}$

so the gradient of the altitude $= m_{AD} = -8$ (because $m_1 \times m_2 = -1$).

The altitude has gradient -8 and passes through $(2, -4)$.

Using $y - b = m(x - a)$:

$$y - (-4) = -8(x - 2)$$
$$y + 4 = -8x + 16$$
$$8x + y = 12$$

The equation of the altitude is $8x + y - 12 = 0$.

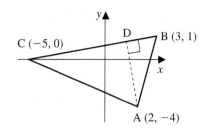

Exercise 1K

1 In each triangle find the equation of the altitude from B.
   (a) P(7, 3), R(−5, −1) and B(1, 6)   **(b)** K(4, −7), H(5, −6) and B(3, 1)
   (c) B(5, −4), U(7, 0) and V(0, −2)   **(d)** A(4, 2), B(5, 3) and C(4, 5)
   (e) P(−4, 2), Q(−4, 6) and B(0, 5)   **(f)** B(1, 6), D(2, 3) and S(3, 3)

2 In triangle DEF find the equation of the altitude from D, where
   D is (4, 5) and EF has equation $y = 3x + 2$.

3 In triangle PKL find the equation of the altitude from L, where L
   is (−6, −8) and PK has equation $3x + y = 0$.

4 In triangle RST find the equation of the altitude from S, where S
   is (6, −1) and RT has equation $2y − 3x + 1 = 0$.

5 Find the equations of **all** the altitudes of the triangles with vertices
   (a) G(1, 2), J(4, 0) and T(3, 1)
   (b) S(−4, 3), E(5, 2) and U(1, 1)
   (c) L(−2, 2), G(−2, 3) and C(4, −1).

Medians of a triangle

A **median** of a triangle is a line from a vertex to the mid-point
of the opposite side. A triangle has three medians.

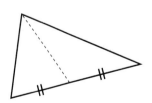

This is how to draw a median of a triangle.

Construct the
perpendicular
bisector of BC.

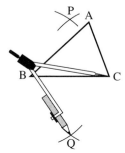

Mark M where
PQ would meet
BC. AM is a
median of
triangle ABC.

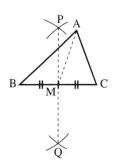

Exercise 1L

1 (a) Draw a triangle. Draw its three medians.
(b) What do you notice about the medians?
(c) Test your conjecture by drawing another triangle and its medians.

2 (a) Draw a triangle. Construct its three medians.
(b) For each median measure the distance from the vertex to the centroid and the distance from the centroid to the mid-point of the opposite side.
(c) Make a conjecture and test it.

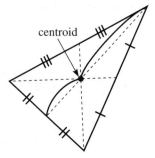

Exercise 1L shows you that the three medians of a triangle are **concurrent**. Their point of intersection is called the **centroid** of the triangle. It is the triangle's 'balancing point'. The centroid is a **point of trisection** of the medians, i.e. it divides each median in the ratio $2:1$.

You need to be able to find the equation of a median. Example 13 shows you how.

Example 13
Triangle ABC has vertices A(3, −7), B(8, 1) and C(4, −3). Find the equation of the median from A.

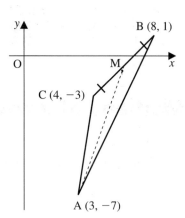

Let M be the mid-point of BC.

The coordinates of M are $\left(\dfrac{8+4}{2}, \dfrac{1+(-3)}{2}\right) = (6, -1)$

The gradient of AM is $m_{AM} = \dfrac{-7-(-1)}{3-6} = 2$

The median has gradient 2 and passes through (3, −7).
Using $y - b = m(x - a)$:

$y - (-7) = 2(x - 3)$
$\qquad y + 7 = 2x - 6$
$\qquad\quad y = 2x - 13$

The equation of the median is $2x - y - 13 = 0$.

Exercise 1M

1 Find the equation of the median from D for a triangle with vertices:
(a) D(4, 5), E(8, −2) and F(2, 0)   **(b)** T(1, −7), R(−4, 7) and D(−1, 3)
(c) U(5, 0), D(2, −2) and S(3, 0)   **(d)** W(−1, 9), P(3, −3) and D(−1, −2)

2 (a) Triangle QER has vertices Q(7, 3), E(9, 0) and R(5, 1). Find the equation of the median which passes through the mid-point of QR.

   (b) Triangle MFP has vertices M(4, −6), F(2, 8) and P(−8, 4). Find the equation of the median which passes through the mid-point of FP.

3 Find the equations of all three medians of triangles with vertices:

   (a) K(3, 7), L(−1, −5) and M(7, 3)   **(b)** H(2, 0), K(8, −2) and U(−4, 6)

   (c) C(6, 2), D(−5, 2) and E(1, −2)   **(d)** Q(−3, 5), H(−5, −2) and F(−7, 4)

Lines in a triangle

Now that you have learnt about the various lines associated with triangles you can use them to solve problems.

Example 14

F, G and H are the points (1, 0), (−4, 3) and (0, −1), respectively. FJ is a median of triangle FGH and HR is an altitude. Find the coordinates of the point of intersection, D, of FJ and HR.

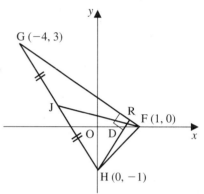

Median

J is the mid-point of GH.

J is the point $\left(\dfrac{-4+0}{2}, \dfrac{3+(-1)}{2}\right) = (-2, 1)$

$m_{JF} = \dfrac{1-0}{-2-1} = -\dfrac{1}{3}$

The median has gradient $-\frac{1}{3}$ and passes through (−2, 1) so

$y - 1 = -\frac{1}{3}(x + 2)$

$3y - 3 = -x - 2$

$\quad 3y = -x + 1$

Altitude

$m_{GF} = \dfrac{3-0}{-4-1} = -\dfrac{3}{5}$

$m_{HR} = \dfrac{5}{3}$

The altitude has gradient $\frac{5}{3}$ and passes through (0, −1) so

$y + 1 = \frac{5}{3}(x - 0)$

$3y + 3 = 5x$

$\quad 3y = 5x - 3$

Solve these equations simultaneously:

$3y = -x + 1$ ①

$3y = 5x - 3$ ②

to give $D\left(\frac{2}{3}, \frac{1}{9}\right)$.

Exercise 1N

1 E, D and V are the points with coordinates $(0, -5)$, $(2, -11)$ and $(8, 1)$, respectively. Find
(a) the equation of EH, the altitude of triangle EDV
(b) the area of triangle EDV.

2 A triangle ABC has vertices A(1, 6), B(4, 0) and C(−2, 0).
(a) Use Pythagoras' theorem to show that the triangle is isosceles.
(b) (i) The altitudes AD and CE intersect at H, where D and E lie on BC and AB, respectively. Find the coordinates of H.
(ii) Hence show that H lies one quarter of the way up DA.

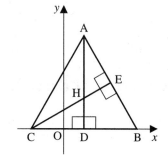

3 A triangle has vertices K(4, 1), L(5, 4) and M(8, 1). Find
(a) the equation of the altitude through L
(b) the equation of the altitude through M
(c) the coordinates of the orthocentre of triangle KLM.

4 P is the point (3, 0), Q is (7, 0) and R is (5, −3). Find
(a) the equation of the median through R
(b) the equation of the median through P
(c) the coordinates of the centroid of triangle PQR.

5 In triangle ABC, A has coordinates (0, 5), B has coordinates (6, 9) and C has coordinates (0, 12). Find
(a) the equation of the perpendicular bisector of AC
(b) the equation of the perpendicular bisector of AB
(c) the coordinates of the circumcentre of triangle ABC
(d) the radius of the circumcircle of triangle ABC.

6 A triangle has vertices L(2, 3), M(0, 2) and U(4, −2).
(a) Find the coordinates of the centroid, G, of triangle LMU.
(b) Find the coordinates of the orthocentre, H, of triangle LMU.
(c) Find the coordinates of the circumcentre, C, of triangle LMU.
(d) Show that C, H and G are collinear.

The line through G, H and C is called the Euler line for triangle LMU.

7 Triangle OGH has vertices at $(0, 0)$, $(10, 0)$ and $(5, 5\sqrt{3})$.
(a) Show that triangle OGH is equilateral.
(b) Choose any point, P, inside the triangle or on one of the sides and calculate the shortest distance from P to each of the sides of triangle OGH.
(c) Add these three distances together.
(d) Repeat **(b)** and **(c)** for another position of P.
(e) What do you notice?
(f) Test your conjecture.

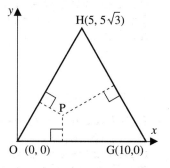

This result is known as Viviani's theorem.

Exercise 1O Mixed questions

1 Two sides of a rectangle have equations $y = 2x$ and $2y + x = 5$.
Find, algebraically, the coordinates of the vertex of the rectangle formed by these sides.

2 The point A has coordinates (1, 6) and the line PQ has equation $2x - 5y - 1 = 0$.
   (a) Find the equation of the line through A perpendicular to PQ.
   (b) Find the coordinates of the point where this line meets PQ.

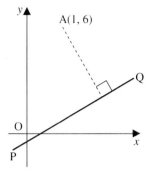

3 A triangle ABC has vertices A(4, 8), B(1, 2) and C(7, 2).
   (a) Show that the triangle is isosceles.
   (b)   **(i)** The altitudes AD and BE intersect at H, where D and E lie on BC and CA respectively. Find the coordinates of H.
      (ii) Hence show that H lies one quarter of the way up DA.
                                                            [Higher]

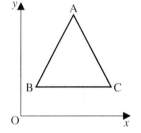

4 OABC is a parallelogram where O is the origin and B is the point (3, 7). OC has equation $y = 6x$ and OA has equation $y = -5x$.
   (a) Find the equations of AB and BC.
   (b) Hence determine the coordinates of A and C.

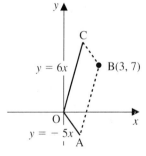

5 ABCD is a square. A is the point with coordinates (3, 4) and ODC has equation $y = \frac{1}{2}x$.
   (a) Find the equation of the line AD.
   (b) Find the coordinates of D.
   (c) Find the area of the square ABCD.   [Higher]

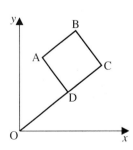

6 PQRS is a parallelogram where P is the point (0, 4) and S is (6, 7). The equations of the diagonals are $y = 7$ and $2y = 3x + 8$.
   (a) Find the coordinates of the centre of symmetry of PQRS.
   (b) Calculate the coordinates of Q and R.

7 (a) In the diagram, A is the point $(-1, 1)$, B is
$(3, 3)$ and C is $(6, 2)$.
The perpendicular bisector of AB has
equation $y + 2x = 4$.
Find the equation of the perpendicular
bisector of BC.
(b) Find the centre of the circle which
passes through A, B and C.   [Higher]

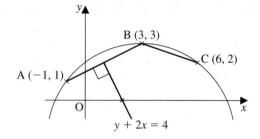

8 A triangle has sides with equations $y = 7x - 6$, $8y - 5 = 3x$ and
$10x - 9y = -52$. Calculate the coordinates of its vertices.

9 P, Q and R have coordinates $(1, -2)$, $(6, 3)$ and $(9, 14)$
respectively and are three vertices of a kite PQRS.
(a) Find the equations of the diagonals of this kite and the
coordinates of the point where they intersect.
(b) Find the coordinates of the fourth vertex S.   [Higher]

10 A, B and C are the points with coordinates $(2, 3)$, $(4, 9)$ and
$(10, -3)$ respectively. Find
(a) the equation of AH, the altitude of triangle ABC;
(b) the area of triangle ABC.   [Higher]

11 RSTU is a rhombus with R the point $(-4, -2)$ and T the point
$(6, -4)$.
(a) Find the equation of the diagonal RT.
(b) Find the equation of the diagonal SU.
(c) If RS has the equation $3y = 2x + 2$ find the coordinates
of S and U.

SUMMARY

(1) The gradient of AB $= m_{AB}$

$$= \frac{\text{Change in } y}{\text{Change in } x}$$

$$= \frac{y_2 - y_1}{x_2 - x_1}$$

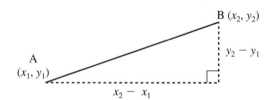

(2) (a) lines that slope
- upwards from left to right have a positive gradient
- downwards from left to right have a negative gradient

(b) lines parallel to the
- x-axis have gradient zero and equations of the form
$y = a$
- y-axis have gradient undefined and equations of the
form $x = b$

(c) parallel lines have equal gradients

(d) the gradient of a line is the tangent of the angle it makes
with the positive direction of the x-axis.

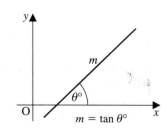

③ If two lines with gradients m_1 and m_2 are perpendicular then $m_1 \times m_2 = -1$.

If $m_1 \times m_2 = -1$ then the lines with gradients m_1 and m_2 are perpendicular.

④ The equation of a straight line with gradient m and y-intercept c is $y = mx + c$.

⑤ $Ax + By + C = 0$ is the **general equation** of a straight line.

⑥ The equation of a straight line with gradient m and passing through (a, b) is $y - b = m(x - a)$.

2 Sets and functions

In mathematics we often use symbols as shorthand for words, for example we use the symbol $=$ to stand for the word equals.

In this unit you will learn some new shorthand symbols which we use to describe sets of numbers or objects.

For example, the mathematical statement $A = \{x : 1 \leqslant x \leqslant 5, x \in \mathbf{R}\}$ is the shorthand for 'A is the set of Real numbers from 1 to 5 inclusive'.

First you need to know some basic definitions.

Set notation

Notation	Example
$\in$ means 'is a member of'	$4 \in \{1, 2, 3, 4\}$
$\notin$ means 'is **not** a member of'	$5 \notin \{1, 2, 3, 4\}$
$\{\ \}$ means 'the empty set', i.e. a set with no members (or elements)	The set of square numbers between 10 and 15 is $\{\ \}$
subset means 'part of a set'	$\{3, 6, 9\}$ is a subset of $\{1, 2, 3, 4, 5, 6, 7, 8, 9\ 10\}$

Some standard sets are
the set of **natural numbers**, $\mathbf{N} = \{1, 2, 3, 4, 5, \ldots\}$

the set of **whole numbers**, $\mathbf{W} = \{0, 1, 2, 3, 4, 5, \ldots\}$

the set of **integers**, $\mathbf{Z} = \{\ldots, -3, -2, -1, 0, 1, 2, 3, \ldots\}$

the set of **rational numbers**, $\mathbf{Q}$, is the set of all numbers that can be written as fractions

the set of **real numbers**, $\mathbf{R}$, is the set of real numbers – rational and irrational.

The relationship between these sets is illustrated in the diagram.

Sets can be defined using 'set-builder' notation.

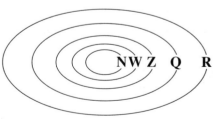

Example 1
List the members of the set P, where $P = \{x : 5 < x < 10, x \in \mathbf{W}\}$.

P is the set of values of x between 5 and 10 that are whole numbers.
$P = \{6, 7, 8, 9\}$.

1 List the following sets:

(a) A, the set of integers between -5 and 5, inclusive.

(b) B, the set of whole numbers less than 10.

2 Which of these statements are true?

(a) $3 \in \mathbf{N}$ (b) $-10 \in \mathbf{W}$ (c) $\frac{1}{2} \notin \mathbf{Q}$

(d) $\sqrt{-9} \in \mathbf{R}$ (e) $-\frac{1}{4} \in \mathbf{Z}$ (f) $\mathbf{W}$ is a subset of $\mathbf{N}$.

(g) $\{5, 10, 15, \ldots\}$ is a subset of $\mathbf{W}$.

(h) The set of prime numbers between 8 and 12 is $\{\ \}$.

(i) When $x \in \mathbf{Q}$ and $27x^2 = 3$ the solution set for x is $\{\ \}$.

3 List the sets defined by:

(a) $P = \{x : x < 5,\ x \in \mathbf{W}\}$ (b) $L = \{x : -2 \leqslant x \leqslant 4,\ x \in \mathbf{Z}\}$

(c) $S = \{x : 5 < x < 20,\ x\ \text{prime}\}$ (d) $V = \{x : 3x + 1 \leqslant 0,\ x \in \mathbf{W}\}$

(e) $M = \{x : x^2 + 2x + 3 = 0,\ x \in \mathbf{R}\}$ (f) $B = \{x : \sin x° > 2,\ x \in \mathbf{W}\}$

(g) $G = \{x : \tan x° = 0,\ 0 \leqslant x \leqslant 360,\ x \in \mathbf{R}\}$ (h) $K = \{x : x = 3p - 1,\ p = \pm 5\}$

Functions and mappings

> A **function** or mapping from a set A to a set B is a rule that relates each element in set A to one and only one element in set B.
>
> The set of elements in set A is called the **domain**.
> The set of images in set B is called the **range**.

A function can be described by
- a formula for f(x)
- an arrow diagram
- a graph

Example 2

The function f, defined by f$(x) = x^2 + 3x$, has domain $\{-2, -1, 0, 1, 2, 3\}$.

(a) Find the range.   (b) Draw an arrow diagram   (c) Draw a graph.

(a) Use the formula for f(x)

f$(-2) = 4 - 6 = -2$

f$(-1) = 1 - 3 = -2$

f$(0) = 0 + 0 = 0$

f$(1) = 1 + 3 = 4$

f$(2) = 4 + 6 = 10$

(b)

Set A   Set B

$-2 \bullet$

$-1 \bullet \rightarrow \bullet\ -2$

$0 \bullet \rightarrow \bullet\ 0$

$1 \bullet \rightarrow \bullet\ 4$

$2 \bullet \rightarrow \bullet\ 10$

(c)

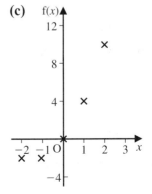

Exercise 2B

1 $g(x) = x^2 + 1$, $x \in \{-3, -2, -1, 0, 1, 2, 3\}$.

  (a) State the range.

  (b) Show the function as an arrow diagram.

  (c) Draw a graph of the function.

2 $f(x) = x^2 - x - 12$ and $x \in \{1, 2, 3, 4\}$.

  (a) State the range.

  (b) Show the function as an arrow diagram.

3 (a) For the function $h(x) = 3^x$ with domain $\{3, 2, 1, 0, -1, -2, -3\}$ list the set of images.

  (b) What element would need to be included in the domain if 81 was in the range?

4 A function is defined by $f(x) = \sin x°$ with domain $\{x: 0 \leqslant x \leqslant 360, x \in \mathbf{R}\}$.

  (a) Find f(0), f(30), f(45), f(60) and f(90).

  (b) If $f(a) = -1$ find a.

  (c) Describe the range using set-builder notation.

5 For the function $g(x) = x^2 + 1$, whose domain is a subset of $\mathbf{Z}$, list **all** the possible elements in the domain if the **range** is $\{1, 5, 10, 17, 26\}$.

6 The function $f(x) = x^2 - 2x - 3$ has domain $\{x: -1 \leqslant x \leqslant 4, x \in \mathbf{R}\}$. Find values of x such that $f(x) = 0$.

7 The displacement in metres, s(t), for a car as it accelerates from rest is given by $s(t) = 16t + \frac{1}{2}t^2$, where t is the time in seconds after it starts.

  (a) Give a possible domain for t.

  (b) How far has the car travelled after 10 seconds?

  (c) Calculate the average speed of the car between $t = 6$ and $t = 10$.

8 Which of the following graphs illustrate functions?

(a)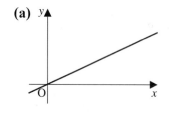

(b)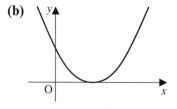

(c)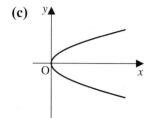

(d)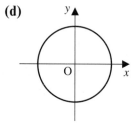

(e)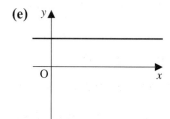

(f)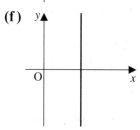

Composition of functions

$h(x) = 2x + 5$ can be thought of as being composed of two functions.

The 'multiply by 2' function is denoted by f and the 'add 5' function is denoted by g.

The composite function, h, says 'first multiply by 2 then add 5'.

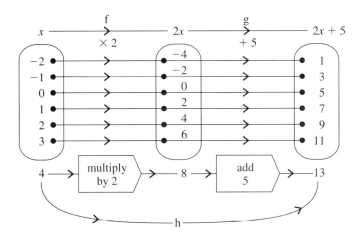

A composite function can be written in the form $h(x) = g(f(x))$ and is read as 'g of f of x'.

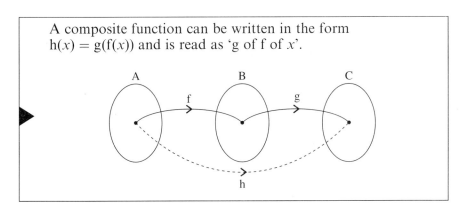

The composite function, h, is sometimes called a function of a function.

Example 3
Write $h(x) = x^2 - 1$ as a composition of two functions, f and g.

First function: 'square each element from the domain', i.e. $f(x) = x^2$.
Second function: 'subtract 1 from each answer', i.e. $g(x) = x - 1$.

Example 4
Given $f(x) = 3x$, $g(x) = x + 1$ and $h(x) = g(f(x))$:

(a) evaluate $g(f(2))$ **(b)** find a formula for $h(x)$.

(a) $g(f(2)) = g(6) = 6 + 1 = 7$ **(b)** $h(x) = g(f(x)) = g(3x) = 3x + 1$.

Example 5

If $f(x) = x^2 - 2$ and $g(x) = \dfrac{1}{x}$ ($x \neq 0$, since $\dfrac{1}{x}$ is undefined for

$x = 0$), find a formula for

(a) $h(x) = f(g(x))$ **(b)** $k(x) = g(f(x))$

(a) $h(x) = f(g(x)) = f\left(\dfrac{1}{x}\right) = \left(\dfrac{1}{x}\right)^2 - 2 = \dfrac{1}{x^2} - 2$, $x \neq 0$

(b) $k(x) = g(f(x)) = g(x^2 - 2) = \dfrac{1}{x^2 - 2}$, $x \neq \pm\sqrt{2}$

> ▶   In general $f(g(x)) \neq g(f(x))$.

Exercise 2C

1 For each function $h(x)$, where $h(x) = g(f(x))$, write formulae for
the first function, f, and the second function, g.

(a) $h(x) = 3x - 2$ **(b)** $h(x) = x^2 + 7$ **(c)** $h(x) = 5x^3$

(d) $h(x) = \frac{1}{2}(x + 2)$ **(e)** $h(x) = (x - 6)^2$ **(f)** $h(x) = 3(2x + 1)$

2 f and g are functions on the set of integers. $f(x) = x + 1$ and
$g(x) = 3x$.

(a) Copy and complete this diagram for the integers 3 to -3:

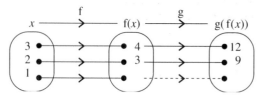

(b) Complete: $h(x) = g(f(x)) = g(x + 1) = $

3 f and g are functions on the set **R**. $f(x) = 2x + 1$ and $g(x) = 3x$.

(a) Evaluate (i) $g(f(2))$, (ii) $g(f(1))$, (iii) $g(f(-1))$ and (iv) $g(f(-2))$.

(b) State a formula for $g(f(x))$.

4 $f(x) = x + 2$ and $g(x) = \dfrac{1}{3x}$, $x \neq 0$.

(a) Find the value of (i) $f(g(2))$ and (ii) $g(f(2))$.

(b) Find formulae for (i) $h(x) = f(g(x))$ and (ii) $k(x) = g(f(x))$.

5 For each pair of functions write a formula for $h(x) = f(g(x))$.

(a) $f(x) = x + 1$, $g(x) = 3x$ **(b)** $f(x) = 2x + 1$, $g(x) = 4x$

(c) $f(x) = x - 2$, $g(x) = x^2$ **(d)** $f(x) = x^2$, $g(x) = x + 4$

(e) $f(x) = 4x$, $g(x) = \sin x$ **(f)** $f(x) = 2^x$, $g(x) = x - 5$

6 For each pair of functions in question 5 write a formula for
$k(x) = g(f(x))$.

7 Find formulae for $f(g(x))$ and $g(f(x))$ where $f(x) = x^2$ and
$g(x) = \cos x$, $x \in \mathbf{R}$.

8 The functions f and g, defined on suitable domains, are given by
$$f(x) = \frac{1}{x^2 - 4} \text{ and } g(x) = x + 1.$$
(a) Find an expression for $h(x)$, where $h(x) = f(g(x))$.
Give your answer as a single fraction.
(b) State a suitable domain for h.

9 A function f is defined on the set of real numbers by
$$f(x) = \frac{1 - x}{x}, (x \neq 0).$$
Find, in its simplest form, an expression for $f(f(x))$.

10 On a suitable set of real numbers, functions f and g are defined
by $f(x) = \frac{1}{x + 3}$ and $g(x) = \frac{1}{x} - 3$. Find $f(g(x))$ in its simplest
form.

Inverse of a function

> A function in which the elements of two sets are paired so
> that each element of set A corresponds to one element of set
> B, and vice versa, is called a **one-to-one correspondence**.

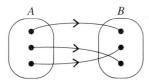

> When a function f is a one-to-one correspondence from set A
> to set B, another function, f^{-1}, exists that maps from set B to
> set A. This function is called the **inverse** of f.

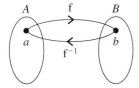

For each element $f(a) = b$ and $f^{-1}(b) = a$.
The range of f is the domain of f^{-1}. The domain of f is the range of f^{-1}.

> $f^{-1}(f(x)) = f(f^{-1}(x)) = x$

Example 6
If $f(x) = 2x$, find $f^{-1}(x)$.

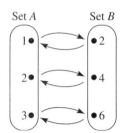

Set A   Set B

$f^{-1}(x) = \frac{1}{2}x$.

Example 7
If $f(x) = x + 5$, find $f^{-1}(x)$.

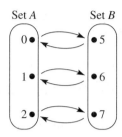

Set A   Set B

$f^{-1}(x) = x - 5$.

Example 8
If $f(x) = 2x + 1$, find $f^{-1}(x)$.

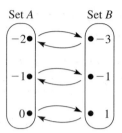

Set A   Set B

$f^{-1}(x) = \frac{1}{2}(x - 1)$, i.e.
subtract 1, then divide by 2.

Exercise 2D

1 Which arrow diagrams illustrate a function that could have an inverse? Write formulae for each function and its inverse.

(a)
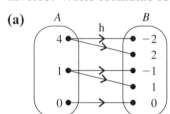

(b)
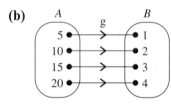

(c)
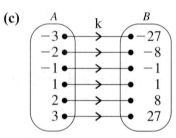

2 For each function f, the domain and range are the set of real numbers. Find a formula for the inverse function f^{-1}.

(a) $f(x) = x + 99$

(b) $f(x) = 10x$

(c) $f(x) = \frac{1}{4}x$

(d) $f(x) = x - \frac{1}{2}$

(e) $f(x) = 2x + 5$

(f) $f(x) = 3x - 1$

(g) $f(x) = \frac{x}{3} - 2$

(h) $f(x) = \frac{1}{2}(x + 9)$

(i) $f(x) = x^3 - 1$

3 For each function find (i) $f^{-1}(x)$, (ii) $f(f^{-1}(x))$ and (iii) $f^{-1}(f(x))$.

(a) $f(x) = 2x - 3$

(b) $f(x) = 5 - 3x$

(c) $f(x) = \frac{x + 1}{2}$

4 For $f(x) = x^2$, $-2 < x < 2$, $x \in \mathbf{Z}$

(a) State the range.

(b) Explain why an inverse function does not exist.

5 $f(x) = 2x - 1$, $g(x) = 3 - 2x$ and $h(x) = \frac{1}{4}(5 - x)$.

(a) Find a formula for $k(x)$, where $k(x) = f(g(x))$.

(b) Find a formula for $h(k(x))$.

(c) What is the connection between the functions h and k?

Graphs of inverses

Is there a relationship between the graph of a function and the graph of its inverse? Try the following exercise and see if you can find a relationship.

Exercise 2E

1 Draw the graphs of each function and its inverse on the same diagram. For each function $x \in \mathbf{R}$.

   (a) $f(x) = 2x$ and $f^{-1}(x) = \frac{1}{2}x$

   (b) $f(x) = x + 5$ and $f^{-1}(x) = x - 5$

   (c) $f(x) = 2x + 1$ and $f^{-1}(x) = \frac{1}{2}(x - 1)$

   (d) $f(x) = x^3$ and $f^{-1}(x) = \sqrt[3]{x}$

2 (a) On each of the diagrams from question 1 draw the line $y = x$.

   (b) Make a conjecture about the graph of a function and the graph of its inverse.

Exercise 2E, shows you that:

> To find the graph of an inverse function reflect the graph of the function in the line $y = x$.
>
>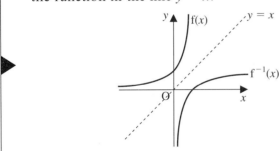

Exercise 2F

1 Copy each sketch and draw the inverse of each function.

   (a) 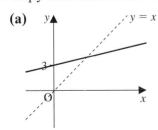 **(b)** 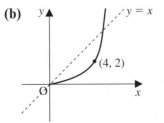 **(c)** 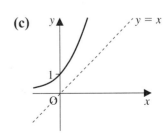

2 Draw the graph of each function and on the same diagram sketch its inverse.

   (a) $f(x) = 5x$ **(b)** $f(x) = 3x + 5$ **(c)** $f(x) = x^3 + 10$

Exponential functions

▶ $f(x) = a^x$, $x \in \mathbf{R}$, is called an **exponential function** to base a, $a \in \mathbf{R}$, $a \neq 0$

Example 9
Draw the graph of $f(x) = 2^x$, $x \in \mathbf{R}$.

Calculate some values of $f(x)$

x	$f(x) = 2^x$
-2	$2^{-2} = \frac{1}{4}$
-1	$2^{-1} = \frac{1}{2}$
0	$2^0 = 1$
1	$2^1 = 2$
2	$2^2 = 4$
3	$2^3 = 8$

Draw the graph:
Since the points plotted appear to lie on a smooth curve we can assume that 2^x exists for all real values of x.

$f(x) = 2^x$ is an example of an exponential function. It has base 2.

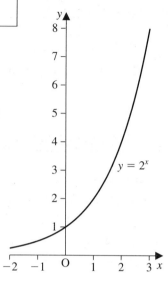

Exercise 2G

1 (a) Draw the graph of $f(x) = 2^x$ for $x \in \{-2, -1, 0, 1, 2, 3\}$. Use 2 mm paper and a scale of 2 cm to 1 unit for x and 2 cm to 5 units for $f(x)$. Join the points with a smooth curve to give the graph of $f(x) = 2^x$ for $x \in \mathbf{R}$.

(b) On the same diagram draw the graph of $g(x) = 3^x$ for x, $-2 \leqslant x \leqslant 3$, $x \in \mathbf{R}$.

(c) Which point lies on the graphs of both $f(x) = 2^x$ and $g(x) = 3^x$?

(d) Which point lies on the graphs of all exponential functions $f(x) = a^x$, $a > 0$? Explain.

2 Draw the graph of $k(x) = 10^x$ for $-2 \leqslant x \leqslant 2$.

3 (a) Use Table 1 to help draw the graph of $f(x) = 2^x$ for $-2 \leqslant x \leqslant 3$.
Use a scale of 1 cm to 1 unit for both axes.
Extend the x-axis to 8 and the y-axis to -3.

(b) On the diagram you have drawn for $f(x) = 2^x$ use Table 2 to help draw the graph of its inverse, $f^{-1}(x)$.

Table 1	
x	$f(x) = 2^x$
-2	$\frac{1}{4}$
-1	$\frac{1}{2}$
0	1
1	2
2	4
3	8

Table 2	
x	$f^{-1}(x)$
$\frac{1}{4}$	-2
$\frac{1}{2}$	-1
1	0
2	1
4	2
8	3

Logarithmic functions

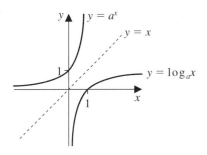

▶ The inverse function of $f(x) = a^x$ is called the
logarithmic function to base a written as $\log_a x$.

▶ If $f(x) = a^x$, then $f^{-1}(x) = \log_a x$.
If $f(x) = \log_a x$, then $f^{-1}(x) = a^x$.

Exercise 2H

1 Sketch the graphs of each pair of functions on the same diagram.
   (a) $g(x) = 3^x$ and $g^{-1}(x) = \log_3 x$.
   (b) $k(x) = 10^x$ and $k^{-1}(x) = \log_{10} x$.

2 On a diagram, with the same scales, draw graphs of $f(x) = 2^x$ and
$g(x) = (\frac{1}{2})^x$ for $-2 \leqslant x \leqslant 3$ and $x \in \mathbf{R}$.

   Hint: $(\frac{1}{2})^x = 2^{-x}$, e.g. $(\frac{1}{2})^3 = \dfrac{1}{2^3} = 2^{-3}$.

Exercise 2I Mixed questions

1 $f(x) = 2x - 1$, $g(x) = 3 - 2x$ and $h(x) = \frac{1}{4}(5 - x)$.
   (a) Find a formula for $k(x)$ where $k(x) = f(g(x))$
   (b) Find a formula for $h(k(x))$.
   (c) What is the connection between the functions h and k?

   [Higher]

2 (a) $f(x) = 4x^2 - 3x + 5$.
   Show that $f(x + 1)$ simplifies to $4x^2 + 5x + 6$ and find a
   similar expression for $f(x - 1)$.
   Hence show that $\frac{1}{2}(f(x + 1) - f(x - 1))$ simplifies to $8x - 3$.

   (b) $g(x) = 2x^2 + 7x - 8$.
   Find an expression for $\frac{1}{2}(g(x + 1) - g(x - 1))$.

   (c) By examining your answers for **(a)** and **(b)** write the
   simplified expression for

   $\frac{1}{2}(h(x + 1) - h(x - 1))$ where $h(x) = 3x^2 + 5x - 1$.   [Higher]

3 The diagram illustrates three
functions f, g and h.
The functions f and g are defined by

$f(x) = 2x + 5$, $g(x) = x^2 - 3$

The function h is such that whenever

$f(p) = q$ and $g(q) = r$ then $h(p) = r$.

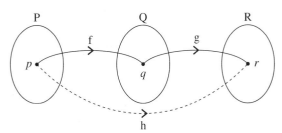

   (a) If $q = 7$ find the values of p and r.
   (b) Find a formula for $h(x)$ in terms of x.   [Higher]

4 Functions f and g, defined on suitable domains, are given by
$f(x) = 2x$ and $g(x) = \sin x + \cos x$.
Find $f(g(x))$ and $g(f(x))$.   [Higher]

5 A function f is defined on the set of real numbers by

$$f(x) = \frac{x}{1-x}.$$

Find, in its simplest form, an expression for $f(f(x))$.   [Higher]

6 On a suitable set of real numbers, functions f and g are defined by

$$f(x) = \frac{1}{x+2} \text{ and } g(x) = \frac{1}{x} - 2.$$

Find $f(g(x))$ in its simplest form.   [Higher]

7 The functions f and g, defined on suitable domains, are given by

$$f(x) = \frac{1}{x^2 - 4} \text{ and } g(x) = 2x + 1.$$

(a) Find an expression for $h(x)$, where $h(x) = g(f(x))$
Give your answer as a single fraction.
(b) State a suitable domain for h.   [Higher]

SUMMARY

① A **function** or mapping from a set A to a set B is a rule that relates
each element in set A to one and only one element in set B.
The set of elements in set A is called the **domain**.
The set of images in set B is called the **range**.

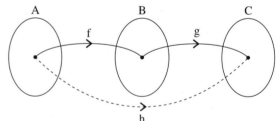

② A composite function can be written
in the form $h(x) = g(f(x))$ and is read
as 'g of f of x'.

③ In general $f(g(x)) \neq g(f(x))$.

④ A function in which the elements of two sets are paired so that
each element of set A corresponds to one element of set B, and
vice versa, is called a **one-to-one correspondence**.

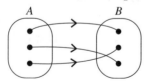

⑤ When a function f is a one-to-one correspondence from set A to
set B, another function, f^{-1}, exists that maps from set B to set A.
This function is called the **inverse** of f.

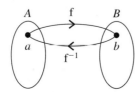

(6) $f^{-1}(f(x)) = f(f^{-1}(x)) = x$

(7) To find the graph of an inverse function reflect the graph of the function in the line $y = x$.

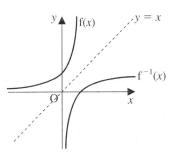

(8) $f(x) = a^x$, $x \in \mathbf{R}$, is called an **exponential function** to base a, $a \in \mathbf{R}$, $a \neq 0$.

(9) The inverse function of $f(x) = a^x$ is called the **logarithmic function** to base a, written as $\log_a x$.

(10) If $f(x) = a^x$, then $f^{-1}(x) = \log_a x$.
   If $f(x) = \log_a x$, then $f^{-1}(x) = a^x$.

3 Graphs of functions

Scientists often carry out experiments to see whether or not two variables are linked, for example, the mass attached to the end of a spring and the length of a spring. Usually they will plot the two variables on a graph to see if there is a relationship. In many cases the graphs have a familiar shape which can be related to a standard graph. Then the relationship between the variables can be found more easily.

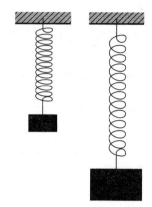

Standard graphs

The aim of this section is to improve your skills in identifying functions from their graphs.

First we will revise some of the graphs met at Standard Grade.

Exercise 3A

1 Pair each function with an appropriately shaped graph.

(a) $y = x$ (b) $y = x^2$ (c) $y = x^3$

(d) $y = \dfrac{1}{x}$ (e) $y = \sqrt{x}$ (f) $y = \sin x^\circ$

(g) $y = \cos x^\circ$ (h) $y = \tan x^\circ$ (i) $y = 2^x$

(i)
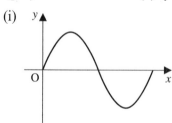

(ii)
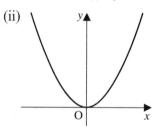

(iii)
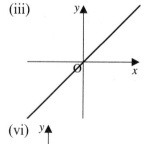

(iv)
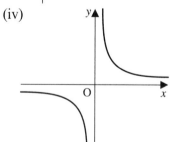

(v)
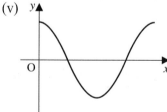

(vi)
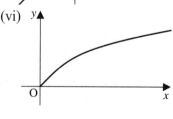

(vii)
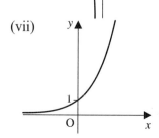

(viii)
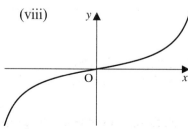

(ix)
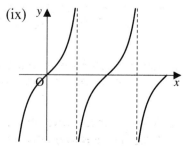

Graphs of $y = f(x) + a$

This exercise will help you find out how to sketch a curve of the form $y = f(x) + a$ from the basic curve, $y = f(x)$.

Exercise 3B

For this exercise, assume that $x \in \mathbf{R}$.

1 (a) Copy and complete:

x	-3	-2	-1	0	1	2	3
$2x$	-6						
$2x + 3$	-3						
$2x - 2$	-8						

(b) On one diagram draw graphs of $y = 2x$, $y = 2x + 3$ and $y = 2x - 2$ for $-3 \leqslant x \leqslant 3$.

2 (a) Copy and complete:

x	-3	-2	-1	0	1	2	3
x^2							
$x^2 + 2$							
$x^2 - 3$							

(b) On one diagram draw graphs of $y = x^2$, $y = x^2 + 2$ and $y = x^2 - 3$ for $-3 \leqslant x \leqslant 3$.

3 (a) Copy and complete:

x	0	30	60	90	...	330	360
$\sin x°$	0	0.5	0.87				
$\sin x° + 2$	2						
$\sin x° - 1$							

(b) On one diagram draw graphs of $y = \sin x°$, $y = \sin x° + 2$ and $y = \sin x° - 1$ for $0 \leqslant x \leqslant 360$.

4 On one diagram sketch graphs of $y = x^3$, $y = x^3 + 10$ and $y = x^3 - 5$, for $-2 \leqslant x \leqslant 2$.

5 On one diagram sketch graphs of $y = -x^2 + 2x$, $y = -x^2 + 2x + 5$ and $y = -x^2 + 2x - 2$, for $-3 \leqslant x \leqslant 3$.

6 Make a conjecture about the relationship between the graphs of $f(x)$, $f(x) + a$ and $f(x) - a$.

Sketching graphs of $y = f(x) + a$

Exercise 3B, shows you that:

To obtain the graph of $y = f(x) + a$,
slide $y = f(x)$ **vertically**
    upwards for $a > 0$
downwards for $a < 0$.

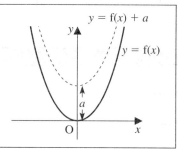

Exercise 3C

1 Describe the transformation of these graphs:

(a) $y = \frac{1}{2}x$ to $y = \frac{1}{2}x + 3$ (b) $y = x^3$ to $y = x^3 + 20$

(c) $y = x^2 - 5x + 6$ to $y = x^2 - 5x + 4$ (d) $y = \sin x°$ to $y = \sin x° + 5$

(e) $y = 10^x$ to $y = 10^x + 2$ (f) $y = f(x)$ to $y = f(x) - b$

(g) $y = x^3 - 6x - 2$ to $y = x^3 - 6x - 3$

2 Part of the graph of $f(x) = x^2 - 2x$ is shown.
  (a) Identify the coordinates of A, B and C.
  (b) Sketch the graph of $y = f(x) + 1$ and state the
     coordinates of the images of A, B and C.

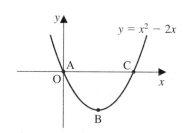

3 Part of the graph of $y = f(x)$ is shown.
  (a) Copy the graph and on the same diagram
     sketch graphs of the related functions $y = f(x) + 1$
     and $y = f(x) - 3$.
  (b) Annotate the sketches with the coordinates
     of both sets of images of A, B, C and D.

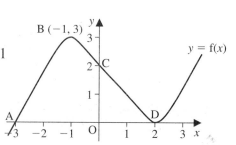

4 Part of the graph of $y = f(x)$ is shown.
  Also shown are the graphs of two
  related functions.
  Find the values of k and n.

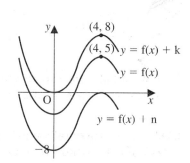

Graphs of $y = f(x + a)$

This exercise will help you find out how to sketch a curve of the form $y = f(x + a)$ from the basic curve, $y = f(x)$.

Exercise 3D

For this exercise, assume that $x \in \mathbf{R}$.

1 (a) Copy and complete:

x	-3	-2	-1	0	1	2
$2x$	-6	-4				
$2(x + 3)$	0	2				
$2(x - 1)$	-8					

(b) On one diagram draw graphs of $y = 2x$, $y = 2(x + 3)$ and $y = 2(x - 1)$ for $-3 \leqslant x \leqslant 2$.

2 (a) Copy and complete:

x	-3	-2	-1	0	1	2	3
x^2							
$(x + 2)^2$							
$(x - 2)^2$							

(b) On one diagram draw graphs of $y = x^2$, $y = (x + 2)^2$ and $y = (x - 2)^2$ for $-3 \leqslant x \leqslant 3$.

3 (a) Copy and complete:

x	0	30	60	90	120	150	$\ldots$	330	360
$\sin x°$	0	0.5	0.87						
$\sin (x + 30)°$	0.5	0.87							
$\sin (x - 60)°$	-0.87	-0.5							

(b) On one diagram draw graphs of $y = \sin x°$, $y = \sin (x + 30)°$ and $y = \sin (x - 60)°$ for $0 \leqslant x \leqslant 360$.

4 On one diagram sketch graphs of $y = x^2$, $y = (x + 3)^2$ and $y = (x - 4)^2$, for $-5 \leqslant x \leqslant 5$.

5 On one diagram sketch graphs of $y = x^3$, $y = (x + 2)^3$ and $y = (x - 3)^3$, for $-4 \leqslant x \leqslant 4$.

6 Make a conjecture about the relationship between the graphs of $f(x)$, $f(x + a)$ and $f(x - a)$.

Sketching graphs of $y = f(x + a)$

Exercise 3D, shows you that:

To obtain the graph of $y = f(x + a)$, **slide** $y = f(x)$ **horizontally** to the left for $a > 0$ to the right for $a < 0$.

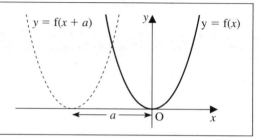

Exercise 3E

1 Describe the transformation of these graphs:

   (a) $y = \frac{1}{4}x$ to $y = \frac{1}{4}(x + 3)$ **(b)** $y = x^3$ to $y = (x - 4)^3$

   (c) $y = \cos x^\circ$ to $y = \cos(x + 15)^\circ$ **(d)** $y = \sqrt{x}$ to $\sqrt{(x - 1)}$

   (e) $y = 5^x$ to $y = 5^{(x+2)}$ **(f)** $y = \tan x^\circ$ to $y = \tan(x - 30)^\circ$

   (g) $y = f(x)$ to $y = f(x + 3)$ **(h)** $y = f(x)$ to $y = f(x - b)$

2 Part of the graph of $f(x) = x^2 + 4x$ is shown.
   (a) Identify the coordinates of A, B and C.
   (b) Sketch the graph of $y = f(x - 5)$ and state the coordinates of the images of A, B and C.

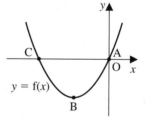

3 Part of the graph of $y = f(x)$ is shown.
   (a) Copy the graph and on the same diagram sketch graphs of the related functions $y = f(x + 4)$ and $y = f(x - 2)$.
   (b) Annotate the sketches with the coordinates of both sets of images of A, B, C and D.

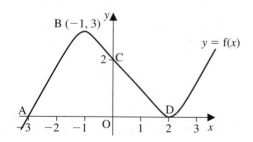

4 Part of the graph of $y = f(x)$ is shown. Also shown are the graphs of two related functions. Find the values of k and n.

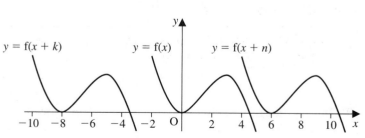

5 *Express $x^2 + 6x + 9$ in the form $(x + p)^2$.
   Hence sketch the graph of $y = x^2 + 6x + 9$.

---

*You can find out more about Completing the square on page 325.

Graphs of $y = -f(x)$

This exercise will help you find out how to sketch a curve of the form $y = -f(x)$ from the basic curve, $y = f(x)$.

Exercise 3F

For this exercise, assume that $x \in \mathbf{R}$.

1 (a) Copy and complete:

x	-3	-2	-1	0	1	2	3
$2x$	-6	-4					
$-2x$	6						

(b) On one diagram draw graphs of $y = 2x$ and $y = -2x$ for $-3 \leqslant x \leqslant 3$.

2 (a) Copy and complete:

x	-3	-2	-1	0	1	2	3
x^2	9						
$-x^2$	-9						

(b) On one diagram draw graphs of $y = x^2$ and $y = -x^2$ for $-3 \leqslant x \leqslant 3$.

3 (a) Copy and complete:

x	0	30	60	90	120	...	330	360
$\sin x°$	0	0.5	0.87					
$-\sin x°$	0	-0.5						

(b) On one diagram draw graphs of $y = \sin x°$ and $y = -\sin x°$ for $0 \leqslant x \leqslant 360$.

4 Sketch the graphs of each pair of functions on one diagram
  (a) $y = x^2 - 2x$ and $y = 2x - x^2$
  (b) $y = x^2 + 2x - 3$ and $y = 3 - 2x - x^2$
  (c) $y = x^3$ and $y = -x^3$
  (d) $y = \cos x°$ and $y = -\cos x°$

5 Make a conjecture about the relationship between the graphs of $f(x)$ and $-f(x)$.

Sketching graphs of $y = -f(x)$

Exercise 3F, shows you that:

> To obtain the graph of $y = -f(x)$, **reflect** $y = f(x)$ **in the x-axis**.

Exercise 3G

1 Sketch the graphs of $y = f(x)$ and $y = -f(x)$ on one diagram.

(a) $f(x) = 3x$ (b) $f(x) = 3x^2 + 2$ (c) $f(x) = -x^2 - 5$

(d) $f(x) = x^3 + 10$ (e) $f(x) = 4^x$ (f) $f(x) = (x + 3)(x - 2)$

2 Part of the graph of $y = f(x)$ is shown.

(a) Copy the graph and on the same diagram sketch the graph of $y = -f(x)$.

(b) Annotate the sketch with the coordinates of the images of A, B, C and D.

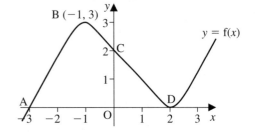

3 Part of the graph of $y = g(x)$ is shown. Copy the graph and on the same diagram sketch the graph of $y = -g(x)$.

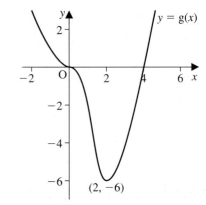

4 Part of the graph of $y = f(x)$ is shown.

(a) Copy the graph and on the same diagram sketch the graph of $y = -f(x) + 2$.

(b) Copy the graph and on the same diagram sketch the graph of $y = -f(x + 2)$.

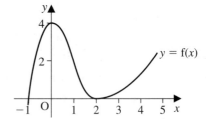

Graphs of $y = f(-x)$

This exercise will help you find out how to sketch a curve of the form $y = f(-x)$ from the basic curve, $y = f(x)$.

Exercise 3H

For this exercise, assume that $x \in \mathbf{R}$.

1 (a) Copy and complete:

x	-3	-2	-1	0	1	2	3
$2x + 3$	-3	-1	1				
$2(-x) + 3$	9	7					

(b) On one diagram draw graphs of $y = 2x + 3$ and $y = -2x + 3$ for $-3 \leqslant x \leqslant 3$.

2 (a) Copy and complete:

x	-4	-3	-2	-1	0	1	2	3	4
$(x+1)(x-3)$	21	12	5						
$(-x+1)(-x-3)$	5	0							

(b) On one diagram draw graphs of $y = (x+1)(x-3)$ and $y = (-x+1)(-x-3)$ for $-4 \leqslant x \leqslant 4$.

3 (a) Copy and complete:

x	-3	-2	-1	0	1	2	3
$(2+x)(1+x)$							
$(2-x)(1-x)$							

(b) On one diagram draw graphs of $y = (2+x)(1+x)$ and $y = (2-x)(1-x)$ for $-3 \leqslant x \leqslant 3$.

4 Sketch the graphs of each pair of functions on one diagram
  (a) $y = x$ and $y = -x$
  (b) $y = -3x + 1$ and $y = 3x + 1$
  (c) $y = x^2 + 4x + 4$ and $y = (-x)^2 + 4(-x) + 4$
  (d) $y = x^2 + 6x + 5$ and $y = x^2 - 6x + 5$

5 Make a conjecture about the relationship between the graphs of $f(x)$ and $f(-x)$.

Sketching graphs of $y = f(-x)$

Exercise 3H, shows you that:

> ▶ To obtain the graph of $y = f(-x)$, **reflect** $y = f(x)$ **in the y-axis**.

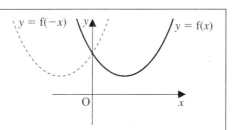

Exercise 3I

1 Sketch the graphs of $y = f(x)$ and $y = f(-x)$ on one diagram.
  (a) $f(x) = 2x + 5$ **(b)** $f(x) = (x-1)^2$ **(c)** $f(x) = x^3$
  (d) $f(x) = \sin x°$ **(e)** $f(x) = 3^x$ **(f)** $f(x) = \cos x°$

2 Part of the graph of $y = f(x)$ is shown.
  (a) Copy the graph and on the same diagram sketch the graph of the related function $y = f(-x)$.
  (b) Annotate the sketch with the coordinates of the images of A, B, C and D.

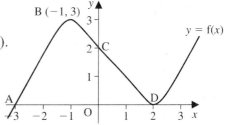

3 Sketch the graph of $y = \sin x°$ for $0 \leqslant x \leqslant 360$, $x \in \mathbf{R}$, and on the same diagram sketch the graph of $y = \sin(-x)°$.

4 Part of the graph of $y = h(x)$ is shown.
   (a) Copy the graph and on the same diagram sketch the graph of the related function $y = h(-x)$.
   (b) Annotate the sketch with the coordinates of the images of A, B, C and D.

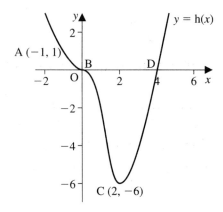

5 (a) Sketch the graph of $y = 2^x$ and on the same diagram the graph of $y = \left(\frac{1}{2}\right)^x$ (hint: $\frac{1}{2} = 2^{-1}$).
   (b) Make a statement about the relationship between the graphs of $y = a^x$ and $y = \left(\frac{1}{a}\right)^x$.

Graphs of $y = kf(x)$

This exercise will help you find out how to sketch a graph of the form $y = kf(x)$ from the basic curve, $y = f(x)$.

Exercise 3J

For this exercise, assume that $x \in \mathbf{R}$.

1 (a) Copy and complete:

x	-3	-2	-1	0	1	2	3
$x^2 - 3$	6	1					
$2(x^2 - 3)$	12	2					
$3(x^2 - 3)$	18	3					

   (b) On one diagram draw graphs of $y = x^2 - 3$, $y = 2(x^2 - 3)$ and $y = 3(x^2 - 3)$ for $-3 \leqslant x \leqslant 3$.

2 (a) Copy and complete:

x	-1	0	1	2	3	4	5
$x^2 - 4x + 3$	8	3					
$3(x^2 - 4x + 3)$	24	9					

   (b) On one diagram draw graphs of $y = x^2 - 4x + 3$ and $y = 3(x^2 - 4x + 3)$ for $-1 \leqslant x \leqslant 5$.

3 (a) Copy and complete:

x	0	30	60	90	120	$\ldots$	330	360
$\sin x°$	0	0.5	0.87					
$2\sin x°$	0	1.0	1.74					

(b) On one diagram draw graphs of $y = \sin x°$ and $y = 2\sin x°$ for $0 \leqslant x \leqslant 360$.

4 On one diagram sketch graphs of $y = (x+1)(x+5)$ and $y = 2(x+1)(x+5)$ for $-7 \leqslant x \leqslant 1$.

5 On one diagram sketch graphs of $y = \cos x°$ and $y = 3\cos x°$.

6 Make a conjecture about the relationship between the graphs of $f(x)$ and $kf(x)$.

Sketching graphs of $y = k\mathbf{f}(x)$

Exercise 3J, shows you that:

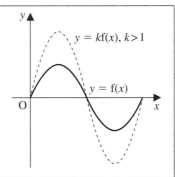

To obtain the graph of $y = kf(x)$, **stretch or compress** $y = f(x)$ **vertically** by a factor of k:

  stretch for $k > 1$
  compress for $k < 1$.

Exercise 3K

1 Copy each graph and, on the same diagram, sketch the graph of the given related function.
Annotate the sketches with the coordinates of the images of A, B, C, D and E.

(a) $y = 3f(x)$

(b) $y = \frac{1}{2}f(x)$

(c) $y = 2f(x)$

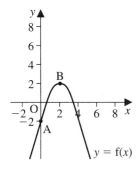

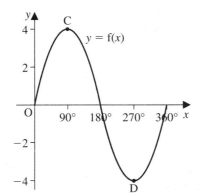

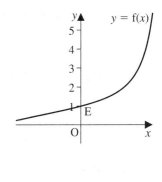

Graphs of $y = f(kx)$

This exercise will help you find out how to sketch a graph of the form $y = f(kx)$ from the basic curve, $y = f(x)$.

Exercise 3L

For this exercise, assume that $x \in \mathbf{R}$.

1 (a) Copy and complete:

x	-3	-2	-1	0	1	2	3
$x^2 - 4$	5	0					
$(2x)^2 - 4$	32	12					

(b) On one diagram draw graphs of $y = x^2 - 4$ and $y = 4x^2 - 4$ for $-3 \leqslant x \leqslant 3$.

2 (a) Copy and complete:

x	-1	0	1	2	3	4	5
$x^2 - 4x$	5	0					
$(2x)^2 - 4(2x)$	12	0					

(b) On one diagram draw graphs of $y = x^2 - 4x$ and $y = 4x^2 - 8x$ for $-1 \leqslant x \leqslant 5$.

3 (a) Copy and complete:

x	0	30	60	90	120	$\ldots$	330	360
$\cos x^\circ$	1	0.87	0.5					
$\cos (2x)^\circ$	1	0.5	-0.5					

(b) On one diagram draw graphs of $y = \cos x^\circ$ and $y = \cos (2x)^\circ$ for $0 \leqslant x \leqslant 360$.

4 On one diagram sketch graphs of $y = 8 - 2x - x^2$ and $y = 8 - 4x - 4x^2$ for $-6 \leqslant x \leqslant 4$.
(Note that $y = 8 - 4x - 4x^2$ can be written as $y = 8 - 2(2x) - (2x)^2$.)

5 On one diagram draw graphs of $y = \sin x^\circ$ and $y = \sin 2x^\circ$ for $0 \leqslant x \leqslant 360$.

6 Make a conjecture about the relationship between the graphs of $y = f(x)$ and $y = f(kx)$.

Sketching graphs of $y = f(kx)$

Exercise 3K, shows you that:

> To obtain the graph of $y = f(kx)$, **stretch** or **compress** $y = f(x)$ **horizontally** by a factor of k:
>
> ▶   compress for $k > 1$
>   stretch for $k < 1$.

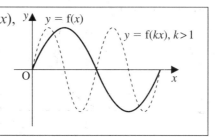

Exercise 3M

1 Copy each graph and, on the same diagram, sketch the graph of the given related function.
Annotate the sketches with the coordinates of the images of A, B, C and D.

(a) $y = f(3x)$ **(b)** $y = f(5x)$ **(c)** $y = f\left(\dfrac{x}{2}\right)$

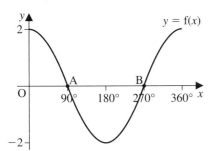
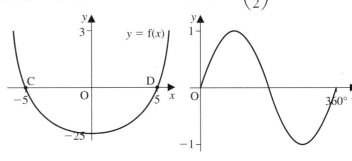

Graphs of related exponential functions

The equation of an exponential function can be determined from two points on its graph.

Example 1

Part of the graph of $y = a^x + b$ is shown.
Find the values of a and b.

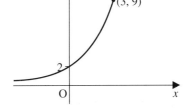

Since $(0, 2)$ lies on the curve then

$$2 = a^0 + b$$
$$= 1 + b$$

so $b = 1$

$(3, 9)$ also lies on the curve hence

$$9 = a^3 + b$$
$$9 = a^3 + 1$$
$$a^3 = 8$$

so $a = 2$

Hence $y = 2^x + 1$

Exercise 3N

1 Find the value of a in the following:

  (i)   (ii)

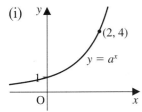
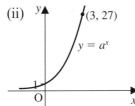

2 Use the graphs in question 1 to help sketch the graphs of

    (a) $y = 2^x - 1$ **(b)** $y = 3^x + 1$

3 Find the value of a and b in the following:

(i)
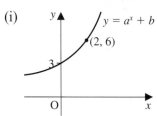

(ii)
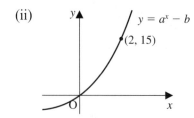

(iii)
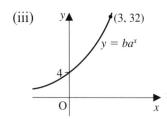

(iv)
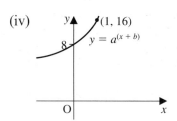

4 Sketch the graph of each function showing the y intercept and the coordinates of one other point.

    (a) $y = 2^x + 4$ **(b)** $y = 3^x - 2$ **(c)** $y = 3^{(x-2)}$ **(d)** $y = 2^{(x+3)}$

Graphs of logarithmic functions

For the exponential function $y = 3^x$, since $y = 1$ when $x = 0$ and $y = 3$ when $x = 1$ then $(0, 1)$ and $(1, 3)$ lie on the graph of $y = 3^x$.

The inverse function, $y = \log_3 x$, is a reflection of $y = 3^x$ in the line $y = x$.

Hence $(1, 0)$ and $(3, 1)$ lie on the graph of $y = \log_3 x$, so $\log_3 1 = 0$ and $\log_3 3 = 1$.
In general, since $a^0 = 1$ and $a^1 = a$ then:
$\log_a 1 = 0$ and $\log_a a = 1$.

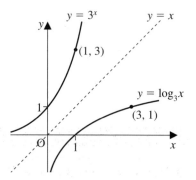

Example 2

Part of the graph of $y = \log_a x$ is shown.
Find the value of a.

Since $y = 1$ when $x = 5$, $1 = \log_a 5$
so $a = 5$, since $\log_5 5 = 1$.
Hence $y = \log_5 x$.

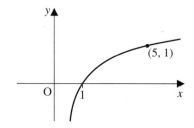

Exercise 3O

1 Find the value of a in each function.

(i)

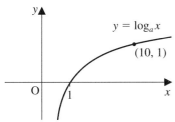

(ii)

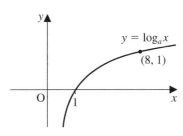

2 (a) Sketch the graph of the function $y = \log_5 x$, showing the coordinates of two points that lie on the curve.
(b) On the same diagram sketch $y = \log_5 x + 1$.
(c) On the same diagram sketch $y = \log_5(x - 4)$.

3 Each sketch shows part of a logarithmic function. Find the value of k in each case.

(a)

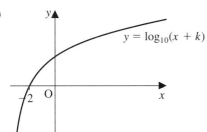

(b)

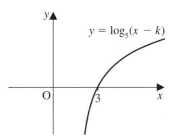

(c)

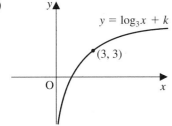

Exercise 3P Mixed questions

1 Part of the graph of $y = f(x)$ is shown. On separate diagrams sketch the graphs of

(a) $y = f(-x)$ **(b)** $y = -f(x)$
(c) $y = f(x) + 2$ **(d)** $y = f(-x) + 2$

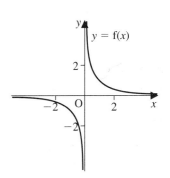

2 The graph of a quadratic function is shown. On separate diagrams sketch the graphs of

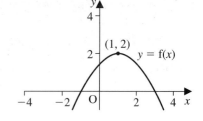

(a) $y = f(x) - 2$ **(b)** $y = f(x - 2)$

(c) $y = -f(x)$ **(d)** $y = f(-x)$

(e) $y = 3 - f(x)$

3 The graph of $y = a^x$, $a > 0$, is shown. Draw separate sketches to show the graphs of

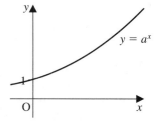

(a) $y = -a^x$ **(b)** $y = a^x - 1$

[Higher]

4 The graph of $y = f(x)$ is shown. On separate diagrams sketch the graphs of

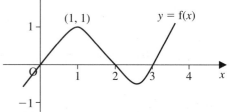

(a) $y = f(x) + 1$ **(b)** $y = f(x + 1)$

(c) $y = -f(x) + 1$ **(d)** $y = -f(x + 2)$

5 The graph of $y = f(x)$ is shown. On separate diagrams sketch the graphs of

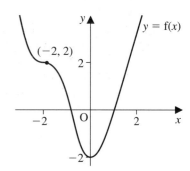

(a) $y = f(x) - 2$ **(b)** $y = 2f(x)$

(c) $y = f(2x)$ **(d)** $y = -2f(x)$

6 Part of the graph of $y = f(x)$ is shown in the diagram. On separate diagrams, sketch the graphs of

(i) $y = f(x - 1)$ **(ii)** $y = -f(x) - 2$

indicating on each graph the images of A, B, C and D.

[Higher]

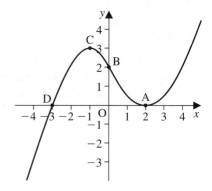

7 The sketch shows the graph of $y = f(x)$ for $-2 \leqslant x \leqslant 4$.
The function $g(x)$ has the line $x = 4$ as an axis of symmetry
and $g(x) = f(x)$ for $-2 \leqslant x \leqslant 4$. On separate sketches, indicate
(a) $y = g(x)$ for $-2 \leqslant x \leqslant 10$
(b) $y = -2g(x)$ for $0 \leqslant x \leqslant 8$ [Higher]

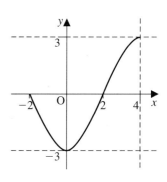

8 The diagram shows the graph of $y = f(x)$.

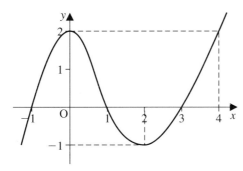

Sketch the graph of $y = 2 - f(x)$.   [Higher]

9 The first diagram shows a sketch of part of the
graph of $y = f(x)$ where $f(x) = (x - 2)^2 + 1$.
The graph cuts the y-axis at A and has a
minimum turning point at B.
(a) Write the coordinates of A and B.
(b) The second diagram shows the graph of $y = f(x)$
and $y = g(x)$ where $g(x) = 5 + 4x - x^2$. $g(x)$ can
be written in the form $m + n \times f(x)$ where m and
n are constants. Write the values of m and n.
                [Higher]

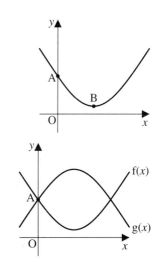

10 The diagram shows a sketch of the graphs of the quadratic
functions $y = f(x)$ and $y = -f(x + \frac{1}{2})$.
(a) If $f(x)$ has a stationary value of $(1, 0)$ find $f(x)$.
(b) Find the coordinates of the point A where the
graph of $y = -f(x + \frac{1}{2})$ cuts the y-axis.   [Higher]

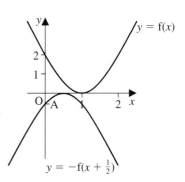

11 Pairs of graphs of related functions are shown. For each, give the
function represented by the dashed curve.

(a)
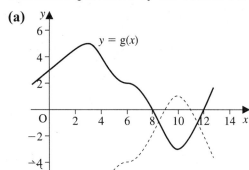

(b)
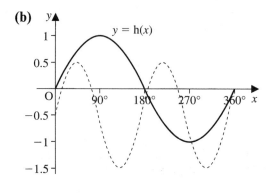

(c)
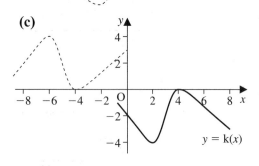

(d)
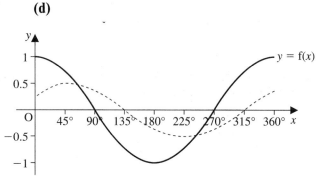

12 Make a copy of this graph of $y = \log_{10} x$. On your copy,
sketch the graph of $y = \log_{10}(x - 2)$.

[Higher]

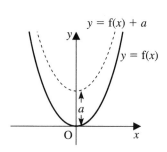

SUMMARY

① To obtain the graph of $y = f(x) + a$,
   slide $y = f(x)$ vertically

   upwards for $a > 0$
   downwards for $a < 0$.

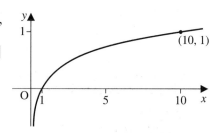

② To obtain the graph of $y = f(x + a)$,
   slide $y = f(x)$ horizontally

   to the left for $a > 0$
   to the right for $a < 0$.

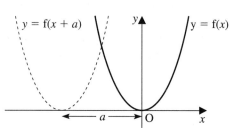

③ To obtain the graph of $y = -f(x)$, **reflect** $y = f(x)$ **in the x-axis**.

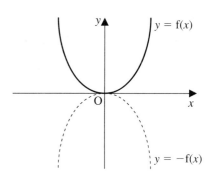

④ To obtain the graph of $y = f(-x)$, **reflect** $y = f(x)$ **in the y-axis**.

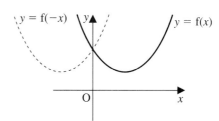

⑤ To obtain the graph of $y = kf(x)$, **stretch** or **compress** $y = f(x)$ **vertically** by a factor of k:

    stretch for $k > 1$
compress for $k < 1$.

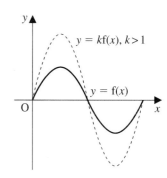

⑥ To obtain the graph of $y = f(kx)$, **stretch** or **compress** $y = f(x)$ **horizontally** by a factor of k:

compress for $k > 1$
    stretch for $k < 1$.

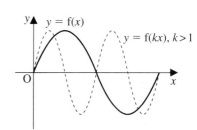

4 Trigonometry: graphs and equations

Many experiments, such as the motion of a simple pendulum, produce a trigonometric graph.

In this unit you will learn the general features of trigonometric graphs.
You will need to use these features to solve problems involving trigonometry.

*Motion of a
simple pendulum*

Period and amplitude

▶ A graph which consists of a repeated pattern is described as **periodic**.

The graphs shown below are of **periodic functions**:

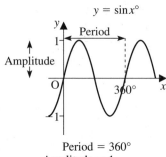

Period = 360°
Amplitude = 1

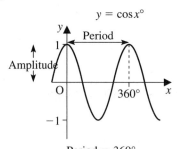

Period = 360°
Amplitude = 1

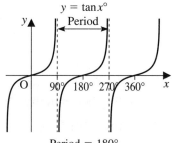

Period = 180°
Amplitude cannot be measured

▶ The horizontal extent of the basic pattern is called the **period**.
Half of the vertical extent is called the **amplitude**.

Example 1

Find the period and amplitude of the function $y = 3 \sin 4x° - 2$ which is shown in the diagram.

Since the wave pattern is repeated 4 times in 360°, the period

$$= \frac{360°}{4} = 90°$$

The graph of $y = 3 \sin 4x° - 2$ is stretched by a factor of 3 vertically.
Since the vertical extent is 6 units, the amplitude is 3.

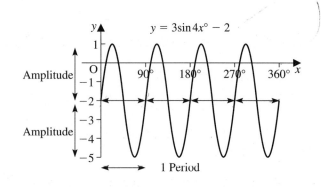

Exercise 4A

1 For each function state (i) the period and (ii) the amplitude, where it exists.

(a)
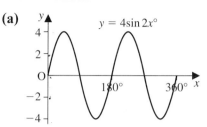
$y = 4\sin 2x°$

(b)
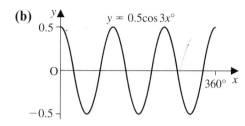
$y = 0.5\cos 3x°$

(c)
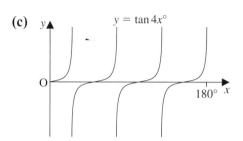
$y = \tan 4x°$

(d)
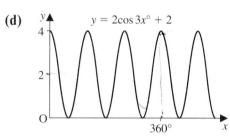
$y = 2\cos 3x° + 2$

(e)
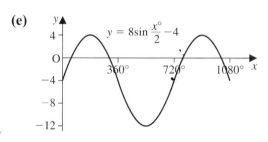
$y = 8\sin \dfrac{x°}{2} - 4$

(f)
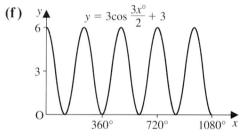
$y = 3\cos \dfrac{3x°}{2} + 3$

2 For the functions $y = p\sin qx°$ and $y = p\cos qx°$, use your answers from question 1 to state the relationship between
(a) p and the amplitude of the function
(b) q and the period of the function.

3 For each function state (i) the period and (ii) the amplitude, where it exists.

(a) $y = 4\sin x°$ **(b)** $y = \cos 3x° + 1$ **(c)** $y = \tan 2x°$

(d) $y = 5\cos 2x° - 3$ **(e)** $y = 4\sin \dfrac{x°}{3}$ **(f)** $y = 0.5\sin \dfrac{x°}{4} + 1$

Graphs of trigonometric functions

Exercise 4A shows you that:

> For $y = a\sin bx°$ and $y = a\cos bx°$
>
> Amplitude $= a$ and period $= \dfrac{360°}{b}$
>
> For $y = a\tan bx°$
>
> Amplitude cannot be measured, period $= \dfrac{180°}{b}$

We often need to sketch graphs of trigonometric functions to help us solve problems.

This example is a reminder of the techniques learnt in Chapter 3, Graphs of functions.

Example 2

Sketch the graph of $y = 2\sin 3x° + 1 \ (0 \leqslant x \leqslant 360)$.

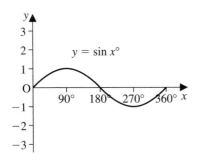

Step 1
Start with the graph of $y = \sin x°$.

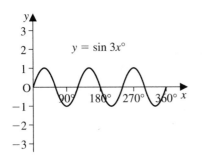

Step 2
Squeeze horizontally
by a factor of $\frac{1}{3}$.

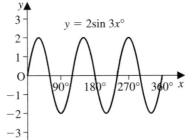

Step 3
Stretch vertically
by a factor of 2.

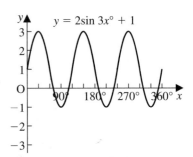

Step 4
Slide vertically
1 unit upwards.

Exercise 4B

For this exercise, assume that $x \in \mathbf{R}$.

1 Sketch and annotate the graph of each of the following functions:

   ✓ **(a)** $y = 3\sin 2x° + 1 \ (0 \leqslant x \leqslant 360)$ ✓**(b)** $y = 2\cos 4x° \ (0 \leqslant x \leqslant 360)$

   ✓ **(c)** $y = 4\cos 3x° - 2 \ (0 \leqslant x \leqslant 360)$ ✓**(d)** $y = 4\sin \dfrac{x°}{2} - 1 \ (0 \leqslant x \leqslant 720)$

   ✓ **(e)** $y = \cos 3x° + 1 \ (0 \leqslant x \leqslant 360)$ ✓**(f)** $y = 4\cos(x - 90)° \ (0 \leqslant x \leqslant 360)$

✓ **2** Sketch and annotate the graph of each function:

   ✓ **(a)** $y = \sin(x - 30)° + 4 \ (0 \leqslant x \leqslant 360)$ ✓**(b)** $y = \cos(x - 45)° - 1 \ (0 \leqslant x \leqslant 360)$

   ✓ **(c)** $y = 2\cos(x + 30)° + 1 \ (0 \leqslant x \leqslant 360)$ ✓ **(d)** $y = 3\sin(x + 60)° - 2 \ (0 \leqslant x \leqslant 360)$

   ✓ **(e)** $y = \sin(x + 45)° \ (0 \leqslant x \leqslant 360)$

3 Write a trigonometric function represented by each graph.

(a)

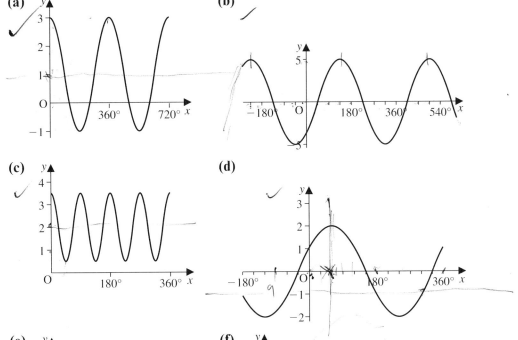

(b)

(c)

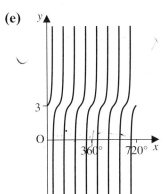

(d)

(e)

(f)

4 The graph of the function $y = 4\sin(x - 60)°$ is shown. Find the values of a, b, c and d.

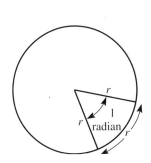

$y = 4\sin(x - 60)°$

Radians

Degrees are not the only units used to measure angles. It is often useful to measure angles in radians.

The following construction defines a radian:
- Draw a large circle.
- Measure the radius.
- Mark an arc, with the same length as the radius, on the circumference.
- Join each end of the arc to the centre of the circle.

> The angle subtended at the centre of a circle by an arc equal in length to the radius is **1 radian**.

To find the relationship between degrees and radians, consider the circumference of a circle.

Complete circumference $= 2\pi r$.

So the radius will fit on the circumference 2π times.

So there are 2π radians in a complete turn.

A complete revolution is 2π radians so $360° = 2\pi$ radians.

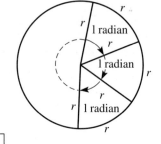

> π radians $= 180°$

This relationship can be used to convert between degrees and radians using proportion.

Note: Angles are measured in radians unless the degree sign (°) is shown.

Example 3

Convert $120°$ to radians.

Degrees	Radians
180°	π
60°	$\dfrac{\pi}{3}$
120°	$\dfrac{2\pi}{3}$

Example 4

Convert $\dfrac{5\pi}{9}$ radians to degrees.

Radians	Degrees
π	180°
$\dfrac{\pi}{9}$	20°
$\dfrac{5\pi}{9}$	100°

Exercise 4C

1 Convert to radians
  (a) $90°$ **(b)** $60°$ **(c)** $225°$ **(d)** $330°$ **(e)** $160°$

2 Convert to degrees
  (a) $\dfrac{\pi}{3}$ radians **(b)** $\dfrac{\pi}{4}$ radians **(c)** $\dfrac{4\pi}{3}$ radians **(d)** $\dfrac{5\pi}{6}$ radians **(e)** $\dfrac{9\pi}{5}$ radians

3 Evaluate
  (a) $\sin\dfrac{\pi}{6}$ **(b)** $\cos\dfrac{5\pi}{6}$ **(c)** $\tan\dfrac{\pi}{4}$ **(d)** $\cos\dfrac{2\pi}{3}$

4 (a) Sketch the graph of $y = \sin x$ for $0 \leqslant x \leqslant 2\pi$, $x \in \mathbf{R}$.
  (b) State the coordinates of the maximum and minimum turning points.

5 Identify a trigonometric function represented by each graph.

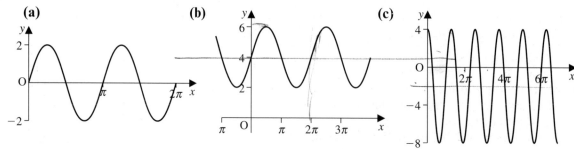

Special angles and triangles

It is useful to know the exact values of common trigonometric ratios
such as $\sin 60°$, $\cos 30°$, etc., because exact values allow us to
calculate accurate answers to problems. To find these exact values,
we examine the angles in an equilateral triangle.

Triangle DHG is equilateral with each side
2 units long.
HM is an axis of symmetry of the triangle
and therefore it bisects DG at right angles.

Using Pythagoras' theorem:

$HM^2 = HD^2 - DM^2$

$HM = \sqrt{2^2 - 1^2} = \sqrt{3}$ units

$\sin 60° = \dfrac{HM}{DH} = \dfrac{\sqrt{3}}{2}$

The **exact** value of $\sin 60°$ is $\dfrac{\sqrt{3}}{2}$.

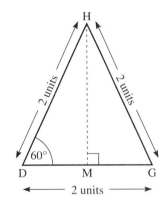

Exercise 4D

1 From the diagram above find the **exact** value of
  (a) $\cos 60°$ **(b)** $\tan 60°$

2 (a) What is the size of angle DHM in the diagram above?
  (b) Write the **exact** value of
    (i) $\sin 30°$ (ii) $\cos 30°$ (iii) $\tan 30°$

3 Triangle RLW is a right-angled isosceles triangle with LW and
  RW of length 1 unit.
  (a) What is the size of angle LRW?
  (b) Use Pythagoras' theorem to calculate the length of LR.
  (c) Write the **exact** value of
    (i) $\sin 45°$ (ii) $\cos 45°$ (iii) $\tan 45°$

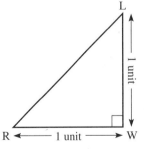

4 Triangle ABC is right-angled at B. Angle BAC is $x°$ and can be
  varied.

  (a) If x is reduced towards 0 and the length of AB is kept
    constant, what happens to the length of
    (i) BC   (ii) AC?
  (b) As x approaches 0 write what happens to the value of
    (i) $\sin x°$ (ii) $\cos x°$ (iii) $\tan x°$
  (c) Write down the value of
    (i) $\sin 0°$ (ii) $\cos 0°$ (iii) $\tan 0°$

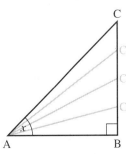

5 Triangle FGH is right-angled at H. Angle FGH is $x°$
and can be varied.

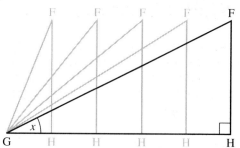

  (a) If x is increased towards 90 and the length
     of FH is kept constant, what happens to the
     length of
     (i) GH   (ii) GF?

  (b) As x approaches 90 write down what
     happens to the value of
     (i) $\sin x°$ (ii) $\cos x°$ (iii) $\tan x°$

  (c) Write down the value of
     (i) $\sin 90°$ (ii) $\cos 90°$

Using exact values

Using the results obtained in Exercise 4D, we can complete a table
of **exact** values of the trigonometric ratios.

	$0°$	$30°$	$45°$	$60°$	$90°$
	0	$\dfrac{\pi}{6}$	$\dfrac{\pi}{4}$	$\dfrac{\pi}{3}$	$\dfrac{\pi}{2}$
sin	0	$\dfrac{1}{2}$	$\dfrac{1}{\sqrt{2}}$	$\dfrac{\sqrt{3}}{2}$	1
cos	1	$\dfrac{\sqrt{3}}{2}$	$\dfrac{1}{\sqrt{2}}$	$\dfrac{1}{2}$	0
tan	0	$\dfrac{1}{\sqrt{3}}$	1	$\sqrt{3}$	undefined

We can use these exact values to solve trigonometrical problems. In
doing this you should remember the following relationships:

$$\frac{\pi}{2}$$
$$(90°)$$

2nd quadrant   1st quadrant
Sine positive   *All positive*

$\pi(180°)$ ————————————————— $(0°)0$

Tangent positive   *Cosine positive*
3rd quadrant   4th quadrant

$$(270°)$$
$$\frac{3\pi}{2}$$

Angles are normally measured **anticlockwise** from 0.

Negative angles are measured **clockwise** from 0.

In order to find an exact value, first rewrite an angle in terms of its
associated acute angle.

Example 5
What is the exact value of

(a) $\sin 300°$

(b) $\cos(-135)°$

(c) $\tan\dfrac{11\pi}{4}$

(a)

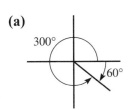

$\sin 300° = -\sin 60°$

$= -\dfrac{\sqrt{3}}{2}$

(b)

225°   45°

$-135°$

$\cos(-135)° = \cos 225°$

$= -\cos 45°$

$= -\dfrac{1}{\sqrt{2}}$

(c)

$\dfrac{11\pi}{4}$

$\dfrac{\pi}{4}$

$\tan\dfrac{11\pi}{4} = \tan\dfrac{3\pi}{4}$

$= \tan\dfrac{\pi}{4}$

$= -1$

Example 6
Calculate the **exact** length of the side marked x in the triangle below.

$\sin 60° = \dfrac{x}{10}$

$x = 10\sin 60°$

$= 10 \times \dfrac{\sqrt{3}}{2}$

$= 5\sqrt{3}\,\text{m}$

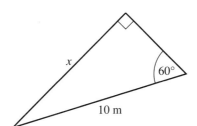

60°

10 m

Exercise 4E

1 Find the **exact** value of

(a) $\sin 135°$ **(b)** $\tan 210°$ **(c)** $\cos\dfrac{5\pi}{4}$ **(d)** $\tan\dfrac{2\pi}{3}$ **(e)** $\cos 240°$

(f) $\cos(-120°)$ **(g)** $\tan(-135°)$ **(h)** $\sin\left(-\dfrac{\pi}{6}\right)$ **(i)** $\cos\left(-\dfrac{2\pi}{3}\right)$ **(j)** $\tan\left(-\dfrac{7\pi}{6}\right)$

(k) $\sin\dfrac{9\pi}{4}$ **(l)** $\cos\dfrac{11\pi}{3}$ **(m)** $\sin(-480°)$ **(n)** $\tan 675°$ **(o)** $\cos\left(-\dfrac{25\pi}{6}\right)$

2 Find, in its simplest form, the **exact** value of

(a) $2\sin 150° \cos 300°$

(b) $\sin^2 210° + \cos^2 330°$

(c) $\cos^2\dfrac{4\pi}{3} - \sin^2\dfrac{4\pi}{3}$

(d) $\dfrac{1}{\sin\dfrac{7\pi}{4}}$

3 Calculate the **exact** length of the side marked x in each triangle.

(a)

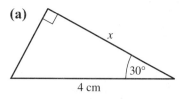

(b)

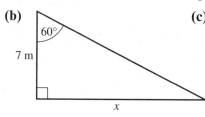

(c)

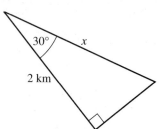

4 Triangle ABC is right-angled at B and BD is an altitude.
  (a) Calculate the exact length of
      (i) BD   (ii) AD
      (iii) DC   (iv) AC
      (v) BC
  (b) Show that
      (i) $BD^2 = AD \times DC$
      (ii) $AB^2 = AD \times AC$
      (iii) $BC^2 = AC \times DC$

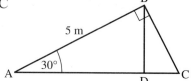

Solving problems using exact values

We can use exact values to solve more complex problems. It is usually helpful to sketch a diagram to illustrate the trigonometry of the problem.

Example 7

An oil tanker is sailing north. At 0115 hours a lighthouse is due east of the tanker. By 0230 hours the lighthouse is 10 km from the tanker on a bearing of 150°. Calculate the exact speed of the tanker.

On the diagram, L is the position of the lighthouse, T_1 is the position of the tanker at 0115 hours and T_2 is the position of the tanker at 0230 hours.

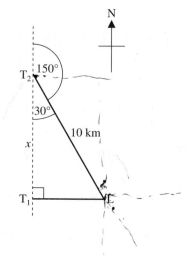

In right-angled triangle T_1T_2L

$$\cos 30° = \frac{x}{10}$$

$$x = 10 \cos 30°$$

$$= 10 \frac{\sqrt{3}}{2}$$

$$= 5\sqrt{3} \text{ km}$$

$$\text{Speed} = \frac{\text{Distance}}{\text{Time}} = \frac{5\sqrt{3}}{1\frac{1}{4}} = \frac{5\sqrt{3}}{\frac{5}{4}} = 5\sqrt{3} \times \frac{4}{5} = 4\sqrt{3} \text{ km/hour.}$$

The exact speed of the tanker is $4\sqrt{3}$ km/hour.

Exercise 4F

1 Two boats, *Lively Lady* and *Saucy Sue*, leave port at the same time. *Lively Lady* sails due west at a speed of 5 km/hour and *Saucy Sue* sails on a bearing of 210°. After 4 hours *Saucy Sue* is due south of *Lively Lady*. Calculate the exact value of
  (a) the distance between the two boats after 4 hours' sailing
  (b) *Saucy Sue*'s speed.

2 A house is 9 m wide and 12 m long. The roof space is a triangular prism and the rafters make angles of 60° and 30° with the horizontal.
  Calculate the exact values of
  (a) the lengths of the rafters
  (b) the cross-sectional area of the roof space
  (c) the volume of the roof space.

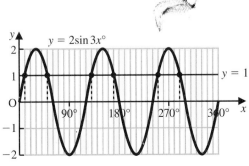

3 A plot of land, ABCD, is shown in the diagram. Calculate the exact value of
  (a) the length of the diagonal BD
  (b) the area of triangle ABD
  (c) the length of AB.

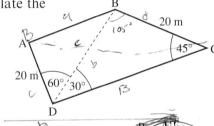

4 Part of a reciprocating engine is shown in the diagram. As the crank, PC, rotates about C the slide, S, moves along a horizontal shaft SC. PC is 1 m long.
  (a) Calculate the exact length of the connecting rod, PS, if angle PSC is 30° when angle PCS is 45°.
  (b) Calculate the distance from S to C when angle SPC is 90°.
  (c) Calculate the size of angle SCP when SC is $\frac{1}{2}(\sqrt{5}-1)$ m.

Graphical solution of equations

To solve an equation of the type $f(x) = g(x)$ graphically we need to sketch both functions and identify the x-coordinate of the point(s) of intersection. Because trigonometric functions are periodic there are often multiple answers.

Example 8
Solve $2 \sin 3x° = 1 \, (0 \leqslant x \leqslant 360)$ for x.

In this example $f(x) = 2 \sin 3x°$ and $g(x) = 1$.
First, we draw the graphs of $y = 2 \sin 3x°$ and $y = 1$, from $x = 0°$ to 360°, on the same diagram.

The graphs intersect when $2 \sin 3x° = 1$.

So the solutions are $x° = 10°, 50°, 130°, 170°, 250°$ and $290°$.

Example 9

Solve $4\cos\dfrac{x}{3} = 0 \ (0 \leqslant x \leqslant 2\pi)$

Draw the graph of $y = 4\cos\dfrac{x}{3}$ between $x = 0$ and 2π radians.

The graph cuts the x-axis where $4\cos\dfrac{x}{3} = 0$.

So the solution is $x = 1.5\pi = \dfrac{3\pi}{2}$ radians.

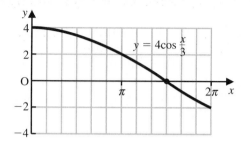

Exercise 4G

1 Use the graph in Example 8 to solve
  (a) $2\sin 3x° = -1 \ \ (0 \leqslant x \leqslant 360)$
  (c) $2\sin 3x° = 2 \ \ (0 \leqslant x \leqslant 360)$
  (b) $2\sin 3x° = 0 \ \ (0 \leqslant x \leqslant 360)$
  (d) $2\sin 3x° = -2 \ \ (0 \leqslant x \leqslant 360)$

2 Use the graph in Example 9 to solve
  (a) $4\cos\dfrac{x}{3} = 4 \ \ (0 \leqslant x \leqslant 2\pi)$
  (b) $4\cos\dfrac{x}{3} = 2 \ \ (0 \leqslant x \leqslant 2\pi)$

  (c) $4\cos\dfrac{x}{3} = -2 \ \ (0 \leqslant x \leqslant 2\pi)$
  (d) $4\cos\dfrac{x}{3} = -4 \ \ (0 \leqslant x \leqslant 2\pi)$

3 Solve
  (a) $\sin 3x° = 1 \ \ (0 \leqslant x \leqslant 180)$
  (b) $2\sin 3x° = -1 \ \ (-180 \leqslant x \leqslant 0)$
  (c) $4\cos\dfrac{x}{3} = 2 \ \ (0 \leqslant x \leqslant 4\pi)$

4 Solve graphically
  (a) $\sin 2x° = 0.5 \ \ (0 \leqslant x \leqslant 180)$
  (b) $2\cos x = \sqrt{3} \ \ (-\pi \leqslant x \leqslant \pi)$

  (c) $\tan 2\theta = 1 \ \ (0 \leqslant \theta \leqslant 2\pi)$
  (d) $6\sin\dfrac{x}{2} - 1 = 2 \ \left(-\dfrac{\pi}{4} \leqslant x \leqslant \dfrac{\pi}{2}\right)$

5 The graph shows the depth, d m, of water in a harbour t hours after midnight. The depth of water can be modelled approximately by the function $d = \cos 30t° + 1$.
  (a) From the graph find the value of a.
  (b) At what times are high and low tide?
  (c) A boat anchored in the harbour has a draught of 1.5 m. Between which hours will it be afloat?

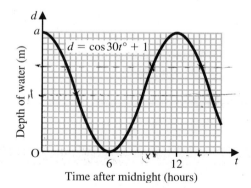

6 Solve graphically:
  (a) $\sin 3x° = 0.2 \ \ (0 \leqslant x \leqslant 180)$
  (b) $3\cos 2x = 0.65 \ \ (-\pi \leqslant x \leqslant \pi)$

  (c) $2\tan t° - 3 = 0 \ \ (0 \leqslant t \leqslant 720)$
  (d) $0.3\cos\dfrac{x}{6} + 0.14 = 0 \ \ (-\pi \leqslant x \leqslant 2\pi)$

Algebraic solution of equations

A more accurate solution of trigonometric equations can be achieved using algebraic methods.

Example 10

Solve for x, $2\sin 4x° + \sqrt{3} = 0$ for $0 \leqslant x \leqslant 180$.

$$2\sin 4x° + \sqrt{3} = 0$$
$$2\sin 4x° = -\sqrt{3}$$
$$\sin 4x° = -\frac{\sqrt{3}}{2}$$

Since $\sin 4x°$ is negative there will be solutions in the third and fourth quadrants.

Also since $0 \leqslant x \leqslant 180$ then $0 \leqslant 4x \leqslant 720$.

The associated acute angle is $\sin^{-1}\frac{\sqrt{3}}{2} = 60°$

In the third quadrant, $4x° = 240°$
In the fourth quadrant, $4x° = 300°$
There are further solutions at $(240 + 360)°$ and $(300 + 360)°$

So $4x° = 240°$ or $300°$ or $600°$ or $660°$
$\quad x° = 60°$ or $75°$ or $150°$ or $165°$

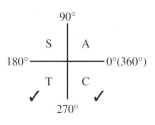

Example 11

Solve $\tan^2 x° = 3$ $(0 \leqslant x \leqslant 360)$

$$\tan^2 x° = 3$$
$$\tan x° = \pm\sqrt{3}$$

When $\tan x° = +\sqrt{3}$ then $x° = 60°$ or $240°$
When $\tan x° = -\sqrt{3}$ then $x° = 120°$ or $300°$
$x° = 60°, 120°, 240°, 300°$

$\tan x° = \sqrt{3}$ has solutions in the first and third quadrants.

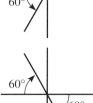

$\tan x° = -\sqrt{3}$ has solutions in the second and fourth quadrants.

Example 12

Solve $3\sin^2 x° - 4\sin x° + 1 = 0$ $(0 \leqslant x \leqslant 360)$

$(3\sin x° - 1)(\sin x° - 1) = 0$
$3\sin x° - 1 = 0$ or $\sin x° - 1 = 0$
$\sin x° = \frac{1}{3}$ $\qquad$ or $\sin x° = 1$
$x° = 19.5°, 160.5°$ or $\quad x° = 90°$
$x° = 19.5°, 90°, 160.5°$

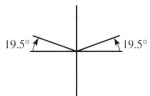

$\sin x° = \frac{1}{3}$ has solutions in the first and second quadrants.
$\sin^{-1}\frac{1}{3} = 19.5°$

Exercise 4H

1 Solve

(a) $\sqrt{3}\tan x° = 1$ $(0 \leqslant x \leqslant 360)$

(b) $\sqrt{2}\cos x° - 1 = 0$ $(0 \leqslant x \leqslant 180)$

(c) $4 = 5 - \tan 2x$ $(0 \leqslant x \leqslant \pi)$

(d) $2\cos 3x° + 1 = 0$ $(0 \leqslant x \leqslant 360)$

(e) $1 - \sqrt{2}\sin 6t = 0$ $(0 \leqslant t \leqslant \pi)$

(f) $4\tan 3z° + 4 = 0$ $(0 \leqslant z \leqslant 90)$

2 Solve

(a) $\sin^2 x° - 1 = 0$ $(0 \leqslant x \leqslant 360)$

(b) $3 \tan^2 x° - 1 = 0$ $(0 \leqslant x \leqslant 360)$

(c) $2 \cos^2 x = 1$ $(0 \leqslant x \leqslant 2\pi)$

(d) $4 \sin^2 x° - 1 = 0$ $(0 \leqslant x \leqslant 360)$

3 Solve

(a) $\sin x° = 0.92$ $(0 \leqslant x \leqslant 360)$

(b) $2 \tan x° = 1.36$ $(0 \leqslant x \leqslant 720)$

(c) $3 \cos x° + 1 = 0.766$ $(0 \leqslant x \leqslant 540)$

(d) $5 \cos x - 2 = -0.72$ $(0 \leqslant x \leqslant 2\pi)$

(e) $4 \sin t + 2 = -0.35$ $(0 \leqslant t \leqslant 4\pi)$

(f) $1 - \tan z° = -0.53$ $(0 \leqslant z \leqslant 540)$

4 Solve

(a) $5 \sin 2x° = 2.5$ $(0 \leqslant x \leqslant 360)$

(b) $10 \cos 3x° = 9.6$ $(0 \leqslant x \leqslant 360)$

5 Use factorisation when solving

(a) $\tan^2 x° + \tan x° = 0$ $(0 \leqslant x \leqslant 360)$

(b) $8 \sin^2 x° + 2 \sin x° - 3 = 0$ $(0 \leqslant x \leqslant 360)$

(c) $6 \sin^2 x + \sin x - 1 = 0$ $(0 \leqslant x \leqslant 2\pi)$

(d) $12 \cos^2 x - 5 \cos x - 2 = 0$ $(0 \leqslant x \leqslant \pi)$

Algebraic solution of compound angle equations

Algebraic solutions of trigonometric equations can be extended to problems involving compound angles such as $(3x + 45)°$, $(2x - 30)°$, etc.

Example 13

Solve for x, $4 \tan (3x + 45)° = -2.5$, $0 \leqslant x \leqslant 180$

$$4 \tan (3x + 45)° = -2.5$$
$$\tan (3x + 45)° = -0.625$$

Since $\tan (3x + 45)°$ is negative there are solutions in the second and fourth quadrants.

Also since $0 \leqslant x \leqslant 180$ then $45 \leqslant 3x + 45 \leqslant 585$

The associated acute angle is $\tan^{-1} 0.625 = 32°$
In the second quadrant, $(3x + 45)° = 180° - 32° = 148°$
In the fourth quadrant, $(3x + 45)° = 360° - 32° = 328°$
Another solution in the range is $(3x + 45)° = 148° + 360° = 508°$
So $3x° + 45° = 148°$ or $328°$ or $508°$
and $\qquad x° = 34.3°$ or $94.3°$ or $154.3°$

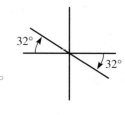

Example 14

Solve algebraically $2 \sin \left(2x - \dfrac{\pi}{3} \right) = 1$, $0 \leqslant x \leqslant 2\pi$

$$2 \sin \left(2x - \frac{\pi}{3} \right) = 1$$

$$\sin \left(2x - \frac{\pi}{3} \right) = \frac{1}{2}$$

Since $\sin \left(2x - \dfrac{\pi}{3} \right)$ is positive there are solutions in the first and second quadrants.

Also since $0 \leqslant x \leqslant 2\pi$ then $-\dfrac{\pi}{3} \leqslant 2x - \dfrac{\pi}{3} \leqslant \dfrac{13\pi}{3}$

The associated acute angle is $\sin^{-1}\dfrac{1}{2} = \dfrac{\pi}{6}$

so $2x - \dfrac{\pi}{3} = \dfrac{\pi}{6}$ or $\dfrac{5\pi}{6}$ or $\left(\dfrac{\pi}{6} + 2\pi\right)$ or $\left(\dfrac{5\pi}{6} + 2\pi\right)$

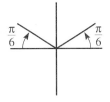

$2x = \dfrac{3\pi}{6}$ or $\dfrac{7\pi}{6}$ or $\dfrac{15\pi}{6}$ or $\dfrac{19\pi}{6}$

$x = \dfrac{\pi}{4}$ or $\dfrac{7\pi}{12}$ or $\dfrac{15\pi}{12}$ or $\dfrac{19\pi}{12}$

Exercise 4I

1 Solve for x where $0 \leqslant x \leqslant 360$
  (a) $2\cos(x + 60)^\circ = \sqrt{3}$ **(b)** $5\sin(2x - 20)^\circ = 3$

2 Solve for x where $0 \leqslant x \leqslant 2\pi$
  (a) $3\tan\left(2x + \dfrac{\pi}{2}\right) = 3$ **(b)** $2\cos\left(2x - \dfrac{\pi}{4}\right) = 1$

3 Solve
  (a) $8\tan(x + 30)^\circ = 3.5$ $(0 \leqslant x \leqslant 360)$
  (b) $3\cos(x - 45)^\circ = 2.7$ $(0 \leqslant x \leqslant 180)$
  (c) $\sin(2t + 60)^\circ = 0.5$ $(0 \leqslant t \leqslant 180)$
  (d) $5\cos(6r - 20)^\circ + 3 = 7.25$ $(0 \leqslant r \leqslant 90)$

4 A ball is attached to the end of a piece of elastic and allowed to bounce up and down.
  At time t seconds the distance of the ball from its support, h metres, is $h = 4\cos 12t^\circ + 3$. At what times between $t = 0$ and $t = 90$ will

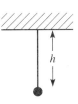

  (a) $h = 2.5$ and
  (b) $h = 3.75$?

Exercise 4J Mixed questions

1 For each function (i) state its period, (ii) state its amplitude and (iii) sketch its graph.
  (a) $y = 3\cos 5x^\circ + 1$ $(0 \leqslant x \leqslant 90)$
  (b) $y = \frac{1}{2}\sin 2x^\circ$ $(0 \leqslant x \leqslant 360)$

2 For each graph (i) state its period, (ii) state its amplitude if it exists and (iii) write down its function.

(a)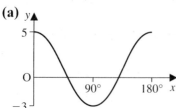

(b)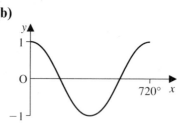

(c)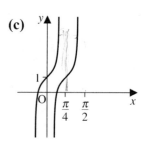

3 Convert to degrees

(a) $\dfrac{3\pi}{8}$ radians   **(b)** $\dfrac{7\pi}{6}$ radians   **(c)** $\dfrac{12\pi}{5}$ radians

4 Convert to radians

(a) $270°$ **(b)** $150°$ **(c)** $315°$

5 Write the **exact** value of

(a) $\sin 315°$ **(b)** $\tan \dfrac{7\pi}{6}$ **(c)** $\cos(-150)°$

6 Find, in its simplest form, the **exact** value of

(a) $\cos^2 210° - \sin^2 30°$ **(b)** $\sin \dfrac{\pi}{3} \sin \dfrac{5\pi}{4}$ **(c)** $1 - 2\sin^2 300°$

7 The diagram shows a sketch of the graph

of $y = \sin\left(2x - \dfrac{\pi}{6}\right)$, $0 \leqslant x \leqslant \pi$, and the

straight line $y = 0.5$.
These graphs intersect at P and Q.
Find algebraically the coordinates
of P and Q.   [Higher]

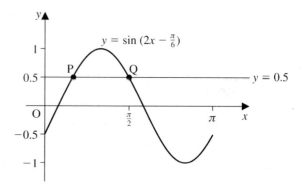

8 Use the graph to solve
  (a) $3\sin 4x° = 2$ $(0 \leqslant x \leqslant 180)$
  (b) $1 - 3\sin 4x° = 0$ $(0 \leqslant x \leqslant 90)$
  (c) $3\sin 4x° - 2 = 1$ $(0 \leqslant x \leqslant 180)$

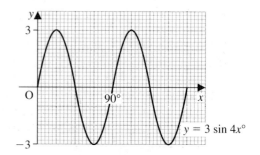

9 Solve

  (a) $\sin 3x° = 0.32 \quad (0 \leqslant x \leqslant 90)$

  (b) $4\tan(6\theta - 120)° = -3 \quad (0 \leqslant \theta \leqslant 180)$

  (c) $2 + 3\cos(4t - 30)° = 5 \quad (0 \leqslant t \leqslant 90)$

  (d) $8\cos\left(2\phi + \dfrac{\pi}{6}\right) + 3 = 2 \quad (0 \leqslant \phi \leqslant \pi)$

  (e) $4\sin^2 x = 1 \quad (0 \leqslant x \leqslant 2\pi)$

  (f) $1 - 3\tan^2 x° = 0 \quad (0 \leqslant x \leqslant 180)$

  (g) $2\cos^2 t° - 3\cos t° + 1 = 0 \quad (0 \leqslant t \leqslant 360)$

  (h) $4\sin^2 z° + 4\sin z° - 3 = 0 \quad (0 \leqslant z \leqslant 360)$

10 The diagram opposite shows the graph of a sine function from $0°$ to $90°$.

  (a) State the equation of the graph.

  (b) The line with equation $y = -1.5$ intersects the curve at A and B. Find the coordinates of A and B.

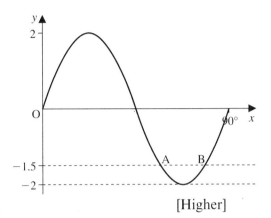

[Higher]

11 The sketch represents part of the graph of a trigonometric function of the form $y = p\sin(x + r)° + q$. It crosses the axes at $(0, s)$ and $(t, 0)$ and has turning points at $(50, -2)$ and $(u, 4)$.

  (a) Write down values of p, q, r and u

  (b) Find the values for s and t.   [Higher]

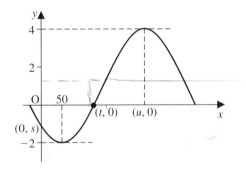

12 The minimum depth, d ft, of water in a harbour t hours after midnight can be approximated by the function
$d(t) = 35 + 15\cos 0.5t$ where $0 \leqslant t \leqslant 24$.

  (a) A ship with a draught of 25 ft is in harbour at midnight. By what time must it leave to prevent grounding?

  (b) What is the next time it can return to the harbour?

13 The alarm in a noisy factory is a siren whose volume, θ decibels, fluctuates so that at time t minutes after starting it is given by the function $\theta(t) = 20\sin 6t + 70$. The average noise level in the factory is $\theta = 75$.

  (a) What are the maximum and minimum volumes of the siren?

  (b) For what percentage of each cycle is the alarm siren audible over the background factory noise?

  (c) New regulations are introduced whereby the siren must be audible over the background noise for 45% of the time it is sounding. What value of the amplitude of θ would allow this regulation to be met?

14 The Water Board of a local authority discovered it was able to represent the approximate amount of water $W(t)$, in millions of gallons, stored in a reservoir t months after 1st May 1988 by the formula

$$W(t) = 1.1 - \sin\frac{\pi t}{6}$$

The board then predicted that under normal conditions this formula would apply for three years.

(a) Draw and label sketches of the graphs of $y = \sin\dfrac{\pi t}{6}$ and $y = -\sin\dfrac{\pi t}{6}$, for $0 \leqslant t \leqslant 36$ on the same diagram.

(b) On a separate diagram and using the same scale on the t-axis as you used in part (a), draw a sketch of the graph of
$$W(t) = 1.1 - \sin\frac{\pi t}{6}.$$

(c) On the 1st April 1990 a serious fire required an extra $\frac{1}{4}$ million gallons of water from the reservoir to bring the fire under control.
Assuming that the previous trend continues from the new lower level, when will the reservoir run dry if water rationing is not imposed? [Higher]

SUMMARY

(1) A graph which consists of a repeated pattern is described as **periodic**.

(2) The horizontal extent of the basic pattern is called the **period**. Half of the vertical extent is called the **amplitude**.

(3) For $y = a \sin bx°$ and $y = a \cos bx°$

Amplitude $= a$ and period $= \dfrac{360°}{b}$

For $y = a \tan bx°$

Amplitude cannot be measured, period $= \dfrac{180°}{b}$

(4) The angle subtended at the centre of a circle by an arc equal in length to the radius is **1 radian**.

(5) π radians $= 180°$

(6)

	0°	30°	45°	60°	90°
	0	$\dfrac{\pi}{6}$	$\dfrac{\pi}{4}$	$\dfrac{\pi}{3}$	$\dfrac{\pi}{2}$
sin	0	$\dfrac{1}{2}$	$\dfrac{1}{\sqrt{2}}$	$\dfrac{\sqrt{3}}{2}$	1
cos	1	$\dfrac{\sqrt{3}}{2}$	$\dfrac{1}{\sqrt{2}}$	$\dfrac{1}{2}$	0
tan	0	$\dfrac{1}{\sqrt{3}}$	1	$\sqrt{3}$	undefined

5 Recurrence relations

Recurring problems

This bacteria population doubles in size every 20 minutes.
How many bacteria will there be in 24 hours' time?

This chapter shows you how to use algebra to solve problems like this quickly.

First try to solve these problems without the help of algebra.

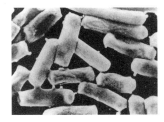

Clostridium botulinum
produces the most deadly known toxin and is usually caught from canned fish.

Exercise 5A

1 £1000 is invested at an interest rate of 5% per annum.
  (a) What is the value of the investment after 4 years?
  (b) After how many years will the investment be worth £1500?

2 Under laboratory conditions a population of bacteria grows at a rate of 15% per day. At the start of the first day of an experiment the initial population was 100.
  (a) What is the size of the population after 3 days?
  (b) How long will it take for the population to double in size?

3 A health report states that the level of certain harmful gases in the atmosphere should be no more than 110 units. The environmental health department has recorded a level of 150 units of harmful gases in High Street. They plan to reduce this level by 5% per annum.
  (a) How many years will it take to reduce the gases to a safe level?
  (b) If the reduction was 8% per annum, how long would it take to reduce the gases to a safe level?

4 At the beginning of 1998 the population of Ethiopia was 56 million. At that time, the rate of population increase was 3% per annum. If this rate remains constant, what will the population be at the start of the year 2003?

5 An oil tanker has run aground and spilled 25 000 tonnes of oil. It is estimated that the natural action of the sea can reduce the amount of oil by 40% per week.
  (a) How long will it take the natural action of the sea to reduce the amount of oil to less than 1000 tonnes?
  (b) After how many more weeks will the amount of oil be reduced to less than 100 tonnes?

Using recurrence relations to solve problems

To answer question 1 on page 69, you probably generated a
sequence of numbers like this:

| Start value | First year | Second year | Third year | Fourth year | |
| 1000 | 1050 | 1102.50 | 1157.625 | 1215.50625 | ... |

Each number in the sequence is called a term.
You can use algebra to represent the terms like this:

| $u_0 = 1000$ | $u_1 = 1050$ | $u_2 = 1102.50$ | $u_3 = 1157.625$ | $u_4 = 1215.50625$ | ... |

Notice that if you label the starting value u_0 then the 1st term is u_1,
the 2nd is u_2, the 3rd is u_3 and the 4th is u_4.

In general, the nth term is u_n.

In the above example, notice that each term is 5% greater than the
one before it, so

$u_1 = 1.05u_0$, $u_2 = 1.05u_1$, $u_3 = 1.05u_2$, $u_4 = 1.05u_3$, and so on.

In general, $u_{n+1} = 1.05u_n$.

This pattern is called a **recurrence relation** because the pattern $1.05u_n$
recurs.

> A recurrence relation describes a sequence in which each term
> is a function of previous terms.

Example 1
The value of an endowment policy increases at a rate of 6% per
annum. If the initial value of the policy is £8000, find a recurrence
relation for the value of the policy.
Use this to calculate the value after 4 years.

Each term will be 6% greater than the one before it therefore the
recurrence relation is $u_{n+1} = 1.06u_n$. We know that $u_0 = 8000$ so

$u_1 = 1.06 \times 8000 \qquad = 8480$
$u_2 = 1.06 \times 8480 \qquad = 8988.80$
$u_3 = 1.06 \times 8988.80 \quad = 9528.128$
$u_4 = 1.06 \times 9528.128 = 10\,099.81568$

The value of the endowment policy after 4 years is £10 099.82.

Exercise 5B

1 The value of a house appreciates by 3% per annum. Its value at
the beginning of 1999 was £150 000.
   (a) Find a recurrence relation for the value of the house.
   (b) Calculate the expected value of the house at the beginning of
   the year 2006.

2 An art dealer bought a painting for £2.5 million at the beginning of 1998. She expects the value to rise by 5% per annum.
   (a) Find a recurrence relation for the value of the painting.
   (b) Calculate the expected value of the painting at the beginning of the year 2003.

3 The value of a car depreciates by 20% per annum. Its value at the beginning of 1999 was £12 000.
   (a) Find a recurrence relation for the value of the car.
   (b) Calculate the expected value of the car at the beginning of the year 2002.

4 It is estimated that a strain of flu will infect 5% of healthy people per week if no treatment is given.
   (a) Each week, what percentage of people remains healthy?
   (b) Find a recurrence relation for the number of healthy people.
   (c) For a population of 5000 people, how many will still be healthy after 3 weeks?
   (d) How long will it take for half the initial population to become infected?

More complex recurrence relations

We can also use recurrence relations to solve problems involving constant terms as well as variable terms.

Example 2
A patient is injected with 160 ml of a drug. Every 6 hours 25% of the drug passes out of her bloodstream. To compensate, a further 20 ml dose is given every 6 hours.

(a) Find a recurrence relation for the amount of drug in the bloodstream.
(b) Use your answer to calculate the amount of drug remaining after 24 hours.

Initial dose, $u_0 = 160$ ml. Every six hours 25% leaves the bloodstream therefore 75% remains and a further 20 ml dose is added.

(a) The recurrence relation is

$$u_{n+1} = 0.75u_n + 20, \quad \text{and} \quad u_0 = 160\text{ ml}.$$

(b) 20 ml of the drug is injected every 6 hours so after 24 hours four injections will have been made:

$u_1 = 0.75 \times 160 + 20 \quad = 140$
$u_2 = 0.75 \times 140 + 20 \quad = 125$
$u_3 = 0.75 \times 125 + 20 \quad = 113.75$
$u_4 = 0.75 \times 113.75 + 20 = 105.3125$

The amount of drug remaining in the bloodstream after 24 hours is 105 ml (to the nearest ml).

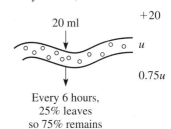
Every 6 hours, 20 ml is added
20 ml +20
u
0.75u
Every 6 hours, 25% leaves so 75% remains

Exercise 5C

1 A family have taken out a mortgage for £50 000 on a house. The interest charged on this sum is 6.5% per annum. They have agreed to pay back £4500 each year. How much will the family owe after
   (a) 3 years   **(b)** 5 years?

2 An industrial complex has requested permission to dump 40 units per week of chemical waste into a sea loch. It is estimated that the natural action of the sea will remove 20% of the waste per week. How many units of chemical waste will there be in the loch after
   (a) 2 weeks   **(b)** 4 weeks?

3 A warehouse restocks by ordering 5% of the existing stock at the beginning of each month. During each month 1000 items are distributed from the warehouse. If the existing stock is 5000 items, will the warehouse ever run out of stock?

4 Sea lice are affecting the salmon on a fish farm. It is estimated that each year 40% of the population will die if no cure can be found. Each year the farm is restocked with 100 salmon. If the original salmon population was 400 find the remaining population after
   (a) 2 years   **(b)** 5 years

5 Tom is given £50 on his thirteenth birthday and £25 on each birthday after. He invests each of these gifts in a building society which pays interest at a rate of 4% per annum.
   (a) Find a recurrence relation for the amount in his building society.
   (b) Calculate the expected balance in the account on his eighteenth birthday.

6 A car designer has calculated that petrol evaporates from a tank at a rate of 5% per week. The tank was initially filled with 35 litres of petrol. If she adds 1.5 litres each week
   (a) find a recurrence relation for the volume of petrol in the tank
   (b) calculate the volume of petrol in the tank after 5 weeks.

7 The air pressure in the front tyre of a mountain bike was 50 p.s.i. Each week 15% of the air pressure was lost but then air was pumped in to raise the pressure by 2 p.s.i. The manufacturer recommends that the air pressure within the tyre should not drop below 30 p.s.i.
   (a) Find a recurrence relation for the air pressure in the tyre.
   (b) Calculate the air pressure in the tyre after 3 weeks.
   (c) Does the pressure ever fall below the manufacturer's recommendation?

8 The population of mice at a breeding centre rises at a rate of 8% per month. Each month 100 mice are sold to pet shops. The initial population was 500.
   (a) Find a recurrence relation for the number of mice at the centre.
   (b) How many mice are there in the centre after 4 months?
   (c) How long will it take before the centre runs out of mice?

9 A job advertisement offers a starting salary of £25 000 with an annual percentage increase of 4% plus an annual increment of £2000.
   (a) Find a recurrence relation for the total annual salary.
   (b) Calculate the expected salary 8 years after starting.

10 Each day during July 50 kg of Tayberries ripen. Fruit pickers estimate that 80% of ripe fruit is picked daily. The estimated weight of ripe fruit on 1st July 1998 was 3000 kg.
   (a) Find a recurrence relation for the weight of ripe fruit.
   (b) What is the estimated weight of ripe fruit available on 9th July?

11 A second-hand car depreciates in value by 16% each year. A mechanic estimates that he can increase the value of a car by £250 with routine maintenance. If a car's value in August 1999 was £8000, calculate its estimated value in August 2005.

Linear recurrence relations

A sequence defined by:

▶ $u_{n+1} = au_n + b, \ a \neq 0$

is called a **linear recurrence relation**.

Notice that $u_{n+1} = au_n + b$ has the same form as the equation of a straight line, i.e. $y = mx + c$.

Example 3

A sequence is defined by the recurrence relation $u_{n+1} = 0.6u_n + 5$, $u_0 = 8$.

Calculate the value of u_3 and find the smallest value of n for which $u_n > 12$.

$u_{n+1} = 0.6u_n + 5$, $u_0 = 8$
  $u_1 = 0.6 \times 8 + 5$ $= 9.8$
  $u_2 = 0.6 \times 9.8 + 5$ $= 10.88$
  $u_3 = 0.6 \times 10.88 + 5$ $= 11.528$
  $u_4 = 0.6 \times 11.528 + 5$ $= 11.9168$
  $u_5 = 0.6 \times 11.9168 + 5$ $= 12.15008$, which is greater than 12

$u_3 = 11.528$ and $n = 5$ for $u_n > 12$.

Exercise 5D

1 For each recurrence relation find u_3.
   (a) $u_{n+1} = 0.25u_n + 6, \ u_0 = 3$ (b) $u_{n+1} = 0.5u_n - 15, \ u_0 = 10$
   (c) $u_{n+1} = 2u_n + 100, \ u_0 = -4$ (d) $u_{n+1} = -2u_n + 7, \ u_0 = 4$
   (e) $u_{n+1} = -u_n + 5, \ u_0 = 1$ (f) $u_{n+1} = -0.4u_n - 20, \ u_0 = -1$

2 A sequence is defined by the recurrence relation
   $u_{n+1} = 0.25u_n + 6, \ u_0 = 100$.
   (a) Calculate the value of u_3.
   (b) Find the smallest value of n for which $u_n < 9$.

3 A sequence is defined by the recurrence relation
   $u_{n+1} = 1.5u_n + 10, \ u_0 = 100$.
   (a) Calculate the value of u_4.
   (b) Find the smallest value of n for which $u_n > 1000$.
   (c) How many terms of this sequence lie between 1000 and 2000?

4 A sequence is defined by the recurrence relation
$u_n = 0.9u_{n-1} + 360$, $u_0 = 2$.
  (a) Calculate the value of u_2.
  (b) Find the smallest value of n for which $u_n > 1500$.
  (c) If $u_0 = 1$, find the smallest value of n for which $u_n > 1500$.

5 A sequence is defined by the recurrence relation
$u_n = 1.1u_{n-1} - 20$, $u_1 = 100$.
  (a) Calculate the value of u_5.
  (b) Find the smallest value of n for which
      (i) $u_n < 0$ (ii) $u_n < -50$.

Investigating long-term effects

In this section you will investigate what happens when a linear recurrence relation is extended to include a large number of terms.

Example 4
An industrial complex has requested permission to dump 50 units per week of chemical waste into a sea loch. It is estimated that the natural action of the sea will remove 40% of waste per week. What is the long-term effect in terms of waste residue?

Let u_n be the number of units of waste in the loch after n weeks.

$u_0 = 0$ and $u_{n+1} = 0.6u_n + 50$

$u_0 = 0$,	$u_1 = 50$,	$u_2 = 80$, $u_3 = 98$
$u_4 = 108.8$,	$u_5 = 115.28$,	$u_6 = 119.168\ldots$,

$u_{15} = 124.941\,226\,9$, $u_{16} = 124.964\,736\,1$, $u_{17} = 124.978\,841\,7$

The waste seems to be approaching a limit of 125 units therefore the long-term effect will be a residue of 125 units of waste in the sea loch.

Exercise 5E

1 Assuming an initial level of waste of 0 units, and that 50 units are dumped each week, investigate the long-term effect if the rate of removal of waste is:
  (a) 30%   **(b)** 50%   **(c)** 60%

2 Assuming an initial level of waste of 0 units and a removal rate of 40% per week, investigate the long-term effect if the amount of waste dumped weekly is:
  (a) 25 units   **(b)** 100 units   **(c)** 200 units

3 Assuming a removal of 40% per week, and that 50 units are dumped weekly, investigate the long-term effect if the initial level of waste is:
  (a) 100 units   **(b)** 200 units   **(c)** 125 units

Example 5

A family has a mortgage of £60 000. The interest is charged at 8% per annum. They repay £7000 each year. What happens to the loan over time?

Let u_n be the outstanding loan after n years.

$u_{n+1} = 1.08u_n - 7000$ and $u_0 = 60000$

$u_0 = 60000,$ $u_1 = 57800,$ $u_2 = 54424,$

$u_3 = 52857.92,$ $u_4 = 50086.55,$ $u_5 = 47093.48\ldots,$

$\ldots,$ $u_{15} = 265.35,$ $u_{16} = -6713.42$

The value of the loan changes from positive to negative during the 16th year so it must have been paid back during the 16th year.

Exercise 5F

1 Assuming a mortgage of £60 000 and repayments of £7000 per annum, investigate the long-term effect on the loan if the interest rate is:
   (a) 2%   **(b)** 5%   **(c)** 15%

2 Assuming a mortgage of £60 000 and an interest rate of 8% per annum, investigate the long-term effect on the loan if the annual repayment is:
   (a) £15 000   **(b)** £10 000   **(c)** £4000

3 Assuming an interest rate of 8% per annum and repayments of £7000 per annum, investigate the long-term effect if the mortgage is:
   (a) £30 000   **(b)** £50 000   **(c)** £150 000

Convergence and divergence

You can plot sequences graphically to show up patterns.
For example, if we plot graphs for the pollution and mortgage problems in Exercises 5E and 5F, two quite different patterns emerge.

The graphs for the pollution problems show sequences that are convergent, i.e. the sequences approach a particular value called the limit. We sometimes call this 'tending to a limit':

Pollution problem

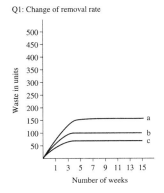

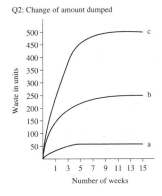

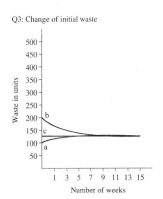

The graphs for questions 1 and 2 show sequences that tend to different limits. The graph for question 3 shows a sequence that tends to the same limit from different starting values.

The graphs for the mortgage problems show sequences that diverge, i.e. they do not tend to a limit:

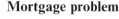

Mortgage problem

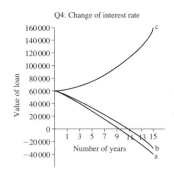
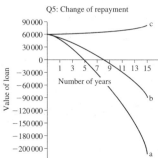
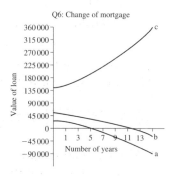

Investigating $u_{n+1} = au_n + b$

You can tell whether a sequence will converge or diverge from its recurrence relation.

The following questions will help you find out how.

Exercise 5G

1 (a) Investigate the long-term effect of altering a in the recurrence relation $u_{n+1} = au_n + 1$, with $u_0 = 2$ for the following values of a:

    (i) 3   (ii) 2   (iii) 1   (iv) 0.5   (v) 0.25
    (vi) 0.1   (vii) -0.1 (viii) -0.8 (ix) -1 (x) -2

(b) Make a conjecture.
(c) Test your conjecture.

2 (a) Investigate the long-term effect of altering b in the recurrence relation $u_{n+1} = 0.2u_n + b$, with $u_0 = 1$ for the following values of b:

    (i) -2 (ii) -1 (iii) -0.5 (iv) 0.5
    (v) 1   (vi) 2   (vii) 3   (viii) 4

(b) Make a conjecture.
(c) Test your conjecture.

3 (a) Investigate the long-term effect of altering u_0 in the recurrence relation $u_{n+1} = 0.2u_n + 4$ for the following values of u_0:

    (i) 100   (ii) 50   (iii) 2   (iv) 1
    (v) 0.5   (vi) -0.5 (vii) -1 (viii) -25

(b) Make a conjecture.
(c) Test your conjecture.

The limit of a recurrence relation

Exercise 5G shows you that:

> For linear recurrence relation $u_{n+1} = au_n + b$:
>
> if $-1 < a < 1$ then u_n tends to a limit.
>
> if u_n tends to a limit, L, then $L = \dfrac{b}{1-a}$

Proof

If a limit L exists then we can write $\lim_{n \to \infty} u_n = L$ and therefore L is the limit of the sequence u_n as n becomes very large.

Since $\lim_{n \to \infty} u_n = L$, then $\lim_{n \to \infty} u_{n+1} = L$, therefore

$$u_{n+1} = au_n + b$$

becomes

$$L = aL + b$$

$$L - aL = b$$

$$(1-a)L = b$$

$$L = \frac{b}{1-a}$$

Example 6

Find the first six terms and the limit of the recurrence relation $u_{n+1} = 0.6u_n + 12$ when $u_0 = 20$.

The first six terms are:

$u_1 = 24$, $u_2 = 26.4$, $u_3 = 27.84$, $u_4 = 28.704$, $u_5 = 29.2224$, $u_6 = 29.53344$.

$a = 0.6$, so $-1 < a < 1$ and therefore a limit exists.

$$L = \frac{b}{1-a} \qquad \text{or} \qquad L = 0.6L + 12$$

$$= \frac{12}{1-0.6} \qquad\qquad\qquad L - 0.6L = 12$$

$$\qquad\qquad\qquad\qquad\qquad 0.4L = 12$$

$$= 30 \qquad\qquad\qquad\qquad\qquad L = 30$$

To be sure you have found the limit, you need only check that $u_n = u_{n+1} = L$.

Check: when $u_n = 30$ then $u_{n+1} = 0.6 \times 30 + 12$

$$= 30$$

As $u_n = u_{n+1} = 30$, the limit is 30.

Exercise 5H

1 Find the first five terms and the limit, if it exists, for each recurrence relation.

(a) $u_{n+1} = 0.2u_n + 4$, $u_0 = 6$
(b) $u_{n+1} = 0.2u_n + 4$, $u_0 = 10$
(c) $u_{n+1} = 0.2u_n + 8$, $u_0 = 5$
(d) $u_{n+1} = 0.2u_n + 12$, $u_0 = 5$
(e) $u_{n+1} = 0.1u_n + 10$, $u_0 = 6$
(f) $u_n = 0.25u_{n-1} + 100$, $u_1 = 160$
(g) $u_{n+1} = 3u_n + 1$, $u_0 = 2$
(h) $u_{n+1} = -0.5u_n + 6$, $u_0 = 4$
(i) $u_n = -0.1u_{n-1} + 5$, $u_1 = 1$
(j) $u_{n+1} = -u_n + 10$, $u_0 = 1$

2 A sequence is defined by the recurrence relation
$$u_{n+1} = 0.75u_n + 15, \ u_0 = 75.$$
(a) Calculate the value of u_2.
(b) What is the smallest value of n for which $u_n < 64$?
(c) Find the limit of this sequence as $n \to \infty$.

3 A sequence is defined by the recurrence relation
$$u_n = 0.4u_{n-1} + 1500, \ u_1 = 600.$$
(a) Calculate the value of u_2.
(b) What is the smallest value of n for which $u_n > 2400$?
(c) Find the limit of this sequence as $n \to \infty$.

4 Local authority health inspectors are concerned about the standard of drinking water in a reservoir. An upper limit of 60 mg/l of nitrates in water is acceptable for safe drinking. A company wants to discharge nitrates at a rate of 30 mg/l each week into the reservoir. Treatment works remove 45% of the nitrates from the reservoir each week. Before any discharges the level of nitrates was found to be 25 mg/l.
(a) Write a recurrence relation to describe this situation.
(b) Should the local authority permit the company to discharge this amount of nitrates?
(c) If purification could remove 55% of nitrates each week, would the drinking water be safe?

5 A research biologist is investigating the use of parasites to control aphids in a greenhouse. She has discovered that the parasites kill 75% of aphids present each day. From experience the researcher knows that the population of aphids will increase by 500 daily. At the start of the trials it is estimated that there are 1000 aphids present. If the number of aphids remains below 600 the trials have been successful and the parasite could be sold to the public. Can the researcher claim success for these trials?

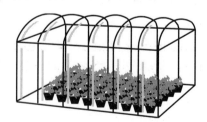

6 Once a week the cleansing department removes litter from a public park. These cleaning operations remove 90% of the litter present. Each week the public drop 25 kg of litter.
(a) In the long run what will happen to the mass of litter in the park?
(b) If litter bins are strategically placed it is found that only 10 kg of litter is dropped per week in the park. How will this affect the litter problem in the long run?

7 In a small highland village it is estimated that the population drops by 5% each year. A land deal has been arranged to persuade people to return to the village. This results in 15 people returning each year. If the original population was 200 and the population keeps dropping at a steady rate, what is the long-term effect on the population?

8 A local remand centre holds 350 prisoners at present. It has been estimated that this number will increase by 15% each month. During any month 50 prisoners are released. The centre is considered overcrowded if the number of inmates is greater than 400. Will the centre ever be overcrowded if this situation continues?

9 In a sales drive a building society is trying to gain new customers. In any 6 month period it estimates that it loses 1.5% of its customers to competitors and attracts 7000 new customers. It has 0.5 million customers at the start of its sales drive.
   (a) How many customers will the building society have after 4 years?
   (b) What would happen to the number of customers in the long term if this situation continued?
   (c) How many new customers would the society have to attract in each 6 month period to maintain 0.5 million customers?

10 A forestry company owns 100 hectares of woodland. Each hectare contains 60 mature trees. To maintain stocks the company needs to have 1500 mature trees at any one time. It estimates that 25% of mature trees are felled each month, while 300 trees reach maturity over the same period of time. Will stocks be maintained at an acceptable level?

Solving recurrence relations to find *a* and *b*

Instead of being given values for a and b, you may need to use several values of u_n to find a and b. The method is straightforward: you need to find and solve two simultaneous equations.

Example 7
A recurrence relation is defined by $u_{n+1} = au_n + b$.
If $u_1 = 5$, $u_2 = 9.5$ and $u_3 = 20.75$, find the values of a and b.

$$u_{n+1} = au_n + b \qquad\qquad u_{n+1} = au_n + b$$
$$u_2 = au_1 + b \qquad\qquad u_3 = au_2 + b$$
$$9.5 = 5a + b \qquad\qquad 20.75 = 9.5a + b$$

Solving the simultaneous equations gives $a = 2.5$ and $b = -3$.

Exercise 5I

1 A recurrence relation is defined by $u_{n+1} = au_n + b$. In each of the following cases find the values of a and b.
   (a) $u_1 = 10$, $u_2 = 35$, $u_3 = 47.5$ **(b)** $u_1 = 2$, $u_2 = 4$, $u_3 = 14$

(c) $u_1 = 100,\ u_2 = 0,\ u_3 = -50$ (d) $u_1 = -1,\ u_2 = 1,\ u_3 = -1$

(e) $u_1 = 25,\ u_2 = -90,\ u_3 = 370$ (f) $u_3 = 8,\ u_4 = 21,\ u_5 = 47$

(g) $u_7 = 50,\ u_8 = -10,\ u_9 = -22$ (h) $u_{11} = 0.8,\ u_{12} = 10.2,\ u_{13} = 12.55$

(i) $u_{n+1} = 16,\ u_{n+2} = 4,\ u_{n+3} = 1$ (j) $u_{n+1} = 99,\ u_{n+2} = -12.1,\ u_{n+3} = -23.21$

2 The first three terms of the linear recurrence relation
$u_n = au_{n-1} + b$ are 12, 10 and 8 respectively. Find the values of a
and b.

3 A girl's parents invested a fixed sum of money in a special bank
account at the beginning of each year following her 16th
birthday. The interest rate over the period of investment
remained constant and no money was withdrawn. The amount in
the account at the end of three consecutive years was £328,
£504.40 and £689.62, respectively. What was the interest rate and
the amount invested each year?

4 A department store offers a budget account to its customers.
Each month interest is charged on any outstanding debt, while a
fixed sum has to be repaid at the end of each month. A customer
had an outstanding debt on three consecutive months of £500,
£460 and £419.20. Find the interest rate and the fixed sum repaid
each month.

Linked recurrence relations

Problems involving two different but linked variables can often be
solved using recurrence relations. The following example shows you
how.

Example 8

Cool Car Rental Plc has an office at Glasgow Airport and one at
Edinburgh Airport. The total number of cars stored at the depots is
100. Experience has shown that 85% of the cars rented at Glasgow
are returned there each week while the remainder are returned to the
Edinburgh depot. Of the cars rented at Edinburgh 55% are returned
there each week while the remaining 45% are returned to Glasgow.
What is the optimum number of cars which should
be based at each depot?

Let g_n = the number of cars stored at Glasgow and

$\quad e_n$ = the number of cars stored at Edinburgh.

$\quad e_n + g_n = 100$

$g_{n+1} = 0.85g_n + 0.45e_n,\ e_n = 100 - g_n$

$g_{n+1} = 0.85g_n + 0.45(100 - g_n)$

$\qquad = 0.85g_n + 45 - 0.45g_n$

$\qquad = 0.4g_n + 45$

$a = 0.4$ so $-1 < a < 1$ and therefore a limit exists. The limit is:

$$L = \frac{b}{1-a}$$
$$= \frac{45}{1-0.4}$$
$$= 75$$

Glasgow should be allocated 75 cars and Edinburgh should be allocated 25 cars.

Exercise 5J

1 The All American Fly and Drive Company has a depot in Washington and one in New York. The total number of cars stored at the depots is 200. Experience has shown that 30% of the cars hired at Washington are returned there each week while the remainder are returned to the New York depot. Of the cars hired at New York 90% are returned there each week while the remaining 10% are returned to Washington.
  (a) If W_n denotes the number of cars at the Washington depot after n weeks, show that $W_{n+1} = 0.2W_n + 20$.
  (b) What is the optimum number of cars which should be based at each depot?

2 The population of Scotland is approximately 5 million. Each year since 1990, 30% of the rural community has moved to an urban environment, while 2% of urban dwellers have moved to the country. Demographers are concerned with the long-term effect on the population if this pattern continues.
  (a) If R_n denotes the rural population, in millions, after n years, show that $R_{n+1} = 0.68R_n + 0.1$.
  (b) What would be the long-term effect on the rural population if this pattern were to continue?

3 Canmore High School has 80 members of staff. All members of staff travel to work by car. A survey by pupils has concluded that 20% of those staff who drive one day are passengers the next day and that 10% of those who are passengers one day drive the next day.
  (a) Find a recurrence relation to describe the number of drivers each day.
  (b) What is the least number of cars travelling to the school each day?

4 Two building societies share 100 000 customers. Society A estimates that it loses 20% of its customers to Society B each year, while Society B estimates that it loses 30% of its customers to Society A each year. If this situation continued how many customers would each society have in the long run?

5 Medical research scientists are testing a drug on 250 volunteers. Each volunteer is given two bottles of tablets marked Drug E and Drug D. One of the drugs is a placebo and the other is the drug being tested. Volunteers are not told which drug is which. Each week 18% of those who thought Drug E was effective change their mind and choose Drug D. Of those who thought Drug D was effective 32% change their mind and choose Drug E.

(a) Of the 250 volunteers how many chose Drug E in the long run?

(b) The trial is considered a success if 90% of the volunteers choose the same drug. Was the trial successful?

Special sequences

There are some common sequences, some of which have special names. It is useful to know these and the following exercise introduces them.

Exercise 5K

1 Consider the recurrence relation $u_{n+1} = u_n + 5$. The sequence is:

$u_1, u_2 = u_1 + 5, u_3 = u_2 + 5$
$$= (u_1 + 5) + 5$$
$$= u_1 + (2 \times 5)$$

(a) Express the next three terms of this sequence in terms of u_1.

(b) Express u_8 in terms of u_1.

(c) Express u_n in terms of u_1.

2 Consider the recurrence relation $u_{n+1} = u_n + b$.

(a) Express the first four terms of the sequence in terms of u_1 and b.

(b) Express u_8 in terms of u_1 and b.

(c) Express u_n in terms of u_1 and b.

This type of recurrence relation is called an **arithmetic sequence**.

3 Consider the recurrence relation $u_{n+1} = 2u_n$. The sequence is:

$u_1 = u_1, u_2 = 2u_1, u_3 = 2u_2$
$$= 2 \times 2u_1$$
$$= 2^2 u_1$$

(a) Express the next three terms of this sequence in terms of u_1.

(b) Express u_8 in terms of u_1.

(c) Express u_n in terms of u_1.

4 Consider the recurrence relation $u_{n+1} = au_n$.

(a) Express the first four terms of the sequence in terms of u_1 and a.

(b) Express u_n in terms of u_1 and a.

This type of recurrence relation is called an **geometric sequence**.

5 Consider the recurrence relation $u_{n+2} = u_{n+1} + u_n$. Write the first ten terms of this sequence when $u_1 = 1$ and $u_2 = 1$.

This type of recurrence relation is called a **Fibonacci sequence** after the Italian mathematician who discovered it.

5L Mixed questions

1 A sequence is defined by the recurrence relation
   $$u_{n+1} = 0.75u_n + 4, \; u_0 = 20$$
   (a) Calculate the value of u_2.
   (b) What is the smallest value of n for which $u_n < 17$?
   (c) Find the limit of this sequence as $n \to \infty$.

2 A car designer has calculated that water escapes from an engine's cooling system at a rate of 10% per month. The system was initially filled with 36 litres of coolant. If she adds 4 litres each month,
   (a) find a recurrence relation to describe this
   (b) calculate the volume of coolant in the system after 6 months.
   (c) If the volume of coolant drops below 28 litres the engine will overheat. Is the engine in any danger of overheating?

3 The sum of £1000 is placed in an investment account on January 1st and, thereafter, £100 is placed in the account on the first day of each month.
   ● Interest at the rate of 0.5% per month is credited to the account on the last day of each month.
   ● This interest is calculated on the amount in the account on the first day of the month.
   (a) How much is in the account on June 30th?
   (b) On what date does the account first exceed £2000?
   (c) Find a recurrence relation which describes the amount in the account, explaining your notation carefully.   [Higher]

4 On the day of his thirteenth birthday, a boy is given a sum of money to invest and instructions not to withdraw any money until after his eighteenth birthday. The money is invested and compound interest of 9% per annum is added each following birthday. By what percentage will the investment have increased when he withdraws his money just after his eighteenth birthday?   [Higher]

5 (a) At 12 noon a hospital patient is given a pill containing 50 units of antibiotic.
   By 1p.m. the number of units in the patient's body has dropped by 12%.
   By 2p.m. a further 12% of the units remaining in the body at 1p.m. is lost.
   If this fall-off rate is maintained, find the number of units of antibiotic remaining at 6p.m.
   (b) A doctor considers prescribing a course of treatment which involves a patient taking one of these pills every 6 hours over a long period of time.
   The doctor knows that more than 100 units of this antibiotic in the body is regarded as too dangerous.
   Should the doctor prescribe this course of treatment or not? Give reasons for your answer.   [Higher]

6 A department store offers a budget account to its customers. Each month interest is charged on any outstanding debt, while a fixed sum has to be repaid at the end of each month. A customer had an outstanding debt on three consecutive months of £750, £690 and £628.80. Find the interest rate and the fixed sum repaid each month.

7 Central Scotland Car Hire have a depot at Glasgow Airport and
one at Edinburgh Airport. The total number of cars stored at the
depots is 150. Experience has shown that 70% of the cars hired
at Glasgow Airport are returned there each week while the
remainder are returned to the Edinbugh depot. Of the cars hired
at Edinburgh Airport 60% are returned there each week while
the remainder are returned to Glasgow.
(a) If G_n denotes the number of cars at the Glasgow depot after
n weeks, show that $G_{n+1} = 0.3G_n + 60$
(b) What is the optimum number of cars which should be stored
at each depot?

SUMMARY

① A recurrence relation describes a sequence in which each term is
a function of previous terms.

② A sequence defined by $u_{n+1} = au_n + b$, $a \neq 0$ is called a **linear
recurrence relation**.

③ For a linear recurrence relation $u_{n+1} = au_n + b$:

If $-1 < a < 1$ then u_n tends to a limit

If u_n tends to a limit, L, then $L = \dfrac{b}{1 - a}$.

6 Differentiation

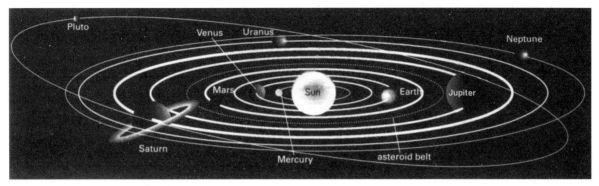

Solar system (not to scale).

Calculus was developed in the seventeenth century by Sir Isaac Newton (1642–1727) and Gottfried Leibniz (1646–1716) who disagreed fiercely over who originated it. Calculus provides a tool for solving problems involving motion. For example, methods obtained from calculus are used to study the orbits of the planets, to calculate the flight path of a rocket and to predict the path of a particle through an electromagnetic field. In fact, calculus can be used to study any situation where a rate of increase or decrease is involved.

Distance–time graphs

As you will remember from Standard Grade, distance–time graphs can be used to calculate speed.

Exercise 6A

1 The graph shows the movement of a car over time.
   (a) Describe the car's journey.
   (b) What is the average speed during
      (i) the first 10 minutes
      (ii) the second 10 minutes
      (iii) the last 10 minutes
      (iv) the first 20 minutes
      (v) the full 30 minutes?
   (c) What is the actual speed
      (i) 5 minutes from the start
      (ii) 15 minutes from the start
      (iii) 25 minutes from the start
      (iv) at any time during the first 10 minutes?
   (d) Is it likely that a car could travel in this manner?

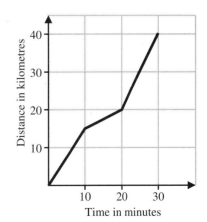

2 (a) From the graph what is the average speed
during the first
(i) 10 minutes   (ii) 20 minutes   (iii) 30 minutes?
(b) Why is it difficult to calculate the speed exactly
5 minutes from the start?

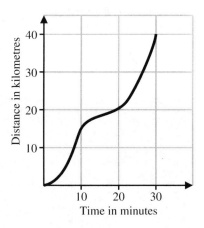

Calculating instantaneous speed

The slope of the graph in question 1 implies that a car could travel
at a constant speed and then change instantaneously to a different
constant speed. This is not realistic and a gradual change of speed is
much more likely. This is shown in the second question.

Question 2(b) involves calculating an **instantaneous** speed, i.e. the
rate of change of distance with respect to time. Problems that
involve rate of change are studied in **differential calculus**. Examples
of such problems include the rate of a chemical reaction, the growth
rate of an infectious disease, the rate of heat loss and the rate of
growth of investments.

Example 1
The diagram shows a distance–time graph. On this
graph, distance $= f(t) = t^2$, where $t =$ time.
What is the speed exactly 2 seconds from the start?

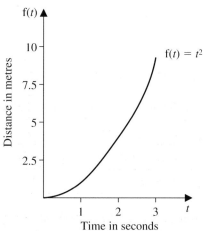

While this is difficult to answer immediately, it is
possible to calculate the speed over a period of
time close to the 2 second mark.

$$\text{Average speed between} \atop \text{2 seconds and 3 seconds} = \frac{\text{change in distance}}{\text{change in time}}$$

$$= \frac{f(3) - f(2)}{3 - 2}$$

$$= \frac{3^2 - 2^2}{1}$$

$$= \frac{9 - 4}{1}$$

$$= 5\,\text{m/s}$$

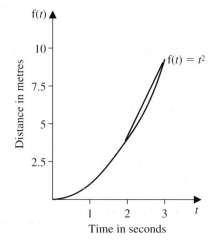

Average speed between
2 seconds and 2.5 seconds
$$= \frac{\text{change in distance}}{\text{change in time}}$$
$$= \frac{f(2.5) - f(2)}{2.5 - 2}$$
$$= \frac{6.25 - 4}{0.5}$$
$$= 4.5 \, \text{m/s}$$

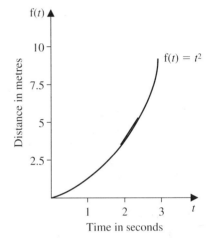

Average speed between
2 seconds and 2.25 seconds
$$= \frac{\text{change in distance}}{\text{change in time}}$$
$$= \frac{f(2.25) - f(2)}{2.25 - 2}$$
$$= \frac{5.0625 - 4}{0.25}$$
$$= 4.25 \, \text{m/s}$$

This process can be repeated, reducing the time intervals as shown below.

time interval	2–3	2–2.5	2–2.25	2–2.1	2–2.01	2–2.001	2–2.0001
change in distance	5	2.25	1.0625	0.41	0.0401	0.004001	0.00040001
change in time	1	0.5	0.25	0.1	0.01	0.001	0.0001
average speed	5	4.5	4.25	4.1	4.01	4.001	4.0001

Reducing the time interval gives a closer approximation to the instantaneous speed at 2 seconds. As the change in time tends to zero, the speed tends to a limit of 4 m/s at 2 seconds.

Exercise 6B

1 Using the method outlined above, find the instantaneous speed at 3 seconds.

time interval	3–4	3–3.5	3–3.25	3–3.1	3–3.01	3–3.001	3–3.0001
change in distance							
change in time	1						
average speed							

2 Find the instantaneous speed at 4 seconds.

3 (a) Use the results obtained above to complete this table.

time (s)	2	3	4
instantaneous speed (m/s)	4		

(b) Make a conjecture about the instantaneous speed at t seconds for $f(t) = t^2$.

(c) Test your conjecture.

The derived function

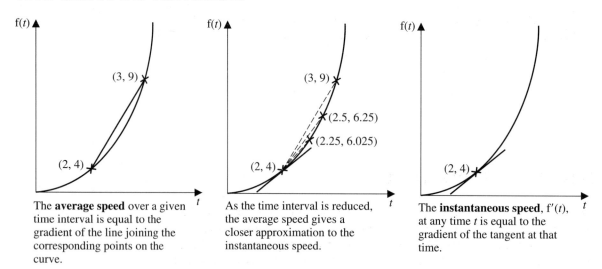

The **average speed** over a given time interval is equal to the gradient of the line joining the corresponding points on the curve.

As the time interval is reduced, the average speed gives a closer approximation to the instantaneous speed.

The **instantaneous speed**, $f'(t)$, at any time t is equal to the gradient of the tangent at that time.

From the results tabulated in question 3, you should notice that when the distance is given by $f(t) = t^2$, the instantaneous speed, or the rate of change of distance with respect to time, is $2t$.

> The rate of change can be written as $f'(t)$ and is called the **derived function**.

The method of finding the derived function in exercise 6B above can be used to calculate instantaneous speeds.

The results can be shown in a table:

distance $f(t)$	t^2	t^3	t^4	t^5		t^n
speed $f'(t)$	$2t$	$3t^2$	$4t^3$	$5t^4$		nt^{n-1}

In general

> If $f(t) = t^n$ then $f'(t) = nt^{n-1}$

Example 2

For $f(t) = t^4$, calculate the speed when $t = 2$.

$f(t) = t^4$

$f'(t) = 4t^3$

Therefore, when $t = 2$, $f'(2) = 4 \times 2^3 = 32$

The speed is $32 \, \text{m/s}$ at 2 seconds.

Exercise 6C

1 Find $f'(t)$ and hence calculate the speed for each of the following:

(a) $f(t) = t^3$ at $t = 4$ (b) $f(t) = t^2$ at $t = 10$

(c) $f(t) = t^5$ at $t = 3$ (d) $f(t) = t^6$ at $t = 2$

(e) $f(t) = t^4$ at $t = 10$ (f) $f(t) = t^{10}$ at $t = 1$

(g) $f(t) = t^{\frac{3}{2}}$ at $t = 4$ (h) $f(t) = \sqrt{t^5}$ at $t = 4$

The derivative of x^n

As we saw in the previous section, the gradient of a tangent may be used to calculate the instantaneous speed, or rate of change, from a graph of distance versus time. In the same way, in general terms the gradient of a tangent may be used to calculate the instantaneous rate of change of any function.

On the graph $y = f(x)$ A is the point $(x, f(x))$ and B is the point $((x + h), f(x + h))$.

Following the same process used to find the speed from the distance–time graph,

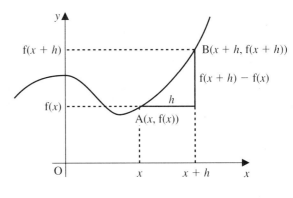

the gradient of the line AB $= \dfrac{\text{change in } y}{\text{change in } x}$

$= \dfrac{f(x + h) - f(x)}{(x + h) - x}$

$= \dfrac{f(x + h) - f(x)}{h}$

The gradient of the tangent at A is derived by reducing the interval h towards 0. As h tends to 0, $\dfrac{f(x + h) - f(x)}{h}$ tends to a limit. This limit is the gradient of the tangent at A, i.e. $f'(x)$. This can be written as:

$$\blacktriangleright \quad f'(x) = \lim_{h \to 0} \frac{f(x + h) - f(x)}{h}$$

> f′(x) is called the **derived function** or the **derivative** of f(x).
> The derivative of a function represents:
> - the rate of change of the function
> - the gradient of the tangent to the graph of the function

The process of deriving f′(x) from f(x) is called **differentiation**.

Using the above formula to derive f′(x) is called **differentiating from first principles**.

For example, the following proofs show how f′(x) is derived from first principles for $f(x) = x^2$ and $f(x) = x^3$.

If $f(x) = x^2$ then $f'(x) = 2x$ If $f(x) = x^3$ then $f'(x) = 3x^2$

Proof   ***Proof***

$$f'(x) = \lim_{h \to 0} \frac{f(x+h) - f(x)}{h} \qquad f'(x) = \lim_{h \to 0} \frac{f(x+h) - f(x)}{h}$$

$$= \lim_{h \to 0} \frac{(x+h)^2 - x^2}{h} \qquad\qquad = \lim_{h \to 0} \frac{(x+h)^3 - x^3}{h}$$

$$= \lim_{h \to 0} \frac{x^2 + 2hx + h^2 - x^2}{h} \qquad = \lim_{h \to 0} \frac{x^3 + 3hx^2 + 3h^2x + h^3 - x^3}{h}$$

$$= \lim_{h \to 0} \frac{2hx + h^2}{h} \qquad\qquad = \lim_{h \to 0} \frac{3hx^2 + 3h^2x + h^3}{h}$$

$$= \lim_{h \to 0} \frac{h(2x + h)}{h} \qquad\qquad = \lim_{h \to 0} \frac{h(3x^2 + 3hx + h^2)}{h}$$

$$= \lim_{h \to 0} 2x + h \qquad\qquad = \lim_{h \to 0} 3x^2 + 3hx + h^2$$

$$= 2x \qquad\qquad\qquad\qquad = 3x^2$$

 These proofs may be confirmed by examining the graphs of $f(x) = x^2$ and $f(x) = x^3$.

From the points plotted in each case, you can see that f′(x) is a straight line for $f(x) = x^2$ and has a quadratic shape for $f(x) = x^3$.

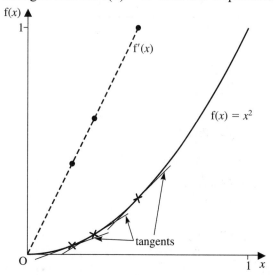

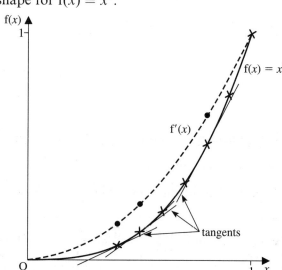

From similar graphs the following results are obtained:

f(x)	x^2	x^3	x^4	x^5
f'(x)	$2x$	$3x^2$	$4x^3$	$5x^4$

In general terms:

> ▶ If $f(x) = x^n$ then $f'(x) = nx^{n-1}$, where n is a rational number

Note that before differentiating, you need to express the function in the form x^n.

Example 3

For each of the following functions find $f'(x)$

(a) $f(x) = x^6$ (b) $f(x) = x^{-2}$ (c) $f(x) = x^{\frac{5}{3}}$

(d) $f(x) = x^{-\frac{1}{2}}$ (e) $f(x) = \dfrac{1}{x}$ (f) $f(x) = \sqrt{x}$

(a) $f'(x) = 6x^5$ (b) $f'(x) = -2x^{-3}$ (c) $f'(x) = \frac{5}{3}x^{\frac{2}{3}}$

(d) $f'(x) = -\frac{1}{2}x^{-\frac{3}{2}}$ (e) $f(x) = x^{-1}$ (f) $f(x) = x^{\frac{1}{2}}$

$\qquad\qquad\qquad\qquad\quad f'(x) = -1x^{-2} \qquad\quad f'(x) = \frac{1}{2}x^{-\frac{1}{2}}$

$\qquad\qquad\qquad\qquad\qquad = -\dfrac{1}{x^2} \qquad\qquad\quad = \dfrac{1}{2\sqrt{x}}$

✓ Exercise 6D

Find the derivative of each of the following.

1 x^5 **2** x^7 **3** x^8 **4** x^{10} **5** x^{50}

6 x^{100} **7** x^{-3} **8** x^{-4} **9** x^{-10} **10** x^{-50}

11 x^{-100} **12** $x^{\frac{4}{3}}$ **13** $x^{\frac{5}{2}}$ **14** $x^{\frac{1}{2}}$ **15** $x^{\frac{2}{3}}$

16 $x^{-\frac{1}{3}}$ **17** $x^{-\frac{2}{3}}$ **18** $x^{-\frac{4}{3}}$ **19** x **20** 1

21 $\sqrt[3]{x}$ **22** $\sqrt[4]{x}$ **23** $\sqrt[5]{x}$ **24** $\sqrt{x^3}$ **25** $\sqrt[3]{x^2}$

26 $\sqrt{x^5}$ **27** $\sqrt[3]{x^4}$ **28** $\dfrac{1}{x^4}$ **29** $\dfrac{1}{x^{10}}$ **30** $\dfrac{1}{x^{50}}$

31 $\dfrac{1}{x^{\frac{5}{3}}}$ **32** $\dfrac{1}{x^{\frac{7}{4}}}$ **33** $\dfrac{1}{x^{\frac{3}{4}}}$ **34** $\dfrac{1}{x^{\frac{7}{2}}}$ **35** $\dfrac{1}{\sqrt{x}}$

36 $\dfrac{1}{\sqrt[3]{x}}$ **37** $\dfrac{1}{\sqrt{x^3}}$ **38** $\dfrac{1}{\sqrt[3]{x^2}}$ **39** $\dfrac{1}{\sqrt[3]{x^4}}$ **40** $\dfrac{1}{\sqrt{x^5}}$

Rate of change

The rate of change of a function, $f'(x)$, can be evaluated for any value of x.

Example 4

If $f(x) = x^4$,
find the value of $f'(2)$.

$f(x) = x^4$
$f'(x) = 4x^3$
$f'(2) = 4 \times 2^3$
$\quad = 32$

The value of $f'(2)$ is 32.

Example 5

Find the rate of change of $f(x) = x^{-1}$ at $x = 4$.

$f(x) = x^{-1}$
$f'(x) = -1x^{-2}$
$\quad = -\dfrac{1}{x^2}$

$f'(4) = \dfrac{-1}{4^2} = -\frac{1}{16}$

The rate of change of $f(x) = x^{-1}$ at $x = 4$ is $-\frac{1}{16}$.

Example 6

Find the gradient of the tangent to the curve $f(x) = x^2$ at $x = 5$.

$f(x) = x^2$
$f'(x) = 2x$
$f'(5) = 2 \times 5 = 10$

The gradient of the tangent at $x = 5$ is 10.

Example 7

Smoke from a factory chimney travels $\sqrt{t}$ km in t hours.
Calculate the speed (rate of change) of the smoke after 4 hours.

The distance travelled by the smoke is $d(t) = \sqrt{t}$

$$= t^{\frac{1}{2}}$$

$$d'(t) = \frac{1}{2} t^{-\frac{1}{2}}$$

$$= \frac{1}{2\sqrt{t}}$$

After 4 hours, $t = 4$ therefore $\quad d'(4) = \dfrac{1}{2 \times \sqrt{4}}$

$$= \frac{1}{4}$$

The speed of the smoke after 4 hours is $\frac{1}{4}$ km/h.

Exercise 6E

1 For $f(x) = x^3$, find the value of
   (a) $f'(2)$ **(b)** $f'(3)$ **(c)** $f'(\frac{1}{3})$ **(d)** $f'(-2)$
   (e) the rate of change of f at $x = 4$
   (f) the rate of change of f at $x = \frac{1}{2}$
   (g) the derivative of f at $x = 5$
   (h) the gradient of f at $x = -\frac{1}{4}$

2 (a) If $f(x) = x^2$, find $f'(3)$ **(b)** If $g(x) = x^5$, find $g'(2)$

  (c) If $h(t) = t^{-1}$, find $h'(3)$ **(d)** If $r(x) = \sqrt{x}$, find $r'(9)$

  (e) If $s(t) = \sqrt{t^3}$, find $s'(4)$ **(f)** If $t(x) = \dfrac{1}{\sqrt{x}}$, find $t'(4)$

3 Find the rate of change of

  (a) x^4 at $x = 2$ **(b)** x^6 at $x = -1$

  (c) $\dfrac{1}{x^4}$ at $x = \dfrac{1}{2}$ **(d)** $\sqrt[3]{x^4}$ at $x = 8$

4 Find the gradient of the tangent to each curve at the given value of x.

  (a) $f(x) = x^3$ at $x = 4$ **(b)** $f(x) = \dfrac{1}{x^2}$ at $x = -1$

  (c) $f(x) = \sqrt[3]{x}$ at $x = \frac{1}{8}$ **(d)** $f(x) = \dfrac{1}{x^3}$ at $x = 2$

5 The distance a rocket travels in the initial stages of lift-off is calculated using the formula $d(t) = t^3$. Calculate the speed of the rocket 10 seconds after lift-off.

6 The value of an investment is calculated using $V(t) = \sqrt{t^3}$, where V is the value and t is the time in years. Calculate the growth rate (rate of change) of the investment after 9 years.

Derivative of ax^n

We can also find the derivatives of multiples of x^n.
The values in the following tables can be derived from the graphs by evaluating the gradient of the tangents.

$f(x)$	x^2	$2x^2$	$3x^2$	ax^2
$f'(1)$	2	4	6	$2a$
$f'(2)$	4	8	12	$4a$
$f'(x)$	$2x$	$4x$	$6x$	$2ax$

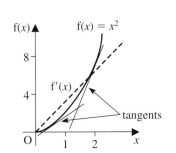

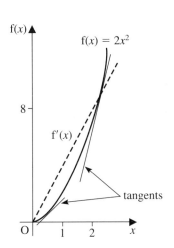

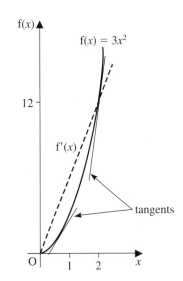

f(x)	x^3	$2x^3$	$3x^3$	ax^3
f'(1)	3	6	9	$3a$
f'(2)	12	24	36	$12a$
f'(x)	$3x^2$	$6x^2$	$9x^2$	$3ax^2$

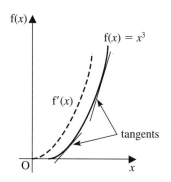

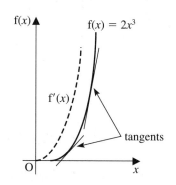

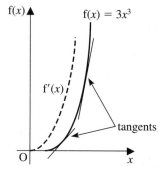

From these results we can obtain a general formula:

> If $f(x) = ax^n$ then $f'(x) = anx^{n-1}$, where a is a constant and n is a rational number.

Similarly, the following can be derived:

> If $f(x) = g(x) + h(x)$ then $f'(x) = g'(x) + h'(x)$

Example 8

For each of the following functions find $f'(x)$.

(a) $f(x) = 3x^4$ (b) $f(x) = x^4 - 5x^3 - 4x^2 + x + 3$

(c) $f(x) = \dfrac{5}{x^2}$ (d) $f(x) = \dfrac{1}{2x^3}$ (e) $f(x) = \dfrac{x}{3} + \dfrac{2}{x}$

(a) $f'(x) = 3 \times 4x^3$ (b) $f'(x) = 4x^3 - 15x^2 - 8x + 1$

      $= 12x^3$

(c) $f(x) = 5x^{-2}$ (d) $f(x) = \dfrac{1}{2}x^{-3}$ (e) $f(x) = \dfrac{1}{3}x + 2x^{-1}$

    $f'(x) = 5 \times (-2)x^{-3}$

        $= -10x^{-3}$ $f'(x) = \dfrac{1}{2} \times (-3)x^{-4}$ $f'(x) = \dfrac{1}{3} - 2x^{-2}$

        $= \dfrac{-10}{x^3}$ $= \dfrac{-3}{2x^4}$ $= \dfrac{1}{3} - \dfrac{2}{x^2}$

Exercise 6F

Find the derivative of each of the following:

1 $3x^5$ **2** $5x^2$ **3** $10x^5$ **4** $4x^{-3}$

5 $\frac{1}{2}x^6$ **6** $\frac{3}{4}x^9$ **7** $50x^{10}$ **8** $\dfrac{3}{x^3}$

9 $\dfrac{2}{x^4}$ **10** $\dfrac{1}{2x^3}$ **11** $\dfrac{3}{2x^4}$ **12** $3\sqrt{x}$

13 $4\sqrt{x^3}$ **14** $\frac{1}{2}\sqrt[3]{x^2}$ **15** $\dfrac{2}{\sqrt{x}}$ **16** $\dfrac{3}{2\sqrt{x}}$

17 $\dfrac{3}{4x^{\frac{3}{2}}}$ **18** $\dfrac{10}{3x^{\frac{5}{2}}}$ **19** $x^4 + x^3 + x^2 + x + 1$

20 $2x^3 - 4x^2 + 6$ **21** $\frac{1}{2}x^3 - \frac{1}{3}x^2 + \frac{1}{4}$ **22** $3x^2 + \sqrt[3]{x}$

23 $3x^3 - \dfrac{1}{4x^2}$ **24** $2x^5 + \dfrac{2}{\sqrt{x}}$ **25** $4x^2 + \dfrac{6}{\sqrt[3]{x}}$

26 $\dfrac{x}{4} + \dfrac{4}{x}$ **27** $x^2 - 5 - \dfrac{1}{x^2}$

Derivatives of products and quotients

We can also find the derivatives of more complicated expressions. Before differentiating a function we have to express it as the sum of individual terms.

Example 9
Find the derivative of each of the following:

(a) $f(x) = (x - 2)(x + 4)$ **(b)** $f(x) = \sqrt{x}(x^3 + \sqrt{x})$ **(c)** $f(x) = \dfrac{x^2 - 2x + 1}{\sqrt{x}}$

(a) $f(x) = x^2 + 2x - 8$

$f'(x) = 2x + 2$

(b) $f(x) = x^{\frac{7}{2}} + x$

$f'(x) = \frac{7}{2}x^{\frac{5}{2}} + 1$

$= 7\sqrt{x^5} + 1$

(c) $f(x) = x^{\frac{3}{2}} - 2x^{\frac{1}{2}} + x^{-\frac{1}{2}}$

$f'(x) = \frac{3}{2}x^{\frac{1}{2}} - 2 \times \frac{1}{2}x^{-\frac{1}{2}} + \left(-\frac{1}{2}\right)x^{-\frac{3}{2}}$

$= \dfrac{3x^{\frac{1}{2}}}{2} - \dfrac{1}{x^{\frac{1}{2}}} - \dfrac{1}{2x^{\frac{3}{2}}}$

$= \dfrac{3x^2 - 2x - 1}{2\sqrt{x^3}}$

Exercise 6G

Find the derivative of each of the following:

1 $(x + 3)(x + 4)$ **2** $(x - 2)(x + 1)$ **3** $(2x + 3)(3x + 1)$

4 $(x + 3)^2$ **5** $(x + 2)(x + 1)(x + 4)$ **6** $(x^2 + 2)(x^2 + 5)$

7 $\sqrt{x}(x^2 - \sqrt{x})$ **8** $\sqrt{x}(\sqrt{x} + 1)$ **9** $\dfrac{1}{x}\left(1 - \dfrac{1}{x}\right)$

10 $\left(\dfrac{1}{x} + 1\right)^2$ **11** $\left(\dfrac{1}{x} + x\right)^2$ **12** $\left(\sqrt{x} + \dfrac{1}{\sqrt{x}}\right)^2$

13 $\left(\dfrac{1}{x^2} - x^2\right)^2$ **14** $\dfrac{1}{\sqrt{x}}\left(\dfrac{1}{\sqrt{x}} - 1\right)$ **15** $\left(x + \dfrac{1}{x}\right)\left(x - \dfrac{1}{x}\right)$

16 $\left(\dfrac{1}{\sqrt{x}} - \sqrt{x}\right)\left(\dfrac{1}{\sqrt{x}} + \sqrt{x}\right)$ **17** $\dfrac{x - 1}{x}$ **18** $\dfrac{x^2 + 2x + 1}{x}$

19 $\dfrac{x^3 - 2x^2 + 5}{x^2}$

20 $\dfrac{x + 1}{\sqrt{x}}$

21 $\dfrac{3 + 2x}{x^2}$

22 $\dfrac{x^2 - 1}{2x}$

23 $\dfrac{3 - x^2}{x^4}$

24 $\dfrac{3x^2 + 4x + 1}{4x^2}$

25 $\dfrac{(x + 1)(x - 2)}{x^3}$

26 $\dfrac{x^2 - 4x}{x\sqrt{x}}$

27 $\dfrac{(1 + 2x)^2}{\sqrt{x}}$

Applications of derivatives

Differentiation can be used to solve real-life problems.

Example 10

A designer of an artificial ski-slope describes the shape of the slope by the function $h(d) = \dfrac{4d - 2d^{\frac{3}{2}}}{\sqrt{d}}$, where d is the horizontal distance in metres and $h(d)$ is the height in metres. Calculate the gradient of the slope 4 metres horizontally from the start of the slope.

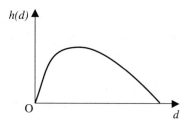

$$h(d) = \frac{4d - 2d^{\frac{3}{2}}}{\sqrt{d}}$$

$$= \frac{4d}{d^{\frac{1}{2}}} - \frac{2d^{\frac{3}{2}}}{d^{\frac{1}{2}}}$$

$$= 4d^{\frac{1}{2}} - 2d$$

$$h'(d) = 2d^{-\frac{1}{2}} - 2$$

$$= \frac{2}{\sqrt{d}} - 2$$

$$h'(4) = \frac{2}{\sqrt{4}} - 2$$

$$= \frac{2}{2} - 2$$

$$= -1$$

The gradient of the slope 4 metres after the start of the slope is -1.

Exercise 6H

1 Given $f(x) = 6x^{\frac{3}{2}}$, find the value of
   (a) $f'(1)$ **(b)** $f'(4)$ **(c)** $f'(\frac{1}{4})$ **(d)** $f'(0)$
   (e) the rate of change of f at $x = 4$
   (f) the derivative of f at $x = 3$
   (g) the rate of change of f at $x = \frac{1}{4}$

2 (a) If $f(x) = x^3 + 4x^2 + 1$, find $f'(2)$.

(b) If $g(x) = 4x^5 - 2x^3 - x$, find $g'(-2)$.

(c) If $h(x) = (x^2 + 1)(x - 1)$, find $h'(3)$.

(d) If $r(x) = \dfrac{\sqrt{x} + 1}{\sqrt{x}}$, find $r'(4)$.

3 Find the rate of change of

(a) $5x^3 - 2x^4$ at $x = 2$

(b) $4\sqrt[3]{x} - \dfrac{2}{\sqrt[3]{x}}$ at $x = 8$

(c) $\dfrac{1}{2x^2} + 5x^3$ at $x = -1$.

4 Find the gradient of the tangent to each curve at the given value of x.

(a) $f(x) = 2x^3 - x^2$ at $x = 3$

(b) $f(x) = \dfrac{3 - 2x}{x^2}$ at $x = -1$

(c) $f(x) = x^{\frac{1}{2}}\left(x^{\frac{1}{2}} - x^{-\frac{1}{2}}\right)$ at $x = 1$.

5 The height, h, of a ball thrown upwards is calculated using the formula $h(t) = 20t - t^2$ where t is the time in seconds after projection.

(a) Calculate the rate of change of height at

    (i) 5 seconds   (ii) 10 seconds

(b) Describe the movement of the ball after 10 seconds.

6 The distance, d metres, travelled on a roller-coaster is calculated using the formula $d(t) = 10t^2 - 5t$, where t is the time in seconds after the start of the ride. Calculate the speed of a car on the roller-coaster 3 seconds after the start of the ride.

7 The circumference C cm, of the largest ripple on the surface of a pond after a stone hits it is given by $C(t) = 2\pi\sqrt{t}$, where t is the time in seconds after the start of the experiment. Calculate the rate of change of the circumference 4 seconds after the stone hits the water.

8 The volume of air, V cm^3, in an artificial lung as it is inflated is calculated using the function $V(t) = 4t^3 + \frac{1}{2}t^2$, where t is the time in seconds from the start of inflation. Find the rate of change of the volume when $t = \frac{1}{2}$.

9 The current I amps in an electrical circuit is given by $I(R) = \dfrac{200}{R}$, where R is the resistance in ohms. Find the rate of change of I with respect to R when the resistance is 10 ohms.

10 The volume of water, in millilitres, which overflows from a weir is calculated using $V(h) = 5h^{\frac{3}{2}}$, where h is the height, in millimetres, of the water above the weir.

Calculate the rate of overflow when the height above the weir is 900 millimetres.

11 The pulse rate, in beats per minute, of a runner t minutes after starting to run is given by $p(t) = 60 + \frac{1}{2}t^2 - t$, for $t \leqslant 10$. Find the rate of change of the pulse rate of the runner 6 minutes after starting.

12 The number of bacteria $N(t)$, in a certain culture is calculated using the formula $N(t) = 4t^3 + 400t + 1000$, where t is the time in hours from the start of the growth. Calculate the growth rate of this culture when $t = 5$.

13 The amount of a drug, in milligrams, in the bloodstream at any time, t minutes, after administering the drug is given by $A(t) = 400\sqrt{t} - 25t$.
 (a) Find the rate of change of the drug in the bloodstream 64 minutes after being injected.
 (b) Explain your answer.

14 The position of a particle, relative to its starting position, is given by $s(t) = t^3 + 6t^2 + 8t - 20$, where t is the time in seconds and $s(t)$ is the distance in centimetres.
 (a) Calculate the speed of the particle when $t = 5$.
 (b) Acceleration is defined as the rate of change of the speed.
  (i) Find a function to describe the acceleration in this case.
  (ii) What is the acceleration when $t = 5$?

Leibniz notation

Instead of writing the derivative as $f'(x)$, we can use the Leibniz notation. This is a geometric notation that helps to stress that we are dealing with a change in x by using the term Δx instead of the symbol h. In Leibniz notation Δx denotes a small change in x and Δy denotes a small change in y.

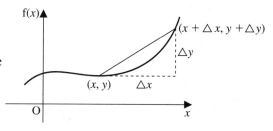

For any function $y = f(x)$ the gradient of the **chord** between (x, y) and $(x + \Delta x, y + \Delta y)$ is $\dfrac{\Delta y}{\Delta x}$.

The gradient of the **tangent** at (x, y) is $\displaystyle\lim_{\Delta x \to 0} \dfrac{\Delta y}{\Delta x}$. This is normally written as $\dfrac{dy}{dx}$.

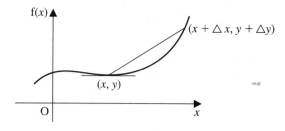

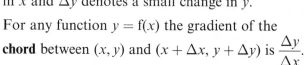

$$\frac{dy}{dx} = f'(x)$$

The derivative of a function, i.e. either $\dfrac{dy}{dx}$ or $f'(x)$, represents

• the rate of change of the function
• the gradient of the tangent at a point.

Example 11

Find the derivative of $y = 3x^4 - 5x^2 - 3x + 6$.

$$y = 3x^4 - 5x^2 - 3x + 6$$

$$\frac{dy}{dx} = 12x^3 - 10x - 3$$

Example 12

Find the rate of change of $y = 4\sqrt{t}$ at $t = 9$.

$$y = 4\sqrt{t} = 4t^{\frac{1}{2}}$$

$$\frac{dy}{dt} = 2t^{-\frac{1}{2}}$$

$$= \frac{2}{\sqrt{t}}$$

At $t = 9$, $\dfrac{dy}{dt} = \dfrac{2}{\sqrt{9}} = \dfrac{2}{3}$

Example 13

Differentiate $r = 8p^{\frac{1}{2}} - p$ with respect to p.

$$r = 8p^{\frac{1}{2}} - p$$

$$\frac{dr}{dp} = 4p^{-\frac{1}{2}} - 1$$

$$= \frac{4}{\sqrt{p}} - 1$$

Example 14

Find the gradient of the tangent to the curve $y = \dfrac{(x + 3)(x - 5)}{x^2}$ at $x = 5$.

$$y = \frac{x^2 - 2x - 15}{x^2}$$

$$= 1 - \frac{2}{x} - \frac{15}{x^2}$$

$$= 1 - 2x^{-1} - 15x^{-2}$$

$$\frac{dy}{dx} = 2x^{-2} + 30x^{-3}$$

$$= \frac{2}{x^2} + \frac{30}{x^3}$$

When $x = 5$, $\dfrac{dy}{dx} = \dfrac{2}{25} + \dfrac{30}{125}$

$$= \frac{40}{125} = \frac{8}{25}$$

The gradient of the tangent to the curve is $\dfrac{8}{25}$.

Exercise 6I

1 Find the derivative of each of the following with respect to the relevant variable:

(a) $7x^5 + 3x^2 - 9x + 7$ (b) $2x^{\frac{1}{2}} - 5x^{\frac{1}{3}}$ (c) $u + \dfrac{3}{u^2}$ (d) $\dfrac{1}{x} + \dfrac{7}{x^3}$

(e) $x(x^3 - x)$ (f) $\left(\dfrac{3}{s^2} - s\right)^2$ (g) $\dfrac{(x+1)(x-8)}{2x^2}$ (h) $\dfrac{(2-5g)^2}{\sqrt{g}}$

2 For the function $y = 2x^3$ find the value of

(a) $\dfrac{dy}{dx}$ at $x = 1$ (b) the derivative of y at $x = 4$ (c) the rate of change of y at $x = \frac{1}{9}$.

3 (a) $y = (r^2 + 1)(r - 3)$, find $\dfrac{dy}{dr}$ at $r = -3$. **(b)** $y = \dfrac{x+3}{x}$, find $\dfrac{dy}{dx}$ at $x = -1$.

4 Find the gradient of the tangent to the curve:

(a) $y = 3x^2 - 7$ at $x = 4$ (b) $y = (2x - 3)(x - 1)$ at $x = 3$ (c) $y = \dfrac{6 + x^3}{x^2}$ at $x = 36$.

5 The number of cells in a primitive organism is calculated using the formula $C = 5t^2 + 20t + 500$, where t is the time in hours from the start of the growth. Calculate the rate of growth of the organism 7 hours after the start of growth.

Equations of tangents

> Since a tangent is a straight line, its equation may be given by $y - b = m(x - a)$.
> Hence to find the equation of the tangent at any point on a curve we need to determine:
> - the coordinates (a, b) of the point
> - the gradient, m, at that point.

Example 15

Find the equation of the tangent to $y = \sqrt{x^3}$ at $x = 9$.

$$y = \sqrt{x^3} = x^{\frac{3}{2}}$$

$$\frac{dy}{dx} = \frac{3}{2}x^{\frac{1}{2}} = \frac{3}{2}\sqrt{x}$$

At $x = 9$, $y = 9^{\frac{3}{2}} = 27$

and $\dfrac{dy}{dx} = \dfrac{3}{2}\sqrt{9} = \dfrac{9}{2}$

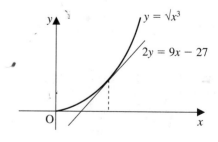

The straight line through $(9, 27)$ with gradient $\frac{9}{2}$ has equation

$$y - b = m(x - a)$$
$$y - 27 = \tfrac{9}{2}(x - 9)$$
$$2y = 9x - 27$$

Therefore the equation of the tangent to $y = \sqrt{x^3}$ at $x = 9$ is $2y = 9x - 27$.

Exercise 6J

1 Find the equation of the tangent to the curve:

    (a) $y = x^3$ at $(2, 8)$ **(b)** $y = x^2 + 3x$ at $(1, 4)$ **(c)** $y = 3x - x^3$ at $x = 1$

    (d) $y = \dfrac{2}{x}$ at $x = -2$ **(e)** $y = 5\sqrt{x}$ at $x = 16$ **(f)** $y = x + \dfrac{1}{x}$ at $x = 2$

    (g) $y = \dfrac{x - 1}{x}$ at $x = -1$ **(h)** $y = x^2(x + 4)$ at $x = 3$ **(i)** $y = \dfrac{1}{x^3}$ at $x = -2$

2 **(a)** Find the equations of the tangents to $y = 2x^2$ at $x = 1$ and $x = -1$.

    (b) Find the point of intersection of the tangents.

3 **(a)** Show there is only one tangent to the curve $y = 3x^2 + 5x$ with gradient 11.

    (b) Find the equation of this tangent.

4 The curve $y = (x - 1)(x^2 + 7)$ meets the x-axis at P and the y-axis at Q. Find the equations of the tangents at P and Q.

5 **(a)** Find the equation of the tangent to the curve $y = x^3 - 2x^2 + 7$ at $(2, 7)$.

    (b) Find the point where the tangent cuts the curve again.

6 The gradient of a tangent to the curve $y = x^4 + 1$ is 32. Find the point of contact of the tangent.

7 Find the point of contact on the curve $y = x^2 + 3x + 5$ at which the tangent has gradient 9.

8 **(a)** Find the points of contact on the curve $y = x^3 - 4x$ for tangents with gradient 8.

    (b) Find the equations of these tangents.

Increasing and decreasing functions

If the value of a function $f(x)$ increases as x increases, the graph is said to be increasing.

If the value of a function $f(x)$ decreases as x increases, the graph is said to be decreasing.

Exercise 6K

1 From the graph it can be seen that the curve $y = x^2 - 4x + 7$ has a turning point at $x = 2$.

    (a) Find $\dfrac{\mathrm{d}y}{\mathrm{d}x}$.

    (b) Copy and complete the table.

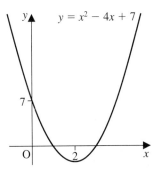

x	-2	-1	0	1	2	3	4	5	6
value of $\dfrac{\mathrm{d}y}{\mathrm{d}x}$			-4		0				
		Graph decreasing				Graph increasing			

(c) What do you notice about the value of $\dfrac{dy}{dx}$ when the graph is

(i) increasing (ii) decreasing?

2 The curve $y = 2x - x^2$ has a turning point at $x = 1$.

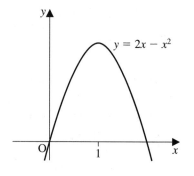

(a) Find $\dfrac{dy}{dx}$.

(b) Copy and complete the table.

x	−2	−1	0	1	2	3	4
value of $\dfrac{dy}{dx}$						−4	
	Graph increasing				Graph decreasing		

(c) What do you notice about the value of $\dfrac{dy}{dx}$ when the graph is

(i) increasing   (ii) decreasing?

3 From the graph, the curve $y = x^3 - 12x^2 + 36x$
has turning points at $x = 2$ and $x = 6$.

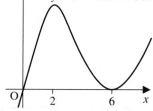

(a) Find $\dfrac{dy}{dx}$.

(b) Copy and complete the table.

x	−1	0	1	2	3	4	5	6	7	8
$\dfrac{dy}{dx}$					−9					
	Graph				Graph			Graph		

(c) What do you notice about the value of $\dfrac{dy}{dx}$ when the graph is

(i) increasing (ii) decreasing?

4 (a) Copy and complete the table for the function $y = 54x - 2x^3$.

x	−6	−5	−4	−3	−2	−1	0	1	2	3	4	5	6
$\dfrac{dy}{dx}$							48						

(b) What can you say about the graph of $y = 54x - 2x^3$ for
(i) $x < -3$ (ii) $-3 < x < 3$ (iii) $x > 3$?

From the previous exercise, you should notice that:

For any curve:

If $\dfrac{dy}{dx} > 0$ then y is increasing.

▶ If $\dfrac{dy}{dx} < 0$ then y is decreasing.

or

If f$'(x) > 0$ then f(x) is increasing.
If f$'(x) < 0$ then f(x) is decreasing.

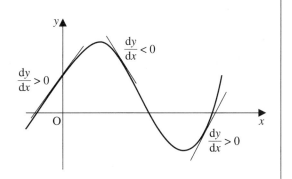

The shape of curves

The derivative of a function may be used to identify the shape of its curve.

Example 16
Find the interval for which the function $y = 3x^2 + 2x - 5$ is increasing.

$$y = 3x^2 + 2x - 5$$

$$\frac{dy}{dx} = 6x + 2$$

The function is increasing when $\dfrac{dy}{dx} > 0$

i.e. when $6x + 2 > 0$
$$6x > -2$$
$$x > -\tfrac{1}{3}$$

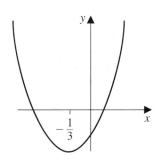

Example 17
Find the intervals in which the function f$(x) = x^3 - 3x^2 + 8$ is increasing and decreasing.

$$\text{f}(x) = x^3 - 3x^2 + 8$$
$$\text{f}'(x) = 3x^2 - 6x$$
$$= 3x(x - 2)$$

Increasing: f$'(x) > 0$ Decreasing: f$'(x) < 0$
$\qquad\qquad 3x^2 - 6x > 0$ $\qquad\qquad\qquad 3x^2 - 6x < 0$
$\qquad\qquad 3x(x - 2) > 0$ $\qquad\qquad\qquad 3x(x - 2) < 0$
$\qquad\qquad x < 0$ or $x > 2$ $\qquad\qquad\qquad 0 < x < 2$

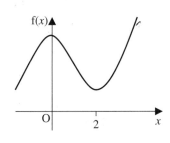

The graph of this function must therefore be as shown opposite.

Example 18

Show algebraically that the function $f(x) = x^3 - 3x^2 + 3x - 10$ is never decreasing.

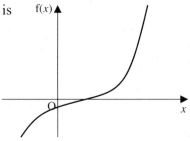

$f(x) = x^3 - 3x^2 + 3x - 10$

$f'(x) = 3x^2 - 6x + 3$

$\quad\quad = 3(x-1)^2$

$(x-1)^2 \geqslant 0$ for all x

Hence $3(x-1)^2 \geqslant 0$ for all x and so $f(x)$ is never decreasing.

Exercise 6L

1 For each function state whether it is increasing or decreasing:

   (a) $f(x) = x^2 - 6x$ at $x = 5$ **(b)** $y = x^3 - 3x^2 + 8$ at $x = 4$

   (c) $f(x) = 3x^2 - x^3$ at $x = -2$ **(d)** $y = 5x^4 + x^2$ at $x = -1$

   (e) $f(x) = x^6 + 4x^3 + 9$ at $x = 1$ **(f)** $y = 4x^8 + 5x^4 - 6x$ at $x = 0$

2 For each function find the intervals in which it is increasing and decreasing.

   (a) $y = x^2 + 3$ **(b)** $f(x) = x^2 - 5x$ **(c)** $y = 4x^2 + 5x + 7$

   (d) $y = x^3 - 6x^2 + 5$ **(e)** $f(x) = 6x - x^3$ **(f)** $y = 3x^3 - 4x$

   (g) $y = x^4 - 2x^2 + 8$ **(h)** $f(x) = 6x^3 + 8x^2 - 1$ **(i)** $y = 2x^4 - 4x^2 - 12$

3 Show that the function $f(x) = \dfrac{x^3}{3}$ is never decreasing.

4 Show that $y = \frac{1}{3}x^3 + x^2 + x + 5$ is never decreasing.

5 Show that $y = -4x - 2x^2 - \dfrac{x^3}{3}$ is never increasing.

6 Show that $y = \frac{2}{3}x^3 - 10x^2 + 50x + 5$ is never decreasing.

7 Show that for all values of x, $f(x) = \dfrac{1}{5}x^5 + \dfrac{2}{3}x^3 + x$ is increasing.

8 An artificial ski-slope is described by the function
$h = 3 - 8d - 4d^2 - \frac{2}{3}d^3$, where d is the horizontal distance and h is the height of the slope. Show that the slope is all downhill.

9 For the function $f(x) = x^3 - 3x$:

   (a) Find $f'(x)$.

   (b) Find $f'(-1)$ and $f'(1)$.

   (c) What can you say about the tangents to $f(x)$ at -1 and 1?

Stationary points

If $f'(x) = 0$ when $x = a$, then $f(x)$ is neither increasing nor decreasing.

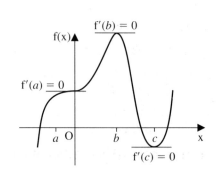

The tangent is horizontal and $f(a)$ is a stationary value.
The coordinates of the stationary point are $(a, f(a))$.

Stationary points occur when $f'(x) = 0$.

The nature of a stationary point depends on the gradient on either side of it. Stationary points may be one of the following types:

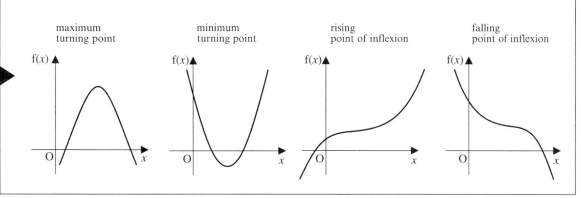

Example 19

Find the stationary points on the curve $f(x) = 2x^3 - 9x^2 + 12x$ and determine their nature.

$$f(x) = 2x^3 - 9x^2 + 12x$$

$$f'(x) = 6x^2 - 18x + 12$$

Stationary points occur when $f'(x) = 0$

$$6x^2 - 18x + 12 = 0$$

$$6(x^2 - 3x + 2) = 0$$

$$6(x - 1)(x - 2) = 0$$

$$x - 1 = 0 \text{ or } x - 2 = 0$$

$$x = 1 \qquad x = 2$$

$$f(1) = 5 \qquad f(2) = 4$$

The stationary points are at $(1, 5)$ and $(2, 4)$.

Consider the gradient, $f'(x)$, in the neighbourhood of each stationary point.

If $f'(x)$ is positive $(+)$ then the graph is increasing $(/)$.

If $f'(x)$ is negative $(-)$ then the graph is decreasing $(\backslash)$.

Using a table to condense the working:

x	1^-	1	1^+
$f'(x)$	+	0	−
slope	/	—	\

x	2^-	2	2^+
$f'(x)$	−	0	+
slope	\	—	/

Maximum turning point at $(1, 5)$ Minimum turning point at $(2, 4)$

Example 20

Find the stationary points on the curve $y = 4x^3 - x^4$ and determine their nature.

$$y = 4x^3 - x^4$$

$$\frac{dy}{dx} = 12x^2 - 4x^3$$

Stationary points occur when $\frac{dy}{dx} = 0$

$$12x^2 - 4x^3 = 0$$
$$4x^2(3 - x) = 0$$
$$4x^2 = 0 \text{ or } 3 - x = 0$$
$$x = 0 \qquad x = 3$$
$$y = 0 \qquad y = 27$$

The stationary points are at $(0, 0)$ and $(3, 27)$.

x	0^-	0	0^+
$\dfrac{dy}{dx}$	$+$	0	$+$
slope	/	—	/

Rising point of inflexion at $(0, 0)$

x	3^-	3	3^+
$\dfrac{dy}{dx}$	$+$	0	$-$
slope	/	—	\

Maximum turning point at $(3, 27)$

Exercise 6M

Find the stationary points on each of the following curves and determine their nature:

1 $y = x^2 - 6x$
2 $f(x) = 9 - x^2$
3 $y = (5 - x)^2$
4 $y = 3x - x^3$
5 $f(x) = x(x - 3)^2$
6 $y = x^3 - 12x + 3$
7 $y = x^3(x - 4)$
8 $f(x) = 2x^3 - 3x^2 - x + 5$
9 $y = x^3(2 - x)$

Curve sketching

> In order to sketch the graph of a function we need to find
> - the y-intercept
> - the x-intercept
> - the stationary points and their nature
> - the behaviour of the curve for large positive and negative x.

Example 21

Sketch the curve $y = x^3 - 3x^2$.

y-intercept
The curve cuts the y-axis when $x = 0$ and $y = 0^3 - 3 \times 0^2 = 0$.

The y-intercept is at $(0, 0)$.

x-intercept

The curve cuts the *x*-axis when $y = 0$

$$0 = x^3 - 3x^2$$
$$0 = x^2(x - 3)$$
$$x = 0 \quad \text{or} \quad x = 3$$

The *x*-intercepts are at $(0, 0)$ and $(3, 0)$.

Stationary points

$y = x^3 - 3x^2$ therefore $\dfrac{dy}{dx} = 3x^2 - 6x.$

For stationary values $\dfrac{dy}{dx} = 0$

$$3x^2 - 6x = 0$$
$$3x(x - 2) = 0$$
$$x = 0 \quad \text{or} \quad x = 2$$

When $x = 0$, $y = 0$

When $x = 2$, $y = 2^3 - 3 \times 2^2 = -4$

Stationary points occur at $(0, 0)$ and $(2, -4)$.

x	0^-	0	0^+
$\dfrac{dy}{dx}$	$+$	0	$-$
slope	/	—	\

x	2^-	2	2^+
$\dfrac{dy}{dx}$	$-$	0	$+$
slope	\	—	/

Maximum turning point at $(0, 0)$ Minimum turning point at $(2, -4)$

Large positive and negative x

As $x \to -\infty$, $x^3 - 3x^2 \to x^3 \to -\infty$

As $x \to +\infty$, $x^3 - 3x^2 \to x^3 \to +\infty$

Hence graph is

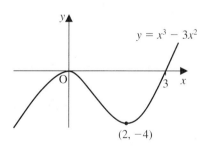

Exercise 6N

Sketch and annotate fully:

1 $f(x) = x^2 + 4x - 5$ **2** $y = x(x - 3)^2$ **3** $f(x) = x^3 - x^2$

4 $y = (x - 2)(x + 3)^2$ **5** $y = 8 + 2x^2 - x^4$ **6** $y = 4x^3(3 - x)$

7 $f(x) = 2x^2 - x^4$ **8** $y = x^3 + 3x^2$ **9** $f(x) = x^2(8 - x^2)$

Closed intervals

For each graph below the maximum and minimum values within a
closed interval are given.

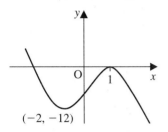

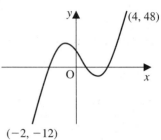

For the interval
$-2 \leqslant x \leqslant 1$
minimum value is -12
maximum value is 0

For the interval
$-1 \leqslant x \leqslant 3$
minimum value is -2
maximum value is 18

For the interval
$-2 \leqslant x \leqslant 4$
minimum value is -12
maximum value is 48

> ▶ In a closed interval the maximum and minimum values of a
> function are either at a stationary point or at an end point of
> the interval.

Example 22
Find the maximum and minimum values of $f(x) = 4x^3 - x^2 - 4x + 1$
in the closed intervals (a) $-1 \leqslant x \leqslant 2$ (b) $-1 \leqslant x \leqslant 1$.

$f'(x) = 12x^2 - 2x - 4$

Stationary points occur when $f'(x) = 0$

$$12x^2 - 2x - 4 = 0$$
$$2(3x - 2)(2x + 1) = 0$$
$$x = \tfrac{2}{3} \quad \text{or} \quad x = -\tfrac{1}{2}$$
$$f\left(\tfrac{2}{3}\right) = -\tfrac{25}{27} \quad f\left(-\tfrac{1}{2}\right) = \tfrac{9}{4}$$

Stationary points occur at $\left(\tfrac{2}{3}, -\tfrac{25}{27}\right)$ and $\left(-\tfrac{1}{2}, \tfrac{9}{4}\right)$.

x	$-\tfrac{1}{2}^-$	$-\tfrac{1}{2}$	$-\tfrac{1}{2}^+$
$f'(x)$	$+$	0	$-$
slope	╱	───	╲

Maximum turning point at $\left(-\tfrac{1}{2}, \tfrac{9}{4}\right)$

x	$\tfrac{2}{3}^-$	$\tfrac{2}{3}$	$\tfrac{2}{3}^+$
$f'(x)$	$-$	0	$+$
slope	╲	───	╱

Minimum turning point at $\left(\tfrac{2}{3}, -\tfrac{25}{27}\right)$

Using this information we can sketch the graph of
the function:

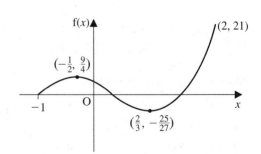

(a) For $-1 \leqslant x \leqslant 2$: $\quad f(-1) = 0, \quad f(2) = 21$
    Hence, minimum value is $-\tfrac{25}{27}$
    $\qquad$ maximum value is 21

(b) For $-1 \leqslant x \leqslant 1$: $\quad f(-1) = 0, \quad f(1) = 0$
    Hence, minimum value is $-\tfrac{25}{27}$
    $\qquad$ maximum value is $\tfrac{9}{4}$

Exercise 6O

1 For each function find the maximum and minimum values within the given closed intervals.

(a) $y = 8x^3 - 3x^2$
$-2 \leqslant x \leqslant 1$

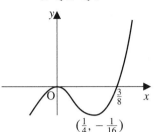

(b) $f(x) = x(x - 3)^2$
$-2 \leqslant x \leqslant 5$

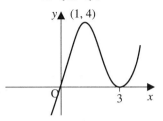

(c) $y = 5x^3 - 3x^5$
$-2 \leqslant x \leqslant 3$

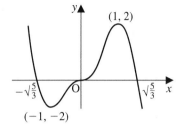

2 For each function find the maximum and minimum values within the given closed interval.

(a) $f(x) = 2x^3$
$-3 \leqslant x \leqslant 3$

(b) $y = 5 - 2x^2 - x^3$
$-2 \leqslant x \leqslant 1$

(c) $f(x) = x^3 + x^2 - 16x - 16$
$-3 \leqslant x \leqslant 3$

(d) $y = 2x^2 - x^4$
$-0.5 \leqslant x \leqslant 0.5$

(e) $f(x) = x^3(8 - x)$
$-1 \leqslant x \leqslant 7$

(f) $f(x) = 3x - x^3$
$-2 \leqslant x \leqslant 1$

Graph of the derived function

We can sketch the graph of the derived function, $f'(x)$, by looking at the features of the graph of $f(x)$. The following graph of $f(x)$ has a maximum turning point at $(a, f(a))$, a minimum turning point at $(b, f(b))$ and a rising point of inflexion at $(c, f(c))$.

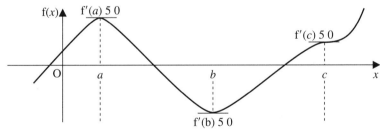

If we look at the gradients of the tangents at the stationary points and on either side of them, we can determine the nature of $f'(x)$:

	$x < a$	$x = a$	$a < x < b$	$x = b$	$b < x < c$	$x = c$	$x > c$
$f'(x)$	+ve	zero	−ve	zero	+ve	zero	+ve

Using this information we can then sketch the graph of $f'(x)$:

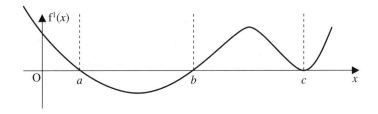

Standard functions

It is useful to learn what the graphs of f(x) and f'(x) look like for different functions.

Type of function

Quadratic   Cubic   Quartic

Derived function

Straight line   Quadratic   Cubic

Example 23

From the graph of the cubic function f(x) shown below, sketch the graph of the derived function.

From the graph of f(x) we can determine the following for f'(x):

	$x < 1$	$x = 1$	$1 < x < 3$	$x = 3$	$x > 3$
f'(x)	−ve	zero	+ve	zero	−ve

Hence the graph of the derived function is as shown opposite.

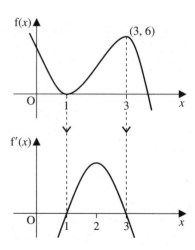

Exercise 6P

For each function sketch the graph of its derived function.

1 Quadratic function

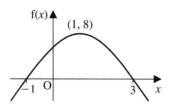

2 Quadratic function

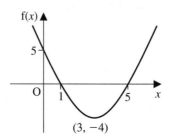

3 Cubic function

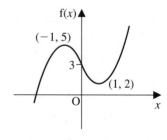

4 Cubic function

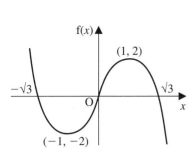

(1, 2)

$-\sqrt{3}$ $\sqrt{3}$

$(-1, -2)$

5 Quartic function

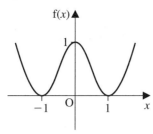

1

-1 O   1

6 Quartic function

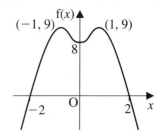

$(-1, 9)$ $(1, 9)$

8

-2 O   2

7 Cubic function

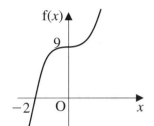

9

-2 O

8 Cubic function

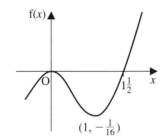

O $1\frac{1}{2}$

$(1, -\frac{1}{16})$

9 Quintic function

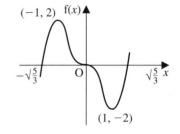

$(-1, 2)$

$-\sqrt{\frac{5}{3}}$ O $\sqrt{\frac{5}{3}}$

$(1, -2)$

Optimization: Maxima and minima

Without differentiation we would need to plot most functions to find their maximum and minimum values.

By finding stationary points we can easily identify and determine these values.

Example 24

The glass front of a carriage clock has breadth x cm.
The jeweller has used 16 cm of gold leaf to edge the perimeter of the glass.

(a) Find, in terms of x, expressions for the height of the glass front and the area of the glass.
(b) Find the dimensions of the rectangle that give the maximum area.
(c) Calculate the maximum area.

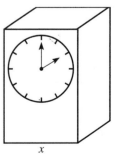

(a)   Perimeter $= 2h + 2b$

$$16 = 2h + 2x$$

Hence, $h = 8 - x$

Area $= h \times b$

$$= x(8 - x)$$

Area, $A(x) = 8x - x^2$

(b) $A(x) = 8x - x^2$

$A'(x) = 8 - 2x$

At the stationary points $A'(x) = 0$

$$8 - 2x = 0$$
$$x = 4$$

We can confirm that the stationary point at $x = 4$ is a maximum by looking at the gradient on either side of it:

x	4^-	4	4^+
$A'(x)$	$+$	0	$-$
slope	/	—	\

Maximum occurs when $x = 4$, therefore the dimensions that give the maximum area are breadth 4 cm, height 4 cm.

(c) $A(x) = 8x - x^2$

$A(4) = 8(4) - 4^2$

$\qquad = 16\,\text{cm}^2$

The maximum area is $16\,\text{cm}^2$.

Exercise 6Q

1 The base of a rectangular display case has length x cm and perimeter 36 cm.
  (a) Find, in terms of x, an expression for the area of the base.
  (b) Find the dimensions of the base that give the maximum area.
  (c) Calculate the maximum area.

2 An architect uses 25 m of antique tiling to frame a window. If the architect designs a window with breadth x m find:
  (a) an expression for the area of the window
  (b) the maximum area of window that can be created.

3 The diagram shows a parallelogram ABCD drawn inside rectangle PQRS.
  (a) Show that the area of ABCD is given by
    $A = 60 - 16x + 2x^2$.
  (b) Find the minimum area of ABCD.

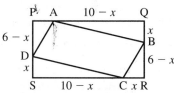

4 The minimum enclosure for a family of guinea pigs is $8\,\text{m}^2$. For a rectangular enclosure of breadth x m find:
  (a) an expression for the perimeter of the enclosure
  (b) the dimensions of the enclosure that will give the minimum perimeter.

5 100 m of decorative edging is used to section off a rectangular rose bed against a wall.
  (a) Using x m for the breadth of the rose bed find an expression for the area of the bed.
  (b) What is the maximum possible area of the rose bed?

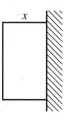

6 A square piece of card of side 30 cm has a square of side x cm cut from each corner. An open box is formed by turning up the sides.
  (a) Show that the volume, V, of the box may be expressed as $900x - 120x^2 + 4x^3$.
  (b) Find the maximum volume of the box.

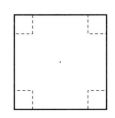

7 The cross-section of a building constructed inside a parabolic framework is shown in the diagram.
  (a) Given that PQ is $2x$ m show that the shaded area is $6x - 2x^3$ square metres.
  (b) Find the maximum cross-sectional area of the building.

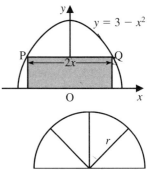

8 A semi-circular window of radius r cm is divided into sectors, each of area 125 cm^2.
  (a) Show that the perimeter of each sector is $P = 2\left(r + \dfrac{125}{r}\right)$
  (b) Find the minimum value of P.

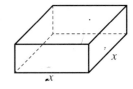

Further applications

In many cases the solution to a problem cannot be found directly from the information provided. Often an expression must be found for a value that is provided and this expression then used to obtain a function that can be differentiated.

Example 25
The volume of the square-based glass display case shown is 500 cm^3. The length of the base is x cm. The base of the case is not made of glass.

(a) Show that the area of glass in the case is $A(x) = x^2 + \dfrac{2000}{x}$.

(b) Find the dimensions of the case that minimise the use of glass and calculate this minimum area.

(a) Area of glass required = area of the top + area of the four sides
$$= x^2 + 4 \times (x \times \text{height})$$

To find the area we need first to find an expression in x for the height. This can be achieved using the formula for the volume of a cuboid:
$$V = \text{length} \times \text{breadth} \times \text{height}$$
$$500 = x \times x \times h$$
$$h = \frac{500}{x^2}$$

Total area of glass, $A(x) =$ area of the top + area of the four sides
$$= x^2 + 4xh$$
$$= x^2 + \left(4x \times \frac{500}{x^2}\right)$$
$$= x^2 + \frac{2000}{x}$$

(b) By finding a minimum stationary point for $A(x)$, we can obtain the value of x for which the area is a minimum.

For a stationary point $A'(x) = 0$

$$A'(x) = 2x - \frac{2000}{x^2} = 0$$

$$2x = \frac{2000}{x^2}$$

$$2x^3 = 2000$$

$$x^3 = 1000$$

$$x = 10$$

This must be confirmed as a minimum stationary point:

x	10^-	10	10^+
$A'(x)$	$-$	0	$+$
slope	$\searrow$	$-$	$\nearrow$

Hence a minimum occurs when $x = 10$.

When $x = 10$, length $= 10\,$cm, breadth $= 10\,$cm and, from the formula for the volume of the case, height $= 5\,$cm.

The minimum area of glass $= A(10) = 10^2 + (4 \times 10 \times 5)$
$$= 300\,\text{cm}^2.$$

Exercise 6R

1 An open box with a square base has volume $256\,\text{cm}^3$.
   (a) Taking x as the length of the base, show that the surface area of the box is $x^2 + \dfrac{1024}{x}$.
   (b) Find the dimensions of the box that will minimise the surface area and calculate this area.

2 A cuboid of volume $1125\,\text{cm}^3$ has length equal to three times the breadth.
   (a) Show that the surface area of the cuboid may be expressed as $6x^2 + \dfrac{3000}{x}$.
   (b) Find the dimensions of the cuboid that give the minimum surface area.

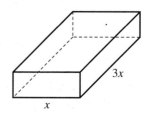

3 The cost, in £ millions, of pumping water at a hydroelectric station is related to the radius of the pipe carrying the water.

For a pipe of radius r m the cost is given by $C = r + \dfrac{9}{r} + 7$.

Find the radius which minimises the cost and calculate this cost.

4 A ship has a 200 km journey to make at a constant speed. At

x km/h the cost of the journey, in £, will be $\left(x^2 + \dfrac{4000}{x}\right)$ per hour.

(a) Find an expression for:
  (i) the time taken for the journey
  (ii) the total cost of the trip.

(b) Find the speed that minimises the cost of the journey and calculate this minimum cost.

5 A cylindrical can of radius x cm has volume 144 cm^3. The cost of producing the can is determined by its surface area.

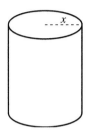

(a) Show that the height of the can is $h = \dfrac{144}{\pi x^2}$

(b) Find an expression for the surface area of the can.
(c) Find the dimensions that will minimise the cost of production.

Exercise 6S Mixed questions

1 Find the derivative of each function.

(a) $f(x) = 4x^2 - \dfrac{3}{x}$ **(b)** $y = 5\sqrt{x} + 7$

(c) $f(x) = \dfrac{6x^3 - x^2 + 5}{x}$ **(d)** $y = \dfrac{x(x-5)}{\sqrt{x}}$

2 Differentiate s with respect to t for

(a) $s = 3t^4 - 5t^2 - 9$ **(b)** $s = 4t^{\frac{5}{2}}$

(c) $s = \dfrac{(t^2 + t)^2}{t}$ **(d)** $s = t(t-4)^2$

3 Find the rate of change of

(a) $y = \dfrac{6}{x}$ at $x = 3$ **(b)** $f(x) = 4\sqrt{x} + 6x$ at $x = 16$

(c) $y = \dfrac{x^3 - x}{x^2}$ at $x = -2$ **(d)** $f(x) = \dfrac{3}{\sqrt{x}}$ at $x = 9$

4 Find the equation of the tangent to the curve $y = 3x^3 - x + 6$ at $x = 2$.

5 Find the stationary points on each of the following curves and determine their nature:
(a) $f(x) = x^3 - x^2$ **(b)** $y = 3x^3 + 2x^2 - 6x + 7$
(c) $f(x) = x^2(x^2 - 2x)$ **(d)** $y = x^3(x - 1)$

6 Find the x-coordinate of each of the points on the curve
$y = x^3 - \dfrac{3x^2}{2} - 36x + 12$ at which the tangent is parallel to the
x-axis.

7 Find the intervals in which $y = x^4 - 2x^2$ is increasing.

8 (a) Show that $f(x) = x^3 - 5$ is never decreasing.
  (b) Show that $f(x) = 10 - 2x^3$ is never increasing.

9 Sketch the graph of each of the following functions:
  (a) $f(x) = 2x^3 - 3x^2 - 36x$ **(b)** $y = 8x^3 - x^4$

10 Find the maximum and minimum values of $f(x) = 3x^2 - x^3$ in the closed interval $-2 \leqslant x \leqslant 1$.

11 For each function, $f(x)$, sketch the graph of $f'(x)$.
  (a) $f(x)$ is a quadratic function   **(b)** $f(x)$ is a cubic function

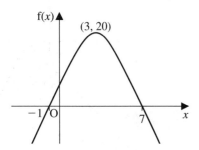
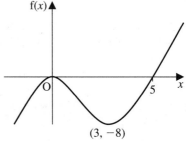

12 The diagram shows the curve $y = 8 - x^3$. Line AB is a tangent at A and intersects the curve at B. Find the coordinates of B.

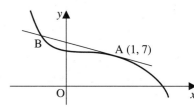

13 In the diagram, a winding river has been modelled by the curve $y = x^3 - x^2 - 6x - 2$ and a road has been modelled by the straight line AB. The road is a tangent to the river at the point $A(1, -8)$. Find the equation of the tangent at A and hence find the coordinates of B.   [Higher]

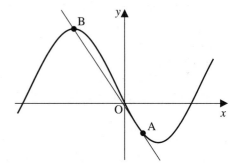

14 (a) The diagram shows a part of the curve with equation $y = 2x^2(x - 3)$. Find the coordinates of the stationary points on the graph and determine their nature.
  (b) State the range of values of k for which $y = k$ intersects the graph in three distinct points.   [Higher]

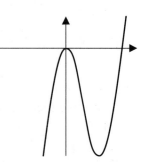

15 Given that $y = 2x^2 + x$, find $\dfrac{dy}{dx}$ and hence show that

$$x\left(1 + \frac{dy}{dx}\right) = 2y.$$ [Higher]

16 The gradient of the tangent to the curve $y = ax^2 + b$ is 16 at the point (2, 23). Find a and b.

17 For a ship travelling at x km/h the running cost in £ is $\left(x^2 + \dfrac{13500}{x}\right)$ per hour. Find the speed that minimises the cost of a 300 km journey.

18 Staff in a hotel are paid £6 an hour. If the hotel is understaffed the lost profit is £$\dfrac{216}{x}$ per hour, where x is the number of employees. What staffing level will minimise the total staffing cost per hour?

19 A yacht club is designing its new flag. The flag is to consist of a red triangle on a yellow rectangular background.
In the yellow rectangle ABCD, AB measures 8 units and AD is 6 units. E and F lie on BC and CD, x units from B and C as shown in the diagram.
  (a) Show that the area, H square units, of the red triangle AEF is given by $H(x) = 24 - 4x + \frac{1}{2}x^2$.
  (b) Hence find the greatest and least possible values of the area of triangle AEF.   [Higher]

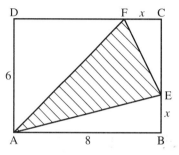

20 $P = xy$ and $2x + 5y = 100$.
  (a) Express P as a function of x.
  (b) Find the maximum value of P.
  (c) State the values of x and y that give the maximum value of P.

21 A rectangular block has a square base of side x cm. Its surface area is $150\,\text{cm}^2$.
  (a) Show that the volume of the block is $\frac{1}{2}(75x - x^3)\,\text{cm}^3$.
  (b) Find the dimensions of the block that maximise its volume.
  (c) What is the maximum volume?

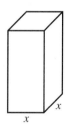

22 A circular piece of card with a sector removed is folded to form a cone. The slanted height of the cone is 12 cm and the vertical height is h cm.

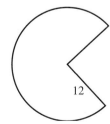
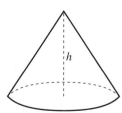

  (a) Show that the volume of the cone, $V\,\text{cm}^3$, is given by the expression $V = \frac{1}{3}\pi h(144 - h^2)$.

  (b) Find the maximum volume.
     (Volume of a cone $= \frac{1}{3}\pi r^2 h$)

23 Diagram 1 is an artist's impression of a new warehouse based on the architect's plans. The warehouse is in the shape of a cuboid and is supported by three identical parabolic girders spaced 30 metres apart.
With coordinate axes as shown in diagram 2, the shape of each girder can be described by the equation $y = 9 - \frac{1}{4}x^2$.

(a) Given that AB is $2x$ metres long, show that the shaded area in diagram 2 is $(18x - \frac{1}{2}x^3)$ square metres.

(b) The architect wished to fit into the girders the cuboid warehouse which had the maximum volume. Find the value of this maximum volume.   [Higher]

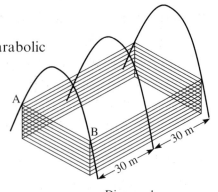

Diagram 1

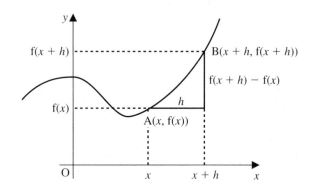

Diagram 2

SUMMARY

(1) The rate of change of a function f(t) can be written as f$'$(t) and is called the **derived function**.

(2) If f(t) = t^n then f$'$(t) = nt^{n-1}

(3) $f'(x) = \lim\limits_{h \to 0} \dfrac{f(x+h) - f(x)}{h}$

(4) The derivative of a function represents:
- the rate of change of the function
- the gradient of the tangent to the function.

(5) If f(x) = x^n then f$'$(x) = nx^{n-1}, where n is a rational number.

(6) If f(x) = ax^n then f$'$(x) = anx^{n-1}, where a is a constant and n is a rational number.

(7) If f(x) = g(x) + h(x) then f$'$(x) = g$'$(x) + h$'$(x)

(8) $\dfrac{dy}{dx} = f'(x)$

9 Since a tangent is a straight line, its equation may be given by

$y - b = m(x - a)$.

Hence to find the equation of the tangent at any point on a curve we need to determine:

- the coordinates (a, b) of the point
- the gradient, m, at that point.

10 For any curve:

If $\dfrac{dy}{dx} > 0$ in a given interval then y is strictly increasing in that interval.

If $\dfrac{dy}{dx} < 0$ in a given interval then y is strictly decreasing in that interval.

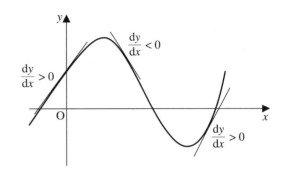

or

If $f'(x) > 0$ in a given interval then $f(x)$ is strictly increasing in that interval.

If $f'(x) < 0$ in a given interval then $f(x)$ is strictly decreasing in that interval.

11 Stationary points occur when $f'(x) = 0$.

12 The nature of a stationary point depends on the gradient on either side of it. Stationary points may be one of the following types:

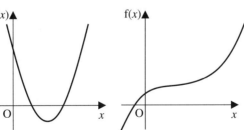

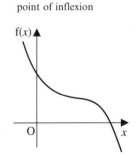

maximum turning point   minimum turning point   rising point of inflexion   falling point of inflexion

13 In order to sketch the graph of a function we need to find:

- the y-intercept
- the x-intercept
- the stationary points and their nature
- the behaviour of the curve for large positive and negative x.

14 In a closed interval the maximum and minimum values of a function are either at a stationary point or at an end point of the interval.

Revision exercise 1A

1 Find the equation of the line joining the points P(2, −1) and Q(4, −9).

2 The vertices of a triangle are A(−1, 1), B(4, 0) and C(1, 6). Find the equation of the altitude of triangle ABC, drawn from A.

3 The line $y = 3x - 1$ makes an angle of $a°$ with the x-axis. Find the value of a.

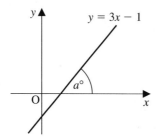

4 The diagonals of a polygon have equations $y = 2x + 1$ and $y = 3x - 2$. Find the point of intersection of the diagonals.

5 A chord of a circle passes through the points P(−2, −3) and Q(6, 1). Find the equation of the diameter of the circle perpendicular to this chord.

6 P is the point (3, 7) and Q is (7, −1).
  (a) Find the equation of the line PQ.
  (b) Find the equation of the line parallel to PQ through the point R(−1, 2).

7 The curve $y = 2x^2 + x - 1$ meets the line $y = x + 1$ at two points. Find the coordinates of both points.

8 M is the point (a, a^2), N is $(3b, 9b^2)$. Find the gradient of MN in its simplest form.

9 In triangle LMN, L is (−1, −2), M is (5, 2) and N is (1, 8).
  (a) Find the equation of the median through N.
  (b) Find the equation of the altitude through L.

10 The diagram shows the curve $y = f(x)$. Sketch the graph of $y = -f(x)$.

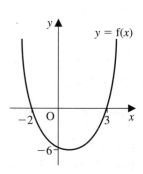

11 The graph of $y = f(x)$ is shown. On separate diagrams sketch the graph of
   (a) $y = f(x) + 3$ **(b)** $y = f(x - 2)$

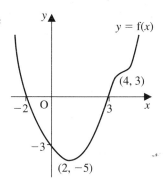

12 The diagram shows the parabola $y = f(x)$. Sketch the parabola with equation $y = -f(x) + 2$.

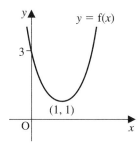

13 The diagram shows the graph of $y = f(x)$, where $f(x) = p \cos x$.
   (a) State the value of p.
   (b) The line $y = 2$ intersects the curve at A, B and C.
      Find the coordinates of A, B and C.

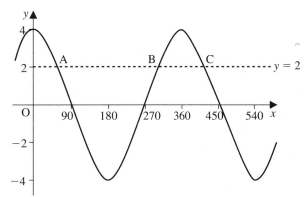

14 The diagram shows the graph of $y = f(x)$, where $f(x) = p \sin (x + q)$.
   (a) State the values of p and q.
   (b) Find the coordinates of A and B.
   (c) Sketch the function $y = 2f(x)$.

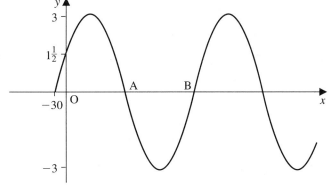

15 Solve $2 \sin 3x° - 1 = 0$ for $0 \leqslant x \leqslant 180$.

16 Solve the equation $2 \cos^2 x = \frac{3}{2}$ for $0 \leqslant x \leqslant \pi$.

17 Find the value of x between 180 and 270 which satisfies the equation $\sqrt{2} \cos (2x - 30)° - 1 = 0$.

18 For the equation $y = 2 + \sin 2x$, find the values of x for which $y = 2.5$, where $0 \leqslant x \leqslant 2\pi$.

19 Find the derivative of each of the following with respect to the relevant variable:

    (a) $4x^3 - 5x^{\frac{1}{2}}$ **(b)** $(2p^2 + 1)(p - 3)$ **(c)** $\dfrac{7r^3 + 2r^2 - 3}{r^2}$

20 Find $f'(x)$ for:

    (a) $f(x) = \frac{1}{2}x^3 + 9$ **(b)** $f(x) = \sqrt{x^5} - \dfrac{1}{x}$ **(c)** $f(x) = \dfrac{3}{5x^3} + 2x^6$

21 For each curve, find the equation of the tangent at the given point.

    (a) $y = 4x^3 - 2x^2$ at $x = 2$ **(b)** $y = \sqrt{x} - 2$ at $x = 4$

22 For each function

    (i) find where the curve meets the axes
    (ii) find the stationary points and the nature of each
    (iii) sketch the curve.

    (a) $f(x) = 4x^3 - 12x^2$ **(b)** $y = (x - 1)^2(x + 2)$

23 A sequence is defined by the recurrence relation $u_{n+1} = 0.7u_n + 4$, $u_0 = 2$.

    (a) Find the value of u_3.
    (b) Does this sequence tend to a limit? Justify your answer.
    (c) Find the limit as $n \to \infty$.

24 A sequence is defined by $u_{n+1} = 0.8u_n - 2$, $u_0 = 5$.

    (a) Calculate u_5.
    (b) Find the limit of the sequence if it exists, as $n \to \infty$.

25 The value of a property appreciates by 4% per annum. For a property valued at £220 000 at the beginning of 1998 find

    (a) a recurrence relation for the value of the property
    (b) the expected value at the beginning of 2005.

26 Each evening park rangers manage to clear 85% of the litter dropped in a park during the day. Approximately 2 kg of litter is dropped daily.

    (a) If there is 4 kg of litter in the park just before cleaning on a Monday evening, how much litter will there be after cleaning on Thursday?
    (b) If this trend continues how much litter will there be in the park?

Revision exercise 1B

1 In the diagram, A is the point $(7, 0)$, B is $(-3, -2)$ and C is $(-1, 8)$. The median CE and the altitude BD intersect at J.

   (a) Find the equations of CE and BD.

   (b) Find the coordinates of J.   [Higher]

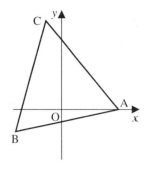

2 The diagram opposite shows a sketch of the function f with a point of inflection at $(-1, -2)$ and a maximum turning point at $(3, 4)$. Sketch the graph of the derived function f'.

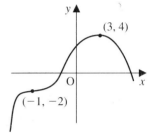

3 For what values of x is the function $f(x) = x^3 - 6x^2 - 15x - 12$ decreasing?

4 Some environmentalists are concerned that the presence of chemical nitrates in drinking water presents a threat to health. The World Health Organisation recommends an upper limit of 50 milligrams per litre (mg/l) for nitrates in drinking water, although it regards levels up to 100 mg/l as safe.

A sub-committee of a Local Water Authority is considering a proposal affecting a small loch which supplies a nearby town with drinking water. The proposal is that a local factory be permitted to make a once-a-week discharge of effluent into the loch, provided that a cleaning treatment of the loch is carried out before each discharge of effluent.

The Water Engineer has presented the following data:

   1. The present nitrate level in the loch is 20 mg/l.
   2. The cleaning treatment removes 55% of the nitrates from the loch.
   3. Each discharge of effluent will result in an addition of 26 mg/l to the nitrate presence in the loch.

and advises the sub-committee that the proposal presents no long-term danger from nitrates to the drinking water supply.

   (a) Show the calculations you would use to check the engineer's advice.

   (b) Is the engineer's advice acceptable?   [Higher]

5 The diagram shows the graphs of the functions $y = f(x)$ and $y = g(x)$. A is the point $(-2, 0)$, B is $(0, -5)$, C is $(0, 3)$ and D is $(4, 0)$. State the range of values of x for which
  (a) $f(x) \leqslant 0$ (b) $f(x) \leqslant g(x)$

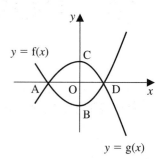

6 The diagram shows the plans for a proposed new racing circuit. The designer wishes to introduce a slip road at B for cars wishing to exit from the circuit to go into the pits. The designer needs to ensure that the two sections of road touch at B in order that drivers may drive straight on when they leave the circuit.

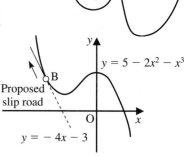

Relative to appropriate axes, the part of the circuit circled above is shown below. This part of the circuit is represented by a curve with equation $y = 5 - 2x^2 - x^3$ and the proposed slip road is represented by a straight line with equation $y = -4x - 3$.
  (a) Find algebraically the coordinates of B.
  (b) Justify the designer's decision that this direction for the slip road does allow drivers to go straight on.

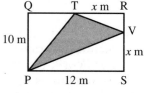

[Higher]

7 The diagram shows a gardener's design for a rectangular garden. The lawn is represented by triangle PTV.
PS is 12 metres, PQ is 10 metres and both TR and VS are x metres.
  (a) Show that the area, A square metres of lawn PTV is given by $A(x) = 60 - 6x + \frac{1}{2}x^2$.
  (b) Hence find the maximum area of the lawn PTV.

8 The cost, £P million, of laying one kilometre of pipe for a water main is calculated by means of the formula

$$P = \frac{4000}{9a} + 4a$$

where a is the cross-sectional area of the pipe in square metres.
  (a) What is the cross-sectional area of the most economical pipe to use? (Answer to the nearest tenth of a square metre.)
  (b) Calculate the minimum cost of laying one kilometre of pipe. (Answer to the nearest £ million.)   [Higher]

9 The diagram shows a sketch of the parabola $y = f(x)$.
  (a) Copy the sketch of $y = f(x)$. On your diagram, draw the parabola with equation $y = -f(x) + 3$.
  (b) State the value of x for which $3 - f(x) \geqslant 0$.
  (c) If $g(x) = 3 - f(x)$, express $g(x)$ in terms of x.   [Higher]

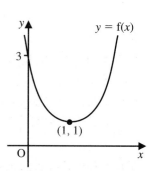

7 Polynomials

What is a polynomial?

Expressions like $3x^4 + 2x^3 - 6x^2 + 11$ and $m^6 - 4m^3 + m^2 - 2$ are called **polynomials**. $(5x - 4)(x + 3)$ is also a polynomial since it can be written as $5x^2 + 11x - 12$.

The **degree** of a polynomial is the value of the highest power, e.g.

$3x^4 + 2x^3 - 6x^2 + x + 11$ is a polynomial of degree 4
$m^6 - 4m^3 + m^2 - 2$ is a polynomial of degree 6

In the polynomial $7x^3 - 5x^2 + x - 4$, the **coefficient** of x^3 is 7.
In the polynomial $5m^4 - m^2 + 5m$, the coefficient of m^2 is -1.

In general, $a_n x^n + a_{n-1} x^{n-1} + a_{n-2} x^{n-2} + \ldots + a_0$ is a polynomial of degree n, where n is a whole number and $a_n, \ldots, a_0$ are coefficients with $a_n \neq 0$.

> ▶ A **root** of a polynomial function, f(x), is a value of x for which f(x) = 0.

Example 1
Express each polynomial as a product of factors.
(a) $5x^3 - 10x$ (b) $9x^2 - 16$ (c) $6x^2 - 7x - 5$

(a) $5x^3 - 10x$ (b) $9x^2 - 16$ (c) $6x^2 - 7x - 5$
   $= 5x(x^2 - 2)$ $= (3x + 4)(3x - 4)$ $= (2x + 1)(3x - 5)$

Example 2
Find the roots of $3x^2 - 12 = 0$.

$$3x^2 - 12 = 0$$
$$3(x^2 - 4) = 0$$
$$3(x - 2)(x + 2) = 0$$
Therefore $x - 2 = 0$ or $x + 2 = 0$
         so $x = 2$ or $x = -2$

Hence the roots of f(x) = $3x^2 - 12$ are 2 and -2.

Example 3
Evaluate f(x) = $3x^3 - 2x^2 + 6x - 4$ for $x = 2$.

f(x) = $3x^3 - 2x^2 + 6x - 4$
f(2) = $3(2^3) - 2(2^2) + 6(2) - 4$
     = $24 - 8 + 12 - 4$
     = 24

Note: For this function, if $x = h$, f(h) = $3h^3 - 2h^2 + 6h - 4$

Nov 29/2
2013

1 State the degree of each polynomial.

   (a) $x^4 + 2x^3 - x - 5$ **(b)** $4t^5 - t - 6$ **(c)** $y + 4$

   (d) $3x^7 - 4x^5 + 7x^4 - 11$ **(e)** $p^{11} - 1$

2 Arrange each polynomial in order of descending powers of x and state its degree.

   (a) $2x + 5x^3 - 3x^2 + 9$ **(b)** $12 + 4x^2 - 9x^4$

   (c) $(x + 4)(x - 7)$ **(d)** $(x + 2)(x - 3)(x + 5)$

3 In each polynomial state the coefficient of (i) x^3 and (ii) x.

   (a) $5x^4 + 7x^3 - 2x^2 + 4x - 1$ **(b)** $6x^3 + 3x^2 - 2x + 11$

   (c) $x^3 + x^2 - x$ **(d)** $2x^4 + 7x + 19$

   (e) $x(x + 4)(x - 1)$ **(f)** $(x - 3)(2x + 3)$

4 Factorise each polynomial.

   (a) $12t + 16$ **(b)** $8m^2 + 20m$ **(c)** $25p^2 - 49$

   (d) $x^2 + 9x + 18$ **(e)** $x^2 + 2x - 35$ **(f)** $36m^2 - 81$

   (g) $2x^2 - 15x - 8$ **(h)** $100p^4 - 64q^2$ **(i)** $12x^2 - 13x - 14$

5 Find the roots of each polynomial.

   (a) $f(x) = x^2 - 16$ **(b)** $f(t) = 6t^2 - 2t$

   (c) $f(m) = m^2 + 10m + 21$ **(d)** $f(s) = 6s^2 + 7s - 3$

6 Find $f(3)$ for each polynomial.

   (a) $f(x) = x^2 + 6$ **(b)** $f(p) = 3p^2 + 2p - 11$

   (c) $f(t) = t^4 - t^3 + 4t^2 + 2t + 1$ **(d)** $f(a) = 4a^3 - 5a^2 + 2$

7 Find the value of each polynomial for the given value of x.

   (a) $x^3 + 7x^2 - 4x + 2$, $x = 2$ **(b)** $4x^2 - 6x + 2$, $x = 1$

   (c) $7x^4 - 20x^2 + 15x + 2$, $x = -2$

8 Calculate

   (a) $f(-1)$ when $f(x) = 3x^2 + x$ **(b)** $f(0)$ when $f(x) = 9x^{11} - 12$

   (c) $f(0.5)$ when $f(x) = x^3 - 4x^2$ **(d)** $f(2)$ when $f(x) = (x + 3)^2(x - 1)$

Nested form

A polynomial function arranged in descending powers of x may be expressed in **nested form**, for example:

$$\begin{aligned} f(h) &= ah^4 + bh^3 + ch^2 + dh + e \\ &= (ah^3 + bh^2 + ch + d)h + e \\ &= ((ah^2 + bh + c)h + d)h + e \\ &= (((ah + b)h + c)h + d)h + e \end{aligned}$$

We can also use the nested form to evaluate polynomials.

Example 4

Use nested form to evaluate $f(x) = 2x^4 + 3x^3 - 10x^2 - 5x + 7$ when $x = 4$.

$$f(x) = 2x^4 + 3x^3 - 10x^2 - 5x + 7$$
$$= (((2x + 3)x - 10)x - 5)x + 7$$

$f(4) = (((2 \times 4 + 3)4 - 10)4 - 5)4 + 7$	multiply 2 by 4 then add 3
$= ((11 \times 4 - 10)4 - 5)4 + 7$	multiply 11 by 4 then subtract 10
$= (34 \times 4 - 5)4 - 5)4 + 7$	multiply 34 by 4 then subtract 5
$= 131 \times 4 + 7$	multiply 131 by 4 then add 7
$= 531$	

A convenient layout for this calculation is:

Example 5

Calculate $f(-3)$ for $f(x) = 2x^4 - 5x^3 + 6x + 3$.

Hence $f(-3) = 282$.

Note: A missing power has coefficient zero.

Exercise 7B

1 Use the nested form to evaluate
  (a) $f(3)$ when $f(x) = 2x^2 + 4x + 6$
  (b) $f(5)$ when $f(x) = 5x^4 + 3x^3 + 7x^2 - 2x + 3$
  (c) $f(-2)$ when $f(x) = 3x^5 + 2x^3 + 6x^2 + 5x - 8$
  (d) $f(10)$ when $f(x) = 7x^6 + 3x^2 - 9x + 11$

2 Find the value of each polynomial for the given value.
  (a) $4x^3 - 3x^2 - 6x + 9$, $x = 7$ **(b)** $8x^6 + 7x^5 - 3x^4 - 2x^2 + x + 1$, $x = -1$
  (c) $5x^4 + 2x^2 + x - 11$, $x = 2$ **(d)** $2x^5 - 3x^4 + 2x^3 - 4x^2 + 5x - 10$, $x = 3$
  (e) $3m^3 + m^2 - 12$, $m = -3$ **(f)** $r^4 + 2r^3 - 3r^2 + 2$, $r = 4$

Division by $(x - a)$

We can divide polynomials using the same method as used for simple division.

In the numeric division calculation $35 \div 8$

$$8 \overline{)35} \quad \text{4 rem 3}$$

8 is the **divisor**, 4 is the **quotient** and 3 is the **remainder**.

Conversely, $35 = 8 \quad \times \quad 4 \quad + \quad 3$
$$\qquad\qquad\;\; \uparrow \qquad\quad \uparrow \qquad\quad \uparrow$$
$$\qquad\quad\;\; \text{divisor} \quad \text{quotient} \quad \text{remainder}$$

In the algebraic division algorithm $(5x^3 + 2x^2 + 8x - 2) \div (x - 2)$

$$
\begin{array}{r}
5x^2 + 12x + 32 \text{ rem } 62 \\
x - 2 \overline{\smash{\big)}\, 5x^3 + 2x^2 + 8x - 2} \\
\underline{5x^3 - 10x^2} \\
12x^2 + 8x \\
\underline{12x^2 - 24x} \\
32x - 2 \\
\underline{32x - 64} \\
62
\end{array}
$$

$(x - 2)$ is the divisor, $(5x^2 + 12x + 32)$ is the quotient and 62 is the remainder.

Hence, $5x^3 + 2x^2 + 8x - 2 = (x - 2)(5x^2 + 12x + 32) + 62$.

An alternative method uses the nested form.

Calculating f(2) for this polynomial:

$$
\begin{array}{c|cccc}
2 & 5 & 2 & 8 & -2 \\
  &   & 10 & 24 & 64 \\
\hline
  & 5 & 12 & 32 & \mathbf{62}
\end{array}
$$

divisor   coefficients of the quotient   remainder

Hence $f(2) = 62$

Comparing the two methods we can see that
- the remainder on dividing by $x - 2$ has the same value as f(2)
- the values of the last line are the coefficients of the quotient
- the degree of the quotient is one less than the original polynomial.

This method is called **synthetic division**.

When $ax^3 + bx^2 + cx + d$ is divided by $x - h$, the quotient and remainder can be found by synthetic division:

$$
\begin{array}{c|cccc}
h & a & b & c & d \\
  &   & ah & ah^2 + bh & ah^3 + bh^2 + ch \\
\hline
  & a & ah + b & ah^2 + bh + c & ah^3 + bh^2 + ch + d = \text{f}(h)
\end{array}
$$

The quotient is $ax^2 + (ah + b)x + (ah^2 + bh + c)$ and the remainder is $ah^3 + bh^2 + ch + d$.

Example 6

Use synthetic division to find the quotient and remainder for
$(4x^3 - 7x^2 + 11) \div (x + 2)$.

$$
\begin{array}{c|cccc}
-2 & 4 & -7 & 0 & 11 \\
 & & -8 & 30 & -60 \\
\hline
 & 4 & -15 & 30 & \mathbf{-49}
\end{array}
$$

The quotient is $(4x^2 - 15x + 30)$ and the remainder is -49.
Hence $4x^3 - 7x^2 + 11 = (x + 2)(4x^2 - 15x + 30) - 49$.

Example 7

Express $(4x^4 + 2x^3 - 6x^2 + 3) \div (2x - 1)$ in the form
$(2x - 1)\,Q(x) + R$, where $Q(x)$ is the quotient and R is the
remainder.

Since $2x - 1$ is the divisor, we evaluate the polynomial for the
corresponding root, $x = \frac{1}{2}$:

$$
\begin{array}{c|ccccc}
\frac{1}{2} & 4 & 2 & -6 & 0 & 3 \\
 & & 2 & 2 & -2 & -1 \\
\hline
 & 4 & 4 & -4 & -2 & \mathbf{2}
\end{array} = f\left(\tfrac{1}{2}\right)
$$

Hence, $f(x) = \left(x - \frac{1}{2}\right)\left(4x^3 + 4x^2 - 4x - 2\right) + 2$

$\qquad\quad = \left(x - \frac{1}{2}\right)2\left(2x^3 + 2x^2 - 2x - 1\right) + 2$

$\qquad\quad = (2x - 1)\left(2x^3 + 2x^2 - 2x - 1\right) + 2$

To state the function in
the required form, take
out a common factor of
2 from the quotient and
multiply the divisor by 2.

Exercise 7C

1 For each calculation identify the divisor, the quotient and the
remainder.
   (a) $16 \div 5$ **(b)** $28 \div 6$ **(c)** $\frac{43}{7}$ **(d)** $\frac{106}{9}$ **(e)** $\frac{36}{9}$

2 Use synthetic division to find the quotient and remainder in each
calculation.
   (a) $(2x^2 + 3x + 4) \div (x - 1)$ **(b)** $(x^3 + 6x^2 + 3x + 1) \div (x - 2)$
   (c) $(x^3 + 4x^2 - 3x - 11) \div (x + 4)$ **(d)** $(3x^3 - 7x^2 + 5x + 4) \div (x + 3)$
   (e) $(x^3 - 11x + 10) \div (x + 5)$ **(f)** $(x^4 - x^2 + 7) \div (x + 1)$

3 For each of the calculations **(a)** to **(c)**:
  (i) use synthetic division to calculate the quotient and remainder.
  (ii) express $f(x)$ in the form $f(x) = (x - h)Q(x) + R$, where $Q(x)$ is
     the quotient and R is the remainder.
  (a) $(4x^3 + 5x^2 - x - 22) \div (x - 2)$
  (b) $(6x^5 - 4x^2 + x + 1) \div (x + 4)$
  (c) $(8x^6 - 3x^5 - 2x + 9) \div (x - 4)$

4 Express each function in the form $f(x) = (ax - b)\,Q(x) + R$,
where $Q(x)$ is the quotient and R is the remainder.
  (a) $(4x^2 + 6x - 20) \div (2x - 1)$ **(b)** $(6x^3 + 16x^2 - 21x + 17) \div (3x - 1)$
  (c) $(10x^2 + 19x - 3) \div (2x + 1)$ **(d)** $(12x^3 - 17x^2 + 2) \div (3x - 2)$
  (e) $(4x^3 - 10x^2 + 14x - 15) \div (2x - 5)$ **(f)** $(25x^3 + 11x + 4) \div (5x + 2)$

Remainder theorem

In the synthetic division method we saw that on dividing f(x) by
($x - h$), f(h) is the remainder.

> ▶ If a polynomial f(x) is divided by ($x - h$) the remainder is f(h).

Proof
f(x) = ($x - h$) Q(x) + R, where Q(x) is the quotient and R is the
remainder.
For $x = h$, f(h) = ($h - h$) Q(h) + R
$$= (0 \times Q(h)) + R$$
$$= R$$
Therefore f(x) = ($x - h$) Q(x) + f(h)

Example 8
Find the quotient and remainder when f(x) = $3x^3 - 5x + 7$ is divided
by $x + 2$ and express the result in the form f(x) = ($x + 2$) Q(x) + f(h).

Since $x + 2$ is the divisor, we evaluate f(-2):

-2	3	0	-5	7
		-6	12	-14
	3	-6	7	**-7**

Hence f(x) = ($x + 2$) ($3x^2 - 6x + 7$) $- 7$.

Exercise 7D

Express each function in the form f(x) = ($ax - b$) Q(x) + f(h)

1 $(5x^3 - 8x^2 - 2x + 11) \div (x - 5)$ 2 $(3x^4 + 2x^2 - 8x - 9) \div (x + 3)$
3 $(2x^4 + 3x^2 - 90) \div (x + 1)$ 4 $(3x^5 - 2x^3 - x^2 + 4x - 6) \div (x + 4)$
5 $(2x^3 - x^2 - 1) \div (2x + 3)$ 6 $(6x^2 - 11x + 8) \div (3x - 4)$
7 $(x^3 + 2x^2 + 3) \div (3x + 2)$ 8 $(8x^4 + 6x^2 - 6x - 1) \div (2x - 1)$

Factor theorem

We can use the Remainder theorem to factorise polynomials.

> ▶ If f(h) = 0 then $x - h$ is a factor of f(x).
> Conversely, if ($x - h$) is a factor of f(x) then f(h) = 0.

Proof
For any function f(x) = ($x - h$) Q(x) + f(h),
if f(h) = 0 then f(x) = ($x - h$) Q(x).

Hence $(x - h)$ is a factor of f(x).
Conversely, if $(x - h)$ is a factor of f(x) then f$(x) = (x - h)$ Q(x).
Hence f$(h) = (h - h)$ Q$(h) = 0$.

Example 9
Show that $(x - 4)$ is a factor of $2x^4 - 9x^3 + 5x^2 - 3x - 4$.

If $(x - 4)$ is a factor of $2x^4 - 9x^3 + 5x^2 - 3x - 4$, f$(4)$ will be zero so we evaluate f(4):

4	2	-9	5	-3	-4	
		8	-4	4	4	
	2	-1	1	1	**0**	so f$(4) = 0$

Since f$(4) = 0$, $(x - 4)$ is a factor of $2x^4 - 9x^3 + 5x^2 - 3x - 4$.
Hence f$(x) = (x - 4)(2x^3 - x^2 + x + 1)$.

Example 10
Factorise fully $2x^3 + 5x^2 - 28x - 15$.

To find the roots consider factors of -15, i.e. ± 1, ± 3, ± 5 and ± 15.
Evaluating f(3):

3	2	5	-28	-15	
		6	33	15	
	2	11	5	**0**	so $(x - 3)$ is a factor.

Hence f$(x) = (x - 3)(2x^2 + 11x + 5)$
$\qquad\quad = (x - 3)(x + 5)(2x + 1)$

Exercise 7E

1 Show that $(x - 3)$ is a factor of $x^3 + 2x^2 - 14x - 3$.

2 Show that $(x + 5)$ is a factor of $2x^3 + 7x^2 - 9x + 30$.

3 Show that $(x + 2)$ and $(x - 4)$ are factors of $x^3 + 7x^2 - 26x - 72$.

4 Show that $(2x - 1)$ is a factor of $2x^3 + 5x^2 - x - 1$.

5 Show that $(3x + 2)$ is a factor of $6x^3 - 29x^2 - 40x - 12$.

6 Identify the factors of $2x^3 + 9x^2 + 11x + 2$.

7 Factorise fully:
   (a) $x^3 - 2x^2 - 11x + 12$
   (b) $5x^3 - 16x^2 - 47x + 10$
   (c) $3x^3 + 28x^2 + 51x + 14$
   (d) $3x^3 - 9x^2 - 12x + 36$
   (e) $x^4 - 7x^2 - 18$
   (f) $x^4 + 3x^3 - 9x^2 - 23x - 12$
   (g) $2x^4 + x^3 - 38x^2 - 79x - 30$
   (h) $3x^4 - 13x^3 - 32x^2 + 12x$

Finding a polynomial's coefficients

We can also use the factor theorem to find unknown coefficients in polynomials.

Example 11

If $(x + 3)$ is a factor of $2x^4 + 6x^3 + px^2 + 4x - 15$, find the value of p.

Since we know $x + 3$ is a factor we first evaluate $f(-3)$ using synthetic division:

$$
\begin{array}{r|rrrrr}
-3 & 2 & 6 & p & 4 & -15 \\
 & & -6 & 0 & -3p & 9p - 12 \\
\hline
 & 2 & 0 & p & -3p + 4 & \mathbf{9p - 27}
\end{array}
$$

Since $(x + 3)$ is a factor the remainder must be 0,

therefore $9p - 27 = 0$

so $p = 3$

Example 12

Find the values of a and b if $(x - 2)$ and $(x + 4)$ are factors of $x^4 + ax^3 - x^2 + bx - 8$.

First we evaluate $f(2)$ and $f(-4)$ using synthetic division:

$$
\begin{array}{r|rrrrr}
2 & 1 & a & -1 & b & -8 \\
 & & 2 & 2a + 4 & 4a + 6 & 8a + 2b + 12 \\
\hline
 & 1 & a + 2 & 2a + 3 & 4a + b + 6 & \mathbf{8a + 2b + 4}
\end{array}
$$

Since $(x - 2)$ is a factor the remainder must be 0, therefore $8a + 2b + 4 = 0$.

$$
\begin{array}{r|rrrrr}
-4 & 1 & a & -1 & b & -8 \\
 & & -4 & -4a + 16 & 16a - 60 & -64a - 4b + 240 \\
\hline
 & 1 & a - 4 & -4a + 15 & 16a + b - 60 & \mathbf{-64a - 4b + 232}
\end{array}
$$

Since $(x + 4)$ is a factor the remainder must be 0, therefore $-64a - 4b + 232 = 0$.

Solving these simultaneous equations:

$$8a + 2b = -4$$
$$64a + 4b = 232$$

gives $a = 5$ and $b = -22$.

Exercise 7F

1 Find the value of p in each polynomial if

   (a) $(x - 7)$ is a factor of $x^3 - 3x^2 - px + 147$.

   (b) $(x + 5)$ is a factor of $3x^4 + 15x^3 - px^2 - 9x + 5$.

   (c) $(2x - 1)$ is a factor of $2x^4 - x^3 + px - 6$.

2 Find the values of p and q if
   (a) $(x - 3)$ and $(x + 1)$ are factors of $x^3 + px + q$.
   (b) $(x + 2)$ and $(x - 5)$ are factors of $x^4 + px^2 + qx - 40$.
   (c) $(x + 3)$ and $(x + 7)$ are factors of $x^4 + px^3 + 30x^2 + 11x + q$.

3 (a) When $x^4 - 3x^3 + px - 5$ is divided by $(x - 3)$ the remainder is 16. Find p.
   (b) When $x^5 + px^3 + 2x^2 - 6x - 8$ is divided by $(x + 2)$ the remainder is 4. Find p.

4 If $(x + 2)$ is a factor of $x^3 + px^2 - x - 2$ find p and the other factors when p has this value.

5 The same remainder is found when $x^3 - 4x^2 + 5x + q$ and $x^2 + 3x + 5$ are divided by $x + 1$. Find q.

Solving polynomial equations

Being able to factorise polynomial expressions helps you solve any polynomial equation.

Example 13
Find the roots of $x^3 - 4x^2 + x + 6 = 0$.

To find the roots consider factors of 6 ($\pm 6, \pm 3, \pm 2, \pm 1$) and evaluate f(3):

3	1	-4	1	6
		3	-3	-6
	1	-1	-2	**0**

$$x^3 - 4x^2 + x + 6 = 0$$
$$(x - 3)(x^2 - x - 2) = 0$$
$$(x - 3)(x + 1)(x - 2) = 0$$
Hence, $x - 3 = 0$ or $x + 1 = 0$ or $x - 2 = 0$
so $x = 3$ or $x = -1$ or $x = 2$
The roots are -1, 2 and 3.

Note: If we draw the graph of $f(x) = x^3 - 4x^2 + x + 6$ we can see that the roots of the equation occur where $f(x)$ cuts the x-axis.

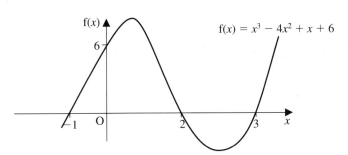

Exercise 7G

1 Show that 5 is a root of $x^3 - 10x^2 + 11x + 70 = 0$ and find the other roots.

2 Find the roots of
   (a) $x^3 + 4x^2 + x - 6 = 0$
   (b) $x^3 - 3x + 2 = 0$
   (c) $x^3 - 3x^2 - 49x - 45 = 0$
   (d) $x^4 + 4x^3 - 17x^2 - 24x + 36 = 0$

3 Solve
   (a) $x^3 + 2x^2 - 5x - 6 = 0$
   (b) $x^3 + 6x^2 + 3x - 10 = 0$
   (c) $x^4 - 4x^3 - 7x^2 + 22x + 24 = 0$
   (d) $x^4 + 4x^3 - 17x^2 - 24x + 36 = 0$

4 Find the roots of
   (a) $2x^3 + 5x^2 - 4x - 3 = 0$
   (b) $3x^3 + 7x^2 - 18x + 8 = 0$
   (c) $6x^3 - 11x^2 - 19x - 6 = 0$
   (d) $2x^3 + 19x^2 + 59x + 60 = 0$

5 Find where the graph of $y = x^3 + x^2 - x + 2$ cuts the x-axis.

6 (a) Given that $(x - 9)$ is a factor of $6x^3 - 53x^2 - kx + 9$, find k.
   (b) Solve f$(x) = 0$ for this value of k.

Functions from graphs

The equation of a polynomial may be established from its graph:

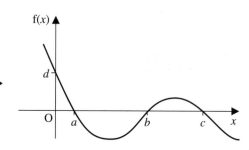

f$(x) = k(x - a)(x - b)(x - c)$ is the general equation for the family of curves. k can be found by substituting $(0, d)$.

Example 14

From the graph find an expression for f(x).

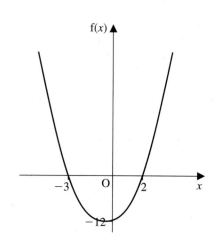

The graph has zeros at $x = -3$ and $x = 2$ so
when f$(x) = 0$, $x = -3$ or $x = 2$

i.e. $x + 3 = 0$ and $x - 2 = 0$

Since a family of parabolas cuts the x-axis at $x = -3$ and $x = 2$, we can say that

$k(x + 3)(x - 2) = 0$, where k is a constant

f$(x) = k(x + 3)(x - 2)$

From the graph, f$(0) = -12$

so $k(0 - 2)(0 + 3) = -12$

$$-6k = -12$$
$$k = 2$$

Hence $f(x) = 2(x + 3)(x - 2)$
$$= 2x^2 + 2x - 12$$

Example 15

From the graph find an expression for $f(x)$.

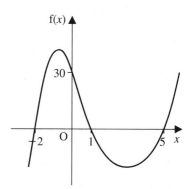

The graph has zeros at $x = -2$, $x = 1$ and $x = 5$ so
when $f(x) = 0$, $x = -2$ or $x = 1$ or $x = 5$

i.e. $x + 2 = 0$, $x - 1 = 0$ and $x - 5 = 0$

Since a family of curves cuts the x-axis at $x = -2$, $x = 1$ and
$x = 5$, we can say that

$k(x + 2)(x - 1)(x - 5) = 0$, where k is a constant
$f(x) = k(x + 2)(x - 1)(x - 5)$

From the graph, $f(0) = 30$
so $k(0 + 2)(0 - 1)(0 - 5) = 30$
$$10k = 30$$
$$k = 3$$

Hence $f(x) = 3(x + 2)(x - 1)(x - 5)$
$$= 3x^3 - 12x^2 - 21x + 30$$

Exercise 7H

From each graph find an expression for $f(x)$.

1

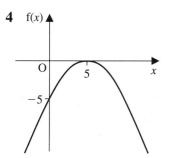

2

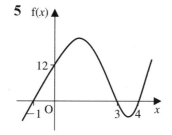

3

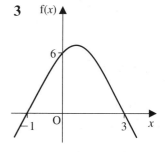

4

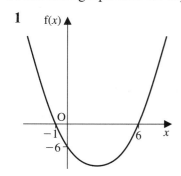

5

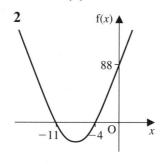

6

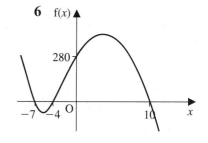

7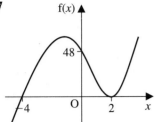

8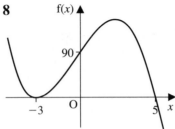

9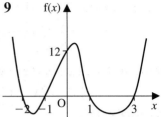

10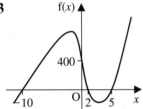

11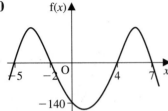

12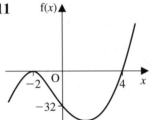

13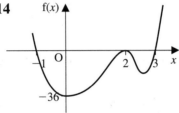

14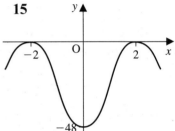

15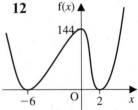

Curve sketching

The factor theorem can be used when sketching the graphs of polynomials.

Example 16

Sketch the graph of $y = x^3 - x^2 - 8x + 12$.

y-intercept
The curve cuts the y-axis when $x = 0$ and $y = 12$, so the y-intercept is at $(0, 12)$.

x-intercept
The curve cuts the x-axis when $y = 0$

i.e. when $x^3 - x^2 - 8x + 12 = 0$.

Using synthetic division, evaluate f(2), a factor of 12:

$$
\begin{array}{c|cccc}
2 & 1 & -1 & -8 & 12 \\
  &   & 2 & 2 & -12 \\
\hline
  & 1 & 1 & -6 & \mathbf{0}
\end{array}
$$

$(x - 2)(x^2 + x - 6) = 0$
$(x - 2)(x + 3)(x - 2) = 0$
$x = 2$ or $x = -3$

The graph cuts the x-axis at $(2, 0)$ and $(-3, 0)$.

Stationary points

$y = x^3 - x^2 - 8x + 12$ therefore $\dfrac{dy}{dx} = 3x^2 - 2x - 8$.

For stationary values $\dfrac{dy}{dx} = 0$

$$3x^2 - 2x - 8 = 0$$
$$(x - 2)(3x + 4) = 0$$

$x = 2$ or $x = -\frac{4}{3}$

When $x = 2$, $y = 8 - 4 - 16 + 12 = 0$

When $x = -\frac{4}{3}$, $y = -\frac{64}{27} - \frac{16}{9} + \frac{32}{3} + 12 = 18\frac{14}{27}$

Stationary points occur at $\left(-\frac{4}{3}, 18\frac{14}{27}\right)$ and $(2, 0)$.

x	$-\frac{4}{3}^-$	$-\frac{4}{3}$	$-\frac{4}{3}^+$
$\dfrac{dy}{dx}$	$+$	0	$-$
slope	/	—	\

x	2^-	2	2^+
$\dfrac{dy}{dx}$	$-$	0	$+$
slope	\	—	/

Maximum turning point at $\left(-\frac{4}{3}, 18\frac{14}{27}\right)$ Minimum turning point at $(2, 0)$

Large positive and negative x

As $x \to -\infty$, $x^3 - x^2 - 8x + 12 \to x^3 \to -\infty$.

As $x \to +\infty$, $x^3 - x^2 - 8x + 12 \to x^3 \to +\infty$.

Hence graph is

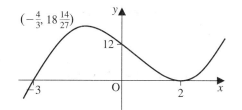

Exercise 7I

Sketch and annotate fully:

1 $y = x^3 + x^2 - 5x + 3$ **2** $y = x^3 + 3x^2 - 9x + 15$ **3** $y = x^3 - 3x - 2$

4 $y = x^3 - 2x^2 - 4x + 8$ **5** $y = 4x^3 - x^2 - 4x + 1$ **6** $y = x^4 - 5x^2 + 4$

7 $y = x^4 + 8x^3 + 18x^2 - 27$ **8** $y = x^3 - 12x - 16$ **9** $y = 3x - 12x^2 - x^3$

Approximate roots

When the roots of $f(x) = 0$ are not rational we can find approximate values by an iterative process.

> A root of a polynomial lies between $x = a$ and $x = b$ if
> $f(a) > 0$ and $f(b) < 0$ or if $f(a) < 0$ and $f(b) > 0$.
>
>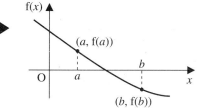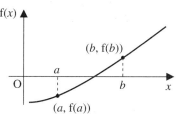

Example 17

For the function $f(x) = x^3 - 4x^2 - 2x + 7$ show there is a real root between 1 and 2. Find this root to two decimal places.

Evaluate $f(1)$ and $f(2)$:

$f(1) = 2$, which is positive and so the graph is above the x-axis at this point.

$f(2) = -5$, which is negative and so the graph is below the x-axis at this point.

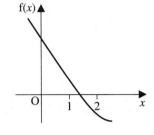

Hence, the graph crosses the x-axis between 1 and 2.

To find the approximate root we evaluate $f(x)$ for values of x between 1 and 2:

x	$f(x)$	Root lies between
1	2	
2	-5	1 and 2
1.3	-1.63	1 and 1.3
1.2	0.568	1.2 and 1.3
1.25	0.203	1.25 and 1.3
1.28	-0.016	1.25 and 1.28
1.27	0.057	1.27 and 1.28
1.275	0.020	1.275 and 1.28

From the last line of the table we can see that the root is 1.28 to two decimal places.

Exercise 7J

1 (a) Show that $x^3 + 2x^2 - 5 = 0$ has a root between 1 and 2.
   (b) Find this root to two decimal places.

2 (a) Show that $y = x^3 - 3x^2 - 6 = 0$ has a root between 3 and 4.
   (b) Find this root to two decimal places.

3 (a) Verify that the curve $y = x^3 - 3x^2 - 9x - 3$ has roots between -2 and -1, between -1 and 0, and between 4 and 5.
   (b) Find the positive root to two decimal places.

4 Find, to two decimal places, the root of $x^3 - 3x^2 + 5x - 4 = 0$ that lies between 1 and 2.

5 Use the diagram opposite to find, to two decimal places, the positive root of the equation $x^3 - 6x^2 - 2 = 0$.

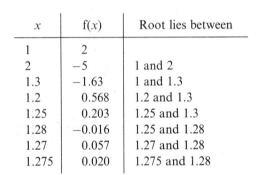

6 The line $y = 2x - 3$ intersects the curve $y = x^3 - 7x + 6$ between $x = 1$ and $x = 2$. Find the x-coordinate of this point of intersection.

7 The line $y = 4x - 9$ intersects the curve $y = x^3 - x^2 - 14x + 24$ between $x = 2$ and $x = 3$. Find the x-coordinate of this point of intersection.

Exercise 7K Mixed questions

1 The tangent to the curve $y = x^3 - 7x + 6$ at the point $(-1, 12)$ has equation $y + 4x = 8$. Find the coordinates of the other point of intersection of the tangent and the curve.

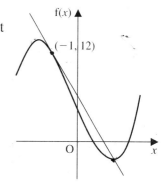

2 For each of the functions **(a)** to **(c)** find d and the other zeros of the function.
   (a) $y = 2x^3 - 5x^2 + x + d$ cuts the x-axis at $(2, 0)$.
   (b) $y = 2x^3 + x^2 - 25x + d$ cuts the x-axis at $(-4, 0)$.
   (c) $y = 3x^3 - 8x^2 - dx - 10$ cuts the x-axis at $(5, 0)$.

3 The graph of a cubic function crosses the x-axis at $x = 1$, $x = 2$ and $x = 3$. It crosses the y-axis at $y = -12$. Find the equation of the function.

4 The diagram shows part of the graph of the curve with equation $f(x) = x^3 + x^2 - 16x - 16$.
   (a) Factorise $f(x)$.
   (b) Write down the coordinates of the four points where the curve crosses the x- and y-axes.
                                                    [Higher]

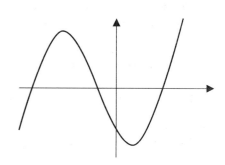

5 $(x - 1)$ and $(x + 4)$ are factors of $f(x) = 2x^3 + 5x^2 + px + q$.
   (a) Find p and q.
   (b) Hence, solve $f(x) = 0$.

6 Solve $x^3 + 11x^2 + 23x - 35 = 0$.

7 (a) The function f is defined by $f(x) = x^3 - 2x^2 - 5x + 6$.
The function g is defined by $g(x) = x - 1$.
Show that $f(g(x)) = x^3 - 5x^2 + 2x + 8$.

(b) Factorise fully $f(g(x))$.

(c) The function k is such that $k(x) = \dfrac{1}{f(g(x))}$.

For what values of x is the function k not defined?   [Higher]

8 Show that the equation $x^3 - 4x^2 + 5 = 0$ has a root between 1 and 2, and find the value of this root to two decimal places.

9 (a) (i) On $\frac{1}{2}$ cm squared paper, draw the graph of $y = x^3$,
where $-3 \leqslant x \leqslant 3$ and $x \in \mathbf{R}$.

(ii) On the same diagram, draw the graph of $y = 6x + 1$.

(b) State the number of roots which the equation $x^3 = 6x + 1$ has in the interval $-3 \leqslant x \leqslant 3$.

(c) Calculate the value of the positive root, correct to 3 significant figures.   [Higher]

10 The line $y = 3x - 16$ intersects the curve $y = x^3 - 12x^2 + 41x - 30$ between $x = 5$ and $x = 6$. Find the x-coordinate of this point of intersection.

11 In a windsurfing competition one competitor's course, relative to appropriate axes, is shown opposite. The y and x axes represent north and east respectively.

Each surfer has to sail north of a buoy at $(-2, 30)$ and south of one at $(2, -12)$. Did this surfer complete the course correctly?

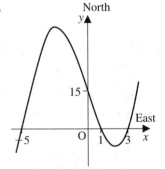

12 The diagram opposite is a sketch of the graph of a cubic function $y = f(x)$. If $y = -16$ is a tangent to the curve, find the formula for $f(x)$.   [Higher]

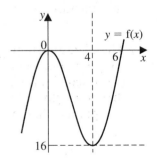

13 (a) Show that $(x - 1)$ is a factor of $f(x) = x^3 - 6x^2 + 9x - 4$ and find the other factors.

(b) Write down the coordinates of the points at which the graph of $y = f(x)$ meets the axes.

(c) Find the stationary points of $y = f(x)$ and determine the nature of each.

(d) Sketch the graph of $y = f(x)$.

(e) Use the graph of $y = f(x)$ to find the number of solutions of the equation $f(x) = -x$.   [Higher]

SUMMARY

(**1**) A root of a polynomial function, $f(x)$, is a value of x for which $f(x) = 0$.

(**2**) When $ax^3 + bx^2 + cx + d$ is divided by $x - h$, the quotient and remainder can be found by synthetic division:

$$
\begin{array}{c|cccc}
h & a & b & c & d \\
& \searrow{+h}\, ah & \searrow{+h}\, ah^2 + bh & \searrow{+h}\, ah^3 + bh^2 + ch & \\
\hline
& a & ah + b & ah^2 + bh + c & ah^3 + bh^2 + ch + d \;= f(h)
\end{array}
$$

The quotient is $ax^2 + (ah + b)x + (ah^2 + bh + c)$ and the remainder is $ah^3 + bh^2 + ch + d$.

(**3**) The remainder theorem:
If a polynomial $f(x)$ is divided by $(x - h)$ the remainder is $f(h)$.

(**4**) The factor theorem:
If $f(h) = 0$ then $(x - h)$ is a factor of $f(x)$.
Conversely, if $(x - h)$ is a factor of $f(x)$ then $f(h) = 0$.

(**5**) The equation of a polynomial may be established from its graph:

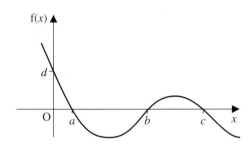

$f(x) = k(x - a)(x - b)(x - c)$ is the general equation for the family of curves. k can be found by substituting $(0, d)$.

(**6**) A root of a polynomial lies between $x = a$ and $x = b$
if $f(a) > 0$ and $f(b) < 0$ or if $f(a) < 0$ and $f(b) > 0$.

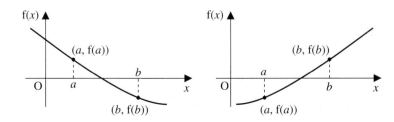

 Quadratic functions

This algebraic expression is a polynomial of degree 2:

$$x^2 + 2x + 1$$

The highest power of x is 2.
The coefficient of x^2 is non-zero.

Expressions like this in which the highest power of x is x^2 (x-squared) are also called **quadratics** (think of the old word for a square: quad).

In this unit you will learn about quadratic functions and their graphs. The graph of a quadratic is easily recognised because of its distinctive shape, which is either $\bigcup$ or $\bigcap$.

This shape is called a parabola.

The path of a projectile such as a ball or an arrow moving under the influence of gravity is a parabola:

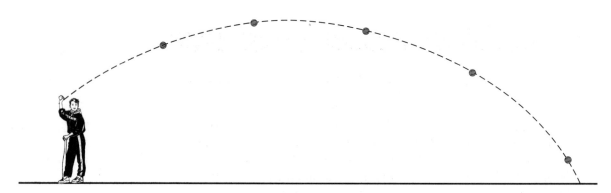

You may come across quadratics in many different forms:

- quadratic expression: $x^2 + 3x + 2$
- quadratic function: $f(x) = x^2 + 3x + 2$
- quadratic mapping: $f : x \rightarrow x^2 + 3x + 2$
- quadratic graph: $y = x^2 + 3x + 2$
- quadratic equation: $x^2 + 3x + 2 = 0$
- quadratic inequation: $x^2 + 3x + 2 > 0$
- quadratic formula: $x = \dfrac{-b \pm \sqrt{b^2 - 4ac}}{2a}$

Graphs of quadratic functions

The next exercise will help you decide which way up the parabola will be.

Exercise 8A

1 Sketch the graph of each function:
   (a) $y = 3x^2$ **(b)** $y = 2x^2 + 1$ **(c)** $y = x^2 + 3x + 2$

2 Sketch the graph of each function:
   (a) $y = -2x^2$ **(b)** $y = -3x^2 + 2$ **(c)** $y = -x^2 + x$

3 Make a conjecture about the shape of the graphs of
   $y = ax^2 + bx + c$ and $y = -ax^2 + bx + c$.

Exercise 8A shows you that:

> The graph of a quadratic function $y = ax^2 + bx + c$ is a
> **parabola**.
> If $a > 0$ the parabola is $\cup$ shaped and the turning point is a
> minimum.
> If $a < 0$ the parabola is $\cap$ shaped and the turning point is a
> maximum.

Exercise 8B

1 (a) Draw the graph of $y = x^2 + 2x - 8$ for $-5 \leqslant x \leqslant 3$ and find
     (i) the coordinates of the points where the graph cuts the
        x-axis
     (ii) the equation of the axis of symmetry of the parabola.
  (b) Explain how to find the equation of the axis of symmetry.
  (c) Which particular point on the parabola does the axis of
     symmetry pass through?

2 For the parabola $y = (x + 2)(x - 6)$ find
  (a) the coordinates of the points where it cuts the x-axis
  (b) the equation of the axis of symmetry
  (c) the coordinates of the point of intersection of the axis of
     symmetry and the parabola.

3 State the equation of the axis of symmetry of each parabola.
  (a)   **(b)**   **(c)**

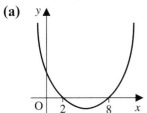
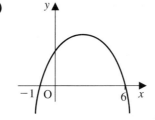
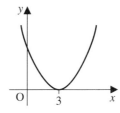

4 A parabola cuts the x-axis at $(-3, 0)$ and $(4, 0)$. State the
  equation of the axis of symmetry.

Sketching quadratic functions

> To sketch and annotate a parabola $y = ax^2 + bx + c$ we need to identify where possible:
> - whether the shape is $\cup$ $(a > 0)$ or $\cap$ $(a < 0)$
> - the coordinates of the y intercept, $(0, c)$
> - the zeros of the function by solving $ax^2 + bx + c = 0$
> - the equation of the axis of symmetry
> - the coordinates of the turning point.

Example 1
Sketch the graph of $y = 5 - 4x - x^2$.

The coefficient of x^2 is negative, so the parabola is $\cap$ shaped.

When $x = 0$, $y = 5$, therefore the y-intercept is $(0, 5)$.

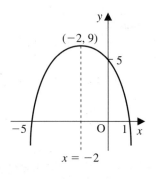

When $y = 0$, $5 - 4x - x^2 = 0$

$$(5 + x)(1 - x) = 0$$
$$x = -5 \text{ or } x = 1$$

Therefore, the zeros are -5 and 1.

The equation of the axis of symmetry is $x = \dfrac{-5 + 1}{2}$

$$x = -2$$

When $x = -2$, $y = 9$, therefore there is a maximum turning point at $(-2, 9)$.

Example 2
Find the equation of the parabola in the form $y = ax^2 + bx + c$ that passes through $(-2, 0)$, $(4, 0)$ and $(0, -16)$.

$y = 0$ when $x = -2$ and $y = 0$ when $x = 4$

so $x + 2 = 0$ and $x - 4 = 0$.

Since a family of parabolas cut the x-axis at $x = -2$ and $x = 4$, we can say that

$y = k(x + 2)(x - 4)$ where k is a constant.

Check that $y = k(x^2 - 2x - 8)$ passes through $(0, -16)$,

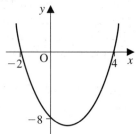

so $\qquad -16 = -8k$

$$k = 2$$

so the equation is $y = 2x^2 - 4x - 16$.

Exercise 8C

1 Sketch and annotate the graphs of:
   (a) $y = x^2 + 6x + 8$
   (b) $y = x^2 + 2x - 15$
   (c) $y = x^2 - 2x - 24$
   (d) $y = x^2 + 5x$

(e) $y = x^2 - 16$

(f) $y = 10 + 3x - x^2$

(g) $y = 4x - x^2$

(h) $y = x^2 - 100$

(i) $y = 9 - x^2$

(j) $y = -15 + 8x - x^2$

2 For each parabola
   (i) find the equation of the axis of symmetry
   (ii) state the nature of the turning point and its coordinates.

(a) $y = x^2 - 8x + 12$

(b) $y = 7 + 6x - x^2$

(c) $y = 3 - 2x - x^2$

(d) $y = x^2 + 10x$

3 With the help of a sketch, find the equation of the parabola of the form $y = x^2 + bx + c$ that passes through

(a) $(2, 0)$ and $(3, 0)$

(b) $(-2, 0)$ and $(4, 0)$

(c) $(-5, 0)$ and $(-1, 0)$

(d) $(0, 0)$ and $(7, 0)$

4 With the help of a sketch find the equations of the parabolas passing through the following points:

(a) $(2, 0)$, $(-2, 0)$ and $(0, -12)$

(b) $(3, 0)$, $(-3, 0)$ and $(0, 18)$

(c) $(2, 0)$, $(4, 0)$ and $(0, -8)$

(d) $(-2, 0)$, $(-4, 0)$ and $(0, -4)$

5 Find the equation of the parabola that passes through $(0, 0)$, $(6, 0)$ and $(3, -27)$.

6 Sketch a graph for $y = ax^2 + bx + c$ when

(a) $a > 0$

(b) $a < 0$

(c) $a > 0$ and $c = 0$

(d) $a < 0$ and $b = 0$

Completing the square

The coordinates of the turning point of a quadratic can also be found by completing the square.

This is particularly useful for parabolas that do not cut the x-axis.

Example 3

Find the equation of the axis of symmetry and the coordinates of the turning point of $y = 2x^2 - 8x + 9$.

First complete the square:
$y = 2(x^2 - 4x + \frac{9}{2})$
$y = 2(x^2 - 4x + 4 - 4 + \frac{9}{2})$
$y = 2[(x - 2)^2 + \frac{1}{2}]$
$y = 2(x - 2)^2 + 1$

Since it is a square, the lowest value that $2(x - 2)^2$ can be is zero.

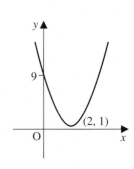

Hence the minimum value of y is 1 and this occurs when $x = 2$. The axis of symmetry is $x = 2$ and there is a minimum turning point at $(2, 1)$.

Example 4

Find the equation of the axis of symmetry and the coordinates of the turning point of $y = 7 + 6x - x^2$.

First complete the square:

$y = 7 + 6x - x^2$

$y = -x^2 + 6x + 7$

$y = -[x^2 - 6x - 7]$

$y = -[x^2 - 6x + 9 - 9 - 7]$

$y = -[(x + 3)^2 - 16]$

$y = 16 - (x - 3)^2$

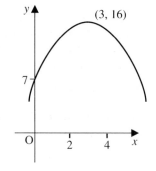

Since it is a square, the lowest value that $(x - 3)^2$ can be is zero.

Hence the maximum value of y is 16 and this occurs when $x = 3$. The axis of symmetry is $x = 3$ and there is a maximum turning point at (3, 16).

> ▶ When the equation $y = ax^2 + bx + c$ is written in the form $y = a(x + p)^2 + q$ the axis of symmetry is $x = -p$ and the turning point is at $(-p, q)$.

Exercise 8D

1 For each function state:
   (i)   whether the turning point is a minimum or maximum
   (ii) the equation of the axis of symmetry
   (iii) the coordinates of the turning point.

   (a) $y = (x + 3)^2 - 2$ **(b)** $y = (5 - x)^2 + 1$
   (c) $y = 8 - (x + 3)^2$ **(d)** $y = (2x + 3)^2 - 4$
   (e) $y = \left(x - \frac{1}{2}\right)^2 + 1$ **(f)** $y = 10 - 2(2x - 3)^2$

2 Use the method of completing the square to sketch and annotate each graph.

   (a) $y = x^2 - 4x + 4$ **(b)** $y = 3 + 2x - x^2$
   (c) $y = x^2 + 2x + 5$ **(d)** $y = 8 - 2x - x^2$
   (e) $y = x^2 + 4x + 7$ **(f)** $y = x^2 - 12x$
   (g) $y = 3x^2 - 6x + 4$ **(h)** $y = 6 - x - 2x^2$

3 Without drawing the graphs, match each equation 1 to 5 with one of the statements A to E.

   (1) $y = x^2 + 3x - 10$ **(2)** $y = x^2 - 1$
   (3) $y = (x + 1)^2$ **(4)** $y = x^2 - 2x$
   (5) $y = 3 + 2x - x^2$

   A   The curve has a maximum turning point.
   B   The curve passes through the origin.
   C   The curve has the x-axis as a tangent.
   D   The curve is symmetrical about the y-axis.
   E   The curve has an axis of symmetry with equation $x = -1.5$.

4 Find the coordinates of the turning point of each parabola.

(a) $y = x^2 + 6x - 7$ (b) $y = x^2 - 6x + 14$

(c) $y = 16 - x^2$ (d) $y = 4x - x^2$

(e) $y = 2x^2 - 8x + 9$ (f) $y = -18 - 8x - x^2$

5 Find the equation of a parabola that has

(a) a minimum turning point at $(2, -5)$ (b) a minimum turning point at $(-3, 7)$

(c) a maximum turning point at $(1, 12)$ (d) a maximum turning point at $(3, -4)$

6 Express $x^2 + 2x + 9$ in the form $(x + a)^2 + b$ and hence state the

maximum value of $\dfrac{16}{x^2 + 2x + 9}$.

Solving quadratic equations

> Quadratic equations may be solved by
> - using the graph
> - factorising
> - completing the square
> - using the quadratic formula.

Example 5

Solve $6x^2 + x - 15 = 0$.

$6x^2 + x - 15 = 0$ factorises to

$(2x - 3)(3x + 5) = 0$

$2x - 3 = 0$ or $3x + 5 = 0$

$x = \frac{3}{2}$ or $x = -\frac{5}{3}$

Example 6

Solve $x^2 - 4x - 1 = 0$.

$x^2 - 4x - 1$ does not factorise so complete the square:

$x^2 - 4x - 1 = 0$

$\quad x^2 - 4x = 1$

$x^2 - 4x + 4 = 1 + 4$

$\quad (x - 2)^2 = 5$

$\quad (x - 2) = \pm\sqrt{5}$

$x = 2 + \sqrt{5}$ or $x = 2 - \sqrt{5}$

Exercise 8E

1 Factorise and solve:

(a) $t^2 + 8t + 12 = 0$ (b) $w^2 + 2w - 15 = 0$

(c) $z^2 + 12z - 13 = 0$ (d) $25 - 10f + f^2 = 0$

    (e) $a^2 - 6a - 16 = 0$ **(f)** $h^2 + 14h + 49 = 0$

    (g) $-1 + 2k - k^2 = 0$ **(h)** $x^2 - 25 = 0$

    (i) $3y^2 + 8y + 4 = 0$ **(j)** $10d^2 - 11d - 6 = 0$

    (k) $2x^2 + 18x + 28 = 0$ **(l)** $20 - 15a - 5a^2 = 0$

2 Complete the square and solve:

    (a) $x^2 + 6x + 7 = 0$ **(b)** $x^2 + 2x - 1 = 0$

    (c) $x^2 + 8x + 1 = 0$ **(d)** $x^2 + 3x + \frac{1}{4} = 0$

    (e) $x^2 = -10x - 22$ **(f)** $2x^2 + 2x - 1 = 0$

    (g) $2x^2 = 3x + 6$ **(h)** $5x^2 - 30x - 18 = 0$

3 Solve:

    (a) $x^2 - 15x + 36 = 0$ **(b)** $x^2 + 9 = 11$

    (c) $x^2 - 2x - 8 = 0$ **(d)** $x^2 - 6x + 4 = 0$

    (e) $5x^2 - 17 = 8$ **(f)** $x^2 + 48x - 100 = 0$

    (g) $x^2 - 4x - 7 = 0$ **(h)** $x^2 - 10x - 25 = 0$

    (i) $3x^2 - 8x + 5 = 0$ **(j)** $(x + 8)^2 - 23 = 0$

    (k) $x^2 + 20x - 10 = 0$ **(l)** $x^2 - x - 6 = 0$

    (m) $3x^2 + 6x + 2 = 0$ **(n)** $x^2 + bx + c = 0$

Quadratic inequations

> A quadratic inequation can be solved using a sketch of the quadratic function.

We can then easily see where the graph is positive or negative.

Example 7

Find the values of x for which

(a) $12 - 5x - 2x^2 > 0$ **(b)** $12 - 5x - 2x^2 < 0$

First sketch the graph of $y = 12 - 5x - 2x^2$. The graph has a y-intercept of 12.

Then factorise: $(4 + x)(3 - 2x) = 0$

The function has zeros at -4 and $\frac{3}{2}$.

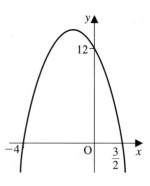

(a) From the graph, the value of $12 - 5x - 2x^2$ is positive (i.e. **above** the x-axis) when $-4 < x < \frac{3}{2}$.

(b) From the graph, the value of $12 - 5x - 2x^2$ is negative, (i.e. **below** the x-axis) when $x < -4$ or $x > \frac{3}{2}$.

Exercise 8F

1 Solve:

    (a) $9 - x^2 = 0$ **(b)** $9 - x^2 > 0$ **(c)** $9 - x^2 < 0$

2 Solve:

    (a) $x^2 + 3x - 4 = 0$ **(b)** $x^2 + 3x - 4 < 0$ **(c)** $x^2 + 3x - 4 > 0$

3 Solve:

(a) $x^2 - x - 6 > 0$

(b) $2 + x - x^2 > 0$

(c) $x^2 + 3x - 10 < 0$

(d) $36 \geqslant x^2$

(e) $x^2 - 5x < 0$

(f) $3x < x^2$

(g) $8 + 2x - x^2 \leqslant 0$

(h) $2x^2 + 11x + 5 \geqslant 0$

(i) $8 + 18x > 5x^2$

(j) $4x^2 - 4x > -1$

The quadratic formula

The quadratic formula allows us to find the relationship between the roots of the quadratic equation $ax^2 + bx + c = 0$ and its coefficients a, b and c.

> If $ax^2 + bx + c = 0$ then $x = \dfrac{-b \pm \sqrt{b^2 - 4ac}}{2a}$, $a \neq 0$.

Proof

$$ax^2 + bx + c = 0$$

$$a\left[x^2 + \frac{b}{a}x + \frac{c}{a}\right] = 0$$

$$a\left[\left(x^2 + \frac{b}{a}x + \frac{b^2}{4a^2}\right) - \frac{b^2}{4a^2} + \frac{c}{a}\right] = 0$$

$$a\left[\left(x + \frac{b}{2a}\right)^2 - \frac{(b^2 - 4ac)}{4a^2}\right] = 0$$

$$a\left(x + \frac{b}{2a}\right)^2 - \frac{a(b^2 - 4ac)}{4a^2} = 0$$

$$a\left(x + \frac{b}{2a}\right)^2 - \frac{(b^2 - 4ac)}{4a} = 0$$

$$a\left(x + \frac{b}{2a}\right)^2 = \frac{b^2 - 4ac}{4a}$$

$$\left(x + \frac{b}{2a}\right)^2 = \frac{b^2 - 4ac}{4a^2}$$

$$x + \frac{b}{2a} = \pm\frac{\sqrt{b^2 - 4ac}}{2a}$$

$$x = \frac{-b}{2a} \pm \frac{\sqrt{b^2 - 4ac}}{2a}$$

$$x = \frac{-b \pm \sqrt{b^2 - 4ac}}{2a}$$

The value(s) of x are called the **roots** of the equation.

Example 8

Solve $2x^2 - 5x + 1 = 0$ rounding the roots to two decimal places.

Using the quadratic formula with $a = 2$, $b = -5$ and $c = 1$:

$$x = \frac{5 \pm \sqrt{25 - 8}}{4}$$

$$x = \frac{5 \pm 4.123}{4}$$

$$x = \frac{9.123}{4} \text{ or } x = \frac{0.877}{4}$$

$$x = 2.28 \text{ or } x = 0.22$$

Example 9

Solve $x^2 + 2x + 9 = 0$.

Using the quadratic formula with $a = 1$, $b = 2$ and $c = 9$:

$$x = \frac{-2 \pm \sqrt{4 - 36}}{2}$$

$$x = \frac{-2 \pm \sqrt{-32}}{2}$$

Since $\sqrt{-32}$ is not a real number there are no real roots.

Exercise 8G

1 Find the roots of each equation, where they exist, to two decimal places:

    (a) $y^2 + 7y + 5 = 0$ **(b)** $x^2 - 6x + 3 = 0$

    (c) $p^2 = 2p + 5$ **(d)** $2w^2 + 12w + 9 = 0$

    (e) $5x^2 = 4 - 3x$ **(f)** $2z^2 - 3z + 4 = 0$

2 Show graphically and algebraically that:

    (a) $x^2 - 6x + 8 = 0$ has two roots

    (b) $x^2 - 6x + 9 = 0$ has one root

    (c) $x^2 - 6x + 10 = 0$ has no real roots.

3 Use the quadratic formula to solve each equation and complete the table. Describe the nature of the roots as either 'real and equal' or 'real and unequal' or 'non-real'.

Equation	Roots	Nature of the roots	$b^2 - 4ac$
(a) $x^2 - 4x + 3 = 0$	1, 3	real and unequal	4
(b) $4x^2 - 9x + 2 = 0$			
(c) $x^2 + 2x + 1 = 0$			
(d) $x^2 - x - 5 = 0$			
(e) $x^2 - 5 = 0$			
(f) $x^2 + 2x + 3 = 0$			
(g) $x^2 - 6x + 9 = 0$			
(h) $2x^2 + x + 3 = 0$			
(i) $9x^2 + 6x + 1 = 0$			

4 Use the results from the table in question 3 to complete these statements:

   (a) If $b^2 - 4ac > 0$ the roots are _____ .

   (b) If $b^2 - 4ac = 0$ the roots are _____ .

   (c) If $b^2 - 4ac < 0$ the roots are _____ .

The discriminant

Exercise 8G shows you that:

> For the quadratic equation $ax^2 + bx + c = 0$, $b^2 - 4ac$ is called the **discriminant**.
>
> ▶ • if $b^2 - 4ac > 0$, the roots are real and unequal
> • if $b^2 - 4ac = 0$, the roots are real and equal
> • if $b^2 - 4ac < 0$, the roots are non-real.

Example 10

Find the nature of the roots of $4x^2 - 12x + 9 = 0$.

$a = 4$, $b = -12$ and $c = 9$.

$$\text{The discriminant} = b^2 - 4ac = (-12)^2 - (4 \times 4 \times 9)$$
$$= 144 - 144$$
$$= 0$$

The discriminant is zero therefore the roots are real and equal.

Exercise 8H

1 Find the discriminant of each equation and state the nature of the roots.

   (a) $3x^2 - 7x + 2 = 0$ **(b)** $2x^2 - 3x + 4 = 0$

   (c) $x^2 - 6x + 9 = 0$ **(d)** $7x^2 + 5x - 1 = 0$

   (e) $2x^2 + x - 1 = 0$ **(f)** $4x^2 - 7x + 3 = 0$

2 For each equation state the nature of the roots.

   (a) $x^2 + 4x - 5 = 0$ **(b)** $x^2 - 3x + 4 = 0$

   (c) $3x^2 - 6x + 3 = 0$ **(d)** $3x^2 - 5x + 1 = 0$

   (e) $x^2 + 8x + 16 = 0$ **(f)** $3x^2 + x + 3 = 0$

Using the discriminant

We can use the discriminant to find unknown coefficients in a quadratic equation.

Example 11

Find p given that $2x^2 + 4x + p = 0$ has real roots.

$a = 2$, $b = 4$, $c = p$.

For real roots $b^2 - 4ac \geqslant 0$, so

$$16 - 8p \geqslant 0$$
$$16 \geqslant 8p$$
$$p \leqslant 2$$

The equation has real roots when $p \leqslant 2$.

Example 12

Find q given that $x^2 + (q - 3)x + q = 0$ has non-real roots.

$a = 1$, $b = q - 3$, $c = q$.

For non-real roots $b^2 - 4ac < 0$, so

$$(q - 3)^2 - 4q < 0$$
$$q^2 - 6q + 9 - 4q < 0$$
$$q^2 - 10q + 9 < 0$$
$$(q - 9)(q - 1) < 0$$

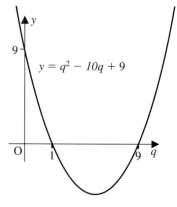

$y = q^2 - 10q + 9$

From the graph of $(q - 9)(q - 1)$, this is true when $1 < q < 9$ therefore the equation has non-real roots when $1 < q < 9$.

Example 13

Show that the roots of $(k - 2)x^2 - (3k - 2)x + 2k = 0$ are always real.

$a = k - 2$, $b = -(3k - 2)$, $c = 2k$

$$
\begin{aligned}
b^2 - 4ac &= [-(3k - 2)]^2 - 4(k - 2)2k \\
&= 9k^2 - 12k + 4 - 8k^2 + 16k \\
&= k^2 + 4k + 4 \\
&= (k + 2)^2
\end{aligned}
$$

Since $(k + 2)^2$ is a square it has a minimum value of zero, therefore $b^2 - 4ac \geqslant 0$ and so the roots of the equation are always real.

Exercise 8I

1 For each equation find the value(s) for p so that the roots are equal.

(a) $x^2 - 8x + p = 0$ (b) $px^2 + 6x + 18 = 0$

(c) $x^2 - 2px + 9 = 0$ (d) $2x^2 + 2px + p^2 - 8 = 0$

(e) $x^2 + (p - 5)x + 4p = 0$ (f) $px^2 - 10x + p = 0$

(g) $x^2 = p(2x - 5)$ (h) $x^2 + 2p + 1 = 2(p - 1)x$

(i) $(x - 1)(x - p) = 0$ (j) $(p + 1)x^2 + 3p = 2(p + 3)x$

2 For what values of k does each equation have real roots?

(a) $x^2 - 4x + k = 0$ (b) $2x^2 + 20x + k = 0$

(c) $kx^2 - 2x + 1 = 0$ (d) $kx^2 + (2k - 3)x + k = 0$

(e) $k(x^2 - x + 1) = 1$ (f) $x(x - 4) + 2 = k(2x - 3k)$

3 Find k given that $kx^2 + (2k + 1)x + k = 0$ has equal roots.

4 Given that k is a real number, show that the roots of the following equations are always real:

(a) $kx^2 + 3x + 3 = k$ (b) $x^2 + 2(k + 1)x + 2k + 1 = 0$

(c) $\dfrac{x^2 - 2x + 21}{3x - 7} = 2k$ (d) $x = \dfrac{2k(x - 2) - 4}{x - 4}$

5 Show that $x(x - 3) = p^2 - 2$ always has real roots if p is real.

6 Show that $px^2 + qx - p = 0$ always has real roots if p and q are real.

7 Show that the roots of $(x - p)(x - q) = r^2$ are real for all values of p, q and r.

8 Calculate the least value of p so that the graph of $y = 4x^2 - px + 25$ does not cut or touch the x-axis.

Condition for tangency

To determine whether a straight line cuts, touches or does not meet a curve the equation of the line is substituted into the equation of the curve. When a quadratic equation results, the discriminant can be used to find the number of points of intersection.

Two points of intersection

$y = x^2 + 3x + 2$ and $y = x + 2$ meet where

$$x^2 + 3x + 2 = x + 2$$
$$x^2 + 2x = 0$$

Discriminant $= 4$ therefore the two roots are real and unequal.

Hence there are two distinct points of intersection.

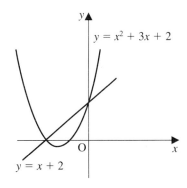

One point of intersection

$y = x^2 + 3x + 2$ and $y = x + 1$ meet where

$$x^2 + 3x + 2 = x + 1$$
$$x^2 + 2x + 1 = 0$$

Discriminant $= 0$ therefore these are equal roots.

Hence there is only one point of intersection and the line is a **tangent** to the parabola.

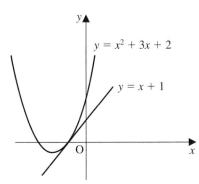

No points of intersection

$y = x^2 + 3x + 2$ and $y = x - 5$ meet where

$x^2 + 3x + 2 = x - 5$
$x^2 + 2x + 7 = 0$

Discriminant $= -24$ therefore there are no real roots.

Hence the line does not meet the parabola.

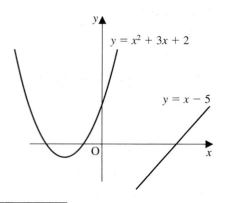

> For a quadratic equation formed when the equation of a
> straight line is substituted into the equation of a parabola:
> - if $b^2 - 4ac > 0$, the line intersects the curve at two places
> - if $b^2 - 4ac = 0$, the line is a tangent to the curve
> - if $b^2 - 4ac < 0$, the line does not intersect the curve.

Example 14

Prove that the line $y = 2x - 1$ is tangent to the parabola $y = x^2$ and find the point of intersection.

The line and parabola meet where $x^2 = 2x - 1$,
therefore $x^2 - 2x + 1 = 0$.

$b^2 - 4ac = (-2)^2 - 4 = 0$, so there is one point of intersection.

Hence the line is a tangent.

The line and parabola meet where

$$x^2 - 2x + 1 = 0$$
so $(x - 1)(x - 1) = 0$
so $x = 1$.

The point of intersection is $(1, 1)$.

Example 15

Find the equation of the tangent to $y = x^2 + 1$ that has gradient 2.

A straight line with gradient 2 will have an equation of the form $y = 2x + k$.

$y = 2x + k$ meets $y = x^2 + 1$ where $x^2 + 1 = 2x + k$

$x^2 - 2x + (1 - k) = 0$

Tangency implies equal roots therefore $b^2 - 4ac = 0$.

$a = 1$, $b = -2$ and $c = 1 - k$:

$$b^2 - 4ac = (-2)^2 - 4(1 - k) = 0$$
$$4 - 4 + 4k = 0$$
$$4k = 0$$
$$k = 0$$

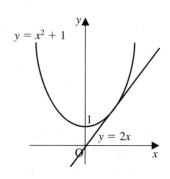

The equation of the tangent is $y = 2x$.

Example 16

Find the equations of the tangents from $(0, -2)$ to the curve $y = 8x^2$.

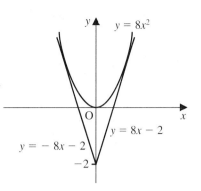

All lines that pass through $(0, -2)$ are of the form $y = mx - 2$.

The line and the parabola meet where $8x^2 = mx - 2$
$$8x^2 - mx + 2 = 0$$

Tangency implies equal roots therefore $b^2 - 4ac = 0$.

$a = 8$, $b = -m$ and $c = 2$:

$$b^2 - 4ac = m^2 - 64 = 0$$
$$m^2 = 64$$
$$m = \pm 8$$

The equations of the two tangents are $y = 8x - 2$ and $y = -8x - 2$.

Exercise 8J

1 For each of the following, prove that the line is a tangent to the parabola and find the point of contact.

(a) $y = x - 4$ and $y = x^2 - 3x$
(b) $y = 2x$ and $y = x^2 + 1$
(c) $y = 4x$ and $y = x^2 + 4$
(d) $y = x - \frac{1}{4}$ and $y = x^2$
(e) $y = 8x - 2$ and $y = 8x^2$
(f) $y + 8x + 8 = 0$ and $y = 2x^2$

2 Find c such that the line $y = 2x + c$ is a tangent to the parabola $y = x^2 - 4x$ and find the coordinates of the point of contact.

3 Given its gradient, find the equation of the tangent to each parabola.

(a) $y = x^2$, $m_{\text{tan}} = 2$
(b) $y = 3x^2$, $m_{\text{tan}} = -2$
(c) $y = x^2 + 1$, $m_{\text{tan}} = 2$
(d) $y = 2x^2 + 5$, $m_{\text{tan}} = 4$
(e) $y = x - x^2$, $m_{\text{tan}} = 3$
(f) $y = x^2 + x - 2$, $m_{\text{tan}} = 1$

4 The line $y = mx - 1$ is a tangent to $y = x^2 - 4x + 3$. Find two values for m.

5 Find the equations of the tangent from the given point to each parabola.

(a) $(0, -1)$, $y = x^2$
(b) $(0, -1)$, $y = x^2 + 3$
(c) $(0, 1)$, $y = -4x^2$

6 A horizontal line is a tangent to the parabola $y = x^2 - 2x - 3$. Find the equation of this tangent and the coordinates of the point of contact.

Exercise 8K Mixed questions

1 Sketch the curves

(a) $y = 2x^2 + x - 3$ (b) $y = 8 - 2x - x^2$

2 For each parabola state its equation in the form $y = ax^2 + bx + c$.

(a) 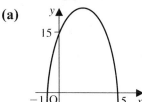   (b) 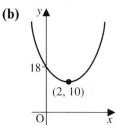   (c)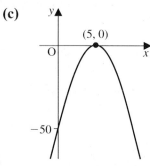

3 Find the equation of the axis of symmetry for the graph of
$y = 4x^2 - 4x - 15$.

4 Solve the equations

(a) $5x^2 - 3x - 1 = 0$ (b) $4x^2 - 5x = 2$

5 Solve

(a) $x^2 - x - 6 < 0$ (b) $2x^2 \leqslant 15 - 7x$

6 Express $f(x) = (2x - 1)(2x + 5)$ in the form $a(x + b)^2 + c$.

[Higher]

7 Express $13 + 4x - 2x^2$ in the form $a + b(x + c)^2$.

8 State the nature of the roots of the equation $3x^2 - 2x + 9 = 0$.

9 Show, by using the discriminant, that the roots of
$12x^2 - 29x + 15 = 0$ are real and unequal.

10 The roots of the equation $(x - 1)(x + k) = -4$ are equal. Find
the values of k.   [Higher]

11 (a) Show that the function $f(x) = 2x^2 + 8x - 3$ can be written in
the form $f(x) = a(x + b)^2 + c$ where a, b and c are constants.

(b) Hence, or otherwise, find the coordinates of the turning point
of the function f.   [Higher]

12 Given that k is a real number, show that the roots of the
equation $kx^2 + 3x + 3 = k$ are always real numbers.

[Higher]

13 Find c such that the line $y = x + c$ is a tangent to the curve
$y = x^2 - 3x$ and find the coordinates of the point of contact.

14 Calculate the least positive integer value of k so that the graph
of $y = kx^2 - 8x + k$ does not cut or touch the x-axis.

[Higher]

SUMMARY

(1) The graph of a quadratic function $y = ax^2 + bx + c$ is a **parabola**.
If $a > 0$ the parabola is $\cup$ shaped and the turning point is a minimum.
If $a < 0$ the parabola is $\cap$ shaped and the turning point is a maximum.

(2) To sketch and annotate a parabola $y = ax^2 + bx + c$ we need to identify where possible
- whether the shape is $\cup$ $(a > 0)$ or $\cap$ $(a < 0)$
- the coordinates of the y-intercept, $(0, c)$
- the zeros of the function by solving $ax^2 + bx + c = 0$
- the equation of the axis of symmetry
- the coordinates of the turning point.

(3) When the equation $y = ax^2 + bx + c$ is written in the form $y = a(x + p)^2 + q$, the axis of symmetry is $x = -p$ and the turning point is at $(-p, q)$.

(4) Quadratic equations may be solved by
- using the graph
- factorising
- completing the square
- using the quadratic formula.

(5) A quadratic inequation can be solved using a sketch of the quadratic function.

(6) If $ax^2 + bx + c = 0$ then $x = \dfrac{-b \pm \sqrt{b^2 - 4ac}}{2a}, a \neq 0$.

(7) For the quadratic equation $ax^2 + bx + c = 0$, $b^2 - 4ac$ is called the discriminant.
- if $b^2 - 4ac > 0$, the roots are real and unequal
- if $b^2 - 4ac = 0$, the roots are real and equal
- if $b^2 - 4ac < 0$, the roots are non-real.

(8) For a quadratic equation formed when the equation of a straight line is substituted into the equation of a parabola:
- if $b^2 - 4ac > 0$, the line intersects the curve at two places
- if $b^2 - 4ac = 0$, the line is a tangent to the curve
- if $b^2 - 4ac < 0$, the line does not intersect the curve.

9 Integration

Area under a curve

Calculus can be divided into two basic parts: differentiation and integration. In Chapter 6 differentiation was introduced by considering distance–time graphs showing the movement of a car over time. Using speed–time graphs we can calculate the distance travelled and so introduce integration.

Example 1

A car is travelling along a motorway at a constant speed of 30 metres per second. How far does the car travel in 5 seconds?

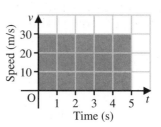

The distance travelled can be found by calculating the area under the speed–time graph.

Area $= 5 \times 30$
$ = 150$
Distance travelled $= 150$ metres

Exercise 9A

In each speed-time graph calculate the distance represented by the shaded area.

1
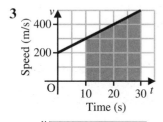

2
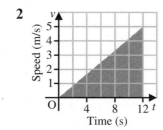

3
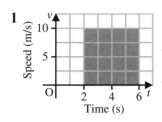

4
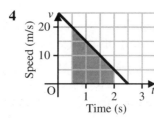

5
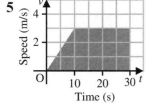

6
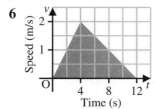

7 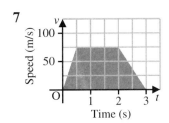   **8**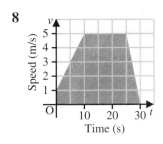

Approximating the area under a curve

This is the speed–time graph for an aeroplane taking off. The distance travelled during the first 3 seconds is represented by the shaded area. You can find an approximate value for the area by counting squares. Alternatively, you can find upper and lower bounds for the area using rectangles. To do this we first need to find the speed at intervals of, say, 0.5 seconds using $v = 2t^2$:

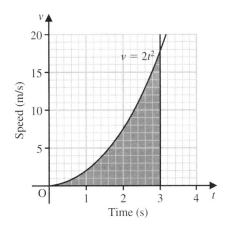

t	0	0.5	1	1.5	2	2.5	3
v	0	0.5	2	4.5	8	12.5	18

Using these values we can plot rectangles either below or above the graph of $v = 2t^2$.

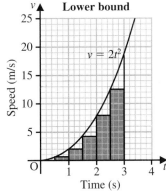

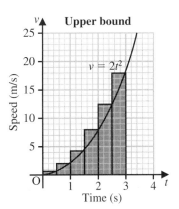

The **lower bound** of the area under the graph is the sum of the areas of the rectangular strips drawn to the right of the curve

$$\text{Area} = 0.5 \times (0 + 0.5 + 2 + 4.5 + 8 + 12.5)$$
$$= 13.75 \, \text{unit}^2$$

The **upper bound** of the area under the graph is the sum of the areas of the rectangular strips drawn to the left of the curve.

$$\text{Area} = 0.5 \times (0.5 + 2 + 4.5 + 8 + 12.5 + 18)$$
$$= 22.75 \, \text{unit}^2$$

The actual area under the graph lies between 13.75 unit^2 and 22.75 unit^2.

Reducing the width of each interval increases the number of rectangles and brings the bounds closer together:

Number of rectangles	6	12	24	48	96	300
Lower bound	13.75	15.8125	16.8906	17.4414	17.7197	17.9101
Upper bound	22.75	20.3125	19.1406	18.5666	18.2822	18.0901

Both the lower bound and the upper bound converge to 18 as the number of rectangles is increased, therefore the area under the graph of $v = 2t^2$ between $t = 0$ and $t = 3$ is 18 unit^2.

Exercise 9B

1 (a) Extend the table of values for $v = 2t^2$ to include $t = 3.5$ and $t = 4$.

   (b) Calculate the upper and lower bounds for the area between $t = 0$ and $t = 4$ using rectangles of width 0.5.

2 Use rectangles of width 0.5 to calculate upper and lower bounds for the area under the graph of $y = 3x^2$ between $x = 0$ and
   (a) $x = 1$ (b) $x = 2$ (c) $x = 3$ (d) $x = 4$

3 Use the bounds for each example in question 2 to estimate, correct to the nearest whole number, a value for each area.

Area under $y = (n + 1)x^n$

By increasing the number of rectangles in question 3 of Exercise 9B the area values can be found more accurately.

> ▶ The area between the graph of a function, $y = f(x)$, and the x-axis, starting at $x = 0$, is called the **area function** $A(x)$.

In the diagram $A(4)$ is shaded for the function $y = 3x^2$.

x	0	1	2	3	4
$A(x)$	0	1	8	27	64

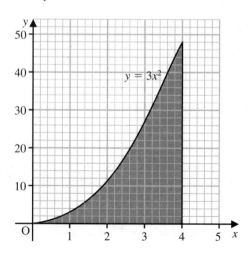

Try the following exercise and see if you can find a general formula for $A(x)$.

Exercise 9C

1 (a) From the table above, find a formula for the area function, $A(x)$, of the graph $y = 3x^2$.
  (b) Use the tables below to find a formula for the area function of
  (i) $y = 4x^3$ (ii) $y = 5x^4$

x	0	1	2	3	4
$A(x)$	0	1	16	81	256

x	0	1	2	3	4
$A(x)$	0	1	32	243	1024

2 (a) Identify the pattern and complete the table.

y	$3x^2$	$4x^3$	$5x^4$	$6x^5$	$9x^8$	$21x^{20}$
$A(x)$	x^3	x^4	x^5			

  (b) Make a conjecture about the area function for the graph of $y = (n+1)x^n$.

From Exercise 9C, you should notice that:

> ▶ The area function for $y = (n+1)x^n$ is $A(x) = x^{(n+1)}$ $(n \neq -1)$.

Example 2
Calculate the area under the graph of $y = 8x^7$ between $x = 0$ and $x = 3$.

Area function for $y = 8x^7$ is $A(x) = x^8$.
Area between $x = 0$ and $x = 3$ is $A(3) = 3^8 = 6561$ unit^2.

Example 3
Calculate the area under the graph of $y = 3x^2$ between $x = 2$ and $x = 3$.

Area function for $y = 3x^2$ is $A(x) = x^3$.
Area between $x = 2$ and $x = 3$ can be calculated as
(area between $x = 0$ and $x = 3$) − (area between $x = 0$ and $x = 2$).
$$A(3) - A(2) = 3^3 - 2^3$$
$$= 19 \text{ unit}^2.$$

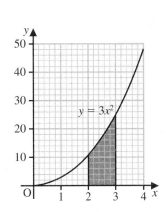

Exercise 9D

1 Write the area function $A(x)$, for
  (a) $y = 12x^{11}$ **(b)** $y = 15x^{14}$ **(c)** $y = 10x^9$ **(d)** $y = 100x^{99}$

2 Calculate the area under the graph of
  (a) $y = 5x^4$ between $x = 0$ and $x = 2$ **(b)** $y = 7x^6$ between $x = 0$ and $x = 3$
  (c) $y = 11x^{10}$ between $x = 0$ and $x = 1$ **(d)** $y = 12x^{11}$ between $x = 0$ and $x = 0.5$.

3 Calculate the area under the graph of $y = 2x$ between $x = 0$ and $x = 10$
  (a) geometrically   **(b)** using the area function of $y = 2x$.

4 Calculate the area under the graph of
  (a) $y = 3x^2$ between $x = 4$ and $x = 10$ **(b)** $y = 2x$ between $x = 0$ and $x = 2$
  (c) $y = 4x^3$ between $x = 1$ and $x = 4$ **(d)** $y = 7x^6$ between $x = 1$ and $x = 2$
  (e) $v = 9t^8$ between $t = 0$ and $t = 1$ **(f)** $a = 5t^4$ between $t = 1$ and $t = 2$.

5 A car accelerates so that its speed, v m/s after t seconds, is given by $v = 2t$. Calculate the distance travelled between $t = 4$ and $t = 6$ seconds.

Anti-differentiation

▶ The reverse process to differentiation is called **anti-differentiation**.

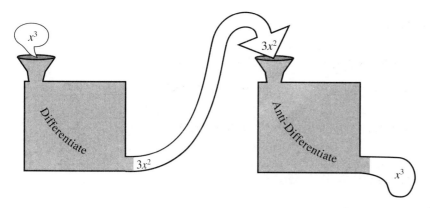

The derivative of $f(x) = x^3$ is $f'(x) = 3x^2$.   ⇔   An anti-derivative of $f'(x) = 3x^2$ is $f(x) = x^3$.

The derivative of $f(x) = x^{-4}$ is $f'(x) = -4x^{-5}$.   ⇔   An anti-derivative of $f'(x) = -4x^{-5}$ is $f(x) = x^{-4}$.

The derivative of $f(x) = x^{\frac{3}{4}}$ is $f'(x) = \frac{3}{4}x^{-\frac{1}{4}}$.   ⇔   An anti-derivative of $f'(x) = \frac{3}{4}x^{-\frac{1}{4}}$ is $f(x) = x^{\frac{3}{4}}$.

Exercise 9E

1 Find an anti-derivative of
  (a) $f'(x) = 4x^3$ **(b)** $f'(x) = 8x^7$ **(c)** $f'(x) = 12x^{11}$
  (d) $f'(x) = 7x^6$ **(e)** $f'(x) = 17x^{16}$ **(f)** $f'(x) = 23x^{22}$
  (g) $f'(x) = -2x^{-3}$ **(h)** $f'(x) = -9x^{-10}$ **(i)** $f'(x) = -6x^{-7}$

(j) $f'(x) = -5x^{-6}$ (k) $f'(x) = -12x^{-13}$ (l) $f'(x) = -14x^{-15}$

(m) $f'(x) = \frac{3}{2}x^{\frac{1}{2}}$ (n) $f'(x) = \frac{7}{4}x^{\frac{3}{4}}$ (o) $f'(x) = \frac{1}{4}x^{-\frac{3}{4}}$

(p) $f'(x) = -\frac{1}{2}x^{-\frac{3}{2}}$ (q) $f'(x) = -\frac{4}{5}x^{-\frac{9}{5}}$ (r) $f'(x) = -\frac{8}{3}x^{-\frac{11}{3}}$

Indefinite integrals

The process of finding anti-derivatives is called **integration**. The following exercise will help you see what happens when x^n is integrated.

Exercise 9F

1 (a) Differentiate each function where C is a constant.

    (i) $f(x) = x^4$, $f(x) = x^4 + 1$, $f(x) = x^4 + 7$ and $f(x) = x^4 + C$

    (ii) $f(x) = x^6$, $f(x) = x^6 + 5$, $f(x) = x^6 - 4$ and $f(x) = x^6 + C$

    (iii) $f(x) = x^{-3}$, $f(x) = x^{-3} - 1$, $f(x) = x^{-3} + 9$ and $f(x) = x^{-3} + C$

(b) (i) What is the derivative function of $f(x) = x^n + C$?

    (ii) What is the anti-derivative of $f'(x) = nx^{n-1}$?

Finding integrals

From Exercise 9F you should notice that:

If $f'(x) = nx^{n-1}$ then $f(x) = x^n + C$ where C is called the **constant of integration**.

The **integral** is written $\int x^n \, dx$ and is read as 'the indefinite integral of x^n with respect to x'.

Since $\dfrac{d}{dx}(x^n + C) = nx^{n-1}$ then $\int nx^{n-1} \, dx = x^n + C$

and since $\dfrac{d}{dx}\left(\dfrac{x^{n+1}}{n+1} + C\right) = x^n$ then $\int x^n \, dx = \dfrac{x^{n+1}}{n+1} + C$

$$\blacktriangleright \quad \int x^n \, dx = \frac{x^{n+1}}{n+1} + C \quad (n \neq -1)$$

Example 4

Find $\int x^6 \, dx$.

$$\int x^6 \, dx = \frac{x^{6+1}}{6+1} + C$$

$$= \frac{1}{7}x^7 + C$$

Example 5

Find $\int t^{-4} \, dt$.

$$\int t^{-4} \, dt = \frac{t^{-4+1}}{-4+1} + C$$

$$= -\frac{1}{3}t^{-3} + C$$

$$= -\frac{1}{3t^3} + C$$

Exercise 9G

1 Integrate, expressing answers with positive powers:

(a) $\int x^3 \, dx$ (b) $\int x^7 \, dx$ (c) $\int x \, dx$

(d) $\int r^5 \, dr$ (e) $\int t^{15} \, dt$ (f) $\int \theta^{25} \, d\theta$

(g) $\int x^{-2} \, dx$ (h) $\int x^{-6} \, dx$ (i) $\int x^{-7} \, dx$

(j) $\int u^{-9} \, du$ (k) $\int \phi^{-17} \, d\phi$ (l) $\int z^{-31} \, dz$

(m) $\int x^{\frac{5}{2}} \, dx$ (n) $\int x^{\frac{7}{4}} \, dx$ (o) $\int x^{\frac{8}{3}} \, dx$

(p) $\int x^{\frac{3}{4}} \, dx$ (q) $\int \psi^{\frac{5}{8}} \, d\psi$ (r) $\int p^{-\frac{2}{3}} \, dp$

Rules of integration

There are two rules we can use when integrating more complex expressions:

When a is a constant

$$\int a x^n \, dx = a \int x^n \, dx = \frac{a x^{n+1}}{n+1} + C \quad (n \neq -1)$$

$$\int (f(x) + g(x)) \, dx = \int f(x) \, dx + \int g(x) \, dx$$

Example 6

Find $\int 6x^3 \, dx$

$\int 6x^3 \, dx = 6 \int x^3 \, dx$

$\qquad = 6\dfrac{x^4}{4} + C$

$\qquad = \dfrac{3}{2} x^4 + C$

Example 7

Find $\int 4t^{-\frac{3}{2}} \, dx$

$\int 4t^{-\frac{3}{2}} \, dx = 4 \int t^{-\frac{3}{2}} \, dx$

$\qquad = 4\dfrac{t^{-\frac{1}{2}}}{-\frac{1}{2}} + C$

$\qquad = -8t^{-\frac{1}{2}} + C = -\dfrac{8}{t^{\frac{1}{2}}} + C$

Example 8

Find $\int 6 \, dx$

$\int 6 \, dx = \int 6x^0 \, dx$

$\qquad = 6 \int x^0 \, dx$

$\qquad = 6x + C$

Example 9

Find $\int (3x^2 - 2x^{\frac{1}{2}}) \, dx$

$\int (3x^2 - 2x^{\frac{1}{2}}) \, dx = 3 \int x^2 \, dx - 2 \int x^{\frac{1}{2}} \, dx$

$\qquad = 3\dfrac{x^3}{3} - 2\dfrac{x^{\frac{3}{2}}}{\frac{3}{2}} + C$

$\qquad = x^3 - \dfrac{4}{3} x^{\frac{3}{2}} + C$

Exercise 9H

1 Find

(a) $\int 5x^2 \, dx$ (b) $\int 2x^6 \, dx$ (c) $\int 9 \, dx$ (d) $\int -3 \, dx$

(e) $\int 9x^{-3} \, dx$ (f) $\int 4t^{-2} \, dt$ (g) $\int -4s^{-7} \, ds$ (h) $\int -8x^{-11} \, dx$

(i) $\int 7x^{\frac{3}{5}} \, dx$ (j) $\int -50\theta^{\frac{4}{3}} \, d\theta$ (k) $\int 10y^{-\frac{3}{7}} \, dy$ (l) $\int -7s^{-\frac{6}{5}} \, ds$

2 Find

(a) $\int (x^4 + x^3)\, dx$ (b) $\int (x^9 + x^2)\, dx$ (c) $\int (x^5 - x^4)\, dx$

(d) $\int (x^3 + x^{-4})\, dx$ (e) $\int (x^{-2} - x^{-7})\, dx$ (f) $\int (t^{-3} + t^{-6})\, dt$

(g) $\int (-x^4 + x^{\frac{3}{2}})\, dx$ (h) $\int (\theta^{\frac{5}{6}} - \theta^{-2})\, d\theta$ (i) $\int (s^{-\frac{9}{5}} - s^{-\frac{2}{5}})\, ds$

(j) $\int (t^7 + t^{-2} - t^{-3})\, dt$ (k) $\int (k^{\frac{5}{2}} + k^{\frac{3}{2}} + k^{\frac{1}{2}})\, dk$ (l) $\int (z^4 + z^{-\frac{4}{9}} - z^{-7})\, dz$

3 Find

(a) $\int (3x^7 + 2x^2)\, dx$ (b) $\int (-6x^8 + 9)\, dx$

(c) $\int (4x^3 + 7x^{-2})\, dx$ (d) $\int (5r^{\frac{3}{2}} - 9r + 3)\, dr$

(e) $\int (2f + 2 + f^{-2})\, df$ (f) $\int (-15s^{-2} + 10s^{-\frac{5}{2}} + 5s^{-3})\, ds$

Further integrals

As with differentiation, before integrating all terms must be written in the form ax^n, where a is a constant.

Example 10

Find $\displaystyle\int \frac{dx}{\sqrt{x}}$

$$\int \frac{dx}{\sqrt{x}} = \int x^{-\frac{1}{2}}\, dx$$

$$= \frac{x^{\frac{1}{2}}}{\frac{1}{2}} + C$$

$$= 2x^{\frac{1}{2}} + C$$

Example 11

Find $\int (t + 3)^2\, dt$

$$\int (t + 3)^2\, dt = \int (t^2 + 6t + 9)\, dt$$

$$= \frac{t^3}{3} + 6\frac{t^2}{2} + 9t + C$$

$$= \frac{1}{3}t^3 + 3t^2 + 9t + C$$

Example 12

Find $\displaystyle\int \frac{s + \sqrt{s} + \sqrt[3]{s}}{s}\, ds$

$$\int \frac{s + s^{\frac{1}{2}} + s^{\frac{1}{3}}}{s}\, ds = \int \left(\frac{s}{s} + \frac{s^{\frac{1}{2}}}{s} + \frac{s^{\frac{1}{3}}}{s} \right) ds$$

$$= \int (s^0 + s^{-\frac{1}{2}} + s^{-\frac{2}{3}})\, ds$$

$$= s + 2s^{\frac{1}{2}} + 3s^{\frac{1}{3}} + C$$

Exercise 9I

1 Find the following integrals:

(a) $\displaystyle\int \frac{dx}{x^2}$ (b) $\displaystyle\int \frac{4}{x^6}\, dx$ (c) $\int \sqrt[3]{x}\, dx$ (d) $\int 2\sqrt[4]{x^3}\, dx$

(e) $\displaystyle\int \frac{dx}{\sqrt[8]{x^5}}$ **(f)** $\displaystyle\int \frac{-5}{\sqrt[3]{x^5}}\, dx$ **(g)** $\displaystyle\int (x-2)^2\, dx$ **(h)** $\displaystyle\int (5+3x)^2\, dx$

(i) $\displaystyle\int (t+1)^3\, dt$ **(j)** $\displaystyle\int s(s^3 - s^5)\, ds$ **(k)** $\displaystyle\int \frac{x+5x^7}{x}\, dx$ **(l)** $\displaystyle\int \frac{f^2 + f^5}{f^2}\, df$

(m) $\displaystyle\int \frac{4+v^4}{v^3}\, dv$ **(n)** $\displaystyle\int \frac{y^6 - 1}{y^{\frac{3}{2}}}\, dy$ **(o)** $\displaystyle\int \frac{5+p^{\frac{1}{2}} - p^{\frac{3}{4}}}{\sqrt{p}}\, dp$ **(p)** $\displaystyle\int r(r+2)(r-4)\, dr$

(q) $\displaystyle\int \frac{\theta(1-\theta^3)}{30^{\frac{3}{2}}}\, d\theta$ **(r)** $\displaystyle\int 3\sqrt{t}(2t - t^3)\, dt$ **(s)** $\displaystyle\int \left(z - \frac{1}{z}\right)^2\, dz$ **(t)** $\displaystyle\int \left(\sqrt{g} + \frac{1}{3g}\right)^2\, dg$

The area function and integration

The following exercise will help you find the relationship between the area function and the anti-derivative.

Exercise 9J

1 (a) Remember that the area function for the graph of $y = (n+1)x^n$ is $A(x) = x^{n+1}$. Copy and complete

$f(x)$	$A(x)$	Anti-derivative of $f(x)$
$2x$	x^2	$x^2 + C$
$3x^2$		
$4x^3$		
$5x^4$		

(b) Make a conjecture relating the area function of the graph and the anti-derivative of a function.

Definite integrals

From Exercise 9J you should notice that:

The area function of the graph of $y = f(x)$ is the anti-derivative of $f(x)$ (apart from the arbitrary constant).

The notation for the area between the graph of $y = f(x)$ and the x-axis from $x = a$ to $x = b$ is $\displaystyle\int_a^b f(x)\, dx$.

This is called a **definite integral**. a and b are the **lower** and **upper limits of integration**, respectively.

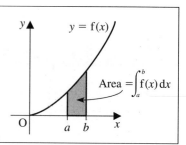

The area between the graph of $y = f(x)$ and the x-axis from $x = a$ to $x = b$ can be calculated as the area from $x = 0$ to $x = b$ **minus** the area from $x = 0$ to $x = a$.

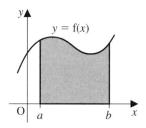

Example 13

Write the shaded area in the diagram as a definite integral.

$$\text{Area} = \int_1^2 (x^2 + 1)\, dx$$

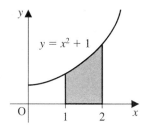

Example 14

Find $\int_2^3 3x^2\, dx$.

The area function for the graph of $y = 3x^2$ is $A(x) = x^3$.

$$\int_2^3 3x^2\, dx = \int_0^3 3x^2\, dx - \int_0^2 3x^2\, dx$$
$$= A(3) - A(2)$$
$$= 3^3 - 2^3$$
$$= 19 \text{ unit}^2$$

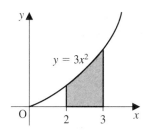

Exercise 9K

1 Write the shaded area as a definite integral.

(a)

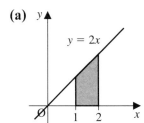

(b)

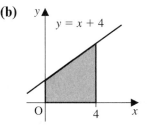

(c)

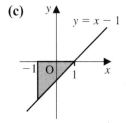

(d)

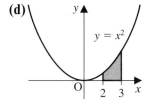

(e)

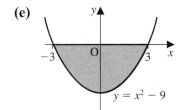

(f)

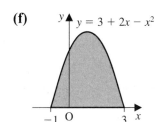

2 Sketch the area represented by the definite integral.

(a) $\displaystyle\int_0^3 2x\,\mathrm{d}x$ (b) $\displaystyle\int_1^2 (x+3)\,\mathrm{d}x$ (c) $\displaystyle\int_{-1}^0 (2x-1)\,\mathrm{d}x$

(d) $\displaystyle\int_3^4 x^2\,\mathrm{d}x$ (e) $\displaystyle\int_{-2}^2 (x^2+1)\,\mathrm{d}x$ (f) $\displaystyle\int_{-1}^2 (x^2-1)\,\mathrm{d}x$

3 Evaluate the definite integral of (a) to (d) by
- making a sketch
- writing down the appropriate area function
- calculating the definite integral as a difference of areas.

(a) $\displaystyle\int_1^5 3x^2\,\mathrm{d}x$ (b) $\displaystyle\int_1^2 4x^3\,\mathrm{d}x$ (c) $\displaystyle\int_{-2}^2 7x^6\,\mathrm{d}x$ (d) $\displaystyle\int_{-3}^{-2} 3x^2\,\mathrm{d}x$

Fundamental theorem of calculus

If $F(x)$ is the anti-derivative of $f(x)$ then

$$\int_a^b f(x)\,\mathrm{d}x = F(b) - F(a) \quad (a \leqslant x \leqslant b)$$

This provides the link between differentiation and integration.

Note: $\displaystyle\int_a^b f(x)\,\mathrm{d}x = (F(b)+C) - (F(a)+C) = F(b) - F(a)$

Example 15

Evaluate $\displaystyle\int_1^3 (x^2 + 2x)\,\mathrm{d}x$.

$$\int_1^3 (x^2 + 2x)\,\mathrm{d}x = \left[\frac{x^3}{3} + x^2\right]_1^3$$

$$= \left(\frac{3^3}{3} + 3^2\right) - \left(\frac{1^3}{3} + 1^2\right)$$

$$= 18 - \frac{4}{3}$$

$$= 16\tfrac{2}{3}\,\text{unit}^2$$

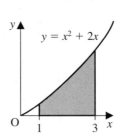

Example 16

Find the positive value of z for which $\displaystyle\int_1^z (1+2x)\,\mathrm{d}x = 4$,

$$\int_1^z (1+2x)\,\mathrm{d}x = [x + x^2]_1^z = 4$$

$$(z + z^2) - (1 + 1) = 4$$

$$z^2 + z - 6 = 0$$

$$(z - 2)(z + 3) = 0$$

Therefore $z = 2$ or -3. The positive value of z is 2.

Exercise 9L

1 Evaluate

(a) $\int_1^3 x^2 \, dx$ **(b)** $\int_3^5 x^3 \, dx$ **(c)** $\int_{-1}^1 x^4 \, dx$ **(d)** $\int_0^2 x^7 \, dx$

(e) $\int_2^5 (x^2 + 3x) \, dx$ **(f)** $\int_0^3 (x^3 + 1) \, dx$ **(g)** $\int_{-3}^{-1} (9 - x^2) \, dx$ **(h)** $\int_{-2}^1 (t^4 + 4) \, dt$

2 Evaluate

(a) $\int_1^4 x^{\frac{1}{2}} \, dx$ **(b)** $\int_4^9 x^{\frac{1}{2}} \, dx$ **(c)** $\int_1^8 x^{\frac{2}{3}} \, dx$

(d) $\int_0^1 t^{\frac{2}{3}} \, dt$ **(e)** $\int_1^2 x^{-3} \, dx$ **(f)** $\int_1^2 x^{-5} \, dx$

(g) $\int_{-4}^{-1} \theta^{-2} \, d\theta$ **(h)** $\int_{-2}^{-1} v^{-4} \, dv$ **(i)** $\int_0^1 (x^{\frac{1}{2}} + x^{\frac{2}{3}}) \, dx$

(j) $\int_1^2 (2x^{-2} - x^{-3}) \, dx$ **(k)** $\int_1^4 (3y^{\frac{3}{2}} - 5y^{-2}) \, dy$ **(l)** $\int_4^{100} (1 - 3u^{-\frac{1}{2}}) \, du$

3 Evaluate

(a) $\int_9^{16} \sqrt{x} \, dx$ **(b)** $\int_1^3 \frac{5}{x^2} \, dx$ **(c)** $\int_8^{27} 6\sqrt[3]{x} \, dx$

(d) $\int_{16}^{625} \frac{4}{\sqrt[4]{x}} \, dx$ **(e)** $\int_2^3 (x + 2)^2 \, dx$ **(f)** $\int_0^4 (r + 3)(r + 2) \, dr$

(g) $\int_2^3 (3 - s)(1 + s) \, ds$ **(h)** $\int_{10}^{20} z(z + 5) \, dz$ **(i)** $\int_1^3 \left(u^2 + \frac{1}{u^2} \right) \, du$

(j) $\int_{-4}^{-2} \frac{1 - t^3}{t^2} \, dt$ **(k)** $\int_1^4 (\sqrt{t} - 2)^2 \, dt$ **(l)** $\int_1^{25} \frac{y^2 - \sqrt{y}}{y} \, dy$

4 Find the positive value of z for which

(a) $\int_0^z x^2 \, dx = 9$ **(b)** $\int_0^z \left(x + \frac{1}{2} \right) dx = 10$ **(c)** $\int_2^z (6x - 5) \, dx = 10$

(d) $\int_0^z 3\sqrt{x} \, dx = 2$ **(e)** $\int_z^{2z} (1 + 2x) \, dx = 24$ **(f)** $\int_{-z}^{3z} (4x + 7) \, dx = 120$

Areas above and below the x-axis

When finding the area under a curve, it is important to draw a sketch. The following exercise will help you see why.

1 (a) Sketch the graph of the functions (a) to (c) and shade the areas represented by each definite integral. Evaluate the definite integrals.

    (a) $y = 4x$:   (i) $\displaystyle\int_{-2}^{0} 4x \, dx$,   (ii) $\displaystyle\int_{0}^{3} 4x \, dx$

    (b) $y = x^2 - 2x$:   (i) $\displaystyle\int_{0}^{2} (x^2 - 2x) \, dx$,   (ii) $\displaystyle\int_{2}^{5} (x^2 - 2x) \, dx$

    (c) $y = x^3 + 8$:   (i) $\displaystyle\int_{-3}^{-2} (x^3 + 8) \, dx$,   (ii) $\displaystyle\int_{2}^{3} (x^3 + 8) \, dx$

2 Using your working in question 1, make a conjecture about areas above and below the x-axis.

3 (a) Evaluate $\displaystyle\int_{-2}^{3} 2x \, dx$.

    (b) Using the formula for the area of a triangle, calculate the areas marked C and D in the diagram.

    (c) Explain why the **total** shaded area in (b) differs from the definite integral in (a).

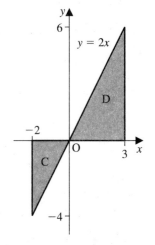

From exercise 9M you should notice that:

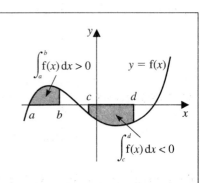

When calculated by integration:

- areas above the x-axis are positive
- areas below the x-axis are negative.

When calculating the area between a curve and the x-axis:

- make a sketch
- calculate areas above and below the x-axis **separately**
- ignore negative signs and add.

Example 17
Calculate the total shaded area in the diagram.

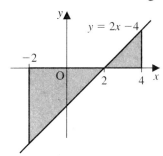

$$\text{Area below } x\text{-axis} = \int_{-2}^{2} (2x - 4)\, dx = [x^2 - 4x]_{-2}^{2} = (4 - 8) - (4 + 8)$$

$$= -16$$

$$\text{Area above } x\text{-axis} = \int_{2}^{4} (2x - 4)\, dx = [x^2 - 4x]_{2}^{4} = (16 - 16) - (4 - 8)$$

$$= 4$$

Total area $= 16 + 4 = 20\,\text{unit}^2$

Example 18
Calculate the area enclosed by the graph of $y = x^2 - 1$ and the x-axis as shown in the diagram.

The graph cuts the x-axis at $(-1, 0)$ and $(1, 0)$.

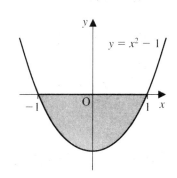

$$\int_{-1}^{1} (x^2 - 1)\, dx = \left[\frac{x^3}{3} - x\right]_{-1}^{1}$$

$$= \left(\frac{1}{3} - 1\right) - \left(\frac{-1}{3} - (-1)\right) = -\frac{4}{3}$$

$$\text{Area} = \frac{4}{3}\,\text{unit}^2$$

Example 19
Calculate the total shaded area in the diagram.

The graph of $y = 8 - 2x - x^2$ cuts the x-axis where $8 - 2x - x^2 = 0$.
$(4 + x)(2 - x) = 0$ so $x = 2$ or $x = -4$.

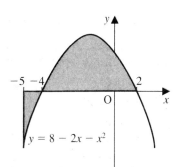

$$\text{Area below } x\text{-axis} = \int_{-5}^{-4} (8 - 2x - x^2)\, dx$$

$$= \left[8x - x^2 - \frac{x^3}{3}\right]_{-5}^{-4} = -3\tfrac{1}{3}\,\text{unit}^2$$

$$\text{Area above } x\text{-axis} = \int_{-4}^{2} (8 - 2x - x^2)\, dx$$

$$= \left[8x - x^2 - \frac{x^3}{3}\right]_{-4}^{2} = 36\,\text{unit}^2$$

Total area $= 3\tfrac{1}{3} + 36 = 39\tfrac{1}{3}\,\text{unit}^2$

Exercise 9N

1 Calculate the total shaded area in each graph.

(a)
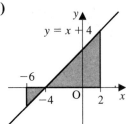

(b)
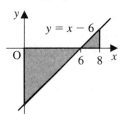

(c)
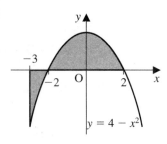

2 For each of the following graphs find where the graph cuts the
x-axis and calculate the total shaded area.

(a)
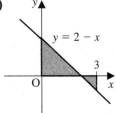

(b)
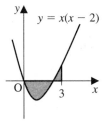

(c)
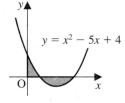

3 Calculate the total area between the graph of the function, the
x-axis and the given lines.
(a) $y = 2x - 6$, $x = 0$, $x = 5$ **(b)** $y = 6 - 4x$, $x = -1$, $x = 2$
(c) $y = x(3 - x)$, $x = -2$, $x = 2$ **(d)** $y = x(x - 1)(x + 2)$, $x = -1$, $x = 2$

4 Calculate the area enclosed by the graph of each function and the
x-axis.
(a) $y = 4 - x^2$ **(b)** $y = x(x + 5)$ **(c)** $y = x^3 - 4x$
(d) $y = x^2 - 5x + 6$ **(e)** $y = 18 + 9x - 2x^2$ **(f)** $y = x^3 - x^2$

Area between two graphs

As well as using integration to find the area between a curve and the
x-axis, we can also use it to find the area between two curves.

Example 20
Calculate the area enclosed by the graphs of the functions
$y = 4 - x^2$ and $y = x + 2$.

The graphs intersect at $(-2, 0)$ and $(1, 3)$.

Calculate the area between the upper graph and the x-axis:

$$\int_{-2}^{1} (4 - x^2)\, dx = \left[4x - \frac{x^3}{3} \right]_{-2}^{1}$$

$$= \left(4 - \frac{1}{3} \right) - \left(-8 - \frac{-8}{3} \right)$$

$$= 9 \text{ unit}^2$$

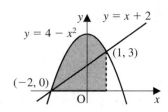

Calculate the area between the lower graph and the x-axis:

$$\int_{-2}^{1} (x + 2)\,dx = \left[\frac{x^2}{2} + 2x\right]_{-2}^{1}$$

$$= \left(\frac{1}{2} + 2\right) - \left(\frac{(-2)^2}{2} + (-4)\right)$$

$$= 4.5$$

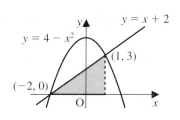

By subtraction, the area between the graphs $= 9 - 4.5 = 4.5\,\text{unit}^2$.

Exercise 9O

1 Calculate the shaded area on each graph.

(a) 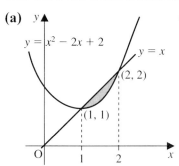 **(b)** 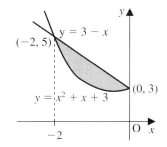 **(c)**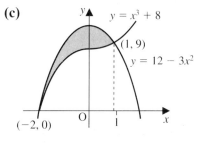

2 (a) (i) For $g(x) = x - (x^2 - 2x + 2)$ calculate $\displaystyle\int_{1}^{2} g(x)\,dx$.

    (ii) For $h(x) = (3 - x) - (x^2 + x + 3)$ calculate $\displaystyle\int_{-2}^{0} h(x)\,dx$.

    (iii) For $j(x) = (12 - 3x^2) - (x^3 + 8)$ calculate $\displaystyle\int_{-2}^{1} j(x)\,dx$.

(b) Compare your answers with those for question 1.

Calculating the area between two graphs

The area enclosed between the curves $y = f(x)$ and $y = g(x)$ from $x = a$ to $x = b$ is given by

$$\int_{a}^{b} f(x)\,dx - \int_{a}^{b} g(x)\,dx = \int_{a}^{b} (f(x) - g(x))\,dx$$

when $f(x) \geqslant g(x)$ and $a \leqslant x \leqslant b$.

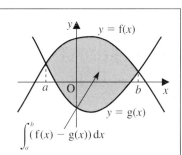

Example 21

Calculate the area enclosed by the graphs of $y = 4 - x^2$ and $y = 6 - \dfrac{3}{2}x^2$.

The graphs intersect at $(-2, 0)$ and $(2, 0)$.

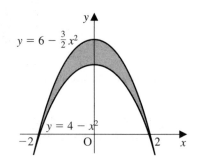

$$\text{Area} = \int_{-2}^{2}\left(\left(6 - \frac{3}{2}x^2\right) - (4 - x^2)\right)dx = \int_{-2}^{2}\left(2 - \frac{x^2}{2}\right)dx$$

$$= \left[2x - \frac{x^3}{6}\right]_{-2}^{2} = \left(4 - \frac{8}{6}\right) - \left(-4 + \frac{8}{6}\right) = 5\tfrac{1}{3}\,\text{unit}^2$$

Example 22

Calculate the area enclosed by the graphs of the functions $g(x) = x + 3$ and $f(x) = 6 - x - x^2$.

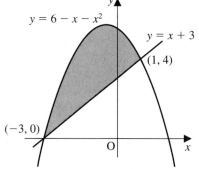

The graphs intersect where

$$x + 3 = 6 - x - x^2$$
$$x^2 + 2x - 3 = 0$$
$$(x + 3)(x - 1) = 0$$
so $x = -3$ or $x = 1$

$$\text{Area} = \int_{-3}^{1}\left((6 - x - x^2) - (x + 3)\right)dx = \int_{-3}^{1}(3 - 2x - x^2)\,dx$$

$$= \left[3x - x^2 - \frac{x^3}{3}\right]_{-3}^{1} = (3 - 1 - \tfrac{1}{3}) - (-9 - 9 + \tfrac{27}{3}) = 10\tfrac{2}{3}\,\text{unit}^2$$

Exercise 9P

1 Calculate the shaded area in each graph.

(a)

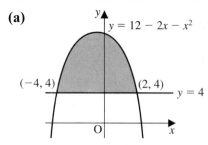

(b)

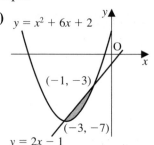

(c)

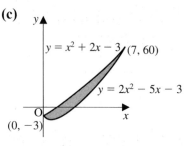

2 Calculate the area enclosed by each pair of graphs:

(a) $y = 12 - 2x - x^2$ and $y = 4$

(b) $y = 7$ and $y = x^2 - 5x + 13$

(c) $y = 2x - 1$ and $y = x^2 + 6x + 2$

(d) $y = 7 + x - x^2$ and $y = -2x - 3$

(e) $y = x^2 + 2x - 3$ and $y = 2x^2 - 5x - 3$

(f) $y = 7 + 6x - x^2$ and $y = 3x^2 - 5x + 4$

3 The diagram shows the shape of an earring. Calculate its area.

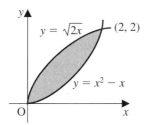

4 The cover of a stunt kite has the shape shown in the diagram. Calculate its area.

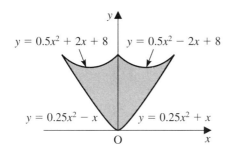

5 A concrete drainage channel is made of concrete blocks shaped as shown in the diagram. Each block has cross-sectional dimensions 2 m by 1.5 m and is 5 m long. By taking a scale of 10 cm to 1 unit and coordinate axes as shown, the channel through which water flows has the equation $y = 2 + \frac{3}{20}x^2$. Calculate the volume of concrete required to make each block.

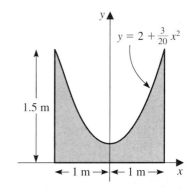

6 Two particles are released at the same time. The first has a speed of v m/s at time t seconds given by $v = 10t - t^2$. The second has a speed given by $v = 0.5t^2$.
   (a) During the first 5 seconds of their motion which particle travels further and by how much?
   (b) How long after their release will they have travelled the same distance?

Differential equations

Equations like $\dfrac{dy}{dx} = x^2 - 7$ and $\dfrac{ds}{dt} = t^2 + 3t + 5$ are called differential equations and they are usually solved by integration. Additional information is often required to allow us to evaluate the constant of integration.

Example 23

A sprinter accelerates so that her speed for the first t seconds after the gun is $v = 3t^2$. How far will she have travelled after 2 seconds?

The distance that she travels in t seconds is s metres, therefore the derived function is:

$$v = \frac{\mathrm{d}s}{\mathrm{d}t} = 3t^2$$

We can find the actual function for the distance, s, by integration:

$$s = \int 3t^2 \, \mathrm{d}t$$

$$s = t^3 + C$$

$s = t^3 + C$ gives a family of functions each of which satisfies the differential equation. To solve the problem it is necessary to identify which member of the family to use.

Since the sprinter has not moved when the gun is fired $s = 0$ when $t = 0$.

Substitute in $s = t^3 + C$

$$0 = 0^3 + C$$

so $\qquad C = 0$

Hence $\qquad s = t^3$

So, when $t = 2$, $s = 8$ metres.

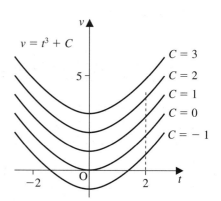

Exercise 9Q

1 Find the solution to each differential equation and sketch four members of each family.

(a) $\dfrac{\mathrm{d}s}{\mathrm{d}t} = 6t$ $\qquad$ (b) $\dfrac{\mathrm{d}s}{\mathrm{d}t} = 3t^2$ $\qquad$ (c) $\dfrac{\mathrm{d}s}{\mathrm{d}t} = 4t + 1$

2 Find the solutions of these differential equations:

(a) $\dfrac{\mathrm{d}s}{\mathrm{d}t} = 4t$ if $s = 0$ when $t = 0$ $\qquad$ (b) $\dfrac{\mathrm{d}s}{\mathrm{d}t} = 5t^2$ if $s = 4$ when $t = 1$

(c) $\dfrac{\mathrm{d}s}{\mathrm{d}t} = 6t^2 + t - 2$ if $s = 0$ when $t = 2$ $\qquad$ (d) $\dfrac{\mathrm{d}s}{\mathrm{d}t} = 3\sqrt{t}$ if $s = 1$ when $t = 4$

3 Find the equation of the function $y = \mathrm{f}(x)$ for which

(a) $\dfrac{\mathrm{d}y}{\mathrm{d}x} = 2$ and the graph passes through the point $(0, 3)$.

(b) $\dfrac{\mathrm{d}y}{\mathrm{d}x} = 4 - 3x$ and the graph passes through the point $(-1, 1)$.

(c) $\dfrac{\mathrm{d}y}{\mathrm{d}x} = \dfrac{1}{5}x^2$ and the graph passes through the point $(0, 4)$.

4 The gradient of a tangent to a curve is given by $\dfrac{dy}{dx} = 2x - 3$.

   If the curve passes through the point $(4, 4)$, find its equation.

5 The gradient of a tangent to a curve is given by $\dfrac{dy}{dx} = 6x - \dfrac{5}{x^2}$.

   The curve passes through the point $(1, 6)$. Find its equation.

6 A stone is dropped into a still pond and creates a series of circular ripples. The area, $A\,\text{m}^2$, of disturbed water increases at a rate of $9\sqrt{t}$ m/s, where t is the time in seconds.

   $\left(\text{Rate of change of area is given by } \dfrac{dA}{dt}\right).$

   (a) Calculate the area of the pond covered by the ripples after 9 seconds.
   (b) Calculate the radius of the outer ripple at this time.

Exercise 9R Mixed questions

1 For each of the following
   (i) evaluate the integral
   (ii) draw a sketch to illustrate the integral as an area.

   (a) $\displaystyle\int_1^4 (2 + 3x)\,dx$ **(b)** $\displaystyle\int_0^6 (4 - x^2)\,dx$

2 Find

   (a) $\displaystyle\int (5x^{-2} - 3 + 2x^2)\,dx$ **(b)** $\displaystyle\int x^2 \left(\dfrac{7}{x^4} + \dfrac{2}{x^2} + 4\right)\,dx \ (x \neq 0)$

   (c) $\displaystyle\int \dfrac{6 - x}{\sqrt{x}}\,dx \ \text{ for } x > 0$

3 Evaluate

   (a) $\displaystyle\int_1^5 \dfrac{x - 2}{3}\,dx$ **(b)** $\displaystyle\int_{-2}^{-1} \left(x + 4 - \dfrac{3}{x^3}\right)\,dx$

   (c) $\displaystyle\int_2^3 (x - 4)^2\,dx$ **(d)** $\displaystyle\int_{-1}^2 x(x - 2)\,dx$

4 (a) Evaluate $\displaystyle\int_{-1}^5 (x^2 - 2x - 3)\,dx$.

   (b) Draw a sketch to explain your answer.

5 Calculate the area enclosed by the graph of the function and the x-axis.
   (a) $y = x^2 - 25$ **(b)** $y = 2x^2 - x - 1$

6 Find the area of the region completely enclosed by the graphs of the functions
   (a) $y = x$ and $y = 1 - 2x^2$ **(b)** $y = 2x^2$ and $y = x^2 - x + 6$

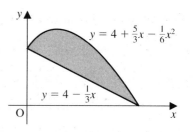

7 When building a road beside a vertical rockface engineers often use wire mesh to cover the rockface. This helps to prevent rocks and debris falling on the road. The shaded region of the diagram opposite represents a part of such a rockface. This shaded region is bound by a parabola and a straight line.

The equation of the parabola is $y = 4 + \frac{5}{3}x - \frac{1}{6}x^2$ and the equation of the line is $y = 4 - \frac{1}{3}x$. Find the area of mesh required for this part of the rockface. [Higher]

8 The area under the graph of $y = 4 + 2x$ from $x = 0$ to $x = 4$ is divided into two equal parts by the line $x = k$. Find the value of k.

9 A particle moves in a straight line with a constant acceleration a m/s^2. At time $t = 0$, the particle's velocity is u m/s.

   (a) Using the differential equation $a = \dfrac{dy}{dt}$, show that the velocity v, at time t is $v = u + at$.

   (b) The distance travelled by the particle in t seconds is s metres. Use the differential equation $v = \dfrac{ds}{dt}$ to show that the distance travelled from its initial position is $s = ut + \frac{1}{2}at^2$.

10 The graph of a function passes through the point $(2, 1)$ and the gradients of the tangents to the graph are given by $\dfrac{dy}{dx} = 2 - 5x$. Calculate the equation of the function.

11 The cargo space of a small bulk carrier is 60 m long. The shaded part of the diagram represents the uniform cross-section of this space. It is shaped like a parabola with equation $y = \frac{1}{4}x^2$, $-6 \leqslant x \leqslant 6$, between the lines $y = 1$ and $y = 9$. Find the area of this cross-section and hence find the volume of cargo that this ship can carry. [Higher]

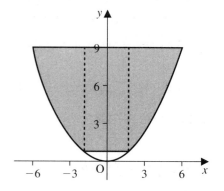

12 The diagram shows two curves with equations $y = x^2$ and $y^2 = x$. The area completely enclosed between these two curves is divided in half by the line with equation $x = k$.

   (a) Represent these two equal areas by two separate integrals each involving k.

   (b) Equate the integrals and show that k is given by the equation $2k^3 - 4k^{\frac{3}{2}} + 1 = 0$.

   (c) Use the substitution p^2 for k^3 to find the value of k. [Higher]

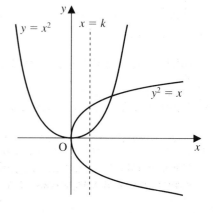

13 The velocity–time graph of a particle is shown. At $t = 0$ the particle is at rest.

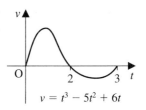

$v = t^3 - 5t^2 + 6t$

   (a) Between $t = 0$ and $t = 2$ the particle moves to the right. Describe how its speed changes during this time.

   (b) Describe its direction and speed between $t = 2$ and $t = 3$.

   (c) Calculate the total distance travelled between $t = 0$ and $t = 3$.

   (d) Calculate how far the particle is away from the origin at $t = 3$.

14 After strenuous exercise the rate of oxygen consumption, $R\,\mathrm{cm^3/min}$, is given by the formula $R = \dfrac{58}{\sqrt{t}}$, where t is the time elapsed since completing the exercise. What volume of oxygen is used up during the first 5 minutes after exercise?

15 A wound heals so that the rate of decrease of its area, A, is $2\sqrt{t}\,\mathrm{mm^2/day}$ where t is the time (in days) since the wound was inflicted. A wound has an initial area of $40\,\mathrm{mm^2}$.

   (a) Find a formula for A in terms of t.

   (b) How long will this wound take to heal completely?

Note: rate of decrease of area is $-\dfrac{\mathrm{d}A}{\mathrm{d}t}$.

SUMMARY

(1) The area between the graph of a function, $y = f(x)$, and the x-axis, starting at $x = 0$, is called the **area function** $A(x)$.

(2) The area function $y = (n + 1)x^n$ is $A(x) = x^{(n+1)}$ $(n \neq -1)$.

(3) The reverse process to differentiation is called **anti-differentiation**.

(4) $\displaystyle\int x^n\,\mathrm{d}x = \dfrac{x^{(n+1)}}{(n+1)} + C\ (n \neq -1)$.

(5) When a is a constant

$$\int ax^n\,\mathrm{d}x = a\int x^n\,\mathrm{d}x = \dfrac{ax^{n+1}}{n+1} + C\ (n \neq -1)$$

$$\int (f(x) + g(x))\,\mathrm{d}x = \int f(x)\,\mathrm{d}x + \int g(x)\,\mathrm{d}x$$

(6) The notation for the area between the graph of $y = f(x)$ and the x-axis from $x = a$ to $x = b$ is $\displaystyle\int_a^b f(x)\,\mathrm{d}x$.

This is called a **definite integral**. a and b are the **lower** and **upper limits of integration**, respectively.

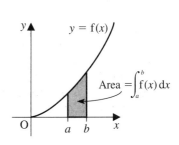

Area $= \displaystyle\int_a^b f(x)\,\mathrm{d}x$

⑦ The Fundamental Theorem of Calculus.
If $F(x)$ is the anti-derivative of $f(x)$ then

$$\int_a^b f(x)\,dx = F(b) - F(a)\ (a \leqslant x \leqslant b)$$

⑧ When calculated by integration
- areas above the x-axis are positive
- areas below the x-axis are negative.

When calculating the area between a curve and the x-axis
- make a sketch
- calculate areas above and below the x-axis **separately**
- ignore negative signs and add.

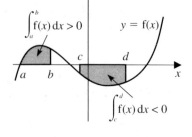

⑨ The area enclosed between the curves $y = f(x)$ and $y = g(x)$ from $x = a$ to $x = b$ is given by

$$\int_a^b f(x)\,dx - \int_a^b g(x)\,dx = \int_a^b (f(x) - g(x))\,dx$$

when $f(x) \geqslant g(x)$ and $a \leqslant x \leqslant b$.

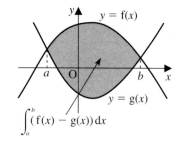

10 3–D trigonometry

In civil engineering it is often necessary to calculate angles and lengths in three-dimensional structures. In this unit the angle between a line and a plane and the angle between two planes will be defined so that 3–D problems can be solved.

Angle between a line and a plane

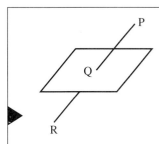

PR is a line which intersects the plane at Q.

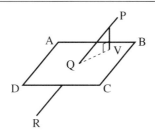

PV is perpendicular to the plane. The angle between the line PQ and the plane is angle PQ̂V

Example 1
ABCDEFGH is a cube. State the point of intersection of and name the angle between
(a) line DE and the plane EFGH
(b) line EC and the plane EFGH
(c) line DB and the plane BCGF.

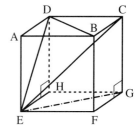

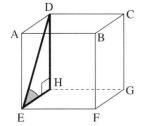

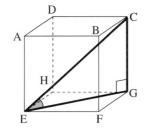

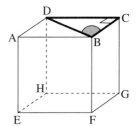

(a) E is the point of intersection.
The required angle is DÊH, since DH is perpendicular to plane EFGH.

(b) E is the point of intersection.
The required angle is CÊG, since CG is perpendicular to plane EFGH.

(c) B is the point of intersection.
The required angle is DB̂C, since DC is perpendicular to plane BCGF.

Exercise 10A

1 PQRSTUVW is a cuboid. Name the point of intersection of and the angle between
  (a) WR and PQRS
  (b) PV and TWVU
  (c) WQ and WVRS.

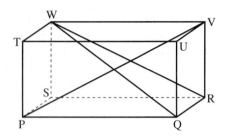

2 ASDEF is a right, square-based pyramid. Name the angle between
  (a) AS and SDEF
  (b) AE and SDEF
  (c) AM and SDEF where M is the mid-point of DE.

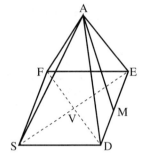

Calculation of the angle between a line and a plane

Now that we can identify the angle between a line and a plane we can calculate the size of such angles.

Example 2

ABCDEF is a wedge with DCEF perpendicular to ABCD.
ABCD and DCEF are rectangles.
Calculate the angle between
(a) AF and ABCD   **(b)** AE and ABCD

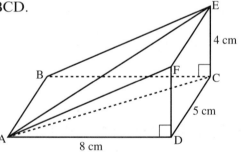

(a) The required angle is $\widehat{FAD}$.

$$\tan \widehat{FAD} = \tfrac{4}{8} = 0.5$$
$$\widehat{FAD} = 26.6°$$

(b) The required angle is $\widehat{EAC}$.
Pythagoras' theorem in triangle ADC gives:

$$AC = \sqrt{8^2 + 5^2} = \sqrt{89}$$
$$\tan \widehat{EAC} = \tfrac{4}{\sqrt{89}} = 0.424$$
$$\widehat{EAC} = 23.0°$$

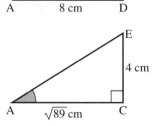

Exercise 10B

1 OJKLM is a right, square-based pyramid.
Calculate the angle between
(a) OL and the base
(b) OQ and the base where Q is the
mid-point of JM.

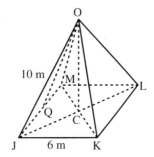

2 WEPJKN is a triangular-based prism.
PWE is an equilateral triangle.
Calculate the angle between PK
and the plane WEKJ.

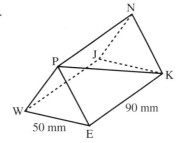

3 RSTU is a regular tetrahedron. M is the
mid-point of SU and C divides TM in the
ratio 2 : 1. Calculate the angle between the
edge RT and the base plane STU.

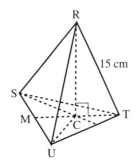

Angle between two planes

Plane ABCD and plane PQRS intersect in the line FG.
K is any point on the line FG.
KW and KT are lines perpendicular to the line FG.
The angle between the planes is WK̂T.

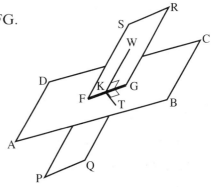

Example 3

VKLMN is a square-based pyramid with all other faces equilateral triangles.

R and S are the mid-points of MN and KL respectively.

(a) State the line where planes VMN and KLMN intersect.

(b) Name the angle between these planes.

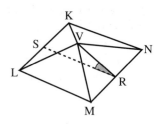

(a) VMN and KLMN meet in line NM.

(b) VR is perpendicular to NM and SR is also perpendicular to NM. The required angle between the planes is $\widehat{VRS}$.

Exercise 10C

1 ABCDEFGH is a cuboid. State the line of intersection and name an angle between

(a) plane EFGH and plane ABGH

(b) plane ABGH and plane BCGF.

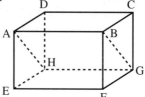

2 ABCDEFGHJKLM is a right regular hexagonal-based prism. Name an angle between the planes

(a) GHJKLM and ABKL

(b) JKDC and KLED

(c) GHBA and ABCDEF.

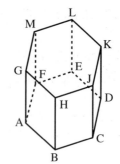

3 RQKB is a rectangle. FRB and FBK are right-angled triangles. Name the angles between the planes

(a) FBK and FBR

(b) FRB and RBKQ

(c) FQK and RBKQ.

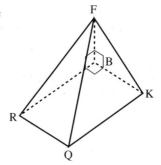

Calculation of the angle between two planes

Now that we can identify the angle between two planes we can calculate the size of such angles.

Example 4

TFBH is a pyramid with FBH an equilateral triangle and T
vertically above F. Calculate the size of the angle between the planes
THB and FHB.

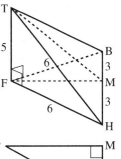

TH = TB, hence triangle THB is isosceles.
Planes THB and FHB meet in the line BH.

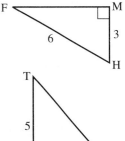

Let M be the mid-point of BH.
TM and FM are perpendicular to BH and
$\widehat{\text{TMF}}$ is the angle between planes THB and FBH.

$\text{FM} = \sqrt{6^2 - 3^2} = \sqrt{27} = 3\sqrt{3}$

$\tan\widehat{\text{TMF}} = \frac{5}{3\sqrt{3}}$

$\widehat{\text{TMF}} = 43.9°$

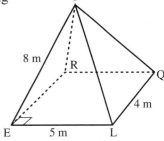

Exercise 10D

1 PELQR is a rectangular-based pyramid with each of the sloping
faces an isosceles triangle of side 8 m.
  (a) In the triangle EPL calculate the length of the altitude
   from P.
  (b) Calculate the angle between the planes EPL and ELQR.
  (c) Calculate the angle between plane PLQ and the base of
   the pyramid.

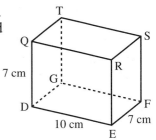

2 DEFGQRST is a cuboid with dimensions 10 cm by 7 cm by 7 cm.
  (a) Calculate the size of the angle between the planes DRSG and
   DEFG.
  (b) Calculate the size of the acute angle between the diagonal
   planes DRSG and EFTQ.

3 ABCDEFGH is a cube of edge 10 cm.
  (a) Calculate the length of AH.
  (b) Show that triangle HAC is equilateral.
  (c) Calculate the length of altitude HM of triangle HAC.
  (d) Calculate the size of the angle between planes HAC and
   ABCD.
  (e) Calculate the size of the angle between planes HAC and
   FAC.

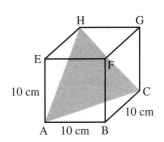

4 The roof of a building, 20 m long by 12 m broad, is made from two congruent equilateral triangles and two congruent trapezia. Calculate
  (a) the height of the roof section
  (b) the size of the angle between one of the trapezoidal sections and the horizontal
  (c) the size of the angle between the two trapezoidal sections.

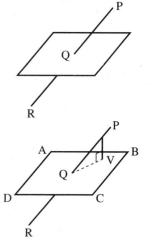

5 The angle between two faces of a solid is called a dihedral angle. Solid shapes whose faces are congruent, regular polygons are called Platonic solids. A cube is a Platonic solid with square faces. Two Platonic solids with equilateral triangular faces are the tetrahedron and octahedron. By taking each edge to be 1 unit long, calculate the dihedral angle for
  (a) a tetrahedron   **(b)** an octahedron

SUMMARY

① PR is a line which intersects the plane at Q.

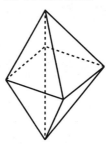

PV is perpendicular to the plane.
The angle between the line PQ and the plane
is angle PQV.

② Plane ABCD and plane PQRS intersect in the line FG.

K is any point on the line FG.
KW and KT are lines perpendicular to the line FG.
The angle between the planes is WKT.

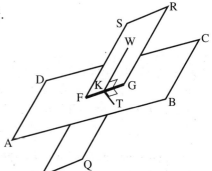

11 Addition formulae

Compound angles

When the graph of $y = \sin \alpha$ is displaced by β units horizontally its equation becomes $y = \sin(\alpha \pm \beta)$. Angles such as $(\alpha + \beta)$ are called **compound angles**.

This chapter shows you how to '**expand**' trigonometric functions like $\sin(\alpha + \beta)$ and write them in terms of functions such as $\sin \alpha$ and $\cos \alpha$. The collective name for such expansions is **addition formulae**.

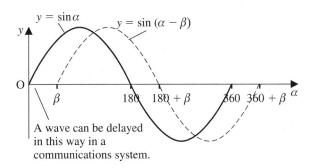

A wave can be delayed in this way in a communications system.

1 (a) Copy and complete the table for the given values of α and β.

α	β	$\sin \alpha$	$\sin \beta$	$\sin \alpha + \sin \beta$	$\sin(\alpha + \beta)$
$30°$	$60°$				
$90°$	$45°$				
$\dfrac{\pi}{6}$	$\dfrac{\pi}{6}$				

(b) Is $\sin(\alpha + \beta) = \sin \alpha + \sin \beta$ for all values of α and β?

2 In triangle ABC, $\sin \theta = \dfrac{AB}{x}$

$$AB = x \sin \theta$$

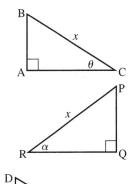

(a) In triangle PQR find PQ in terms of x and α.

(b) In triangle DEF find DE in terms of x and β.

3 For triangle ABC, $AB = x \sin \theta$

$$AC = x \cos \theta$$

Area of triangle ABC $= \frac{1}{2}(AB \times AC)$

$$= \frac{1}{2}x^2 \sin \theta \cos \theta$$

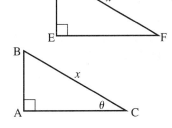

Find similar expressions for the areas of triangles PQR and DEF in question 2.

4 (a) (i) In triangle BCD show that $CD = a \cos \beta$.

(ii) Prove that the area of triangle $CDA = \frac{1}{2} ab \sin \alpha \cos \beta$.

(b) (i) Show that CD can also be written as $b \cos \alpha$.

(ii) Prove that the area of triangle $CDB = \frac{1}{2} ab \sin \beta \cos \alpha$.

(c) Show that the area of triangle $ABC = \frac{1}{2} ab \sin(\alpha + \beta)$.

(d) The area of triangle ABC is
(area of triangle CDA) + (area of triangle CDB).
Show that $\sin(\alpha + \beta) = \sin \alpha \cos \beta + \cos \alpha \sin \beta$

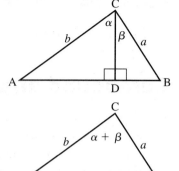

Formula for $\sin(\alpha + \beta)$

Question 4 above demonstrates that for all angles $(\alpha + \beta)$:

$$\sin(\alpha + \beta) = \sin \alpha \cos \beta + \cos \alpha \sin \beta$$

This result is called an **expansion** of $\sin(\alpha + \beta)$. It expresses the relationship between a compound angle and its two constituent angles and helps us to simplify or evaluate trigonometric expressions of this form.

Example 1
Expand (i) $\sin(P + Q)$ and (ii) $\sin(x + 30)°$.

(i) $\sin(P + Q) = \sin P \cos Q + \cos P \sin Q$

(ii) $\sin(x + 30)° = \sin x° \cos 30° + \cos x° \sin 30°$

$$= \sin x° \times \frac{\sqrt{3}}{2} + \cos x° \times \frac{1}{2}$$

$$= \frac{1}{2}(\sqrt{3} \sin x° + \cos x°)$$

Example 2
Show that $\sin(x + y) = \sin x \cos y + \cos x \sin y$, for $x = 30°$ and $y = 60°$.

L.H.S. $= \sin(x + y)$ R.H.S. $= \sin x \cos y + \cos x \sin y$

$\quad = \sin(30 + 60)°$ $\quad = \sin 30° \cos 60° + \cos 30° \sin 60°$

$\quad = \sin 90°$ $\quad = \frac{1}{2} \times \frac{1}{2} + \frac{\sqrt{3}}{2} \times \frac{\sqrt{3}}{2}$

$\quad = 1$ $\quad = \frac{1}{4} + \frac{3}{4}$

$\quad = 1$

Hence, $\sin(x + y) = \sin x \cos y + \cos x \sin y$, for $x + 30°$ and $y = 60°$.

Example 3
Find the exact value of $\sin 75°$.

$\sin 75° = \sin(45 + 30)°$

$\quad = \sin 45° \cos 30° + \cos 45° \sin 30°$

$\quad = \frac{1}{\sqrt{2}} \times \frac{\sqrt{3}}{2} + \frac{1}{\sqrt{2}} \times \frac{1}{2}$

$\quad = \frac{\sqrt{3}}{2\sqrt{2}} + \frac{1}{2\sqrt{2}}$

$\quad = \frac{(\sqrt{3}+1)}{2\sqrt{2}}$

Exercise 11B

1 Expand each of the following:
    (a) $\sin(X + Y)^{\circ}$ **(b)** $\sin(c + 45)^{\circ}$
    (c) $\sin(S + 2T)$ **(d)** $\sin(3\beta + 2\alpha)$

2 Verify that $\sin(\alpha + \beta) = \sin \alpha \cos \beta + \cos \alpha \sin \beta$ for the following values of α and β:
    (a) $\alpha = 45^{\circ}, \beta = 45^{\circ}$ **(b)** $\alpha = \dfrac{\pi}{3}, \beta = \dfrac{\pi}{6}$

    (c) $\alpha = 90^{\circ}, \beta = 30^{\circ}$ **(d)** $\alpha = \dfrac{2\pi}{3}, \beta = \dfrac{\pi}{3}$

3 Find the exact value of **(a)** $\sin 105^{\circ}$ and **(b)** $\sin \dfrac{7\pi}{12} \left(\dfrac{7\pi}{12} = \dfrac{\pi}{3} + \dfrac{\pi}{4} \right)$.

4 Simplify
    (a) $\sin K \cos L + \cos K \sin L$ **(b)** $\sin 15^{\circ} \cos 45^{\circ} + \cos 15^{\circ} \sin 45^{\circ}$
    (c) $\sin \dfrac{\pi}{4} \cos \dfrac{\pi}{2} + \cos \dfrac{\pi}{4} \sin \dfrac{\pi}{2}$ **(d)** $\sin \dfrac{\pi}{6} \cos \dfrac{\pi}{6} + \cos \dfrac{\pi}{6} \sin \dfrac{\pi}{6}$

5 (a) Find the exact value of $\sin A$, $\cos A$, $\sin B$ and $\cos B$ for the triangles shown.
    (b) Hence find the exact value of $\sin(A + B)$.

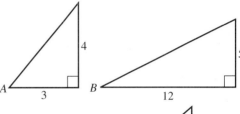

6 Given that P and Q are acute angles with $\sin P = \frac{3}{5}$ and $\sin Q = \frac{8}{17}$, show that $\sin(P + Q) = \frac{77}{85}$.

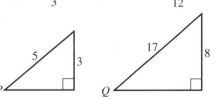

7 Given that X and Y are acute angles with $\cos X = \frac{12}{13}$ and $\tan Y = \frac{3}{4}$, find the exact value of $\sin(X + Y)$.

Formula for $\sin(\alpha - \beta)$

We can use the expansion of $\sin(\alpha + \beta)$ to show that:

▶ $\sin(\alpha - \beta) = \sin \alpha \cos \beta - \cos \alpha \sin \beta$

To prove that this expansion is true you need to remember that:

$\sin(-x) = -\sin x$ and $\cos(-x) = \cos x$

Proof
$$\begin{aligned}
\sin(\alpha - \beta) &= \sin(\alpha + (-\beta)) \\
&= \sin \alpha \cos(-\beta) + \cos \alpha \sin(-\beta) \\
&= \sin \alpha \cos \beta - \cos \alpha \sin \beta
\end{aligned}$$

$\sin(\alpha - \beta) = \sin \alpha \cos \beta - \cos \alpha \sin \beta$

Exercise 11C

1 Expand each of the following:

   (a) $\sin(X - Y)°$
   (b) $\sin(c - 30)°$
   (c) $\sin(2A - B)$
   (d) $\sin(3\beta - 4\alpha)$

2 Verify that $\sin(\alpha - \beta) = \sin\alpha\cos\beta - \cos\alpha\sin\beta$ for the following values of α and β:

   (a) $\alpha = 90°$, $\beta = 30°$
      (b) $\alpha = \dfrac{\pi}{3}$, $\beta = \dfrac{\pi}{6}$

   (c) $\alpha = 135°$, $\beta = 45°$
      (d) $\alpha = \dfrac{5\pi}{6}$, $\beta = \dfrac{2\pi}{3}$

3 Expressing $15°$ as $(45 - 30)°$, find the exact value of $\sin 15°$.

4 (a) Verify that $\dfrac{\pi}{3} - \dfrac{\pi}{4} = \dfrac{\pi}{12}$.

   (b) By writing $\dfrac{\pi}{12}$ as $\dfrac{\pi}{3} - \dfrac{\pi}{4}$, find the exact value of $\sin\dfrac{\pi}{12}$.

5 Simplify

   (a) $\sin S\cos T - \cos S\sin T$
      (b) $\sin 70°\cos 40° - \cos 70°\sin 40°$

   (c) $\sin\dfrac{3\pi}{4}\cos\dfrac{\pi}{4} - \cos\dfrac{3\pi}{4}\sin\dfrac{\pi}{4}$
   (d) $\sin(\theta + 30)°\cos(\theta + 45)° - \cos(\theta + 30)°\sin(\theta + 45)°$

6 (a) Find the exact value of $\sin A$, $\cos A$, $\sin B$ and $\cos B$ for the triangles shown.

   (b) Hence find the exact value of $\sin(A - B)$.

7 Find the exact value of $\sin(P - Q)$.

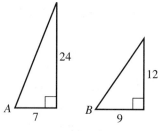

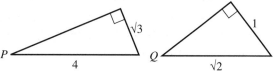

8 Given that A and B are acute angles with $\sin A = \frac{4}{5}$ and $\sin B = \frac{7}{25}$, show that

   (a) $\sin(A - B) = \frac{3}{5}$
      (b) $\sin(A + B) = \frac{117}{125}$

9 Given that A and B are acute angles with $\sin A = \frac{\sqrt{3}}{2}$ and $\sin B = \frac{1}{2}$, show that

   (a) $\sin(A - B) = \frac{1}{2}$
      (b) $\sin(A + B) = 1$

10 The gradient of OA is $\frac{3}{4}$ and the gradient of OB is $\frac{12}{5}$. Prove that $\sin AOB = \frac{33}{65}$.

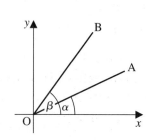

Formulae for $\cos(\alpha \pm \beta)$

Expansions for $\cos(\alpha \pm \beta)$ can be derived from the expressions for $\sin(\alpha \pm \beta)$. The expanded formulae are:

▶ $\cos(\alpha + \beta) = \cos \alpha \cos \beta - \sin \alpha \sin \beta$
$\cos(\alpha - \beta) = \cos \alpha \cos \beta + \sin \alpha \sin \beta$

To prove that these expansions are true you need to remember that:

$$\sin\left(\frac{\pi}{2} - x\right) = \cos x \text{ and } \cos\left(\frac{\pi}{2} - x\right) = \sin x$$

Proof
$$\cos(\alpha + \beta) = \sin\left(\frac{\pi}{2} - (\alpha + \beta)\right)$$

$$= \sin\left(\left(\frac{\pi}{2} - \alpha\right) - \beta\right)$$

$$= \sin\left(\frac{\pi}{2} - \alpha\right)\cos \beta - \cos\left(\frac{\pi}{2} - \alpha\right)\sin \beta$$

$$= \cos \alpha \cos \beta - \sin \alpha \sin \beta$$

$$\cos(\alpha - \beta) = \cos(\alpha + (-\beta))$$
$$= \cos \alpha \cos(-\beta) - \sin \alpha \sin(-\beta)$$
$$= \cos \alpha \cos \beta + \sin \alpha \sin \beta$$

To recap, the four expanded addition formulae are:

$$\sin(\alpha + \beta) = \sin \alpha \cos \beta + \cos \alpha \sin \beta$$
$$\sin(\alpha - \beta) = \sin \alpha \cos \beta - \cos \alpha \sin \beta$$
$$\cos(\alpha + \beta) = \cos \alpha \cos \beta - \sin \alpha \sin \beta$$
$$\cos(\alpha - \beta) = \cos \alpha \cos \beta + \sin \alpha \sin \beta$$

Exercise 11D

1 Expand each of the following:
  (a) $\cos(X - Y)°$ **(b)** $\cos(c + 60)°$ **(c)** $\cos(2A + B)$ **(d)** $\cos(3\beta - 2\alpha)$

2 Verify that $\cos(\alpha + \beta) = \cos \alpha \cos \beta - \sin \alpha \sin \beta$ for the following values of α and β:
  (a) $\alpha = 90°, \beta = 30°$ **(b)** $\alpha = \dfrac{\pi}{3}, \beta = \dfrac{\pi}{6}$

3 Verify that $\cos(\alpha - \beta) = \cos \alpha \cos \beta + \sin \alpha \sin \beta$ for the following values of α and β:
  (a) $\alpha = 90°, \beta = 30°$ **(b)** $\alpha = \dfrac{\pi}{3}, \beta = \dfrac{\pi}{6}$

4 Expressing $15°$ as $(60 - 45)°$, find the exact value of $\cos 15°$.

5 (a) Verify that $\dfrac{7\pi}{12} = \left(\dfrac{\pi}{3} + \dfrac{\pi}{4}\right)$.

   (b) Find the exact value of (i) $\cos \dfrac{7\pi}{12}$ and (ii) $\sin \dfrac{7\pi}{12}$.

6 Simplify
   (a) $\cos P \cos Q - \sin P \sin Q$ **(b)** $\cos 75° \cos 45° - \sin 75° \sin 45°$

   (c) $\cos A \cos B + \sin A \sin B$ **(d)** $\cos \dfrac{3\pi}{4} \cos \dfrac{\pi}{4} + \sin \dfrac{3\pi}{4} \sin \dfrac{\pi}{4}$

   (e) $\sin x \cos y - \sin y \cos x$ **(f)** $\cos 75° \sin 45° + \sin 75° \cos 45°$

7 (a) Find the exact value of $\sin A$, $\cos A$, $\sin B$ and $\cos B$ for the triangles shown.
   (b) Hence find the exact value of
       (i) $\cos (B - A)$ (ii) $\cos (A + B)$
       (iii) $\sin (A + B)$ (iv) $\sin (B - A)$

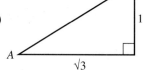
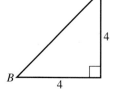

8 A and B are acute angles with $\sin A = \frac{4}{5}$ and $\sin B = \frac{3}{5}$.
   (a) Show that
       (i) $\cos (A - B) = \frac{24}{25}$ (ii) $\sin (A - B) = \frac{7}{25}$
       (iii) $\cos (A + B) = 0$ (iv) $\sin (A + B) = 1$
   (b) State the value of $A + B$.

9 The gradients of OA and OB are $\frac{1}{3}$ and 3 respectively. Show that $\cos \text{AOB} = \frac{3}{5}$.

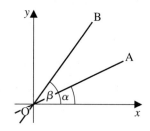

Trigonometric identities

The addition formulae we have now established help us to prove complex trigonometric identities.

Example 4
Prove that $\cos (90 + x)° = -\sin x°$

$$\text{L.H.S.} = \cos (90 + x)°$$
$$= \cos 90° \cos x° - \sin 90° \sin x°$$
$$= 0 \times \cos x° - 1 \times \sin x°$$
$$= -\sin x°$$
$$= \text{R.H.S.}$$

Example 5

Prove that $\dfrac{\sin(\alpha+\beta)}{\cos\alpha\cos\beta} = \tan\alpha + \tan\beta$

L.H.S. $= \dfrac{\sin(\alpha+\beta)}{\cos\alpha\cos\beta} = \dfrac{\sin\alpha\cos\beta + \cos\alpha\sin\beta}{\cos\alpha\cos\beta}$

$\qquad = \dfrac{\sin\alpha\cos\beta}{\cos\alpha\cos\beta} + \dfrac{\cos\alpha\sin\beta}{\cos\alpha\cos\beta}$

$\qquad = \dfrac{\sin\alpha}{\cos\alpha} + \dfrac{\sin\beta}{\cos\beta}$

$\qquad = \tan\alpha + \tan\beta$

$\qquad = $ R.H.S.

Exercise 11E

1 Verify each of the following by expanding the left-hand side:
   (a) $\sin(90 - x)° = \cos x°$ (b) $\sin(180 - x)° = \sin x°$
   (c) $\sin(180 + x)° = -\sin x°$ (d) $\sin(360 - x)° = -\sin x°$

2 Prove that
   (a) $\sin(\alpha+\beta) + \sin(\alpha-\beta) = 2\sin\alpha\cos\beta$
   (b) $\sin(\alpha+\beta) - \sin(\alpha-\beta) = 2\cos\alpha\sin\beta$

3 Verify each of the following by expanding the left-hand side:
   (a) $\cos(90 - x)° = \sin x°$ (b) $\cos(180 - x)° = -\cos x°$
   (c) $\cos(360 - x)° = \cos x°$ (d) $\cos(180 + x)° = -\cos x°$

4 Prove that
   (a) $\cos(\alpha+\beta) + \cos(\alpha-\beta) = 2\cos\alpha\cos\beta$
   (b) $\cos(\alpha-\beta) - \cos(\alpha+\beta) = 2\sin\alpha\sin\beta$

5 Prove that
   (a) $\dfrac{\sin(\alpha-\beta)}{\cos\alpha\cos\beta} = \tan\alpha - \tan\beta$ (b) $\dfrac{\cos(\alpha+\beta)}{\cos\alpha\cos\beta} = 1 - \tan\alpha\tan\beta$

6 Prove that
   (a) $\sin(x+y)\sin(x-y) = \sin^2 x - \sin^2 y$
   (b) $\cos(x+y)\cos(x-y) = \cos^2 y - \sin^2 x$

7 Prove that
   (a) $(\cos\theta + \cos\omega)^2 + (\sin\theta + \sin\omega)^2 = 2[1 + \cos(\theta - \omega)]$
   (b) $(\cos\theta + \sin\omega)^2 + (\sin\theta - \cos\omega)^2 = 2[1 - \sin(\theta - \omega)]$

8 Find the minimum value of each of the following.
   (a) $\sin\alpha\cos\beta + \cos\alpha\sin\beta$ (b) $\sin\alpha\cos\beta - \cos\alpha\sin\beta$
   (c) $\cos\alpha\cos\beta - \sin\alpha\sin\beta$ (d) $\cos\alpha\cos\beta + \sin\alpha\sin\beta$

Applications of addition formulae

Addition formulae help us to

- simplify expressions that are to be differentiated or integrated
- calculate angle size and side length in structures
- solve equations.

Example 6

For the diagram opposite show that $\cos \text{LMN} = \dfrac{\sqrt{5}}{5}$.

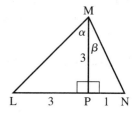

$LM = \sqrt{18} = 3\sqrt{2}$, $MN = \sqrt{10}$

$\cos\alpha = \dfrac{3}{3\sqrt{2}} = \dfrac{1}{\sqrt{2}}$, $\sin\alpha = \dfrac{1}{\sqrt{2}}$, $\cos\beta = \dfrac{3}{\sqrt{10}}$, $\sin\beta = \dfrac{1}{\sqrt{10}}$

$\cos \text{LMN} = \cos(\alpha + \beta)$

$\qquad = \cos\alpha\cos\beta - \sin\alpha\sin\beta$

$\qquad = \dfrac{1}{\sqrt{2}} \times \dfrac{3}{\sqrt{10}} - \dfrac{1}{\sqrt{2}} \times \dfrac{1}{\sqrt{10}}$

$\qquad = \dfrac{2}{\sqrt{20}}$

$\qquad = \dfrac{2}{2\sqrt{5}}$

$\qquad = \dfrac{1}{\sqrt{5}}$

$\qquad = \dfrac{\sqrt{5}}{5}$

Exercise 11F

1 For the diagram opposite show that $\sin \text{QPS} = \frac{63}{65}$.

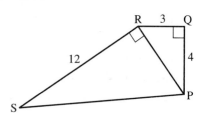

2 A light beam is reflected from a mirror as shown in the diagram.
   (a) Express y in terms of x.
   (b) Prove that $\sin y° = \sin 2x°$.

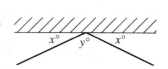

3 Show that $\cos(a + 120)° + \sin(a + 30)° = 0$.

4 Two telephone poles, AB and CD, are situated 9 m apart. They are held by wires that are fixed to the ground at E. Calculate the exact value of cos AEC.

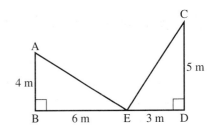

5 The diagram shows part of the frame of a mountain bike. Triangle ABD is an equilateral triangle of side 400 mm. BC = DC = 600 mm.
(a) By applying the cosine rule, prove that $\cos\alpha = \frac{1}{3}$.

(b) Hence show that $\cos ABC = \frac{(1 - 2\sqrt{6})}{6}$.

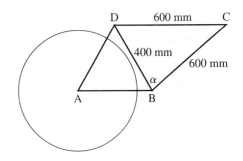

6 Show that, for triangle RST, $t = \dfrac{r\sin(\alpha + \beta)}{\sin\alpha}$.

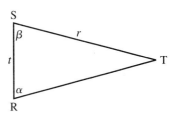

7 The support for a hanging basket is designed with two supporting struts, LN and LK, as shown in the diagram.
(a) Find angle KLN in terms of α and β.

(b) Hence show that $KN = \dfrac{LN\sin(\beta - \alpha)}{\sin\alpha}$.

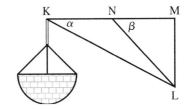

8 The diagram shows part of the metal structure of a bridge. Calculate the exact value of sin XOY.

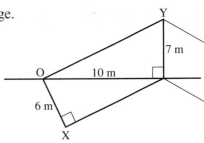

9 (a) By expressing $\tan(\alpha + \beta)$ as $\dfrac{\sin(\alpha + \beta)}{\cos(\alpha + \beta)}$, prove that

$$\tan(\alpha + \beta) = \frac{\tan\alpha + \tan\beta}{1 - \tan\alpha\tan\beta}.$$

(b) Prove that $\tan(\alpha - \beta) = \dfrac{\tan\alpha - \tan\beta}{1 + \tan\alpha\tan\beta}$.

Formulae involving 2α

We can also use the addition formulae to rewrite expressions that involve 2α. Expanding $\sin 2\alpha$ and $\cos 2\alpha$ gives the expressions:

$$\sin 2\alpha = 2\sin \alpha \cos \alpha$$

$$\cos 2\alpha = \cos^2 \alpha - \sin^2 \alpha$$
$$= 2\cos^2 \alpha - 1$$
$$= 1 - 2\sin^2 \alpha$$

These results are referred to as double-angle formulae because the angle on the left of the equation (2α) is double that on the right of the equation (α).

To prove that these expressions are true you need to remember that:
$\sin^2 \alpha + \cos^2 \alpha = 1$

Proof
$$2\alpha = (\alpha + \alpha)$$
Hence $\cos 2\alpha = \cos (\alpha + \alpha)$
$$= \cos \alpha \cos \alpha - \sin \alpha \sin \alpha$$
$$= \cos^2 \alpha - \sin^2 \alpha$$
Also, $\cos 2\alpha = \cos^2 \alpha - \sin^2 \alpha$
$$= \cos^2 \alpha - (1 - \cos^2 \alpha)$$
$$= 2\cos^2 \alpha - 1$$
In addition, $\cos 2\alpha = \cos^2 \alpha - \sin^2 \alpha$
$$= (1 - \sin^2 \alpha) - \sin^2 \alpha$$
$$= 1 - 2\sin^2 \alpha$$

See question 1 in Exercise 11G for the proof of the $\sin 2\alpha$ expression.

Example 7
Given that θ is acute with $\tan \theta = \frac{4}{3}$, calculate $\sin 2\theta$ and $\cos 2\theta$.

$\sin 2\theta = 2\sin \theta \cos \theta$ $\cos 2\theta = \cos^2 \theta - \sin^2 \theta$
$\quad = 2 \times \frac{4}{5} \times \frac{3}{5}$ $\quad = \left(\frac{3}{5}\right)^2 - \left(\frac{4}{5}\right)^2$
$\quad = \frac{24}{25}$ $\quad = -\frac{7}{25}$

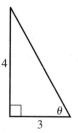

Exercise 11G

1 By writing $2\alpha = (\alpha + \alpha)$, prove that $\sin 2\alpha = 2\sin \alpha \cos \alpha$.

2 Expand each of the following.
   (a) $\sin 2x°$ **(b)** $\cos 2y°$ **(c)** $\sin 2\beta$ **(d)** $\cos 2\beta$

3 By expressing 4β as $2(2\beta)$, write each of the following in terms of $\sin 2\beta$ and $\cos 2\beta$:
   (a) $\sin 4\beta$ **(b)** $\cos 4\beta$

4 **(a)** Express $\sin 6X$ in terms of $\sin 3X$ and $\cos 3X$.
  (b) Express $\cos 6X$ in terms of $\sin 3X$ and $\cos 3X$.

5 Write $\cos 10x$ in terms of
  (a) $\cos 5x$ and $\sin 5x$ **(b)** $\cos 5x$ only   **(c)** $\sin 5x$ only

6 By expressing α as $2\left(\dfrac{\alpha}{2}\right)$, write each of the following in terms of

  $\sin\dfrac{\alpha}{2}$ and $\cos\dfrac{\alpha}{2}$:
  (a) $\sin\alpha$ **(b)** $\cos\alpha$

7 Given that P is an acute angle and $\sin P = \frac{3}{5}$
  (a) show that $\sin 2P = \frac{24}{25}$.
  (b) find the exact value of $\cos 2P$.

8 Given that X is an acute angle with $\cos X = \frac{12}{13}$, calculate the
  exact value of
  (a) $\sin 2X$ **(b)** $\cos 2X$

9 Given that θ is an acute angle with $\tan\theta = \frac{1}{2}$, calculate the exact
  value of
  (a) $\sin 2\theta$ **(b)** $\cos 2\theta$

10 Express each of the following in terms of $\sin 2A$ or $\cos 2A$:
   (a) $2\sin A\cos A$ **(b)** $1 - 2\sin^2 A$ **(c)** $\cos^2 A - \sin^2 A$ **(d)** $\sin^2 A - \cos^2 A$

11 Find the exact value of each of the following:
   (a) $2\cos^2 15° - 1$ **(b)** $2\sin 15°\cos 15°$ **(c)** $1 - 2\sin^2 22.5°$
   (d) $2\sin^2 15° - 1$ **(e)** $2\sin 60°\cos 60°$ **(f)** $1 - 2\cos^2 60°$

12 The diagram shows a kite whose leading diagonal forms the
   diameter of a circle. Find the exact value of
   (a) $\sin$ XOY   **(b)** $\cos$ XOY

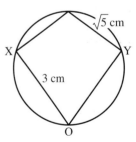

13 By expressing 3θ as $(2\theta + \theta)$ prove that
   (a) $\sin 3\theta = 3\sin\theta - 4\sin^3\theta$ **(b)** $\cos 3\theta = 4\cos^3\theta - 3\cos\theta$

14 The diagram shows two adjacent spokes of a bicycle wheel with
   centre P.
   (a) Use the sine rule to show that

   $$\frac{r}{\cos\dfrac{\omega}{2}} = \frac{p}{\sin\omega}$$

   (b) Hence show that $p = 2r\sin\dfrac{\omega}{2}$.

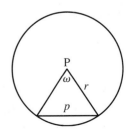

Trigonometric equations

Double-angle formulae often occur in trigonometric equations. We can solve these equations by substituting in the expressions derived in the previous sections. As a general rule you should use $\cos 2\alpha = 2\cos^2 \alpha - 1$ if $\cos \alpha$ also appears in the equation and use $\cos 2\alpha = 1 - 2\sin^2 \alpha$ if $\sin \alpha$ also appears in the equation.

Example 8

Solve the equation $\sin 2x° - \sin x° = 0$ for $0 \leqslant x \leqslant 360$.

$$\sin 2x - \sin x = 0$$
$$2\sin x \cos x - \sin x = 0$$
$$\sin x(2\cos x - 1) = 0$$

$\sin x° = 0$ or $2\cos x° - 1 = 0$

$\sin x° = 0$ or $\cos x° = \dfrac{1}{2}$

$x = 0, 180$ or $x = 60, 300$

Example 9

Solve the equation $\cos 2x - \cos x = 0$ for $0 \leqslant x \leqslant 2\pi$.

$$\cos 2x - \cos x = 0$$
$$2\cos^2 x - 1 - \cos x = 0$$
$$2\cos^2 x - \cos x - 1 = 0$$
$$(2\cos x + 1)(\cos x - 1) = 0$$
$$2\cos x + 1 = 0 \text{ or } \cos x - 1 = 0$$

$$\cos x = \dfrac{-1}{2} \text{ or } \cos x = 1$$

$$x = \dfrac{2\pi}{3}, \dfrac{4\pi}{3} \text{ or } x = 0, 2\pi$$

$$x = 0, \dfrac{2\pi}{3}, \dfrac{4\pi}{3}, 2\pi$$

Exercise 11H

1 Solve the following equations for $0 \leqslant x \leqslant 360$:

(a) $\sin 2x° + \sin x° = 0$

(b) $\sin 2x° + \cos x° = 0$

(c) $\cos 2x° - \sin x° = 0$

(d) $\cos 2x° - 3\sin x° - 1 = 0$

(e) $\cos 2x° + \cos x° = 0$

(f) $\cos 2x° + \cos x° + 1 = 0$

(g) $\cos 2x° + 5\cos x° + 4 = 0$

(h) $\cos 2x° - 4\sin x° + 5 = 0$

(i) $\cos 2x° + 3\cos x° - 1 = 0$

(j) $2\cos 2x° + \cos x° - 1 = 0$

(k) $2 - \cos 2x° = 5\cos x°$

(l) $5\cos 2x° = \cos x° - 2$

2 Solve the following equations for $0 \leqslant \alpha \leqslant 2\pi$.

(a) $\sin 2\alpha + \sin \alpha = 0$ (b) $\sin 2\alpha - \cos \alpha = 0$

(c) $\cos 2\alpha + \cos \alpha = 0$ (d) $2\cos 2\alpha + 1 = 0$

(e) $\cos 2\alpha = \cos \alpha$ (f) $\cos 2\alpha = 1 + \sin \alpha$

3 The diagram shows the graphs of $f(x) = 4\sin 2x°$ and $g(x) = 2\sin x°$ for $0 \leqslant x \leqslant 360$.

(a) Solve algebraically the equation $4\sin 2x° = 2\sin x°$.

(b) Hence find the coordinates of points A and B.

(c) For what values of x in the interval $0 \leqslant x \leqslant 360$ is $4\sin 2x° \geqslant 2\sin x°$?

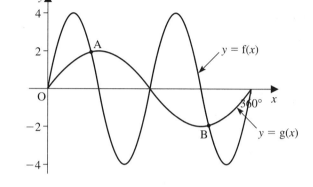

4 The diagram shows the graph of $h(x) = \cos 2x$ and $k(x) = 1 - 3\cos x$ for $0 \leqslant x \leqslant 2\pi$.

(a) Solve algebraically the equation $\cos 2x = 1 - 3\cos x$.

(b) Hence find the coordinates of points A and B.

(c) For what values of x in the interval $0 \leqslant x \leqslant 2\pi$ is $\cos 2x < 1 - 3\cos x$?

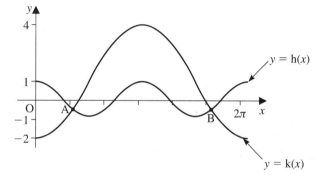

5 The diagram shows the graphs of $f(x) = a\sin bx°$ and $g(x) = c\sin x°$ for $0 \leqslant x \leqslant 360$.

(a) State the values of a, b and c.

(b) Solve, algebraically, the equation $f(x) = g(x)$.

(c) Find the coordinates of the points of intersection of the graphs for $0 \leqslant x \leqslant 360$.

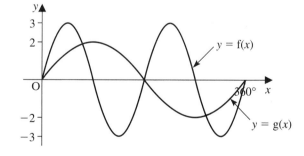

6 For the following graphs of trigonometrical functions find
  (i) the equation of each graph.
  (ii) algebraically the points of intersection of the graphs.

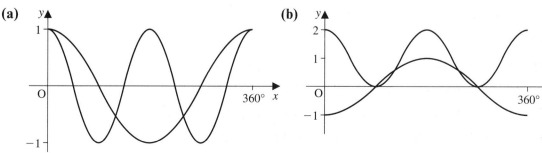

(a)

(b)

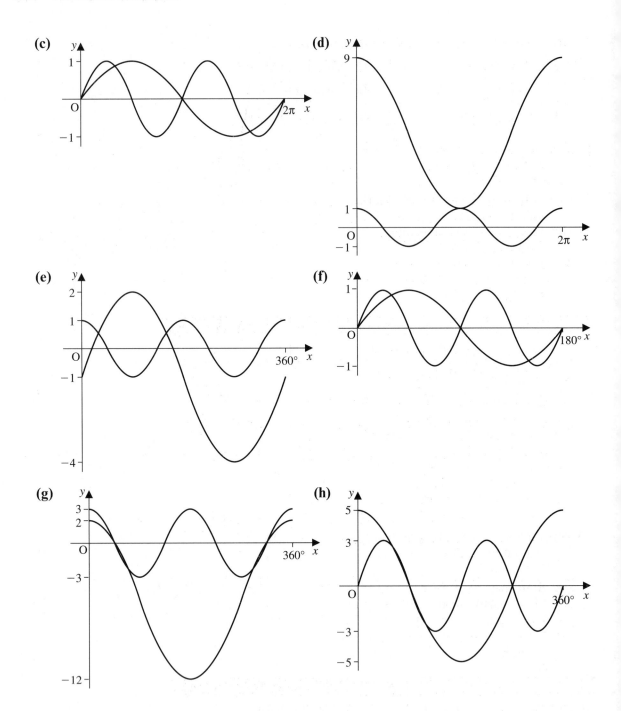

Formulae for cos²x and sin²x

The double-angle formulae $\cos 2\alpha = 2\cos^2\alpha - 1$ and $\cos 2\alpha = 1 - 2\sin^2\alpha$ can be rearranged to make $\cos^2\alpha$ and $\sin^2\alpha$ the subjects of the formulae. This allows us to solve equations involving $\sin^2 x$ or $\cos^2 x$ or both.

$$\cos^2\alpha = \tfrac{1}{2}(1 + \cos 2\alpha)$$
$$\sin^2\alpha = \tfrac{1}{2}(1 - \cos 2\alpha)$$

Proof

$\cos 2\alpha = 2\cos^2 \alpha - 1$

$\cos 2\alpha + 1 = 2\cos^2 \alpha$

$\frac{1}{2}(\cos 2\alpha + 1) = \cos^2 \alpha$

$\cos^2 \alpha = \frac{1}{2}(1 + \cos 2\alpha)$

Proof

$\cos 2\alpha = 1 - 2\sin^2 \alpha$

$\cos 2\alpha - 1 = -2\sin^2 \alpha$

$1 - \cos 2\alpha = 2\sin^2 \alpha$

$\sin^2 \alpha = \frac{1}{2}(1 - \cos 2\alpha)$

Example 10

Express $2\cos^2 x - 3\sin^2 x$ in terms of $\cos 2x$.

$$2\cos^2 x - 3\sin^2 x = 2 \times \frac{1}{2}(1 + \cos 2x) - 3 \times \frac{1}{2}(1 - \cos 2x)$$
$$= 1 + 1\cos 2x - \frac{3}{2} + \frac{3}{2}\cos 2x$$
$$= -\frac{1}{2} + \frac{5}{2}\cos 2x$$
$$= \frac{1}{2}(5\cos 2x - 1)$$

Exercise 11I

1 Use the formulae for $\cos^2 x$ and $\sin^2 x$ to express each of the following without a squared term:

   (a) $\cos^2 \beta$ **(b)** $\sin^2 \beta$ **(c)** $\cos^2 A$ **(d)** $\sin^2 A$

   (e) $\cos^2 2x$ **(f)** $\sin^2 2p$ **(g)** $\cos^2\left(\dfrac{x}{2}\right)$ **(h)** $\sin^2\left(\dfrac{x}{2}\right)$

2 Using $\cos^2 \alpha = \frac{1}{2}(\cos 2\alpha + 1)$ and $\sin^2 \alpha = \frac{1}{2}(1 - \cos 2\alpha)$, show that $\cos^2 \alpha + \sin^2 \alpha = 1$.

3 Express each of the following in terms of $\cos 2x$:

   (a) $2\cos^2 x$ **(b)** $2\sin^2 x$ **(c)** $4\cos^2 x$ **(d)** $\frac{1}{2}\sin^2 x$

   (e) $\cos^4 x$ **(f)** $\sin^4 x$ **(g)** $4\cos^2 x$ **(h)** $8\sin^2 x$

4 Prove that

   (a) $(2\cos \alpha + 1)(2\cos \alpha - 1) = 1 + 2\cos 2\alpha$

   (b) $\sin^4 x = \frac{1}{8}(\cos 4x - 4\cos 2x + 3)$

   (c) $\cos^4 x = \frac{1}{8}(\cos 4x + 4\cos 2x + 3)$

Exercise 11J Mixed questions

1 Given that $\sin A = \frac{3}{5}$ and $\sin B = \frac{\sqrt{3}}{4}$ and that A and B are acute angles, find the exact value of

   (a) $\sin(A + B)$ **(b)** $\cos(A + B)$

2 Given that $\sin C = \frac{1}{\sqrt{3}}$ find the exact value of $\cos C$ and $\sin 2C$.

3 Given that $\cos \theta = \frac{5}{13}$ find the exact value of $\sin \theta$ and $\cos 2\theta$.

4 (a) Expand $\sin(x + 150)°$ and $\cos(x + 120)°$.

   (b) Hence find the exact value of
      $\cos x° - \sin(x + 150)° + \cos(x + 120)°$.

5 The diagram shows the roof truss for a new stand at a football stadium. Find the exact value of cos ABC.

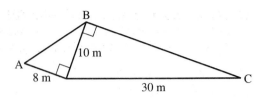

6 A transport engineer has been set the task of designing new bicycle stands for the city centre. The diagram shows part of his design. H is the hub (centre) of the wheel, LO is the diameter of the wheel along the line of the front forks and triangle OMN is the stand. The diameter of the test wheel is 650 mm. Show that $\cos \text{LOM} = -\frac{16}{65}$.

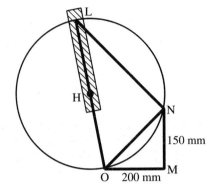

7 The diagram shows two telegraph poles, AB and ED, with support wires pegged at a single point C. Find the exact value of
(a) cos ACB **(b)** sin ECD
(c) cos ACE **(d)** sin ACE

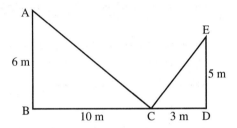

8 Solve the following equations for $0 \leqslant x \leqslant 360$.
(a) $\cos 2x° - 3\cos x° + 2 = 0$ **(b)** $\sin 2x° - 2\cos x° = 0$
(c) $\cos 2x° = 4\sin x° - 5$ **(d)** $\cos 2x° = 1 - 2\sin x°$

9 Solve the following equations for $0 \leqslant \theta < 2\pi$.
(a) $\cos 2\theta + 3\sin \theta - 2 = 0$ **(b)** $\cos 2\theta - 4\cos \theta - 5 = 0$
(c) $\cos 2\theta = \cos \theta - 1$ **(d)** $\sin 2\theta = 3\sin \theta$

10 The diagram shows the graph of $f(x) = 3\sin 2x°$ and the line $y = 2$ for $0 \leqslant x \leqslant 360$.
(a) Find the points of intersection of $f(x)$ and the line $y = 2$.
(b) In the interval $0 \leqslant x \leqslant 360$, for what values of x is $3\sin 2x° > 2$?

11 The diagram shows the graph of $f(x) = \cos 2x°$ and $g(x) = 1 - \sin x°$ for $0 \leqslant x \leqslant 360$.
(a) Solve algebraically the equation $\cos 2x° = 1 - \sin x°$.
(b) Hence find the coordinates of points A and B.
(c) In the interval $0 \leqslant x \leqslant 90$, for what values of x is $\cos 2x° < 1 - \sin x°$?

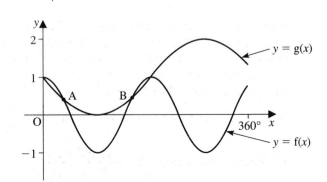

12 The diagram shows △ABC with AB = 13 and angle C = 90°.
D lies on AC such that DC = 4 and angle DBC = 30°. If angle
ABD = $x°$, find the **exact** value of sin $x°$.   [Higher]

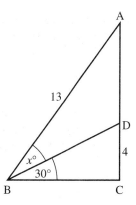

13 (a) For the triangle shown opposite show that
sin (180 − $(x + y)$) = sin $(x + y)$.

(b) Hence use the sine rule to show that for this triangle
$$b = \frac{a \sin (x + y)}{\sin x}.$$

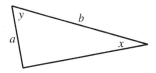

14 The profile of a one-person tent is shown in the diagram
opposite.

(a) Prove that AB = $\dfrac{h}{\tan \beta} + \dfrac{h}{\tan \alpha}$.

(b) Hence prove that AB = $\dfrac{h \sin (\alpha + \beta)}{\sin \alpha \sin \beta}$.

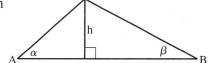

15 A ship is sailing due north at a constant speed. When at position
A, a lighthouse L is observed on a bearing of $a°$. One hour later,
when the ship is at position B, the lighthouse is on a bearing of
$b°$. The shortest distance between the ship and the lighthouse
during this hour was d miles.

(a) Prove that AB = $\dfrac{d}{\tan a°} - \dfrac{d}{\tan b°}$.

(b) Hence prove that AB = $\dfrac{d \sin (b - a)°}{\sin a° \sin b°}$.

(c) Calculate the shortest distance from the ship to the
lighthouse when the bearings $a°$ and $b°$ are 060° and 135°
respectively and the constant speed of the ship is 14 miles per
hour.   [Higher]

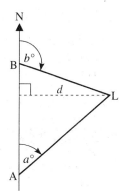

16 A tent is being tested for strength in high winds.
Two guy ropes, EG and EH, are attached to the pole
as shown in the diagram. Angles θ and ϕ and distance d
are altered during the test.

(a) Find the size of angle GEH in terms of θ and ϕ.

(b) Use the sine rule to show that EG = $\dfrac{d \sin \theta}{\sin (\phi - \theta)}$.

(c) Hence prove that EF = $\dfrac{d \sin \theta \sin \phi}{\sin (\phi - \theta)}$.

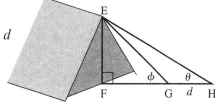

17 Triangle XYZ is isosceles.

    (a) Prove that $x = \dfrac{y \sin 2\alpha}{\cos \alpha}$.

    (b) Hence show that $x = 2y \sin \alpha$.

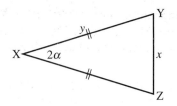

18 The diagram shows an isosceles triangle PQR in which PR = QR and angle PQR = $x°$.

    (a) Show that $\dfrac{\sin x°}{p} = \dfrac{\sin 2x°}{r}$.

    (b) (i) State the value of $x°$ when $p = r$.

        (ii) Use the fact that $p = r$, solve the equation in **(a)** above to justify your stated value of $x°$.

        [Higher]

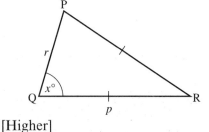

19 Show that, for the triangle ABC shown, $a = \dfrac{b \sin \lambda}{\cos(\theta - \lambda)}$.

    [Higher]

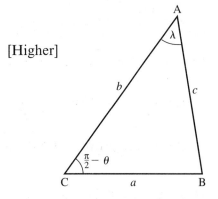

20 Prove the following identities:

    (a) $6 \sin \alpha \cos \alpha = 3 \sin 2\alpha$ **(b)** $(\sin \alpha + \cos \alpha)^2 = 1 + \sin 2\alpha$

    (c) $\left(\sin \tfrac{1}{2}\alpha - \cos \tfrac{1}{2}\alpha\right)^2 = 1 - \sin \alpha$ **(d)** $\cos^4 \alpha - \sin^4 \alpha = \cos 2\alpha$

    (e) $\dfrac{\sin 2x}{1 + \cos 2x} = \tan x$ **(f)** $\dfrac{1 - \cos 2x}{1 + \cos 2x} = \tan^2 x$

SUMMARY

① $\sin(\alpha + \beta) = \sin \alpha \cos \beta + \cos \alpha \sin \beta$

② $\sin(\alpha - \beta) = \sin \alpha \cos \beta - \cos \alpha \sin \beta$

③ $\cos(\alpha + \beta) = \cos \alpha \cos \beta - \sin \alpha \sin \beta$

   $\cos(\alpha - \beta) = \cos \alpha \cos \beta + \sin \alpha \sin \beta$

④ $\sin 2\alpha = 2 \sin \alpha \cos \alpha$

⑤ $\cos 2\alpha = \cos^2 \alpha - \sin^2 \alpha$

         $= 2 \cos^2 \alpha - 1$

         $= 1 - 2 \sin^2 \alpha$

⑥ $\cos^2 \alpha = \tfrac{1}{2}(1 + \cos 2\alpha)$

   $\sin^2 \alpha = \tfrac{1}{2}(1 - \cos 2\alpha)$

12 The circle

This chapter shows you how to solve problems involving circles using the equation of a circle in several different forms.

The distance between two points

The exercise will help you find the formula for the distance between two points. You will need this later to find the radius of a circle.

Exercise 12A

1 (a)

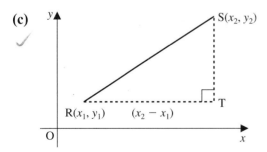

Find the lengths of AC and BC, and calculate the length of AB.

(b)

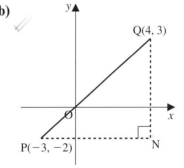

Find the lengths of of PN and QN, and calculate the length of PQ.

(c)

The length of RT is $(x_2 - x_1)$. State the length of ST and write an expression for the length of RS.

From the exercise you should have found that:

> The distance between (x_1, y_1) and (x_2, y_2) is
> $\sqrt{(x_2 - x_1)^2 + (y_2 - y_1)^2}$. This is known as the **distance formula**.

Example 1

Calculate the distance between A(−3, 3) and B(1, 7).

$$AB = \sqrt{(1-(-3))^2+(7-3)^2}$$
$$= \sqrt{(16+16)}$$
$$= \sqrt{32}$$
$$= 4\sqrt{2}$$

Exercise 12B

1 Calculate the distance between
  (a) C(2, 3) and D(5, 7)   **(b)** G(1, 0) and H(7, 8)
  (c) S(−2, 1) and T(3, 13)   **(d)** K(−6, −4) and L(3, −16)

2 Triangle PQR has vertices P(−3, 6), Q(9, 2) and R(6, −7).
Calculate the length of each side and show that the triangle is
right angled.

3 KLMN has vertices K(−4, 7), L(4, 1), M(0, −7) and N(−8, −1).
Show that the opposite sides of this shape are equal.

4 F(−5, −1), G(2, 8) and H(5, −3) are vertices of a triangle.
Prove that the triangle is isosceles but **not** equilateral.

5 Prove that triangle STU with vertices S(−6, 0), T(−3, 4) and
U(5, −2) is right angled.

The equation of a circle

From exercise 12C you should be able to work out the equation of a
basic circle.

Exercise 12C

1 (a) Plot these points on a coordinate diagram:
      (5, 0), (4, 3), (3, 4), (0, 5), (−3, 4), (−4, 3), (−5, 0),
      (−4, −3), (−3, −4), (0, −5), (3, −4), (4, −3).
  (b) Check that the points lie on the circumference of a circle.
     Find its centre and radius.
  (c) For each point calculate $x^2 + y^2$ and suggest a rule linking
     the coordinates of every point (x, y) on the circumference of
     this circle with its radius.

2 (a) Plot these points on a coordinate diagram:
      (13, 0), (12, 5), (5, 12), (0, 13), (−5, 12), (−12, 5),
      (−13, 0), (−12, −5), (−5, −12), (0, −13), (5, −12), (12, −5).
  (b) Check that the points lie on the circumference of a circle.
     Find its centre and radius.
  (c) For each point calculate $x^2 + y^2$ and suggest a rule for points
     on the circumference of this circle.

The equation of a circle, centre the origin and radius *r*

A circle is defined as the locus of all points P(x, y) that are a constant distance (radius) from a given point (centre).

From exercise 12C you should notice that:

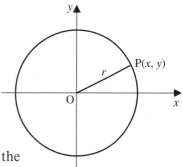

> ► The equation of a circle with centre (0, 0) and radius *r* is $x^2 + y^2 = r^2$.

Proof
P(x, y) is any point on the circumference of a circle with centre the origin and radius *r*.

For every position of P, $OP = r$

From the distance formula, $OP^2 = x^2 + y^2$

so $x^2 + y^2 = r^2$

Hence $x^2 + y^2 = r^2$ is the equation of a circle with centre the origin and radius *r*.

Example 2
Write the equation of a circle with centre the origin and radius $6\sqrt{2}$.

The equation of the circle is $x^2 + y^2 = r^2$
$$x^2 + y^2 = \left(6\sqrt{2}\right)^2$$
$$x^2 + y^2 = 72$$

Example 3
Show that the point A$\left(-3, \sqrt{7}\right)$ lies on the circle $x^2 + y^2 = 16$.

When $x = -3$ and $y = \sqrt{7}$, $x^2 + y^2 = (-3)^2 + \left(\sqrt{7}\right)^2$
$$= 9 + 7$$
$$= 16$$

Hence A lies on the circle $x^2 + y^2 = 16$

Exercise 12D

1 Write the equation of the circle with centre the origin and radius
   (a) 4   **(b)** 7   **(c)** 9   **(d)** 12   **(e)** t

2 Write the equation of the circle with centre (0, 0) and passing through
   (a) (6, 8)   **(b)** (0, −3)   **(c)** (3, 5)   **(d)** (−2, 1)

3 State the radius of each circle.
   (a) $x^2 + y^2 = 49$ **(b)** $x^2 + y^2 = 5$ **(c)** $x^2 + y^2 = 225$
   (d) $x^2 + y^2 = 27$ **(e)** $x^2 + y^2 = \frac{9}{4}$ **(f)** $x^2 + y^2 = 0.25$

4 The lines $x = 7$, $y = 7$, $x = -7$ and $y = -7$ are tangents to a circle. Find the equation of the circle.

5 A circle passes through the vertices of a rectangle whose sides have equations $x = 12$, $x = -12$, $y = 9$ and $y = -9$. Find the equation of the circle.

6 The treble ring on a dart board can be represented by the circle $x^2 + y^2 = 100$. If the double ring has a radius 1.6 times that of the treble, find its equation.

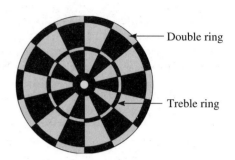

Double ring

Treble ring

7 Which point lies on the circumference of which circle?
K(5, 3) L(7, −4) M(−2, 8) N(−6, −6) P(4, $\sqrt{12}$) Q($\sqrt{9}$, −$\sqrt{6}$)
(a) $x^2 + y^2 = 68$ (b) $x^2 + y^2 = 15$ (c) $x^2 + y^2 = 34$
(d) $x^2 + y^2 = 72$ (e) $x^2 + y^2 = 28$ (f) $x^2 + y^2 = 65$

8 Find two values for each letter.
(a) $(a, 4)$ lies on $x^2 + y^2 = 41$ (b) $(-3, q)$ lies on $x^2 + y^2 = 58$
(c) (w, w) lies on $x^2 + y^2 = 200$ (d) $(t, 2t)$ lies on $x^2 + y^2 = 5$
(e) $(r, r+1)$ lies on $x^2 + y^2 = 5$ (f) $(p+1, p-1)$ lies on $x^2 + y^2 = 6$

9 (a) For each point on the diagram calculate $x^2 + y^2$.
(b) The equation of this circle is $x^2 + y^2 = 36$. Write an inequation describing the coordinates of points which lie
  (i) inside the circle
  (ii) outside the circle.

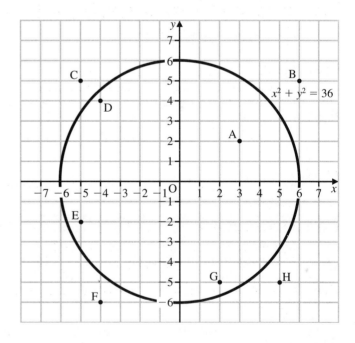

10 State whether each point lies inside, outside or on the circumference of the given circle.
(a) $(2, 5)$, $x^2 + y^2 = 30$ (b) $(-5, 7)$, $x^2 + y^2 = 12$
(c) $(0, -1)$, $x^2 + y^2 = 1$ (d) $(-3, -3)$, $x^2 + y^2 = 20$
(e) $(8, -9)$, $x^2 + y^2 = 145$ (f) $(\frac{1}{2}, -\frac{1}{4})$, $x^2 + y^2 = \frac{5}{16}$

Circles with other centres

The equation of a circle with a centre that is not the origin is a little harder to spot. The following questions will help you to find it.

Exercise 12E

1 (a) Plot these points on a coordinate diagram:
$(12, 3)$, $(10, 9)$, $(2, 13)$, $(-4, 11)$, $(-8, 3)$, $(-6, -3)$, $(2, -7)$, $(8, -5)$

(b) Check that the points lie on the circumference of a circle. Find the centre and radius of this circle.

(c) For each point on the circumference find $(x - 2)^2 + (y - 3)^2$ and suggest a rule linking the coordinates of every point (x, y) on the circumference of this circle with its radius.

2 (a) Plot these points on a coordinate diagram:
$(12, -2)$, $(4, 10)$, $(-1, 11)$, $(-13, 3)$, $(-14, -2)$, $(-6, -14)$, $(-1, -15)$, $(11, -7)$

(b) For each point on the circumference find $(x + 1)^2 + (y + 2)^2$ and suggest a rule for points on the circumference of this circle.

The equation of a circle with centre (*a*, *b*) and radius *r*

From the above exercise, you should notice that:

> The equation of a circle with centre (a, b) and radius r is
> $$(x - a)^2 + (y - b)^2 = r^2$$

Proof
$P(x, y)$ is any point on the circumference of a circle with centre $C(a, b)$ and radius r.

For every position of P, $CP = r$
From the distance formula, $CP^2 = (x - a)^2 + (y - b)^2$
so $(x - a)^2 + (y - b)^2 = r^2$

Hence $(x - a)^2 + (y - b)^2 = r^2$ is the equation of a circle with centre (a, b) and radius r.

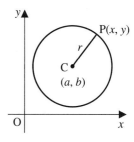

Example 4
Write the equation of the circle with centre $(3, -5)$ and radius $2\sqrt{3}$.

The equation of the circle is $(x - a)^2 + (y - b)^2 = r^2$
$$(x - 3)^2 + (y + 5)^2 = \left(2\sqrt{3}\right)^2$$
$$(x - 3)^2 + (y + 5)^2 = 12$$

Example 5
Show that the point B(7, −3) lies on the circle
$(x − 2)^2 + (y + 5)^2 = 29$.

When $x = 7$ and $y = -3$, $(x − 2)^2 + (y + 5)^2 = (7 − 2)^2 + (−3 + 5)^2$
$$= 5^2 + 2^2$$
$$= 29$$

Therefore B lies on the circle $(x − 2)^2 + (y + 5)^2 = 29$.

Exercise 12F

1 Write the equation of the circle with the given centre and radius.
Leave your answer in the form $(x − a)^2 + (y − b)^2 = r^2$.

   (a) (4, 1), $r = 4$ **(b)** (3, 3), $r = 6$ **(c)** (0, −9), $r = 8$

   (d) (−5, 2), $r = \sqrt{7}$ **(e)** (−7, −1), $r = 2\sqrt{5}$ **(f)** (p, q), $r = s$

2 State the centre and radius of each circle.

   (a) $(x − 8)^2 + (y − 3)^2 = 100$ **(b)** $(x − 6)^2 + (y + 6)^2 = 25$

   (c) $(x + 1)^2 + (y − 12)^2 = 40$ **(d)** $(x + 7)^2 + y^2 = 169$

3 A circle with centre G(7, −2) passes through the point K(−2, 10).
Calculate the radius and find the equation of the circle.

4 AB is the diameter of a circle where A is (9, 5) and B is (−1, −7).
Find the equation of the circle.

5 A circle has the equation $(x − 3)^2 + (y + 9)^2 = 144$. A smaller
concentric circle has a radius one-third that of the larger one.
Find the equation of the smaller circle.

6 Find the equation of a circle with centre (−8, 5) and which has
the y-axis as a tangent.

7 The lines $x = 11$, $x = −3$, $y = 6$ and $y = −8$ are tangents to a
circle. Find the equation of the circle.

8 Which point lies on the circumference of which circle?

   C(1, 1), D(1, 2), E(5, 8), F(−2, −3), O(0, 0), G(−5, 7)

   (a) $(x − 2)^2 + (y − 4)^2 = 25$ **(b)** $(x + 5)^2 + y^2 = 49$

   (c) $(x + 2)^2 + (y − 9)^2 = 73$ **(d)** $(x + 4)^2 + (y + 10)^2 = 116$

   (e) $x^2 + (y + 7)^2 = 20$ **(f)** $(x − 1)^2 + (y − 1)^2 = 1$

9 (a) For each point (x, y) in the diagram calculate
$(x - 2)^2 + (y - 1)^2$

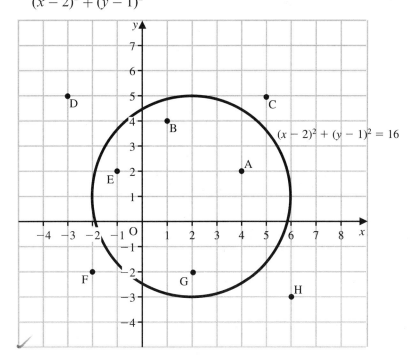

(b) The equation of the circle is $(x - 2)^2 + (y - 1)^2 = 16$. Write
an inequation describing the coordinates of points which lie
  (i) inside the circle
  (ii) outside the circle.

10 State whether each point lies inside, outside or on the circumference
of the given circle.

(a) $(2, 6)$, $(x - 1)^2 + (y + 1)^2 = 10$ **(b)** $(5, -3)$, $(x - 4)^2 + (y - 1)^2 = 20$
(c) $(-7, -9)$, $(x + 3)^2 + (y + 5)^2 = 30$ **(d)** $(-8, 10)$, $(x + 2)^2 + (y - 6)^2 = 52$
(e) $(0, -5)$, $(x - 3)^2 + (y + 7)^2 = 9$ **(f)** $(2, 2)$, $(x - 1)^2 + (y - 1)^2 = 2$

The expanded form of the equation of a circle

The equation of a circle, $(x - a)^2 + (y - b)^2 = r^2$, can be written in
an expanded form. You must be able to recognise this expanded
form and know how to determine the radius and the coordinates of
the centre of the circle from it.

Example 6
The equation of a circle is $(x - 2)^2 + (y - 3)^2 = 25$.
Write the equation without brackets.

$$(x - 2)^2 + (y - 3)^2 = 25$$
$$x^2 - 4x + 4 + y^2 - 6y + 9 - 25 = 0$$
$$x^2 + y^2 - 4x - 6y - 12 = 0$$

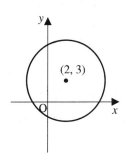

Example 7

Show that $x^2 + y^2 + 6x - 2y - 15 = 0$ is the equation of a circle.
Find the centre and radius of the circle.

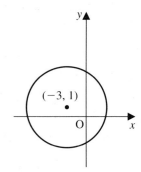

$$x^2 + y^2 + 6x - 2y - 15 = 0$$

Complete the squares: $x^2 + 6x + y^2 - 2y \qquad = 15$

$$x^2 + 6x + 9 + y^2 - 2y + 1 = 15 + 9 + 1$$
$$(x + 3)^2 + (y - 1)^2 \qquad = 25$$
$$(x - (-3))^2 + (y - 1)^2 \qquad = 5^2$$

Hence the equation represents a circle with centre $(-3, 1)$ and radius 5.

Exercise 12G

1 Find the equation of each circle with the given centre and radius.
Write your answer without brackets in its simplest form.

  (a) $(1, 2)$, $r = 4$ **(b)** $(3, 4)$, $r = 6$ **(c)** $(5, -1)$, $r = 3$
  (d) $(-4, 2)$, $r = 2$ **(e)** $(-5, -5)$, $r = 1$ **(f)** $(0, -7)$, $r = 8$

2 Show that each equation represents a circle and for each find the
centre, find the radius and draw a sketch.

  (a) $x^2 + y^2 - 4x - 6y + 9 = 0$ **(b)** $x^2 + y^2 + 2x + 8y + 1 = 0$
  (c) $x^2 + y^2 + 6x - 2y + 6 = 0$ **(d)** $x^2 + y^2 - 10x + 10y + 1 = 0$
  (e) $x^2 + y^2 - 8x - 6y = 0$ **(f)** $x^2 + y^2 - 6x = 0$
  (g) $x^2 + y^2 + 12y = 0$ **(h)** $x^2 + y^2 - 2ax - 2by = 0$

The general equation of a circle

Now that we are familiar with the expanded form of
$(x - a)^2 + (y - b)^2 = r^2$ we can write the general equation of a circle:

> $x^2 + y^2 + 2gx + 2fy + c = 0$ (where g, f and c are constants)
> is the **general equation** of a circle with centre $(-g, -f)$
> and radius $\sqrt{g^2 + f^2 - c}$, provided $g^2 + f^2 - c > 0$.

This equation allows us to find the centre and radius of any circle.

Proof

$$x^2 + y^2 + 2gx + 2fy + c = 0$$
$$x^2 + 2gx + y^2 + 2fy = -c$$
$$x^2 + 2gx + g^2 + y^2 + 2fy + f^2 = -c + g^2 + f^2$$
$$(x + g)^2 + (y + f)^2 = g^2 + f^2 - c$$
$$(x - (-g))^2 + (y - (-f))^2 = g^2 + f^2 - c$$

This is the equation of a circle with centre $(-g, -f)$ and radius
$\sqrt{g^2 + f^2 - c}$.

Example 8
Find the radius and the centre of the circle with equation
$x^2 + y^2 - 6x + 2y - 6 = 0$.

Using the general equation of a circle, $x^2 + y^2 + 2gx + 2fy + c = 0$:
$2g = -6$, therefore $g = -3$
$2f = 2$,   therefore $f = 1$
$c = -6$

The centre of the circle is $(-g, -f)$, i.e. $(3, -1)$.

The radius of the circle is $\sqrt{g^2 + f^2 - c}$

$$= \sqrt{(-3)^2 + 1^2 - (-6)}$$
$$= \sqrt{16}$$
$$= 4$$

Exercise 12H

1 For each circle find
   (i) the values of g, f and c (ii) the centre   (iii) the radius.
   (a) $x^2 + y^2 + 6x + 2y - 6 = 0$ **(b)** $x^2 + y^2 + 6x + 6y + 2 = 0$
   (c) $x^2 + y^2 + 8x - 4y + 11 = 0$ **(d)** $x^2 + y^2 - 2x - 12y - 12 = 0$
   (e) $x^2 + y^2 - 4x - 8y - 5 = 0$ **(f)** $x^2 + y^2 + 10x - 8y - 8 = 0$
   (g) $x^2 + y^2 - 18x + 2y - 18 = 0$ **(h)** $x^2 + y^2 + 12x + 16y = 0$
   (i) $x^2 + y^2 - 10x + 24y = 0$ **(j)** $x^2 + y^2 - 4y + 3 = 0$
   (k) $x^2 + y^2 + x - 2y - 1 = 0$ **(l)** $x^2 + y^2 = 81$

2 Find the general equation of each circle.
   (a)   **(b)**   **(c)**

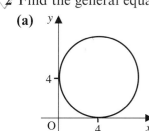
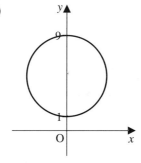
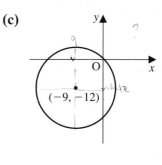

3 Match each statement to one of the circle equations (a) to (f).
   A   The centre is $(5, -2)$.   **B**   The radius is 13.
   C   The diameter is 18.   **D**   It is concentric with $x^2 - y^2 = 1$
   E   The centre is $(-7, 0)$ and the circumference of the circle passes through the origin.
   F   The end-points of a diameter are $(2, 5)$ and $(-4, -3)$.
   (a) $x^2 + y^2 - 12x - 14y + 4 = 0$ **(b)** $x^2 + y^2 + 2x - 2y - 23 = 0$
   (c) $x^2 + y^2 - 10x + 4y + 13 = 0$ **(d)** $x^2 + y^2 + 14x = 0$
   (e) $x^2 + y^2 = 400$ **(f)** $x^2 + y^2 - 24x + 10y = 0$

4 For each equation
   (i) calculate $g^2 + f^2 - c$ (ii) explain why it does not represent a circle.
   (a) $x^2 + y^2 - 6x - 4y + 14 = 0$ (b) $x^2 + y^2 + 2x - 8y + 20 = 0$
   (c) $x^2 + y^2 + 10x + 2y + 26 = 0$ (d) $x^2 + y^2 + 25 = 0$

5 Identify each equation which represents a circle and calculate its radius.
   (a) $x^2 + y^2 + 2x + 12y + 1 = 0$ (b) $x^2 + y^2 + 4x - 2y + 5 = 0$
   (c) $x^2 + y^2 - 8x + 16y - 1 = 0$ (d) $x^2 + y^2 - 6x - y + 10 = 0$
   (e) $x^2 + y^2 + 20x + 19 = 0$ (f) $x^2 + y^2 + 2x + 2y = 47$
   (g) $x^2 + y^2 - 6x - 10y - 2 = 0$ (h) $x^2 + y^2 + 6.25 = 0$

6 (a) Find the centre C and the radius of the circle
         $x^2 + y^2 + 10x - 6y + 9 = 0$.
   (b) Calculate the distance between C and A(8, 3).
   (c) Sketch the circle and draw a tangent from A to meet the
         circle at B. Calculate the length of AB.

7 Which of the points A(4, 10), B(−10, 3) and C(11, −7) lie on the
   circumference of the circle $x^2 + y^2 + 2x + 4y - 164 = 0$?

8 The point (2, −3) lies on the circumference of the circle
   $x^2 + y^2 - 4x - 8y + c = 0$. Find the value of c.

9 (a) Write each equation in general form and state the coefficient
         of x^2 and the coefficient of y^2.
         (i) $(x - 8)^2 + (y - 3)^2 = 100$ (ii) $(x - 6)^2 + (y + 6)^2 = 25$
         (iii) $x^2 + (y + 7)^2 = 20$ (iv) $(x + 7)^2 + y^2 = 169$
   (b) For an equation to represent a circle it must be able to be
         written in the form $(x - a)^2 + (y - b)^2 = r^2$. Write this
         equation without brackets in its simplest form and state the
         coefficient of x^2 and the coefficient of y^2.

10 Arrange each of the equations (a) to (d) in the form $x^2 + y^2 + 2gx + 2fy + c = 0$.
   Find the centre and radius of each circle.
   (a) $2x^2 + 2y^2 = 32$ (b) $5x^2 + 5y^2 + 10x + 40y + 5 = 0$
   (c) $\frac{1}{3}x^2 + \frac{1}{3}y^2 = 3$ (d) $\frac{1}{4}x^2 + \frac{1}{4}y^2 + x + \frac{1}{2}y = 0$

11 Identify each equation which represents a circle and find its centre and radius.
   (a) $4x^2 + 4y^2 = 9$ (b) $x^2 + 4y^2 + 6x + 8y + 9 = 0$
   (c) $\frac{1}{4}x^2 + \frac{1}{4}y^2 = 1$ (d) $x^2 + 8x - 16y - 1 = 0$
   (e) $3x^2 + 3y^2 + 6x - 12y = 0$ (f) $\frac{1}{2}x^2 + \frac{1}{2}y^2 - 18 = 0$
   (g) $x^2 - y^2 - 2x + 2y - 2 = 0$ (h) $5x^2 + 5y^2 = 30y$
   (i) $\frac{1}{4}x^2 + \frac{1}{4}y^2 + x + 5y = 10$ (j) $x^2 + y^2 + 2xy - 6 = 0$

12 Machinery in a flour mill has wheel A driving wheel B
   by means of a chain. With coordinate axes as shown,
   wheel A has radius 10 units and touches both axes.
   (a) Find the equation of wheel A.
   (b) If wheel B has equation $x^2 + y^2 + 28x + 147 = 0$ and
         1 unit represents 9 cm calculate
         (i) the distance between the centres of the wheels.
         (ii) the smallest gap between the wheels.

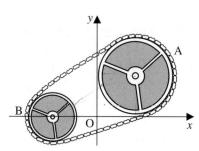

good one!

13 Some of Scotland's Iron Age Celts lived in crannogs or lake dwellings. The people reached their circular island homes by wading across an underwater causeway. The causeway ran in a straight line towards the centre of the island.

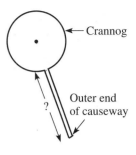

With suitable axes and taking the origin at the outer end of the causeway, the equation of the circle occupied by a crannog is $x^2 + y^2 - 22y + 85 = 0$. If one unit represents $5\,\mathrm{m}$, calculate the distance in metres from the outer end of the causeway to the edge of the crannog.

14 A(4, 8), B(2, 4) and C(10, 0) are points on the circumference of a circle.
   (a) Show that triangle ABC is right angled at B.
   (b) Explain why P(7, 4) is the centre of the circle.
   (c) Calculate the length of the radius.
   (d) Find the equation of the circle.

15 Circle A has equation $x^2 + y^2 - 10x - 12y + 36 = 0$. Circle B has equation $x^2 + y^2 + 8x + 12y - 48 = 0$.
   (a) Find the centre and radius of each circle.
   (b) Show that the circles touch externally.
   (c) Find the coordinates of the point of contact of the circles.

16 Three circles touch externally as shown in the diagram. The centres are collinear and the equations of the two smaller circles are $x^2 + y^2 + 20x - 16y + 139 = 0$ and $x^2 + y^2 - 28x + 48y + 747 = 0$.
   Find the equation of the large circle.

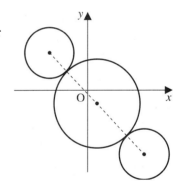

Intersection of a line and a circle

The following exercise will show you that:

> ▶ A straight line and a circle can have two, one or no points of intersection.

Exercise 12I

1 (a) Sketch the circle $x^2 + y^2 = 25$ and the lines $x = -3$, $x = 5$ and $x = 8$ on the same diagram.
   (b) For each line state the number of points of intersection with the circle.
   (c) Find the coordinates of each point of intersection.

2 (a) Sketch the circle $x^2 + y^2 = 64$ and the lines $y = 2$, $y = 8$ and $y = 12$ on the same diagram.
   (b) For each line state the number of points of intersection with the circle.
   (c) Find the coordinates of each point of intersection.

To find the coordinates of the point(s) of intersection in more complicated cases, use the following method:

Example 9

Find where the line $y = 2x$ meets the circle $x^2 + y^2 = 45$.

To find which points are common to both the line and the circle, substitute $2x$ for y in the circle equation.

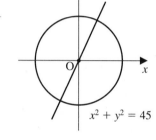

$$x^2 + (2x)^2 = 45$$
$$x^2 + 4x^2 = 45$$
$$5x^2 = 45$$
$$x^2 = 9$$
$$x = \pm 3$$

When $x = 3$ When $x = -3$
    $y = 2 \times 3$ $y = 2 \times (-3)$
    $y = 6$ $y = -6$

The line and the circle meet at $(3, 6)$ and $(-3, -6)$.

Example 10

Find where the line $y = 2x + 8$ meets the circle $x^2 + y^2 + 4x + 2y - 20 = 0$.

Substituting $(2x + 8)$ for y in the circle equation

$$x^2 + (2x + 8)^2 + 4x + 2(2x + 8) - 20 = 0$$
$$x^2 + 4x^2 + 32x + 64 + 4x + 4x + 16 - 20 = 0$$
$$5x^2 + 40x + 60 = 0$$
$$5(x^2 + 8x + 12) = 0$$
$$5(x + 2)(x + 6) = 0$$
$$x = -2 \quad \text{or} \quad x = -6$$

When $x = -2$ When $x = -6$
    $y = 2 \times (-2) + 8$ $y = 2 \times (-6) + 8$
    $y = 4$ $y = -4$

The line and the circle meet at $(-2, 4)$ and $(-6, -4)$.

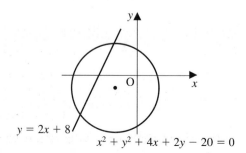

Exercise 12J

1 For each system of equations
   (i) make a sketch
   (ii) find the points of intersection of the line and the circle.

(a) $x^2 + y^2 = 72$
$y = x$

(b) $x^2 + y^2 = 250$
$y = 3x$

(c) $x^2 + y^2 = 32$
$x + y = 0$

(d) $x^2 + y^2 = 125$
$x = 2y$

(e) $x^2 + y^2 = 26$
$x - 5y = 0$

(f) $x^2 + y^2 = 68$
$x + 4y = 0$

(g) $(x - 3)^2 + (y - 4)^2 = 1$
$y = x$

(h) $(x + 2)^2 + (y - 1)^2 = 25$
$y = -3x$

2 For each system of equations
   (i) make a sketch
   (ii) find the points of intersection of the line and the circle.

(a) $x^2 + y^2 = 25$
$y = x - 1$

(b) $x^2 + y^2 = 85$
$y = 2x + 5$

(c) $x^2 + y^2 = 9$
$y = 3 - x$

(d) $x^2 + y^2 = 10$
$x = 2y - 5$

(e) $x^2 + y^2 = 2$
$x = y - 2$

(f) $(x + 1)^2 + (y - 2)^2 = 20$
$y = x + 1$

3 Find the points of intersection of these lines and circles.
   (a) $y = x + 3$ and $x^2 + y^2 + 4x - 8y + 11 = 0$
   (b) $x + y = 1$ and $x^2 + y^2 - 2x - 4y + 1 = 0$
   (c) $x = 2y + 6$ and $x^2 + y^2 - 6x + 8y = 0$
   (d) $x - 2y - 8 = 0$ and $x^2 + y^2 - 12x + 6y + 29 = 0$
   (e) the y-axis and $x^2 + y^2 - 24x - 25 = 0$
   (f) the x-axis and $x^2 + y^2 - 6x - 16y - 27 = 0$

4 The circle $x^2 + y^2 - 8x - 2y - 8 = 0$ cuts the y-axis at P and Q.
Find the length of PQ.

5 The circle $x^2 + y^2 - 8x - 8y + 7 = 0$ cuts the x-axis at G and H.
Find the equation of the circle which has GH as a diameter.

Tangents to circles

When a straight line meets a circle at one point only the line is said
to be a **tangent** to the circle.

Example 11
Show that the line $3x + y = -10$ is a tangent to the circle
$x^2 + y^2 - 8x + 4y - 20 = 0$.

Rearrange $3x + y = -10$ to give $y = -3x - 10$.

Substitute $y = -3x - 10$ for y in the circle equation:

$x^2 + (-3x - 10)^2 - 8x + 4(-3x - 10) - 20 = 0$
$x^2 + 9x^2 + 60x + 100 - 8x - 12x - 40 - 20 = 0$
$$10x^2 + 40x + 40 = 0$$

At this point there are two alternative methods of solution:

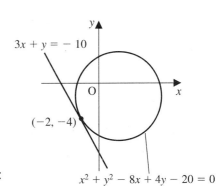

Method 1

$$10(x^2 + 4x + 4) = 0$$
$$10(x + 2)(x + 2) = 0$$
$$x = -2 \text{ or } x = -2$$
$$y = -4 \text{ or } y = -4$$

The line is a tangent because there is only one point of contact, i.e. $(-2, -4)$.

Method 2

$$\text{Discriminant} = b^2 - 4ac$$
$$= 40^2 - 4 \times 10 \times 40$$
$$= 0$$

Since the discriminant is zero the equation has two equal roots and therefore only one point of contact. So $3x + y = 10$ is a tangent to the circle.

Example 12

Find the equations of the tangents from the point $(0, -4)$ to the circle $x^2 + y^2 = 8$.

Equation of tangent $y - b = m(x - a)$
$$y + 4 = mx$$
$$y = mx - 4$$

Substitute $y = mx - 4$ for y in the circle equation
$$x^2 + y^2 = 8$$
$$x^2 + (mx - 4)^2 = 8$$
$$x^2 + m^2x^2 - 8mx + 16 = 8$$
$$(1 + m^2)x^2 - 8mx + 8 = 0$$
$$a = 1 + m^2 \quad b = -8m \quad c = 8$$

For tangency $b^2 - 4ac = 0$
$$64m^2 - 32(1 + m^2) = 0$$
$$32m^2 = 32$$
$$m = \pm 1$$

Equations of tangents are $y = x - 4$ and $y = -x - 4$.

Exercise 12K

1 Find the point of intersection of these lines and circles.

(a) $x = 8$, $x^2 + y^2 = 64$
(b) $y = 11$, $x^2 + y^2 = 121$
(c) $y = 6$, $x^2 + y^2 + 6x - 27 = 0$
(d) $y - x = 2$, $x^2 + y^2 = 2$
(e) $y = 2x + 8$, $x^2 + y^2 + 4x + 2y = 0$
(f) $2x - y = 4$, $x^2 + y^2 - 2x - 6y + 5 = 0$
(g) $x + 3y = -1$, $x^2 + y^2 + 10x + 4y + 19 = 0$

2 Show that these lines are tangents to the given circles.

(a) $y = x + 6$
$x^2 + y^2 + 2x - 2y - 6 = 0$
(b) $y = x - 10$
$x^2 + y^2 + 4x + 8y - 12 = 0$

3 Show that $y + 3x + 10 = 0$ is a tangent to the circle $x^2 + y^2 - 8x + 4y - 20 = 0$ and find the point of contact.

4 (a) Show that the line $y - 9 = 0$ is a tangent to the circles $x^2 + y^2 = 81$ and $x^2 + y^2 - 24x - 10y + 153 = 0$, and find each point of contact.

(b) Calculate the length of the common tangent.

5 A quadratic equation is always formed when finding the points
of intersection of a line and a circle.
Describe the value of its discriminant if the line and circle
(a) meet at two distinct points. (b) meet at one point. (c) do not meet.

6 Use the discriminant method to find if the line and circle
(i) meet at two points, (ii) meet at one point or (iii) do not meet.
(a) $x + y = -2$ (b) $y = x - 1$
$\quad x^2 + y^2 - 6x - 8y = 0$ $\quad x^2 + y^2 + 8x - 4y - 29 = 0$
(c) $y = 3x + 10$ (d) $3x - 2y + 2 = 0$
$\quad x^2 + y^2 - 8x - 4y - 20 = 0$ $\quad x^2 + y^2 = 36$

7 Find the equations of the tangents from the given point to the
given circle:
(a) $(0, 5)$: $x^2 + y^2 = 16$ (b) $(0, 2)$: $x^2 + y^2 - 8x - 4y + 16 = 0$

Equations of tangents

The equation of a tangent at a point on a
circle can be found from its gradient and
the coordinates of the point of contact
using the relationship

$m_{\text{tan}} \times m_{\text{rad}} = -1$

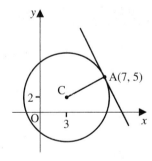

Example 13

Show that A(7, 5) lies on the circle $x^2 + y^2 - 6x - 4y - 12 = 0$ and
find the equation of the tangent at A.

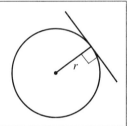

At A(7, 5),

$x^2 + y^2 - 6x - 4y - 12 = 49 + 25 - 42 - 20 - 12 = 0$

Hence A(7, 5) lies on the circle.

The centre of the circle is C(3, 2).

$m_{\text{CA}} = \dfrac{5 - 2}{7 - 3} = \dfrac{3}{4}$

$m_{\text{rad}} \times m_{\text{tan}} = -1$

so $\qquad m_{\text{tan}} = -\dfrac{4}{3}$

The equation of the tangent at A is $(y - 5) = -\frac{4}{3}(x - 7)$

$$3(y - 5) = -4(x - 7)$$
$$4x + 3y - 43 = 0$$

Exercise 12L

1 Show that the point R(−12, −5) lies on the circle $x^2 + y^2 = 169$. Find the equation of the tangent to the circle at R.

2 Find the equation of the tangent to $x^2 + y^2 - 2x - 10y + 17 = 0$ at the point (1, 8).

3 Find the equation of the tangent to $x^2 + y^2 + 10x - 8y - 17 = 0$ at the point (2, 1).

4 Find the equations of the tangents to $x^2 + y^2 + 6x - 4y - 24 = 0$ at the points P(3, 1) and Q(−9, 3).

5 **(a)** Find the equations of the tangents to the circle $x^2 + y^2 = 100$ at its points of intersection with the x-axis.
   (b) Find the equations of the tangents to the circle $x^2 + y^2 = 100$ at the points P(6, −8) and Q(6, 8).
   (c) Find the angle the tangent at P makes with the positive direction of the x-axis and the acute angle between it and the tangent at Q.

6 The design for part of a large wrought-iron gate shows a circle with diameter 120 cm and four straight rods of equal length. The structure is braced by two short vertical rods each 12 cm long. Coordinate axes have been drawn so that the design is symmetrical about the axes. Other dimensions are shown in the diagram.
   (a) Find the equation of the rod AB.
   (b) Find the equation of the circular section.
   (c) Prove that the rod AB is a tangent to the circle and find the coordinates of B.

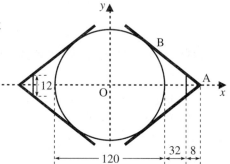

Exercise 12M Mixed questions

1 A bakery firm makes gingerbread men each 14 cm high with a circular 'head' and 'body'. The equation of the 'body' is $x^2 + y^2 - 10x - 12y + 45 = 0$ and the line of centres is parallel to the y-axis. Find the equation of the 'head'. **[Higher]**

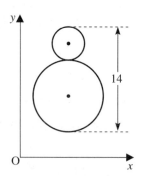

2 This diagram shows a computer-generated display of a game of noughts and crosses. Relative to the coordinate axes that have been added to the display, the 'nought' at A is represented by a circle with equation $(x - 2)^2 + (y - 2)^2 = 4$.
   (a) Find the centre of the circle at B.
   (b) Find the equation of the circle at B. **[Higher]**

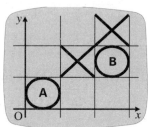

3 The point (0, 2) is the mid-point of a chord of the circle
$x^2 + y^2 + 10x + 6y - 66 = 0$. Find the equation of the chord.

4

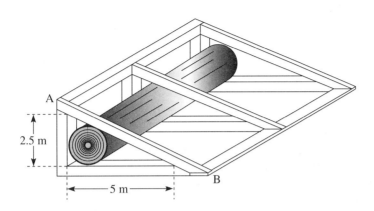

A cylindrical tank of radius 1 m is to be housed in the roof space
of a factory. The roof is in the shape of a right triangular prism
5 m wide and 2.5 m high. The tank has to rest on the horizontal
girders and is fixed against the vertical girders. With suitable axes
and the origin at the join of the vertical and horizontal girders
find:

(a) the equation of the outer rim of the front end of the
cylinder.

(b) the equation of the front roof girder, AB.

The architect has calculated that the tank will just fit under the
roof girders. Is he right? Explain.

5

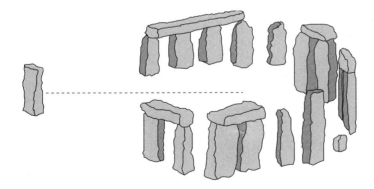

An ancient stone circle has a processional pathway from the
heelstone to the centre of the stone circle. In the picture above,
the heelstone is on the left and the dotted line represents the
processional pathway.
With suitable axes and using the heelstone as the origin, the
equation of the stone circle is $x^2 + y^2 - 8x - 6y + 21 = 0$.
Given that 1 unit represents 15 m, calculate the distance in metres
from the heelstone to the nearest point on the edge of the circle.

[Higher]

6 An ear-ring is to be made from silver
wire and is designed in the shape of two
touching circles with two tangents to the
outer circle, as shown in diagram 1.

Diagram 1

Diagram 2 shows a drawing of this ear-ring
related to the coordinate axes. The circles touch
at $(0, 0)$. The equation of the inner circle is
$x^2 + y^2 + 3y = 0$. The outer circle intersects the
y-axis at $(0, -4)$. The tangents meet the y-axis
at $(0, -6)$. Find the total length of silver wire
required to make this ear-ring.   [Higher]

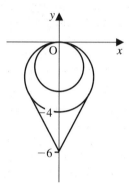

Diagram 2

7 When newspapers were printed by lithograph, the newsprint
had to run over three rollers, illustrated in the diagram by
three circles. The centres A, B and C of the three circles are
collinear.

The equations of the circumferences of the outer circles are
$(x + 12)^2 + (y + 15)^2 = 25$ and $(x - 24)^2 + (y - 12)^2 = 100$.
Find the equation of the central circle.   [Higher]

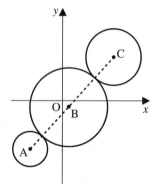

8 A circular roundabout has to be built close to an old wall.
With suitable axes and the origin at the centre of the
roundabout the equation of the outer boundary of the
roundabout is $x^2 + y^2 = 225$. All units are in metres.
The equation of the wall is $4x + 3y = 100$. There has to be
a gap of more than 5 m between the wall and the
roundabout. Is this in fact the case? Explain.

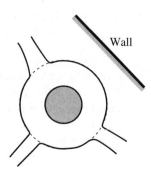

9 Warships are manoeuvering during a naval exercise. With units in miles and suitable coordinate axes, the frigates Ajax and Bristol are stationary at A(8, 8) and B(16, 32) respectively.

(a) Find the equation of the perpendicular bisector of AB.

(b) The destroyer Delta is also stationary at a point D, which is in the same quadrant and equidistant from the axes. Delta's radar has a circular sweep and can just pick up Ajax and Bristol at the limit of radar range. Find the coordinates of Delta's position.

(c) Find the equation of the circle that forms the limit of Delta's radar sweep.

(d) An enemy ship is sailing on a bearing of approximately 008° in a straight line, which can be represented by the equation $7x - y = 72$.

Will the enemy ship be picked up on Delta's radar? Give a reason for your answer.

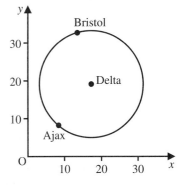

10 In the equation $y + 2x = p$, p can be replaced by two integers to give the equations of two tangents to the circle $x^2 + y^2 - 2x - 4y = 0$.

(a) Find both values for p.

(b) State the equations of the tangents and find their points of contact, A and B, with the circle.

(c) Find the equation of diameter AB.

SUMMARY

① The distance between (x_1, y_1) and (x_2, y_2) is

$\sqrt{(x_2 - x_1)^2 + (y_2 - y_1)^2}$. This is known as the **distance formula**.

② The equation of a circle with centre $(0, 0)$ and radius r is $x^2 + y^2 = r^2$.

③ The equation of a circle with centre (a, b) and radius r is $(x - a)^2 + (y - b)^2 = r^2$.

④ $x^2 + y^2 + 2gx + 2fy + c = 0$ (where g, f and c are constants) is the **general equation** of a circle with centre $(-g, -f)$ and radius $\sqrt{g^2 + f^2 - c}$, provided $g^2 + f^2 - c > 0$.

⑤ A straight line and a circle can have two, one or no points of intersection.

⑥ The equation of a tangent at a point on a circle can be found from its gradient and the coordinates of the point of contact using the relationship: $m_{rad} \times m_{tan} = -1$

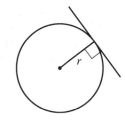

Revision exercise 2A

1 Show that $(x + 3)$ is a factor of $2x^3 + 7x^2 + 2x - 3$. Hence, factorise the polynomial fully.

2 Find p if $(x + 3)$ is a factor of $x^3 - x^2 + px + 15$.

3 One root of the equation $2x^3 - px^2 - 17x + 30 = 0$ is 2. Find the value of p and the other roots of the equation.

4 The curve $y = 3x^3 + x^2 - 5x + d$ cuts the x-axis at $(1, 0)$. Find the value of d.

5 Solve $2x^3 + 5x^2 - x - 6 = 0$.

6 Find the roots of $x^4 - 2x^3 - 4x^2 + 2x + 3 = 0$.

7 Find where the curve $y = 2x^3 + 3x^2 - 18x + 8$ cuts the x-axis.

8 (a) Write down the coordinates of the centre of the circle with equation $x^2 + y^2 - 4x - 6y + 9 = 0$.
(b) Find the equation of the tangent to this circle at the point A(2, 5).

9 Given that $\sin P = \frac{4}{5}$ and $\cos Q = \frac{12}{13}$ and that P and Q are acute angles, find the exact value of $\sin(P - Q)$.

10 Find the values of k for which the equation $2x^2 + 4x + k = 0$ has real roots.

11 Calculate the shaded area in the diagram.

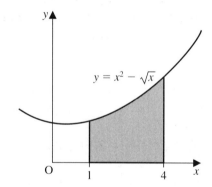

12 $x - 2$ is a factor of $3x^3 - kx^2 + 4$. Find
(a) the value of k
(b) the other factors of $3x^3 - kx^2 + 4$ for this value of k.

13 Solve $x^2 - 5x - 6 \geqslant 0$.

14 Find the exact solutions of the equation
$4\cos^2 x - 3 = 0, \ 0 \leqslant x \leqslant 2\pi$.

15 Find $\displaystyle\int \left(2\sqrt{x} + 4 + \frac{1}{x^5}\right) dx$.

16 Find the equation of the tangent at the point $(1, -3)$ on the circle $x^2 + y^2 + 2x + 4y = 0$.

17 Evaluate $\displaystyle\int_1^9 \left(2t + \frac{4}{\sqrt{t}}\right) dt$.

18 Given that $\tan \theta = \dfrac{7}{\sqrt{15}}$, where $0 < \theta < \dfrac{\pi}{2}$, find the **exact** value of $\sin 2\theta$.

19 (a) Find the coordinates of the points of intersection of the curves with equations $y = 3x$ and $y = x^2 - 5x$.
   (b) Find the area completely enclosed between these two curves.

20 Solve $5 \sin 2x° - 3 \cos x° = 0$ for $0 \leqslant x \leqslant 180$.

21 Solve algebraically the equation
$3 \cos 2x° + 4 \cos x° + 1 = 0$, $0 \leqslant x < 360$.

22 A curve for which $\dfrac{dy}{dx} = 7 - 8x^3$ passes through the point $(2, 15)$.

Express y in terms of x.

23 The roots of the equation $(x + 2)(x - k) = -9$ are equal. Find the values of k.

24 Given that $\sin A = \dfrac{2}{\sqrt{5}}$ and that $0 < A < \dfrac{\pi}{2}$, find the exact value of

   (a) $\cos A$ **(b)** $\cos 2A$

25 The straight line $y = x$ cuts the circle
$x^2 + y^2 - 6x - 2y - 24 = 0$ at A and B.
   (a) Find the coordinates of A and B.
   (b) Find the equation of the circle which has AB as diameter.   [Higher]

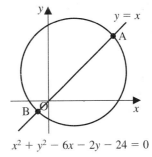

$x^2 + y^2 - 6x - 2y - 24 = 0$

26 Express $x^2 + 2x - 9$ in the form $(x + a)^2 + b$ and hence state the maximum value of $\dfrac{1}{x^2 + 2x - 9}$.

27 The equation $x^2 + y^2 + 2px - 8y + 25 = 0$ represents a circle. Find possible ranges of values for p.

28 AB is a tangent at B to the circle with centre C and equation $(x - 2)^2 + (y - 2)^2 = 25$.
The point A has coordinates $(10, 8)$.
Find the area of triangle ABC.   [Higher]

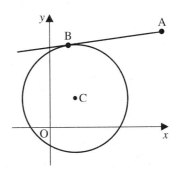

29 By writing $165°$ as $(120° + 45°)$ show that the **exact** value of
$\cos 165°$ is $\dfrac{-\sqrt{2}(1 + \sqrt{3})}{4}$.

Revision exercise 2B

1 The diagram shows part of the graph of $f(x) = x^3 - 3x + 2$.

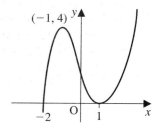

(a) Factorise $f(x)$.

(b) Write down the coordinates of the points where $f(x)$ cuts the axes.

(c) Find the coordinates of the stationary points of $f(x)$ and justify their nature.

2 (a) Show that the equation of the circle which passes through the points $(0, 0)$, $(4, 0)$ and $(0, -2)$ is $x^2 + y^2 - 4x + 2y = 0$.

(b) Show that the line with equation $y = 2x - 10$ is a tangent to this circle and state the coordinates of the point of contact.

[Higher]

3 A new company of music publishers intends to adopt the shape of a harp as its trademark, as shown in Diagram 1.

To reproduce this trademark accurately, the graphs of $y = 3x^3 - 12x^2 + 13x$ and $y = x$ are drawn, as shown in Diagram 2.

(a) Show that the straight line $y = x$ is a tangent to the curve at T.

(b) Calculate the area of the trademark.

[Higher]

Diagram 1

Diagram 2

4 The line with equation $3x + y = k$ is a tangent to the circle $x^2 + y^2 - 6x + 8y + 15 = 0$.

(a) Find the **two** possible values for k.

(b) Find the equation of the diameter joining the points of contact.

5 A function f is defined by the formula $f(x) = x^2(x - 4)$, $x \in \mathbf{R}$.

(a) Write down the coordinates of the points where the curve with equation $y = f(x)$ meets the coordinate axes.

(b) Find the stationary points of $y = f(x)$ and determine the nature of each of them.

(c) Sketch the curve $y = f(x)$.

(d) Find the area completely enclosed by the curve $y = f(x)$ and the x-axis.

6 Use exact values of the trigonometric ratios to show that

$$\tan 120° = \frac{2 \tan 60°}{1 - \tan^2 60°}.$$

7 (a) The point A(2, 2) lies on the parabola $y = x^2 + px + q$.
Find the relationship between p and q.

(b) The tangent to the parabola at A is the line $y = x$.
Find the value of p.
Hence find the equation of the parabola.

(c) Using your answers for p and q, find the value of the
discriminant of $x^2 + px + q = 0$.
What feature of the sketch is confirmed by this value?

[Higher]

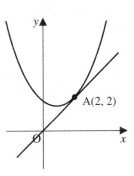

8 Diagram 1 shows a rectangular sheet of transparent plastic
moulded into a parabolic shape and pegged to the ground to
form a cover for growing plants. Triangular metal frames are
placed over the cover to support it and prevent it blowing away
in the wind.
Diagram 2 shows an end view of the cover and the triangular
frame related to the origin O and axes Ox and Oy.
(All dimensions are given in centimetres.)

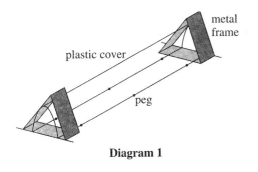

Diagram 1

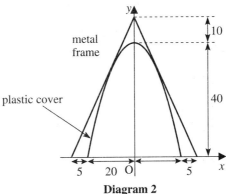

Diagram 2

(a) Show that the equation of the parabolic end is $y = 40 - \dfrac{x^2}{10}$,
$-20 \leqslant x \leqslant 20$.

(b) Show that the triangular frame touches the cover without
disturbing the parabolic shape.   [Higher]

9 Find the possible values of p for which the line $x + y + p = 0$ is
a tangent to the circle $x^2 + y^2 = 8$.

10 (a) Show that for the isosceles triangle opposite,
$$\frac{b}{\sin \theta^\circ} = \frac{a}{\cos \dfrac{\theta^\circ}{2}}.$$

(b) Hence, or otherwise, show that
$$b = 2a \sin \frac{\theta^\circ}{2}.$$ [Higher]

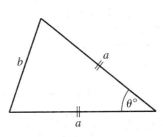

11 A sports club awards trophies in the form of paperweights bearing the club crest.

Diagram 1 shows the front view of one of these paperweights. Each is made from two different types of glass. The two circles are concentric and the base line is a tangent to the inner circle.

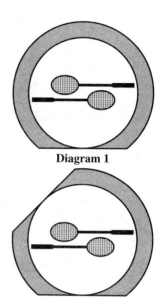

Diagram 1

(a) Relative to x, y coordinate axes, the equation of the outer circle is $x^2 + y^2 - 8x + 2y - 19 = 0$ and the equation of the base line is $y = -6$.

Show that the equation of the inner circle is $x^2 + y^2 - 8x + 2y - 8 = 0$.

(b) An alternative form of the paperweight is made by cutting off a piece of glass from the original design along a second line with equation $3x - 4y + 9 = 0$ as shown in Diagram 2.

Show that this line is a tangent to the inner circle and state the coordinates of the point of contact.

[Higher]

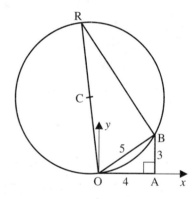

Diagram 2

12 P is the point with coordinates $(\sin(x + 30)°, \cos(x - 30)°)$ and Q has coordinates $(\sin(x - 30)°, \cos(x + 30)°)$.

Find, in its simplest form, an expression for the gradient of the line PQ. [Higher]

13 The right-angled triangle OAB with sides of length 3 cm, 4 cm and 5 cm is placed with one vertex at the origin O as shown in the diagram.

A circle centre C and diameter RO of length 13 cm is drawn and passes through O and B. What is the gradient of the line RO?

[Higher]

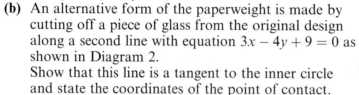

13 Vectors

Vectors and scalars

In order to deal with direction in space we need to introduce the idea of a vector.

> A **vector** is a quantity with both magnitude (size) and direction.

For example

- the force applied to a snooker ball

- the velocity of an aeroplane

- the acceleration due to gravity.

A **scalar** is a quantity with magnitude only. For example
- the mass of a teacher
- the time taken to read this page
- the speed of a car.

A vector can be represented geometrically using a directed line segment. The length of the line represents the magnitude of the vector. The direction is indicated by an arrow.

For example

- the velocity of a wind blowing towards the north east with speed 40 km/h

- the velocity of a river flowing towards the south east with speed 10 km/h

- a force of 200 newtons needed to move a car.

40 units

10 units

200 units

Components

A vector is named either using the letters at the end of the directed line segment $\overrightarrow{AB}$ or using a bold letter **u**.

This vector is named $\overrightarrow{AB}$ or **u**

A vector may also be represented by its **components**:

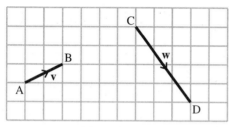

$$\overrightarrow{AB} = \mathbf{v} = \begin{pmatrix} 2 \\ 1 \end{pmatrix} \qquad \overrightarrow{CD} = \mathbf{w} = \begin{pmatrix} 3 \\ -4 \end{pmatrix}$$

These are know as **column vectors**.

Magnitude

The **magnitude** of a vector is represented by its length and is written $|\mathbf{u}|$ or $|\overrightarrow{AB}|$. It can be calculated using Pythagoras' theorem.

Example 1

Find $|\mathbf{u}|$ if $\mathbf{u} = \begin{pmatrix} -3 \\ 4 \end{pmatrix}$

$$|\mathbf{u}| = \sqrt{(-3)^2 + 4^2}$$
$$= 5 \text{ units}$$

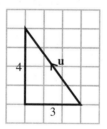

If $\overrightarrow{PQ} = \begin{pmatrix} a \\ b \end{pmatrix}$ then $|\overrightarrow{PQ}| = \sqrt{a^2 + b^2}$

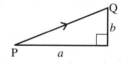

Exercise 13A

1 List two further examples of (i) vector quantities and (ii) scalar quantities.

2 State the components of each vector.

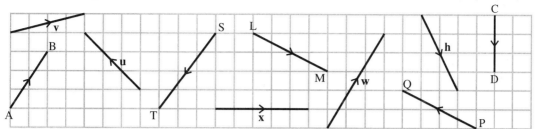

3 Calculate the magnitude of each vector, leaving answers as surds in simplest form where necessary.

$$\mathbf{v} = \begin{pmatrix} 5 \\ 12 \end{pmatrix} \quad \mathbf{w} = \begin{pmatrix} 3 \\ -4 \end{pmatrix} \quad \mathbf{p} = \begin{pmatrix} 3 \\ -6 \end{pmatrix} \quad \overrightarrow{AB} = \begin{pmatrix} 4 \\ -4 \end{pmatrix} \quad \overrightarrow{CD} = \begin{pmatrix} -2 \\ -4 \end{pmatrix} \quad \overrightarrow{EF} = \begin{pmatrix} 8 \\ 2 \end{pmatrix}$$

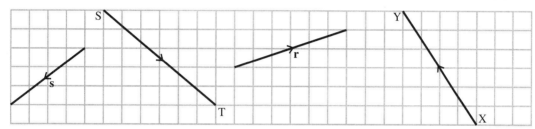

4 Vector **h** represents the velocity (in km/h) of a hang-glider. Calculate the speed of the hang-glider.

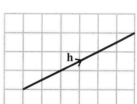

Scale: 1 square = 1 km

5 Vector **v** represents the velocity (in km/h) of a boat. Calculate the speed of the boat.

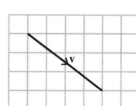

Scale: 1 square = 2 km

Equal vectors

Vectors with the same magnitude and direction are **equal**.

$$\mathbf{v} = \mathbf{u} = \mathbf{w} = \begin{pmatrix} 1 \\ 2 \end{pmatrix}$$

Equal vectors have equal components.

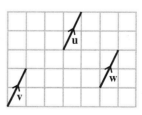

For vectors

$$\mathbf{u} = \begin{pmatrix} a \\ b \end{pmatrix} \text{ and } \mathbf{v} = \begin{pmatrix} c \\ d \end{pmatrix}, \text{ if } \mathbf{u} = \mathbf{v} \text{ then } a = c \text{ and } b = d.$$

20/7/16

Exercise 13B

1 (a) State the components of each vector.
  (b) Name the vector equal to
      (i) **u**   (ii) **s**   (iii) **t**

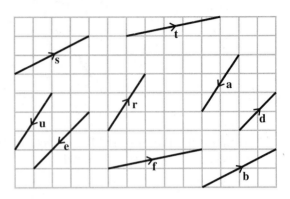

2 Which of the following can be represented by the same vector:
  a boat travelling
  (a) north east at 10 km/h
  (b) at 10 km/h on a bearing of 135°
  (c) north east at 5 km/h
  (d) at 10 km/h on a bearing of 045°?

3 $\mathbf{u} = \begin{pmatrix} 3x \\ y+6 \end{pmatrix}$, $\mathbf{v} = \begin{pmatrix} 12 \\ -2 \end{pmatrix}$ and $\mathbf{u} = \mathbf{v}$. Find x and y.

4 $\mathbf{r} = \begin{pmatrix} p+2 \\ q-4 \end{pmatrix}$, $\mathbf{s} = \begin{pmatrix} q \\ -p \end{pmatrix}$ and $\mathbf{r} = \mathbf{s}$. Find p and q.

Addition of vectors

We can add two vectors to produce a **resultant** vector.

Example 2

In the diagram the canoe is travelling at 4 km/h at right angles to the bank. If it meets a downstream current of 3 km/h, what happens to the canoe?

Let **v** represent the velocity of the canoe and **u** represent the velocity of the current. The resultant velocity can be represented by adding the vectors as shown. Note that the vectors are added nose-to-tail.

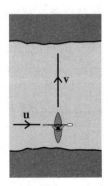

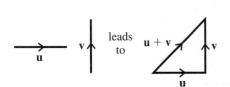

Any two vectors can be added in this way.

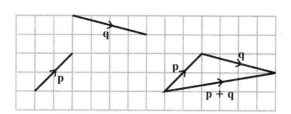

Let $\overrightarrow{AB} = \begin{pmatrix} 3 \\ 4 \end{pmatrix}$ and $\overrightarrow{BC} = \begin{pmatrix} 2 \\ -5 \end{pmatrix}$

then $\overrightarrow{AB} + \overrightarrow{BC} = \overrightarrow{AC}$

$\begin{pmatrix} 3 \\ 4 \end{pmatrix} + \begin{pmatrix} 2 \\ -5 \end{pmatrix} = \begin{pmatrix} 5 \\ -1 \end{pmatrix}$

so $\overrightarrow{AC} = \begin{pmatrix} 5 \\ -1 \end{pmatrix}$

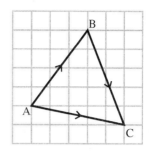

> For vectors **u** and **v**, if $\mathbf{u} = \begin{pmatrix} a \\ b \end{pmatrix}$ and $\mathbf{v} = \begin{pmatrix} c \\ d \end{pmatrix}$ then
>
> $\mathbf{u} + \mathbf{v} = \begin{pmatrix} a + c \\ b + d \end{pmatrix}.$

Exercise 13C

1 Draw the resultant vector $\mathbf{u} + \mathbf{v}$ for each pair of vectors and write the components of **u** and **v**.

(a)

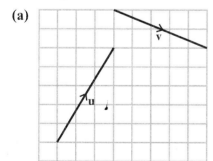

(b)

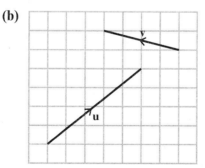

(c)

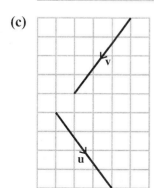

(d)

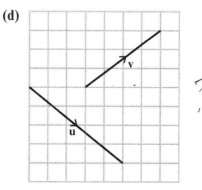

2 Find the components of $\mathbf{u} + \mathbf{v}$ when

(a) $\mathbf{u} = \begin{pmatrix} 2 \\ 5 \end{pmatrix}$ and $\mathbf{v} = \begin{pmatrix} 3 \\ -6 \end{pmatrix}$ (b) $\mathbf{u} = \begin{pmatrix} 5 \\ 8 \end{pmatrix}$ and $\mathbf{v} = \begin{pmatrix} -9 \\ 4 \end{pmatrix}$

(c) $\mathbf{u} = \begin{pmatrix} -3 \\ -2 \end{pmatrix}$ and $\mathbf{v} = \begin{pmatrix} 7 \\ -6 \end{pmatrix}$ (d) $\mathbf{u} = \begin{pmatrix} 0 \\ -7 \end{pmatrix}$ and $\mathbf{v} = \begin{pmatrix} -4 \\ 4 \end{pmatrix}$

(e) $\mathbf{u} = \begin{pmatrix} -7 \\ -5 \end{pmatrix}$ and $\mathbf{v} = \begin{pmatrix} -6 \\ 8 \end{pmatrix}$ (f) $\mathbf{u} = \begin{pmatrix} 0 \\ 0 \end{pmatrix}$ and $\mathbf{v} = \begin{pmatrix} 0 \\ 1 \end{pmatrix}$

3 For each pair of vectors
  (i) draw a representative of $\mathbf{p} + \mathbf{q}$
  (ii) state the components of $\mathbf{p} + \mathbf{q}$
  (iii) calculate $|\mathbf{p} + \mathbf{q}|$.

(a) $\mathbf{p} = \begin{pmatrix} 2 \\ 3 \end{pmatrix}$ and $\mathbf{q} = \begin{pmatrix} 4 \\ 1 \end{pmatrix}$ (b) $\mathbf{p} = \begin{pmatrix} 3 \\ 2 \end{pmatrix}$ and $\mathbf{q} = \begin{pmatrix} 2 \\ -1 \end{pmatrix}$

(c) $\mathbf{q} = \begin{pmatrix} -3 \\ 4 \end{pmatrix}$ and $\mathbf{q} = \begin{pmatrix} 4 \\ -1 \end{pmatrix}$ (d) $\mathbf{p} = \begin{pmatrix} 4 \\ -2 \end{pmatrix}$ and $\mathbf{q} = \begin{pmatrix} 3 \\ -2 \end{pmatrix}$

4 (a) For the parallelogram shown opposite name the vector equal to
  (i) $\overrightarrow{AB} + \overrightarrow{BC}$ (ii) $\overrightarrow{AD} + \overrightarrow{DC}$
(b) What can be said about the vectors $\mathbf{v} + \mathbf{u}$ and $\mathbf{u} + \mathbf{v}$?

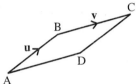

5 Using the diagram below draw a representative of the resultant vector for each of the following:

(a) $\mathbf{u} + \mathbf{v}$ (b) $\mathbf{v} + \mathbf{w}$ (c) $(\mathbf{u} + \mathbf{v}) + \mathbf{w}$ (d) $\mathbf{u} + (\mathbf{v} + \mathbf{w})$

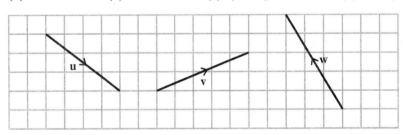

(e) What can be said about $(\mathbf{u} + \mathbf{v}) + \mathbf{w}$ and $\mathbf{u} + (\mathbf{v} + \mathbf{w})$?

6 In the regular hexagon shown opposite
$\overrightarrow{AB} + \overrightarrow{FE} = \overrightarrow{AB} + \overrightarrow{BC} = \overrightarrow{AC}$.
Find a vector equal to
(a) $\overrightarrow{AB} + \overrightarrow{BC}$ (b) $\overrightarrow{AB} + \overrightarrow{BC} + \overrightarrow{CD}$ (c) $\overrightarrow{FE} + \overrightarrow{ED}$
(d) $\overrightarrow{FA} + \overrightarrow{ED}$ (e) $\overrightarrow{ED} + \overrightarrow{DC} + \overrightarrow{EF}$

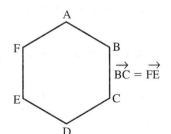

$\overrightarrow{BC} = \overrightarrow{FE}$

7 Find p and q in each vector equation.

(a) $\begin{pmatrix} 2 \\ 3 \end{pmatrix} + \begin{pmatrix} p \\ q \end{pmatrix} = \begin{pmatrix} 4 \\ 7 \end{pmatrix}$ (b) $\begin{pmatrix} 5 \\ -1 \end{pmatrix} + \begin{pmatrix} p \\ q \end{pmatrix} = \begin{pmatrix} 3 \\ -4 \end{pmatrix}$ (c) $\begin{pmatrix} p \\ 5 \end{pmatrix} + \begin{pmatrix} 4 \\ q \end{pmatrix} = \begin{pmatrix} 10 \\ -8 \end{pmatrix}$

8 A canoe travelling at a velocity of 6 m/s meets a current at right angles. If the velocity of the current is 2.5 m/s calculate
  (a) the resultant speed of the canoe
  (b) the angle between the resultant and the original direction.

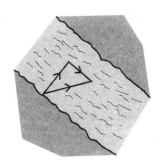

9 A bird is flying due south at a speed of 15 km/h. The wind blows from the west at a speed of 20 km/h.
  (a) Draw a diagram to show the resultant velocity of the bird
  (b) Calculate the resultant speed and bearing of the bird's flight.

The zero vector

If $\overrightarrow{AB} = \begin{pmatrix} 1 \\ 2 \end{pmatrix}$ then $\overrightarrow{BA} = \begin{pmatrix} -1 \\ -2 \end{pmatrix}$, as shown in the diagram.

$$\overrightarrow{AB} + \overrightarrow{BA} = \begin{pmatrix} 1 \\ 2 \end{pmatrix} + \begin{pmatrix} -1 \\ -2 \end{pmatrix} = \begin{pmatrix} 0 \\ 0 \end{pmatrix}$$

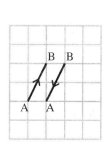

> $\begin{pmatrix} 0 \\ 0 \end{pmatrix}$ is called the **zero vector**, written **0**.
>
> ▶ $\overrightarrow{BA}$ is the **negative** of $\overrightarrow{AB}$.
>
> For any vector **u**, $\mathbf{u} + (-\mathbf{u}) = \mathbf{0}$. If $\mathbf{u} = \begin{pmatrix} a \\ b \end{pmatrix}$ then $-\mathbf{u} = \begin{pmatrix} -a \\ -b \end{pmatrix}$.

Subtraction of vectors

For vectors **u** and **v**, if $\mathbf{u} = \begin{pmatrix} 6 \\ 5 \end{pmatrix}$ and $\mathbf{v} = \begin{pmatrix} 2 \\ 4 \end{pmatrix}$

then $\mathbf{u} - \mathbf{v} = \mathbf{u} + (-\mathbf{v}) = \begin{pmatrix} 6 \\ 5 \end{pmatrix} + \begin{pmatrix} -2 \\ -4 \end{pmatrix} = \begin{pmatrix} 4 \\ 1 \end{pmatrix}$

or $\mathbf{u} - \mathbf{v} = \begin{pmatrix} 6 \\ 5 \end{pmatrix} - \begin{pmatrix} 2 \\ 4 \end{pmatrix} = \begin{pmatrix} 4 \\ 1 \end{pmatrix}$

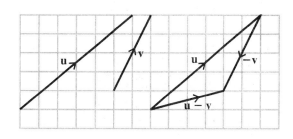

> For vectors **u** and **v**, if
>
> ▶ $\mathbf{u} = \begin{pmatrix} a \\ b \end{pmatrix}$ and $\mathbf{v} = \begin{pmatrix} c \\ d \end{pmatrix}$, then $\mathbf{u} - \mathbf{v} = \begin{pmatrix} a - c \\ b - d \end{pmatrix}$

Exercise 13D

1 Find x and y in each vector equation.

(a) $\begin{pmatrix} 2 \\ 3 \end{pmatrix} + \begin{pmatrix} x \\ y \end{pmatrix} = \begin{pmatrix} 0 \\ 0 \end{pmatrix}$ (b) $\begin{pmatrix} 5 \\ -1 \end{pmatrix} + \begin{pmatrix} x \\ y \end{pmatrix} = \begin{pmatrix} 0 \\ 0 \end{pmatrix}$ (c) $\begin{pmatrix} x \\ -5 \end{pmatrix} + \begin{pmatrix} 4 \\ y \end{pmatrix} = \begin{pmatrix} 0 \\ 0 \end{pmatrix}$

2 Write the negative of each vector.

(a) $\begin{pmatrix} 2 \\ 3 \end{pmatrix}$ (b) $\begin{pmatrix} -5 \\ -7 \end{pmatrix}$ (c) $\begin{pmatrix} -5 \\ 2 \end{pmatrix}$ (d) $\begin{pmatrix} x \\ y \end{pmatrix}$ (e) $\begin{pmatrix} 2x \\ y \end{pmatrix}$ (f) $\begin{pmatrix} -a \\ -b \end{pmatrix}$

3 Find the components of $\mathbf{u} - \mathbf{v}$ when

(a) $\mathbf{u} = \begin{pmatrix} 10 \\ 8 \end{pmatrix}, \mathbf{v} = \begin{pmatrix} 9 \\ 7 \end{pmatrix}$ (b) $\mathbf{u} = \begin{pmatrix} -5 \\ -8 \end{pmatrix}, \mathbf{v} = \begin{pmatrix} -2 \\ 5 \end{pmatrix}$ (c) $\mathbf{u} = \begin{pmatrix} 6 \\ 9 \end{pmatrix}, \mathbf{v} = \begin{pmatrix} -3 \\ -2 \end{pmatrix}$

4 For each pair of vectors
   (i) draw a representative of $\mathbf{p} - \mathbf{q}$
   (ii) state the components of $\mathbf{p} - \mathbf{q}$
   (iii) calculate $|\mathbf{p} - \mathbf{q}|$.

(a) $\mathbf{p} = \begin{pmatrix} 2 \\ 4 \end{pmatrix}$ and $\mathbf{q} = \begin{pmatrix} 2 \\ 1 \end{pmatrix}$ (b) $\mathbf{p} = \begin{pmatrix} -1 \\ -3 \end{pmatrix}$ and $\mathbf{q} = \begin{pmatrix} -1 \\ -5 \end{pmatrix}$

(c) $\mathbf{p} = \begin{pmatrix} 4 \\ -1 \end{pmatrix}$ and $\mathbf{q} = \begin{pmatrix} -3 \\ 4 \end{pmatrix}$ (d) $\mathbf{p} = \begin{pmatrix} 3 \\ 6 \end{pmatrix}$ and $\mathbf{q} = \begin{pmatrix} 4 \\ -2 \end{pmatrix}$

5 ABCD is a parallelogram. If $\overrightarrow{AB} = \mathbf{u}$ and $\overrightarrow{BC} = \mathbf{v}$, name the directed line segment that represents
   (a) $\mathbf{v} - \mathbf{u}$ (b) $\mathbf{u} - \mathbf{v}$
   (c) What do you notice about your answers to (a) and (b)?

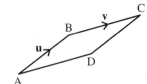

6 Use the diagram opposite to name the directed line segment that represents
   (a) $\mathbf{p} - \mathbf{r}$ (b) $\mathbf{r} - \mathbf{p}$ (c) $\mathbf{t} - \mathbf{q}$ (d) $\mathbf{s} - \mathbf{t}$
   (e) $\mathbf{p} - \mathbf{r} - \mathbf{q}$ (f) $\mathbf{t} + \mathbf{r} - \mathbf{p}$ (g) $\mathbf{s} - \mathbf{p} + \mathbf{q}$

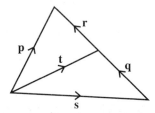

7 Use the diagram in question 6 to find the directed line segment that represents $\mathbf{x}$ in each of these vector equations:
   (a) $\mathbf{x} + \mathbf{p} = \mathbf{r}$ (b) $\mathbf{x} - \mathbf{s} = \mathbf{q}$ (c) $\mathbf{x} + \mathbf{r} = \mathbf{p}$ (d) $\mathbf{x} - \mathbf{s} = -\mathbf{t}$

Multiplication by a scalar

A force represented by vector $\mathbf{f}$ moves a trolley of mass 10 kg. If the mass is doubled the force must be doubled to have the same effect. This force can be represented by $\mathbf{f} + \mathbf{f}$ or $2\mathbf{f}$.

2$\mathbf{f}$ has the same direction as $\mathbf{f}$ but has twice its magnitude.

Vector $\mathbf{u}$ multiplied by a scalar k, where $k > 0$, gives vector $k\mathbf{u}$ with the same direction as $\mathbf{u}$ and magnitude $k|\mathbf{u}|$.

If vector $\mathbf{v} = \begin{pmatrix} x \\ y \end{pmatrix}$ then $k\mathbf{v} = \begin{pmatrix} kx \\ ky \end{pmatrix}$ and vector $k\mathbf{v}$ is parallel to vector $\mathbf{v}$.

▶ Hence if $\mathbf{u} = k\mathbf{v}$ then $\mathbf{u}$ is parallel to $\mathbf{v}$.

Conversely if $\mathbf{u}$ is parallel to $\mathbf{v}$ then $\mathbf{u} = k\mathbf{v}$.

Exercise 13E

1 The diagram shows vectors $\mathbf{u}$, $\mathbf{v}$ and $2\mathbf{u}$.

(a) Draw representatives of
   (i) $3\mathbf{u}$ (ii) $2\mathbf{v}$ (iii) $3\mathbf{v}$ (iv) $\frac{1}{2}\mathbf{v}$

(b) State the components of each vector in part (a).

(c) State the components of (i) $k\mathbf{u}$ (ii) $k\mathbf{v}$

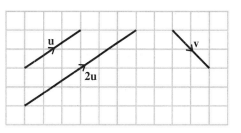

2 Using the diagram in question 1 draw representatives of
   (i) $\mathbf{u}$ (ii) $2\mathbf{u}$ (iii) $3\mathbf{u}$ (iv) $-2\mathbf{u}$ (v) $-3\mathbf{u}$

3 If vector $\mathbf{u} = \begin{pmatrix} -8 \\ 6 \end{pmatrix}$ and vector $\mathbf{v} = \begin{pmatrix} 12 \\ 10 \end{pmatrix}$ write down the

components of

(a) $3\mathbf{u}$ (b) $4\mathbf{v}$ (c) $\frac{1}{2}\mathbf{u}$

(d) $\frac{3}{4}\mathbf{v}$ (e) $3\mathbf{u} + 4\mathbf{v}$ (f) $3\mathbf{u} - 4\mathbf{v}$

4 Vector $\mathbf{v} = \begin{pmatrix} -3 \\ 2 \end{pmatrix}$. Which of the following vectors are parallel to vector $\mathbf{v}$?

$\mathbf{p} = \begin{pmatrix} 3 \\ -2 \end{pmatrix}$ $\mathbf{q} = \begin{pmatrix} 2 \\ -3 \end{pmatrix}$ $\mathbf{r} = \begin{pmatrix} -6 \\ 4 \end{pmatrix}$ $\mathbf{s} = \begin{pmatrix} 9 \\ -6 \end{pmatrix}$ $\mathbf{t} = \begin{pmatrix} 4.5 \\ 3 \end{pmatrix}$ $\mathbf{u} = \begin{pmatrix} -9 \\ -6 \end{pmatrix}$

5 The diagram shows a metalwork lattice. Copy and complete:

(a) $\overrightarrow{AE} = 4\,\overrightarrow{AI}$

(b) $\overrightarrow{HD} = \ldots \overrightarrow{AB}$

(c) $\overrightarrow{GL} = \ldots \overrightarrow{GC}$

(d) $\overrightarrow{LM} = \ldots \overrightarrow{MC}$

(e) $\overrightarrow{FB} = \ldots \overrightarrow{FM}$

(f) $\overrightarrow{GJ} = \ldots \overrightarrow{GC}$

(g) $2\overrightarrow{GL} + 2\overrightarrow{MI} = \ldots$

(h) $3\overrightarrow{EK} + \overrightarrow{HI} = \ldots \overrightarrow{ED} + \ldots \overrightarrow{CA}$

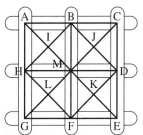

Unit vectors

> For any vector **v** there exists a parallel vector **u** of magnitude 1 unit. This is called a **unit vector**.

Example 3
Find the components of the unit vector, **u**, parallel to vector **v**, if $\mathbf{v} = \begin{pmatrix} 3 \\ 4 \end{pmatrix}$.

$$|\mathbf{v}| = \sqrt{3^2 + 4^2}$$
$$= 5$$

so the unit vector $\mathbf{u} = \frac{1}{5}\mathbf{v}$

$$= \frac{1}{5}\begin{pmatrix} 3 \\ 4 \end{pmatrix}$$

$$= \begin{pmatrix} \frac{3}{5} \\ \frac{4}{5} \end{pmatrix}$$

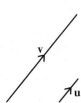

Exercise 13F

1 Find the components of the unit vector parallel to each vector:

(a) $\mathbf{p} = \begin{pmatrix} -3 \\ 4 \end{pmatrix}$ **(b)** $\mathbf{q} = \begin{pmatrix} 12 \\ 5 \end{pmatrix}$ **(c)** $\mathbf{r} = \begin{pmatrix} -8 \\ -6 \end{pmatrix}$ **(d)** $\mathbf{s} = \begin{pmatrix} -4 \\ -3 \end{pmatrix}$

2 A is the point (3, 4) and B is the point (5, 2).
  (a) Write down the components of
     (i) $\overrightarrow{OA}$ (ii) $\overrightarrow{OB}$
     (iii) $\overrightarrow{AB}$ (iv) $\overrightarrow{OB} - \overrightarrow{OA}$
  (b) What do you notice about your answers?

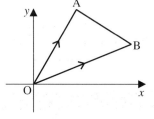

Position vectors

> $\overrightarrow{OA}$ is called the **position vector** of the point A relative to origin O, written **a**.
>
> $\overrightarrow{OB}$ is called the position vector of the point B, written **b**.

From question 2 in Exercise 13F, you should have noticed that:
$$\overrightarrow{AB} = \overrightarrow{AO} + \overrightarrow{AB}$$
$$= -\mathbf{a} + \mathbf{b}$$
$$= \mathbf{b} - \mathbf{a}$$

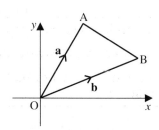

> $\overrightarrow{AB} = \mathbf{b} - \mathbf{a}$ where $\mathbf{a}$ and $\mathbf{b}$ are the position vectors of A and B.

Example 4

If P and Q have coordinates (4, 8) and (2, 3), respectively, find the components of $\overrightarrow{PQ}$.

$$\overrightarrow{PQ} = \mathbf{q} - \mathbf{p}$$

$$= \begin{pmatrix} 2 \\ 3 \end{pmatrix} - \begin{pmatrix} 4 \\ 8 \end{pmatrix} = \begin{pmatrix} -2 \\ -5 \end{pmatrix}$$

Exercise 13G

1 A is the point $(-10, 5)$ and B is the point $(6, -4)$.
   (a) Write down the components of position vectors $\mathbf{a}$ and $\mathbf{b}$.
   (b) Find the components of $\overrightarrow{AB}$.

2 For each pair of points (i) find the components of $\overrightarrow{PQ}$ and (ii) calculate $|\overrightarrow{PQ}|$:
   (a) P(1, 4), Q(4, 8)   (b) P(−3, 5), Q(9, 0)
   (c) P(−8, −4), Q(−10, 6)   (d) P(5, −2), Q(0, −12)

Collinearity

You saw in Chapter 1, The straight line, how you tell if points are collinear. In this exercise you will use vectors to show that points are collinear.

Exercise 13H

1 (a) Plot the points A(2, 1), B(3, 3) and C(6, 9) on a Cartesian diagram.
   (b) Find the components of (i) $\overrightarrow{AB}$ and (ii) $\overrightarrow{BC}$.
   (c) Express $\overrightarrow{BC}$ in terms of $\overrightarrow{AB}$.
   (d) What can be said about AB and BC?
   (e) How are points A, B and C related?

> Points are said to be **collinear** if they lie on a straight line.
>
> If $\overrightarrow{AB} = k\overrightarrow{BC}$, where k is a scalar, then AB is parallel to BC.
>
> If B is also a point common to both AB and BC then A, B and C are collinear.

Example 5

Prove that the points A(2, 4), B(8, 6) and C(11, 7) are collinear.

$$\overrightarrow{AB} = \mathbf{b} - \mathbf{a} \qquad\qquad\qquad \overrightarrow{BC} = \mathbf{c} - \mathbf{b}$$

$$= \begin{pmatrix} 8 \\ 6 \end{pmatrix} - \begin{pmatrix} 2 \\ 4 \end{pmatrix} \qquad\qquad = \begin{pmatrix} 11 \\ 7 \end{pmatrix} - \begin{pmatrix} 8 \\ 6 \end{pmatrix}$$

$$= \begin{pmatrix} 6 \\ 2 \end{pmatrix} \qquad\qquad\qquad = \begin{pmatrix} 3 \\ 1 \end{pmatrix}$$

$$\overrightarrow{AB} = \begin{pmatrix} 6 \\ 2 \end{pmatrix} = 2 \begin{pmatrix} 3 \\ 1 \end{pmatrix} = 2\overrightarrow{BC}$$

$\overrightarrow{AB} = 2\overrightarrow{BC}$ so $\overrightarrow{AB}$ is parallel to $\overrightarrow{BC}$.

B is a point common to both AB and BC, so A, B and C are **collinear**.

Exercise 13I

1 Which of the following sets of points are collinear?

(a) P(2, 3), Q(5, 5), R(13, 9)   (b) S(−3, 7), T(4, 10), U(2, −5)

(c) X(4, 6), Y(6, 2), Z(10, −6)   (d) A(1, 5), B(2, 4), C(−1, 7)

(e) D(2, 7), E(−4, 4), F(−2, 5)   (f) K(2, −1), L(−4, 2), M(−2, 1)

2 At 1300 hours the ferry Carrième is located at the point (−5, −2). One hour later it is located at (−1, 0). If the ferry continues on the same course, will it collide with the fishing vessel Bàtabeag anchored at the point (1, 1)?

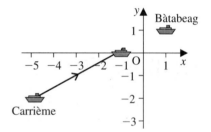

3 The stretch of pipeline between Borall and Poruit has three manholes for access with coordinates A(−3, 4), B(5, −2) and $C\left(11, -6\tfrac{1}{2}\right)$. Do these manholes lie in a straight line?

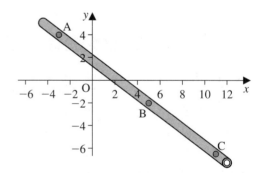

4 An engineer can check a theodolite for accuracy by sighting three pegs laid out in a straight line. Can he use pegs placed at (4, 5), $\left(1\tfrac{1}{2}, 2\right)$ and (−6, −11) to check the instrument?

5 An infrared burglar alarm has to pass through three collinear points in a room to operate properly. If these points can be represented on a coordinate diagram as (5, 1), (3, 5) and (0, 10), will the alarm operate properly?

Section formula

The section formula can be used to divide a line in a given ratio.
This exercise will help you find the formula.

Exercise 13J

1 A is the point (5, 8) and B is the point (9, 16). Find the coordinates of M, the mid-point of AB.

2 Copy and complete each set of statements for the following diagrams.

(a)
$$\overrightarrow{OM} = \overrightarrow{OA} + \overrightarrow{AM}$$
$$= \overrightarrow{OA} + \tfrac{1}{2}\overrightarrow{AB}$$
$$= \mathbf{a} + \tfrac{1}{2}(\mathbf{b} - \mathbf{a})$$
$$= \mathbf{a} + \tfrac{1}{2}\mathbf{b} - \tfrac{1}{2}\mathbf{a}$$
$$= \ldots \mathbf{a} + \ldots \mathbf{b}$$

M divides AB in the ratio 1:1

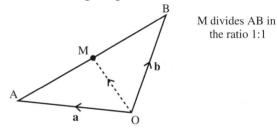

(b)
$$\overrightarrow{OS} = \overrightarrow{OA} + \overrightarrow{AS}$$
$$= \overrightarrow{OA} + \ldots \overrightarrow{AB}$$
$$= \mathbf{a} + \ldots (\ldots - \ldots)$$
$$= \mathbf{a} + \ldots - \ldots$$
$$= \ldots \mathbf{a} + \ldots \mathbf{b}$$

S divides AB in the ratio 1:2

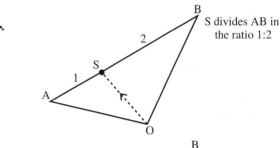

(c)
$$\overrightarrow{OT} = \overrightarrow{OA} + \overrightarrow{AT}$$
$$= \overrightarrow{OA} + \ldots \overrightarrow{AB}$$
$$= \mathbf{a} + \ldots (\ldots - \ldots)$$
$$= \mathbf{a} + \ldots - \ldots$$
$$= \ldots \mathbf{a} + \ldots \mathbf{b}$$

T divides AB in the ratio 3:2

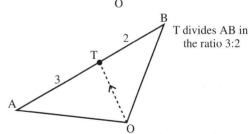

3 Make a conjecture about **p** the position vector of point P that divides AB in the ratio
(a) 5:4
(b) $m:n$.

From Exercise 13J, you should notice that:

> If **p** is the position vector of the point P that divides AB in the ratio $m:n$ then
>
> ▶ $$\mathbf{p} = \frac{n}{m+n}\mathbf{a} + \frac{m}{m+n}\mathbf{b}$$
>
>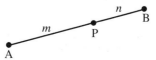

This is called the **section formula**.

Proof

$$\overrightarrow{OP} = \overrightarrow{OA} + \overrightarrow{AP}$$

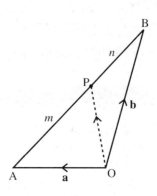

$$= \overrightarrow{OA} + \frac{m}{m+n} \overrightarrow{AB}$$

$$= \mathbf{a} + \frac{m}{m+n} (\mathbf{b} - \mathbf{a})$$

$$= \mathbf{a} + \frac{m}{m+n} \mathbf{b} - \frac{m}{m+n} \mathbf{a}$$

$$= \frac{(m+n)\mathbf{a}}{m+n} + \frac{m\mathbf{b}}{m+n} - \frac{m\mathbf{a}}{m+n}$$

$$= \frac{n}{m+n} \mathbf{a} + \frac{m}{m+n} \mathbf{b}$$

Example 6

A and B have coordinates (3, 2) and (7, 14), respectively. Find the coordinates of the point P that divides AB in the ratio 1 : 3.

$$\mathbf{p} = \tfrac{3}{4}\mathbf{a} + \tfrac{1}{4}\mathbf{b}$$

$$= \tfrac{1}{4}(3\mathbf{a} + \mathbf{b})$$

$$= \tfrac{1}{4}\left(3\begin{pmatrix}3\\2\end{pmatrix} + \begin{pmatrix}7\\14\end{pmatrix}\right)$$

$$= \tfrac{1}{4}\begin{pmatrix}16\\20\end{pmatrix} = \begin{pmatrix}4\\5\end{pmatrix}$$

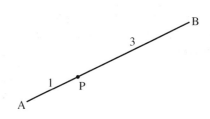

P has coordinates (4, 5).

Exercise 13K

1 Given that P divides AB in the given ratio, find the coordinates of P in each case.
  (a) A(5, 3), B(−5, 8), AP : PB = 1 : 4
  (b) A(−2, 4), B(−5, −2), AP : PB = 1 : 2
  (c) A(4, −6), B(−1, 9), AP : PB = 2 : 3
  (d) A(7, 0), B(−5, 6), AP : PB = 2 : 1

2 A and B have coordinates (−1, 5) and (4, 10), respectively. Find P if AP : PB is 3 : 2.

3 R, S and T have coordinates (6, 7), (10, 13) and (16, 22), respectively. Prove that R, S and T are collinear and give the ratio in which S divides RT.

4 Prove that P(−7, −3), Q(−4, 1) and R(2, 9) are collinear and find the ratio PQ : QR.

5 The centroid of a triangle is the point of intersection of the medians of the triangle. The centroid divides each median in the ratio $2:1$. If the vertices of a triangle are A$(-3, 2)$, B$(5, -1)$ and C$(4, -1)$, find

(a) the coordinates of M, the mid-point of BC

(b) the coordinates of the centroid.

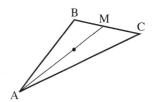

6 $\overrightarrow{FG}$ and $\overrightarrow{GH}$ can be represented by the vectors $\begin{pmatrix} -5 \\ 8 \end{pmatrix}$ and $\begin{pmatrix} x \\ 12 \end{pmatrix}$.

Given that F, G and H are collinear find

(a) the value of x

(b) the ratio in which G divides FH.

7 A is the point $(2, 2)$, B is $(4, 7)$, C is $(0, 4)$ and D is $(-2, -1)$.

X is a point such that $\overrightarrow{AX} = \frac{1}{2}\overrightarrow{AC}$.

(a) Prove that $\overrightarrow{DX} = \frac{1}{2}\overrightarrow{DB}$.

(b) What kind of shape is ABCD?

Three-dimensional coordinates

In the real world points in space can be located using a three-dimensional coordinate system. For example, air traffic controllers find the location of a plane by its height as well as its grid reference.

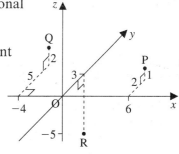

Example 7

Write the coordinates of points P, Q and R using three-dimensional coordinates.

P is the point $(6, 2, 1)$, Q is the point $(-4, 5, 2)$ and R is the point $(0, 3, -5)$.

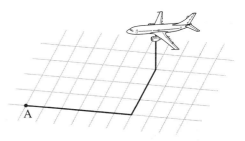

1 For each diagram write the coordinates of P.

(a) 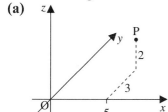   **(b)** 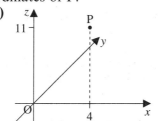   **(c)**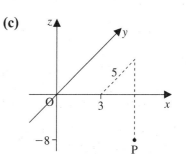

2 State the coordinates of each vertex of the cuboid.

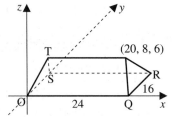

3 The roof of a house is constructed from two congruent isosceles triangles and two congruent trapezia, as illustrated in the diagram. State the coordinates of each corner of the roof.

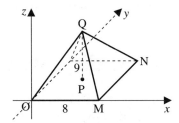

4 State the coordinates of each vertex of the square-based pyramid shown in the diagram.

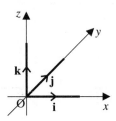

Three-dimensional vectors

Vectors in three-dimensional space are defined by three components.
For example, the velocity of an aircraft taking off can be illustrated as:

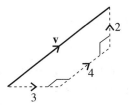

This is written as the vector $\mathbf{v} = \begin{pmatrix} 3 \\ 4 \\ 2 \end{pmatrix}$. This is called the **component form**.

> A vector may also be defined in terms of $\mathbf{i}$, $\mathbf{j}$ and $\mathbf{k}$, where $\mathbf{i}$, $\mathbf{j}$ and $\mathbf{k}$ are unit vectors in the x, y and z directions, respectively:
>
> In component form these vectors are written as
>
> $\mathbf{i} = \begin{pmatrix} 1 \\ 0 \\ 0 \end{pmatrix}$, $\mathbf{j} = \begin{pmatrix} 0 \\ 1 \\ 0 \end{pmatrix}$ and $\mathbf{k} = \begin{pmatrix} 0 \\ 0 \\ 1 \end{pmatrix}$.

Any vector may be expressed as a combination of its components:

So $\mathbf{v} = \begin{pmatrix} 3 \\ 4 \\ 2 \end{pmatrix}$ can be written:

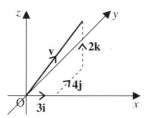

$\mathbf{v} = 3\mathbf{i} + 4\mathbf{j} + 2\mathbf{k}$

Exercise 13M

1 Express **s**
  (a) in terms of **i**, **j** and **k**
  (b) in component form.

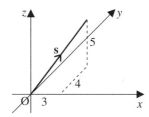

2 Express each vector in component form:
  (a) $\mathbf{v} = 2\mathbf{i} + 5\mathbf{j} + 7\mathbf{k}$
  (b) $\overrightarrow{BC} = 6\mathbf{i} - 4\mathbf{j} + 3\mathbf{k}$
  (c) $\mathbf{w} = 5\mathbf{i} - 2\mathbf{k}$
  (d) $\overrightarrow{FG} = -7\mathbf{k}$

3 Express each vector in terms of **i**, **j** and **k**:

  (a) $\mathbf{p} = \begin{pmatrix} 5 \\ 3 \\ 4 \end{pmatrix}$
  (b) $\overrightarrow{LM} = \begin{pmatrix} 6 \\ -4 \\ -1 \end{pmatrix}$
  (c) $\mathbf{q} = \begin{pmatrix} -3 \\ 0 \\ 4 \end{pmatrix}$
  (d) $\overrightarrow{RT} = \begin{pmatrix} 0 \\ 1 \\ 0 \end{pmatrix}$

4 If $\mathbf{p} = 2\mathbf{i} + 3\mathbf{j} + \mathbf{k}$ and $\mathbf{q} = \mathbf{i} + 2\mathbf{j} - 2\mathbf{k}$, express in component form:
  (a) $\mathbf{p} + \mathbf{q}$
  (b) $\mathbf{q} - \mathbf{p}$
  (c) $3\mathbf{p} - \mathbf{q}$
  (d) $2\mathbf{p} + 3\mathbf{q}$

Properties of 3–D vectors

The properties of two-dimensional vectors can also be applied to three-dimensional vectors.

Magnitude

If $\overrightarrow{AD} = \begin{pmatrix} 4 \\ 2 \\ 5 \end{pmatrix}$, $AD^2 = AC^2 + CD^2$

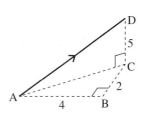

$$\begin{aligned} AD^2 &= (AB^2 + BC^2) + CD^2 \\ &= 4^2 + 2^2 + 5^2 \\ |\overrightarrow{AD}| &= \sqrt{16 + 4 + 25} \\ &= \sqrt{45} \\ &= 3\sqrt{5} \text{ units} \end{aligned}$$

> If $\overrightarrow{PQ} = \begin{pmatrix} a \\ b \\ c \end{pmatrix}$ then $|\overrightarrow{PQ}| = \sqrt{a^2 + b^2 + c^2}$

Addition

$$\begin{pmatrix} 2 \\ 3 \\ -1 \end{pmatrix} + \begin{pmatrix} 4 \\ -2 \\ 5 \end{pmatrix} = \begin{pmatrix} 6 \\ 1 \\ 4 \end{pmatrix}$$

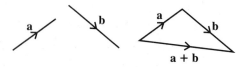

If $\mathbf{u} = \begin{pmatrix} a \\ b \\ c \end{pmatrix}$ and $\mathbf{v} = \begin{pmatrix} p \\ q \\ r \end{pmatrix}$ then $\mathbf{u} + \mathbf{v} = \begin{pmatrix} a+p \\ b+q \\ c+r \end{pmatrix}$

Negative vector

If $\overrightarrow{CD} = \begin{pmatrix} -3 \\ 2 \\ 7 \end{pmatrix}$ then $\overrightarrow{DC} = \begin{pmatrix} 3 \\ -2 \\ -7 \end{pmatrix}$

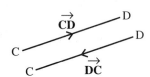

If $\mathbf{u} = \begin{pmatrix} a \\ b \\ c \end{pmatrix}$ then $-\mathbf{u} = \begin{pmatrix} -a \\ -b \\ -c \end{pmatrix}$

Subtraction

$$\begin{pmatrix} 4 \\ -2 \\ 5 \end{pmatrix} - \begin{pmatrix} -3 \\ -4 \\ 6 \end{pmatrix} = \begin{pmatrix} 7 \\ 2 \\ -1 \end{pmatrix}$$

If $\mathbf{u} = \begin{pmatrix} a \\ b \\ c \end{pmatrix}$ and $\mathbf{v} = \begin{pmatrix} p \\ q \\ r \end{pmatrix}$

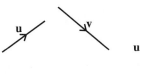

then $\mathbf{u} - \mathbf{v} = \begin{pmatrix} a \\ b \\ c \end{pmatrix} - \begin{pmatrix} p \\ q \\ r \end{pmatrix} = \begin{pmatrix} a-p \\ b-q \\ c-r \end{pmatrix}$

Multiplication by a scalar

$$3 \begin{pmatrix} 4 \\ -3 \\ 2 \end{pmatrix} = \begin{pmatrix} 12 \\ -9 \\ 6 \end{pmatrix}$$

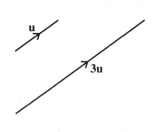

If $\mathbf{u} = \begin{pmatrix} a \\ b \\ c \end{pmatrix}$ then $k\mathbf{u} = \begin{pmatrix} ka \\ kb \\ kc \end{pmatrix}$

Position vectors

The position vector of a three-dimensional point A is $\overrightarrow{OA}$, usually written $\mathbf{a}$.

$$\overrightarrow{OA} = \mathbf{a} = \begin{pmatrix} 3 \\ 4 \\ 6 \end{pmatrix}$$

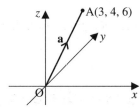

If R is (2, −5, 1) and S is (4, 1, −3)

then $\overrightarrow{RS} = \mathbf{s} - \mathbf{r}$

$$= \begin{pmatrix} 4 \\ 1 \\ -3 \end{pmatrix} - \begin{pmatrix} 2 \\ -5 \\ 1 \end{pmatrix} = \begin{pmatrix} 2 \\ 6 \\ -4 \end{pmatrix}$$

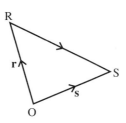

▶ $\overrightarrow{AB} = \mathbf{b} - \mathbf{a}$, where $\mathbf{a}$ and $\mathbf{b}$ are position vectors of A and B, respectively.

Section formula

If A is (4, −6, 12), B(4, 4, −3) and P divides $\overrightarrow{AB}$ in the ratio 3 : 2 then

$\mathbf{p} = \frac{2}{5}\mathbf{a} + \frac{3}{5}\mathbf{b}$

$= \frac{1}{5}(2\mathbf{a} + 3\mathbf{b})$

$= \frac{1}{5}\left(\begin{pmatrix} 8 \\ -12 \\ 24 \end{pmatrix} + \begin{pmatrix} 12 \\ 12 \\ -9 \end{pmatrix} \right)$

$= \frac{1}{5}\begin{pmatrix} 20 \\ 0 \\ 15 \end{pmatrix} = \begin{pmatrix} 4 \\ 0 \\ 3 \end{pmatrix}$

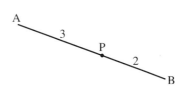

i.e. P is the point (4, 0, 3).

If P divides AB in the ratio $m:n$ then $\mathbf{p} = \dfrac{n}{m+n}\mathbf{a} + \dfrac{m}{m+n}\mathbf{b}$.

Exercise 13N

1 Write the components of each vector.

(a)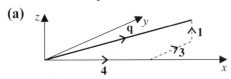

(b) $\mathbf{r} = 4\mathbf{i} + 6\mathbf{j} - 8\mathbf{k}$

(c) $\overrightarrow{OM}$ given M(2, −5, 6)

(d) $\overrightarrow{FG}$ given F(2, 4, −6) and G(−3, 2, 5)

2 Calculate the magnitude of each vector, leaving the answer in surd form where necessary.

(a) $\mathbf{p} = \begin{pmatrix} 2 \\ -5 \\ 3 \end{pmatrix}$

(b) $\overrightarrow{UV} = \begin{pmatrix} 5 \\ -1 \\ -1 \end{pmatrix}$

(c) $\mathbf{r} = 2\mathbf{i} - 3\mathbf{j} + 5\mathbf{k}$

(d)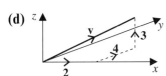

(e) $\overrightarrow{PQ}$ given P(2, 5, 5) and Q(3, −1, −1)

(f) $\mathbf{s}$ given S$(\sqrt{2}, 3, \sqrt{5})$

(g) $\mathbf{x} = \sqrt{3}\mathbf{i} + 7\mathbf{j} - \mathbf{k}$

3 $\mathbf{u} = 3\mathbf{i} - 4\mathbf{j} + 2\mathbf{k}$ and $\mathbf{v} = a\mathbf{i} + 5\mathbf{j} - \mathbf{k}$. If $|\mathbf{u}| = |\mathbf{v}|$ find a.

4 Write the negative of each vector.

(a) $\mathbf{v} = \begin{pmatrix} 3 \\ -6 \\ 7 \end{pmatrix}$

(b) $\overrightarrow{CD} = \begin{pmatrix} 7 \\ -7 \\ -8 \end{pmatrix}$

(c) $\mathbf{f} = \mathbf{i} + 8\mathbf{j} - \mathbf{k}$

(d) $\mathbf{g} = \sqrt{2}\mathbf{i} - 2\sqrt{2}\mathbf{j} + \mathbf{k}$

5 Find $\mathbf{p} + \mathbf{q}$ and $\mathbf{p} - \mathbf{q}$ when

(a) $\mathbf{p} = 2\mathbf{i} + 3\mathbf{j} + \mathbf{k}$, $\mathbf{q} = 4\mathbf{i} - 5\mathbf{j} - 3\mathbf{k}$

(b) $\mathbf{p} = \begin{pmatrix} 2 \\ 5 \\ 3 \end{pmatrix}$, $\mathbf{q} = \begin{pmatrix} -5 \\ 6 \\ 1 \end{pmatrix}$

6 Peter Pan is suspended by three wires with forces $\begin{pmatrix} 4 \\ 2 \\ 3 \end{pmatrix}$, $\begin{pmatrix} 3 \\ -7 \\ 5 \end{pmatrix}$

and $\begin{pmatrix} -2 \\ 5 \\ 8 \end{pmatrix}$ acting on them. By adding, find the resultant force.

7 PQRS is a parallelogram with vertices $P(2, 3, -1)$, $Q(6, 5, -4)$ and $R(7, 4, 1)$. Find the coordinates of S.

8 Find $\overrightarrow{PQ}$ if

(a) $\overrightarrow{PR} = \begin{pmatrix} -3 \\ 2 \\ -3 \end{pmatrix}$ and $\overrightarrow{RQ} = \begin{pmatrix} 4 \\ 4 \\ 6 \end{pmatrix}$

(b) $\overrightarrow{PW} = \begin{pmatrix} -1 \\ -1 \\ 7 \end{pmatrix}$ and $\overrightarrow{WQ} = \begin{pmatrix} 3 \\ 10 \\ 3 \end{pmatrix}$

9 Solve the vector equation for a and b: $\begin{pmatrix} 2 \\ b \\ 3 \end{pmatrix} + \begin{pmatrix} a \\ 5 \\ 4 \end{pmatrix} = \begin{pmatrix} b \\ 2a \\ 7 \end{pmatrix}$

10 (a) If $\mathbf{u} = \begin{pmatrix} 3 \\ 4 \\ -6 \end{pmatrix}$, find $3\mathbf{u}$.

(b) If $\mathbf{v} = \begin{pmatrix} -1 \\ 0 \\ 3 \end{pmatrix}$, find $4\mathbf{v}$.

11 If $\mathbf{p} = \begin{pmatrix} -3 \\ 2 \\ 6 \end{pmatrix}$, $\mathbf{q} = \begin{pmatrix} 6 \\ -1 \\ 6 \end{pmatrix}$ and $\mathbf{r} = \begin{pmatrix} 2 \\ 0 \\ -3 \end{pmatrix}$,

express in component form:

(a) $\mathbf{p} + 2\mathbf{q}$ (b) $3\mathbf{r} - \mathbf{p}$ (c) $5\mathbf{p} + 2\mathbf{q} - \mathbf{r}$ (d) $\mathbf{p} - 2\mathbf{q} + 4\mathbf{r}$

12 If $\mathbf{f} = \begin{pmatrix} -1 \\ 4 \\ 3 \end{pmatrix}$ and $\mathbf{g} = \begin{pmatrix} 5 \\ 5 \\ -2 \end{pmatrix}$, solve each vector equation for $\mathbf{v}$.

(a) $\mathbf{f} + \mathbf{v} = \mathbf{g}$ (b) $\mathbf{v} = 2\mathbf{f} + \mathbf{g}$ (c) $2\mathbf{v} + \mathbf{f} = \mathbf{g} + 3\mathbf{f}$

13 P is $(7, -10, 3)$ and Q is $(2, -3, -9)$. Find the components of $\overrightarrow{PQ}$.

14 F is $(3, 5, -5)$ and G is $(-1, -1, 5)$. Find the components of $\overrightarrow{FG}$.

15 P is $(2, -3, 5)$, Q is $(9, -6, 9)$ and R is $(23, -12, 17)$.
 (a) Show that P, Q and R are collinear.
 (b) Find PQ:QR.

16 A laser beam is directed through a filter to its target. The coordinates of the source, filter and target are $S(2, -5, -6)$, $F(8, -6, -4)$ and $T(20, -8, 0)$, respectively. Show that they are properly aligned.

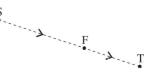

17 At 1300 hours the submarine Paxman is located by sonar at the point $(-5, -2, 9)$. One hour later it is located at $(-1, 0, -3)$. If it continues on the same course will it hit the fishing vessel, Neptune, located at point $(1, 1, 0)$?

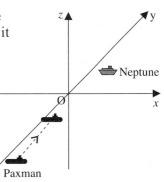

18 The points $A(-1, 4, 8)$, $B(1, 2, 3)$ and $C(5, y, z)$ are collinear. Find the values of y and z.

19 P is $(-2, 4, -1)$ and R is $(8, -1, 19)$. Find the coordinates of T if $\dfrac{PT}{TR} = \dfrac{2}{3}$.

20 Points A and B have coordinates $(1, -5, 7)$ and $(13, 19, -5)$, respectively. Find the coordinates of P such that P divides $\overrightarrow{AB}$ in the ratio
 (a) $1:1$ **(b)** $1:2$ **(c)** $2:1$ **(d)** $3:1$ **(e)** $1:5$

21 A helicopter flies on a straight line at a constant speed. It takes 3 minutes to fly from A to B and 2 minutes to fly from B to C. Relative to coordinate axes, A is the point $(2, 4, 7)$ and C is $(2, 9, -3)$. Find the coordinates of B.

22 For the points $P(2, 0, -2)$, $Q(-4, -4, -4)$ and $R(2, -4, 2)$:
 (a) Find the coordinates of
  (i) M, the mid-point of PR
  (ii) N, the mid-point of QR
  (iii) L, the mid-point of PQ
  (iv) C, which divides $\overrightarrow{QM}$ in the ratio $2:1$.
 (b) Show that P, C and N are collinear.
 (c) Does RL pass through point C?
 (d) What can you say about the medians of this triangle?

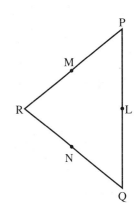

23 The tops of three pylons on a ski tow have coordinates
P(−5, 6, −5), Q(7, −2, −1) and R(10, −4, 0). Show that the tops
are collinear and find the ratio in which Q divides PR.

24 A marble base for a statue is formed from a cube of side 7 m. It
is placed relative to coordinate axes as shown in the diagram.
A, B and C divide ST, UT and PT, respectively, in the ratio 3 : 4.
(a) Find the coordinates of A, B and C.
(b) If the corner of the cube is cut off along the plane defined by
ABC find the surface area of the block.

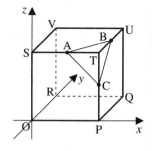

The scalar product

So far our work on vectors has covered addition, subtraction and
multiplication by a scalar. We now consider a form of vector
multiplication.

> For two vectors **a** and **b** the **scalar product**
> is defined as $\mathbf{a}.\mathbf{b} = |\mathbf{a}|\,|\mathbf{b}|\cos\theta$, where θ is the
> angle between **a** and **b**, $0 \leqslant \theta \leqslant 180°$.

The scalar product is also known as the **dot product**.

Note: (i) The vectors point away from the vertex.
Note: (ii) The scalar product is **not** a vector, it is a scalar.

Example 8
Find the scalar product for vectors **a** and **b** when $|\mathbf{a}| = 4$ units,
$|\mathbf{b}| = 5$ units for **(a)** $\theta = 45°$ **(b)** $\theta = 90°$.

(a) $\mathbf{a}.\mathbf{b} = |\mathbf{a}|\,|\mathbf{b}|\cos\theta$
$= 4 \times 5 \times \cos 45°$
$= 20 \times \dfrac{1}{\sqrt{2}}$
$= \dfrac{20}{\sqrt{2}}$
$= 10\sqrt{2}$

(b) $\mathbf{a}.\mathbf{b} = |\mathbf{a}|\,|\mathbf{b}|\cos\theta$
$= 4 \times 5 \times \cos 90°$
$= 20 \times 0$
$= 0$

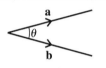

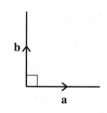

> If **a** and **b** are **perpendicular** then $\mathbf{a}.\mathbf{b} = 0$.

1 Calculate **a.b** for each pair of vectors.

(a)

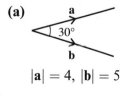

$|\mathbf{a}| = 4,\ |\mathbf{b}| = 5$

(b)

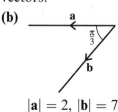

$|\mathbf{a}| = 2,\ |\mathbf{b}| = 7$

(c)

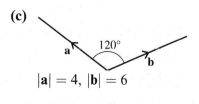

$|\mathbf{a}| = 4,\ |\mathbf{b}| = 6$

(d)

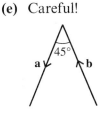

$|\mathbf{a}| = 5, \ |\mathbf{b}| = 8$

(e) Careful!

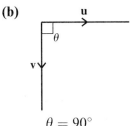

$|\mathbf{a}| = 7, \ |\mathbf{b}| = 8$

(f)

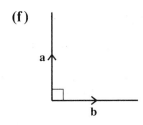

$|\mathbf{a}| = 6, \ |\mathbf{b}| = 5$

2 For each diagram below state whether the scalar product will be positive, negative or zero.

(a)

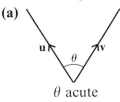

θ acute

(b)

$\theta = 90°$

(c)

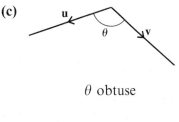

θ obtuse

3 The unit vectors in the x, y and z direction are **i**, **j** and **k**, respectively. Find the value of
    (a) i.j   **(b) i.k**   **(c) k.j**   **(d) i.i**   **(e) j.j**

Component form of a scalar product

> If $\mathbf{a} = \begin{pmatrix} a_1 \\ a_2 \\ a_3 \end{pmatrix}$ and $\mathbf{b} = \begin{pmatrix} b_1 \\ b_2 \\ b_3 \end{pmatrix}$ then $\mathbf{a.b} = a_1 b_1 + a_2 b_2 + a_3 b_3$

Proof
In triangle OAB

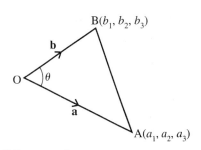

$\overrightarrow{AB} = \mathbf{b} - \mathbf{a}$

$|\mathbf{a}|^2 = |OA|^2 = a_1^2 + a_2^2 + a_3^2$

$|\mathbf{b}|^2 = |OB|^2 = b_1^2 + b_2^2 + b_3^2$

$|\overrightarrow{AB}|^2 = |\mathbf{b} - \mathbf{a}|^2 = (b_1 - a_1)^2 + (b_2 - a_2)^2 + (b_3 - a_3)^2$

Applying the cosine rule, $AB^2 = OA^2 + OB^2 - 2 \times OA \times OB \times \cos\theta$

$(b_1 - a_1)^2 + (b_2 - a_2)^2 + (b_3 - a_3)^2$

$\qquad = (a_1^2 + a_2^2 + a_3^2) + (b_1^2 + b_2^2 + b_3^2) - 2|\mathbf{a}|\,|\mathbf{b}|\cos\theta$

$(b_1^2 - 2b_1 a_1 + a_1^2) + (b_2^2 - 2b_2 a_2 + a_2^2) + (b_3^2 - 2b_3 a_3 + a_3^2)$

$\qquad = a_1^2 + a_2^2 + a_3^2 + b_1^2 + b_2^2 + b_3^2 - 2|\mathbf{a}|\,|\mathbf{b}|\cos\theta$

$-2|\mathbf{a}|\,|\mathbf{b}|\cos\theta = -2b_1 a_1 - 2b_2 a_2 - 2b_3 a_3$

$2|\mathbf{a}|\,|\mathbf{b}|\cos\theta = 2a_1 b_1 + 2a_2 b_2 + 2a_3 b_3$

$|\mathbf{a}|\,|\mathbf{b}|\cos\theta = a_1 b_1 + a_2 b_2 + a_3 b_3$

So $\mathbf{a.b} = a_1 b_1 + a_2 b_2 + a_3 b_3$

Example 9

Find **u.w** for vectors $\mathbf{u} = \begin{pmatrix} 1 \\ 3 \\ -4 \end{pmatrix}$ and $\mathbf{w} = \begin{pmatrix} 2 \\ 6 \\ 2 \end{pmatrix}$.

$$\mathbf{u.w} = u_1 w_1 + u_2 w_2 + u_3 w_3$$
$$= 1 \times 2 + 3 \times 6 + (-4) \times 2$$
$$= 2 + 18 - 8$$
$$= 12$$

Exercise 13P

1 Calculate the scalar product for each pair of vectors.

(a) $\mathbf{a} = \begin{pmatrix} 4 \\ 3 \\ 6 \end{pmatrix}$, $\mathbf{b} = \begin{pmatrix} 7 \\ 3 \\ 2 \end{pmatrix}$ (b) $\mathbf{p} = \begin{pmatrix} 5 \\ 5 \\ 6 \end{pmatrix}$, $\mathbf{q} = \begin{pmatrix} 6 \\ 2 \\ -3 \end{pmatrix}$ (c) $\overrightarrow{AB} = \begin{pmatrix} 1 \\ -4 \\ -2 \end{pmatrix}$, $\overrightarrow{AC} = \begin{pmatrix} 8 \\ 9 \\ -5 \end{pmatrix}$

(d) $\mathbf{m} = 2\mathbf{i} + 5\mathbf{j} + 7\mathbf{k}$ (e) $\mathbf{f} = 4\mathbf{i} + 2\mathbf{j} - 3\mathbf{k}$ (f) $\mathbf{s} = \mathbf{i} + \mathbf{j} - \mathbf{k}$
    $\mathbf{n} = 4\mathbf{i} + 2\mathbf{j} + 2\mathbf{k}$ $\mathbf{g} = 8\mathbf{i} - 6\mathbf{j} + 3\mathbf{k}$ $\mathbf{t} = \mathbf{i} - \mathbf{j} - \mathbf{k}$

2 In each diagram find
  (i) the components of $\overrightarrow{AB}$ and $\overrightarrow{AC}$ (ii) $\overrightarrow{AB}.\overrightarrow{AC}$

(a)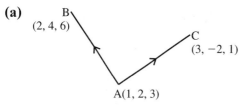

(b)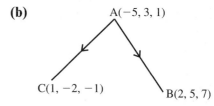

(c)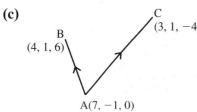

3 P is the point (2, 5, −4), Q is (3, 4, 3) and R is (−4, 5, 1). Find
  (a) $\overrightarrow{PQ}.\overrightarrow{PR}$ (b) $\overrightarrow{RP}.\overrightarrow{RQ}$ (c) $\overrightarrow{QR}.\overrightarrow{QP}$

4 ABC is an equilateral triangle with coordinates A(−1, 3, 6),
  B(1, 3, 4) and C(−1, 5, 4).
  (a) Write in component form (i) $\overrightarrow{AB}$, (ii) $\overrightarrow{BC}$ and (iii) $\overrightarrow{AC}$
  (b) Find $\overrightarrow{AB}.\overrightarrow{AC}$ and $\overrightarrow{BC}.\overrightarrow{BA}$
  (c) Why should $\overrightarrow{AB}.\overrightarrow{AC} = \overrightarrow{BC}.\overrightarrow{BA} = \overrightarrow{CA}.\overrightarrow{CB}$?

Angle between vectors

The scalar product may be used to find the angle between two vectors.

We have already seen that $\mathbf{a.b} = |\mathbf{a}|\,|\mathbf{b}|\cos\theta$ and $\mathbf{a.b} = a_1b_1 + a_2b_2 + a_3b_3$,

therefore $\qquad |\mathbf{a}|\,|\mathbf{b}|\cos\theta = a_1b_1 + a_2b_2 + a_3b_3$

or

$$\blacktriangleright \quad \cos\theta = \frac{a_1b_1 + a_2b_2 + a_3b_3}{|\mathbf{a}|\,|\mathbf{b}|} \quad \text{or} \quad \cos\theta = \frac{\mathbf{a.b}}{|\mathbf{a}|\,|\mathbf{b}|}$$

Example 10
Calculate the angle, θ, between vectors $\mathbf{p} = 3\mathbf{i} + 2\mathbf{j} + 5\mathbf{k}$ and $\mathbf{q} = 4\mathbf{i} + \mathbf{j} + 3\mathbf{k}$.

$$\mathbf{p} = \begin{pmatrix} 3 \\ 2 \\ 5 \end{pmatrix} \text{ and } \mathbf{q} = \begin{pmatrix} 4 \\ 1 \\ 3 \end{pmatrix}$$

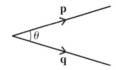

Therefore $\quad |\mathbf{p}| = \sqrt{3^2 + 2^2 + 5^2} = \sqrt{38}$

$\qquad\qquad |\mathbf{q}| = \sqrt{4^2 + 1^2 + 3^2} = \sqrt{26}$

and $\quad \mathbf{p.q} = 3 \times 4 + 2 \times 1 + 5 \times 3$

$\qquad\qquad = 29$

$\cos\theta = \dfrac{\mathbf{p.q}}{|\mathbf{p}|\,|\mathbf{q}|}$

$\qquad = \dfrac{29}{\sqrt{38}\sqrt{26}}$

$\qquad = 0.923$

$\quad \theta = 22.7°$

The angle between $\mathbf{p}$ and $\mathbf{q}$ is $22.7°$, since $0 \leqslant \theta \leqslant 180°$.

Exercise 13Q

1 Calculate the angle between each pair of vectors

(a) $\mathbf{a} = \begin{pmatrix} 4 \\ 3 \\ 6 \end{pmatrix}$, $\mathbf{b} = \begin{pmatrix} 7 \\ 3 \\ 2 \end{pmatrix}$ (b) $\mathbf{p} = \begin{pmatrix} 5 \\ 5 \\ 6 \end{pmatrix}$, $\mathbf{q} = \begin{pmatrix} 6 \\ 2 \\ -3 \end{pmatrix}$ (c) $\overrightarrow{AB} = \begin{pmatrix} 1 \\ -4 \\ -2 \end{pmatrix}$, $\overrightarrow{AC} = \begin{pmatrix} 8 \\ 9 \\ 5 \end{pmatrix}$

(d) $\mathbf{m} = 2\mathbf{i} + 5\mathbf{j} + 7\mathbf{k}$ (e) $\mathbf{f} = 4\mathbf{i} + 2\mathbf{j} - 3\mathbf{k}$ (f) $\mathbf{s} = \mathbf{i} + \mathbf{j} - \mathbf{k}$

$\quad\mathbf{n} = 4\mathbf{i} + 2\mathbf{j} + 2\mathbf{k}$ $\quad\mathbf{g} = 8\mathbf{i} - 6\mathbf{j} + 3\mathbf{k}$ $\quad\mathbf{t} = \mathbf{i} - \mathbf{j} - \mathbf{k}$

2 P is the point $(-3, -4, 6)$ and Q is the point $(2, 6, -8)$.

Use the vectors $\overrightarrow{OP}$ and $\overrightarrow{OQ}$ to calculate angle POQ.

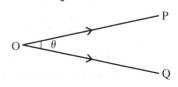

3 F is (1, −2, 5) and G is (3, 4, −1). Calculate angle FOG.

4 For the points L(2, 3, 5), M(5, −1, 6) and N(1, 5, −4)

    (a) state the components of $\overrightarrow{LM}$ and $\overrightarrow{LN}$

    (b) calculate the angle θ between $\overrightarrow{LM}$ and $\overrightarrow{LN}$.

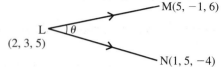

5 For the points R(2, 2, 5), S(2, −5, 7) and T(2, 3, −5) find $R\widehat{S}T$.

6 For the points A(1, 7, 13), B(1, 3, 7) and C(2, −3, 9) find $A\widehat{B}C$.

Perpendicular vectors

Given $|\mathbf{a}| \neq 0$ and $|\mathbf{b}| \neq 0$ and $\mathbf{a}.\mathbf{b} = 0$,

then $\cos\theta = \dfrac{0}{|\mathbf{a}|\,|\mathbf{b}|} = 0$

hence $\theta = 90°$.

> If $\mathbf{a}.\mathbf{b} = 0$ then $\mathbf{a}$ and $\mathbf{b}$ are perpendicular.

Example 11

$\mathbf{a} = 3\mathbf{i} + 2\mathbf{j} - \mathbf{k}$ and $\mathbf{b} = \mathbf{i} - 4\mathbf{j} - 5\mathbf{k}$. Show that $\mathbf{a}$ and $\mathbf{b}$ are perpendicular.

$$\begin{aligned}
\mathbf{a}.\mathbf{b} &= 3 \times 1 + 2 \times (-4) + (-1) \times (-5) \\
&= 3 + (-8) + 5 \\
&= 0
\end{aligned}$$

Hence $\mathbf{a}$ and $\mathbf{b}$ are perpendicular.

Exercise 13R

1 Given $\mathbf{a} = \begin{pmatrix} 2 \\ -3 \\ 5 \end{pmatrix}$ and $\mathbf{b} \begin{pmatrix} 1 \\ 4 \\ 2 \end{pmatrix}$, show that $\mathbf{a}$ and $\mathbf{b}$ are perpendicular.

2 $\mathbf{m} = \begin{pmatrix} 5 \\ 3 \\ 4 \end{pmatrix}$, $\mathbf{n} = \begin{pmatrix} -2 \\ -3 \\ 5 \end{pmatrix}$ and $\mathbf{p} = \begin{pmatrix} 6 \\ 1 \\ 3 \end{pmatrix}$. Which two vectors are perpendicular?

3 Show that the triangle with vertices L(5, 7, −5), M(4, 7, −3) and N(2, 7, −4) is right-angled at M.

4 Triangle PQR has vertices P(1, 0, 0), Q(1, 1, 1) and R(0, 1, 1). Which angle is a right angle?

5 $\mathbf{r} = -3\mathbf{i} + \mathbf{j} + 5\mathbf{k}, \mathbf{s} = 2\mathbf{i} - 4\mathbf{j} + 2\mathbf{k}$. Prove that $\mathbf{r}$ and $\mathbf{s}$ are perpendicular.

6 $\mathbf{m} = 2\mathbf{i} + 4\mathbf{j} - \mathbf{k}, \mathbf{n} = 3\mathbf{i} - 2\mathbf{j} + p\mathbf{j}$. If $\mathbf{m}$ and $\mathbf{n}$ are perpendicular, what is the value of p?

7 The vector $a\mathbf{i} + b\mathbf{j} + \mathbf{k}$ is perpendicular to both $3\mathbf{i} - 4\mathbf{j} + 6\mathbf{k}$ and $-5\mathbf{i} + 2\mathbf{k} + 4\mathbf{j}$. Find the values of a and b.

8 The vector $a\mathbf{i} + b\mathbf{j} - \mathbf{k}$ is perpendicular to both $-2\mathbf{i} + 5\mathbf{j} + 4\mathbf{k}$ and $5\mathbf{i} - 4\mathbf{j} + 7\mathbf{k}$. Find the values of a and b.

Applications

Vector geometry can be used to solve a variety of problems.

Exercise 13S

1 L is the point $(2, -2, 6)$, M is $(5, 1, 10)$ and N is $(14, 10, 22)$.
 (a) Show that L, M and N are collinear.
 (b) Find the ratio in which M divides LN.

2 PQRS is a quadrilateral with vertices $P(8, -2, 6)$, $Q(16, 6, -2)$,
 $R(0, 8, 8)$ and $S(-8, 0, 16)$.
 (a) Find the coordinates of M, the mid-point of PQ.
 (b) Find the coordinates of N, which divides RM in the ratio $2:1$.
 (c) Show that Q, N and S are collinear and find the ratio in
   which N divides QS.

3 A perspex prism is used to split light. The diagram
 shows the position of the prism with respect to axes
 Ox, Oy and Oz. LP is parallel to Oz and PQ is
 parallel to Ox. Calculate angle LMN.

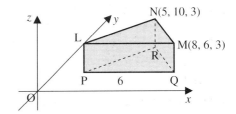

4 $\mathbf{r} = 8\mathbf{i} - \mathbf{j} + 3\mathbf{k}$ and $\mathbf{s} = 6\mathbf{i} + 4\mathbf{j} - \mathbf{k}$.

 (a) Find the components of $\mathbf{r} + \mathbf{s}$ and $\mathbf{r} - \mathbf{s}$.
 (b) Calculate the angle between $\mathbf{r} + \mathbf{s}$ and $\mathbf{r} - \mathbf{s}$.

5 The diagram shows a box kite positioned on the x, y and z axes.
 PQ is a support strut.
 (a) Write the components of $\overrightarrow{PQ}$.
 (b) Calculate $|\overrightarrow{PQ}|$.
 (c) Calculate angle OPQ.

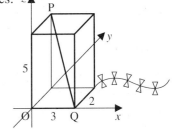

6 The rectangular frame for a satellite dish is
 positioned as shown, with support struts
 OE and OA.
 (a) Find the coordinates of E, the point of
   intersection of the diagonals.
 (b) Find the angle between OE and OA.

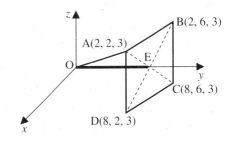

7 The diagram shows the position of an aircraft, A, and two transmitters, T_1 and T_2, relative to the control tower, C.

A(5, 9, 14)

T_2(10, 7, 10)

T_1(−3, 5, 6)

C(0, 0, 0)

Scale: 1 unit to 10 km

(a) Calculate the distance between the transmitters.
(b) Calculate angle T_1CT_2.
(c) Prove that at this moment the beams T_1A and T_2A are perpendicular.
(d) Four minutes before this the plane was at (5, 12, 18). Find the speed of the plane.

Properties of the scalar product

In the next exercise you will investigate the commutative and distributive laws for vectors.

Exercise 13T

1 (a) For vectors $\mathbf{u} = \begin{pmatrix} 2 \\ 3 \\ 4 \end{pmatrix}$ and $\mathbf{v} = \begin{pmatrix} 7 \\ 5 \\ -4 \end{pmatrix}$ calculate $\mathbf{u}.\mathbf{v}$ and $\mathbf{v}.\mathbf{u}$.

(b) Make a conjecture about $\mathbf{u}.\mathbf{v}$ and $\mathbf{v}.\mathbf{u}$ for any vectors $\mathbf{u}$ and $\mathbf{v}$.
(c) Test your conjecture.

2 For vectors $\mathbf{p} = \begin{pmatrix} 3 \\ 5 \\ 1 \end{pmatrix}$, $\mathbf{q} = \begin{pmatrix} -5 \\ 6 \\ 4 \end{pmatrix}$ and $\mathbf{r} = \begin{pmatrix} 7 \\ -2 \\ -4 \end{pmatrix}$:

(a) calculate $\mathbf{q} + \mathbf{r}$ and $\mathbf{p}.(\mathbf{q} + \mathbf{r})$
(b) calculate $\mathbf{p}.\mathbf{q} + \mathbf{p}.\mathbf{r}$ and $\mathbf{p}.\mathbf{q} + \mathbf{q}.\mathbf{r}$.
What do you notice?

From the exercise, you should notice that:

▶ For vectors $\mathbf{a}$ and $\mathbf{b}$, $\mathbf{a}.\mathbf{b} = \mathbf{b}.\mathbf{a}$

Proof
$\mathbf{a}.\mathbf{b} = a_1b_1 + a_2b_2 + a_3b_3$
$= b_1a_1 + b_2a_2 + b_3a_3$
$= \mathbf{b}.\mathbf{a}$

▶ For vectors **a**, **b** and **c**, **a**.(**b** + **c**) = **a**.**b** + **b**.**c**

Proof

$$\mathbf{a} = \begin{pmatrix} a_1 \\ a_2 \\ a_3 \end{pmatrix}, \quad \mathbf{b} + \mathbf{c} = \begin{pmatrix} b_1 + c_1 \\ b_2 + c_2 \\ b_3 + c_3 \end{pmatrix}$$

So $\quad \mathbf{a}.(\mathbf{b} + \mathbf{c}) = a_1(b_1 + c_1) + a_2(b_2 + c_2) + a_3(b_3 + c_3)$
$$= a_1 b_1 + a_1 c_1 + a_2 b_2 + a_2 c_2 + a_3 b_3 + a_3 c_3$$
$$= (a_1 b_1 + a_2 b_2 + a_3 b_3) + (a_1 c_1 + a_2 c_2 + a_3 c_3)$$
$$= \mathbf{a}.\mathbf{b} + \mathbf{a}.\mathbf{c}$$

Example 12

Calculate **p**.(**r** + **q**) when $|\mathbf{p}| = 3$, $|\mathbf{r}| = 3$ and $|\mathbf{q}| = 4$.

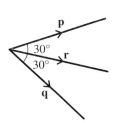

$$\mathbf{p}.(\mathbf{r} + \mathbf{q}) = \mathbf{p}.\mathbf{r} + \mathbf{p}.\mathbf{q}$$
$$= 3 \times 3 \times \cos 30° + 3 \times 4 \times \cos 60°$$
$$= \frac{9\sqrt{3}}{2} + 6$$

Exercise 13U

1 For each diagram calculate **r**.(**s** + **t**).

(a)

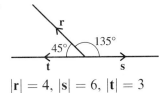

$|\mathbf{r}| = 4$, $|\mathbf{s}| = 6$, $|\mathbf{t}| = 3$

(b)

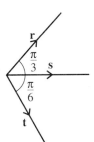

$|\mathbf{r}| = 6$, $|\mathbf{s}| = 6$, $|\mathbf{t}| = 8$

2 $\mathbf{a} = \begin{pmatrix} 2 \\ 4 \\ 3 \end{pmatrix}$, $\mathbf{b} = \begin{pmatrix} 5 \\ 3 \\ 6 \end{pmatrix}$ and $\mathbf{c} = \begin{pmatrix} 5 \\ -6 \\ -1 \end{pmatrix}$. Calculate:

(i) **a**.(**b** + **c**)   (ii) **b**.(**a** + **c**)   (iii) **c**.(**a** − **b**)

3 If **a**.(**b** + **c**) = **a**.**c**, what can you say about vectors **a** and **b**?

4 For vectors **p** and **q** calculate **q**.(**p** + **q**), when $|\mathbf{q}| = 3$ and $|\mathbf{p}| = 4$.

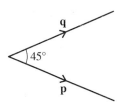

5 $\mathbf{a} = 2\mathbf{i} + 4\mathbf{j} - \mathbf{k}$, $\mathbf{b} = \mathbf{i} - \mathbf{j} + 4\mathbf{k}$ and $\mathbf{c} = 3\mathbf{i} + 2\mathbf{j} + 4\mathbf{k}$.
Evaluate **c**.(**a** + **b**).

6 $\mathbf{p} = 2\mathbf{i} + 3\mathbf{j} + 4\mathbf{k}$, $\mathbf{q} = \mathbf{i} + 3\mathbf{j} + 2\mathbf{k}$ and $\mathbf{r} = 2\mathbf{i} + \mathbf{j} + a\mathbf{k}$.
If **p**.(**q** + **r**) is 6 greater than **q**.(**p** + **r**), find the value of a.

7 In the equilateral triangle shown opposite each side is of length 5 units. Calculate $\mathbf{a}.(\mathbf{a} + \mathbf{b} + \mathbf{c})$.

8 In the isosceles triangle shown opposite $|\mathbf{a}| = 1$. Calculate $\mathbf{a}.(\mathbf{a} + \mathbf{b} + \mathbf{c})$.

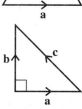

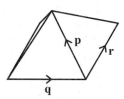

9 In the square-based pyramid shown opposite all the edges are of length 8 units. Evaluate $\mathbf{p}.(\mathbf{q} + \mathbf{r})$.

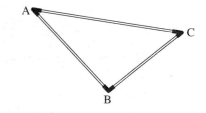

Exercise 13V   Mixed questions

1 A construction toy consists of joints and straws. Part of a construction has joints at A(5, 4, 6), B(2, 1, −3) and C(3, 3, −4).

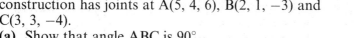

(a) Show that angle ABC is 90°.

(b) If a joint is inserted at D, which divides $\overrightarrow{AB}$ in the ratio 2 : 1, find
  (i) the coordinates of D   (ii) angle ACD.

2 An aircraft flying at a constant speed on a straight flight path takes 2 minutes to fly from A to B and 1 minute to fly from B to C. Relative to a suitable set of axes, A is the point (−1, 3, 4) and B is the point (3, 1, −2). Find the coordinates of the point C.

[Higher]

3 Relative to the top of a hill, three gliders have positions given by R(−1, −8, −2), S(2, −5, 4) and T(3, −4, 6).
Prove that R, S and T are collinear.

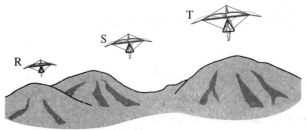

[Higher]

4 A crystal has the shape of an octahedron, as shown in the diagram. Its vertices, relative to coordinate axes, are P(2, −10, 4), Q(12, −6, 8), R(14, 2, 0), S(4, −2, −4), T(−8, 18, 20) and U(24, −26, −16). Show that the space diagonals PR and TU bisect at right angles.

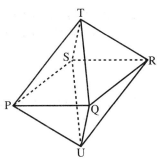

5 A crystal of potash alum is observed, through a microscope, to have the shape of an octahedron as shown in the diagram. Its vertices, relative to a suitable set of coordinate axes, are A(1, −5, 2), B(6, −3, 4), C(7, 1, 0), D(2, −1, −2), E(−4, 9, 10) and F(12, −13, −8).

Show that the space diagonals AC and EF of this crystal bisect each other at right angles.   [Higher]

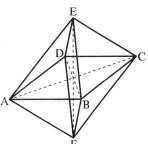

6 (a) Relative to the mutually perpendicular axes Ox, Oy and Oz, the front face of a pyramid is represented by triangle ABC, where A is the point with coordinates (9, 9, 24), B is the point (27, 3, 0), C is the point (3, 27, 0) and M is the mid-point of AC, as shown in the diagram oposite. Find the coordinates of G, which divides BM in the ratio 2 : 1.

(b) Support girders are to be erected from O to G and from O to A. Calculate the size of the angle between the girders.   [Higher]

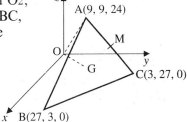

7 The diagram shows the rhombohedral crystal lattice of calcium carbonate. The three oxygen atoms P, Q and R around the carbon atom A have coordinates as shown.

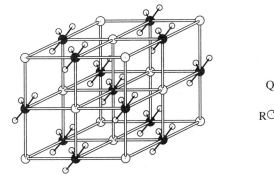

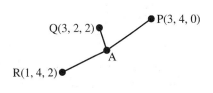

(a) Calculate the size of angle PQR.
(b) M is the mid-point of QR and T is the point which divides PM in the ratio 2 : 1.
   (i) Find the coordinates of T.
   (ii) Show that P, Q and R are equidistant from T.
(c) The coordinates of A are (2, 3, 1).
   (i) Show that P, Q and R are also equidistant from A.
   (ii) Explain why T, and not A, is the centre of the circle through P, Q and R.   [Higher]

8 In the diagram $\overrightarrow{AB}$ and $\overrightarrow{BD}$ are representatives of
vectors **u** and **v**, respectively. $AD:DC = 2:1$.
Find $\overrightarrow{BC}$ in terms of **u** and **v**.

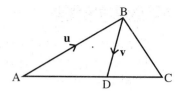

9

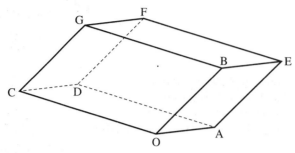

The figure OADCBEFG shown is a sketch of a parallelepiped
which is a solid with six faces, each a parallelogram, having
opposite pairs of faces congruent. Taking O as the origin,

A, B, C have position vectors $\begin{pmatrix} 1 \\ 0 \\ 0 \end{pmatrix}$, $\begin{pmatrix} 2 \\ 1 \\ 2 \end{pmatrix}$, $\begin{pmatrix} -3 \\ 2 \\ 1 \end{pmatrix}$ respectively.

(a) (i) Write down the position vectors of the points D, E and F.
    (ii) Evaluate $\overrightarrow{OF}.\overrightarrow{OD}$ and hence find the acute angle between
        the space diagonal OF and the face diagonal OD.
(b) Show that OF and CE are perpendicular.
(c) Find the position vector of the mid-point of OF and deduce
    that the space diagonals OF and CE bisect each other.

                                                 [Higher]

10 In the tetrahedron ABCD, E, F, G and H are the mid-points of
AB, AC, CD and BD, respectively. Show that EH is parallel to FG.

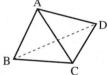

11 PQRS is a rhombus of side 4 units. K,L,M and N are the mid-
points of PQ, QR, RS and SP, respectively. $\overrightarrow{SN}$ is a
representative of vector **u** and $\overrightarrow{SM}$ a representative of vector **v**.
Show that $\overrightarrow{SK}.\overrightarrow{SL} = 5\mathbf{u}.\mathbf{v} + 16$.

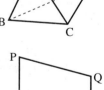

12 Two engines on a rocket exert forces represented by the vectors
$\begin{pmatrix} 6 \\ 10 \\ -3 \end{pmatrix}$ and $\begin{pmatrix} -1 \\ 8 \\ 15 \end{pmatrix}$.

(a) Find the resultant force on the rocket.
(b) The rocket must move onto a course represented by the vector $\begin{pmatrix} -1 \\ 19 \\ 4 \end{pmatrix}$.

    What force must a third engine exert to achieve this?
(c) Calculate the angle between the new course and the original one.

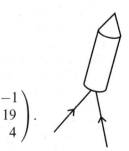

SUMMARY

① A **vector** is a quantity with both magnitude (size) and direction.

② A vector is named either using the letters at the end of the directed line segment $\overrightarrow{AB}$ or using a bold letter **u**,

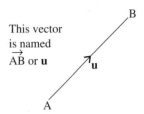

This vector is named $\overrightarrow{AB}$ or **u**

③ A vector may also be represented by its **components**:

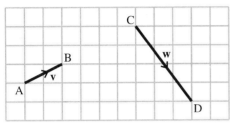

$$\overrightarrow{AB} = \mathbf{v} = \begin{pmatrix} 2 \\ 1 \end{pmatrix} \qquad \overrightarrow{CD} = \mathbf{w} = \begin{pmatrix} 3 \\ -4 \end{pmatrix}$$

These are know as **column vectors**.

④ If $\overrightarrow{PQ} = \begin{pmatrix} a \\ b \end{pmatrix}$ then $|\overrightarrow{PQ}| = \sqrt{a^2 + b^2}$

⑤ For vectors

$\mathbf{u} = \begin{pmatrix} a \\ b \end{pmatrix}$ and $\mathbf{v} = \begin{pmatrix} c \\ d \end{pmatrix}$, if $\mathbf{u} = \mathbf{v}$ then $a = c$ and $b = d$.

⑥ For vectors **u** and **v**, if $\mathbf{u} = \begin{pmatrix} a \\ b \end{pmatrix}$ and $\mathbf{v} = \begin{pmatrix} c \\ d \end{pmatrix}$ then $\mathbf{u} + \mathbf{v} = \begin{pmatrix} a+c \\ b+d \end{pmatrix}$.

⑦ $\begin{pmatrix} 0 \\ 0 \end{pmatrix}$ is called the **zero vector**, written **0**.

$\overrightarrow{BA}$ is the **negative** of $\overrightarrow{AB}$.

For any vector **u**, $\mathbf{u} + (-\mathbf{u}) = \mathbf{0}$. If $\mathbf{u} = \begin{pmatrix} a \\ b \end{pmatrix}$ then $-\mathbf{u} = \begin{pmatrix} -a \\ -b \end{pmatrix}$.

⑧ For vectors **u** and **v**, if

$\mathbf{u} = \begin{pmatrix} a \\ b \end{pmatrix}$ and $\mathbf{v} = \begin{pmatrix} c \\ d \end{pmatrix}$, then $\mathbf{u} - \mathbf{v} = \begin{pmatrix} a-c \\ b-d \end{pmatrix}$

⑨ If vector $\mathbf{v} = \begin{pmatrix} x \\ y \end{pmatrix}$ then $k\mathbf{v} = \begin{pmatrix} kx \\ ky \end{pmatrix}$ and vector k**v** is parallel to vector **v**.

Hence if $\mathbf{u} = k\mathbf{v}$ then **u** is parallel to **v**.

Conversely if **u** is parallel to **v** then $\mathbf{u} = k\mathbf{v}$.

(10) For any vector **v** there exists a parallel vector **u** of magnitude 1 unit. This is called a **unit vector**.

(11) $\overrightarrow{OA}$ is called the **position vector** of the point A relative to origin O, written **a**.

$\overrightarrow{OB}$ is called the position vector of the point B, written **b**.

(12) $\overrightarrow{AB} = \mathbf{b} - \mathbf{a}$ where **a** and **b** are the position vectors of A and B.

(13) Points are said to be **collinear** if they lie on a straight line.

If $\overrightarrow{AB} = k\overrightarrow{BC}$, where k is a scalar, then AB is parallel to BC.

If B is also a point common to both AB and BC then A, B and C are collinear.

(14) If **p** is the position vector of the point P that divides AB in the ratio $m:n$ then

$$\mathbf{p} = \frac{n}{m+n}\mathbf{a} + \frac{m}{m+n}\mathbf{b}$$

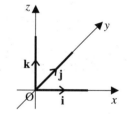

(15) A vector may also be defined in terms of **i**, **j** and **k**. where **i**, **j** and **k** are unit vectors in the x, y and z directions, respectively:

In component form these vectors are written as

$$\mathbf{i} = \begin{pmatrix} 1 \\ 0 \\ 0 \end{pmatrix}, \mathbf{j} = \begin{pmatrix} 0 \\ 1 \\ 0 \end{pmatrix} \text{ and } \mathbf{k} = \begin{pmatrix} 0 \\ 0 \\ 1 \end{pmatrix}.$$

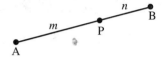

(16) For two vectors **a** and **b** the **scalar product** is defined as $\mathbf{a}.\mathbf{b} = |\mathbf{a}|\,|\mathbf{b}|\cos\theta$, where θ is the angle between **a** and **b**, $0 \leqslant \theta \leqslant 180°$.

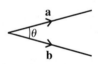

(17) If **a** and **b** are **perpendicular** then $\mathbf{a}.\mathbf{b} = 0$.

If $\mathbf{a}.\mathbf{b} = 0$ then **a** and **b** are perpendicular.

(18) If $\mathbf{a} = \begin{pmatrix} a_1 \\ a_2 \\ a_3 \end{pmatrix}$ and $\mathbf{b} = \begin{pmatrix} b_1 \\ b_2 \\ b_3 \end{pmatrix}$ then $\mathbf{a}.\mathbf{b} = a_1 b_1 + a_2 b_2 + a_3 b_3$

(19) $\cos\theta = \dfrac{a_1 b_1 + a_2 b_2 + a_3 b_3}{|\mathbf{a}|\,|\mathbf{b}|}$ or $\cos\theta = \dfrac{\mathbf{a}.\mathbf{b}}{|\mathbf{a}|\,|\mathbf{b}|}$

(20) For vectors **a** and **b**, $\mathbf{a}.\mathbf{b} = \mathbf{b}.\mathbf{a}$

(21) For vectors **a**, **b** and **c**, $\mathbf{a}.(\mathbf{b} + \mathbf{c}) = \mathbf{a}.\mathbf{b} + \mathbf{b}.\mathbf{c}$

14 Further calculus

Differentiation and integration have so far been confined to simple algebraic functions. We will now extend our study to functions involving trigonometric and complex algebraic expressions.

Differentiation of sin x and cos x

The exercise will help you find out what happens when $\sin x$ and $\cos x$ are differentiated.

Exercise 14A

1 The diagram shows part of the graph of $y = \sin x$.

(a) Tangents have been drawn at
$x = 0, \dfrac{\pi}{2}, \pi, \dfrac{3\pi}{2}$ and 2π.

Find the gradients of the tangents at these points.

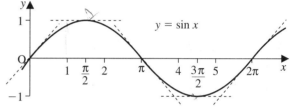

(b) Draw axes with the same scales as those on the diagram.

   (i) Plot the values of the gradient of $y = \sin x$ at $x = 0, \dfrac{\pi}{2}, \pi,$
$\dfrac{3\pi}{2}$ and 2π.

   (ii) Join up the points with a **smooth** curve.

(c) Make a conjecture about the derivative of $\sin x$.

2 Repeat question 1 using the graph of $y = \cos x$ shown opposite.

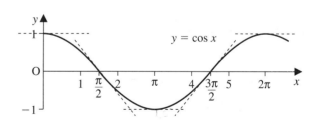

From questions 1 and 2 you should see that:

If $y = \sin x$, $\dfrac{dy}{dx} = \cos x$

If $y = \cos x$, $\dfrac{dy}{dx} = -\sin x$

or

$$\frac{d}{dx}(\sin x) = \cos x \qquad \frac{d}{dx}(\cos x) = -\sin x$$

Note: For these results to be true x must be measured in **radians**.

Example 1
Find $f'(x)$ when $f(x) = 2\sin x$.

If $f(x) = 2\sin x$
$\quad f'(x) = 2\cos x$

Example 2
Find $\dfrac{d}{dx}(3\sin x - 5\cos x)$.

$$\dfrac{d}{dx}(3\sin x - 5\cos x) = 3\cos x - 5(-\sin x)$$
$$= 3\cos x + 5\sin x$$

Exercise 14B

✓**1** Find $f'(x)$ when
(**a**) $f(x) = 4\cos x$ (**b**) $f(x) = -2\sin x$
(**c**) $f(x) = 8\cos x$ (**d**) $f(x) = 2\sin x + \cos x$
(**e**) $f(x) = 6\cos x + 5\sin x$ (**f**) $f(x) = 7\cos x - \sin x$
(**g**) $f(x) = 9\sin x + x^4$ (**h**) $f(x) = 5\cos x - 3x^2$
(**i**) $f(x) = 3\cos x - 10\sin x + 3\sqrt{x}$ (**j**) $f(x) = 2\sin x - 6\cos x + \sqrt[3]{x^2}$

✓ **2** Find
(**a**) $\dfrac{d}{dr}(6\sin r)$ (**b**) $\dfrac{d}{dt}(-3\sin t + 5\cos t)$ (**c**) $\dfrac{d}{d\theta}\left(\cos\theta + 7\sin\theta + \dfrac{3}{\theta^4}\right)$

✓ **3** Find the gradient of the graph of the function
$f(x) = \cos x - \sin x$ at
(**a**) $x = 0$ (**b**) $x = \dfrac{\pi}{4}$ (**c**) $x = \dfrac{\pi}{2}$ (**d**) $x = \dfrac{3\pi}{2}$

4 Use differentiation to show that
(**a**) $y = \sin x$ has a maximum turning point at $\left(\dfrac{\pi}{2}, 1\right)$ and a
minimum turning point at $\left(\dfrac{3\pi}{2}, -1\right)$.

(**b**) $y = \cos x$ has a maximum turning point at $(0, 1)$ and a
minimum turning point at $(\pi, -1)$.

5 Find the equation of the tangent to
(**a**) $y = \sin x$ at the point where $x = \dfrac{\pi}{3}$.

(**b**) $y = 3\cos x$ at the point where $x = \dfrac{\pi}{6}$.

6 For the curve $y = \sin x - \cos x$ $(0 \leqslant x \leqslant 2\pi)$
(**a**) find the y-intercept (**b**) find the zeros
(**c**) find the turning points and their nature (**d**) sketch the curve.

Integration of sin x and cos x

Integration is the reverse process to differentiation, therefore

$$\blacktriangleright \quad \int \cos x \, dx = \sin x + C \qquad \int \sin x \, dx = -\cos x + C$$

Note: For these results to be true x must be measured in **radians**.

Example 3

Find $\int (2 \sin x - \cos x) \, dx$.

$$\int (2 \sin x - \cos x) \, dx$$
$$= -2 \cos x - \sin x + C$$

Example 4

Evaluate $\int_0^{\frac{\pi}{4}} (4 \cos x + \sqrt{2} \sin x) \, dx$.

$$\int_0^{\frac{\pi}{4}} (4 \cos x + \sqrt{2} \sin x) \, dx = \left[4 \sin x - \sqrt{2} \cos x \right]_0^{\frac{\pi}{4}}$$

$$= \left(4 \sin \frac{\pi}{4} - \sqrt{2} \cos \frac{\pi}{4} \right) - (4 \sin 0 - \sqrt{2} \cos 0)$$

$$= \left(\frac{4}{\sqrt{2}} - \frac{\sqrt{2}}{\sqrt{2}} \right) - (0 - \sqrt{2})$$

$$= \frac{4}{\sqrt{2}} - 1 + \sqrt{2}$$

$$= 3\sqrt{2} - 1$$

Exercise 14C

1 Find

(a) $\int 6 \cos x \, dx$

(b) $\int 2 \sin x \, dx$

(c) $\int -3 \sin x \, dx$

(d) $\int (4 \cos \theta + 9 \sin \theta) \, d\theta$

(e) $\int (\cos z - 3 \sin z) \, dz$

(f) $\int (7 \sin t - 12 \cos t) \, dt$

(g) $\int (x^5 + 2 \cos x) \, dx$

(h) $\int (\sqrt{t^3} - \sin t) \, dt$

(i) $\int \left(3 \sin q - 10 \cos q - \frac{5}{q^7} \right) \, dq$

2 Evaluate

(a) $\displaystyle\int_0^{\frac{\pi}{2}} 6\cos x \, dx$

(b) $\displaystyle\int_0^{\frac{\pi}{2}} 2\sin x \, dx$

(c) $\displaystyle\int_{\frac{\pi}{4}}^{\pi} 3\cos\theta \, d\theta$

(d) $\displaystyle\int_0^{\frac{\pi}{4}} (\sin r + 2\cos r) \, dr$

(e) $\displaystyle\int_{\frac{\pi}{3}}^{\frac{\pi}{2}} (4\cos t - 3\sin t) \, dt$

(f) $\displaystyle\int_0^{2\pi} (5\sin\phi + 8\cos\phi) \, d\phi$

(g) $\displaystyle\int_0^{\frac{\pi}{4}} (1 + 2\cos x) \, dx$

(h) $\displaystyle\int_0^{\frac{\pi}{6}} \left(u + \frac{u^2}{2} - \sin u \right) du$

(i) $\displaystyle\int_{-\frac{\pi}{4}}^{\frac{\pi}{4}} (6t + 3\sin t - 3\cos t) \, dt$

3 (a) Find
(i) $\displaystyle\int_0^{\pi} \sin x \, dx$
(ii) $\displaystyle\int_{\pi}^{2\pi} \sin x \, dx$
(iii) $\displaystyle\int_0^{2\pi} \sin x \, dx$

(b) Find the area between the curve $y = \sin x$ and the x-axis from $x = 0$ to $x = 2\pi$.

4 Find the area between the curve $y = \cos x$ and the x-axis from $x = 0$ to $x = \pi$.

5 Calculate the area under the curve

(a) $y = 5\cos x - \sin x$ between $x = 0$ and $x = \dfrac{\pi}{4}$.

(b) $y = 9\sin x + 4\cos x$ between $x = \dfrac{\pi}{2}$ and $x = \dfrac{5\pi}{6}$.

6 Calculate the shaded areas

(a)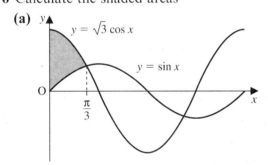

(b)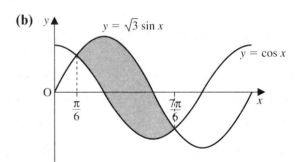

7 A particle is moving in a straight line so that its speed, v m/s, at time t seconds is given by the function $v(t) = t + \sqrt{2}\sin t$.
(a) Find the particle's speed when
　　(i) $t = 0$ seconds　**(ii)** $t = \pi$ seconds　**(iii)** $t = 2\pi$ seconds
(b) **(i)** Find the particle's acceleration at time t.
　　(ii) Find the times when the acceleration is 0, for $0 \leqslant t \leqslant 2\pi$.
　　(iii) Sketch the graph of $v(t)$ for $0 \leqslant t \leqslant 2\pi$.
(c) The particle is at the origin at time $t = 0$.
　　(i) Calculate the function, $s(t)$, representing its distance, s, from the origin at time t.
　　(ii) Calculate the particle's distance from the origin at $t = \dfrac{\pi}{2}$, π and 2π seconds.

Derivative of $(x + a)^n$

We can find the derivative of expressions of the form $(x + a)^n$ by expanding the function and differentiating individual terms.

Example 5

If $y = (x + 4)^3$ find $\dfrac{dy}{dx}$. Factorise your answer fully.

$$y = (x + 4)^3 = (x + 4)(x + 4)^2$$
$$= (x + 4)(x^2 + 8x + 16)$$
$$= x^3 + 8x^2 + 16x + 4x^2 + 32x + 64$$
$$= x^3 + 12x^2 + 48x + 64$$
$$\frac{dy}{dx} = 3x^2 + 24x + 48$$
$$= 3(x^2 + 8x + 16) = 3(x + 4)^2$$

Using the method in Example 5 for the following questions, try to find the general formula for the derivative of $(x + a)^n$.

Exercise 14D

1 Use the method in Example 5 to find $\dfrac{dy}{dx}$ when:

   (a) $y = (x + 2)^2$ **(b)** $y = (x - 5)^2$ **(c)** $y = (x + 1)^3$ **(d)** $y = (x + 2)^3$

2 Make a conjecture about the derivative of $(x + a)^n$.

From questions 1 and 2 you should notice that:

$$\frac{d}{dx}(x + a)^n = n(x + a)^{n-1} \ (n \in \mathbf{Q}, a \in \mathbf{R})$$

Example 6

Find $\dfrac{d}{dx}(x + 5)^8$.

$$\frac{d}{dx}(x + 5)^8 = 8(x + 5)^7$$

Example 7

Differentiate $\dfrac{1}{(x - 5)^2}$.

$$y = \frac{1}{(x - 5)^2} = (x - 5)^{-2}$$
$$\frac{dy}{dx} = -2(x - 5)^{-3} = \frac{-2}{(x - 5)^3}$$

Exercise 14E

1 Differentiate
   (a) $(x + 4)^9$ **(b)** $(x - 3)^3$ **(c)** $(x + 5)^{-2}$

   (d) $\sqrt{x - 3}$ **(e)** $\dfrac{1}{x + 4}$ **(f)** $\sqrt[4]{(x + 3)^3}$

2 Find

(a) $\dfrac{d}{dx}((x+1)^2 + \sin x)$ (b) $\dfrac{d}{dx}(\sqrt{x-4} - \cos x)$ (c) $\dfrac{d}{dt}\left(\sin t + \dfrac{1}{t+8}\right)$

Derivative of $(ax + b)^n$

Now that we have formulated a rule for differentiating $(x + a)^n$ we can obtain another rule for differentiating $(ax + b)^n$.

Example 8

If $y = (2x - 3)^3$ find $\dfrac{dy}{dx}$.

$$y = (2x - 3)^3$$

Expanding brackets $\quad = (2x - 3)(4x^2 - 12x + 9)$

$$= 8x^3 - 24x^2 + 18x - 12x^2 + 36x - 27$$

$$= 8x^3 - 36x^2 + 54x - 27$$

Differentiating $\quad \dfrac{dy}{dx} = 24x^2 - 72x + 54$

Factorising $\quad\quad\quad = 6(4x^2 - 12x + 9) = 6(2x - 3)^2$

Rearranging $\quad\quad\quad = 3(2x - 3)^2 \times 2$

Using the same method try exercise 14F and see if you can find the rule.

Exercise 14F

1 Find $\dfrac{dy}{dx}$ when:

(a) $y = (3x + 5)^2$ (b) $y = (7x + 1)^2$ (c) $y = (2x - 1)^3$ (d) $y = (3x + 5)^3$

2 Make a conjecture about the derivative of $(ax + b)^n$.

From questions 1 and 2 you should see that:

$$\blacktriangleright \quad \dfrac{d}{dx}(ax + b)^n = an(ax + b)^{n-1} \ (n \in \mathbf{Q}, a \in \mathbf{R})$$

Example 9

Differentiate $y = (5x - 7)^4$.

$$y = (5x - 7)^4$$

$$\dfrac{dy}{dx} = 5 \times 4(5x - 7)^3$$

$$= 20(5x - 7)^3$$

Example 10

Differentiate $f(x) = \dfrac{1}{\sqrt{2x + 3}}$.

$$f(x) = \dfrac{1}{\sqrt{2x + 3}} = (2x + 3)^{-\frac{1}{2}}$$

$$f'(x) = 2 \times \left(-\dfrac{1}{2}\right)(2x + 3)^{-\frac{3}{2}}$$

$$= -\dfrac{1}{(2x + 3)^{\frac{3}{2}}}$$

$$= -\dfrac{1}{\sqrt{(2x + 3)^3}}$$

Exercise 14G

1 Differentiate

(a) $y = (4x + 3)^5$

(b) $y = (6x - 1)^8$

(c) $y = (x - 9)^{-3}$

(d) $y = (4 - 6x)^{\frac{3}{4}}$

(e) $y = \sqrt{2x + 5}$

(f) $y = \dfrac{1}{5x - 4}$

(g) $f(x) = (5x - 3)^6$

(h) $f(x) = (7x + 1)^4$

(i) $f(x) = (0.5x + 8)^{10}$

(j) $f(x) = \sqrt{6x + 2}$

(k) $f(x) = \dfrac{1}{(6x - 1)^4}$

(l) $f(x) = \dfrac{1}{\sqrt[5]{(10x + 1)^4}}$

The chain rule

The formula $\dfrac{d}{dx}(ax + b)^n = an(ax + b)^{n-1}$ can be described using functional notation or Leibniz notation.

Using functional notation

Let $h(x) = (ax + b)^n = g(f(x))$ where $f(x) = ax + b$ and $g(x) = x^n$.

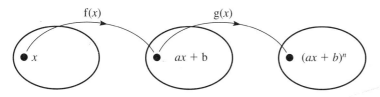

$$f'(x) = a$$
$$g'(x) = nx^{n-1}$$
$$g'(ax + b) = n(ax + b)^{n-1}$$

Since $\quad f(x) = ax + b,\ g'(f(x)) = n(ax + b)^{n-1}$
$$h(x) = (ax + b)^n$$
therefore $\quad h'(x) = an(ax + b)^{n-1}$
$$h'(x) = f'(x) \times g'(f(x))$$

Using Leibniz notation

Let $y = (ax + b)^n$ and $u = ax + b$.

$$y = u^n$$

$$\frac{du}{dx} = a$$

$$\frac{dy}{du} = nu^{n-1} = n(ax + b)^{n-1}$$

$$\frac{dy}{dx} = an(ax + b)^{n-1}$$

hence $\quad \dfrac{dy}{dx} = \dfrac{dy}{du} \times \dfrac{du}{dx}$

These formulae are referred to as the **chain rule**.

> $h'(x) = g'(f(x)) \times f'(x)$ or $\dfrac{dy}{dx} = \dfrac{dy}{du} \times \dfrac{du}{dx}$ is called the **chain rule**.

Example 11

Find $h'(x)$ if $h(x) = \cos\left(2x + \dfrac{\pi}{4}\right)$.

$h(x) = g(f(x))$ where $f(x) = 2x + \dfrac{\pi}{4}$ and $g(x) = \cos x$

$f'(x) = 2$ and $g'(x) = -\sin x$

$h'(x) = g'(f(x)) \times f'(x)$

$$= -\sin\left(2x + \dfrac{\pi}{4}\right) \times 2$$

$$= -2\sin\left(2x + \dfrac{\pi}{4}\right)$$

Example 12

Differentiate $\sqrt{x^2 + 3x}$.

$$y = \sqrt{x^2 + 3x} = (x^2 + 3x)^{\frac{1}{2}}$$

Let $u = x^2 + 3x$ then $y = u^{\frac{1}{2}}$

$$\frac{du}{dx} = 2x + 3 \text{ and } \frac{dy}{du} = \frac{1}{2}u^{-\frac{1}{2}}$$

$$\frac{dy}{dx} = \frac{dy}{du} \times \frac{du}{dx}$$

$$= \frac{1}{2}u^{-\frac{1}{2}} \times (2x + 3)$$

$$= \frac{2x + 3}{2\sqrt{x^2 + 3x}}$$

Example 13

Find the derivative of $\sin^3 x$.

Let $u = \sin x$ then $y = u^3$.

$$\frac{du}{dx} = \cos x \qquad \frac{dy}{du} = 3u^2$$

$$\frac{dy}{dx} = \frac{dy}{du} \times \frac{du}{dx}$$

$$= 3u^2 \times \cos x$$

$$= 3\sin^2 x \cos x$$

Exercise 14H

1 Differentiate
(a) $y = (x^9 + 8x)^3$

(b) $y = (x^3 - 1)^5$

(c) $y = (3 + 2x - x^2)^3$

(d) $h(x) = (2 - 3x)^7$

(e) $h(x) = (2x + 7)^{-\frac{5}{2}}$

(f) $h(x) = \dfrac{4}{\sqrt{4 - 7x}}$

2 Differentiate
(a) $h(x) = \sin(5x + 2)$

(b) $h(x) = \cos(3x - 1)$

(c) $h(x) = \cos(1 - 6x)$

3 Find the derivative of
(a) $\cos^2 x$

(b) $\sin^5 x$

(c) $\dfrac{1}{\cos^2 x}$

4 Differentiate
(a) $2 \sin x$
(b) $\sin 2x$
(c) $\sin^2 x$
(d) $\sin x^2$
(e) $\cos \sqrt{x}$
(f) $\sqrt{\cos x}$

5 Differentiate
(a) $(x^2 - 5)^6$

(b) $\sqrt{(x^2 - 3x + 5)^3}$

(c) $\sin^2(4 - 3\theta)$

(d) $\dfrac{3}{(6r - r^4)^3}$

(e) $\cos\left(\dfrac{2}{t}\right)$

(f) $\cos(\sin \phi)$

Applications

The chain rule allows us to investigate applications involving composite functions.

Example 14
Find the equation of the tangent to the graph of $y = \sqrt{x^2 + 5}$ at the point where $x = 2$.

To find the equation of the tangent we need to determine its gradient and the coordinates of a point on it.

When $x = 2$, $y = \sqrt{2^2 + 5} = 3$, therefore the tangent passes through the point $(2, 3)$.

The gradient of the tangent is given by $f'(2)$
$f(x) = (x^2 + 5)^{\frac{1}{2}}$

$f'(x) = \dfrac{1}{2}(x^2 + 5)^{-\frac{1}{2}} \times 2x = \dfrac{x}{\sqrt{x^2 + 5}}$

$f'(2) = \dfrac{2}{\sqrt{9}} = \dfrac{2}{3}$

The equation of the tangent at $x = 2$ is $y - b = m(x - a)$:

$$y - 3 = \frac{2}{3}(x - 2)$$

$$3y - 9 = 2x - 4$$

$$3y = 2x + 5 \text{ or } 2x - 3y + 5 = 0$$

Exercise 14I

1 Find the equation of the tangent to the graph of $y = \dfrac{2}{x-2}$ at the point where $x = 1$.

2 What are the coordinates of the point(s) on the graph of $y = \dfrac{-4}{x+1}$ where the tangent is parallel to $y = x$?

3 Find the coordinates of the stationary points on
    (a) $f(x) = \cos 2x - \cos x$ $(0 \leqslant x \leqslant 2\pi)$ **(b)** $f(x) = 2 \sin x + \sin 2x$ $(0 \leqslant x \leqslant 2\pi)$

4 (a) Show that the graph of $y = \cos x - x$ is never increasing.
   (b) Determine the coordinates of all stationary points in the interval $0 \leqslant x \leqslant 2\pi$.

5 A particle is moving so that its distance, s metres, from the origin at time t seconds is given by $s = \sin\left(2t - \dfrac{\pi}{4}\right)$.

    (a)   (i) Find an expression for the velocity of the particle.
        (ii) What is the velocity of the particle at $t = 0$?
       (iii) At what times $(0 \leqslant t \leqslant 2\pi)$ is the particle stationary?
    (b)   (i) Find an expression for the particle's acceleration.
       (ii) At what times $(0 \leqslant t \leqslant 2\pi)$ is the acceleration a maximum?

6 $P(x, y)$ is any point on the graph of $y = \dfrac{1}{x}$ and s is the length of OP.

    (a) Show that $s = \sqrt{x^2 + \dfrac{1}{x^2}}$.

    (b) Find the coordinates of the points on the graph of $y = \dfrac{1}{x}$ which are closest to the origin.

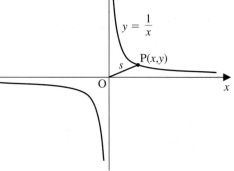

7 (a) Show that if $y = x + \sin^2 x$ then $\dfrac{dy}{dx} = 1 + \sin 2x$.

   (b) Find the position of the stationary points of $y = x + \sin^2 x$ for $0 \leqslant x \leqslant 2\pi$.

   (c) Sketch the graph of $y = x + \sin^2 x$ for $0 \leqslant x \leqslant 2\pi$.

Integrating $(ax + b)^n$

In the preceding section we have shown that:

$$\frac{d}{dx}(ax + b)^n = an(ax + b)^{n-1}$$

Since the term $(ax + b)$ features in both expressions we can assume that the integral of $(ax + b)^n$ will contain the expression $(ax + b)^{n+1}$. Consequently, when integrating such expressions we study the derivative first.

Example 15

Find $\int (x+2)^3\, dx$.

$$\frac{d}{dx}(x+2)^4 = 4(x+2)^3$$

$4(x+2)^3$ is four times greater than the integral sought so

$$\int (x+2)^3\, dx = \frac{(x+2)^4}{4} + C$$

Example 16

Find $\int (2x+3)^4\, dx$.

$$\frac{d}{dx}(2x+3)^5\, dx = 5(2x+3)^4 \times 2$$

$10(2x+3)^4$ is ten times greater than the integral sought so

$$\int (2x+3)^4\, dx = \frac{(2x+3)^5}{2 \times 5} + C$$

$$= \frac{(2x+3)^5}{10} + C$$

Example 17

Find $\int (3x-7)^8\, dx$.

Since $\dfrac{d}{dx}(3x-7)^9 = 27(3x-7)^8$

then $\int (3x-7)^8\, dx = \dfrac{(3x-7)^9}{27} + C$

Example 18

Find $\int_0^4 \sqrt{2x+1}\, dx$.

Since $\dfrac{d}{dx}(2x+1)^{\frac{3}{2}} = 3(2x+1)^{\frac{1}{2}}$

then $\displaystyle\int_0^4 (2x+1)^{\frac{1}{2}}\, dx = \left[\frac{(2x+1)^{\frac{3}{2}}}{3}\right]_0^4$

$$= \frac{9^{\frac{3}{2}}}{3} - \frac{1^{\frac{3}{2}}}{3}$$

$$= 9 - \tfrac{1}{3}$$

$$= 8\tfrac{2}{3}$$

These examples lead to the general formula:

$$\int (ax + b)^n \, dx = \frac{(ax + b)^{n+1}}{a(n + 1)} + C, \quad n \neq -1$$

Exercise 14J

1 Find

(a) $\displaystyle\int (x + 3)^3 \, dx$

(b) $\displaystyle\int (x - 3)^2 \, dx$

(c) $\displaystyle\int (x + 5)^{-3} \, dx$

(d) $\displaystyle\int \sqrt{x - 10} \, dx$

(e) $\displaystyle\int \frac{dt}{(t + 9)^2}$

(f) $\displaystyle\int \frac{dq}{\sqrt{q - 7}}$

2 (a) Find   (i) $\displaystyle\int (2x + 5)^5 \, dx$ (ii) $\displaystyle\int (3x - 8)^2 \, dx$ (iii) $\displaystyle\int (4x - 7)^9 \, dx$

(b) Check your answers by differentiating.

3 Integrate

(a) $(x + 3)^{-2}$

(b) $(2x + 3)^{-3}$

(c) $(1 - 2x)^{\frac{1}{2}}$

(d) $\dfrac{1}{(3x - 1)^2}$

(e) $\dfrac{1}{\sqrt{1 + 2x}}$

(f) $\dfrac{1}{\sqrt[3]{2x - 5}}$

4 Evaluate

(a) $\displaystyle\int_1^2 (3x - 1)^2 \, dx$

(b) $\displaystyle\int_{-1}^1 (6x + 1)^3 \, dx$

(c) $\displaystyle\int_1^2 (2t + 5)^4 \, dt$

5 Calculate the shaded area in the graph.

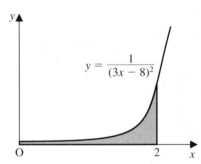

$$y = \frac{1}{(3x - 8)^2}$$

6 Calculate the area between the graph of $y = (2x - 1)^2$, the x-axis and the lines $x = 0$ and $x = \frac{1}{2}$.

7 Calculate the area between the graph of $y = (3 - 2x)^3$, the x-axis and the lines $x = 0$ and $x = 1$.

8 An experimental aeroplane wing has a profile formed by the graphs of the functions $y = \sqrt{2x + 1}$ and $y = \frac{1}{3}x^2 - \frac{1}{2}x - \frac{1}{3}$ between $x = -\frac{1}{2}$ and $x = 4$.
Calculate the cross-sectional area of the wing.

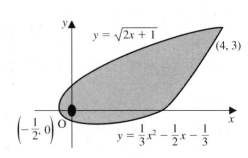

Integrating sin(ax + b) and cos(ax + b)

We already know that when $f(x) = \sin(ax + b)$, $f'(x) = a\cos(ax + b)$.
Since integration is the reverse of differentiation it follows that:

$$\int \cos(ax + b)\, dx = \frac{1}{a}\sin(ax + b) + C$$

$$\int \sin(ax + b)\, dx = -\frac{1}{a}\cos(ax + b) + C$$

Example 19

Find $\int \cos\left(3x + \frac{\pi}{4}\right) dx$.

$$\int \cos\left(3x + \frac{\pi}{4}\right) dx = \frac{1}{3}\sin\left(3x + \frac{\pi}{4}\right)$$

Example 20

Find the area enclosed by the graph of $y = \sin\left(4x + \frac{\pi}{6}\right)$, the x-axis and the lines $x = 0$ and $x = \frac{\pi}{8}$.

$$\text{Area} = \int_0^{\frac{\pi}{8}} \sin\left(4x + \frac{\pi}{6}\right) dx$$

$$= \left[-\frac{1}{4}\cos\left(4x + \frac{\pi}{6}\right) \right]_0^{\frac{\pi}{8}}$$

$$= \left(-\frac{1}{4}\cos\frac{2\pi}{3} \right) - \left(-\frac{1}{4}\cos\frac{\pi}{6} \right)$$

$$= \frac{1}{8} + \frac{\sqrt{3}}{8}$$

$$= \frac{1 + \sqrt{3}}{8}$$

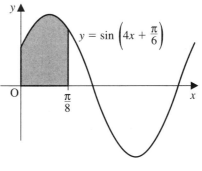

Exercise 14K

1 Find

(a) $\int \sin(3x - 4)\, dx$

(b) $\int \cos 6x\, dx$

(c) $\int \cos(5x + 1)\, dx$

(d) $\int \sin 2x\, dx$

(e) $\int 3\cos\frac{1}{2}x\, dx$

(f) $\int (x + \cos 3x)\, dx$

(g) $\int \sin(2 - 3t)\, dt$

(h) $\int 2\cos(1 - 4s)\, ds$

(i) $\int ((5z + 2)^4 - 2\sin 3z)\, dz$

2 Evaluate

(a) $\int_0^{\frac{\pi}{3}} \cos 2x\, dx$

(b) $\int_0^{\frac{\pi}{4}} \sin t\, dt$

(c) $\int_0^{\frac{\pi}{2}} \sin\left(3t + \frac{\pi}{4}\right) dt$

3 (a) Evaluate $\displaystyle\int_0^{\frac{\pi}{2}} \cos 2x \, dx$.

(b) Find the area enclosed by the graph of $y = \sin 2x$, the x-axis and the lines $x = 0$ and $x = 2\pi$.

4 Calculate the area between the x-axis and the graph of

(a) $y = \cos 3x$ between $x = 0$ and $x = \dfrac{\pi}{6}$.

(b) $y = 3\sin 4x$ between $x = \pi$ and $x = \dfrac{5\pi}{4}$.

5 Calculate the area between the graph of $y = x + \sin 2x$, the x-axis and the lines $x = 0$ and $x = \dfrac{\pi}{2}$.

6 Calculate the shaded area in the diagram opposite.

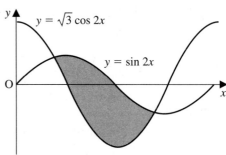

$y = \sqrt{3}\cos 2x$

$y = \sin 2x$

7 (a) Use the identity $\cos 2A = 2\cos^2 A - 1$ to express $\cos^2 x$ in terms of $\cos 2x$. Hence evaluate $\displaystyle\int_0^{\frac{\pi}{2}} \cos^2 x \, dx$.

(b) Express $\sin^2 x$ in terms of $\cos 2x$. Hence evaluate $\displaystyle\int_{\frac{\pi}{6}}^{\frac{\pi}{2}} \sin^2 x \, dx$.

8 Use double-angle formulae to find

(a) $\displaystyle\int (\cos^2 2x - \sin^2 2x) \, dx$ **(b)** $\displaystyle\int \sin 3x \cos 3x \, dx$ **(c)** $\displaystyle\int (1 - \sin^2 4x) \, dx$

Exercise 14L   Mixed questions

1 Differentiate
   (a) $f(x) = 8\sin x$ **(b)** $g(t) = -3\cos t$ **(c)** $f(\theta) = 2\sin\theta + 6\cos\theta$

2 Integrate
   (a) $\displaystyle\int 6\cos x \, dx$ **(b)** $\displaystyle\int 12\sin x \, dx$ **(c)** $\displaystyle\int (5\sin x - 3\cos x) \, dx$

3 Differentiate
   (a) $f(x) = (2x - 7)^{10}$ **(b)** $r(t) = 5\sin 3t$ **(c)** $j(\phi) = \cos 4\phi + 5(2 - 9\phi)^8$

   (d) $u(t) = \sqrt{(6t + 10)^5}$ **(e)** $f(z) = \dfrac{3}{(9z + 4)^2}$ **(f)** $a(v) = \cos(v^2 - 2v)$

   (g) $h(t) = \cos^2 t$ **(h)** $y(x) = 4\sin^5 x - \dfrac{1}{x}$ **(i)** $v(s) = \sqrt{1 - 4s^2} + 3\sin^2 s$

4 Integrate

(a) $\displaystyle \int (6x + 1)^{11}\, dx$

(b) $\displaystyle \int \frac{2\,dt}{(5t - 7)^4}$

(c) $\displaystyle \int (\sin 5t + \cos(-2t))\, dt$

5 Evaluate

(a) $\displaystyle \int_0^1 (4x - 2)^3\, dx$

(b) $\displaystyle \int_0^{\frac{1}{3}} \frac{5\, dx}{(3x + 1)^4}$

(c) $\displaystyle \int_{\frac{\pi}{4}}^{\frac{\pi}{2}} 3 \cos\left(\frac{\pi}{2} - 2x\right) dx$

6 Find the coordinates of the stationary points on the graph of $y = 3 \sin^2 x$ ($0 \leqslant x \leqslant 2\pi$). Hence sketch the graph.

7 Find the equation of the tangent to the curve

(a) $y = \dfrac{1}{2x - 1}$ where $x = 3$

(b) $y = \sin 3\theta$ where $\theta = \dfrac{\pi}{6}$

8 Find the value of $\displaystyle \int_0^{\frac{\pi}{4}} \sin^2 P\, dP$.

9 If $y = 6 \sin x + \sqrt{2} \cos x$ show that $\dfrac{d^2 y}{dx^2} = -y$.

10 Find the value of θ, where $0 < \theta < \dfrac{\pi}{2}$, for which $3 \sin\left(2\theta - \dfrac{\pi}{3}\right)$

has its maximum value.

11 Find, in its simplest form, the **exact** value of $\displaystyle \int_0^1 \sqrt{6 - 2x}\, dx$.

12 (a) Find $\displaystyle \int_0^{\frac{\pi}{2}} \cos 4x\, dx$.

(b) Explain your answer with the help of a sketch.

13 (a) By writing $\cos 3x$ as $\cos(2x + x)$ show that
$\cos 3x = 4 \cos^3 x - 3 \cos x$.

(b) Hence find $\displaystyle \int \cos^3 x\, dx$.

14 An oil production platform, $9\sqrt{3}$ km offshore, is to be connected by a pipeline to a refinery on shore, 100 km down the coast from the platform, as shown in the diagram.

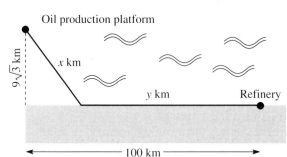

The length of the underwater pipeline is x km and the length of the pipeline on land is y km. It costs £2 million to lay each kilometre of pipeline underwater and £1 million to lay each kilometre of pipeline on land.

(a) Show that the total cost of this pipeline is £$C(x)$ million where $C(x) = 2x + 100 - (x^2 - 243)^{\frac{1}{2}}$.

(b) Show that $x = 18$ gives a minimum cost for this pipeline. Find this minimum cost and the corresponding total length of the pipeline. [Higher]

15 The mean value of a function f between $x = a$ and $x = b$ is given by:

$$\frac{1}{b - a} \int_a^b f(x)\, dx.$$

(a) Use the formula above to show that the mean value of

$f(x) = \sin x$ between $x = 0$ and $x = \pi$ is $\dfrac{2}{\pi}$.

(b) The current, I amperes, flowing in an electric circuit varies over time, t seconds (measured from switch-on), according to the relationship $I(t) = 2 \sin 600t$.

Calculate the mean value of the current flowing in this electric circuit over the first $\frac{1}{300}$th of a second after switch-on. (Answer to two significant figures.) [Higher]

16 An artist has been asked to design a window made from pieces of coloured glass of different shapes. To preserve a balance of colour, each shape must have the **same** area. Three of the shapes used are drawn below.

A   B   C

Relative to the x and y axes the shapes are positioned as shown below. The artist drew the curves accurately by using the equation(s) shown in each diagram.

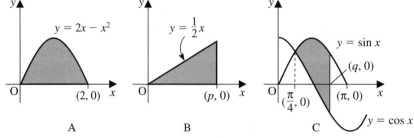

A   B   C

(a) Find the area shaded under $y = 2x - x^2$.

(b) Use the area found in part (a) to find the value of p.

(c) Prove that q satisfies the equation $\cos q + \sin q = 0.081$ and hence find the value of q to two significant figures.

SUMMARY

① $\dfrac{\mathrm{d}}{\mathrm{d}x}(\sin x) = \cos x$

$\dfrac{\mathrm{d}}{\mathrm{d}x}(\cos x) = -\sin x$

② $\displaystyle\int \cos x \, \mathrm{d}x = \sin x + C$

$\displaystyle\int \sin x \, \mathrm{d}x = -\cos x + C$

③ $\dfrac{\mathrm{d}}{\mathrm{d}x}(x + a)^n = n(x + a)^{n-1}$ $(n \in \mathbf{Q}, a \in \mathbf{R})$

④ $\dfrac{\mathrm{d}}{\mathrm{d}x}(ax + b)^n = an(ax + b)^{n-1}$ $(n \in \mathbf{Q}, a \in \mathbf{R})$

⑤ $\mathrm{h}'(x) = \mathrm{g}'(\mathrm{f}(x)) \times \mathrm{f}'(x)$ or $\dfrac{\mathrm{d}y}{\mathrm{d}x} = \dfrac{\mathrm{d}y}{\mathrm{d}u} \times \dfrac{\mathrm{d}u}{\mathrm{d}x}$ is called the **chain rule**.

⑥ $\displaystyle\int (ax + b)^n \, \mathrm{d}x = \dfrac{(ax + b)^{n+1}}{a(n + 1)} + C, \, (n \neq -1)$

⑦ $\displaystyle\int \cos(ax + b) \, \mathrm{d}x = \dfrac{1}{a}\sin(ax + b) + C$

⑧ $\displaystyle\int \sin(ax + b) \, \mathrm{d}x = -\dfrac{1}{a}\cos(ax + b) + C$

15 Exponential and logarithmic functions

Exponential functions

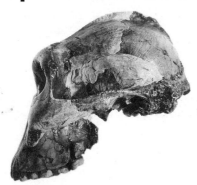

Carbon dating can be used to find the age of remains like these. This technique depends on our knowledge of the rate of decay of the radioactive material carbon-14.

Growth and decay occur all around us. For example, plants grow and decay, bacteria grow and radioactive elements decay. In this chapter we examine ways of expressing growth and decay mathematically.

Indices

In the expression a^b, a is the **base** and b is the index or **exponent**. Calculations involving indices, or exponents, may be done using the x^y, or y^x, key on a calculator.

Example 1

Solve $2^n = 256$

Try: $2^6 = 64$
     $2^7 = 128$
     $2^8 = 256$

Hence, $n = 8$

Example 2

Find the smallest integer value of n such that $4^n > 10\,000$

Try: $4^5 = 1024$, which is less than $10\,000$
     $4^6 = 4096$, which is less than $10\,000$
     $4^7 = 16\,384$, which is greater than $10\,000$

Hence, $n = 7$

Exercise 15A

1 Evaluate
   (a) 6^4 (b) 7^8 (c) $4^{0.5}$ (d) 0.8^6 (e) 4.5^3
   (f) 8^{-4} (g) $11^{-2.6}$ (h) $3.7^{-4.6}$ (i) $43.1^{-1.1}$ (j) $0.98^{-0.5}$

2 Evaluate
   (a) 3^t when $t = 1.5$ (b) 5^{-x} when $x = 3$
   (c) 1.8^{4t} when $t = 0.8$ (d) 15.6^{3m} when $m = -2.1$

3 Solve for n:
   (a) $8^n = 512$ (b) $3^n = 81$ (c) $5^n = 3125$ (d) $20^n = 8000$ (e) $1.5^n = 5.0625$

4 Solve for x, to two significant figures:
  (a) $2^x = 5$ (b) $3^x = 50$ (c) $10^x = 1000$ (d) $6^x = 42$ (e) $5^x = 150$

5 Find the smallest integer value of n such that:
  (a) $3^n > 100$ (b) $2^n > 1200$ (c) $1.5^n > 1000$ (d) $0.8^n < 0.5$ (e) $0.4^n < 0.02$

6 Find the largest integer value of n such that:
  (a) $2^n < 3000$ (b) $5^n < 15\,000$ (c) $1.2^n < 2$ (d) $0.6^n > 0.08$ (e) $2.3^n > 140$

Graphs of a^x

This exercise revises some of the work from Chapter 3, Graphs of functions.

Exercise 15B

1 (a) Complete the table of values for $y = 2^x$.

x	-3	-2	-1	0	1	2	3
y		$\frac{1}{4}$		2			

  (b) Sketch the graph of $y = 2^x$ on a grid with $-3 \leqslant x \leqslant 3$ and $0 \leqslant y \leqslant 64$.
  (c) How does the graph of $y = 2^x$ differ from $y = x^2$?

2 Complete the table of values for each function and sketch each graph on the same diagram as used for question 1.
  (a) $y = 3^x$ (b) $y = 4^x$

x	-3	-2	-1	0	1	2	3
y			$\frac{1}{3}$				27

x	-3	-2	-1	0	1	2	3
y	$\frac{1}{64}$						

3 What do you notice about the graphs of $y = 2^x$, $y = 3^x$ and $y = 4^x$?

4 Using your graphs, find an approximate solution to each equation:
  (a) $2^x = 5.5$ (b) $2^x = 7.8$ (c) $2^x = 0.5$ (d) $3^x = 1.5$ (e) $3^x = 0.2$
  (f) $3^x = 7.8$ (g) $4^x = 0.9$ (h) $4^x = 6.6$ (i) $4^x = 2.2$ (j) $4^x = 1$

5 (a) For each of the following functions complete a table of values for $-3 \leqslant x \leqslant 3$ and sketch the graph of each function on the same diagram.

   (i) $y = \dfrac{1}{2^x}$ (ii) $y = \dfrac{1}{3^x}$ (iii) $y = \dfrac{1}{4^x}$

  (b) What do you notice about these graphs?

6 Using the graphs obtained in question 5 find an approximate solution to each equation:

  (a) $\dfrac{1}{2^x} = 5$ (b) $\dfrac{1}{2^x} = 1.2$ (c) $\dfrac{1}{2^x} = 0.6$ (d) $\dfrac{1}{3^x} = 2.4$ (e) $\dfrac{1}{3^x} = 0.2$

  (f) $\dfrac{1}{3^x} = 8$ (g) $\dfrac{1}{4^x} = 4$ (h) $\dfrac{1}{4^x} = 7.5$ (i) $\dfrac{1}{4^x} = 0.9$ (j) $\dfrac{1}{4^x} = \dfrac{1}{4}$

From Exercise 15B you should notice that:

For $y = a^x$, $a > 1$, the graph

- is always positive
- never crosses the x-axis
- is increasing
- passes through $(0, 1)$.

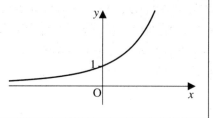

For $y = a^x$, $0 < a < 1$, the graph

- is always positive
- never crosses the x-axis
- is decreasing
- passes through $(0, 1)$.

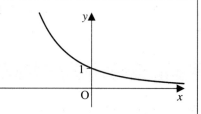

Exponential growth and decay

A function of the form $y = a^x$ is called an **exponential function** to the base a, $a \neq 0$.

$y = 5^x$ is an exponential function with base 5.
$r = 0.1^t$ is an exponential function with base 0.1.

If $a > 1$ then $y = a^x$ is a **growth** function: If $0 < a < 1$ then $y = a^x$ is a **decay** function:

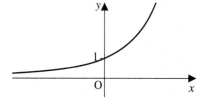
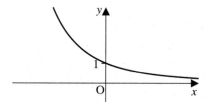

Example 3
The rabbit population on an island increases by 15% per year. How many years will it take for the population to at least double?

Let r_0 be the initial number of rabbits.
After 1 year, $r_1 = 1.15r_0$
    2 years, $r_2 = 1.15r_1 = (1.15)^2 r_0$
    3 years, $r_3 = 1.15r_2 = (1.15)^3 r_0$

Therefore, after n years, $r_n = (1.15)^n r_0$

For the population to at least double, $(1.15)^n \geqslant 2$
Try $1.15^3 = 1.52$
    $1.15^4 = 1.75$
    $1.15^5 = 2.01$
Population will double within 5 years.

Example 4

The efficiency of a machine decreases by 2% per year. When the efficiency drops below 80% the machine is no longer economically viable. For how long will the machine be economically viable?

Let E_0 represent the initial efficiency of the machine.
After 1 year, $E_1 = 0.98E_0$
2 years, $E_2 = 0.98^2E_0$

Therefore, after n years, $E_n = 0.98^n E_0$

The machine is no longer useful if $0.98^n \leqslant 0.8$
$0.98^{10} = 0.820$
$0.98^{11} = 0.801$
$0.98^{12} = 0.785$
After 11 years the machine should be replaced.

Exercise 15C

1 Cells in a petri dish multiply at a rate of 20% per day. Taking C_0 as the initial population:
  (a) find a formula for C_n, the number of cells after n days.
  (b) how long will it take for the number of cells to at least double?

2 Aftershave standing in an open bottle evaporates at a rate of 12% per week.
  (a) Taking V_0 as the initial volume, find a formula for V_n, the volume after n weeks.
  (b) How long will it take to reduce the volume by one half?

3 The population of Metropolis is decreasing by 2% each year.
  (a) Using P_0 for the initial population, find a formula for P_n, the population after n years.
  (b) How many years will it take for the population to drop from 900 000 to below 800 000?

4 The value of an antique vase is increasing by 4% each year. Its initial value was £750.
  (a) How much is it worth after 2 years?
  (b) After how many years will it be worth more than £1000?

5 The number of passes in Higher mathematics increases by 2% per year. How long will it take for the number of passes to increase by at least 25%?

6 A car worth £12 000 in 1997 loses 20% in value each year. What is the car worth in 2004?

7 On a production line 6% of the machines become obsolete each year.
  (a) Assuming no new machines are purchased, how long will it take for half the machines to be out of action?
  (b) If the initial number of machines is 80 predict the number which will require to be replaced in 6 years' time.

8 A radioactive substance has a half-life of 12 years. This means 50% of the substance will decay over a 12-year period.
  (a) How long will it take for a given quantity of the radioactive material to reduce to 10% of its original mass?
  (b) For an initial quantity of 800 grams, how much will be left after 60 years?

9 A car factory has a target of 1.5% increase in output each year.
  (a) Initially production stood at 18 000 cars and 2 years later was 18 515. Was the factory on target during this period?
  (b) If production does increase at this rate how long would it take to achieve a total increase of 10%?

10 A lump sum of £23 000 is invested at a fixed rate of 9% per annum.
  (a) How much interest is accrued after 4 years?
  (b) How long will it take to double the sum invested?
  (c) If interest is added half yearly, how long will it take to double the sum?

The exponential function

For the functions $f(x) = 2^x$ and $f(x) = 3^x$ the graphs of $y = f(x)$ and $y = f'(x)$ may be drawn using the gradients of tangents:

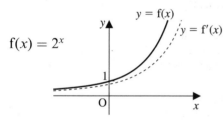

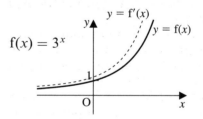

Similarly, for the functions $y = 2.7^x$ and $y = 2.8^x$:

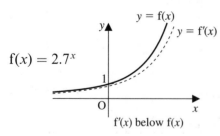

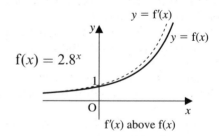

From these graphs we can see that:

- $f'(x)$ is also an exponential function
- $f'(x) = kf(x)$
- a value exists between 2.7 and 2.8 for which $f'(x) = f(x)$.

The value at which $f'(x) = f(x)$ is 2.718... and is denoted by e.
If $f(x) = e^x$, then $f'(x) = e^x$, as shown on the graph opposite.

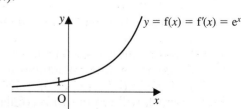

▶ $f(x) = 2.718^x = e^x$ is called the exponential function to the base e.

e^x is sometimes written $\exp(x)$ and most calculators have an e^x key so we can easily calculate exponential functions. The use of the letter e to represent the value 2.718... is attributed to Leonhard Euler, a Swiss mathematician born in 1707. Euler was responsible for much of the notation in use today, including π and $f(x)$. He was one of the most prolific and creative mathematicians of all time.

Exercise 15D

1 Evaluate:
   (a) e^3 **(b)** $e^{3.4}$ **(c)** $e^{-1.2}$ **(d)** $e^{\frac{2}{3}}$ **(e)** $3e^{-2}$

2 Evaluate:
   (a) e^a when $a = 7$ **(b)** e^b when $b = 1.5$
   (c) e^{-t} when $t = 3.2$ **(d)** e^{3m} when $m = 2.5$

3 Solve for x:
   (a) $e^x = 15$ **(b)** $e^x = 0.35$ **(c)** $e^x = 1$ **(d)** $e^x = 4$ **(e)** $e^{2x} = 8$

4 The cell population of a bacterium is determined by $c = 10^6 e^{3t}$, where c is the number of cells and t is the time in days. How many cells are there after 2 days?

5 The mass of a fixed quantity of radioactive substance decays according to the formula $m = 50e^{-0.02t}$, where m is the mass and t is the time in years. What is the mass after 12 years?

Logarithms

For the function $f(x) = 2^x$ an **inverse function**, $f^{-1}(x)$, exists. The inverse function is a reflection in $y = x$.

x	-2	-1	0	1	2	3	4
y	$\frac{1}{4}$	$\frac{1}{2}$	1	2	4	8	16

x	$\frac{1}{4}$	$\frac{1}{2}$	1	2	4	8	16
$f^{-1}(x)$	-2	-1	0	1	2	3	4

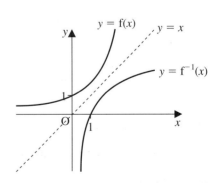

The inverse function of $f(x) = 2^x$ is called the **logarithmic function** of x to the **base** 2, written $f^{-1}(x) = \log_2 x$.

▶ If $y = a^x$ then $x = \log_a y$
   If $y = \log_a x$ then $x = a^y$

For example, since $2^6 = 64$, $\log_2 64 = 6$.

Example 5
Write $5^3 = 125$ in logarithmic form.

$\log_5 125 = 3$

Example 6
Write $y = 7^4$ in logarithmic form.

$\log_7 y = 4$

Example 7
Simplify $\log_3 9$

Since $9 = 3^2$
$\log_3 9 = \log_3 3^2 = 2$

Example 8
Change $3y = \log_u 7$ to exponential form.

$u^{3y} = 7$

Exercise 15E

1 Write in logarithmic form:
  (a) $2^5 = 32$
  (b) $4^3 = 64$
  (c) $10^6 = 1\,000\,000$
  (d) $9^{-\frac{1}{2}} = \frac{1}{3}$
  (e) $y = 7^{11}$
  (f) $x = 12^y$
  (g) $m = n^3$
  (h) $p = 6^{-5}$
  (i) $25^{\frac{1}{2}} = 5$
  (j) $16^0 = 1$
  (k) $8^{\frac{2}{3}} = 4$
  (l) $27^{-\frac{2}{3}} = \frac{1}{9}$

2 Simplify:
  (a) $\log_2 16$
  (b) $\log_5 125$
  (c) $\log_{10} 100\,000$
  (d) $\log_3 81$
  (e) $\log_9 81$
  (f) $\log_{10} 0.01$
  (g) $\log_4 \frac{1}{16}$
  (h) $\log_{36} \frac{1}{6}$

3 Change to exponential form:
  (a) $x = \log_y 3$
  (b) $r = \log_s 5$
  (c) $p = \log_4 q$
  (d) $f = \log_2 g$
  (e) $w = \log_x y$
  (f) $4m = \log_n 6$
  (g) $2a = \log_b c$
  (h) $2h + 1 = \log_h 4$

Laws of logarithms

Logarithms were first advanced as an aid to computation by the Scottish mathematician John Napier, born in 1550. Napier was also famous for his invention of 'Napier's bones', a mechanical system of rods for carrying out the process of multiplication. Today we use electronic calculators to perform the processes for which Napier used logarithms but we still need to know how logarithmic calculations are performed.

There are three rules that apply when using logarithms:

$$\log_a xy = \log_a x + \log_a y$$

Proof
Let $\log_a x = p$ and $\log_a y = q$
Therefore $x = a^p$ and $y = a^q$
Hence $xy = a^p a^q$
$\quad xy = a^{p+q}$
$\log_a xy = p + q$
$\log_a xy = \log_a x + \log_a y$

Example 9
Simplify $\log_2 4 + \log_2 8$

$\log_2 4 + \log_2 8 = \log_2 (4 \times 8)$
$\qquad = \log_2 32$
$\qquad = \log_2 (2^5)$
$\qquad = 5$

$$\log_a \frac{x}{y} = \log_a x - \log_a y$$

Proof

Let $\log_a x = p$ and $\log_a y = q$

Therefore $x = a^p$ and $y = a^q$

Hence $\dfrac{x}{y} = \dfrac{a^p}{a^q}$

$\dfrac{x}{y} = a^{p-q}$

$\log_a \dfrac{x}{y} = p - q$

$\log_a \dfrac{x}{y} = \log_a x - \log_a y$

Example 10

Simplify $\log_6 9 + \log_6 8 - \log_6 2$

$$\log_6 9 + \log_6 8 - \log_6 2 = \log_6 \frac{(9 \times 8)}{2}$$

$$= \log_6 36$$

$$= 2$$

$$\boxed{\quad \log_a x^n = n \log_a x \quad}$$

Proof

Let $\log_a x = p$

Therefore $x = a^p$

Hence $x^n = (a^p)^n$

$x^n = a^{np}$

$\log_a x^n = np$

$\log_a x^n = n \log_a x$

Note: $\log_a a = 1$ since $a^1 = a$

$\log_a 1 = 0$ since $a^0 = 1$

Example 11

Simplify $\frac{1}{4} \log_3 81$

$$\frac{1}{4} \log_3 81 = \log_3 (81^{\frac{1}{4}})$$

$$= \log_3 3$$

$$= 1$$

Exercise 15F

1 Simplify:

    (a) $\log_{10} 2 + \log_{10} 500$

    (b) $\log_3 63 - \log_3 7$

    (c) $\log_4 8 + \log_4 8$

    (d) $\log_2 16 - \log_2 8$

    (e) $\log_3 6 + \log_3 12 - \log_3 8$

    (f) $3 \log_3 9$

    (g) $2 \log_{10} 2 + 2 \log_{10} 5$

    (h) $\log_2 3 + \log_2 2 - \log_2 6 - \log_2 8$

    (i) $2 \log_4 2 - \log_4 \frac{1}{4} - 2 \log_4 4$

    (j) $\log_3 9 - \log_3 \frac{1}{3}$

    (k) $\frac{1}{2} \log_2 16 - \frac{1}{3} \log_2 8$

    (l) $3 \log_{10} 10 + \frac{1}{2} \log_{10} 10$

    (m) $\log_{10} 5 + \log_{10} 8 - \log_{10} 4$

    (n) $\log_3 12 - 2 \log_3 2$

2 If $p = 3 \log_2 \dfrac{q}{r}$ find the value of p when:

    (a) $q = 16, r = 4$

    (b) $q = 80, r = 10$

3 If $f(x) = 2 \log_3 x$ find:

    (a) $f(9)$

    (b) $f(1)$

    (c) $f(\frac{1}{3})$

4 If $f(x) = 3 \log_2 x$ find:

    (a) $f(8)$

    (b) $f(\frac{1}{4})$

    (c) $f(32)$

5 If $\log_a y = \log_a 2 + 3 \log_a x$, express y in terms of x.

6 If $\log_a y = \log_a 7 + 5 \log_a m$, express y in terms of m.

7 If $\log_a r = \log_a s - 2 \log_a t$, express r in terms of s and t.

8 If $3 \log_2 y = \log_2 (x - 1) + 3$ show that $y^3 = 8(x - 1)$.

Logarithmic equations

Using the rules in the previous section we can now solve logarithmic equations.

Example 12

Solve, for $x > 0$, $\log_a x + \log_a 4 = \log_a 8$

$$\log_a x + \log_a 4 = \log_a 8$$
$$\log_a 4x = \log_a 8$$
$$4x = 8$$
$$x = 2$$

Example 13

Solve, for $x > 0$, $\log_2 (3x - 5) - \log_2 (x + 2) = 1$

$$\log_2 (3x - 5) - \log_2 (x + 2) = 1$$
$$\log_2 \left(\frac{3x - 5}{x + 2} \right) = 1$$

Since $\log_2 2 = 1$, $\log_2 \left(\dfrac{3x - 5}{x + 2} \right) = \log_2 2$

$$\frac{3x - 5}{x + 2} = 2$$
$$3x - 5 = 2(x + 2)$$
$$x = 9$$

Example 14

Solve, for $x > 0$, $\log_a (2x + 1) + \log_a (3x - 10) = \log_a 11x$

$$\log_a (2x + 1)(3x - 10) = \log_a 11x$$
$$(2x + 1)(3x - 10) = 11x$$
$$6x^2 - 28x - 10 = 0$$
$$2(3x + 1)(x - 5) = 0$$
$$x = -\tfrac{1}{3}, \; x = 5$$

Hence $x = 5$ since $x > 0$

Exercise 15G

1 Solve, for $x > 0$:

(a) $\log_a 4 + \log_a x = \log_a 12$ **(b)** $\log_a x - \log_a 6 = \log_a 11$ **(c)** $\log_a x + 2 \log_a 5 = \log_a 100$

(d) $\log_p 12 - \log_p x = \log_p 1$ **(e)** $\log_m x - \log_m \tfrac{1}{3} = \log_m 27$ **(f)** $\log_a x^2 + \log_a 2 = \log_a 50$

(g) $\tfrac{1}{2} \log_a x + \log_a 4 = \log_a 20$ **(g)** $\log_a 16 - 3 \log_a x = \log_a 2$ **(i)** $2 \log_a x - \log_a 4 = \log_a 9$

2 Solve, for $x > 0$:

(a) $\log_a (x + 1) + \log_a (x - 1) = \log_a 8$ **(b)** $\log_a (2x + 1) + \log_a (3x) = \log_a 63$

(c) $\log_5 (x + 1) + \log_5 (x - 3) = 1$ **(d)** $\log_7 (x^2 - 1) - \log_7 (x - 1) = 2$

(e) $\log_2 (x - 1) + \log_2 (x + 1) = 3$ **(f)** $\log_9 (x - 4) - \log_9 (x - 8) = \tfrac{1}{2}$

3 Solve, for $x > 0$:

   (a) $\log_a (x - 6) + \log_a (x - 4) = \log_a x$ **(b)** $\log_9 (2x + 5) - \log_9 (x - 5) = \log_9 \dfrac{x}{2}$

   (c) $\log_2 x + \log_2 (3x - 5) = \log_2 10x$ **(d)** $2 \log_a x + \log_a (2x - 6) = \log_a 8x$

4 The difference, n, in decibels, between two sound intensities is

given by the formula $n = 10 \log_{10} \left(\dfrac{S_1}{S_2} \right)$, where S_1 and S_2 are the

sound intensities in phons, $S_1 > S_2$. Shuffling a pack of cards has a
sound intensity of 40 phons. If a clock alarm is 4 decibels greater
than shuffling cards what is the sound intensity of the alarm?

Natural logarithms

Logarithms to the base e are called natural logarithms, written $\log_e x$
or $\ln x$.

> $\log_e x = \ln x$

Example 15

Solve $\ln x = 7$

$\log_e x = 7$
$\quad x = e^7$
$\quad x = 1096.6$

Example 16

Solve $e^x = 9$

Take natural logs of both sides

$\ln e^x = \ln 9$
$\quad x = \ln 9$
$\quad x = 2.2$

Example 17

Solve $4^{2x+1} = 50$

$\ln 4^{2x+1} = \ln 50$
$(2x + 1) \ln 4 = \ln 50$
$2x + 1 = \dfrac{\ln 50}{\ln 4}$
$2x + 1 = 2.82$
$\quad 2x = 1.82$
$\quad\quad x = 0.91$

Example 18

For the formula $P(t) = 50e^{-2t}$:
(a) evaluate $P(0)$
(b) for what value of t is $P(t) = \frac{1}{2} P(0)$?

(a) $P(0) = 50e^{-2(0)} = 50e^0 = 50$
(b) $P(t) = \frac{1}{2} P(0) = 25$

$\quad\quad 50e^{-2t} = 25$
$\quad\quad e^{-2t} = \frac{1}{2}$
$\quad\quad \ln e^{-2t} = \ln \frac{1}{2}$
$\quad\quad -2t = -0.693$
$\quad\quad t = 0.35$

Exercise 15H

1 Solve

   (a) $\ln x = 9$ **(b)** $\ln x = 17$ **(c)** $\ln x = 1.8$ **(d)** $\ln x = 15$ **(e)** $\ln x = 27$

2 Solve

   (a) $e^x = 11$ **(b)** $e^x = 21$ **(c)** $e^{2x} = 16$ **(d)** $e^{4x} = 31$ **(e)** $e^{5x+1} = 20$

3 Solve

   (a) $5^x = 11$ **(b)** $3^x = 19$ **(c)** $7^x = 25$ **(d)** $8^{2x} = 36$ **(e)** $9^{3x+1} = 86$

4 The number of bacteria of a particular strain is given by
$B(t) = 30e^{1.5t}$, where t is the time in hours.
(a) How many bacteria are there at time zero?
(b) How long will it take for the number of bacteria to double?

5 A radioactive material has mass, m, at time t years, given by
$m = m_0e^{-0.01t}$, where m_0 is the initial mass.
(a) If the original mass is 400 g, find the mass after 8 years.
(b) The half-life of the substance is the time taken for half the
mass to decay. Find the half-life of the substance.

6 The pressure in a tyre is falling according to the formula
$P_t = P_0e^{-kt}$, where P_0 is the initial pressure, P_t is pressure at
time t, t is the time in hours and k is a constant.
(a) At time zero the pressure is 60 units, 24 hours later it is 10
units. Find the value of k to two significant figures.
(b) If the pressure falls below 30 units the tyre is unsafe to use.
Is a tyre initially inflated to 50 units still safe to use after 5
hours?

7 For a radioactive substance $A = A_0e^{-kt}$, where A_0 is the initial
amount of the substance, k is a constant and t is the time in
minutes. In 5 minutes, 20 g of this substance is reduced to 18 g.
(a) Find the value of k to two significant figures.
(b) Find the half-life of this substance.

Formulae from experimental data

Results from an experiment may be analysed to find if a formula
connecting the variables exists. For example, if corresponding
readings of two variables x and y are plotted and the graph obtained
is a straight line then x and y are related by the formula $y = mx + c$.

Data from an experiment may result in a graph of the form
shown in the diagram, indicating exponential growth. A graph
such as this implies a formula of the type $y = kx^n$, where k and n
are constants.

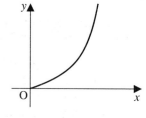

Using logarithms we can express $y = kx^n$ in the form of the equation
of a straight line.

If $\quad y = kx^n$

then $\quad \log y = \log kx^n$

$\quad \log y = \log k + \log x^n$

$\quad \log y = n \log x + \log k$

or $\quad Y = nX + c$, where $Y = \log y$, $X = \log x$ and $c = \log k$

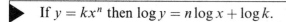

▶ If $y = kx^n$ then $\log y = n \log x + \log k$.

This is a linear equation. Hence, if the graph of $\log y$ against $\log x$
is a straight line, then the formula is of type $y = kx^n$. The straight
line graph may be used to determine k and n.

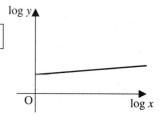

Example 19

Experimental data are given in the table.

x	50.1	194.9	501.2	707.9
y	20.9	46.8	83.2	102.3

(a) Show that y and x are related by the formula $y = kx^n$.
(b) Find the values of k and n, and state the formula that connects x and y.

(a) Taking logs to base 10 of x and y gives:

$\log_{10} x$	1.70	2.29	2.70	2.85
$\log_{10} y$	1.32	1.67	1.92	2.01

If we plot these points, we can see that they lie on straight line. Hence, the formula connecting y and x is of the form $y = kx^n$.

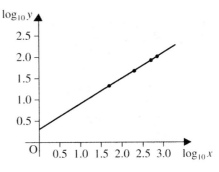

(b) Taking two points on the best-fitting straight line and using the formula $Y = nX + c$, where $Y = \log_{10} y$, $X = \log_{10} x$ and $c = \log_{10} k$:

$$Y = nX + c$$
$$2.01 = n2.85 + c$$
$$1.32 = n1.70 + c$$

Solving these equations simultaneously gives

$n = 0.6$ and $c = 0.3$.

Since $c = \log_{10} k$, $\log_{10} k = 0.3$
$$k = 10^{0.3}$$
$$k = 2$$

Hence $y = 2x^{0.6}$

Exercise 15I

1 For each set of data
   (i) show that the formula connecting y and x is of the form $y = kx^n$.
   (ii) find the value of k and n, and state the formula that connects x and y.

(a)

x	1.26	1.58	2.0	2.5	3.16
y	3.98	7.94	17.78	31.6	63.1

(b)

x	1.0	2.0	3.0	4.0	5.0
y	19	80	177	316	500

(c)

x	10	20	30	40	50
y	20	32.6	43.3	52.9	61.8

(d)

x	1.0	1.5	2.0	3.0	4.0
y	2.50	8.42	20.0	67.5	160

(e)

x	1.2	3.1	4.2	5.5	6.5
y	3.94	16.37	25.8	38.7	49.7

(f)

x	14.1	28.2	63.1	126
y	15.9	6.31	3.16	1.58

2 For each line of best fit shown, $\log_{10} y$ is plotted against $\log_{10} x$. Express y in terms of x.

(a)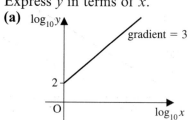

(b)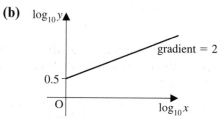

(c)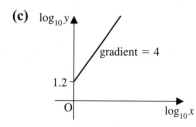

(d)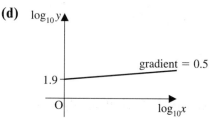

(e)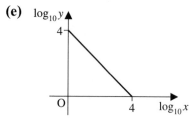

(f)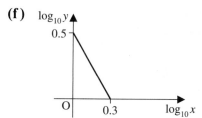

Further formulae from experimental data

Data from an experiment may result in a graph of the form shown in the diagram. A graph such as this may imply a formula of the type $y = ab^x$, where a and b are constants.

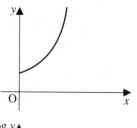

If $y = ab^x$

then $\log y = \log ab^x$

   $\log y = \log a + x \log b$

or $Y = mX + c$, where $Y = \log y$, $m = \log b$ and $c = \log a$

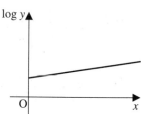

> If $y = ab^x$ then $\log y = \log a + x \log b$

This is a linear equation. Hence, if the graph of $\log y$ against x is a straight line, then the formula is of type $y = ab^x$.
The straight line graph may be used to determine a and b.

Example 20

Experimental data are given in the table.

x	1.0	1.5	2.2	2.5	3.0
y	6.0	8.5	13.8	16.9	24.0

(a) Show that y and x are related by the formula $y = ab^x$.

(b) Find the values of a and b, and state the formula that connects x and y.

(a) Taking logs to base 10 of y gives:

x	1.0	1.5	2.2	2.5	3.0
$\log_{10} y$	0.78	0.93	1.12	1.23	1.38

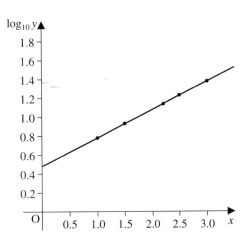

If we plot these points, we can see that they lie on straight line. Hence, the formula connecting y and x is of the form $y = ab^x$.

(b) Taking two points on the best-fitting straight line and using the formula $Y = mx + c$, where $Y = \log_{10} y$, $m = \log_{10} b$ and $c = \log_{10} a$:

$$y = mx + c$$
$$1.38 = m(3.0) + c$$
$$0.78 = m(1.0) + c$$

Solving these equations simultaneously gives

$$m = 0.3 \text{ so } \log_{10} b = 0.3$$
$$b = 2.0$$
$$c = 0.48 \text{ so } \log_{10} a = 0.48$$
$$a = 3.0$$

Hence $y = 3.0(2.0)^x$

Exercise 15J

1 For each set of data
  (i) show that the formula connecting y and x is of the form $y = ab^x$.
  (ii) find the value of a and b, and state the formula that connects x and y.

(a)

x	1	2	3	4	5
y	12	48	192	768	3072

(b)

x	0.5	1.2	3.8	4.1
y	1.79	1.53	0.86	0.80

(c)

x	2.3	3.2	4.6	5.0
y	23.97	52.7	179.52	254.8

(d)

x	1.1	2.3	3.0	4.2	5.1
y	1.87	3.05	4.05	6.59	9.49

(e)

x	0.8	1.3	2.6	3.7
y	0.84	1.15	2.65	5.37

2 For each line of best fit shown, $\log_{10} y$ is plotted against x.
Express y in terms of x.

(a)

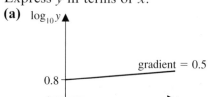

(b)

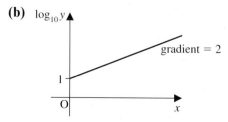

(c)

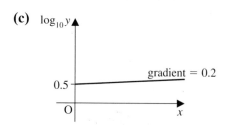

(d)

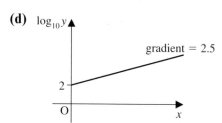

(e)

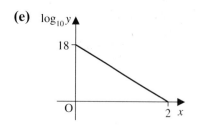

(f)

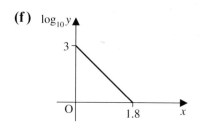

3 For each set of data given
  (i) sketch the graph of $\log_{10} y$ against x
  (ii) determine the formula connecting y and x.

(a)

x	0.5	1.2	3.1	4.2
y	0.1	1.38	23.83	59.27

(b)

x	2.0	3.1	3.8	4.4	5.1
y	0.53	0.24	0.15	0.10	0.06

Related graphs

From the graphs of $y = e^x$ and $y = \ln x$ you can use the techniques learnt in Chapter 3, Graphs of functions, to sketch a number of related graphs.

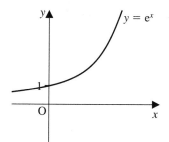

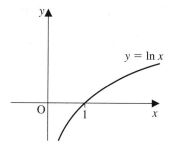

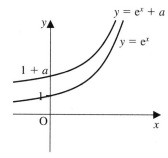

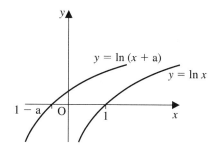

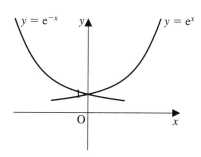

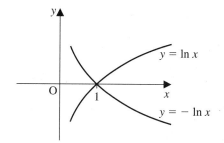

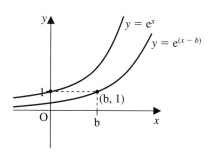

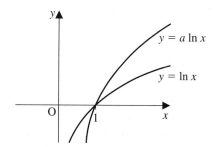

Example 21

The graph of $f(x) = \log_3 x$ is shown opposite.

(a) Sketch the graph of $f(x) = \log_3 x$ and on the same diagram

sketch the graph of $g(x) = \log_3 \dfrac{1}{x}$.

(b) Sketch the graph of $f(x) = \log_3 x$ again, and on the same
diagram sketch the graph of $h(x) = \log_3 3x$.

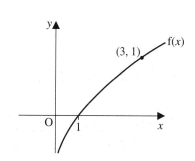

(a) Since $\log\dfrac{1}{x} = \log x^{-1} = -\log x$ the graph of

$g(x) = \log_3\dfrac{1}{x}$ is a reflection in the x-axis of

$f(x) = \log_3 x$

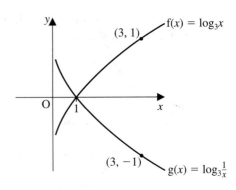

(b) $\begin{aligned} h(x) &= \log_3 3x \\ &= \log_3 3 + \log_3 x \\ &= 1 + \log_3 x \end{aligned}$

When $f(x) = 0$, $1 + \log_3 x = 0$

$\qquad\qquad \log_3 x = -1$

$\qquad\qquad x = 3^{-1} = \tfrac{1}{3}$

So the graph of $h(x)$ is derived from the graph of $f(x)$ shifted vertically by 1 unit.

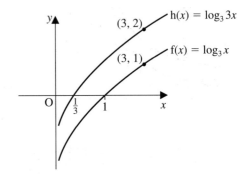

Exercise 15K

1 Make two copies of the sketch of the graph of $f(x) = \log_2 x$.

    (a) On one diagram sketch the graph of $f(x) = \log_2\dfrac{1}{x}$.

    (b) On the other diagram sketch the graph of $f(x) = \log_2 2x$.

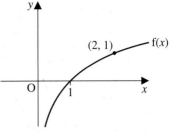

2 Make two copies of the graph of $f(x) = \log_9 x$.
    (a) On one diagram sketch the graph of $f(x) = \log_9 x + 3$.
    (b) On the other diagram sketch the graph of $f(x) = \log_9 81x$.

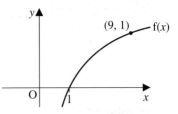

3 Sketch the graph of $y = \log_8 x$.
    On the same diagram:
    (a) sketch the graph of $y = \log_8 (x - 3)$
    (b) sketch the graph of $y = \log_8 8(x - 3)$.

4 Sketch two copies of the graph of $y = \log_5 x$.
    (a) On one diagram sketch the graph of $y = \log_5 (x + 1)$.
    (b) On the other diagram sketch the graph of $y = 3\log_5 x$.

5 A sketch of the graph of $y = \log_6 (x + a)$ is shown opposite. Find the value of a.

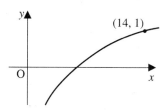

6 A sketch of the graph of $y = \log_{12} (x - a)$ is shown opposite. Find the value of a.

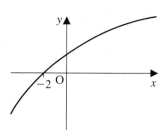

(14, 1)

7 For each pair of functions, sketch the graphs on one diagram:
   (a) $y = e^x$, $y = e^x + 5$ **(b)** $y = e^x$, $y = -e^x$
   (c) $y = e^x$, $y = e^{x-3}$ **(d)** $y = e^x$, $y = 2e^x$

Exercise 15L Mixed questions

1 Solve for x, to two significant figures:
   (a) $4^x = 70$ **(b)** $6^x = 120$ **(c)** $11^x = 5$ **(d)** $1.4^x = 34.5$

2 The population of an urban district is decreasing at the rate of 1.5% per year.
   (a) Taking P_0 as the initial population find a formula for the population, P_n, after n years.
   (b) How long will it take for the population to drop from 350 000 to 300 000?

3 Evaluate:
   (a) $3e^{2.1}$
   (c) $4e^{3t}$ when $t = 0.4$
   (b) $4.2e^{-1.4}$
   (d) $3e^{3x-2}$ when $x = 2.1$

4 Write in logarithmic form:
   (a) $3^8 = 6561$
   (c) $m = 8^{5.2}$
   (b) $x^9 = 19683$
   (d) $r = a^6$

5 Change to exponential form:
   (a) $m = \log_n 4$
   (c) $5n = \log_p 7$
   (b) $q = \log_s r$
   (d) $3h - 1 = \log_a 8$

6 Simplify:
   (a) $\log_4 8 + \log_4 32$ **(b)** $2\log_3 3 - \log_3 81 + \log_3 \frac{1}{9}$ **(c)** $\frac{1}{3}\log_9 27 - \log_9 3$

7 If $4\log_3 y = \log_3 (x^2 - 1) + 3$ show that $y^4 = 27(x^2 - 1)$.

8 Solve, for $x > 0$:
   (a) $\log_4 18 - \log_4 x = \frac{1}{2}$ **(b)** $\log(2x + 1) + \log(3x - 2) = \log(x + 2)$

9 As shown in the diagram opposite, a set of
experimental results gives a straight line graph
when $\log_{10} y$ is plotted against $\log_{10} x$.
The straight line passes through $(0, 1)$ and has
a gradient of 2. Express y in terms of x.   [Higher]

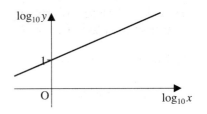

10 (a) On the same diagram, sketch the graphs of $y = \log_{10} x$ and
$y = 2 - x$, where $0 < x < 5$. Write down an approximation
for the x coordinate of the point of intersection.

(b) Find the value of this x coordinate, correct to two decimal
places.   [Higher]

11 (a) For a particular radioactive substance, the mass m (in grams)
at time t (in years) is given by $m = m_0 e^{-0.02t}$, where m_0 is the
original mass. If the original mass is 500 grams, find the
mass after 10 years.

(b) The half-life of any material is the time taken for half of the
mass to decay. Find the half-life of this substance.

(c) Illustrate all of the above information on a graph.
        [Higher]

12 Two sound intensities P_1 and P_2 are said to differ by n decibels
when $n = 10 \log_{10} \dfrac{P_2}{P_1}$
where P_1 and P_2 are measured in phons and $P_2 > P_1$. Rustling
leaves have a typical sound intensity of 30 phons. If the sound
intensity of a fire alarm siren is 6.5 decibels greater than rustling
leaves, what is the sound intensity of the fire alarm siren,
measured in phons?   [Higher]

SUMMARY

① For $y = a^x$, $a > 1$, the graph
- is always positive
- never crosses the x-axis
- is increasing
- passes through $(0, 1)$.

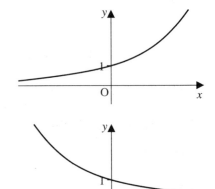

② For $y = a^x$, $0 < a < 1$, the graph
- is always positive
- never crosses the x-axis
- is decreasing
- passes through $(0, 1)$.

③ A function of the form $y = a^x$ is an **exponential function** to the
base a, $a \neq 0$.

④ $f(x) = 2.718^x = e^x$ is called the exponential function to the base e.

(5) If $y = a^x$ then $x = \log_a y$
If $y = \log_a x$ then $x = a^y$

(6) $\log_a xy = \log_a x + \log_a y$

(7) $\log_a \dfrac{x}{y} = \log_a x - \log_a y$

(8) $\log_a x^n = n \log_a x$

(9) $\log_e x = \ln x$.

(10) If $y = kx^n$ then $\log y = n \log x + \log k$.
This is a linear equation. Hence, if the graph of $\log y$ against $\log x$ is a straight line, then the formula is of type $y = kx^n$. The straight line graph may be used to determine k and n.

(11) If $y = ab^x$ then $\log y = \log a + x \log b$
This is a linear equation. Hence, if the graph of $\log y$ against x is a straight line, then the formula is of type $y = ab^x$.
The straight line graph may be used to determine a and b.

16 The wave function

Waves and graphs

Synthesisers generate new sounds by adding together different wave forms. Scientists studying the possibility of wave power look at the effect of adding water waves together. The effects of these waves, and many others in real life, may be represented by trigonometric functions.

To sketch a graph or determine a function that represents the sum of two trigonometric waves you must be familiar with the graphs and functions of single trigonometric wave shapes.

This exercise revises the graphs studied in Chapter 4, Trigonometry.

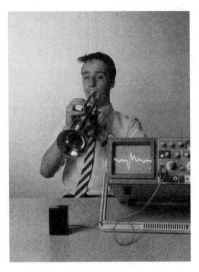

This oscilloscope shows the wave pattern produced by the trumpet.

Exercise 16A

1 The following graphs are of the form $y = a \sin x°$ or $y = b \cos x°$.
  For each graph
    (i) state its equation
    (ii) write the maximum and minimum values.

(a)
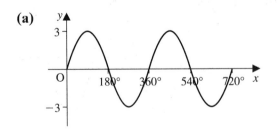

(b)
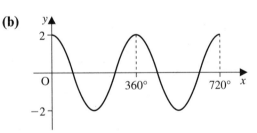

(c)
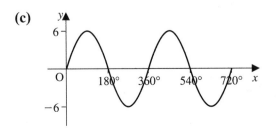

(d)
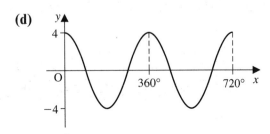

2 The following graphs are of the form $y = \sin(x - \alpha)^\circ$.
  For each graph
  (i) state its equation
  (ii) write the maximum and minimum values.

(a)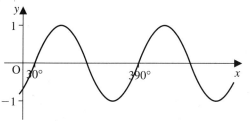

(b)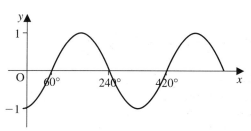

3 The following graphs are of the form $y = \cos(x - \alpha)^\circ$.
  For each graph
  (i) state its equation
  (ii) write the maximum and minimum values.

(a)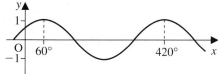

(b)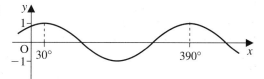

4 The following graphs are of the form $y = c\sin(x - \alpha)^\circ$.
  For each graph
  (i) state its equation
  (ii) write the maximum and minimum values.

(a)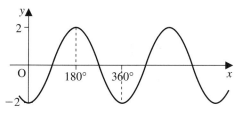

(b)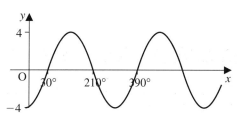

5 The following graphs are of the form $y = d\cos(x - \alpha)^\circ$.
  State the equation of each graph.

(a)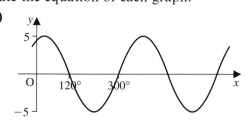

(b)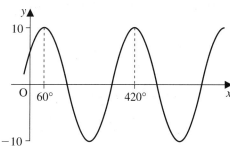

Adding two waves

The diagram shows the graphs of $y = \cos x^\circ$ and $y = \sin x^\circ$.

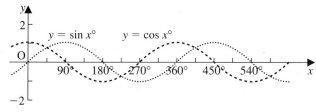

These two functions may be added together to give a new function $y = \cos x° + \sin x°$. A graph of this function may be drawn by adding the y coordinates of the two original functions.

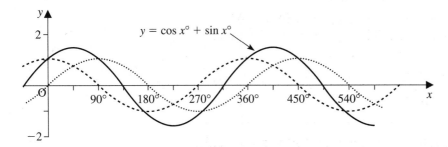

This new function has an amplitude of approximately 1.4 and is a translation 45° to the right of a cosine function. Hence the function may be written as $y = 1.4\cos(x - 45)°$, i.e. $\cos x + \sin x = 1.4\cos(x - 45)°$

Exercise 16B

1 (a) Using a computer package, graphics calculator or table of values sketch each of the sets of graphs (i) to (iv) on the same diagram, for $0 \leqslant x \leqslant 360$.
Use a table of this form if necessary.

$x°$	0	30	60	90	etc.
$y = \cos x°$					
$y = \sin x°$					
$y = \cos x° + \sin x°$					

   (i) $y = 3\cos x°$, $y = 4\sin x°$ and $y = 3\cos x° + 4\sin x°$
   (ii) $y = 8\cos x°$, $y = 6\sin x°$ and $y = 8\cos x° + 6\sin x°$
   (iii) $y = 5\cos x°$, $y = 12\sin x°$ and $y = 5\cos x° + 12\sin x°$
   (iv) $y = 12\cos x°$, $y = 5\sin x°$ and $y = 12\cos x° + 5\sin x°$

(b) Using the graphs drawn, re-write each function of the form $y = a\sin x° + b\cos x°$ as $y = k\cos(x - \alpha)°$.

(c) Copy and complete the following table.

$y = a\cos x° + b\sin x°$	$y = k\cos(x - \alpha)°$	a	b	k	α	$\tan \alpha°$
$y = \cos x° + \sin x°$	$y = 1.4\cos(x - 45)°$	1	1	1.4	45	
$y = 3\cos x° + 4\sin x°$						
$y = 4\cos x° + 3\sin x°$						
$y = 5\cos x° + 12\sin x°$						
$y = 12\cos x° + 5\sin x°$						

(d) Make a conjecture on how to find k and $\alpha°$ given a and b.

(e) Test your conjecture.

Expressing $a \cos x + b \sin x$ in the form $k \cos(x - \alpha)$

Exercise 16B shows us that a combination of sine and cosine functions can be expressed as a single trigonometric function, i.e.

> $a \cos x + b \sin x = k \cos(x - \alpha),$
>
> where $k = \sqrt{a^2 + b^2}$ and $\tan \alpha = \dfrac{b}{a}$

k is the **amplitude** of the function and α is called the **phase angle**.

We can use this single trigonometric equation to simplify calculations.

Proof

Let $a \cos x + b \sin x = k \cos(x - \alpha)$
$$= k(\cos x \cos \alpha + \sin x \sin \alpha)$$
$$= k \cos x \cos \alpha + k \sin x \sin \alpha$$
$$= k \cos \alpha \cos x + k \sin \alpha \sin x$$

Equating like terms gives $a = k \cos \alpha$ and $b = k \sin \alpha$.

$$a^2 + b^2 = k^2 \cos^2 \alpha + k^2 \sin^2 \alpha$$
$$= k^2(\cos^2 \alpha + \sin^2 \alpha)$$
$$= k^2, \text{ since } \cos^2 \alpha + \sin^2 \alpha = 1$$
$$k = \sqrt{a^2 + b^2}, \text{ assuming } k > 0.$$

Also $\dfrac{b}{a} = \dfrac{k \sin \alpha}{k \cos \alpha}$

$$= \dfrac{\sin \alpha}{\cos \alpha}$$

$$= \tan \alpha, \text{ where the quadrant of } \alpha \text{ is determined by } \sin \alpha \text{ and } \cos \alpha.$$

Example 1

Write $4 \cos x° + 3 \sin x°$ in the form $k \cos(x - \alpha)°$, where $0 \leqslant \alpha \leqslant 360$.

$4 \cos x° + 3 \sin x° = k \cos(x - \alpha)°$
$$= k(\cos x° \cos \alpha° + \sin x° \sin \alpha°)$$
$$= k \cos \alpha° \cos x° + k \sin \alpha° \sin x°$$

Hence $k \cos \alpha° = 4$

$k \sin \alpha° = 3$

$\alpha°$ is in the first quadrant as both $\cos \alpha°$ and $\sin \alpha°$ are positive.

$$k = \sqrt{4^2 + 3^2} = 5$$

$\tan \alpha° = \frac{3}{4}$

$\alpha = 36.9$

$4 \cos x° + 3 \sin x° = 5 \cos(x - 36.9)°$

✓	✓✓
Sine positive	All positive
Tangent positive	Cosine positive
	✓

Write each of the following in the form $k\cos(x - \alpha)°$, where $0 \leqslant \alpha \leqslant 360$:

1 $6\cos x° + 8\sin x°$ **2** $5\cos x° + 12\sin x°$ **3** $8\cos x° + 15\sin x°$

4 $2\cos x° + 2\sin x°$ **5** $\cos x° + 2\sin x°$ **6** $2.5\cos x° + 3.5\sin x°$

7 $4\sin x° + 3\cos x°$ **8** $3\sin x° + 5\cos x°$ **9** $1.5\sin x° + 5.5\cos x°$

The difference of two waves

The same formula can be used for an expression written as the difference of two wave shapes.

Example 2

Write $3\cos x° - 2\sin x°$ in the form $k\cos(x - \alpha)°$, where $0 \leqslant \alpha \leqslant 360$.

$$3\cos x° - 2\sin x° = k\cos(x - \alpha)°$$
$$= k(\cos x° \cos \alpha° + \sin x° \sin \alpha°)$$
$$= k\cos \alpha° \cos x° + k\sin \alpha° \sin x°$$

Hence $k\cos \alpha° = 3$
         $k\sin \alpha° = -2$

$\alpha°$ is in the fourth quadrant as $\cos \alpha°$ is positive and $\sin \alpha°$ is negative.

	✓
S	A
T	C
✓	✓✓

$$k = \sqrt{3^2 + (-2)^2} = \sqrt{13}$$
$$\tan \alpha° = -\frac{2}{3}$$
$$\alpha = 326$$
$$3\cos x° - 2\sin x° = \sqrt{13}\cos(x - 326)°$$

1 Write each of the following in the form $k\cos(x - \alpha)°$, where $0 \leqslant \alpha \leqslant 360$:

(a) $3\cos x° - 4\sin x°$ **(b)** $\cos x° - \sin x°$ **(c)** $4\cos x° - 7.5\sin x°$

(d) $2\cos x° - 3\sin x°$ **(e)** $-5\cos x° - 6\sin x°$ **(f)** $-10\cos x° - 7\sin x°$

(g) $5\sin x° - 12\cos x°$ **(h)** $4\sin x° - 6\cos x°$ **(i)** $1.5\sin x° - 2.5\cos x°$

2 Write each of the following in the form $k\cos(x - \alpha)$, where $0 \leqslant \alpha \leqslant 2\pi$:

(a) $\sqrt{3}\cos x - \sin x$ **(b)** $2\sin x - 2\cos x$ **(c)** $\sqrt{3}\sin x + \cos x$

(d) $3\cos x + 3\sin x$ **(e)** $-\cos x - 2\sin x$ **(f)** $3\cos x + 4\sin x$

Expressing $a\cos x + b\sin x$ in other forms

The expression $a\cos x + b\sin x$ may also be written in the form $k\cos(x + \alpha)$, $k\sin(x - \alpha)$ or $k\sin(x + \alpha)$.

Example 3

Write $5\cos x° - 3\sin x°$ in the form $k\sin(x - \alpha)°$, where $0 \leqslant \alpha \leqslant 360$.

$$5\cos x° - 3\sin x° = k\sin(x - \alpha)°$$
$$= k(\sin x° \cos \alpha° - \cos x° \sin \alpha°)$$
$$= k\cos \alpha° \sin x° - k\sin \alpha° \cos x°$$

Hence $\quad k\cos \alpha° = -3$
$$k\sin \alpha° = -5$$

$\alpha°$ is in the third quadrant as both $\cos \alpha°$ and $\sin \alpha°$ are negative.

$$k = \sqrt{(-3)^2 + (-5)^2} = \sqrt{34}$$

$$\tan \alpha° = \frac{-5}{-3}$$

$$\alpha = 239$$

$$5\cos x° - 3\sin x° = \sqrt{34}\sin(x - 239)°$$

Example 4

Write $\cos x + \sqrt{3}\sin x$ in the form $k\cos(x + \alpha)$, where $0 \leqslant \alpha \leqslant 2\pi$.

$$\cos x + \sqrt{3}\sin x = k\cos(x + \alpha)$$
$$= k(\cos x \cos \alpha - \sin x \sin \alpha)$$
$$= k\cos \alpha \cos x - k\sin \alpha \sin x$$

Hence $\quad k\cos \alpha = 1$
$$k\sin \alpha = -\sqrt{3}$$

α is in the fourth quadrant as $\cos \alpha$ is positive and $\sin \alpha$ is negative.

$$k = \sqrt{1^2 + (-\sqrt{3})^2} = 2$$

$$\tan \alpha = \frac{-\sqrt{3}}{1}$$

$$\alpha = \frac{5\pi}{3}$$

$$\cos x + \sqrt{3}\sin x = 2\cos\left(x + \frac{5\pi}{3}\right)$$

Exercise 16E

1 Write each of the following in the form $k\cos(x + \alpha)°$, where $0 \leqslant \alpha \leqslant 360$:

   (a) $1.5\cos x° + 2\sin x°$ **(b)** $2.4\cos x° + \sin x°$ **(c)** $\cos x° + \sin x°$

   (d) $-\cos x° - \sqrt{3}\sin x°$ **(e)** $5\cos x° + 2\sin x°$ **(f)** $-1.3\cos x° - 4.5\sin x°$

2 Write each of the following in the form $k\sin(x - \alpha)°$, where $0 \leqslant \alpha \leqslant 360$:

   (a) $4\cos x° - 3\sin x°$ **(b)** $\cos x° + \sin x°$ **(c)** $8\cos x° - 15\sin x°$

   (d) $2.5\cos x° + 6\sin x°$ **(e)** $3\cos x° - 3\sin x°$ **(f)** $\sqrt{3}\sin x° - \cos x°$

3 Write each of the following in the form $k\sin(x + \alpha)°$, where $0 \leqslant \alpha \leqslant 360$:

   (a) $4\cos x° - 3\sin x°$ **(b)** $\cos x° + \sin x°$ **(c)** $8\cos x° - 15\sin x°$

   (d) $2.5\cos x° + 6\sin x°$ **(e)** $-3\cos x° - 3\sin x°$ **(f)** $-5\cos x° - 3.5\sin x°$

4 Write each of the following in the form $k \sin(x - \alpha)$, where $0 \leqslant \alpha \leqslant 2\pi$:

(a) $\sqrt{3} \cos x + \sin x$ (b) $\cos x - \sin x$ (c) $\cos x - \sqrt{3} \sin x$

(d) $-10 \cos x - 10 \sin x$ (e) $\cos x + 2 \sin x$ (f) $4 \cos x - 3 \sin x$

5 Write each of the following in the form $k \sin(x + \alpha)$, where $0 \leqslant \alpha \leqslant 2\pi$:

(a) $\cos x + \sin x$ (b) $\sqrt{3} \cos x - \sin x$ (c) $\cos x + \sqrt{3} \sin x$

(d) $3 \cos x + 3 \sin x$ (e) $-3 \cos x - \sqrt{2} \sin x$ (f) $2.5 \cos x - 6 \sin x$

Multiple angles

We can also apply the wave function formula to multiple angles.

Example 5

Write $5 \cos 2x° + 12 \sin 2x°$ in the form $k \sin(2x + \alpha)°$, where $0 \leqslant \alpha \leqslant 360$.

$$\begin{aligned}
5 \cos 2x° + 12 \sin 2x° &= k \sin(2x + \alpha)° \\
&= k(\sin 2x° \cos \alpha° + \cos 2x° \sin \alpha°) \\
&= k \cos \alpha° \sin 2x° + k \sin \alpha° \cos 2x°
\end{aligned}$$

Hence $k \cos \alpha° = 12$

$\qquad\qquad k \sin \alpha° = 5$

$\alpha°$ is in the first quadrant as both $\cos \alpha°$ and $\sin \alpha°$ are positive.

$\qquad k = \sqrt{5^2 + 12^2} = 13$

$\tan \alpha° = \frac{5}{12}$

$\qquad \alpha = 22.6$

$5 \cos 2x° + 12 \sin 2x° = 13 \sin(2x + 22.6)°$

✓	✓✓
S	A
T	C
	✓

Exercise 16F

1 Given that $0 \leqslant \alpha \leqslant 360$, express $\cos 2x° + \sin 2x°$ in the form

(a) $k \cos(2x - \alpha)°$ (b) $k \cos(2x + \alpha)°$ (c) $k \sin(2x - \alpha)°$

2 Given that $0 \leqslant \alpha \leqslant 360$, express $\cos 5x° + \sin 5x°$ in the form

(a) $k \cos(5x - \alpha)°$ (b) $k \sin(5x - \alpha)°$ (c) $k \sin(5x + \alpha)°$

3 Given that $0 \leqslant \alpha \leqslant 2\pi$, express $\cos 8\theta + \sin 8\theta$ in the form

(a) $k \cos(8\theta - \alpha)$ (b) $k \cos(8\theta + \alpha)$ (c) $k \sin(8\theta + \alpha)$

Maximum and minimum values

The maximum and minimum values of a function of the form $a \cos x + b \sin x$ may be found by expressing the function as a single trigonometric function.

Example 6

Write $\sin x° - \cos x°$ in the form $k\cos(x - \alpha)°$.
Hence find its maximum value and the value of x at which this
maximum occurs.

$$\sin x° - \cos x° = k\cos(x - \alpha)°$$
$$= k(\cos x° \cos \alpha° + \sin x° \sin \alpha°)$$
$$= k\cos \alpha° \cos x° + k\sin \alpha° \sin x°$$

Hence $k\cos \alpha° = -1$
$\qquad k\sin \alpha° = 1$

$\alpha°$ is in the second quadrant as $\cos \alpha°$ is negative and $\sin \alpha°$ is positive.

$$k = \sqrt{(-1)^2 + 1^2} = \sqrt{2}$$

$$\tan \alpha° = \frac{1}{-1}$$

$$\alpha = 135$$

$$\sin x° - \cos x° = \sqrt{2}\cos(x - 135)°$$

The maximum value of $\cos(x - 135)°$ is 1.
Hence the maximum value of $\sqrt{2}\cos(x - 135)°$ is $\sqrt{2}$.
This maximum occurs when $\cos(x - 135)° = 1$
$$\text{so}\quad (x - 135) = 0$$
$$x = 135$$

The maximum value is $\sqrt{2}$ and occurs when $x = 135$.

✓✓	✓
S	A
T	C
✓	

Exercise 16G

1 Write each of the following in the form $k\cos(x - \alpha)°$, where $0 \leqslant \alpha \leqslant 360$.
   Hence find the maximum value of each expression and when it occurs.
   (a) $6\cos x° + 8\sin x°$ (b) $5\cos x° - 12\sin x°$ (c) $-8\cos x° - 15\sin x°$
   (d) $2\cos x° - 2\sin x°$ (e) $\cos x° + 2\sin x°$ (f) $2.5\cos x° + 3.5\sin x°$

2 (i) Write each of the expressions (a) to (f) in the form $k\cos(\theta - \alpha)$, where $0 \leqslant \theta \leqslant 2\pi$.
   (ii) Find the maximum value and when it occurs.
   (iii) Find the minimum value and when it occurs.
   (a) $\cos \theta + \sin \theta$ (b) $\sin \theta + \sqrt{2}\cos \theta$ (c) $-\sqrt{3}\cos \theta - \sin \theta$
   (d) $\cos \theta + \sqrt{3}\sin \theta$ (e) $27\sin \theta - \sqrt{27}\cos \theta$ (f) $\sqrt{8}\cos \theta - 2\sin \theta$

3 A ripple tank demonstrates the effect of two water waves being
   added together.
   (a) The waves are described by $h = 25\cos t°$ and $h = 15\sin t°$
        ($0 \leqslant t \leqslant 360$), where h is the height in millimetres above still
        water level and t is the time in seconds from the start of the
        demonstration. Express the resultant wave in the form
        $k\cos(t - \alpha)°$.
   (b) Hence find the maximum height of the resultant wave and
        the value of t at which it occurs.

4 A synthesiser adds two sound waves together to make a new sound. The first wave is described by $V = 75 \sin t°$ and the second by $V = 100 \cos t°$, where V is the volume in decibels and t is the time in seconds.
   (a) Express the resultant wave in the form $k \sin (t - \alpha)°$.
   (b) Find the minimum volume of the resultant wave and the value of t at which it occurs.

5 (a) Find the maximum and minimum values of $\cos x° + \sqrt{3} \sin x°$, where $0 \leqslant x \leqslant 360$, and state the values of x at which these occur.
   (b) Hence find the maximum value of $10 + \cos x° + \sqrt{3} \sin x°$.

6 Find the maximum and minimum values of $\sqrt{2} + \sqrt{2} \cos x° + \sqrt{2} \sin x°$, where $0 \leqslant x \leqslant 360$, and state the values of x at which these occur.

7 Find the maximum and minimum values of $\pi + \cos w + 3 \sin w$, where $0 \leqslant w \leqslant 2\pi$, and state the values of w at which these occur.

8 Find the maximum value of $\cos 3x° + \sin 3x°$, where $0 \leqslant x \leqslant 360$, and state the value of x at which this maximum first occurs.

9 Find the minimum value of $4 \cos 36x° + 3 \sin 36x°$, where $0 \leqslant x \leqslant 10$, and state the value of x at which this minimum occurs.

10 Find the maximum value of $50 \cos 4\theta + 50 \sin 4\theta$, where $0 \leqslant \theta \leqslant \pi$, and state both values of θ at which this maximum occurs.

11 The height, h, of the sea in metres above the mean sea level in a harbour may be calculated using the formula
$h = \sqrt{2} \cos 30t° + \sin 30t°$, where t is the time in hours after midnight on 1st January.
   (a) Express the height in the form $k \sin (30t + \alpha)°$.
   (b) Find the maximum and minimum height of the sea.
   (c) At what times did high and low tides first occur?

Solving equations

We can solve equations involving $a \cos x + b \sin x$ by using the wave formula.

Example 7
Solve $\sqrt{3} \cos \theta + \sin \theta = \sqrt{2}$, for $0 \leqslant \theta \leqslant 2\pi$.

$$\sqrt{3} \cos \theta + \sin \theta = k \cos(\theta - \alpha)$$
$$= k(\cos \theta \cos \alpha + \sin \theta \sin \alpha)$$
$$= k \cos \alpha \cos \theta + k \sin \alpha \sin \theta$$

Hence $k \cos \alpha = \sqrt{3}$
$$k \sin \alpha = 1$$

α is in the first quadrant as both $\cos \alpha$ and $\sin \alpha$ are positive.

$$k = \sqrt{(\sqrt{3})^2 + 1^2} = 2$$

$$\tan \alpha = \frac{1}{\sqrt{3}}$$

$$\alpha = \frac{\pi}{6}$$

$\checkmark$	$\checkmark\checkmark$
S	A
T	C

(with $\checkmark$ under A and $\checkmark$ under C)

$$\sqrt{3}\cos\theta + \sin\theta = \sqrt{2}$$

therefore $\quad 2\cos\left(\theta - \dfrac{\pi}{6}\right) = \sqrt{2}$

$$\cos\left(\theta - \frac{\pi}{6}\right) = \frac{\sqrt{2}}{2} = \frac{1}{\sqrt{2}}$$

$$\left(\theta - \frac{\pi}{6}\right) = \frac{\pi}{4} \quad \text{or} \quad \frac{7\pi}{4}$$

$$\theta = \frac{\pi}{4} + \frac{\pi}{6} \quad \text{or} \quad \frac{7\pi}{4} + \frac{\pi}{6}$$

$$\theta = \frac{5\pi}{12} \quad \text{or} \quad \frac{23\pi}{12}$$

Example 8

Solve $2\cos 2x° - 3\sin 2x° = 1$, for $0 \leqslant x \leqslant 360$.

$$
\begin{aligned}
2\cos 2x° - 3\sin 2x° &= k\cos(2x - \alpha)° \\
&= k(\cos 2x° \cos\alpha° + \sin 2x° \sin\alpha°) \\
&= k\cos\alpha° \cos 2x° + k\sin\alpha° \sin 2x°
\end{aligned}
$$

Hence $\quad k\cos\alpha° = 2$

$\quad\quad\quad\ k\sin\alpha° = -3$

$\alpha°$ is in the fourth quadrant as $\cos\alpha°$ is positive and $\sin\alpha°$ is negative.

$$k = \sqrt{2^2 + (-3)^2} = \sqrt{13}$$

$$\tan\alpha° = \frac{-3}{2}$$

$$\alpha = 304$$

$$2\cos 2x° + 3\sin 2x° = 1$$

therefore $\quad \sqrt{13}\cos(2x - 304)° = 1$

$$\cos(2x - 304)° = \frac{1}{\sqrt{13}}$$

since $\quad\quad 0 \leqslant \quad x \quad\ \leqslant 360$

then $\quad\quad -304 \leqslant 2x - 304 \leqslant 416$

$$
\begin{aligned}
(2x - 304) &= -74 \text{ or } -286 \text{ or } 74 \text{ or } 286 \\
2x &= 230 \text{ or } \quad 18 \text{ or } 378 \text{ or } 596 \\
x &= 115 \text{ or } \quad\ 9 \text{ or } 189 \text{ or } 295
\end{aligned}
$$

(side diagram)

$$
\begin{array}{c|c}
\checkmark & \checkmark \\
\text{S} & \text{A} \\
\hline
\text{T} & \text{C} \\
 & \checkmark\checkmark
\end{array}
$$

Exercise 16H

1 Solve each equation for $0 \leqslant x \leqslant 360$.

   (a) $5\cos x° + 12\sin x° = 13$ **(b)** $3\cos x° + 4\sin x° = 5$ **(c)** $\cos x° - \sqrt{3}\sin x° = 1$

   (d) $8\cos x° - 6\sin x° = 5$ **(e)** $2\cos x° + 3\sin x° = -1$ **(f)** $2\cos x° + 2\sin x° - 1 = 0$

2 Solve each equation for $0 \leqslant \theta \leqslant 2\pi$.

    (a) $\cos\theta + \sin\theta = 1$ **(b)** $\cos\theta - \sin\theta = -1$ **(c)** $\cos\theta + \sqrt{3}\sin\theta = 1$

    (d) $\sqrt{2}\cos\theta + \sqrt{2}\sin\theta = 1$ **(e)** $\sqrt{3}\cos\theta - \sin\theta = \sqrt{3}$ **(f)** $\cos\theta - \sqrt{3}\sin\theta = 1$

3 Solve each equation for $0 \leqslant x \leqslant 360$.

    (a) $\cos 2x° + \sin 2x° = -1$ **(b)** $5\cos 2x° - 12\sin 2x° = 2.6$

    (c) $\cos 3x° - 7\sin 3x° = 5$ **(d)** $4\cos\frac{1}{2}x° = 3\sin\frac{1}{2}x° + 2.5$

    (e) $1.2\cos\frac{1}{2}x° = 1 - 0.9\sin\frac{1}{2}x°$ **(f)** $\sqrt{3}\cos 4x° + 2\sin 4x° - 1 = 0$

4 Solve each equation for $0 \leqslant \theta \leqslant 2\pi$.

    (a) $\cos 2\theta + \sin 2\theta = 1$ **(b)** $-\cos 2\theta - \sin 2\theta = 1$ **(c)** $\cos\dfrac{\theta}{2} + \sqrt{3}\sin\dfrac{\theta}{2} = 1$

    (d) $\sqrt{2}\sin\dfrac{\theta}{2} - \sqrt{2}\cos\dfrac{\theta}{2} = 1$ **(e)** $\sqrt{3}\cos 3\theta - \sin 3\theta = \sqrt{3}$ **(g)** $\cos 4\theta - \sqrt{3}\sin 4\theta = 1$

Applications

Many wave shapes, whether occurring as sound, light, water or electrical waves, can be described mathematically by $a\cos x + b\sin x$. We can therefore use this expression to solve a variety of mathematical problems.

Example 9

The formula $d(t) = 450 + 200(\cos 30t° - \sin 30t°)$ gives an approximation to the depth, d, in centimetres, of water in a harbour t hours after midnight.

(a) Express $f(t) = \cos 30t° - \sin 30t°$ in the form $k\cos(30t - \alpha)°$ and state the values of k and α, where $0 \leqslant \alpha \leqslant 360$.

(b) Use your result from part **(a)** to help you sketch the graph of $f(t)$ for $0 \leqslant t \leqslant 12$.

(c) Hence, on a separate diagram, sketch the graph of $d(t)$ for $0 \leqslant t \leqslant 12$.

(d) When is the first 'low water' time at the harbour?

(e) The local fishing fleet needs at least 2 metres depth of water to enter the harbour without risk of running aground. Between what times must the fleet avoid entering the harbour?

(a) $f(t) = \cos 30t° - \sin 30t° = k\cos(30t - \alpha)°$

$$= k(\cos 30t° \cos\alpha° + \sin 30t \sin\alpha°)$$
$$= k\cos\alpha° \cos 30t° + k\sin\alpha° \sin 30t°$$

Hence $k\cos\alpha° = 1$
$$k\sin\alpha° = -1$$

$\alpha°$ is in the fourth quadrant as $\cos\alpha°$ is positive and $\sin\alpha°$ is negative.

$$k = \sqrt{1^2 + (-1)^2} = \sqrt{2}$$

$$\tan\alpha° = \frac{-1}{1}$$

$$\alpha = 315$$

$$\cos x° - \sin x° = \sqrt{2}\cos(30t - 315)°$$

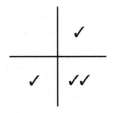

(b)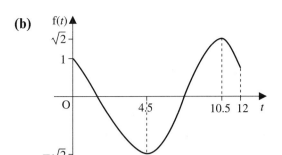

(c)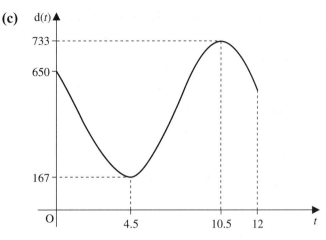

(d) Low water occurs at the minimum value of $d(t)$.

$\cos(30t - 315)° = -1$

since $\quad 0 \leqslant \quad t \quad \leqslant 12$

then $-315 \leqslant 30t - 315 \leqslant 45$

$$30t - 315 = -180$$
$$30t = 135$$
$$t = 4.5$$

Low water first occurs at 4.30 a.m.

(e) $450 + 200(\cos 30t° - \sin 30t°) = 200$

$$200\sqrt{2}\cos(30t - 315)° = 200 - 450$$
$$\cos(30t - 315)° = -0.884$$
$$30t - 315 = -208 \text{ or } -152$$
$$30t = 107 \text{ or } 163$$
$$t = 3.57 \text{ or } 5.43$$

The fleet should avoid entering the harbour between 3.34 a.m. and 5.26 a.m.

Exercise 16I

1 The formula $d(t) = 600 + 100(\cos 30t° - \sin 30t°)$ gives an approximation to the depth, d, in centimetres, of water in a harbour t hours after midnight.

  (a) Express $f(t) = \cos 30t° - \sin 30t°$ in the form $k\cos(30t - \alpha)°$ and state the values of k and α, where $0 \leqslant \alpha \leqslant 360$.

  (b) Use your result from part (a) to help you sketch the graph of $f(t)$ for $0 \leqslant t \leqslant 12$.

  (c) Hence, on a separate diagram, sketch the graph of $d(t)$ for $0 \leqslant t \leqslant 12$.

  (d) When is the first 'low water' time at the harbour?

  (e) The local fishing fleet needs at least 3 metres depth of water to enter the harbour without risk of running aground. Between what times must it avoid entering the harbour?

2 The frequency, f hertz, of the sound of a smoke alarm t seconds after it starts to sound is given by $f = 1000 - 100\sin 180t° + 100\sqrt{3}\cos 180t°$.

   (a) Express f in the form $f = 1000 + k\sin(180t - \alpha)°$ where $k > 0$ and $0 \leqslant \alpha \leqslant 360$.

   (b) Hence, sketch the graph of f for $0 \leqslant t \leqslant 6$.

   (c) If the frequency drops below 1050 hertz, the alarm may not waken inhabitants of a house. Between which times is the alarm sounding below this frequency?

3 An engineer studying wave power models waves in a tank using the formula $h = 2 + \cos 20t° + 0.5\sin 20t°$, where h is the height of the wave in metres and t is the time in seconds after the start of the experiment. The wave is in danger of damaging the apparatus if its height exceeds 3 metres. Between which times is the apparatus in danger of being damaged?

4 The current sent to a light is given by the formula $i = 50 - 10\sin \pi t + 10\cos \pi t$ where i is the current in milliamps and t is the time in seconds after the circuit has been switched on. The light will come on if the current is at least 60 milliamps. Between which times will the light first come on?

Exercise 16J Mixed questions

1 (a) Express $5\sin x° - 10\cos x°$ in the form $k\sin(x - \alpha)°$ where $k > 0$ and $0 \leqslant \alpha < 360$. Find the values of k and α.

   (b) Find the maximum value of $f(x) = 5\sin x° - 10\cos x°$ and state the value at which this maximum occurs.

2 $f(x) = 4\cos x° + 5\sin x°$.

   (a) Express $f(x)$ in the form $k\cos(x - \alpha)°$, where $k > 0$ and $0 \leqslant \alpha \leqslant 360$.

   (b) Hence solve algebraically $f(x) = 2$ for $0 \leqslant x \leqslant 360$.

3 (a) Express $\sin 2x° - \sqrt{3}\cos 2x°$ in the form $k\sin(2x - \alpha)°$, where $k > 0$ and $0 \leqslant \alpha < 90$.

   (b) Find algebraically the values of x between 0 and 180 for which $\sin 2x° - \sqrt{3}\cos 2x° = \sqrt{3}$.

   (c) Find the range of values of x between 0 and 180 for which $\sin 2x° - \sqrt{3}\cos 2x° \leqslant \sqrt{3}$.

4 (a) Express $\sin\theta - \cos\theta$ in the form $k\sin(\theta - \alpha)$, where $k > 0$ and $0 \leqslant \alpha \leqslant 2\pi$.

   (b) Find algebraically the values of x between 0 and 180 for which $\sin\theta - \cos\theta = 1$.

   (c) Find the rage of values of x between 0 and 180 for which $\sin\theta - \cos\theta \leqslant 1$.

5 The expression $20\sin 10T° + 40\cos 10T°$ represents the displacement of a wave after T seconds. This expression can be rewritten in the form $R\sin(10T + \alpha)$ where $R > 0$ and $0 \leqslant \alpha \leqslant 360$.

   (a) Find the values of R and α.

   (b) Write down the amplitude of the wave.

   (c) Use your values of R and α to sketch the graph of $R\sin(10T + \alpha)°$ against T for $0 \leqslant T \leqslant 36$, showing clearly the points where the graph cuts the x-axis and any stationary points.   [Higher]

6 The frequency, f cycles per second, of the sound from a police car siren T seconds after it has been switched on is given by the formula $f = 800 + 50\sqrt{3} \sin \pi T - 50 \cos \pi T$.

This formula can be expressed in the form $f = 800 + R \sin(\pi T - \alpha)$,

where $R > 0$ and $0 < \alpha < \dfrac{\pi}{2}$.

(a) Find the values of R and α.

(b) State the period of this sound.

(c) Use your values of R and α to sketch the graph of f for $0 \leqslant T \leqslant 3$, indicating the end points and any maxima or minima.

(d) The chairman of the local road safety committee has suggested that only when the frequency is higher than 850 cycles per second does the wail of the siren adequately penetrate the protective ear muffs worn by tractor drivers and workers using pneumatic drills or the headphones worn by some cyclists and joggers.

For what fraction of each period is the siren emitting an adequate warning to these people?   [Higher]

7 A builder has obtained a large supply of 4 metre rafters. He wishes to use them to build some holiday chalets. The planning department insists that the gable end of each chalet should be in the form of an isosceles triangle surmounting two squares, as shown in the diagram.

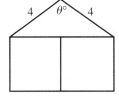

(a) If $\theta°$ is the angle shown in the diagram and A is the area (in square metres) of the gable end, show that
$$A = 8(2 + \sin \theta° - 2 \cos \theta°)$$

(b) Express $8 \sin \theta° - 16 \cos \theta°$ in the form $k \sin(\theta - \alpha)°$.

(c) Find algebraically the value of θ for which the area of the gable end is 30 square metres.   [Higher]

SUMMARY

① $a \cos x + b \sin x$ can be written in the following forms:
- $k \cos(x - \alpha)$
- $k \cos(x + \alpha)$
- $k \sin(x - \alpha)$
- $k \sin(x + \alpha)$

where $k = \sqrt{a^2 + b^2}$ and $\tan \alpha$ can be calculated using a and b. You must first expand $\cos(x \pm \alpha)$ or $\sin(x \pm \alpha)$ and then equate coefficients.

② The maximum and minimum values of $a \cos x + b \sin x$ are given by the maximum and minimum values of any of:
- $k \cos(x - \alpha)$
- $k \cos(x + \alpha)$
- $k \sin(x - \alpha)$
- $k \sin(x + \alpha)$

③ The solutions of the equation $a\cos x + b\sin x = c$ can be obtained from any of the following equations:

- $k\cos(x - \alpha) = c$
- $k\cos(x + \alpha) = c$
- $k\sin(x - \alpha) = c$
- $k\sin(x + \alpha) = c$

Revision exercise 3A

1 Show that the points A(2, −1, 5), B(−1, 2, −1) and C(−3, 4, −5) are collinear and find the ratio in which B divides AC.

2 Calculate the length of the vector, **a**, where
$$\mathbf{a} = 2\mathbf{i} - 4\sqrt{3}\mathbf{j} - 3\sqrt{2}\mathbf{k}.$$

3 The graph illustrates the law $u = kt^n$. Find the values of k and n.

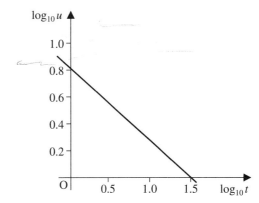

4 Find $\dfrac{dy}{dx}$ when $y = \sin 3x + 4(2x − 3)^4$.

5 Find $\displaystyle\int (4 − x^3 + 2\cos 4x)\, dx$.

6 Find the value of $\displaystyle\int_2^3 \frac{3}{(x − 1)^3}\, dx$

7 Write $5\sin x° − 2\cos x°$ in the form $k\cos(x − \alpha)°$ where $k > 0$ and $0 \leqslant \alpha < 180$.

8 Find the value of $\displaystyle\int_0^{\frac{1}{2}} \sqrt{1 − 2x}\, dx$.

9 The vector $\mathbf{i} + p\mathbf{j} + q\mathbf{k}$ is perpendicular to both the vectors $2\mathbf{i} − 3\mathbf{j} + \mathbf{k}$ and $−\mathbf{i} + 5\mathbf{j} − 2\mathbf{k}$. Find the values of p and q.

10 (a) Express $2\sin 3x − 5\cos 3x$ in the form $k\sin(3x + a)°$ where $k > 0$ and $0 \leqslant a < 360$. Find the values of k and a.
   (b) Find the maximum value of $2 + 2\sin 3x − 5\cos 3x$ and state the value of x for which this maximum occurs.

11 Differentiate $\sin^2 x + 3(2 − 5x)^8$ with respect to x.

12 The diagram shows part of the graph of $y = \log_e (x + k)$. Find the value of k.

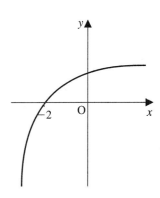

13 (a) Evaluate $\displaystyle\int_0^\pi \sin 2x \; dx$.

   (b) Draw a sketch to explain your answer.

14 The curve $y = f(x)$ passes through the point $\left(\dfrac{3\pi}{4}, -1\right)$ and

   $f'(x) = \sin 4x$. Find $f(x)$.

15 The diagram shows representatives of two vectors, **a** and **b**, meeting at an angle of 60°.
   If $|\mathbf{a}| = 5$ and $|\mathbf{b}| = 3$, evaluate $\mathbf{a}.(\mathbf{a} - \mathbf{b})$.

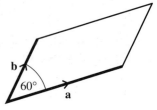

16 Medical researchers studying the growth of a strain of bacteria observe that the number of bacteria present after t hours is given by the formula $N(t) = 40e^{1.5t}$

   (a) State the number of bacteria present at the start of the experiment.

   (b) How many minutes will the bacteria take to double in number?   [Higher]

17 Evaluate $\displaystyle\int_{-2}^0 \sqrt{(4 - 6t)^3} \; dt$.

18 Calculate the area bounded by the curve $y = 5\sin 3x + 2\cos 4x$,

   the x-axis and the lines $x = 0$ and $x = \dfrac{\pi}{4}$.

Revision exercise 3B

1 PQRS is a quadrilateral with vertices P(0, 0, 0), Q(2, 4, 0), R(0, 5, −1) and S(4, −2, 2).
  (a) K, L, M and N are the mid-points of PQ, QR, RS and SP, respectively. Find the coordinates of K, L, M and N.
  (b) What kind of quadrilateral is KLMN? Explain.

2 The diagram shows part of the graphs of $y = \sin x$ and $y = \cos 2x$ $(0 \leqslant x \leqslant 180°)$.
  (a) Solve $\sin x = \cos 2x$ $(0 \leqslant x \leqslant 180°)$.
  (b) Calculate the shaded area.

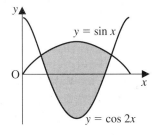

3 PQRS is a quadrilateral with vertices P(−2, −1, −4), Q(1, 5, −7), R(7, 8, 5) and S(7, 2, 17).
  (a) Find the coordinates of T which lies on PR such that PT : TR = 5 : 4.
  (b) Show that Q, T and S are collinear.
  (c) Calculate the size of the acute angle between the diagonals of quadrilateral PQRS. [Higher]

4 Radiocarbon dating is a method of determining the age of some types of archaeological remains. In a sample, which originally contained m_0 grams of carbon 14, there will be m grams of carbon 14 after t years where $m = m_0 e^{-1.2 \times 10^{-4} t}$.
  (a) What mass of carbon 14 will remain in a sample, originally containing 100 mg of it, after 1000 years?
  (b) How old is a sample which originally had 100 mg of carbon 14 and now has 70 mg?
  (c) How long will it take for half of the original quantity of carbon 14 to decay?

5 A body is moving in a straight line so that its distance, x m, from a fixed point is given by $x = 6 \sin 4t + 8 \cos 4t$.
  (a) Express $6 \sin 4t + 8 \cos 4t$ in the form $R \sin (4t + \alpha)$.
  (b) Write down the amplitude of the body's motion.
  (c) Find the times, $0 \leqslant t \leqslant \pi$, when the body is at the extreme of its travel.

6 (a) On the same diagram, sketch the graphs of $y = \log_{10} x$ and $y = 2 - x$ where $0 < x < 5$. Write down an approximation for the x-coordinate of the point of intersection.
  (b) Find the value of this x-coordinate, correct to two decimal places. [Higher]

7 (a) A tractor tyre is inflated to a pressure of 50 units. Twenty-four hours later the pressure has dropped to 10 units. If the pressure, P_t units, after t hours is given by the formula $P_t = P_0 e^{-kt}$, find the value of k, to three decimal places.

(b) The tyre manufacturer advises that serious damage to the tyre will result if it is used when the pressure drops below 30 units.

If a farmer inflates the tyre to 50 units and drives the tractor for 4 hours, can the tractor be driven further without inflating the tyre and without risking serious damage to the tyre?   [Higher]

8 A model crystal was made from a cube of side 3 units by slicing off the corner P to leave a triangular face ABC. Coordinate axes have been introduced as shown in the diagram. The point A divides OP in the ratio $1:2$. Points B and C similarly divide RP and SP, respectively, in the ratio $1:2$.

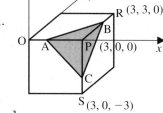

(a) Find the coordinates of A, B and C.
(b) Calculate the area of triangle ABC.
(c) Calculate the percentage increase or decrease in the surface area of the crystal compared with the cube.   [Higher]

9 A particle is moving along the x-axis so that its velocity v m/s at time t seconds is given by $v = 4\cos(3t + 2)$.

(a) Find the times, $0 \leqslant t \leqslant 2\pi$, when the particle is at rest.
(b) Calculate the acceleration of the particle when $t = 2$ seconds.
(c) Calculate the distance travelled by the particle during the first 5 seconds of its motion.

10 A dam is to be built to contain water in a new reservoir. Relative to axes, as shown in the diagram, the inner and outer walls can be represented by parts of the graphs of $y = \dfrac{20}{\sqrt{4-x}} - 10, 0 \leqslant x \leqslant 3$, and $y = 50 - 8x, x \geqslant 5$.

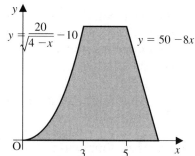

(all dimensions are in metres).
(a) Calculate the height of the dam.
(b) Calculate its cross-sectional area.
(c) If the dam is 80 m long and has a constant cross-section, calculate the volume of material required for its construction.

11 The amplitude, A, of a warning siren, at time t seconds after starting, in a chemical plant can be represented by $A(t) = 1000 + 300(\sin \pi t - \sqrt{3}\cos \pi t)$.

(a) Express $300(\sin \pi t - \sqrt{3}\cos \pi t)$ in the form $R\cos(\pi t + \alpha)$ where $R > 0$ and $0 \leqslant \alpha \leqslant 2\pi$.
(b) What are the values of the period and amplitude of A?
(c) In one part of the plant the amplitude of the noise of machinery is 750 units. When is the warning siren first heard?

12 U^{235} is a radioactive isotope of uranium. It decays into lead according to the law $m = m_0 e^{kt}$ where m_0 is the mass of U^{235} originally present and m is the mass present after t years.

(a) The half-life of U^{235}, i.e. the time taken for half of the isotope to decay, is 7×10^8 years. Find the value of k correct to two significant figures.

(b) A sample of rock contains 20 mg of U^{235}. How long will it be before this is reduced by 0.5 mg?

(c) The age of the Earth is estimated to be 5.25×10^9 years. What fraction of the U^{235} present at its formation is still around today?

13 Triangle OPQ is right-angled at P and is free to rotate about the origin, O. OP is 10 units long and PQ is 4 units.

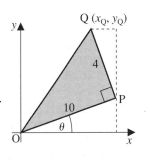

(a) Show that, when OP makes an angle of θ with the x-axis, the y-coordinate of Q is given by $y_Q = 10\sin\theta + 4\cos\theta$.

(b) Express this in the form $R\sin(\theta + \alpha)$ with $R > 0$ and $-\dfrac{\pi}{2} \leqslant \alpha \leqslant \dfrac{\pi}{2}$.

(c) Find a corresponding expression for the x coordinate of Q, x_Q.

(d) As θ varies what are the maximum distances of Q from the x and y axes?

(e) Show, algebraically, that Q lies on the circle with equation $x^2 + y^2 = 116$.

14 Linktown Church is considering designs for a logo for their parish magazine. The 'C' is part of a circle and the centre of the circle is the mid-point of the vertical arm of the 'L'. Since the 'L' is clearly smaller than the 'C', the designer wishes to ensure that the total length of the arms of the 'L' is as long as possible. The designer decides to call the point where the 'L' and 'C' meet A, and chooses to draw coordinate axes so that A is in the first quadrant. With axes as shown, the equation of the circle is $x^2 + y^2 = 20$.

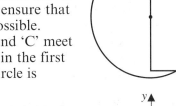

(a) If A has coordinates (x, y), show that the total length T of the arms of the 'L' is given by $T = 2x + \sqrt{20 - x^2}$.

(b) Show that for a stationary value of T, x satisfies the equation $x = 2\sqrt{20 - x^2}$.

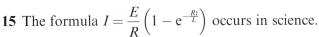

(c) By squaring both sides, solve this equation. Hence find the greatest length of the arms of the 'L'.

[Higher]

15 The formula $I = \dfrac{E}{R}\left(1 - e^{-\frac{Rt}{L}}\right)$ occurs in science.

(a) Show that $t = \log_e\left(\dfrac{E}{E - RI}\right)^{\frac{L}{R}}$

(b) Find the value of t when $E = 240$, e $= 2.72$, $L = 2.6$, $R = 40$ and $I = 1.1$.

[Higher]

Essential skills

This chapter revises skills covered within the Credit course. You do not need to work through all of the chapter but you may find it useful to dip into sections within the chapter at appropriate times when working through the rest of the book.

Algebra

$$(3p)^2 \times 5kp = 9p^2 \times 5kp$$
$$= 9 \times p^2 \times 5 \times k \times p$$
$$= 45 \times p^2 \times k \times p$$
$$= 45 \times p^3 \times k$$
$$= 45kp^3$$

Algebra is used to describe mathematical relationships. We can expand and simplify algebraic expressions by following certain rules.

Adding and subtracting algebraic terms

Algebraic expressions normally follow these conventions:

- terms are ordered according to their powers, usually with the highest power first
- variables within terms are put in alphabetical order
- where possible a negative first term is avoided.

To simplify algebraic expressions we can combine like terms.

Example 1
Simplify $3a^2 + 5ab + 2b^2 - 3b + 4ba + 7a^2$.

$$3a^2 + 5ab + 2b^2 - 3b + 4ba + 7a^2 = 3a^2 + 7a^2 + 5ab + 4ab + 2b^2 - 3b$$
$$= 10a^2 + 9ab + 2b^2 - 3b$$

Exercise 1

1 Simplify where possible:
  (a) $3pq + 5pq$
  (b) $7xy + 2zy$
  (c) $km + 6mk$
  (d) $12cd^2 - 5cd^2$
  (e) $13rs^2 - 8r^2s$
  (f) $7ax^2 + 3bx^2$
  (g) $4v^2w + 3wv^2$
  (h) $9p^2q^2 - q^2p^2$

   (i) $3y^2 - 2y^2 + 7y - y$

   (k) $b^2 + 3b^2 - ab - 2ab$

   (m) $ab + 3xy + 5ab$

   (o) $8xy^2 + xy - 6xy^2$

   (q) $13cd - 20cd + dc$

   (s) $2x^3 + 3x^2 - x^3$

   (j) $r^3 + 2r^3 - 8r + 5r$

   (l) $5x^2 + x^2 - x + x$

   (n) $pq - kl + 7pq$

   (p) $9vw^2 - 7v^3w - vw^2$

   (r) $a^3 + b^3 - a^3b^3$

   (t) $5x^2 + x^3 - 9x^2$

2 Simplify:

   (a) $x^2 + 10 - x^2 + 10$

   (c) $m^2 + m + 1 - m^2 - 2m - 3$

   (e) $a - 2c + 3b - 2b + a + 5c$

   (g) $4x^2 - 5xy - 2xy - x^2$

   (i) $2.7k - 1.3j + 3.3k + 0.9j$

   (k) $4x^2 - 8y^2 - 3xy + 5xy - 2y^2$

   (b) $p^2 + p + p^2 + 2p$

   (d) $-3b^2 + 2b + 4 + b^2 - 2b + 4$

   (f) $-p - r - q + 7p - 4q - r$

   (h) $9s^2 - 5r^2 - 8r^2s^2 - 8s^2$

   (j) $\frac{1}{4}t^2 - s + \frac{1}{2} + \frac{1}{2}t^2 - \frac{1}{2}s + \frac{1}{4}$

   (l) $ab + a^2b - 9ab + 5a^2b + b^2a$

Multiplying and dividing algebraic expressions

We can also multiply and divide algebraic expressions.

Example 2

Simplify

   (a) $(3p)^2 \times 5kp$

   (c) $-9t(st - 5t^2)$

   (b) $24x^2y \div 8y^2x$

   (d) $\dfrac{20x^2 - 5xy}{10x}$

   (a) $\begin{aligned}(3p)^2 \times 5kp &= 9p^2 \times 5kp \\ &= 9 \times p^2 \times 5 \times k \times p \\ &= 45 \times p^2 \times k \times p \\ &= 45 \times p^3 \times k \\ &= 45kp^3\end{aligned}$

   (b) $\begin{aligned}24x^2y \div 8y^2x &= \frac{24x^2y}{8xy^2} \\ &= \frac{3x}{y}\end{aligned}$

   (c) $\begin{aligned}-9t(st - 5t^2) &= -9st^2 + 45t^3 \\ &= 45t^3 - 9st^2\end{aligned}$

   (d) $\begin{aligned}\frac{20x^2 - 5xy}{10x} &= \frac{20x^2y}{10x} - \frac{5xy}{10x} \\ &= 2xy - \frac{y}{2}\end{aligned}$

Exercise 2

1 Simplify:

   (a) $7a \times 3a^2b$

   (d) $ab \times pq$

   (g) $\dfrac{1}{a} \times a$

   (j) $(2b)^2 \times 3b$

   (m) $(7x)^2 \times (-x)^2$

   (p) $\dfrac{3}{(2s)^2} \times 8rs$

   (b) $-8xy \times 4xy$

   (e) $-k \times (-km^2)$

   (h) $r^2 \times \dfrac{p}{r}$

   (k) $5e \times (5f)^2$

   (n) $-4p \times (pqg)^2$

   (q) $\dfrac{1}{x^3} \times x^3y$

   (c) $mn^2 \times m^2n$

   (f) $cd \times (-d^2)$

   (i) $\dfrac{v}{w^2} \times \dfrac{w}{v}$

   (l) $(-g)^2 \times 7fg$

   (o) $\left(\dfrac{1}{a}\right)^3 \times a^2$

   (r) $\dfrac{a}{b^2} \times \dfrac{b}{a^2}$

2 Simplify:

(a) $6ab \div 3a$ (b) $15xy \div 5y$ (c) $36cd \div 9cd$

(d) $7pq^2 \div pq$ (e) $20rs^2 \div 4s^2$ (f) $54f^2g \div 9f$

(g) $12ab^2 \div 4a^2b$ (h) $16uv \div 8uv^2$ (i) $19ab \div ab^2$

(j) $3m^2n \div 18mn$ (k) $7gh^2 \div 14h^3$ (l) $28k^2l^2 \div 7k^2l$

(m) $3tu \div 39t^2u^2$ (n) $33vw^3 \div 11vw$ (o) $42xy^2 \div 6x^2y$

3 Expand:

(a) $3x(5x + 2)$ (b) $7y(y^2 - z)$ (c) $-3a^2(2 - 5a^2)$

(d) $-(9p - q)$ (e) $12r(s^2 + r)$ (f) $-w^2(vw + 1)$

(g) $(13x - 5y)3y$ (h) $(a^2 + b^2)abc$ (i) $(-5d^3 - e^2)e$

(j) $f^2g(3g - 2f)$ (k) $(m^2 + 5n)km$ (l) $-8t^3(u - tu)$

4 Simplify:

(a) $\dfrac{27x + 18}{3}$ (b) $\dfrac{35x^2 - 5y}{5}$ (c) $\dfrac{x^2 - 5x}{x}$

(d) $\dfrac{12ab + a^2}{4a}$ (e) $\dfrac{48p^2q - 16pq}{8p}$ (f) $\dfrac{5r^2s^2 + 7rs^2}{rs}$

(g) $\dfrac{pqr + p^2qr^2}{pqr}$ (h) $\dfrac{14x^3y^2 - 28xy + 7x^2y}{7xy}$

Expanding brackets

We can simplify algebraic expressions by expanding terms in brackets.

Example 3

Expand the following expressions:

(a) $x^2(3x - 4) - 6x - 2(3 - x)^2$ (b) $(2x + 3)(x^2 - 5x + 3)$ (c) $(2x - 5)^3$

(a) $x^2(3x - 4) - 6x - 2(3 - x)^2$

$= x^2(3x - 4) - 6x - 2(9 - 6x + x^2)$ ——————— expand squared bracket

$= 3x^3 - 4x^2 - 6x - 18 + 12x - 2x^2$ ——————— remove brackets

$= 3x^3 - 6x^2 + 6x - 18$ ——————— simplify

(b) $(2x + 3)(x^2 - 5x + 3)$

$= 2x(x^2 - 5x + 3) + 3(x^2 - 5x + 3)$ ——————— multiply terms in the second bracket

$= 2x^3 - 10x^2 + 6x + 3x^2 - 15x + 9$ ——————— by each term from the first

$= 2x^3 - 7x^2 - 9x + 9$ ——————— simplify

(c) $(2x - 5)^3 = (2x - 5)(2x - 5)(2x - 5)$

$= (2x - 5)(4x^2 - 20x + 25)$ ——————— multiply a pair of brackets

$= 2x(4x^2 - 20x + 25) - 5(4x^2 - 20x + 25)$ ——————— multiply second bracket by

$= 8x^3 - 40x^2 + 50x - 20x^2 + 100x - 125$ ——————— each term from the first

$= 8x^3 - 60x^2 + 150x - 125$ ——————— simplify

Exercise 3

1 Expand:
  (a) $(x + 3)(x + 4)$
  (c) $(p - 2)(p - 13)$
  (e) $(4 - s)(8 + s)$
  (g) $(3v - 1)(7v + 4)$
  (i) $2(x + 5)(x + 7)$
  (k) $7(1 - t)(4 - t)$

  (b) $(4 - y)(6 - y)$
  (d) $(r + 5)(r - 6)$
  (f) $(2t + 5)(t - 7)$
  (h) $(2 - 9w)(4 - 3w)$
  (j) $5(a + 2)(a - 9)$
  (l) $-4(m + 2)(m - 10)$

2 Expand:
  (a) $(x + 2)^2$
  (c) $(7 + 2a)^2$
  (e) $(x + 2)(x - 2)$
  (g) $(20 + 7q)(20 - 7q)$
  (i) $5(a - 2)(a + 2)$
  (k) $6(m - n)(m + n)$
  (m) $(b + 5)^2$
  (o) $(8 - k)^2$
  (q) $(9 + 2z)^2$
  (s) $(3p - q)^2$
  (u) $(a + b)^2$
  (w) $(5x - 8y)^2$

  (b) $(3y - 5)^2$
  (d) $(9 - 4q)^2$
  (f) $(3k - 1)(3k + 1)$
  (h) $3(x + 1)(x - 1)$
  (j) $10(3 + p)(3 - p)$
  (l) $2(3k + 4j)(3k - 4j)$
  (n) $(d - 6)^2$
  (p) $(10 + p)^2$
  (r) $(7 - 5v)^2$
  (t) $(5m + 2n)^2$
  (v) $(g - 7h)^2$
  (x) $(6v + 9w)^2$

3 Expand and simplify:
  (a) $x(2x + 4) + 3x - 5(x^2 - 6)$
  (c) $8x(5x - 6) - 3(x + 4)^2$
  (e) $9(a - 6)^2 - a(2a + 3)^2$
  (g) $4f(f - 5)^2 + 20f - 2(3f - 1)^2$
  (i) $-6s(7 + s)^2 + (2s - 6)^2$

  (b) $x^2(5x - 7) + 4x(3x + 2) - x^2$
  (d) $y^2(y + 5) - 7y - (y - 5)^2$
  (f) $25p^2 - (5 - p)^2 + 10p$
  (h) $t^2(9t - 1) - 9(t + 1)^2 + 10t^2$
  (j) $(8 - 2w)^2 - 60 + 10w - (w - 4)^2$

4 Expand and simplify:
  (a) $(x + 1)(x^2 - 2x + 3)$
  (c) $(5a - 2)(3a^2 - 7a + 4)$
  (e) $(7p^2 - 8p - 9)(3p + 6)$
  (g) $(8 + t)(8 - 3t + 3t^2)$
  (i) $(2 + x)(3x^2 + 5x + 1)$
  (k) $(f + 9)(5 - 7f + 4f^2)$
  (m) $2(w + 5)(w^2 - 3w + 1)$
  (o) $5(2 - a)(3a^2 + a - 2)$

  (b) $(2y + 4)(y^2 + 5y - 6)$
  (d) $(b^2 + 5b - 2)(6b - 1)$
  (f) $(1 - q)(5 - 2q + q^2)$
  (h) $(6 - 4s - 2s^2)(9 - 5s)$
  (j) $(6 - d)(7d^2 + 2d - 8)$
  (l) $(2 - 4h - 3h^2)(6h + 9)$
  (n) $3(z^2 + 7z - 2)(2z - 1)$
  (p) $4(1 + b)(7 - 2b - b^2)$

5 Expand and simplify:
  (a) $(k + 4)^3$
  (c) $(p - 1)^3$
  (e) $(a + 2)^3$
  (g) $(2d + 3)^3$
  (i) $(1 + 4x)^3$

  (b) $(3r - 5)^3$
  (d) $(4 + 2q)^3$
  (f) $(b - 1)^3$
  (h) $(5e - 2)^3$

Factorising

Some algebraic expressions can be written as a product of factors.
This is called **factorisation**.

Example 4
Factorise fully:

(a) $3ab^2 + 9ab$ (b) $x^2 + 5x + 6$ (c) $20 - 15a - 5a^2$

(d) $y^2 - 81$ (e) $72 - 2t^2$ (f) $t^4 - 1$

(a)	$3ab^2 + 9ab = 3ab(b + 3)$	common factor
(b)	$x^2 + 5x + 6 = (x + 2)(x + 3)$	quadratic factors
(c)	$20 - 15a - 5a^2 = 5(4 - 3a - a^2)$	common factor then
	$\quad\quad = 5(4 + a)(1 - a)$	quadratic factors
(d)	$y^2 - 81 = (y + 9)(y - 9)$	difference of squares
(e)	$72 - 2t^3 = 2(36 - t^2)$	common factor then
	$\quad\quad = 2(6 + t)(6 - t)$	difference of squares
(f)	$t^4 - 1 = (t^2 + 1)(t^2 - 1)$	difference of squares
	$\quad\quad = (t^2 + 1)(t + 1)(t - 1)$	repeated

Exercise 4

1 Factorise fully:

(a) $5xy + 15y^2$ (b) $7f^2g^2 - fg$

(c) $2pq^2 + 14pq - 7p^2$ (d) $rs^3 - 3rs + 6s^2$

(e) $t^2 + 8t + 12$ (f) $r^2 - 11r + 10$

(g) $y^2 + 6y + 5$ (h) $p^2 - 6p + 8$

(i) $24 - 11s + s^2$ (j) $w^2 + 2w - 15$

(k) $v^2 + 3v - 4$ (l) $15 + 2w - w^2$

(m) $z^2 + 12z - 13$ (n) $-x^2 + 4x - 3$

(o) $25 - 10f + f^2$ (p) $a^2 - 6a - 16$

(q) $x^2 - 8x - 9$ (r) $35 - 2q - q^2$

(s) $b^2 - b - 20$ (t) $h^2 + 14h + 49$

(u) $-1 + 2k - k^2$ (v) $3y^2 + 8y + 4$

(w) $2x^2 + 9x + 4$ (x) $6m^2 + 13m + 5$

(y) $10d^2 - 11d - 6$ (z) $9p^2 + 18p - 16$

2 Factorise fully:

(a) $x^2 - 25$ (b) $a^2 - 1$ (c) $a^2 - 100$

(d) $4p^2 - 9$ (e) $64p^2 - 121$ (f) $36 - 25u^2$

(g) $x^2 - 16y^2$ (h) $49t^2 - 144s^2$ (i) $f^2 - 900g^2$

(j) $5x^2 - 500$ (k) $3w^2 - 243$ (l) $10v^2 - 40$

(m) $12p^2 - 3$ (n) $20 - 45s^2$ (o) $7y^2 - 28z^2$

(p) $27a^2 - 48b^2$ (q) $125d^2 - 45e^2$ (r) $98f^2 - 200g^2$

(s) $v^4 - 16$ (t) $w^4 - 81$ (u) $x^4 - 10\,000$

(v) $7y^4 - 7$ (w) $16a^4 - 1$ (x) $162 - 2b^4$

Completing the square

$x^2 + 8x + 16$ is a **perfect square** because $x^2 + 8x + 16 = (x + 4)^2$.

Example 5
Add a number to make $x^2 - 6x$ a perfect square.

Add 9 to make $x^2 - 6x + 9 = (x - 3)^2$

Example 6
Write $x^2 + 8x + 3$ in the form $(x + p)^2 + q$

$$\begin{aligned}
x^2 + 8x + 3 &= (x^2 + 8x) + 3 && \text{Separate 3 from the other terms}\\
&= (x^2 + 8x + 16) + 3 - 16 && \text{Add 16 to complete the}\\
&&& \text{square and subtract 16 to}\\
&= (x + 4)^2 - 13 && \text{maintain value}
\end{aligned}$$

Example 7
Write $4 + x - x^2$ in the form $p - (x + q)^2$

$$\begin{aligned}
4 + x - x^2 &= -(x^2 - x - 4) && \text{Take a common factor of } -1\\
&= -[(x^2 - x) - 4] && \text{Separate } -4 \text{ from the other terms}\\
&= -[(x^2 - x + \tfrac{1}{4}) - 4 - \tfrac{1}{4}] && \text{Add } \tfrac{1}{4} \text{ to complete the square and}\\
&&& \text{subtract } \tfrac{1}{4} \text{ to maintain value}\\
&= -[(x - \tfrac{1}{2})^2 - 4\tfrac{1}{4}]\\
&= 4\tfrac{1}{4} - (x - \tfrac{1}{2})^2
\end{aligned}$$

Example 8
Write $3x^2 + 6x + 2$ in the form $a(x + p)^2 + q$

$$\begin{aligned}
3x^2 + 6x + 2 &= 3[x^2 + 2x + \tfrac{2}{3}] && \text{Take the coefficient of } x^2\\
&= 3[(x^2 + 2x) + \tfrac{2}{3}] && \text{as a factor}\\
&= 3[(x^2 + 2x + 1) + \tfrac{2}{3} - 1]\\
&= 3[(x + 1)^2 - \tfrac{1}{3}]\\
&= 3(x + 1)^2 - 1
\end{aligned}$$

Exercise 5

1 Add a number to each expression to make a perfect square.

(a) $x^2 + 2x$ (b) $x^2 + 4x$ (c) $y^2 + 12y$

(d) $m^2 - 6m$ (e) $t^2 - 14t$ (f) $w^2 - 20w$

(g) $x^2 + 3x$ (h) $a^2 + a$ (i) $n^2 + 7n$

(j) $r^2 - 9r$ (k) $v^2 - \tfrac{2}{3}v$ (l) $x^2 - \tfrac{1}{2}x$

2 Write each expression in the form $(x + p)^2 + q$.

(a) $x^2 + 6x + 10$ (b) $y^2 - 2y + 3$ (c) $z^2 + 8z - 10$

(d) $a^2 - 10a - 5$ (e) $b^2 + 18b - 81$ (f) $c^2 - 40c + 1$

   (g) $r^2 + 5r - 5$ **(h)** $s^2 + s + 2$ **(i)** $t^2 - 3t - 1$

   (j) $m^2 + \frac{1}{2}m + \frac{1}{4}$ **(k)** $n^2 + 0.6n - 1$ **(l)** $w^2 - 1.6w + 2$

3 Write each expression in the form $p - (x + q)^2$.

   (a) $4 + 2x - x^2$ **(b)** $5 - 4x - x^2$ **(c)** $2 + x - x^2$

   (d) $6 + 3x - x^2$ **(e)** $2x - 6 - x^2$ **(f)** $4x - 6 - x^2$

4 Write each expression in the form $a(x + p)^2 + q$.

   (a) $2x^2 + 4x - 1$ **(b)** $3y^2 + 12y + 5$ **(c)** $5a^2 - 30a - 18$

   (d) $2n^2 + 2n + 1$ **(e)** $4b^2 - 12b - 5$ **(f)** $2m^2 - 3m - 6$

Algebraic fractions

We can add or subtract algebraic fractions by following the same techniques as we use for numerical fractions.

Example 9

Express each of the following as a single fraction and simplify where possible:

(a) $\dfrac{4}{x} - \dfrac{3}{x}$ **(b)** $\dfrac{a}{2} + \dfrac{b}{7}$ **(c)** $\dfrac{4}{5y} - \dfrac{1}{4y}$

(d) $\dfrac{a}{x} - \dfrac{b}{y}$ **(e)** $\dfrac{x+5}{2} + \dfrac{x-2}{3}$

(a) $\dfrac{4}{x} - \dfrac{3}{x} = \dfrac{1}{x}$

(b) $\dfrac{a}{2} + \dfrac{b}{7} = \dfrac{a}{2} \times \dfrac{7}{7} + \dfrac{b}{7} \times \dfrac{2}{2}$

$$= \dfrac{7a}{14} + \dfrac{2b}{14}$$

$$= \dfrac{7a + 2b}{14}$$

(c) $\dfrac{4}{5y} - \dfrac{1}{4y} = \dfrac{4}{5y} \times \dfrac{4}{4} - \dfrac{1}{4y} \times \dfrac{5}{5}$

$$= \dfrac{16}{20y} - \dfrac{5}{20y}$$

$$= \dfrac{11}{20y}$$

(d) $\dfrac{a}{x} - \dfrac{b}{y} = \dfrac{a}{x} \times \dfrac{y}{y} - \dfrac{b}{y} \times \dfrac{x}{x}$

$$= \dfrac{ay}{xy} - \dfrac{bx}{xy}$$

$$= \dfrac{ay - bx}{xy}$$

(e) $\dfrac{x+5}{2} + \dfrac{x-2}{3} = \dfrac{(x+5)}{2} \times \dfrac{3}{3} + \dfrac{(x-2)}{3} \times \dfrac{2}{2}$

$$= \dfrac{3(x+5)}{6} + \dfrac{2(x-2)}{6}$$

$$= \dfrac{3x + 15 + 2x - 4}{6}$$

$$= \dfrac{5x + 11}{6}$$

Exercise 6

1 Express each of the following as a single fraction and simplify where possible:

(a) $\dfrac{e}{5} + \dfrac{2e}{5}$

(b) $\dfrac{5m}{7} - \dfrac{2m}{7}$

(c) $\dfrac{5r}{12} + \dfrac{11r}{12}$

(d) $\dfrac{a}{3} + \dfrac{b}{3}$

(e) $\dfrac{3p}{7} - \dfrac{q}{7}$

(f) $\dfrac{13}{v} - \dfrac{2}{v}$

(g) $\dfrac{8}{w} - \dfrac{9}{w}$

(h) $\dfrac{2a}{u} + \dfrac{3a}{u}$

(i) $\dfrac{a}{x} - \dfrac{b}{x}$

2 Express each of the following as a single fraction and simplify where possible:

(a) $\dfrac{5x}{6} - \dfrac{2x}{3}$

(b) $\dfrac{n}{5} + \dfrac{3n}{20}$

(c) $\dfrac{7u}{8} - \dfrac{5u}{16}$

(d) $\dfrac{p}{4} - \dfrac{q}{2}$

(e) $\dfrac{3x}{25} - \dfrac{y}{5}$

(f) $\dfrac{3a}{22} + \dfrac{3b}{2}$

(g) $\dfrac{1}{a} + \dfrac{3}{2a}$

(h) $\dfrac{5}{3b} - \dfrac{1}{b}$

(i) $\dfrac{3}{4g} + \dfrac{7}{12g}$

(j) $\dfrac{1}{13p} - \dfrac{5}{39p}$

(k) $\dfrac{3}{2x} + \dfrac{1}{2}$

(l) $\dfrac{3}{5} - \dfrac{2}{5a}$

(m) $\dfrac{a}{2} - \dfrac{a}{9}$

(n) $\dfrac{2t}{3} + \dfrac{t}{8}$

(o) $\dfrac{3h}{5} - \dfrac{2h}{7}$

(p) $\dfrac{u}{3} + \dfrac{v}{2}$

(q) $\dfrac{5h}{7} - \dfrac{4k}{9}$

(r) $\dfrac{2c}{3} + \dfrac{3d}{10}$

(s) $\dfrac{4}{5m} - \dfrac{1}{2m}$

(t) $\dfrac{3}{4r} + \dfrac{5}{6r}$

(u) $\dfrac{2}{9t} - \dfrac{3}{4t}$

3 Express each of the following as a single fraction and simplify where possible:

(a) $\dfrac{a}{2} + \dfrac{3}{b}$

(b) $\dfrac{x}{5} - \dfrac{4}{y}$

(c) $\dfrac{7}{r} + \dfrac{s}{9}$

(d) $\dfrac{8}{u} - \dfrac{t}{3}$

(e) $\dfrac{3m}{5} - \dfrac{7}{2n}$

(f) $\dfrac{6}{7v} - \dfrac{2w}{3}$

(g) $\dfrac{c}{p} + \dfrac{d}{q}$

(h) $\dfrac{9}{x} + \dfrac{5}{y}$

(i) $\dfrac{8}{b} - \dfrac{7}{d}$

(j) $\dfrac{p}{e} - \dfrac{3}{f}$

(k) $\dfrac{2a}{7} + \dfrac{9}{3b}$

(l) $\dfrac{5}{9} - \dfrac{x}{2f}$

(m) $\dfrac{x+1}{2} + \dfrac{x-2}{3}$

(n) $\dfrac{a-5}{4} - \dfrac{a+3}{5}$

(o) $\dfrac{q+4}{3} + \dfrac{q-6}{7}$

(p) $\dfrac{w-7}{8} - \dfrac{w-1}{9}$

(q) $\dfrac{t+12}{6} + \dfrac{t}{10}$

(r) $\dfrac{2x+3}{5} + \dfrac{7-x}{9}$

Complex algebraic fractions

We can use the same technique to add or subtract algebraic fractions regardless of how complex they may be.

Example 10

Express as a single fraction:

(a) $\dfrac{3}{x-2} - \dfrac{5}{x}$

(b) $\dfrac{a-5}{a^2+7a+12} + \dfrac{2}{a+4}$

(a) $\dfrac{3}{x-2} - \dfrac{5}{x} = \dfrac{3}{x-2} \times \dfrac{x}{x} - \dfrac{5}{x} \times \dfrac{(x-2)}{(x-2)}$

$= \dfrac{3x}{x(x-2)} - \dfrac{5(x-2)}{x(x-2)}$

$= \dfrac{3x - 5x + 10}{x(x-2)}$

$= \dfrac{-2x + 10}{x(x-2)}$

$= \dfrac{-2(x-5)}{x(x-2)}$

(b) $\dfrac{a-5}{a^2+7a+12} + \dfrac{2}{a+4} = \dfrac{(a-5)}{(a+4)(a+3)} + \dfrac{2}{(a+4)}$

$= \dfrac{(a-5)}{(a+4)(a+3)} + \dfrac{2}{(a+4)} \times \dfrac{(a+3)}{(a+3)}$

$= \dfrac{(a-5)}{(a+4)(a+3)} + \dfrac{2(a+3)}{(a+4)(a+3)}$

$= \dfrac{(a-5) + 2(a+3)}{(a+4)(a+3)}$

$= \dfrac{a - 5 + 2a + 6}{(a+4)(a+3)}$

$= \dfrac{3a + 1}{(a+4)(a+3)}$

Exercise 7

1 Express as a single fraction:

(a) $\dfrac{2}{a+1} + \dfrac{3}{a}$

(b) $\dfrac{4}{w+3} - \dfrac{7}{w}$

(c) $\dfrac{6}{e-5} + \dfrac{9}{e}$

(d) $\dfrac{5}{m} - \dfrac{8}{m+2}$

(e) $\dfrac{1}{r} + \dfrac{9}{r-7}$

(f) $\dfrac{7}{v} - \dfrac{3}{v-9}$

(g) $\dfrac{3}{b+1} + \dfrac{2}{b+3}$

(h) $\dfrac{4}{n-5} + \dfrac{6}{n+2}$

(i) $\dfrac{5}{s+4} - \dfrac{8}{s+7}$

(j) $\dfrac{7}{t-2} - \dfrac{9}{t+5}$

(k) $\dfrac{5}{x-1} + \dfrac{1}{x-7}$

(l) $\dfrac{9}{y-8} - \dfrac{6}{y-5}$

2 Express as a single fraction:

(a) $\dfrac{2}{a^2 - 1} + \dfrac{1}{a + 1}$

(b) $\dfrac{1}{x^2 - 1} - \dfrac{1}{x - 1}$

(c) $\dfrac{1}{b + 3} + \dfrac{3}{b^2 + 4b + 3}$

(d) $\dfrac{2}{w^2 - 2w + 1} + \dfrac{3}{w - 1}$

(e) $\dfrac{1}{p - 2} - \dfrac{3}{p^2 + p - 6}$

(f) $\dfrac{2}{x + 2} - \dfrac{5}{x^2 - 3x - 10}$

(g) $\dfrac{1}{c^2 - 2c + 1} + \dfrac{1}{c^2 - 1}$

(h) $\dfrac{m + 4}{m^2 - 9} - \dfrac{1}{m - 3}$

Indices

There are some rules you need to remember when using indices:

- $a^m \times a^n = a^{m+n}$
- $\dfrac{a^m}{a^n} = a^{m-n}$
- $(a^m)^n = a^{mn}$

- $(ab)^m = a^m b^m$
- $a^{-m} = \dfrac{1}{a^m}$
- $\sqrt[n]{a} = a^{\frac{1}{n}}$

- $\sqrt[n]{a^m} = a^{\frac{m}{n}}$
- $a^0 = 1$
- $a^1 = a$

These rules help us to simplify and evaluate expressions containing indices.

Example 11
Simplify:

(a) $3x^2 \times 5x^7$

(b) $21a^{\frac{1}{2}} \div 7a^{\frac{1}{4}}$

(c) $(8b^{-\frac{1}{2}})^{\frac{2}{3}}$

(a) $3x^2 \times 5x^7$
$= 15x^{2+7}$
$= 15x^9$

(b) $21a^{\frac{1}{2}} \div 7a^{\frac{1}{4}}$
$= 3a^{\frac{1}{2} - \frac{1}{4}}$
$= 3a^{\frac{1}{4}}$
$= 3\sqrt[4]{a}$

(c) $(8b^{-\frac{1}{2}})^{\frac{2}{3}}$
$= 8^{\frac{2}{3}} b^{-\frac{1}{2} \times \frac{2}{3}}$
$= (\sqrt[3]{8})^2 b^{-\frac{1}{3}}$
$= \dfrac{4}{\sqrt[3]{b}}$

Example 12
Evaluate $243^{-\frac{3}{5}}$.

$$243^{-\frac{3}{5}} = \frac{1}{243^{\frac{3}{5}}} = \frac{1}{(\sqrt[5]{243})^3} = \frac{1}{3^3} = \frac{1}{27}$$

Exercise 8

1 Simplify each expression.

(a) $a^5 \times a^4$

(b) $n^{-12} \times n^9$

(c) $c^6 \times c$

(d) $d^{\frac{1}{2}} \times d^3$

(e) $3a^4 \times 5a^3$

(f) $4b^9 \times 2b^{-6}$

(g) $8c^8 \times 7c$

(h) $\dfrac{v^6}{v^2}$

(i) $y^{19} \div y^{-5}$

(j) $\dfrac{k^8}{k}$

(k) $\dfrac{12c^5}{6c^3}$

(l) $\dfrac{48f^{10}}{6f^{-4}}$

(m) $30c^6 \div c^4$

(n) $(c^6)^5$

(o) $(y^7)^{-5}$

(p) $(6h^5)^3$

(q) $(2x^{-2})^5$

(r) $(xy)^5$

(s) $(x^2 y^3)^4$

(t) $(h^3 k^5)^{-8}$

2 Evaluate:

(a) $25^{\frac{1}{2}}$ (b) $16^{\frac{1}{4}}$ (c) $125^{\frac{1}{3}}$ (d) $128^{\frac{1}{7}}$ (e) $8^{\frac{2}{3}}$

(f) $81^{\frac{3}{4}}$ (g) $1000^{\frac{2}{3}}$ (h) $243^{\frac{3}{5}}$ (i) $625^{-\frac{1}{4}}$ (j) $64^{-\frac{5}{6}}$

3 Simplify:

(a) $k^{\frac{1}{2}} \times k^{\frac{1}{4}}$ (b) $t^{\frac{2}{3}} \times t^{\frac{2}{3}}$ (c) $g^{\frac{3}{4}} \times g^{-\frac{1}{4}}$ (d) $\sqrt[3]{y} \times \sqrt[3]{y}$

(e) $4d^{-\frac{1}{2}} \times 5d^{\frac{3}{2}}$ (f) $2\sqrt[3]{e} \times 4\sqrt[3]{e^2}$ (g) $\dfrac{d^{\frac{2}{3}}}{d^{\frac{1}{3}}}$ (h) $d^{\frac{3}{4}} \div d^{\frac{1}{4}}$

(i) $\dfrac{\sqrt[3]{y}}{\sqrt[3]{y}}$ (j) $4d^{\frac{1}{2}} \div 5d^{\frac{3}{2}}$ (k) $\dfrac{4\sqrt[3]{e}}{2\sqrt[3]{e^2}}$ (l) $(4d^{-\frac{1}{2}})^{\frac{3}{2}}$

(m) $(7t)^{-2}$ (n) $(c^3 d^{\frac{1}{2}})^3$ (o) $(x^4 y^2)^{\frac{1}{2}}$ (p) $(s^{\frac{1}{2}} t^{\frac{2}{3}})^{\frac{2}{3}}$

Complex indices

We can simplify and evaluate complex indices by splitting expressions into separate fractions.

Example 13

Express each fraction as a sum of terms.

(a) $\dfrac{x^4 + x^5}{x^2}$ (b) $\dfrac{\sqrt{x} + \sqrt[4]{x^3}}{2\sqrt{x}}$ (c) $\dfrac{(\sqrt{x} - 1)^2}{\sqrt{x}}$

(a) $\dfrac{x^4 + x^5}{x^2} = \dfrac{x^4}{x^2} + \dfrac{x^5}{x^2}$

$\qquad\quad = x^2 + x^3$

(b) $\dfrac{\sqrt{x} + \sqrt[4]{x^3}}{2\sqrt{x}} = \dfrac{x^{\frac{1}{2}} + x^{\frac{3}{4}}}{2x^{\frac{1}{2}}}$

$\qquad\qquad\quad = \dfrac{x^{\frac{1}{2}}}{2x^{\frac{1}{2}}} + \dfrac{x^{\frac{3}{4}}}{2x^{\frac{1}{2}}}$

$\qquad\qquad\quad = \dfrac{x^0}{2} + \dfrac{x^{\frac{1}{4}}}{2}$

$\qquad\qquad\quad = \dfrac{1}{2} + \dfrac{\sqrt[4]{x}}{2}$

(c) $\dfrac{(\sqrt{x} - 1)^2}{\sqrt{x}} = \dfrac{(\sqrt{x} - 1)(\sqrt{x} - 1)}{\sqrt{x}}$

$\qquad\qquad\; = \dfrac{x - 2\sqrt{x} + 1}{\sqrt{x}}$

$\qquad\qquad\; = \dfrac{x^1}{x^{\frac{1}{2}}} - \dfrac{2x^{\frac{1}{2}}}{x^{\frac{1}{2}}} + \dfrac{1}{x^{\frac{1}{2}}}$

$\qquad\qquad\; = x^{\frac{1}{2}} - 2x^0 + \dfrac{1}{x^{\frac{1}{2}}}$

$\qquad\qquad\; = \sqrt{x} - 2 + \dfrac{1}{\sqrt{x}}$

Exercise 9

1 Express each fraction as a sum or difference of terms.

(a) $\dfrac{x^6 + x^7}{x^3}$

(b) $\dfrac{x^{10} - x^{20}}{x^5}$

(c) $\dfrac{x^2 - x^3}{2x^2}$

(d) $\dfrac{2x^4 + 3x^2}{x^6}$

(e) $\dfrac{x^4 - 1}{x^2}$

(f) $\dfrac{x^{\frac{2}{3}} + x^{\frac{3}{4}} + 2}{x^4}$

(g) $\dfrac{x^4 + x^5}{2x^2}$

(h) $\dfrac{x^7 + x^2}{3x^4}$

(i) $\dfrac{2(x^4 - x^6)}{4x^2}$

(j) $\dfrac{\sqrt[3]{x} + x^2}{x}$

(k) $\dfrac{2\sqrt{x} + x^2}{\sqrt{x}}$

(l) $\dfrac{6\sqrt[3]{x} + 2\sqrt[4]{x^5}}{\sqrt[3]{x^4}}$

2 Express each fraction as a sum or difference of terms.

(a) $\dfrac{(x + 2)^2}{x^3}$

(b) $\dfrac{(x + 3)(2x - 1)}{x}$

(c) $\dfrac{(1 - x)^2}{2x}$

(d) $\left(\dfrac{3}{x} - 4\right)^2$

(e) $\dfrac{(x^2 - 5)(x + 5)}{x^2}$

(f) $\left(x + \dfrac{1}{x}\right)\left(x - \dfrac{1}{x}\right)$

(g) $\dfrac{(x - 1)^2}{\sqrt{x}}$

(h) $\dfrac{(x + 2)^2}{x\sqrt{x}}$

(i) $\left(\dfrac{1}{\sqrt{x}} + \sqrt{x}\right)^2$

Surds

An **irrational number** is a number that cannot be written as a common fraction. A **surd** is an irrational root, for example:

- $\sqrt{2}$ **is** a surd
- $\sqrt[3]{25}$ **is** a surd
- $\sqrt{\frac{25}{4}}$ is **not** a surd since $\sqrt{\frac{25}{4}} = \frac{5}{2}$
- $\sqrt[3]{125}$ is **not** a surd since $\sqrt[3]{125} = 5$

Example 14
Solve $x^2 + 1 = 4$ leaving your answer in surd form.

$x^2 + 1 = 4$
$\quad x^2 = 3$
$\quad\ x = \pm\sqrt{3}$

Note: $x = \pm\sqrt{3}$ is an exact answer whereas $x = \pm1.732\,805\ldots$ is only an approximate answer.

Exercise 10

1 Which of these numbers are surds:
$\sqrt{16}$, $\sqrt{65}$, $\sqrt[3]{9}$, $\sqrt[3]{8}$, $\sqrt{1}$, $\sqrt[3]{1}$, $\sqrt{50}$, $\sqrt[3]{33}$, $\sqrt[3]{27}$, $\sqrt{5}$, $\sqrt{1000}$, $\sqrt[3]{-1000}$?

2 Find the **exact** solution of each equation.

   (a) $x^2 - 5 = 9$ **(b)** $x^2 + 6 = 36$ **(c)** $x^3 - 4 = 60$

   (d) $x^2 + 11 = 12$ **(e)** $x^3 - 13 = 26$ **(f)** $x^3 + 20 = 19$

3 For each triangle find the **exact** length of the unknown side.

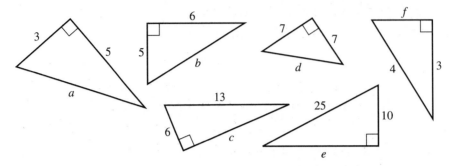

4 Find the **exact** value of each trigonometry ratio.

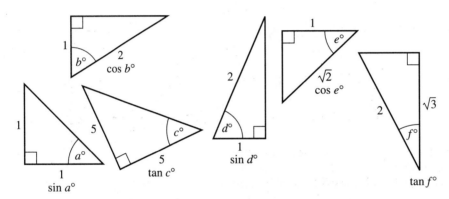

Simplifying surds

A surd can be simplified if it has a factor that is a perfect square, because of the rule:

$$\sqrt{ab} = \sqrt{a} \times \sqrt{b}$$

Surds can be simplified using the normal rules of algebra.

Example 15

Express $\sqrt{18}$ in simplest form.

Find the largest square number that is a factor

$$\sqrt{18} = \sqrt{9 \times 2} = \sqrt{9} \times \sqrt{2} = 3\sqrt{2}$$

Example 16

Simplify $3\sqrt{2} - 5\sqrt{2} + 4\sqrt{5}$.

$$3\sqrt{2} - 5\sqrt{2} + 4\sqrt{5} = -2\sqrt{2} + 4\sqrt{5}$$
$$= 4\sqrt{5} - 2\sqrt{2}$$

Exercise 11

1 Express in simplest form:

(a) $\sqrt{12}$ (b) $\sqrt{20}$ (c) $\sqrt{27}$ (d) $\sqrt{32}$

(e) $\sqrt{45}$ (f) $\sqrt{48}$ (g) $\sqrt{50}$ (h) $\sqrt{63}$

(i) $\sqrt{75}$ (j) $\sqrt{44}$ (k) $\sqrt{98}$ (l) $\sqrt{500}$

(m) $5\sqrt{8}$ (n) $3\sqrt{18}$ (o) $4\sqrt{200}$ (p) $3\sqrt{1000}$

2 Simplify:

(a) $7\sqrt{2} + 3\sqrt{2}$ (b) $9\sqrt{5} - 5\sqrt{5}$ (c) $\sqrt{3} + 6\sqrt{3}$

(d) $4\sqrt{7} - \sqrt{7}$ (e) $9\sqrt{10} - 9\sqrt{10}$ (f) $\sqrt{5} - 8\sqrt{5}$

(g) $3\sqrt{2} - \sqrt{2} + 7\sqrt{2}$ (h) $\sqrt{7} + \sqrt{5} + 2\sqrt{7}$ (i) $2\sqrt{10} - 10\sqrt{2}$

(j) $2\sqrt{5} + 3\sqrt{2} - 2\sqrt{5} - \sqrt{2}$ (k) $-4\sqrt{11} + 8\sqrt{10} - 2\sqrt{11} - 2\sqrt{10}$

3 Calculate the **exact** length of the unknown side in each triangle. Write each answer in its simplest form.

(a) 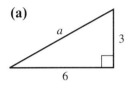   (b) 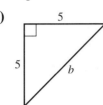   (c) 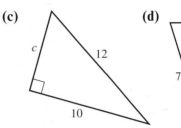   (d)

4 Solve these equations, where necessary leaving the answer as a surd in its simplest form.

(a) $x^2 + 8 = 36$ (b) $x^2 - 15 = 60$ (c) $\frac{1}{2}x^2 + 2 = 51$

(d) $x^2 - 147 = 0$ (e) $x^3 + 12 = 4$ (f) $x^3 - 5 = 49$

Multiplication of surds

Surds can be multiplied using the following rules:

- $\sqrt{a} \times \sqrt{b} = \sqrt{ab}$ - $\sqrt{a} \times \sqrt{a} = a$

Example 17

Simplify:

(a) $\sqrt{8} \times \sqrt{10}$ (b) $(3 + \sqrt{2})(3 - \sqrt{2})$ (c) $(\sqrt{3} + \sqrt{2})^2$

(a) $\sqrt{8} \times \sqrt{10} = \sqrt{8 \times 10}$ or $\sqrt{8} \times \sqrt{10} = \sqrt{4 \times 2} \times \sqrt{2 \times 5}$

$= \sqrt{80}$ $= 2 \times \sqrt{2} \times \sqrt{2} \times \sqrt{5}$

$= \sqrt{16} \times \sqrt{5}$ $= 2 \times 2 \times \sqrt{5}$

$= 4\sqrt{5}$ $= 4\sqrt{5}$

(b) $(3 + \sqrt{2})(3 - \sqrt{2}) = 3 \times 3 - 3 \times \sqrt{2} + \sqrt{2} \times 3 - \sqrt{2} \times \sqrt{2}$

$= 9 - 3\sqrt{2} + 3\sqrt{2} - 2$

$= 7$

(c) $(\sqrt{3} + \sqrt{2})^2 = (\sqrt{3} + \sqrt{2})(\sqrt{3} + \sqrt{2})$
$= \sqrt{3} \times \sqrt{3} + \sqrt{3} \times \sqrt{2} + \sqrt{2} \times \sqrt{3} + \sqrt{2} \times \sqrt{2}$
$= 3 + \sqrt{6} + \sqrt{6} + 2$
$= 5 + 2\sqrt{6}$

Exercise 12

1 Simplify:
    (a) $\sqrt{3} \times \sqrt{3}$ **(b)** $\sqrt{7} \times \sqrt{7}$ **(c)** $\sqrt{2a} \times \sqrt{2a}$
    (d) $\sqrt{4} \times \sqrt{3}$ **(e)** $\sqrt{9} \times \sqrt{2}$ **(f)** $\sqrt{3} \times \sqrt{25}$
    (g) $\sqrt{2} \times \sqrt{5}$ **(h)** $\sqrt{7} \times \sqrt{3}$ **(i)** $\sqrt{11} \times \sqrt{2}$
    (j) $\sqrt{2} \times \sqrt{8}$ **(k)** $\sqrt{12} \times \sqrt{3}$ **(l)** $\sqrt{2} \times \sqrt{50}$
    (m) $\sqrt{2} \times \sqrt{10}$ **(n)** $\sqrt{3} \times \sqrt{6}$ **(o)** $\sqrt{8} \times \sqrt{12}$
    (p) $\sqrt{10} \times \sqrt{20}$ **(q)** $3\sqrt{2} \times 5\sqrt{2}$ **(r)** $3\sqrt{5} \times 5\sqrt{3}$

2 Simplify:
    (a) $\sqrt{2}(1 + \sqrt{2})$ **(b)** $\sqrt{3}(\sqrt{3} - 1)$
    (c) $(1 + \sqrt{5})\sqrt{5}$ **(d)** $\sqrt{7}(5 + \sqrt{7})$
    (e) $\sqrt{2}(3 - 2\sqrt{2})$ **(f)** $(3\sqrt{5} - 2)\sqrt{5}$
    (g) $(\sqrt{3} + 1)(\sqrt{3} - 1)$ **(h)** $(\sqrt{5} - 2)(\sqrt{5} + 2)$
    (i) $(3 + \sqrt{7})(3 - \sqrt{7})$ **(j)** $(\sqrt{5} + \sqrt{2})(\sqrt{5} - \sqrt{2})$
    (k) $(\sqrt{7} - \sqrt{13})(\sqrt{7} + \sqrt{13})$ **(l)** $(2\sqrt{3} + 3\sqrt{2})(2\sqrt{3} - 3\sqrt{2})$
    (m) $(1 + \sqrt{3})^2$ **(n)** $(\sqrt{5} - 2)^2$
    (o) $(\sqrt{2} + \sqrt{7})^2$ **(p)** $(\sqrt{3} - \sqrt{5})^2$

3 (a) Calculate the **exact** area of the rectangle.

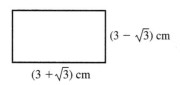

$(3 - \sqrt{3})$ cm
$(3 + \sqrt{3})$ cm

(b) Calculate the **exact** length of the hypotenuse.

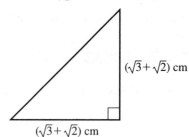

$(\sqrt{3} + \sqrt{2})$ cm
$(\sqrt{3} + \sqrt{2})$ cm

Rationalising denominators

It is sometimes convenient to work with fractions that do not have a surd in the denominator. We can obtain fractions with **rational denominators** by multiplying by $\dfrac{\sqrt{x}}{\sqrt{x}}$ ($= 1$).

Example 18

Express $\dfrac{5}{\sqrt{3}}$ with a rational denominator.

$$\frac{5}{\sqrt{3}} = \frac{5}{\sqrt{3}} \times \frac{\sqrt{3}}{\sqrt{3}} = \frac{5\sqrt{3}}{3}$$

We can also rationalise more complex denominators, e.g. $(3 - \sqrt{2})$, $(\sqrt{3} + \sqrt{5})$, etc.

$(\sqrt{a} + \sqrt{b})$ and $(\sqrt{a} - \sqrt{b})$ are called **conjugate surds**. The product of a pair of conjugate surds is **rational**, i.e.

$$(\sqrt{a} + \sqrt{b})(\sqrt{a} - \sqrt{b}) = (\sqrt{a})^2 - (\sqrt{b})^2 = a - b.$$

We can use this property to simplify more complex denominators.

Example 19

Express with a rational denominator **(a)** $\dfrac{4}{2 - \sqrt{3}}$ and **(b)** $\dfrac{1 - \sqrt{2}}{1 + \sqrt{2}}$

(a) $\dfrac{4}{2 - \sqrt{3}} = \dfrac{4}{2 - \sqrt{3}} \times \dfrac{2 + \sqrt{3}}{2 + \sqrt{3}} = \dfrac{4(2 + \sqrt{3})}{4 - 3} = 8 + 4\sqrt{3}$

(b) $\dfrac{1 - \sqrt{2}}{1 + \sqrt{2}} = \dfrac{1 - \sqrt{2}}{1 + \sqrt{2}} \times \dfrac{1 - \sqrt{2}}{1 - \sqrt{2}} = \dfrac{1 - 2\sqrt{2} + 2}{1 - 2} = \dfrac{3 - 2\sqrt{2}}{-1} = 2\sqrt{2} - 3$

Exercise 13

1 Rationalise the denominators of these fractions:

(a) $\dfrac{1}{\sqrt{2}}$ **(b)** $\dfrac{1}{\sqrt{5}}$ **(c)** $\dfrac{6}{\sqrt{3}}$ **(d)** $\dfrac{8}{\sqrt{2}}$ **(e)** $\dfrac{2}{\sqrt{3}}$

(f) $\dfrac{10}{\sqrt{5}}$ **(g)** $\dfrac{7}{\sqrt{3}}$ **(h)** $\dfrac{3}{\sqrt{5}}$ **(i)** $\dfrac{4}{5\sqrt{2}}$ **(j)** $\dfrac{7}{2\sqrt{5}}$

2 Rationalise the denominator of these fractions then simplify:

(a) $\dfrac{1}{\sqrt{20}}$ **(b)** $\dfrac{1}{\sqrt{50}}$ **(c)** $\dfrac{10}{\sqrt{12}}$ **(d)** $\dfrac{7}{\sqrt{18}}$ **(e)** $\dfrac{2}{\sqrt{75}}$

3 Write these fractions in their simplest form with a rational denominator:

(a) $\dfrac{\sqrt{9}}{\sqrt{2}}$ **(b)** $\dfrac{\sqrt{5}}{\sqrt{3}}$ **(c)** $\sqrt{\dfrac{9}{10}}$ **(d)** $\sqrt{\dfrac{1}{3}}$ **(e)** $\sqrt{\dfrac{3}{5}}$

4 Expand and simplify:

(a) $(5 + \sqrt{3})(5 - \sqrt{3})$ **(b)** $(7 - \sqrt{2})(7 + \sqrt{2})$
(c) $(\sqrt{5} + 4)(\sqrt{5} - 4)$ **(d)** $(\sqrt{2} + \sqrt{3})(\sqrt{2} - \sqrt{3})$
(e) $(\sqrt{7} - \sqrt{5})(\sqrt{7} + \sqrt{5})$ **(f)** $(\sqrt{a} + \sqrt{b})(\sqrt{a} - \sqrt{b})$

5 Rationalise the denominators of these fractions and simplify:

(a) $\dfrac{1}{\sqrt{2} - 1}$ **(b)** $\dfrac{2}{\sqrt{3} - 1}$ **(c)** $\dfrac{8}{\sqrt{5} + 1}$ **(d)** $\dfrac{21}{3 - \sqrt{2}}$

(e) $\dfrac{1}{\sqrt{3} - \sqrt{2}}$ **(f)** $\dfrac{2}{\sqrt{7} + \sqrt{5}}$ **(g)** $\dfrac{1 - \sqrt{3}}{2 - \sqrt{5}}$ **(h)** $\dfrac{4 + \sqrt{5}}{2 + \sqrt{3}}$

Trigonometry

Right-angled triangles

In a right-angled triangle, the trigonometric ratios are defined as:

$$\sin x° = \frac{\text{Opposite}}{\text{Hypotenuse}} = \frac{O}{H} \quad \Big\} \quad \text{SOH}$$

$$\cos x° = \frac{\text{Adjacent}}{\text{Hypotenuse}} = \frac{A}{H} \quad \Big\} \quad \text{CAH}$$

$$\tan x° = \frac{\text{Opposite}}{\text{Adjacent}} = \frac{O}{A} \quad \Big\} \quad \text{TOA}$$

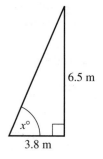

We can use these ratios to find the size of angles or the length of sides in right-angled triangles.

Example 20

A vertical pole 6.5 m long casts a horizontal shadow of 3.8 m. Find the angle of elevation of the sun.

The angle of elevation of the sun is the angle x in the diagram.

$$\tan x° = \frac{6.5}{3.8}$$

$$= 1.711$$

$$x° = 59.7°$$

Example 21

An aircraft on its final approach flies from a height of 400 m at an angle of depression of 9°. Find the distance that the aircraft travels.

From the diagram, the distance the aircraft travels is d.

$$\sin 9° = \frac{400}{d}$$

$$d = \frac{400}{\sin 9°}$$

$$d = 2557 \, \text{m}$$

Exercise 14

1 Calculate x in each of the following diagrams:

(a)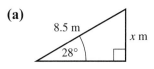

(b)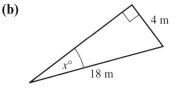

(c)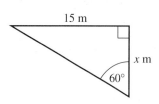

(d)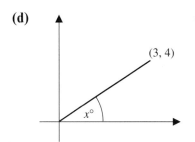

(e)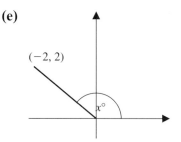

(f)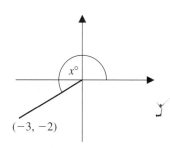

2 A ladder is resting against the top of a wall 2.5 m high. The angle between the ladder and the ground is 75°. Calculate the length of the ladder.

3 A roof truss is shown in the diagram. What is the size of the angle between the sloping side AB and the horizontal?

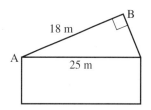

Non right-angled triangles

For non right-angled triangles we have to use a different set of rules to calculate angles, the length of sides and area:

- Cosine rule: $a^2 = b^2 + c^2 - 2bc \cos A$

  or $\qquad \cos A = \dfrac{b^2 + c^2 - a^2}{2bc}$

- Sine rule: $\dfrac{a}{\sin A} = \dfrac{b}{\sin B} = \dfrac{c}{\sin C}$

- Area of triangle: area $= \frac{1}{2} ab \sin C$

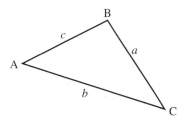

Example 22

The distance between the tee and the flag on a golf hole is 345 m. A golfer slices his tee shot at an angle of 30° to the line between the tee and the flag. His ball travels a distance of 175 m. How far is his ball from the flag?

Draw and label a diagram. Decide which rule to use.
On the diagram, T is the position of the tee, B is the position of the ball and F is the position of the flag. We know the length of two sides of the triangle and the size of one angle so we can use the cosine rule to find the length of the remaining side.

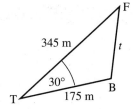

$$t^2 = f^2 + b^2 - 2fb \cos T$$
$$= 175^2 + 345^2 - 2 \times 175 \times 345 \cos 30°$$
$$= 28\,900$$
$$t = \sqrt{28\,900}$$
$$= 170$$

Therefore the ball is 170 m from the flag.

Exercise 15

1 Find x in each of the following triangles:

(a)

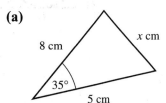

(b)

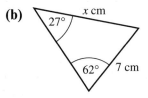

(c)

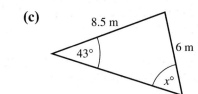

(d)

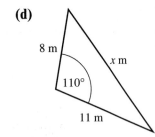

(e)

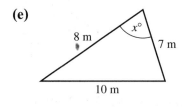

(f)

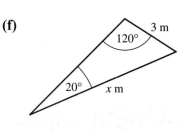

2 In the diagram telegraph pole AB is supported by wires AC and AD. Find
(a) the length of AC.
(b) the height of the pole.

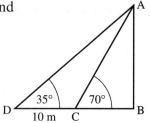

3 Calculate the distance between the tips of the hands of a town hall clock at 2 o'clock if the minute hand is 2.5 m long and the hour hand is 1.5 m long.

Applications

We can use the rules given in the previous two sections to solve a
variety of trigonometric problems.

1 A tunnel under a river is to span a
distance of 800 m and the eastern end
is 15 m lower than the western end.
The tunnel is started at the western end
with a shaft 525 m long at an angle of
depression of 5°. Tunnelling is then
started at the eastern end. What must
the angle of depression ($x°$) be of this
shaft if it is to meet the end of the one
from the west?

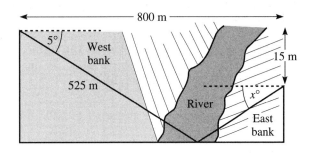

2 PT and PQ are tangents to a circle centre C and
radius 2 units. If QS = 1 unit:
  (a) calculate the length of QR
  (b) calculate the size of angle QCR
  (c) prove that angle QCR = angle TPQ
  (d) calculate the length of PT
  (e) calculate the area of triangle PTQ.

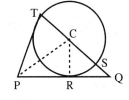

3 A jib crane is shown in the diagram.
Calculate the length of BC.

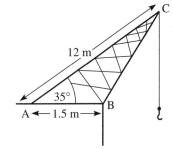

4 An aircraft takes off from Lossiemouth on a submarine
reconnaissance exercise. It flies 1250 km on a bearing of 025°. It
then changes direction to a bearing of 197° and flies for a further
850 km, when it detects a submarine. What is the aircraft's
distance and bearing from Lossiemouth?

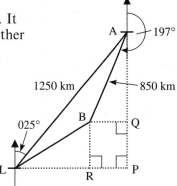

5 A yacht leaves port and sails on a bearing of 204° for 12 miles. It
then changes course and sails for a further 17 miles on a bearing
of 300°. How far is the yacht from the port?

6 The angle of elevation of the top of a tree is 38°. From another point, 12 m closer to the tree, the angle of elevation of the top of the tree is 50°. How high is the tree?

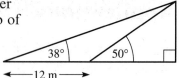

7 A UFO is seen by one person at an angle of elevation of 25° and by another person 15 km closer to it at an elevation of 31°. Calculate the height of the UFO.

8 A lighthouse sits at the edge of a cliff. From a boat at sea the angle of elevation of the top of the lighthouse is 46° and that of the bottom of the lighthouse 44.5°. If the lighthouse is 21 m high, what is the height of the cliff?

Identities

$(a + b)^2 = a(a + b) + ab + b^2$ is called an **identity** because it is true for **all** values of a and b.

To prove that a statement like this is an identity it is necessary to show that the expressions on either side of the equals sign are identical.

Example 23
Prove the identity $(a + b)^2 = a(a + b) + ab + b^2$.

L.H.S. $= (a + b)^2$ R.H.S. $= a(a + b) + ab + b^2$
$= a + 2ab + b^2$ $= a^2 + ab + ab + b^2$
                                                   $= a^2 + 2ab + b^2$

Hence $(a + b)^2 = a(a + b) + ab + b^2$.

Example 24
Prove the identity $\cos^2 x°(1 - \tan^2 x°) = 1 - 2\sin^2 x$
(remember that $\sin^2 x° + \cos^2 x° = 1$ and $\dfrac{\sin x°}{\cos x°} = \tan x°$).

L.H.S. $= \cos^2 x°(1 - \tan^2 x°)$
$= \cos^2 x° - \cos°x° \tan^2 x°$
$= \cos^2 x° - \cos^2 x° \dfrac{\sin^2 x°}{\cos^2 x°}$
$= \cos^2 x° - \sin^2 x°$
$= (1 - \sin^2 x°) - \sin^2 x°$
$= 1 - 2\sin^2 x°$
$= $ R.H.S.

Hence $\cos^2 x°(1 - \tan^2 x°) = 1 - 2\sin^2 x°$.

Exercise 17

1 Prove the following identities:
  (a) $(x + 1)^2 = (x - 1)^2 + 4x$
  (b) $(x - y)^2 = (y - x)^2$
  (c) $(p + 5)(p + 1) = -8 + (p + 3)^2$
  (d) $4(a^2 - 4) = (2a - 4)^2 + 16(a - 2)$
  (e) $(a + b)^2 + (a - b)^2 = 2(a^2 + b^2)$
  (f) $(x + 2)^3 = x^3 + 2(3x^2 + 6x + 4)$
  (g) $(6x - y)^2 - (4x - y)(9x - y) = xy$
  (h) $(px - qy)^2 + (qx + py)^2 = (p^2 + q^2)(x^2 + y^2)$

2 Prove the identities:
  (a) $5\cos^2 x° + 5\sin^2 x° = 5$
  (b) $2\cos^2 x° - 1 = 1 - 2\sin^2 x°$
  (c) $(\cos P° + \sin P°)^2 = 2\sin P° \cos P° + 1$
  (d) $2\sin a° \cos a° + (\cos a° - \sin a°)^2 = 1$
  (e) $(\cos Y° + \sin Y°)(\cos Y° - \sin Y°) = 1 - 2\sin^2 Y°$
  (f) $\cos A° \tan A° = \sin A°$
  (g) $\cos^2 Q° \tan^2 Q° = 1 - \cos^2 Q°$
  (h) $\dfrac{\cos A°}{\sin A°} - \dfrac{\sin A°}{\cos A°} = \dfrac{2\cos^2 A° - 1}{\sin A° \cos A°}$

Specimen
Unit assessment 1(H)

Outcome 1

1 Find the equation of the line which passes through the points
(2, −3) and (4, 5).

2 The line AB makes an angle of 35° with the positive
direction of the x-axis, as shown in the diagram.
Find the gradient of AB.

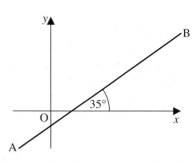

3 (a) Write down the gradient of a line parallel to the line $y = 3x − 5$.
(b) Write down the gradient of a line perpendicular to the line
$y = 3x − 5$.

Outcome 2

4 (a) The graph of $y = f(x)$ is shown in the diagram.
    (i) Sketch the graph of $y = f(x + 3)$.
    (ii) Sketch the graph of $y = −f(x)$.

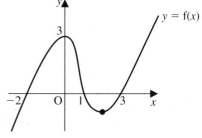

(b) The diagram shows a graph of the form $y = a \sin x°$.
    (i) State the value of a.
    (ii) Sketch the graph of $y = f(x) + 2$.

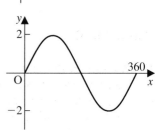

5 (a) The diagram shows a graph of the form $y = b^x$.
    (i) Find the value of b.
    (ii) Sketch the graph of $y = 3^x$.

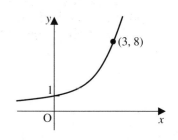

(b) This diagram shows the graph of $y = \log_a x$.

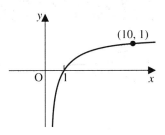

   (i) State the value of a.

   (ii) Sketch the graph of $y = \log_5 x$.
        Show clearly where the graph crosses the x-axis
        and mark the coordinates of one other point which
        it passes through.

6 (a) The functions f and g are defined as $f(x) = 2x^2$ and
        $g(x) = x - 1$. Express $f(g(x))$ in terms of x.

(b) The functions f and g are defined as $f(x) = 4x$ and
        $g(x) = \sin x$. Express $g(f(x))$ in terms of x.

Outcome 3

7 Differentiate the following with respect to x.

   (a) $(x + 3)(x + 5)$

   (b) $\dfrac{x^{\frac{5}{2}} + 1}{x}$

8 The diagram shows a sketch of the curve with equation
   $y = (x + 2)(x - 3)$ with a tangent drawn at the point $(4, 6)$.
   Find the equation of this tangent.

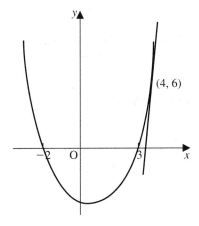

9 Find the coordinates of the stationary points of the curve
   $y = 2x^3 - 3x^2 - 12x + 9$ and determine their nature.

Outcome 4

10 In a controlled experiment, a biologist discovers that 100 aphids
    are born each week. A parasite is introduced which kills 40% of
    the aphids each week.

   (a) If the number of aphids at the start of day n is defined as u_n
         write down a recurrence relation for u_{n+1}.

   (b) Find the limit of this recurrence relation and explain what
         the limit means in the context of the question.

Specimen
Unit assessment 2(H)

Outcome 1

1 (a) Show that $(x - 2)$ is a factor of $3x^3 - 7x^2 + 4$.
  (b) Hence, or otherwise, fully factorise $3x^3 - 7x^2 + 4$.

2 Show that the quadratic equation $6x^2 - 3x + 7 = 0$ has no real roots.

Outcome 2

3 Integrate $\int \left(2x + \dfrac{3}{\sqrt{x}} \right) \, dx$.

4 Calculate the area of the shaded region in the diagram.

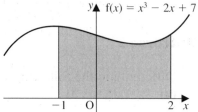

5 Write down the integral which represents the area enclosed by the graphs of $y = 2x$ and $y = 24 - x^2$. Do **not** carry out the integration.

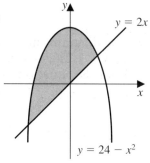

Outcome 3

6 Solve algebraically the equation $2 \sin 3x° = 1$ for $0 \leqslant x \leqslant 180$.

7 The diagram shows the cross-section of an adjustable ramp which is made from two right-angled triangles, ABD and DBC. Angle $DBC = \alpha°$ and angle $ABD = \beta°$.
  (a) Find the exact value of $\sin(\alpha + \beta)°$.
  (b) Hence calculate the height of the ramp.

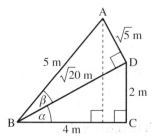

8 (a) Express $\cos x \cos \frac{\pi}{6} - \sin x \sin \frac{\pi}{6}$ in the form $\cos(A + B)$.
  (b) Hence solve $\cos x \cos \frac{\pi}{6} - \sin x \sin \frac{\pi}{6} = \frac{1}{2}$ for $0 \leqslant x \leqslant 2\pi$.

Outcome 4

9 (a) Write down the equation of the circle with radius 5 and centre $(3, -4)$.
  (b) A circle has equation $x^2 + y^2 - 4x + 6y - 3 = 0$. Write down the coordinates of its centre and calculate its radius.

10 Show that the line with equation $2y = 5 - x$ is a tangent to the circle with equation $x^2 + y^2 = 5$.

11 The point A(3, 2) lies on the circle $x^2 + y^2 - 4x - 1 = 0$. Find the equation of the tangent to the circle at A.

Specimen
Unit assessment 3(H)

Outcome 1

1 A(3, −2, −2), P(5, −4, −1) and R(11, −10, 2) are three points in space. Prove that A, P and R are collinear.

2 G is the point (7, −5, 1) and T is the point (1, 1, 7). Find the coordinates of B which divides GT in the ratio 5 : 1.

3 $\overrightarrow{QP} = -5\mathbf{i} + 2\mathbf{j} + 2\mathbf{k}$ and $\overrightarrow{QR} = 2\mathbf{i} + 4\mathbf{j} - 4\mathbf{k}$

    (a) Calculate $\overrightarrow{QP}.\overrightarrow{QR}$

    (b) Find the size of angle PQR.

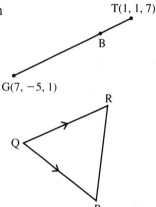

Outcome 2

4 Differentiate   **(a)** $f(x) = 5\sin x$ **(b)** $f(x) = -3\cos x$.

5 (a) Given that $h(x) = (5 - 4x)^5$ find $h'(x)$.

6 Find **(a)** $\int (x-1)^4 \, dx$

      (b) $\int 3\cos x \, dx$

      (c) $\int \frac{2}{3} \sin x \, dx$

Outcome 3

7 (a) Simplify $\log_a 8 + \log_a 2$

    (b) Simplify $2 \log_4 8 - \log_4 16$

8 (a) If $p = 2^{8.6}$ find the approximate value of p.

    (b) Find an expression for the exact value for x if $2^x = 10$

    (c) Given that $\log 10^k = 2.3$, write down an expression for the exact value of k.

    (d) Solve $e^{3x} = 15$

Outcome 4

9 $\sqrt{3}\cos x° + \sin x°$ can be written in the form $k\cos(x - \alpha)°$ where $k > 0$ and $0 < \alpha < 360$. Find the values of k and α.

Specimen Course assessment

PAPER I

Calculators may not be used in this paper.

1 A, B and C are the points $(-2, -3)$ $(2, -2)$ and $(-4, 4)$ respectively. D divides BC in the ratio $1:3$.

   (a) Find the coordinates of D.
   (b) Show that AD is an altitude of triangle ABC.
   (c) E is a point such that BE is a median of triangle ABC. Find the equation of BE.
   (d) Find the coordinates of F, the point of intersection of altitude AD and median BE.

2 A circle is inscribed in a square of side 6 units. The bottom left hand corner of the square has coordinates P(4, 5). Find the equation of the circle.

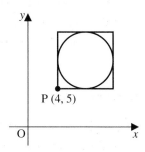

3 A sequence is defined by the recurrence relation $u_{n+1} = 0.7\,u_n + 10$.

   (a) Explain why the sequence has a limit as n tends to infinite.
   (b) Find algebraically the exact value of the limit.

4 **(a)** Show that $(x - 2)$ is a factor of $x^3 - 2x^2 - 4x + 8$.
   (b) Hence find the coordinates of the points of intersection of the graph of $y = x^3 - 2x^2 - 4x + 8$ and the coordinate axes.
   (c) Find the stationary points of $y = x^3 - 2x^2 - 4x + 8$ and determine their nature.
   (d) Sketch the graph of $y = x^3 - 2x^2 - 4x + 8$.

5 Find the value of p so that $(x + 2)$ is a factor of $x^3 + px^2 - 5x + 6$. Hence find the other factors.

6 Find $\dfrac{dy}{dx}$, given that $y = \sqrt{x^2 - 5}$

7 Solve algebraically the equation: $\cos 2\theta = \cos \theta, \ 0 \leqslant \theta \leqslant 2\pi$

8 Two functions f and g are defined on the set of real numbers by:

   $$f(x) = \frac{x}{1 - x}, \ (x \neq 1) \text{ and } g(x) = 5 - 2x$$

   (a) Find, in its simplest form, an expression for $f(g(x))$.
   (b) For what value of x is $f(g(x))$ undefined?

9 **(a)** Show that $(\cos x - \sin x)^2 = 1 - \sin 2x$.

   (b) Hence, find $\displaystyle\int (\cos x - \sin x)^2 \, dx$.

10 The roots of the equation $\dfrac{x^2}{4-x} = p$ are equal. Find the values of p.

11 The diagram opposite shows a sketch of the quartic function f(x) with stationary points at $(0, -2)$ and $(3, 2)$. Sketch the graph of the derived function f$'(x)$.

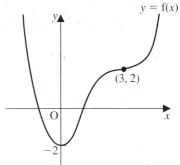

12 The sketch shows part of graph of $y = a \log_3 (x + b)$ Find the values of a and b.

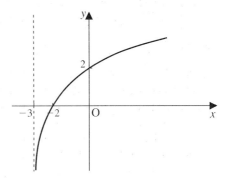

PAPER II

Calculators may be used in this paper.

1 Find the equation of the perpendicular bisector of the line joining P(4, −2) and Q(10, 2).

2 A drug in the body dissipates at the rate of 12% during each 10 minute period from the initial treatment.
   (a) If an initial dose of 50 units is given how much of the dose will still be present in a patient's bloodstream after 1 hour?
   (b) A doctor prescribes this drug to a patient. It is known that in order to be effective a level of at least 50 units must be maintained over the long term, however the drug becomes toxic if the level exceeds 100 units.
   The doctor prescribes 50 units every hour. What is the long term effect of this treatment?

3 A graphic designer is given the task of creating a logo for Blink Eye Shadow.
   The diagram shows the graphs of two curves f(x) = $x^2 - 7x + 10$ and g(x) = $-x^2 + 3x + 10$ intersecting at A and B.

Figure 1

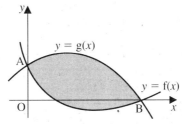

Figure 2

   (a) Find the coordinates of B
   (b) Hence find the area of the shaded part in Figure 2.

4 A, B and C are the points (1, 2, 3), (4, 1, 5) and (5, −4, 1) respectively.
  (a) Prove that triangle OAB is isosceles.
  (b) Calculate the size of angle AOB.
  (c) Prove that triangle ABC is right angled at B and that its area is twice that of triangle OAB.

5 (a) Find the equation of the circle whose centre is C(2, −1) and which passes through the point A(1, 1).
  (b) Find the equation of the tangent to this circle at A.
  (c) Show that this tangent is also a tangent to the circle with equation:

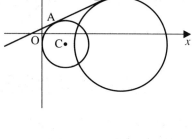

$$x^2 + y^2 - 14x + 2y + 30 = 0$$

and find the point of contact.
  (d) If the tangent touches the second circle at B find the length of the common tangent AB.

6 The depth, d metres, of water in a harbour is given by the formula

$$d = \cos 30t + \sqrt{3}\sin 30t + 3$$

where t is the time in hours after midnight.
  (a) Express d in the form $k\cos(30t - \alpha) + 3$, where $k > 0$ and $0 \leqslant \alpha \leqslant 360$.
  (b) Sketch the graph of d for $0 \leqslant t \leqslant 12$, indicating all relevant points.
  (c) When is the first 'high water' time at the harbour?
  (d) A ship needs at least 4 metres depth of water to enter the harbour. Between what times must it avoid entering the harbour?

7 An open tank with a square base and vertical sides is to have a capacity of 32 cubic metres.
  (a) Taking the length of the square base to be x metres, find an expression for the height h in terms of x.
  (b) Hence show that the surface area, A square metres, of the tank can be written in the form

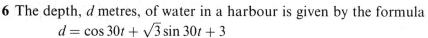

$$A(x) = x^2 + \frac{128}{x}$$

  (c) Find the dimensions of the tank so that the cost of cladding it in copper sheet will be a minimum.

8 The mass M grams of a radioactive isotope after a time t is given by

$$M = M_0 e^{-kt}$$

where M_0 is the initial mass of the isotope and k is a constant.
In 5 days, 10 grams of the isotope are reduced to 8 grams through radioactive decay.
  (a) Find the value of k.
The half-life of a substance is the length of time in which half the substance decays.
  (b) Find the half-life of the radioactive isotope.

9 The diagram shows a circle, centre O, of radius r units. The chord QS is at right angles to the diameter RT.
  (a) Show that $RP = r + r\cos\theta$. Find a similar expression for QP.
  (b) Hence show that the area A of the triangle QRS is given by

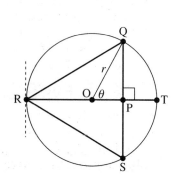

$$A = r^2(\sin\theta + \tfrac{1}{2}\sin 2\theta)$$

  (c) Show that $RS = r\sqrt{2 + 2\cos\theta}$.

Answers

Chapter 1   The straight line

Exercise 1A

1 (i) $\frac{1}{4}$ (ii) $\frac{3}{2}$ (iii) $\frac{1}{3}$ (iv) 5   (v) $-\frac{1}{6}$ (vi) -1
(vii) $-\frac{5}{2}$ (viii) -1

2 (a) gradients are positive   (b) gradients are negative

3 (a) $m_{LM} = \frac{1}{3}$ (b) $m_{TU} = -\frac{3}{13}$

   (c) $m_{HI} = -\frac{11}{3}$ (d) $m_{PQ} = -\frac{1}{10}$

4 (a) $m_{IJ} = 0$; $m_{KL} = 0$ (b) gradients are zero
   (c) IJ $y = 2$; KL $y = -3$

5 $y = -2$

6 (a) $m_{AB} = \frac{6}{0}$; $m_{CD} = \frac{7}{0}$ (b) AB $x = 5$; CD $x = -3$

   (c) $x = 3$

7 (a) (i) $\frac{2}{3}$ (ii) $\frac{2}{3}$ (iii) $\frac{2}{3}$

   (b) gradients are equal
   (c) lines are parallel
   (d) lines with the same gradients are parallel

8 $m_{KL} = \frac{1}{4}$; $m_{LM} = \frac{5}{-3}$; $m_{MN} = \frac{1}{4}$; $m_{NK} = -\frac{5}{3}$

9 (a) $B\widehat{C}D$

   (b) $m_{AB} = \dfrac{y_2 - y_1}{x_2 - x_1}$

   (c) $\tan \theta° = \dfrac{BD}{CD} = \dfrac{BE}{AE} = \dfrac{y_2 - y_1}{x_2 - x_1}$

   (d) gradient of a line = tangent of angle it makes with OX.

10 $63.4°$

Exercise 1B

2 sets (a) and (d) collinear

3 (a) $m_{UV} = \frac{2}{5}$ (b) S

4 (a) -2, top left to bottom right
   (b) $\frac{1}{2}$, bottom left to top right
   (c) -1, top left to bottom right
   (d) $\frac{1}{8}$, bottom left to top right
   (e) $-\frac{5}{13}$, top left to bottom right
   (f) $\frac{8}{0}$, parallel to y-axis
   (g) $-\frac{16}{3}$, top left to bottom right
   (h) 0, parallel to x-axis
   (i) $\frac{12}{0}$, parallel to y-axis
   (j) $\frac{3}{5}$, bottom left to top right

5 (a) $m_{AB} = \frac{1}{3}$; $m_{BC} = 6$; $m_{CD} = \frac{1}{3}$; $m_{DA} = 6$
   (b) opposite sides parallel, ABCD is a parallelogram

6 (a) $45°$ (b) $80.5°$ (c) $60°$
   (d) $135°$ (e) $157.4°$ (f) $90°$

7 x-axis, $(3, 0)$; y-axis, $(0, -6)$

8 $m_{OR} = \frac{5}{3}$; $m_{QR} = -\frac{5}{3}$

9 helicopter flies over plane

10 (a) $m_{KL} = 0$; $m_{LM} = -\frac{4}{3}$; $m_{MN} = 0$; $m_{NK} = -\frac{4}{3}$
   (b) LN, $63.4°$; KM, $153.4°$
   (c) KLMN is a rhombus – opposite sides parallel and diagonals at right angles

Exercise 1C

1 (a) (i) $(-3, 5)$ (ii) $m_{OP} = \frac{3}{5}$; $m_{OP'} = -\frac{5}{3}$ (iii) -1
   (b) (i) $(-1, 8)$ (ii) $m_{AB} = \frac{3}{5}$; $m_{AB'} = -\frac{5}{3}$ (iii) -1

2 (i)

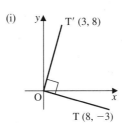

   (ii) $m_{OQ} = \frac{2}{7}$; $m_{OQ'} = -\frac{7}{2}$
   (iii) $m_{OQ} \times m_{OQ'} = -1$

   (i)

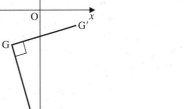

   (ii) $m_{OT} = -\frac{3}{8}$; $m_{OT'} = \frac{8}{3}$
   (iii) $m_{OT} \times m_{OT'} = -1$

3 (a)

   (iii) $m_{EF} = -4$; $m_{EF'} = \frac{1}{4}$
   (iv) $m_{EF} \times m_{EF'} = -1$

   (b)

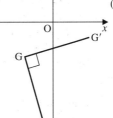

   (iii) $m_{GH} = -4$; $m_{GG'} = \frac{1}{4}$
   (iv) $m_{GH} \times m_{GG'} = -1$

Exercise 1D

1 AB and CD; PQ and VW; LM and JK; RS and GH

2 (a) -1 **(b)** 7 **(c)** $-\frac{1}{5}$

   (d) $-\frac{3}{2}$ **(e)** $\frac{2}{5}$ **(f)** $\frac{7}{3}$

   (g) 0

3 -3

4 1

5 $\frac{5}{3}$

7 $-\frac{1}{4}$

8 No

9 (a) $m_{AC} = -2$; $m_{BD} = \frac{9}{16}$

   (b) No

   (c) No

10 (a) $m_{RQ} = \frac{4}{3}$; $m_{PM} = -\frac{3}{4}$

   (b) PM is an axis of symmetry of the triangle

Exercise 1E

1 (a) $y = 3x + 2$

   (b) $y = 3x + 5$

   (c) $y = 3x$

   (d) $y = 3x - 1$

2

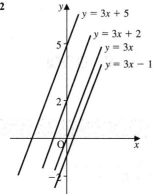

3 (a) $y = -2x + 3$

   (b) $y = -2x + 1$

   (c) $y = -2x - 1$

   (d) $y = -2x - 5$

4 (a)

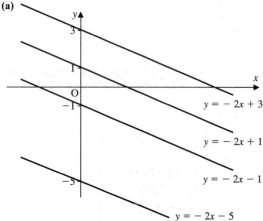

   (b) $y = -2x + c$

5

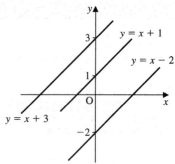

6 (a) (i) $y = 2x - 1$

     (ii) $y = -2x - 1$

     (iii) $y = 3x - 1$

   (b)

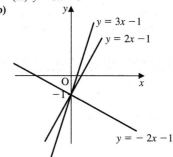

   (c) $y = mx - 1$

7 (a) 5; $(0, 2)$ **(b)** $\frac{1}{2}$; $(0, -4)$ **(c)** -3; $(0, -1)$

   (d) $\frac{1}{4}$; $(0, 3)$ **(e)** 3; $(0, -2)$ **(f)** -1; $(0, 7)$

   (g) $-\frac{2}{3}$; $(0, 3)$ **(h)** $-\frac{3}{2}$; $(0, -\frac{1}{2})$ **(i)** -3; $(0, 0)$

8 (a) no   **(b)** yes   **(c)** no

   (d) yes   **(e)** no   **(f)** no

Exercise 1F

1 (a) $x - 4y - 2 = 0$ **(b)** $3x - 2y - 15 = 0$

   (c) $3x - 4y = 0$

2 (a) $5x + y - 3 = 0$ **(b)** $2x - y - 4 = 0$

   (c) $4x - y - 1 = 0$ **(d)** $x + y - 2 = 0$

   (e) $x - y = 0$ **(f)** $x - 1 = 0$

   (g) $y + 5 = 0$

3 Straight lines:- **(a)**, **(c)**, **(d)**, **(f)**, **(h)**, **(i)**, **(j)**, **(m)**, **(n)**, **(o)**

Exercise 1G

1 (a) $5x - y - 13 = 0$ **(b)** $2x - y + 6 = 0$

   (c) $4x + y - 9 = 0$ **(d)** $x - 4y - 12 = 0$

   (e) $x + 2y - 10 = 0$ **(f)** $y = mx + c$

2 (a) $x - y + 1 = 0$ **(b)** $2x - y - 2 = 0$

   (c) $2x - y + 1 = 0$ **(d)** $x + 2y = 0$

   (e) $x + y + 3 = 0$ **(f)** $x + 3y - 10 = 0$

3 (a) $3x - y - 8 = 0$ **(b)** $2x + y = 0$

   (c) $5x - y + 13 = 0$ **(d)** $3x + y = 0$

   (e) $x = 7$ **(f)** $y = -2$

   (g) $x - 2y + 6 = 0$ **(h)** $x - 2y - 4 = 0$

4 (a) $2x - y + 2 = 0$ **(b)** $x - 2y - 19 = 0$

5 (a) (i) $6x + 5y = 0$ **(ii)** $y = 4x$ **(iii)** $x + 4y - 16.5 = 0$

   (b) $(0.97, 3.88)$

Exercise 1H

1 (a) rhombus
(b) Diagonals of a rhombus bisect each other at right angles
2 (b) They are concurrent

Exercise 1I

1 (a) $x - y + 4 = 0$ **(b)** $5x + y - 24 = 0$
(c) $x - 4y + 11 = 0$ **(d)** $5x + y - 16 = 0$
(e) $20x + 2y - 61 = 0$ **(f)** $x + 11y + 11 = 0$
2 (a) $8x - 2y - 19 = 0;\ 10x - 4y - 13 = 0;\ x - y + 3 = 0$
(b) $y = 2;\ 4x + 2y - 35 = 0;\ 11x - y - 15 = 0$
(c) $6x + 20y + 63 = 0;\ x - 3y + 10 = 0;\ 4x + 26y + 43 = 0$
(d) $20x - 2y - 39 = 0;\ 22x + 4y - 29 = 0;\ x + 3y + 5 = 0$

Exercise 1J

1 (a) kite
(b) Diagonals of a kite are perpendicular
2 (b) They are concurrent

Exercise 1K

1 (a) $3x + y - 9 = 0$ **(b)** $x + y - 4 = 0$
(c) $7x + 2y - 27 = 0$ **(d)** $y = 3$
(e) $y = 5$ **(f)** $x = 1$
2 $x + 3y - 19 = 0$
3 $x - 3y - 18 = 0$
4 $2x + 3y - 9 = 0$
5 (a) $x - y + 1 = 0;\ 2x - y - 8 = 0;\ 3x - 2y - 7 = 0$
(b) $4x + y + 13 = 0;\ 5x - 2y - 21 = 0;\ 9x - y - 8 = 0$
(c) $3x - 2y + 10 = 0;\ 2x - y + 7 = 0;\ y = -1$

Exercise 1L

1 (b) They are concurrent
2 (c) The centroid divides each median in the ratio $2:1$

Exercise 1M

1 (a) $6x + y - 29 = 0$ **(b)** $6x - y + 9 = 0$
(c) $x - y - 4 = 0$ **(d)** $5x - 2y + 1 = 0$
2 (a) $2x + 3y - 18 = 0$ **(b)** $12x + 7y - 6 = 0$
3 (a) $x = 3;\ 5x - 3y - 10 = 0;\ x - 3y + 2 = 0$
(b) $x = 2;\ 5x + 9y - 22 = 0;\ 7x + 9y - 26 = 0$
(c) $x - 4y + 2 = 0;\ 4x + 17y - 14 = 0;\ 8x + y - 6 = 0$
(d) $4x - 3y + 27 = 0;\ x = -5;\ 5x + 6y + 11 = 0$

Exercise 1N

1 (a) $x + 2y + 10 = 0$ **(b)** 30 units^2
2 (b) (i) $(1, \frac{3}{2})$

3 (a) $x = 5$ **(b)** $x + 3y - 11 = 0$
(c) $(5, 2)$
4 (a) $x = 5$ **(b)** $x + 2y - 3 = 0$
(c) $(5, -1)$
5 (a) $2y - 17 = 0$ **(b)** $3x + 2y - 23 = 0$
(c) $(2, \frac{17}{2})$ **(d)** $\frac{1}{2}\sqrt{65}$
6 (a) $(2, 1)$ **(b)** $(\frac{5}{3}, \frac{8}{3})$
(c) $(\frac{13}{6}, \frac{1}{6})$
7 (e) Answer is always $5\sqrt{3}$

Exercise 1O

1 $(1, 2)$
2 (a) $5x + 2y - 17 = 0$ **(b)** $(3, 1)$
3 (b) (i) $(4, \frac{7}{2})$
4 (a) AB, $6x - y - 11 = 0$; BC, $5x + y - 22 = 0$
(b) A $(1, -5)$; C $(2, 12)$
5 (a) $2x + y - 10 = 0$ **(b)** $(4, 2)$
(c) 5 units^2
6 (a) $(2, 7)$ **(b)** Q $(-2, 7)$ R $(4, 10)$
7 (a) $3x - y - 11 = 0$ **(b)** $(3, -2)$
8 $(1, 1), (2, 8), (-7, -2)$
9 (a) $2x - y = 4;\ x + 2y = 12;\ (4, 4)$
(b) $(2, 5)$
10 (a) $x - 2y + 4 = 0$ **(b)** 30 units^2
11 (a) $x + 5y + 14 = 0$ **(b)** $5x - y - 8 = 0$
(c) S $(2, 2)$, U $(0, -8)$

Chapter 2   Sets and functions

Exercise 2A

1 (a) $A = \{-5, -4, -3, -2, -1, 0, 1, 2, 3, 4, 5\}$
(b) $B = \{0, 1, 2, 3, 4, 5, 6, 7, 8, 9\}$
2 (a) and **(g)** are true
3 (a) $P = \{0, 1, 2, 3, 4\}$
(b) $L = \{-2, -1, 0, 1, 2, 3, 4\}$
(c) $S = \{7, 11, 13, 17, 19\}$
(d) $V = \{\ \}$
(e) $M = \{\ \}$
(f) $B = \{\ \}$
(g) $G = \{0, 180, 360\}$
(h) $K = \{-16, 14\}$

Exercise 2B

1 (a) $\{1, 2, 5, 10\}$
(b)

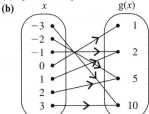

(c)

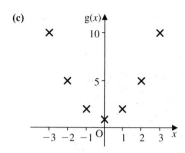

2 (a) $\{-12, -10, -6, 0\}$

(b)

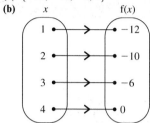

3 (a) $\{27, 9, 3, 1, \frac{1}{3}, \frac{1}{9}, \frac{1}{27}\}$　　**(b)** 4

4 (a) $0; \frac{1}{2}; \frac{1}{\sqrt{2}}; \frac{\sqrt{3}}{2}; 1$　　**(b)** 270

(c) $\{f(x): -1 \leqslant f(x) \leqslant 1, x \in \mathbf{R}\}$

5 $\{-5, -4, -3, -2, 0, 2, 3, 4, 5\}$

6 $-1; 3$

7 (a) $\{t: t \geqslant 0, t \in \mathbf{R}\}$　　**(b)** 210 m

(c) 24 m/s

8 graphs **(a)**, **(b)** and **(e)**

Exercise 2C

1 (a) $f(x) = 3x$, $g(x) = x - 2$　**(b)** $f(x) = x^2$, $g(x) = x + 7$
(c) $f(x) = x^3$, $g(x) = 5x$　**(d)** $f(x) = x + 2$, $g(x) = \frac{1}{2}x$
(e) $f(x) = x - 6$, $g(x) = x^2$　**(f)** $f(x) = 2x + 1$, $g(x) = 3x$

2 (a)

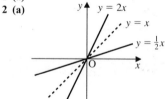

(b) $h(x) = g(f(x)) = g(x + 1) = 3(x + 1)$

3 (a) (i) 15　**(ii)** 9　**(iii)** -3　**(iv)** -9

(b) $g(f(x)) = 3(2x + 1)$

4 (a) (i) $2\frac{1}{6}$　　**(ii)** $\frac{1}{12}$

(b) (i) $h(x) = f(g(x)) = \dfrac{1}{3x} + 2$

(ii) $k(x) = g(f(x)) = \dfrac{1}{3(x + 2)}$

5 (a) $h(x) = 3x + 1$　　**(b)** $h(x) = 8x + 1$
(c) $h(x) = x^2 - 2$　　**(d)** $h(x) = (x + 4)^2$
(e) $h(x) = 4\sin x$　　**(f)** $h(x) = 2^{x - 5}$

6 (a) $k(x) = 3(x + 1)$　　**(b)** $k(x) = 8x + 4$
(c) $k(x) = (x - 2)^2$　　**(d)** $k(x) = x^2 + 4$
(e) $k(x) = \sin 4x$　　**(f)** $k(x) = 2^x - 5$

7 $f(g(x)) = \cos^2 x$; $g(f(x)) = \cos x^2$

8 (a) $h(x) = \dfrac{1}{x^2 + 2x - 3}$

(b) $\{x: x \in \mathbf{R}, x \neq -3, x \neq 1\}$

9 $f(f(x)) = \dfrac{2x - 1}{1 - x}$, $(x \neq 1)$

10 $f(g(x)) = x$

Exercise 2D

1 (b) $g(x) = \frac{1}{5}x$, $g^{-1}(x) = 5x$

(c) $k(x) = x^3$, $k^{-1}(x) = \sqrt[3]{x}$

2 (a) $f^{-1}(x) = x - 99$　　**(b)** $f^{-1}(x) = \dfrac{x}{10}$

(c) $f^{-1}(x) = 4x$　　**(d)** $f^{-1}(x) = x + \frac{1}{2}$
(e) $f^{-1}(x) = \frac{1}{2}(x - 5)$　**(f)** $f^{-1}(x) = \frac{1}{3}(x + 1)$
(g) $f^{-1}(x) = 3(x + 2)$　**(h)** $f^{-1}(x) = 2x - 9$
(i) $f^{-1}(x) = \sqrt[3]{x + 1}$

3 (a) (i) $f^{-1}(x) = \frac{1}{2}(x + 3)$　**(ii)** $f(f^{-1}(x)) = x$
(iii) $f^{-1}(f(x)) = x$

(b) (i) $f^{-1}(x) = \dfrac{5 - x}{3}$　**(ii)** $f(f^{-1}(x)) = x$

(iii) $f^{-1}(f(x)) = x$

(c) (i) $f^{-1}(x) = 2x - 1$　**(ii)** $f(f^{-1}(x)) = x$
(iii) $f^{-1}(f(x)) = x$

4 (a) $\{0, 1, 4\}$
(b) $\{0, 1, 4\}$ cannot map to $\{-2, -1, 0, 1, 2\}$

5 (a) $k(x) = 5 - 4x$　　**(b)** $h(k(x)) = x$
(c) One is the inverse of the other

Exercise 2E

1 (a)
2 (a)

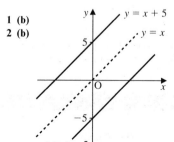

1 (b)
2 (b)

1 (c)
2 (c)

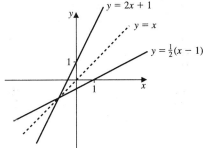

2 (a)

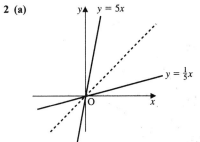

1 (d)
2 (d)

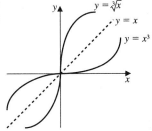

(b)

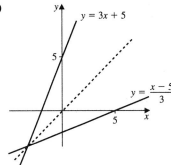

2 (b) One is the reflection of the other in the line $y = x$.

Exercise 2F

1 (a)

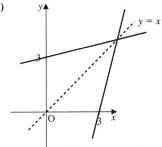

(c)

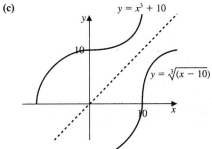

(b)

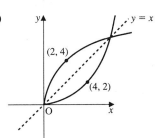

Exercise 2G

1 (a)
(b)

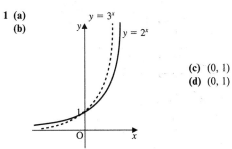

(c) $(0, 1)$
(d) $(0, 1)$

(c)

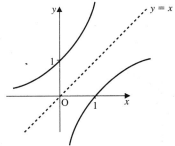

2

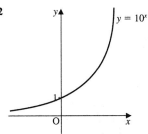

3 (a)
(b)

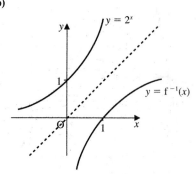

1 (a) $k(x) = 5 - 4x$ **(b)** $h(k(x)) = x$
   (c) inverses
2 (a) $f(x - 1) = 4x^2 - 11x + 12$
   (b) $4x + 7$ **(c)** $6x + 5$
3 (a) $p = 1, r = 46$ **(b)** $h(x) = 4x^2 + 20x + 22$
4 $f(g(x)) = 2\sin x + 2\cos x$, $g(f(x)) = \sin 2x + \cos 2x$

5 $f(f(x)) = \dfrac{x}{1 - 2x}$

6 $f(g(x)) = x$

7 (a) $h(x) = \dfrac{x^2 - 2}{x^2 - 4}$ **(b)** $\{x : x \in \mathbf{R}, x \neq \pm 2\}$

1 (a)

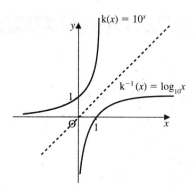

Chapter 3   Graphs of functions

1 (a) (i), (f);   (ii), (b);   (iii), (a);   (iv), (d);   (v), (g);
     (vi), (e);   (vii), (i);   (viii), (c);   (ix), (h)

1 (a)

x	-3	-2	-1	0	1	2	3
$2x$	-6	-4	-2	0	2	4	6
$2x + 3$	-3	-1	1	3	5	7	9
$2x - 2$	-8	-6	-4	-2	0	2	4

(b)

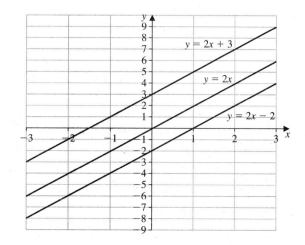

(b)

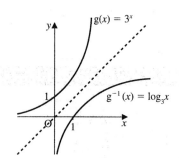

2

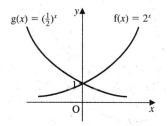

2 (a)

x	-3	-2	-1	0	1	2	3
x^2	9	4	1	0	1	4	9
$x^2 + 2$	11	6	3	2	3	6	11
$x^2 - 3$	6	1	-2	-3	-2	1	6

(b)

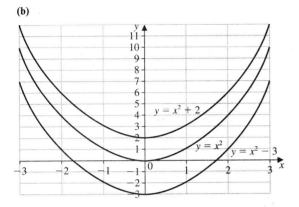

3 (a)

$x°$	0	30	60	90	120	150	180	210	240	270	300	330	360
$\sin x°$	0	0.5	0.87	1.00	0.87	0.5	0	-0.5	-0.87	-1	-0.87	-0.5	0
$\sin x° +2$	2	2.5	2.87	3.00	2.87	2.5	2	1.5	1.13	1	1.13	1.5	2
$\sin x° -1$	-1	-0.5	-0.13	0	-0.13	-0.5	-1	-1.5	-1.87	-2	-1.87	-1.5	-1

(b)

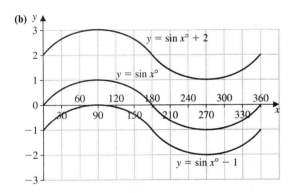

4

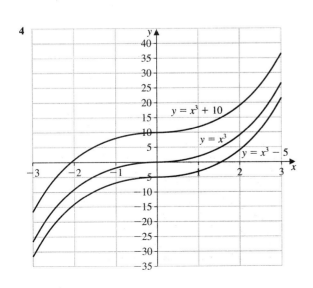

5

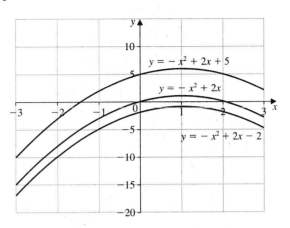

6 The graph of f(x) is slid vertically upwards for f$(x) + a$ and vertically downwards for f$(x) - a$

Exercise 3C

1 (a) $\begin{pmatrix} 0 \\ 3 \end{pmatrix}$ **(b)** $\begin{pmatrix} 0 \\ 20 \end{pmatrix}$

(c) $\begin{pmatrix} 0 \\ -2 \end{pmatrix}$ **(d)** $\begin{pmatrix} 0 \\ 5 \end{pmatrix}$

(e) $\begin{pmatrix} 0 \\ 2 \end{pmatrix}$ **(f)** $\begin{pmatrix} 0 \\ -b \end{pmatrix}$

(g) $\begin{pmatrix} 0 \\ -1 \end{pmatrix}$

2 (a) A $(0, 0)$, B $(1, -1)$, C $(2, 0)$

(b)

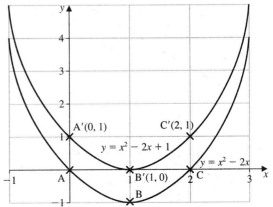

3 (a) (b)

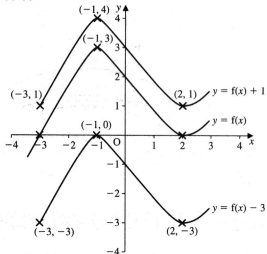

4 $k = 3$, $n = -5$

Exercise 3D

1 (a)

x	-3	-2	-1	0	1	2
$2x$	-6	-4	-2	0	2	4
$2(x + 3)$	0	2	4	6	8	10
$2(x - 1)$	-8	-6	-4	-2	0	2

(b)

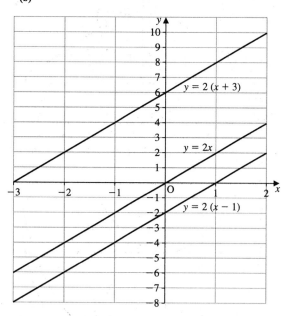

2 (a)

x	-3	-2	-1	0	1	2	3
x^2	9	4	1	0	1	4	9
$(x + 2)^2$	1	0	1	4	9	16	25
$(x - 2)^2$	25	16	9	4	1	0	1

(b)

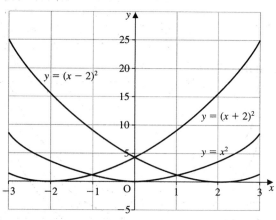

3 (a)

x	0	30	60	90	120	150	180	210	240	270	300	330	360
$\sin x°$	0	0.5	0.87	1	0.87	0.5	0	-0.5	-0.87	-1	-0.87	-0.5	0
$\sin (x + 30)°$	0.5	0.87	1	0.87	0.5	0	-0.5	-0.87	-1	-0.87	-0.5	0	0.5
$\sin (x - 60)°$	-0.87	-0.5	0	0.5	0.87	1	0.87	0.5	0	-0.5	-0.87	-1	-0.87

(b)

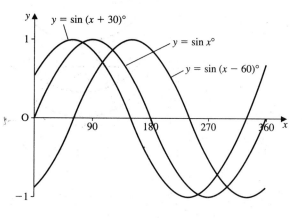

4

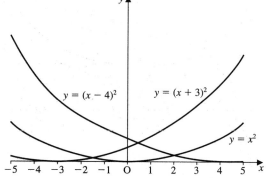

5

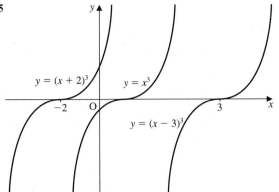

$y = (x + 2)^3$ $y = x^3$ $y = (x - 3)^3$

5

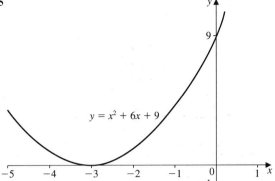

$y = x^2 + 6x + 9$

6 The graph of f(x) is slid horizontally to the left for
f($x + a$) and horizontally to the right for f($x - a$).

Exercise 3E

1 (a) $\begin{pmatrix} -3 \\ 0 \end{pmatrix}$ **(b)** $\begin{pmatrix} 4 \\ 0 \end{pmatrix}$ **(c)** $\begin{pmatrix} -15° \\ 0 \end{pmatrix}$

(d) $\begin{pmatrix} 1 \\ 0 \end{pmatrix}$ **(e)** $\begin{pmatrix} -2 \\ 0 \end{pmatrix}$ **(f)** $\begin{pmatrix} 30° \\ 0 \end{pmatrix}$

(g) $\begin{pmatrix} -3 \\ 0 \end{pmatrix}$ **(h)** $\begin{pmatrix} b \\ 0 \end{pmatrix}$

2 (a) A (0, 0),   B (−2, −4),   C (−4, 0)
(b)

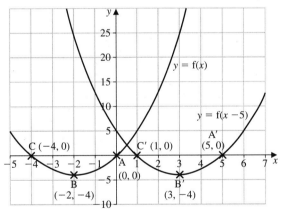

$y = f(x)$
$y = f(x - 5)$
C (−4, 0)   C′ (1, 0)   A′ (5, 0)
A (0, 0)
B (−2, −4)   B′ (3, −4)

3 (a)
(b)

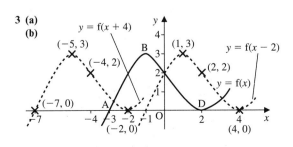

$y = f(x + 4)$ B   (1, 3) $y = f(x - 2)$
(−5, 3)
(−4, 2)   (2, 2)
$y = f(x)$
(−7, 0)   A   D
(−2, 0)   (4, 0)

4 $k = 8, n = -6$

Exercise 3F

1 (a)

x	−3	−2	−1	0	1	2	3
$2x$	−6	−4	−2	0	2	4	6
$-2x$	6	4	2	0	−2	−4	−6

(b)

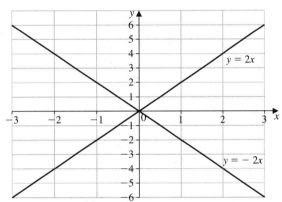

$y = 2x$
$y = -2x$

2 (a)

x	−3	−2	−1	0	1	2	3
x^2	9	4	1	0	1	4	9
$-x^2$	−9	−4	−1	0	−1	−4	−9

(b)

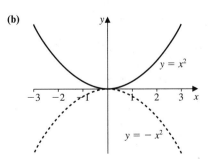

$y = x^2$
$y = -x^2$

3 (a)

x	0	30	60	90	120	150	180	210	240	270	300	330	360
$\sin x°$	0	0.5	0.87	1	0.87	0.5	0	−0.5	−0.87	−1	−0.87	−0.5	0
$-\sin x°$	0	−0.5	−0.87	−1	−0.87	−0.5	0	0.5	0.87	1	0.87	0.5	0

(b)

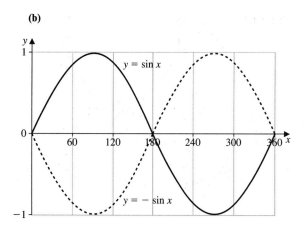

(d)

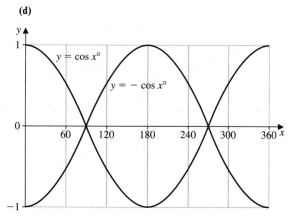

4 (a)

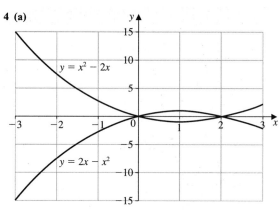

5 The graph of f(x) is reflected in the x-axis to give −f(x).

(b)

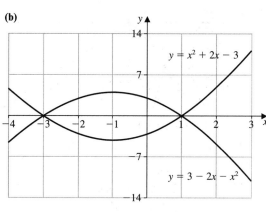

Exercise 3G

1 (a)

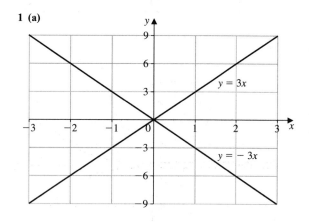

(c)

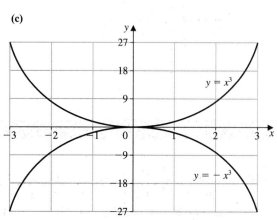

(b)

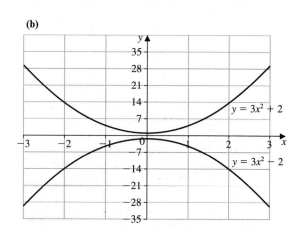

(c)

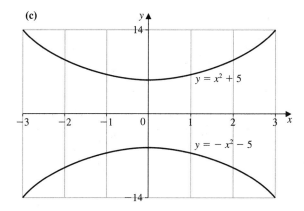

(d)

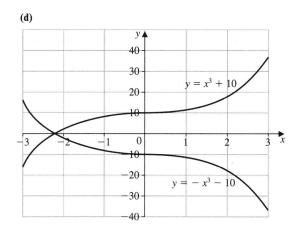

(e)

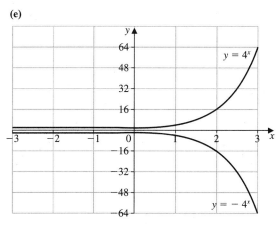

(f)

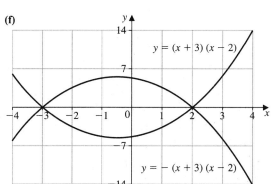

2 (a) (b)

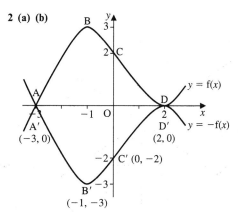

3

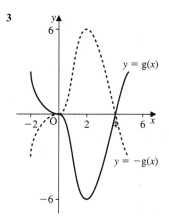

4 (a)

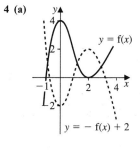

(b)

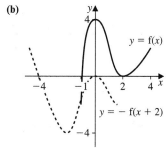

Exercise 3H

1 (a)

x	−3	−2	−1	0	1	2	3
$2x + 3$	−3	−1	1	3	5	7	9
$2(−x) + 3$	9	7	5	3	1	−1	−3

(b)

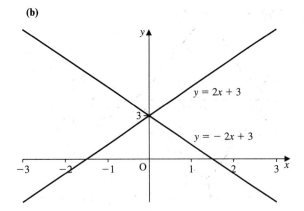

4 (a)

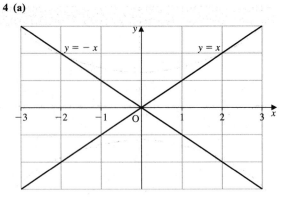

2 (a)

x	-4	-3	-2	-1	0	1	2	3	4
$(x+1)(x-3)$	21	12	5	0	-3	-4	-3	0	5
$(-x+1)(-x+3)$	5	0	-3	-4	-3	0	5	12	21

(b)

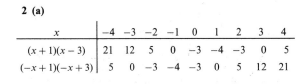

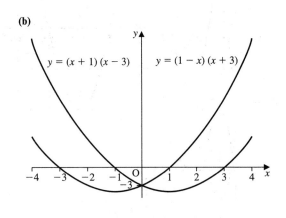

(b)

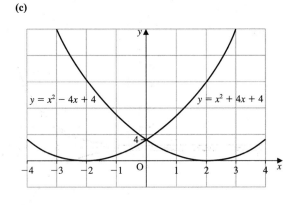

(c)

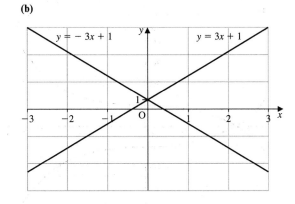

3 (a)

x	-3	-2	-1	0	1	2	3
$(2+x)(1+x)$	2	0	0	2	6	12	20
$(2-x)(1-x)$	20	12	6	2	0	0	2

(b)

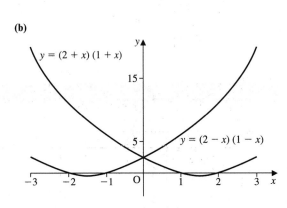

(d)

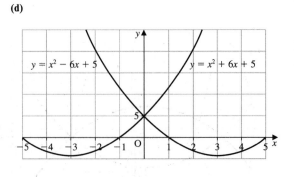

5 The graph of $f(x)$ is reflected in the y-axis to give the graph of $f(-x)$.

Exercise 3I

1 (a)

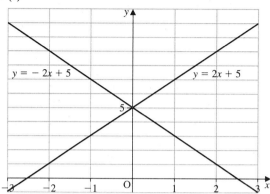

(b)

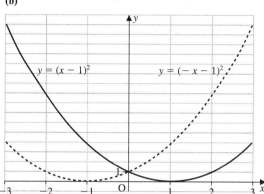

(c)

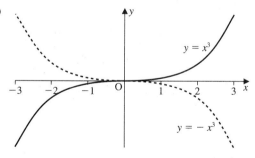

(d)

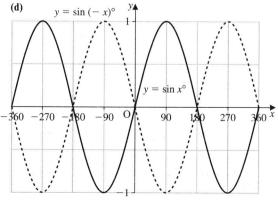

(e)

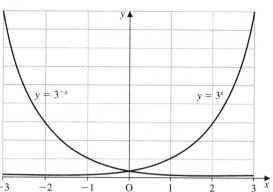

(f)

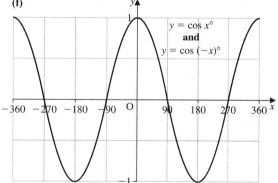

2

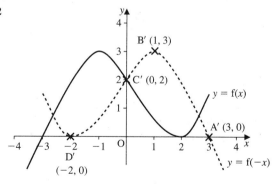

3

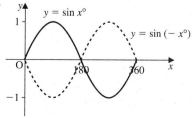

4

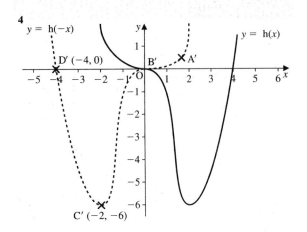

(b)

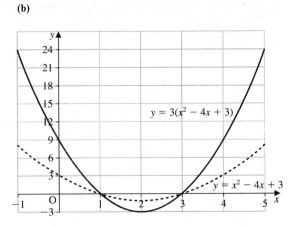

5 (a)

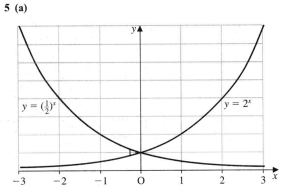

(b) The graph of $y = \left(\dfrac{1}{a}\right)^x$ is the image of the graph of

$y = a^x$ after reflection in the y-axis.

Exercise 3J

1 (a)

x	-3	-2	-1	0	1	2	3
$x^2 - 3$	6	1	-2	-3	-2	1	6
$2(x^2 - 3)$	12	2	-4	-6	-4	2	12
$3(x^2 - 3)$	18	3	-6	-9	-6	3	18

(b)

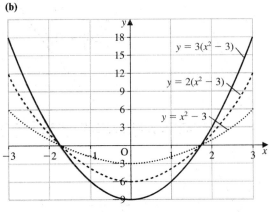

2 (a)

x	-1	0	1	2	3	4	5
$x^2 - 4x + 3$	8	3	0	-1	0	3	8
$3(x^2 - 4x + 3)$	24	9	0	-3	0	9	24

3 (a)

x	0	30	60	90	120	150	180	210	240	270	300	330	360
$\sin x°$	0	0.5	0.87	1	0.87	0.5	0	-0.5	-0.87	-1	-0.87	-0.5	0
$2\sin x°$	0	1.0	1.74	2	1.74	1	0	-1	-1.74	-2	-1.74	-1	0

(b)

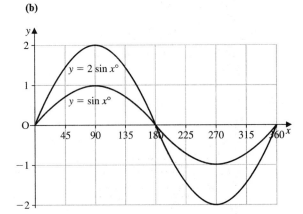

4

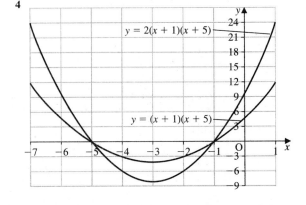

5

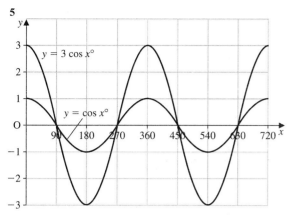

$y = 3 \cos x°$

$y = \cos x°$

6 The graph of f(x) is stretched or compressed vertically to give the graph of kf(x).

Exercise 3K

1 (a)

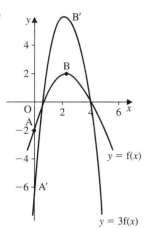

$y = f(x)$

$y = 3f(x)$

(b)

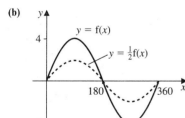

$y = f(x)$

$y = \frac{1}{2}f(x)$

(c)

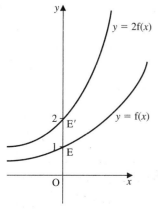

$y = 2f(x)$

$y = f(x)$

Exercise 3L

1 (a)

x	-3	-2	-1	0	1	2	3
$x^2 - 4$	5	0	-3	-4	-3	0	5
$(2x)^2 - 4$	32	12	0	-4	0	12	32

(b)

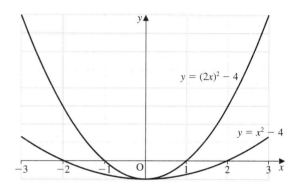

$y = (2x)^2 - 4$

$y = x^2 - 4$

2 (a)

x	-1	0	1	2	3	4	5
$x^2 - 4x$	5	0	-3	-4	-3	0	5
$(2x)^2 - 4(2x)$	12	0	-4	0	12	32	60

(b)

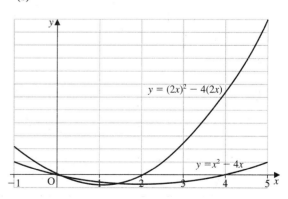

$y = (2x)^2 - 4(2x)$

$y = x^2 - 4x$

3 (a)

x	0	30	60	90	120	150	180	210	240	270	300	330	360
$\cos x°$	1	0.87	0.5	0	-0.5	-0.87	-1	-0.87	-0.5	0	0.5	0.87	1
$\cos 2x°$	1	0.5	-0.5	-1	-0.5	0.5	1	0.5	-0.5	-1	-0.5	0.5	1

(b)

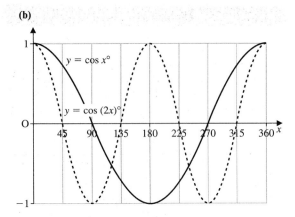

4

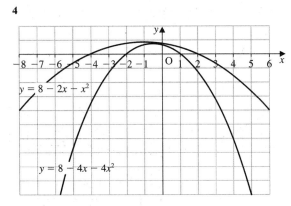

5

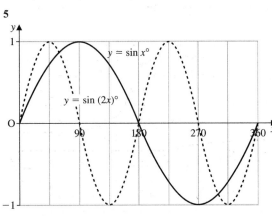

6 The graph of f(x) is stretched or compressed horizontally to give the graph of f(kx)

Exercise 3M

1 (a)

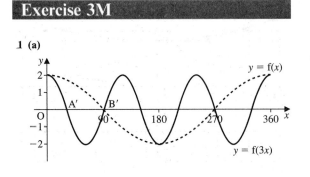

(b)

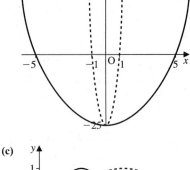

(c)

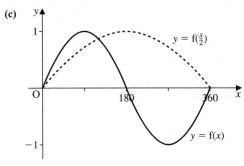

Exercise 3N

1 (a) 2   **(b)** 3

2 (a)

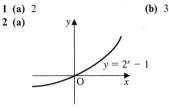

(b)

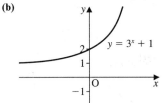

3 (i) 2; 2   **(ii)** 4; 1   **(iii)** 2; 4   **(iv)** 2; 3

4 (a)

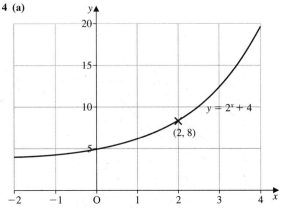

(b)

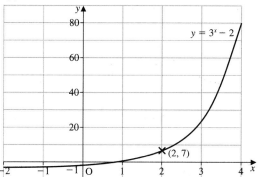

$y = 3^x - 2$

(2, 7)

(c)

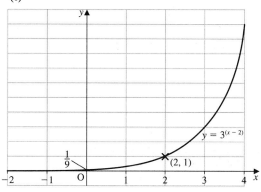

$y = 3^{(x-2)}$

$\frac{1}{9}$

(2, 1)

(d)

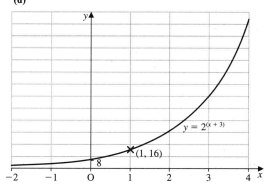

$y = 2^{(x+3)}$

(1, 16)

8

Exercise 3O

1 (i) 10   (ii) 8

2 (a) (b) (c)

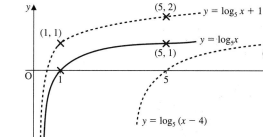

(5, 2) $y = \log_5 x + 1$

(1, 1)

$y = \log_5 x$

(5, 1)

(9, 1)

$y = \log_5 (x - 4)$

3 (a) 3   **(b)** 2   **(c)** 2

Exercise 3P

1 (a)

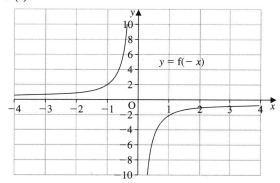

$y = f(-x)$

(b)

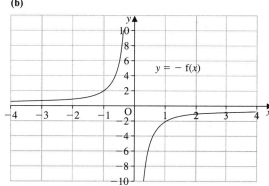

$y = -f(x)$

(c)

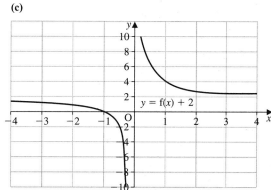

$y = f(x) + 2$

(d)

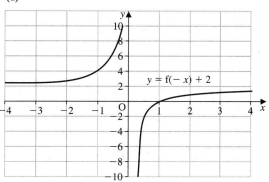

$y = f(-x) + 2$

2 (a)

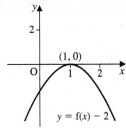

(b)

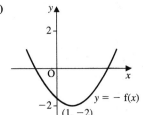

(c)

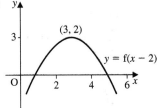

(d)

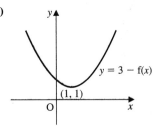

(e)

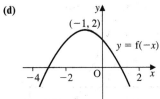

3 (a)

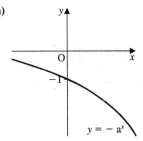

(b)

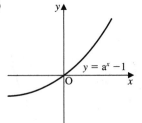

4 (a)

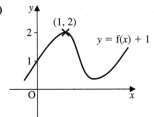

(b)

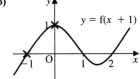

(c)

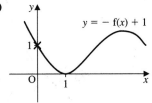

(d)

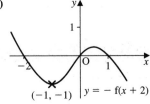

5 (a)

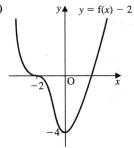

(b)

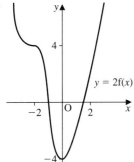

$y = 2f(x)$

(c)

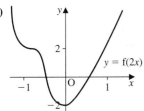

$y = f(2x)$

(d)

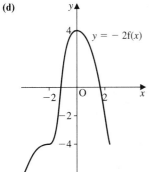

$y = -2f(x)$

6 (i)

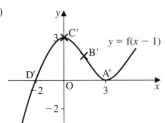

$y = f(x - 1)$

(ii)

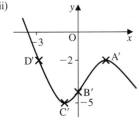

7 (a)

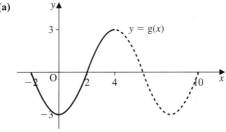

$y = g(x)$

(b)

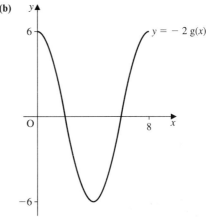

$y = -2 g(x)$

8

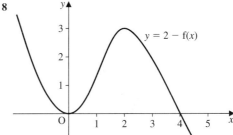

$y = 2 - f(x)$

9 (a) A $(0, 5)$; B $(2, 1)$
  (b) $m = 10$, $n = -1$
10 (a) $y = 2(x - 1)^2$
  (b) $(0, -\frac{1}{2})$
11 (a) $y = -g(x) - 2$
  (b) $y = h(2x) - \frac{1}{2}$
  (c) $y = -k(-x) + 1$
  (d) $y = \frac{1}{2}f(x - 45)$

12

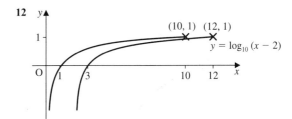

$(10, 1)$ $(12, 1)$

$y = \log_{10}(x - 2)$

Chapter 4
Trigonometry: graphs and equations

Exercise 4A

1 (a) (i) 180°   (ii) 4
  (b) (i) 120°   (ii) 0.5
  (c) (i) 45°   (ii) cannot be measured
  (d) (i) 120°   (ii) 2
  (e) (i) 720°   (ii) 8
  (f) (i) 240°   (ii) 3

2 (a) amplitude $= p$ **(b)** period $= \dfrac{360°}{q}$

3 (a) (i) 360°   (ii) 4
  (b) (i) 120°   (ii) 1
  (c) (i) 90°   (ii) cannot be measured
  (d) (i) 180°   (ii) 5
  (e) (i) 1080°   (ii) 4
  (f) (i) 1440°   (ii) 0.5

Exercise 4B

1 (a)

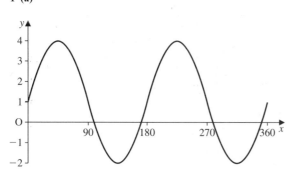

(b)

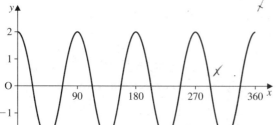

(c)

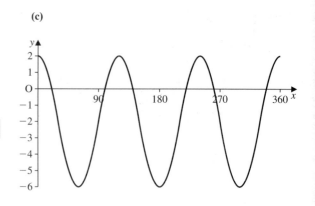

(d)

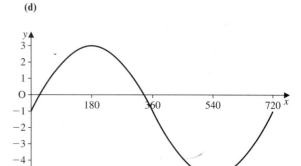

(e)

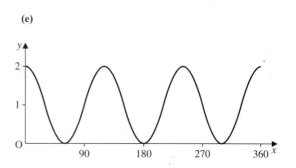

(f)

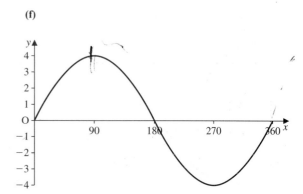

2 (a)

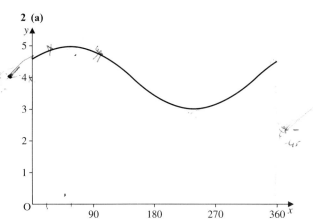

(b)

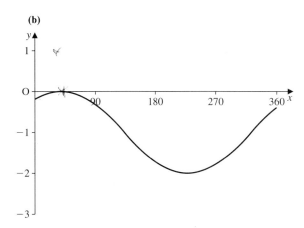

(c)

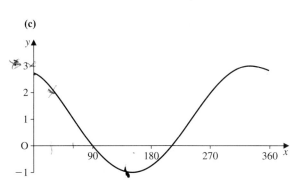

(d)

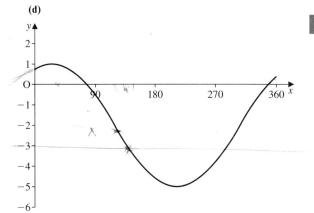

(e)

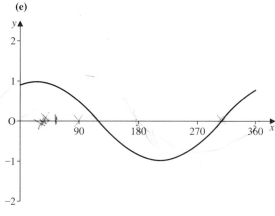

3 (a) $y = 2\cos x° + 1$ **(b)** $y = 5\sin(x - 45)°$
   (c) $y = 1.5\cos 4x° + 2$ **(d)** $y = 2\cos(x - 60)°$
   (e) $y = \tan 2x° + 3$ **(f)** $y = \sin(x - 120)° - 2$

4 $a = 60°,\ b = 240°,\ c = 150°,\ d = 4$

Exercise 4C

1 (a) $\dfrac{\pi}{2}$ **(b)** $\dfrac{\pi}{3}$ **(c)** $\dfrac{5\pi}{4}$ **(d)** $\dfrac{11\pi}{6}$ **(e)** $\dfrac{8\pi}{9}$

2 (a) $60°$ **(b)** $45°$ **(c)** $240°$ **(d)** $150°$ **(e)** $324°$

3 (a) 0.5 **(b)** -0.866 **(c)** 1 **(d)** -0.5

4 (a)

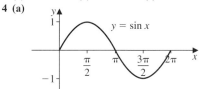

(b) $\text{max.}\left(\dfrac{\pi}{2},\,1\right);\ \text{min.}\left(\dfrac{3\pi}{2},\,-1\right)$

5 (a) $y = 2\sin 2x$ **(b)** $y = 2\sin x + 4$
   (c) $y = 6\cos\frac{3}{2}x - 2$

Exercise 4D

1 (a) $\frac{1}{2}$ **(b)** $\sqrt{3}$

2 (a) $30°$ **(b)** (i) $\frac{1}{2}$ (ii) $\dfrac{\sqrt{3}}{2}$ (iii) $\dfrac{1}{\sqrt{3}}$

3 (a) $45°$ **(b)** $\sqrt{2}$ units   **(c)** (i) $\dfrac{1}{\sqrt{2}}$ (ii) $\dfrac{1}{\sqrt{2}}$ (iii) 1

4 (a) (i)   BC gets closer to zero
      (ii)   AC becomes closer to the length of AB
   (b) (i) $\sin x°$ gets closer to 0
      (ii) $\cos x°$ gets closer to 1
      (iii) $\tan x°$ gets closer to 0
   (c) (i) 0   (ii) 1   (iii) 0

5 **(a)** (i)   GH gets closer to zero
    (ii)   GF becomes closer to the length of FH
  (b) (i) $\sin x°$ approaches 1
    (ii) $\cos x°$ approaches 0
    (iii) $\tan x°$ increases without limit
  (c) (i) 1   (ii) 0

Exercise 4E

1 **(a)** $\dfrac{1}{\sqrt{2}}$ **(b)** $\dfrac{1}{\sqrt{3}}$ **(c)** $-\dfrac{1}{\sqrt{2}}$ **(d)** $-\sqrt{3}$ **(e)** $-\frac{1}{2}$,

  (f) $-\frac{1}{2}$ **(g)** 1   **(h)** $-\frac{1}{2}$ **(i)** $-\frac{1}{2}$ **(j)** $-\dfrac{1}{\sqrt{3}}$

  (k) $\dfrac{1}{\sqrt{2}}$ **(l)** $\frac{1}{2}$ **(m)** $-\dfrac{\sqrt{3}}{2}$ **(n)** -1 **(o)** $\dfrac{\sqrt{3}}{2}$

2 **(a)** $\frac{1}{2}$ **(b)** 1   **(c)** $-\frac{1}{2}$ **(d)** $-\sqrt{2}$

3 (a) $2\sqrt{3}$ cm   **(b)** $7\sqrt{3}$ m   **(c)** $\dfrac{4}{\sqrt{3}}$ km

4 **(a)** (i) $\dfrac{5}{2}$ m   (ii) $\dfrac{5\sqrt{3}}{2}$ m   (iii) $\dfrac{5}{2\sqrt{3}}$

       (iv) $\dfrac{10}{\sqrt{3}}$ (v) $\dfrac{5}{\sqrt{3}}$

Exercise 4F

1 (a) $20\sqrt{3}$ km   **(b)** 10 km/hour

2 **(a)** $\dfrac{9}{2}$ m and $\dfrac{9\sqrt{3}}{2}$ m   **(b)** $\dfrac{81\sqrt{3}}{8}$ m²

  (c) $\dfrac{243\sqrt{3}}{2}$ m³

3 **(a)** $20\sqrt{2}$ m   **(b)** $100\sqrt{6}$ m²   **(c)** $20\sqrt{3} - \sqrt{2}$ m

4 **(a)** $\sqrt{2}$ m   **(b)** $\sqrt{3}$ m   **(c)** 120°

Exercise 4G

1 **(a)** 70°, 110°, 190°, 230°, 310°, 350°
  (b) 0°, 60°, 120°, 180°, 240°, 300°, 360°
  (c) 30°, 150°, 270°
  (d) 90°, 210°, 330°
2 **(a)** 0   **(b)** π
  (c) 2π **(d)** no solution
3 **(a)** 30°, 150°   **(b)** $-10, -50, -130, -170$
  (c) π
4 **(a)** 15°, 75°   **(b)** $-\dfrac{\pi}{6}, \dfrac{\pi}{6}$
  (c) $\dfrac{\pi}{8}, \dfrac{5\pi}{8}, \dfrac{9\pi}{8}, \dfrac{13\pi}{8}$ **(d)** $\dfrac{\pi}{3}$
5 **(a)** 2
  (b) high: 12 00 hours; low: 06 00 hours
  (c) between midnight and 02 00 and between 10 00 and 14 00
6 **(a)** 3.85°, 56.15°, 123.85°, 176.15°
  (b) $-2.47, -0.68, 0.68, 2.47$
  (c) 56.3°, 236.3°, 416.3°, 596.3°
  (d) no solutions

Exercise 4H

1 **(a)** 30°, 210°
  (b) 45°

  (c) $\dfrac{\pi}{8}, \dfrac{5\pi}{8}$

  (d) 40°, 80°, 160°, 200°, 280°, 320°

  (e) $\dfrac{\pi}{24}, \dfrac{\pi}{8}, \dfrac{9\pi}{24}, \dfrac{11\pi}{24}, \dfrac{17\pi}{24}, \dfrac{19\pi}{24}$

  (f) 45°
2 **(a)** 90°, 270°
  (b) 30°, 150°, 210°, 330°

  (c) $\dfrac{\pi}{4}, \dfrac{3\pi}{4}, \dfrac{5\pi}{4}, \dfrac{7\pi}{4}$

  (d) 30°, 150°, 210°, 330°
3 **(a)** 66.93°, 113.07°
  (b) 34.2°, 214.2°, 394.2°, 574.2°
  (c) 94.5°, 265.5°, 454.5°
  (d) 1.31, 4.97
  (e) 3.77, 5.66, 10.05, 11.94
  (f) 56.83°, 236.83°, 416.83°
4 **(a)** 15°, 75°, 195°, 255°
  (b) 5.4°, 114.6°, 125.4°, 234.6°, 245.4°, 354.6°
5 **(a)** 0°, 135°, 180°, 315°, 360°
  (b) 30°, 150°, 228.6°, 311.4°

  (c) $\dfrac{\pi}{9}, \dfrac{8\pi}{9}, \dfrac{7\pi}{6}, \dfrac{11\pi}{6}$

  (d) 0.84, 1.82

Exercise 4I

1 **(a)** 270°, 330°
  (b) 28.5°, 81.5°, 208.5°, 261.5°

2 **(a)** $\dfrac{3\pi}{8}, \dfrac{7\pi}{8}, \dfrac{11\pi}{8}, \dfrac{15\pi}{8}$

  (b) $\dfrac{7\pi}{24}, \dfrac{23\pi}{24}, \dfrac{31\pi}{24}, \dfrac{47\pi}{24}$

3 **(a)** 173.6°, 353.6° **(b)** 19.2°, 70.8°
  (c) 45°, 165°   **(d)** 0.15, 1.01, 1.20, 2.06, 2.24, 3.11
4 **(a)** 8.1, 21.9, 38.1, 51.9, 68.1, 81.9
  (b) 6.6, 23.4, 36.6, 53.4, 66.6, 83.4

Exercise 4J

1 **(a)** (i) 72°   (ii) 3
      (iii)

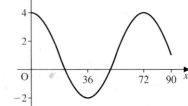

(b) (i) 180   (ii) $\frac{1}{2}$

(iii)

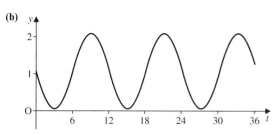

2 (a) (i) 180°   (ii) 4   (iii) $\cos \frac{1}{2}x$

(b) (i) 720°   (ii) 1   (iii) $\cos \dfrac{x}{2}$

(c) (i) $\dfrac{\pi}{2}$ (ii) cannot be measured

   (iii) $y = \tan 2x + 1$

3 (a) 67.5°   **(b)** 210°   **(c)** 432°

4 (a) $\dfrac{3\pi}{2}$ **(b)** $\dfrac{5\pi}{6}$ **(c)** $\dfrac{7\pi}{4}$

5 (a) $-\dfrac{1}{\sqrt{2}}$ **(b)** $\dfrac{1}{\sqrt{3}}$ **(c)** $-\dfrac{\sqrt{3}}{2}$

6 (a) $\frac{1}{2}$ **(b)** $-\dfrac{\sqrt{3}}{2\sqrt{2}}$ **(c)** $-\frac{1}{2}$

7 $P\left(\dfrac{\pi}{6}, 0.5\right); Q\left(\dfrac{\pi}{2}, 0.5\right)$

8 (a) 10.5, 34.5, 100.5, 124.5   **(b)** 5°, 40°
(c) 22.5°, 112.5°
9 (a) 6.22°, 53.78°
(b) 13.9°, 43.9°, 73.9°, 103.9°, 133.9°, 163.9°
(c) 7.5°   **(d)** 0.586, 2.03
(e) $\dfrac{\pi}{6}, \dfrac{5\pi}{6}, \dfrac{7\pi}{6}, \dfrac{11\pi}{6}$ **(f)** 30°, 150°
(g) 0°, 60°, 300°, 360°   **(h)** 30°, 150°
10 (a) $y = 2\sin 4x°$
(b) A(57.2°, −1.5); B(77.9°, −1.5)
11 (a) $p = 3$, $q = 1$, $r = -140$, $u = 230°$
(b) $s = -0.928$; $t = 120.5°$
12 (a) 04 36   **(b)** 10 53
13 (a) max = 90 db; min = 50 db
(b) 42%   **(c)** 31.5

14 (a)
$y = \sin\dfrac{\pi t}{6}$ $y = -\sin\dfrac{\pi t}{6}$

(b)

(c) 28th June 1990

Chapter 5
Recurrence relations

Exercise 5A

1 (a) £1215.51   **(b)** 9 years
2 (a) 152   **(b)** 5 days
3 (a) 7 years   **(b)** 4 years
4 64.9 million
5 (a) 7 weeks   **(b)** 4 weeks more

Exercise 5B

1 (a) $u_{n+1} = 1.03u_n$ **(b)** £184 481.08
2 (a) $u_{n+1} = 1.05u_n$ **(b)** £3.19 million
3 (a) $u_{n+1} = 0.8u_n$ **(b)** £6144
4 (a) 95%   **(b)** $u_{n+1} = 0.95u_n$
(c) 4286   **(d)** 14 weeks

Exercise 5C

1 (a) £46 000.97   **(b)** £42 882.95
2 (a) 97.6 units   **(b)** 134.46 units
3 Yes
4 (a) 304   **(b)** 262
5 (a) $u_{n+1} = 1.04u_n + 25$ **(b)** £196.24
6 (a) $u_{n+1} = 0.95u_n + 1.5$ **(b)** 33.87 litres
7 (a) $u_{n+1} = 0.85u_n + 2$ **(b)** 35.85 p.s.i.
(c) Yes
8 (a) $u_{n+1} = 1.08u_n - 100$ **(b)** 230
(c) 7 months
9 (a) $u_{n+1} = 1.04u_n + 2000$ **(b)** £52 642.68
10 (a) $u_{n+1} = 0.2u_n + 50$ **(b)** 62.5 kg
11 £3823.98

Exercise 5D

1 (a) 7.92   **(b)** −25   **(c)** 668
(d) −11   **(e)** 4   **(f)** −15.136
2 (a) 9.4375   **(b)** 4
3 (a) 587.5   **(b)** 6   **(c)** one
4 (a) 685.62   **(b)** 6   **(c)** 6
5 (a) 53.59   **(b)** (i) 9   (ii) 11

Exercise 5E

1 (a) converges on $166\frac{2}{3}$ units
(b) converges on 100 units
(c) converges on $83\frac{1}{3}$ units

2 (a) converges on 62.5 units
(b) converges on 250 units
(c) converges on 500 units
3 (a) converges on 125
(b) converges on 125
(c) converges on 125

Exercise 5F

1 (a) converges on zero
(b) converges on zero
(c) increases
2 (a) converges on zero
(b) converges on zero
(c) increases
3 (a) converges on zero
(b) converges on zero
(c) increases

Exercise 5G

1 (a) (i), (ii) and (iii) are divergent
(iv) is constant
(v), (vi), (vii) and (viii) are convergent
(ix) alternates between 2 and -1
(x) divergent with alternating positive and negative values
(b) convergent if $-1 < a < 1$
2 (a) all convergent
(b) altering b changes the rate of convergence
3 (a) all converge on 5
(b) altering u_0 does not affect convergence

Exercise 5H

1 (a) 6, 5.2, 5.04, 5.008, 5.0016 .... limit $= 5$
(b) 10, 6, 5.2, 5.04, 5.008 .... limit $= 5$
(c) 5, 9, 9.8, 9.96, 9.992 .... limit $= 10$
(d) 5, 13, 14.6, 14.92, 14.984 .... limit $= 15$
(e) 6, 10.6, 11.06, 11.106, 11.1106 .... limit $= 11\frac{1}{9}$
(f) 160, 140, 135, 133.75, 133.4375 .... limit $= 133\frac{1}{3}$
(g) 2, 7, 22, 67, 202 .... no limit
(h) 4, 4, 4, 4, 4 .... limit $= 4$
(i) 1, 4.9, 4.51, 4.549, 4.5451 .... limit $= 4\frac{6}{11}$
(j) 1, 9, 1, 9, 1 .... no limit
2 (a) $u_2 = 68.4375$ **(b)** 5 **(c)** 60
3 (a) $u_2 = 1740$ **(b)** 5 **(c)** 2500
4 (a) $u_{n+1} = 0.55u_n + 30$
(b) No **(c)** Yes
5 No
6 (a) converges on $27\frac{7}{9}$ kg **(b)** converges on $11\frac{1}{9}$ kg
7 converges on 300
8 Yes
9 (a) 496 203 **(b)** converges on 466 667
(c) 7500
10 No, will drop to 1200

Exercise 5I

1 (a) $a = 0.5, b = 30$ **(b)** $a = 5, b = -6$
(c) $a = 0.5, b = -50$ **(d)** $a = -1, b = 0$
(e) $a = -4, b = 10$ **(f)** $a = 2, b = 5$
(g) $a = 0.2, b = -20$ **(h)** $a = 0.25, b = 10$
(i) $a = 0.25, b = 0$ **(j)** $a = 0.1, b = -22$
2 $a = 1, b = -2$
3 rate $= 5\%$, amount $= £160$
4 rate $= 2\%$, fixed sum $= £50$

Exercise 5J

1 (a) 25 in Washington, 175 in New York
2 (b) would converge on 312 500
3 (a) $D_{n+1} = 0.7D_n + 8$
(b) 27
4 Society A: 60 000; Society B: 40 000
5 (a) 160
(b) No

Exercise 5K

1 (a) $u_4 = u_1 + (3 \times 5)$, $u_5 = u_1 + (4 \times 5)$, $u_6 = u_1 + (5 \times 5)$
(b) $u_8 = u_1 + (7 \times 5)$
(c) $u_n = u_1 + 5(n - 1)$
2 (a) $u_1, u_1 + b, u_1 + 2b, u_1 + 3b$
(b) $u_8 = u_1 + 7b$
(c) $u_n = u_1 + (n - 1)b$
3 (a) $u_4 = 2^3 u_1$, $u_5 = 2^4 u_1$, $u_6 = 2^5 u_1$
(b) $u_8 = 2^7 u_1$
(c) $u_n = 2^{n-1} u_1$
4 (a) $u_2 = au_1$, $u_3 = a^2 u_1$, $u_4 = a^3 u_1$, $u_5 = a^4 u_1$
(b) $u_n = a^{n-1} u_1$
5 $u_1 = 1, u_2 = 1, u_3 = 2, u_4 = 3, u_5 = 5, u_6 = 8, u_7 = 13,$
$u_8 = 21, u_9 = 34, u_{10} = 55$

Exercise 5L

1 (a) 18.25 **(b)** 5 **(c)** 16
2 (a) $u_{n+1} = 0.9u_n + 4, u_0 = 36$
(b) 37.87 litres
(c) No
3 (a) £1537.93
(b) 1st Oct.
(c) $u_{n+1} = 1.005u_n + 100$ where u_{n+1} = amount on 1st of month
u_n = amount on 1st of previous month
4 53.9%
5 (a) 23.22 units
(b) Yes, converges on 93.35 units
6 rate $= 2\%$ per month; repayment $= £75$ per month
7 86 at Glasgow, 64 at Edinburgh

Chapter 6
Differentiation

Exercise 6A

1 (a) The car travels at a constant speed for 10 minutes and then at a slower constant speed for a further 10 minutes. The car then travels for a further 10 minutes at a quicker constant speed.
  (b) (i) 1.5 km/min **(ii)** 0.5 km/min **(iii)** 2 km/min
      (iv) 1 km/min   **(v)** 1.3 km/min
  (c) (i) 1.5 km/min **(ii)** 0.5 km/min **(iii)** 2 km/min
      (iv) 1.5 km/min
  (d) No
2 (a) (i) 1.5 km/min   **(ii)** 1 km/min   **(iii)** 1.3 km/min
  (b) The speed changes continuously

Exercise 6B

1

time in interval	3–4	3–3.5	3–3.25	3–3.1	3–3.01	3–3.001	3–3.0001
change in distance	7	3.25	1.5625	0.61	0.0601	0.006001	0.00060001
change in time	1	0.5	0.25	0.1	0.01	0.001	0.0001
average speed	7	6.5	6.25	6.1	6.01	6.001	6.0001

Speed at 3 seconds = 6 m/s

2 8 m/s
3 (a)

time (s)	2	3	4
instantaneous speed (m/s)	4	6	8

(b) speed = $2t$

Exercise 6C

1 (a) 48   **(b)** 20   **(c)** 405   **(d)** 192
  (e) 4000 **(f)** 10   **(g)** 3   **(h)** 20

Exercise 6D

1 $5x^4$ **2** $7x^6$ **3** $8x^7$
4 $10x^9$ **5** $50x^{49}$ **6** $100x^{99}$
7 $-3x^{-4}$ **8** $-4x^{-5}$ **9** $-10x^{-11}$
10 $-50x^{-51}$ **11** $-100x^{-101}$ **12** $\frac{4}{3}x^{\frac{1}{3}}$
13 $\frac{5}{2}x^{\frac{3}{2}}$ **14** $\frac{1}{2}x^{-\frac{1}{2}}$ **15** $\frac{2}{3}x^{-\frac{1}{3}}$
16 $-\frac{1}{3}x^{-\frac{4}{3}}$ **17** $-\frac{2}{3}x^{-\frac{5}{3}}$ **18** $-\frac{4}{3}x^{-\frac{7}{3}}$
19 1   **20** 0   **21** $\frac{1}{3\sqrt[3]{x^2}}$
22 $\frac{1}{4\sqrt[4]{x^3}}$ **23** $\frac{1}{5\sqrt[5]{x^4}}$ **24** $\frac{3}{2}\sqrt{x}$
25 $\frac{2}{3\sqrt[3]{x}}$ **26** $\frac{5}{2}\sqrt{x^3}$ **27** $\frac{4}{3}\sqrt[3]{x}$

28 $-\dfrac{4}{x^5}$ **29** $-\dfrac{10}{x^{11}}$ **30** $-\dfrac{50}{x^{51}}$
31 $-\dfrac{5}{3x^{\frac{8}{3}}}$ **32** $-\dfrac{7}{4x^{\frac{11}{4}}}$ **33** $-\dfrac{3}{4x^{\frac{7}{4}}}$
34 $-\dfrac{7}{2x^{\frac{9}{2}}}$ **35** $-\dfrac{1}{2\sqrt{x^3}}$ **36** $-\dfrac{1}{3\sqrt[3]{x^2}}$
37 $-\dfrac{3}{2\sqrt{x^5}}$ **38** $-\dfrac{2}{3\sqrt[3]{x^5}}$ **39** $-\dfrac{4}{3\sqrt[3]{x^7}}$
40 $-\dfrac{5}{2\sqrt{x^7}}$

Exercise 6E

1 (a) 12   **(b)** 27   **(c)** $\frac{1}{3}$ **(d)** 12
  (e) 48   **(f)** $\frac{3}{4}$ **(g)** 75   **(h)** $\frac{3}{16}$
2 (a) 6   **(b)** 80   **(c)** $-\frac{1}{9}$ **(d)** $\frac{1}{6}$
  (e) 3   **(f)** $-\frac{1}{16}$
3 (a) 32   **(b)** -6 **(c)** -128 **(d)** $\frac{8}{3}$
4 (a) 48   **(b)** 2   **(c)** $\frac{4}{3}$ **(d)** $-\frac{3}{16}$
5 300
6 $\frac{9}{2}$

Exercise 6F

1 $15x^4$ **2** $10x$ **3** $50x^4$
4 $-12x^{-4}$ **5** $3x^5$ **6** $\frac{27}{4}x^8$
7 $500x^9$ **8** $-\dfrac{9}{x^4}$ **9** $-\dfrac{8}{x^5}$
10 $-\dfrac{3}{2x^4}$ **11** $-\dfrac{6}{x^5}$ **12** $\dfrac{3}{2\sqrt{x}}$
13 $6\sqrt{x}$ **14** $\dfrac{1}{3\sqrt[3]{x}}$ **15** $-\dfrac{1}{\sqrt{x^3}}$
16 $-\dfrac{3}{4\sqrt{x^3}}$ **17** $-\dfrac{9}{8\sqrt{x^5}}$ **18** $-\dfrac{25}{3\sqrt{x^7}}$
19 $4x^3 + 3x^2 + 2x + 1$ **20** $6x^2 - 8x$
21 $\frac{3}{2}x^2 - \frac{2}{3}x$ **22** $6x + \dfrac{1}{3\sqrt[3]{x^2}}$ **23** $9x^2 + \frac{1}{2}x^{-3}$
24 $10x - \dfrac{1}{\sqrt{x^3}}$ **25** $8x - \dfrac{2}{\sqrt[3]{x^4}}$ **26** $\dfrac{1}{4} - \dfrac{4}{x^2}$
27 $2x + \dfrac{2}{x^3}$

Exercise 6G

1 $2x + 7$ **2** $2x - 1$ **3** $12x + 11$
4 $2x + 6$ **5** $3x^2 + 14x + 14$ **6** $4x^3 + 14x$
7 $\frac{5}{2}\sqrt{x^3} - 1$ **8** $1 + \dfrac{1}{2\sqrt{x}}$ **9** $-\dfrac{1}{x^2} + \dfrac{2}{x^3}$
10 $-\dfrac{2}{x^3} - \dfrac{2}{x^2}$ **11** $-\dfrac{2}{x^3} + 2x$ **12** $1 - \dfrac{1}{x^2}$

13. $-\dfrac{4}{x^5} + 4x^3$
14. $-\dfrac{1}{x^2} + \dfrac{1}{2\sqrt{x^3}}$
15. $2x + \dfrac{2}{x^3}$

16. $-\dfrac{1}{x^2} - 1$
17. $\dfrac{1}{x^2}$
18. $1 - \dfrac{1}{x^2}$

19. $1 - \dfrac{10}{x^3}$
20. $\dfrac{1}{2\sqrt{x}} - \dfrac{1}{2\sqrt{x^3}}$
21. $-\dfrac{6}{x^3} - \dfrac{2}{x^2}$

22. $\dfrac{1}{2} + \dfrac{1}{2x^2}$
23. $-\dfrac{12}{x^5} + \dfrac{2}{x^3}$
24. $-\dfrac{1}{x^2} - \dfrac{1}{2x^3}$

25. $-\dfrac{1}{x^2} + \dfrac{2}{x^3} + \dfrac{6}{x^4}$
26. $\dfrac{1}{2\sqrt{x}} + \dfrac{2}{\sqrt{x^3}}$

27. $-\dfrac{1}{2\sqrt{x^3}} + \dfrac{2}{\sqrt{x}} + 6\sqrt{x}$

Exercise 6H

1 (a) 9   (b) 18   (c) $\frac{9}{2}$ (d) 0
   (e) 18   (f) $9\sqrt{3}$ (g) $\frac{9}{2}$
2 (a) 28   (b) 295   (c) 22   (d) $-\frac{1}{16}$
3 (a) -4 (b) $\frac{3}{8}$ (c) 16
4 (a) 48   (b) 8   (c) 1
5 (a) (i) 10 m/s   (ii) 0 m/s   (b) stationary
6 55 m/s
7 $\dfrac{\pi}{2}$ cm/s
8 $3\frac{1}{2}$ cm³/s
9 -2 amp/ohm
10 225 ml/mm
11 5 beats per minute/sec
12 700 bacteria/hour
13 (a) 0   (b) constant amount of drug
14 (a) 143 cm/s
   (b) (i) acceleration = $6t + 12$ (ii) 42 cm/s/s

Exercise 6I

1 (a) $35x^4 + 6x - 9$ (b) $\dfrac{1}{x^{\frac{1}{2}}} - \dfrac{5}{3x^{\frac{2}{3}}}$

(c) $1 - \dfrac{6}{u^3}$ (d) $-\dfrac{1}{x^2} - \dfrac{21}{x^4}$

(e) $4x^3 - 2x$ (f) $-\dfrac{36}{s^5} + \dfrac{6}{s^2} + 2s$

(g) $\dfrac{7}{2x^2} + \dfrac{8}{x^3}$ (h) $-\dfrac{2}{g^{\frac{3}{2}}} - \dfrac{10}{g^{\frac{1}{2}}} + \dfrac{75}{2}g^{\frac{1}{2}}$

2 (a) 6   (b) 96   (c) $\frac{2}{27}$
3 (a) 46   (b) -3
4 (a) 24   (b) 7   (c) $\dfrac{3887}{3888}$
5 90 calls per hour

Exercise 6J

1 (a) $y - 12x + 16 = 0$ (b) $y - 5x + 1 = 0$
(c) $y = 2$ (d) $2y + x + 4 = 0$
(e) $8y - 5x - 80 = 0$ (f) $4y - 3x - 4 = 0$
(g) $y - x - 3 = 0$ (h) $y - 51x + 90 = 0$
(i) $16y + 3x + 8 = 0$

2 (a) $y - 4x + 2 = 0$; $y + 4x + 2 = 0$ (b) $(0, -2)$
3 (b) $y - 11x + 3 = 0$
4 At P: $y - 8x + 8 = 0$; At Q: $y - 7x + 7 = 0$
5 (a) $y - 4x + 1 = 0$ (b) $(-2, -9)$
6 $(2, 17)$
7 $(3, 23)$
8 (a) $(-2, 0)$, $(2, 0)$ (b) $8x - y + 16 = 0$, $8x - y - 16 = 0$

Exercise 6K

1 (a) $2x - 4$
(b)

x	-2	-1	0	1	2	3	4	5	6
$\dfrac{dy}{dx}$	-8	-6	-4	-2	0	2	4	6	8

(c) (i) $\dfrac{dy}{dx} > 0$ (ii) $\dfrac{dy}{dx} < 0$

2 (a) $2 - 2x$
(b)

x	-2	-1	0	1	2	3	4
$\dfrac{dy}{dx}$	6	4	2	0	-2	-4	-6

(c) (i) $\dfrac{dy}{dx} > 0$ (ii) $\dfrac{dy}{dx} < 0$

3 (a) $3x^2 - 24x + 36$
(b)

x	-1	0	1	2	3	4	5	6	7	8
$\dfrac{dy}{dx}$	63	36	15	0	-9	-12	-9	0	15	36

increasing   decreasing   increasing

(c) (i) $\dfrac{dy}{dx} > 0$ (ii) $\dfrac{dy}{dx} < 0$

4 (a)

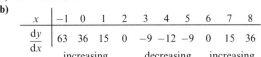

x	-6	-5	-4	-3	-2	-1	0	1	2	3	4	5	6
$\dfrac{dy}{dx}$	-162	-96	-42	0	30	48	54	48	30	0	-42	-96	-162

(b) (i) decreasing   (ii) increasing   (iii) decreasing

Exercise 6L

1 (a) increasing   (b) increasing
(c) decreasing   (d) decreasing
(e) increasing   (f) decreasing
2 (a) decreasing for $x < 0$; increasing for $x > 0$
(b) decreasing for $x < \frac{5}{2}$; increasing for $x > \frac{5}{2}$
(c) decreasing for $x < -\frac{5}{8}$; increasing for $x > -\frac{5}{8}$
(d) increasing for $x < 0$; decreasing for $0 < x < 4$; increasing for $x > 4$
(e) decreasing for $x < -\sqrt{2}$; increasing for $-\sqrt{2} < x < \sqrt{2}$; decreasing for $x > \sqrt{2}$
(f) increasing for $x < -\frac{2}{3}$; decreasing for $-\frac{2}{3} < x < \frac{2}{3}$; increasing for $x > \frac{2}{3}$
(g) decreasing for $x < -1$; increasing for $-1 < x < 0$; decreasing for $0 < x < 1$; increasing for $x > 1$
(h) increasing for $x < -\frac{8}{9}$; decreasing for $-\frac{8}{9} < x < 0$; increasing for $x > 0$
(i) decreasing for $x < -1$; increasing for $-1 < x < 0$; decreasing for $0 < x < 1$; increasing for $x > 1$
9 (a) $3x^2 - 3$ (b) 0, 0   (c) horizontal

Exercise 6M

1 $(3, -9)$ min. TP
2 $(0, 9)$ max. TP
3 $(5, 0)$ max. TP
4 $(-1, -2)$ min. TP; $(1, 2)$ max. TP
5 $(1, 4)$ max. TP; $(3, 0)$ min. TP
6 $(-2, 19)$ max. TP; $(2, -13)$ min. TP
7 $(0, 0)$ falling point of inflexion; $(3, -27)$ min. TP
8 $(1.15, 2.92)$ min. TP; $(-0.15, 5.08)$ max. TP
9 $(0, 0)$ rising point of inflexion; $(1.5, 1.69)$ max. TP

Exercise 6N

1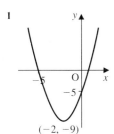
2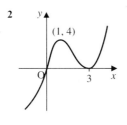
3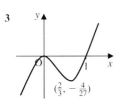
4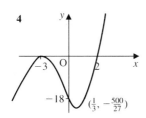
5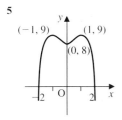
6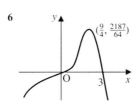
7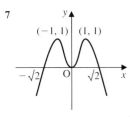
8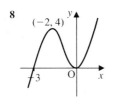
9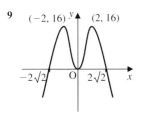

Exercise 6O

1 (a) max. 5; min. -76 (b) max. 20; min. -50
(c) max. 56; min. -594
2 (a) max. 54; min. -54 (b) max. 5; min. 2
(c) max. $\frac{400}{27}$; min. -36 (d) max. 0.4375; min. 0
(e) max. 432; min. -9 (f) max. 2; min. -2

Exercise 6P

1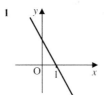
2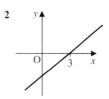
3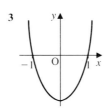
4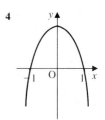
5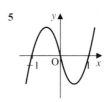
6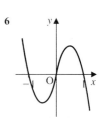
7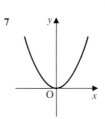
8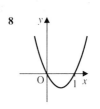
9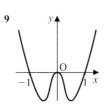

Exercise 6Q

1 (a) $x(18 - x)$ (b) 9 cm by 9 cm   (c) 81 cm²
2 (a) $x(12.5 - x)$ (b) 39.1 m²
3 (b) 28 units²

4 (a) $2x + \dfrac{16}{x}$ **(b)** $\sqrt{8}$ by $\sqrt{8}$

5 (a) $100x - 2x^2$ **(b)** $1250\,\text{m}^2$

6 (b) $2000\,\text{cm}^3$

7 (b) $4\,\text{m}^2$

8 (b) $44.7\,\text{cm}$

Exercise 6R

1 (b) 8 cm by 8 cm by 4 cm; $192\,\text{cm}^2$

2 (b) 6.3 cm by 18.9 cm by 9.45 cm; $714.3\,\text{cm}^2$

3 $r = 3m$; cost $= £13$ million

4 (a) (i) $\dfrac{200}{x}$ **(ii)** $200x + \dfrac{800\,000}{x^2}$

   (b) 20 km/h; £6000

5 (b) $2\pi x^2 + \dfrac{288}{x}$

   (c) $r = \sqrt[3]{\dfrac{72}{\pi}}$, $h = 5.68\,\text{cm}$

Exercise 6S

1 (a) $8x + \dfrac{3}{x^2}$ **(b)** $\dfrac{5}{2\sqrt{x}}$

   (c) $12x - 1 - \dfrac{5}{x^2}$ **(d)** $\dfrac{3}{2}\sqrt{x} - \dfrac{5}{2\sqrt{x}}$

2 (a) $12t^3 - 10t$ **(b)** $10t^{\frac{3}{2}}$

   (c) $3t^2 + 4t + 1$ **(d)** $3t^2 - 16t + 16$

3 (a) $-\frac{2}{3}$ **(b)** $6\frac{1}{2}$

   (c) $1\frac{1}{4}$ **(d)** $-\frac{1}{18}$

4 $y - 35x + 42 = 0$

5 (a) $(0, 0)$ max. TP; $(\frac{2}{3}, -\frac{4}{27})$ min. TP

   (b) $(0.62, 4.76)$ min. TP $(-1.07, 12.03)$ max. TP

   (c) $(0, 0)$ point of inflection; $(\frac{3}{2}, -\frac{27}{16})$ min. TP

   (d) $(0, 0)$ point of inflection; $(\frac{3}{4}, -\frac{27}{256})$ min. TP

6 -3; 4

7 $-1 < x < 0$ and $x > 1$

9

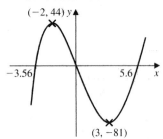

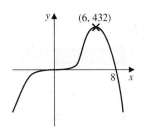

10 max. 20; min. 0

11 (a) 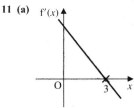 **(b)**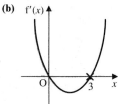

12 B $(-2, 16)$

13 $5x + y + 3 = 0$; B$(-1, 2)$

14 (a) $(0, 0)$ max. TP; $(-2, 8)$ min. TP **(b)** $-8 < k < 0$

15 $\dfrac{dy}{dx} = 4x + 1$

16 $a = 4$; $b = 7$

17 18.9 km/h

18 6

19 (b) greatest $24\,\text{units}^2$; least $16\,\text{units}^2$

20 (a) $20x - \frac{2}{5}x^2$ **(b)** 250 **(c)** $x = 25$; $y = 10$

21 (b) $l = b = h = 5\,\text{cm}$ **(c)** $125\,\text{cm}^3$

22 (b) $696.5\,\text{cm}^3$

23 (b) $2494\,\text{m}^3$

Revision exercise 1A

1 $4x + y = 7$

2 $x - 2y - 1 = 0$

3 $71.6°$

4 $(3, 7)$

5 $2x + y - 3 = 0$

6 (a) $2x + y - 13 = 0$

   (b) $2x + y = 0$

7 $(1, 2)$, $(-1, 0)$

8 $3b + a$

9 (a) $8x + y + 16 = 0$

   (b) $2x + 3y + 4 = 0$

10

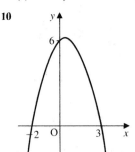

11 (a)

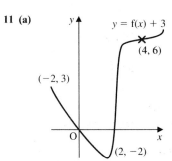

(b)

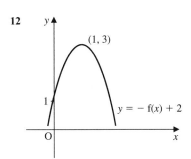

$y = f(x - 2)$

(6, 3)

(4, −5)

(iii)

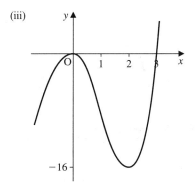

−16

12

(1, 3)

1

$y = -f(x) + 2$

(b) (i) (−2, 0), (2, 0), (1, 0)
   (ii) max. (−1, 4), min (1, 0)

(iii)

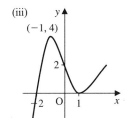

(−1, 4)

2

−2   O   1

13 (a) 4
   (b) A(60°, 2), B(300°, 2), C(420°, 2)
14 (a) $p = 3$, $q = 30°$
   (b) A(150°, 0), B(330°, 0)

(c)

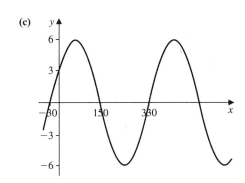

6

3

−30   150   330

−3

−6

15 10°, 50°, 130°, 170°

16 $\dfrac{\pi}{6}, \dfrac{5\pi}{6}$

17 217.5°

18 $\dfrac{\pi}{12}, \dfrac{5\pi}{12}, \dfrac{13\pi}{12}, \dfrac{17\pi}{12}$

19 (a) $12x^2 - \dfrac{5}{2\sqrt{x}}$ **(b)** $6p^2 - 12p + 1$

20 (a) $\frac{3}{2}x^2$ **(b)** $\dfrac{5}{2}x^{\frac{3}{2}} + \dfrac{1}{x^2}$

   (c) $-\dfrac{9}{5x^2} + 12x^5$

21 (a) $40x - y - 56 = 0$ **(b)** $x - 4y - 4 = 0$
22 (a) (i) (0, 0), (3, 0)
   (ii) max. (0, 0), min. (2, −16)

23 (a) 9.446
   (b) Yes, $-1 < 0.7 < 1$
   (c) $13\frac{1}{3}$
24 (a) −6.06784
   (b) −10
25 (a) $u_{n+1} = 1.04u_n$; $u_0 = 220\,000$
   (b) £289 505
26 (a) 0.354 kg
   (b) 2.35 kg

Revision exercise 1B

1 (a) CE: $3x + y - 5 = 0$; BD: $x - y + 1 = 0$
   (b) (1, 2)

2

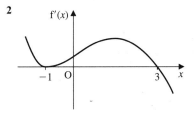

f′(x)

−1   O   3   x

3 $-1 < x < 5$
4 (a) use $u_{n+1} = 0.45u_n + 26$, $u_0 = 20$ to give the sequence
   20, 35, 41.75, 44.79, 47.27 ....
   (b) Yes
5 (a) $-2 < x < 4$ **(b)** $-2 \leqslant x \leqslant 4$
6 (a) (−2, 5)
   (b) Gradient of road and track at $x = -2$ is −4
7 (b) 42 m²
8 (a) 3.3 m²   **(b)** £147 million

9 (a)

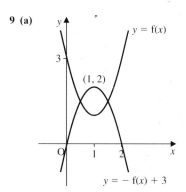

(b) $0 \leqslant x \leqslant 2$ **(c)** $g(x) = -2x(x-2)$

Chapter 7   Polynomials

Exercise 7A

1 (a) 4   **(b)** 5   **(c)** 1
   (d) 7   **(e)** 11
2 (a) $5x^3 - 3x^2 + 2x + 9$, 3
   (b) $-9x^4 + 4x^2 + 12$, 4
   (c) $x^2 - 3x - 28$, 2
   (d) $x^3 + 4x^2 - 11x - 30$, 3
3 (a) (i) 7   **(ii)** 4
   (b) (i) 6   **(ii)** -2
   (c) (i) 1   **(ii)** -1
   (d) (i) 0   **(ii)** 7
   (e) (i) 1   **(ii)** -4
   (f) (i) 0   **(ii)** -3
4 (a) $4(3t + 4)$ **(b)** $4m(2m + 5)$
   (c) $(5p + 7)(5p - 7)$ **(d)** $(x + 6)(x + 3)$
   (e) $(x - 5)(x + 7)$ **(f)** $9(2m + 3)(2m - 3)$
   (g) $(2x + 1)(x - 8)$ **(h)** $4(5p^2 + 4q)(5p^2 - 4q)$
   (i) $(3x + 2)(4x - 7)$
5 (a) ± 4 **(b)** $0, \frac{1}{3}$ **(c)** $-7, -3$ **(d)** $-\frac{3}{2}, \frac{1}{3}$
6 (a) 15   **(b)** 22   **(c)** 97   **(d)** 65
7 (a) 30   **(b)** 0   **(c)** 4
8 (a) 2   **(b)** -12 **(c)** -0.875 **(d)** 25

Exercise 7B

1 (a) 36   **(b)** 3668   **(c)** -106 **(d)** 7 000 221
2 (a) 1192   **(b)** -4 **(c)** 79
   (d) 266   **(e)** -84 **(f)** 338

Exercise 7C

1 (a) 5, 3, 1   **(b)** 6, 4, 4   **(c)** 7, 6, 1
   (d) 9, 11, 7   **(e)** 9, 4, 0
2 (a) $(2x + 5)$, 9   **(b)** $(x^2 + 8x + 19)$, 39
   (c) $(x^2 - 3)$, 1   **(d)** $(3x^2 - 16x + 53)$, -155
   (e) $(x^2 - 5x + 14)$, -60 **(f)** $(x^3 - x^2)$, 7

3 (a) $(x - 2)(4x^2 + 13x + 25) + 28$
   (b) $(x + 4)(6x^4 - 24x^3 + 96x^2 - 388x + 1553) - 6211$
   (c) $(x - 4)(8x^5 + 29x^4 + 116x^3 + 464x^2 + 1856x + 7422) + 29697$
4 (a) $(2x - 1)(2x + 4) - 16$
   (b) $(3x - 1)(2x^2 + 6x - 5)$
   (c) $(2x + 1)(5x + 7) - 10$
   (d) $(3x - 2)(4x^2 - 3x - 2) - 2$
   (e) $(2x - 5)(2x^2 + 7) + 20$
   (f) $(5x + 2)(5x^2 - 2x + 3) - 2$

Exercise 7D

1 $(x - 5)(5x^2 + 17x + 83) + 426$
2 $(x + 3)(3x^3 - 9x^2 + 29x - 95) + 276$
3 $(x + 1)(2x^3 - 2x^2 + 5x - 5)$
4 $(x + 4)(3x^4 - 12x^3 + 46x^2 - 185x + 744) - 2982$
5 $(2x + 3)(x^2 - 2x + 3) - 10$
6 $(3x - 4)(2x - 1) + 4$
7 $(3x + 2)\left(\frac{1}{3}x^2 + \frac{4}{9}x - \frac{8}{27}\right) + 3\frac{16}{27}$
8 $(2x - 1)(4x^3 + 2x^2 + 4x - 1) - 2$

Exercise 7E

6 $(x + 2)(2x^2 + 5x + 1)$
7 (a) $(x - 1)(x + 3)(x - 4)$
   (b) $(x + 2)(5x - 1)(x - 5)$
   (c) $(x + 2)(3x + 1)(x + 7)$
   (d) $3(x - 2)(x - 3)(x + 2)$
   (e) $(x + 3)(x - 3)(x^2 + 2)$
   (f) $(x + 1)^2(x + 4)(x - 3)$
   (g) $(x + 2)(x - 5)(2x + 1)(x + 3)$
   (h) $x(3x - 1)(x + 2)(x - 6)$

Exercise 7F

1 (a) 49   **(b)** 2   **(c)** 12
2 (a) $p = -7, q = -6$
   (b) $p = -15, q = -42$
   (c) $p = 11, q = -21$
3 (a) 7   **(b)** -3
4 $p = 2, (x + 1), (x - 1)$
5 $q = 13$

Exercise 7G

1 $-2, 7$
2 (a) $-3, -2, 1$ **(b)** $-2, 1$
   (c) $-5, -1, 9$ **(d)** $-6, -2, 1, 3$
3 (a) $-3, -1, 2$ **(b)** $-5, -2, 1$
   (c) $-2, -1, 3, 4$ **(d)** $-6, -2, 1, 3$
4 (a) $-3, -\frac{1}{2}, 1$ **(b)** $-4, \frac{2}{3}, 1$
   (c) $-\frac{2}{3}, -\frac{1}{2}, 3$ **(d)** $-4, -3, -\frac{2}{2}$
5 -2
6 (a) 10   **(b)** $-\frac{1}{2}, \frac{1}{3}, 9$

Exercise 7H

1. $f(x) = x^2 - 5x - 6$
2. $f(x) = 2x^2 + 30x + 88$
3. $f(x) = 6 + 4x - 2x^2$
4. $f(x) = -\frac{1}{5}x^2 + 2x - 5$
5. $f(x) = x^3 - 6x^2 + 5x + 12$
6. $f(x) = -x^3 - x^2 + 82x + 280$
7. $f(x) = 3x^3 - 36x + 48$
8. $f(x) = -2x^3 - 2x^2 + 42x + 90$
9. $f(x) = 2x^4 - 2x^3 - 14x^2 + 2x + 12$
10. $f(x) = -\frac{1}{2}x^4 + 2x^3 + \frac{39}{2}x^2 - 43x - 140$
11. $f(x) = 2x^3 - 24x - 32$
12. $f(x) = x^4 + 8x^3 - 8x^2 - 96x + 144$
13. $f(x) = 4x^3 + 12x^2 - 240x + 400$
14. $f(x) = 3x^4 - 18x^3 + 27x^2 + 12x - 36$
15. $f(x) = -3x^4 + 24x^2 - 48$

Exercise 7I

1

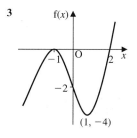

2

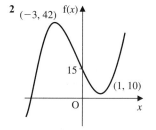

3

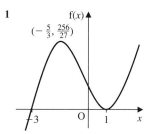

4

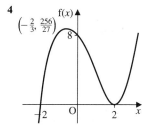

5

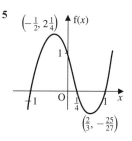

6

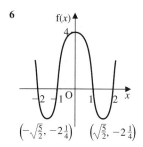

7

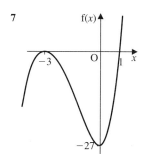

8

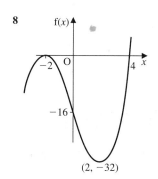

9

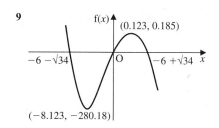

Exercise 7J

1 **(b)** 1.24
2 **(b)** 3.49
3 **(b)** 4.94
4 1.45
5 6.05
6 1.18
7 2.11

Exercise 7K

1 $(2, 0)$
2 **(a)** $d = 2$, $\left(-\frac{1}{2}, 0\right)$, $(1, 0)$
 (b) $d = 12$, $\left(\frac{1}{2}, 0\right)$, $(3, 0)$
 (c) $d = 33$, $\left(-\frac{1}{3}, 0\right)$, $(-2, 0)$
3 $2x^3 - 12x^2 + 22x - 12$
4 **(a)** $(x - 4)(x + 4)(x + 1)$
 (b) $(-4, 0)$, $(-1, 0)$, $(4, 0)$, $(0, -16)$
5 **(a)** $p = -11$, $q = 4$
 (b) -4, $\frac{1}{2}$, 1
6 $-7, -5, 1$
7 **(b)** $(x - 4)(x - 2)(x + 1)$
 (c) $-1, 2, 4$
8 1.38

9 **(a)**

 (b) 3
 (c) 2.53
10 5.15
11 No, does not sail far enough south.
12 $f(x) = \frac{1}{2}x^3 - 3x^2$
13 **(a)** $f(x) = (x - 1)^2(x - 4)$
 (b) $(1, 0)$, $(4, 0)$, $(0, -4)$
 (c) Minimum t.p. $(3, -4)$, maximum t.p. $(1, 0)$

 (d)

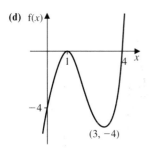

 (e) 3

Exercise 8A

1 **(a)** 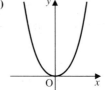 **(b)**

 (c)

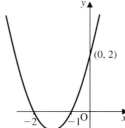

2 **(a)** 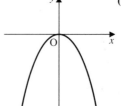 **(b)**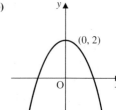

 (c)

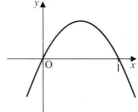

3 If the coefficient of x^2 is positive, the graph is shaped ∪.
 If the coefficient of x^2 is negative, the graph is shaped ∩.

Exercise 8B

1 (a)

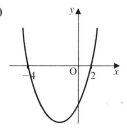

(i) $(-4, 0)$ $(2, 0)$ (ii) $x = -1$

(b) The axis of symmetry is a vertical line which passes mid-way between the points where the graph cuts the x-axis.

(c) Minimum turning point

2 (a) $(-2, 0)$ $(6, 0)$ **(b)** $x = 2$ **(c)** $(2, -16)$

3 (a) $x = 5$ **(b)** $x = 2\frac{1}{2}$ **(c)** $x = 3$

4 $x = \frac{1}{2}$

Exercise 8C

1 (a)

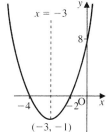

(b)

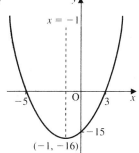

(c)

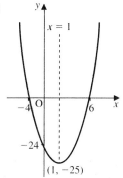

(d)

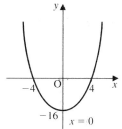

(e)

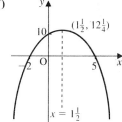

(f)

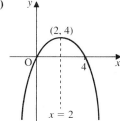

(g)

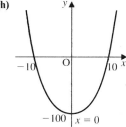

(h)

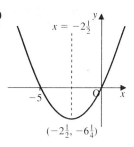

(i)

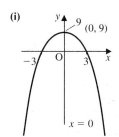

(j)

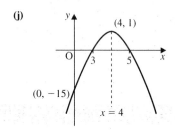

2 (a) (i) $x = 4$ (ii) Minimum $(4, -4)$
  (b) (i) $x = 3$ (ii) Maximum $(3, 16)$
  (c) (i) $x = -1$ (ii) Maximum $(-1, 4)$
  (d) (i) $x = -5$ (ii) Maximum $(-5, -25)$
3 (a) $y = x^2 - 5x + 6$ **(b)** $y = x^2 - 2x - 8$
  (c) $y = x^2 + 6x + 5$ **(d)** $y = x^2 - 7x$
4 (a) $y = 3x^2 - 12$ **(b)** $y = 18 - 2x^2$
  (c) $y = -x^2 + 6x - 8$ **(d)** $y = -\frac{1}{2}x^2 - 3x - 4$
5 $y = 3x^2 - 18x$

6 (a)

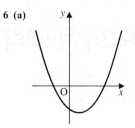

(b)

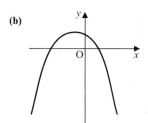

(c)

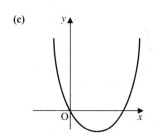

(d)

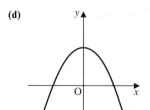

Exercise 8D

1 (a) (i) Min   (ii) $x = -3$ (iii) $(-3, -2)$
  (b) (i) Min   (ii) $x = 5$ (iii) $(5, 1)$
  (c) (i) Max   (ii) $x = -3$ (iii) $(-3, 8)$
  (d) (i) Min   (ii) $x = -1\frac{1}{2}$ (iii) $(-1\frac{1}{2}, -4)$
  (e) (i) Min   (ii) $x = \frac{1}{2}$ (iii) $(\frac{1}{2}, 1)$
  (f) (i) Max   (ii) $x = 1\frac{1}{2}$ (iii) $(1\frac{1}{2}, 10)$

2 (a)

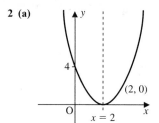

(b)

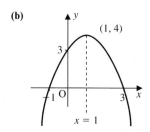

(c)

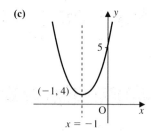

(d)

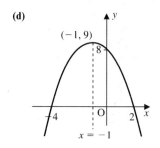

(e)

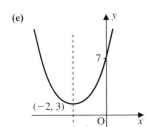

(f)

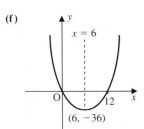

(g)

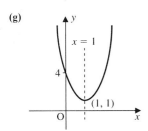

(h)

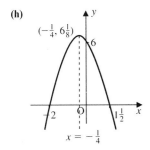

3 (1) E   (2) D   (3) C   (4) B   (5) A
4 (a) $(-3, -16)$ **(b)** $(3, 5)$ **(c)** $(0, 16)$
   (d) $(2, 4)$ **(e)** $(2, 1)$ **(f)** $(-4, -2)$
5 (a) $y = x^2 - 4x - 1$ **(b)** $y = x^2 + 6x + 16$
   (c) $y = 11 + 2x - x^2$ **(d)** $y = -13 + 6x - x^2$
6 2

Exercise 8E

1 (a) $t = -2, t = -6$ **(b)** $w = 3, w = -5$
   (c) $z = 1, z = -13$ **(d)** $f = 5$
   (e) $a = 8, a = -2$ **(f)** $h = -7$
   (g) $k = 1$ **(h)** $x = 5, x = -5$
   (i) $y = -\frac{2}{3}, y = -2$ **(j)** $d = \frac{3}{2}, d = -\frac{2}{5}$
   (k) $x = -2, x = -7$ **(l)** $a = 1, a = -4$
2 (a) $x = -3 + \sqrt{2}, x = -3 - \sqrt{2}$
   (b) $x = -1 + \sqrt{2}, x = -1 - \sqrt{2}$
   (c) $x = -4 + \sqrt{15}, x = -4 - \sqrt{15}$
   (d) $x = \dfrac{-3 + 2\sqrt{2}}{2}, x = \dfrac{-3 - 2\sqrt{2}}{2}$

(e) $x = -5 + \sqrt{3}, x = -5 - \sqrt{3}$
(f) $x = \dfrac{-1 + \sqrt{3}}{2}, x = \dfrac{-1 - \sqrt{3}}{2}$
(g) $x = \dfrac{3 + \sqrt{57}}{4}, x = \dfrac{3 - \sqrt{57}}{4}$
(h) $x = \dfrac{15 + \sqrt{315}}{5}, x = \dfrac{15 - \sqrt{315}}{5}$

3 (a) $x = 3, 12$ **(b)** $x = \pm\sqrt{2}$
   (c) $x = -2, 4$ **(d)** $x = 3 \pm \sqrt{5}$
   (e) $x = \pm\sqrt{5}$ **(f)** $x = -50, 2$
   (g) $x = 2 \pm \sqrt{11}$ **(h)** $x = 5 \pm 5\sqrt{2}$
   (i) $x = 1, \frac{5}{3}$ **(j)** $x = -8 \pm \sqrt{23}$
   (k) $x = -10 \pm \sqrt{110}$ **(l)** $x = -2, 3$
   (m) $x = -1 \pm \frac{1}{3}\sqrt{3}$ **(n)** $x = \dfrac{-b \pm \sqrt{b^2 - 4c}}{2}$

Exercise 8F

1 (a) $x = \pm 3$ **(b)** $-3 < x < 3$
   (c) $x > 3$ or $x < -3$
2 (a) $x = -4, 1$ **(b)** $-4 < x < 1$
   (c) $x < -4$ or $x > 1$
3 (a) $x < -2$ or $x > 3$ **(b)** $-1 < x < 2$
   (c) $-5 < x < 2$ **(d)** $-6 \leqslant x \leqslant 6$
   (e) $0 < x < 5$ **(f)** $x < 0$ or $x > 3$
   (g) $x \leqslant -2$ or $x \geqslant 4$ **(h)** $x \leqslant -5$ or $x \geqslant -\frac{1}{2}$
   (i) $-\frac{2}{5} < x < 4$ **(j)** $x \neq \frac{1}{2}$

Exercise 8G

1 (a) $y = -6.19, -0.81$ **(b)** $x = 0.55, 5.45$
   (c) $p = -1.45, 3.45$ **(d)** $w = -5.12, -0.88$
   (e) $x = -1.24, 0.64$ **(f)** no roots exist

2 (a)

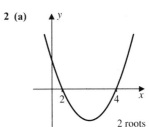

2 roots

(b)

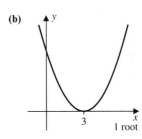

1 root

(c)

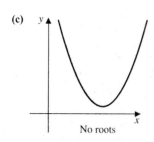

No roots

3	Roots	Nature of roots	$b^2 - 4ac$
(a)	1, 3	real and unequal	4
(b)	$\frac{1}{4}$, 2	real and unequal	49
(c)	-1	real and equal	0
(d)	-1.79, 2.79	real and unequal	21
(e)	-2.24, 2.24	real and unequal	20
(f)	no real roots	non-real	-8
(g)	3	real and equal	0
(h)	no real roots	non-real	-23
(i)	$-\frac{1}{3}$	real and equal	0

4 (a) If $b^2 - 4ac > 0$ the roots are real and unequal
   (b) If $b^2 - 4ac = 0$ the roots are real and equal
   (c) If $b^2 - 4ac < 0$ the roots are non-real

Exercise 8H

1 (a) 25, real and unequal
   (b) -23, non-real
   (c) 0, real and equal
   (d) 53, real and unequal
   (e) 9, real and unequal
   (f) 1, real and unequal

2 (a) real and unequal
   (b) non-real
   (c) real and equal
   (d) real and unequal
   (e) real and equal
   (f) non-real

Exercise 8I

1 (a)	16	**(b)**	$\frac{1}{2}$
(c)	± 3	**(d)**	± 4
(e)	1, 25	**(f)**	± 5
(g)	0, 5	**(h)**	0, 4
(i)	1	**(j)**	$-\frac{3}{2}$, 3

2 (a)	$k \leqslant 4$	**(b)**	$k \leqslant 50$
(c)	$k \leqslant 1$	**(d)**	$k \leqslant \frac{3}{4}$
(e)	$0 \leqslant k \leqslant \frac{4}{3}$	**(f)**	no values

3 $k = -\frac{1}{4}$

8 $p > 20$

Exercise 8J

1 (a)	$(2, -2)$	**(b)**	$(1, 2)$	**(c)**	$(2, 8)$
(d)	$(\frac{1}{2}, \frac{1}{4})$	**(e)**	$(\frac{1}{2}, 2)$	**(f)**	$(-2, 8)$

2 $c = -9$, $(3, -3)$
3 (a)	$y = 2x - 1$	**(b)**	$6x + 3y + 1 = 0$
(c)	$y = 2x$	**(d)**	$y = 4x + 3$
(e)	$y = 3x + 1$	**(f)**	$y = x - 2$

4 $m = 0, -8$
5 (a) $y = 2x - 1$, $y = -2x - 1$
   (b) $y = 4x - 1$, $y = -4x - 1$
   (c) $y = 4x + 1$, $y = -4x + 1$
6 $y = -4$, $(1, -4)$

Exercise 8K

1 (a)   **(b)**

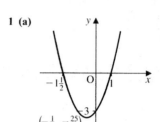
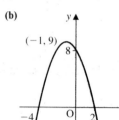

2 (a) $y = -3(x^2 - 4x - 5)$
   (b) $y = 2x^2 - 8x + 18$
   (c) $y = -2x^2 + 20x - 50$
3 $x = \frac{1}{2}$
4 (a) $x = -0.24$, 0.84
   (b) $x = -0.32$, 1.57
5 (a) $-2 < x < 3$
   (b) $-5 \leqslant x \leqslant \frac{3}{2}$
6 $f(x) = 4(x + 1)^2 - 9$
7 $15 - 2(x - 1)^2$
8 Non-real
10 $k = -5, 3$
11 (a) $f(x) = 2(x + 2)^2 - 11$
   (b) $(-2, -11)$
13 $c = -4$, $(2, -2)$
14 $k = 5$

Chapter 9   Integration

Exercise 9A

1 40 m	**2** 30 m	**3** 8000 m
4 18.75 m	**5** 75 m	**6** 12 m
7 168.75 m	**8** 117.5 m	

Exercise 9B

1 (a)

t	3.5	4
v	24.5	32

   (b) 35, 51
2 (a) 0.375, 1.875   **(b)** 5.25, 11.25
   (c) 20.625, 34.125   **(d)** 52.5, 76.5
3 (a) 1   **(b)** 8   **(c)** 27   **(d)** 64

Exercise 9C

1 (a) $A(x) = x^3$ **(b)** (i) x^4 (ii) x^5

2 (a) x^6, x^9, x^{21} **(b)** x^{n+1}

Exercise 9D

1 (a) x^{12} **(b)** x^{15} **(c)** x^{10} **(d)** x^{100}

2 (a) 32 **(b)** 2187 **(c)** 1 **(d)** 0.000244

3 100

4 (a) 936   **(b)** 4   **(c)** 255

   (d) 127   **(e)** 1   **(f)** 31

5 20 m

Exercise 9E

1 (a) x^4 **(b)** x^8 **(c)** x^{12} **(d)** x^7

   (e) x^{17} **(f)** x^{23} **(g)** x^{-2} **(h)** x^{-9}

   (i) x^{-6} **(j)** x^{-5} **(k)** x^{-12} **(l)** x^{-14}

   (m) $x^{\frac{3}{2}}$ **(n)** $x^{\frac{7}{4}}$ **(o)** $x^{\frac{1}{4}}$ **(p)** $x^{-\frac{1}{2}}$

   (q) $x^{-\frac{4}{5}}$ **(r)** $x^{-\frac{8}{3}}$

Exercise 9F

1 (a) (i) $4x^3$ (ii) $6x^5$ (iii) $-3x^{-4}$

   (b) (i) nx^{n-1} (ii) $x^n + C$

Exercise 9G

1 (a) $\dfrac{x^4}{4} + C$ **(b)** $\dfrac{x^8}{8} + C$

   (c) $\dfrac{x^2}{2} + C$ **(d)** $\dfrac{r^6}{6} + C$

   (e) $\dfrac{t^{16}}{16} + C$ **(f)** $\dfrac{\theta^{26}}{26} + C$

   (g) $-\dfrac{1}{x} + C$ **(h)** $-\dfrac{1}{5x^5} + C$

   (i) $-\dfrac{1}{6x^6} + C$ **(j)** $-\dfrac{1}{8u^8} + C$

   (k) $-\dfrac{1}{16\phi^{16}} + C$ **(l)** $-\dfrac{1}{30z^{30}} + C$

   (m) $\dfrac{2x^{\frac{7}{2}}}{7} + C$ **(n)** $\dfrac{4x^{\frac{11}{4}}}{11} + C$

   (o) $\dfrac{3x^{\frac{11}{3}}}{11} + C$ **(p)** $\dfrac{4x^{\frac{7}{4}}}{7} + C$

   (q) $\dfrac{8\psi^{\frac{13}{8}}}{13} + C$ **(r)** $3p^{\frac{1}{3}} + C$

Exercise 9H

1 (a) $\frac{5}{3}x^3 + C$ **(b)** $\dfrac{2x^7}{7} + C$

   (c) $9x + C$ **(d)** $-3x + C$

   (e) $\dfrac{-9}{2x^2} + C$ **(f)** $\dfrac{-4}{t} + C$

   (g) $\dfrac{2}{3s^6} + C$ **(h)** $\dfrac{4}{5x^{10}} + C$

   (i) $\dfrac{35x^{\frac{8}{5}}}{8} + C$ **(j)** $\dfrac{-150\theta^{\frac{7}{3}}}{7} + C$

   (k) $\dfrac{35y^{\frac{4}{7}}}{2} + C$ **(l)** $\dfrac{35}{s^{\frac{1}{5}}} + C$

2 (a) $\dfrac{x^5}{5} + \dfrac{x^4}{4} + C$ **(b)** $\dfrac{x^{10}}{10} + \dfrac{x^3}{3} + C$

   (c) $\dfrac{x^6}{6} - \dfrac{x^5}{5} + C$ **(d)** $\dfrac{x^4}{4} - \dfrac{1}{3x^3} + C$

   (e) $-\dfrac{1}{x} + \dfrac{1}{6x^6} + C$ **(f)** $-\dfrac{1}{2t^2} - \dfrac{1}{5t^5} + C$

   (g) $-\dfrac{x^5}{5} + \dfrac{2x^{\frac{5}{2}}}{5} + C$ **(h)** $\dfrac{6\theta^{\frac{11}{6}}}{11} + \dfrac{1}{\theta} + C$

   (i) $\dfrac{-5}{4s^{\frac{4}{5}}} - \dfrac{5s^{\frac{3}{5}}}{3} + C$ **(j)** $\dfrac{t^8}{8} - \dfrac{1}{t} + \dfrac{1}{2t^2} + C$

   (k) $\dfrac{2k^{\frac{7}{2}}}{7} + \dfrac{2k^{\frac{5}{2}}}{5} + \dfrac{2k^{\frac{3}{2}}}{3} + C$ **(l)** $\dfrac{z^5}{5} + \dfrac{9z^{\frac{5}{9}}}{5} + \dfrac{1}{6z^6} + C$

3 (a) $\dfrac{3}{8}x^8 + \dfrac{2}{3}x^3 + C$ **(b)** $-\dfrac{2}{3}x^9 + 9x + C$

   (c) $x^4 - \dfrac{7}{x} + C$ **(d)** $2r^{\frac{5}{2}} - \dfrac{9r^2}{2} + 3r + C$

   (e) $f^2 + 2f - \dfrac{1}{f} + C$ **(f)** $\dfrac{15}{s} - \dfrac{20}{3s^{\frac{3}{2}}} - \dfrac{5}{2s^2} + C$

Exercise 9I

1 (a) $-\dfrac{1}{x} + C$ **(b)** $-\dfrac{4}{5x^5} + C$

   (c) $\dfrac{3}{4}x^{\frac{4}{3}} + C$ **(d)** $\dfrac{8}{7}x^{\frac{7}{4}} + C$

   (e) $\dfrac{8}{3}x^{\frac{3}{8}} + C$ **(f)** $\dfrac{15}{2x^{\frac{2}{3}}} + C$

   (g) $\dfrac{x^3}{3} - 2x^2 + 4x + C$ **(h)** $25x + 15x^2 + 3x^3 + C$

   (i) $\dfrac{t^4}{4} + t^3 + \dfrac{3t^2}{2} + t + C$ **(j)** $\dfrac{s^5}{5} - \dfrac{s^7}{7} + C$

   (k) $x + \dfrac{5x^7}{7} + C$ **(l)** $f + \dfrac{f^4}{4} + C$

   (m) $\dfrac{-2}{v^2} + \dfrac{v^2}{2} + C$ **(n)** $\dfrac{2y^{\frac{11}{2}}}{11} + \dfrac{2}{y^{\frac{1}{2}}} + C$

   (o) $10p^{\frac{1}{2}} + p - \dfrac{4p^{\frac{5}{4}}}{5} + C$ **(p)** $\dfrac{r^4}{4} - \dfrac{2r^3}{3} - 4r^2 + C$

   (q) $\dfrac{2}{3}\theta^{\frac{1}{2}} - \dfrac{2}{21}\theta^{\frac{7}{2}} + C$ **(r)** $\dfrac{12}{5}t^{\frac{5}{3}} - \dfrac{2}{3}t^{\frac{9}{2}} + C$

   (s) $\dfrac{z^3}{3} - 2z - \dfrac{1}{z} + C$ **(t)** $\dfrac{g^2}{2} + \dfrac{4}{3}g^{\frac{3}{2}} - \dfrac{1}{9g} + C$

Exercise 9J

1 (a)

$f(x)$	$A(x)$	Anti-derivative of $f(x)$
$2x$	x^2	$x^2 + C$
$3x^2$	x^3	$x^3 + C$
$4x^3$	x^4	$x^4 + C$
$5x^4$	x^5	$x^5 + C$

   (b) Differ only by constant C

Exercise 9K

1 (a) $\int_1^2 2x\,dx$ **(b)** $\int_0^4 (x+4)\,dx$
(c) $\int_{-1}^1 (x-1)\,dx$ **(d)** $\int_2^3 x^2\,dx$
(e) $\int_{-3}^3 (x^2-9)\,dx$ **(f)** $\int_{-1}^3 (3+2x-x^2)\,dx$

2 (a)
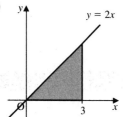
$y = 2x$

(b)
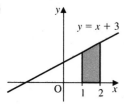
$y = x + 3$

(c)
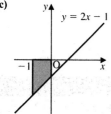
$y = 2x - 1$

(d)
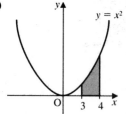
$y = x^2$

(e)
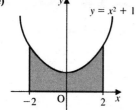
$y = x^2 + 1$

(f)
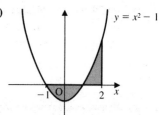
$y = x^2 - 1$

3 (a)
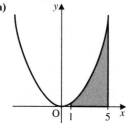
$A(x) = x^3$, 124

(b)
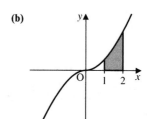
$A(x) = x^4$, 15

(c)
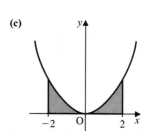
$A(x) = x^7$, 256

(d)
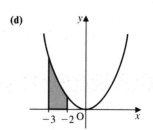
$A(x) = x^3$, 19

Exercise 9L

1 (a) $8\frac{2}{3}$ **(b)** 136   **(c)** $\frac{2}{5}$ **(d)** 32
    (e) $70\frac{1}{2}$ **(f)** $23\frac{1}{4}$ **(g)** $9\frac{1}{3}$ **(h)** $18\frac{3}{5}$

2 (a) $4\frac{2}{3}$ **(b)** $12\frac{2}{3}$ **(c)** $18\frac{3}{5}$ **(d)** $\frac{3}{5}$
    (e) $\frac{3}{8}$ **(f)** $\frac{15}{64}$ **(g)** $\frac{3}{4}$ **(h)** $\frac{7}{24}$
    (i) $1\frac{4}{15}$ **(j)** $\frac{5}{8}$ **(k)** $33\frac{9}{20}$ **(l)** 48

3 (a) $24\frac{2}{3}$ (b) $3\frac{1}{3}$ (c) $292\frac{1}{2}$ (d) 624

   (e) $20\frac{1}{3}$ (f) $85\frac{1}{3}$ (g) $1\frac{2}{3}$ (h) $3083\frac{1}{3}$

   (i) $9\frac{1}{3}$ (j) $6\frac{1}{4}$ (k) $\frac{5}{6}$ (l) 304

4 (a) 3   (b) 4   (c) 3

   (d) 1   (e) $\frac{8}{3}$ (f) 2

Exercise 9M

1 (a) 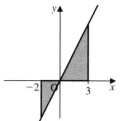   (i) 8   (ii) 18

   (b) 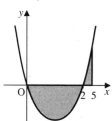   (i) $-1\frac{1}{3}$ (ii) 18

   (c) 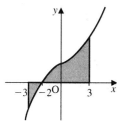   (i) $-8\frac{1}{4}$ (ii) $24\frac{1}{4}$

2 Areas above the x-axis have a positive value; below have a negative value.

3 (a) 5

   (b) $C = 4$, $D = 9$

   (c) Negative area below x-axis cancels out positive area above the x-axis.

Exercise 9N

1 (a) 20   (b) 20   (c) 13

2 (a) $2, 2\frac{1}{2}$ (b) $2, \frac{8}{3}$ (c) $1, 4, 6\frac{1}{3}$

3 (a) 13   (b) 13   (c) 12   (d) $4\frac{7}{12}$

4 (a) $10\frac{2}{3}$ (b) $20\frac{5}{6}$ (c) 8

   (d) $\frac{1}{6}$ (e) $140\frac{5}{8}$ (f) $\frac{1}{12}$

Exercise 9O

1 (a) $\frac{1}{6}$ (b) $1\frac{1}{3}$ (c) $6\frac{3}{4}$

2 (a) (i) $\frac{1}{6}$ (ii) $1\frac{1}{3}$ (iii) $6\frac{3}{4}$

   (b) Answers are the same.

Exercise 9P

1 (a) 36   (b) $1\frac{1}{3}$ (c) $57\frac{1}{6}$

2 (a) 36   (b) $\frac{1}{6}$ (c) $1\frac{1}{3}$

   (d) $57\frac{1}{6}$ (e) $57\frac{1}{6}$ (f) $22\frac{85}{96}$

3 2

4 $26\frac{2}{3}$

5 $20.5\,\text{m}^3$

6 (a) First one by $62\frac{1}{2}\,\text{m}$

   (b) $10\,\text{s}$

Exercise 9Q

1 (a) $3t^2 + C$

   (b) $t^3 + C$

   (c) $2t^2 + t + C$

2 (a) $s = 2t^2$

   (b) $s = \frac{5}{3}t^3 + \frac{7}{3}$

   (c) $s = 2t^3 + \frac{t^2}{2} - 2t - 14$

   (d) $s = 2t^{\frac{3}{2}} - 15$

3 (a) $y = 2x + 3$

   (b) $y = 4x - \frac{3x^2}{2} + 6\frac{1}{2}$

   (c) $\frac{1}{15}x^3 + 4$

4 $y = x^2 - 3x$

5 $y = 3x^2 + \frac{5}{x} - 2$

6 (a) $162\,\text{m}^2$

   (b) $7.2\,\text{m}$

Exercise 9R

1 (a) $28\frac{1}{2}$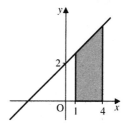

   (b) 48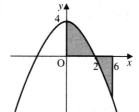

2 (a) $\dfrac{-5}{x} - 3x + \dfrac{2x^3}{3} + C$

   (b) $\dfrac{-7}{x} + 2x + \dfrac{4x^3}{3} + C$

   (c) $12\sqrt{x} - \frac{2}{3}\sqrt{x^3} + C$

3 (a) $\frac{4}{3}$ (b) $3\frac{5}{8}$ (c) $2\frac{1}{3}$ (d) 0

4 (a) 0   (b)

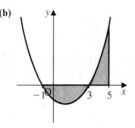

5 (a) $166\frac{2}{3}$ (b) $1\frac{1}{8}$

6 (a) $1\frac{1}{8}$ (b) $20\frac{5}{6}$

7 48

8 2.47

10 $y = 2x - \dfrac{5x^2}{2} + 7$

11 $2080\,\text{m}^3$

12 (a) $\int_0^k (\sqrt{x} - x^2)\,\mathrm{d}x, \ \int_k^1 (\sqrt{x} - x^2)\,\mathrm{d}x$

   (c) 0.44

13 (a) Speed rises then falls to zero

   (b) Moves to the left, speed increasing then falling to zero

   (c) $3\frac{1}{12}$

   (d) $2\frac{1}{4}$

14 $259.4\,\text{cm}^3$

15 (a) $A = 40 - \frac{4}{3}t^{\frac{3}{2}}$

   (b) 9.65 days

Chapter 10
3-D trigonometry

Exercise 10A

1 (a) R; $\angle$WRS   (b) V; $\angle$PVT   (c) W; $\angle$QWR

2 (a) $\angle$ASE   (b) $\angle$AES   (c) $\angle$AMV

Exercise 10B

1 (a) $64.9°$ (b) $71.7°$

2 $24.9°$

3 $54.7°$

Exercise 10C

1 (a) HG; $\angle$BGF

   (b) BG; $\angle$XYC   where X is the mid-point of AH and Y is the mid-point of BG

2 (a) $\angle$BKH or $\angle$ALG   (b) $\angle$JKL   (c) $\angle$HBE

3 (a) $\angle$RBK ($90°$)   (b) $\angle$FBK   (c) $\angle$FKB

Exercise 10D

1 (a) $7.6\,\text{m}$ (b) $74.7°$ (c) $71.2°$

2 (a) $35.0°$ (b) $70.0°$

3 (a) $14.14\,\text{cm}$

   (b) AH = AC = HC (Diagonals of congruent squares)

   (c) $12.25\,\text{cm}$

   (d) $54.7°$

   (e) $70.5°$

4 (a) $9.59\,\text{m}$ (b) $58.0°$ (c) $64.1°$

5 (a) $70.5°$ (b) $109.5°$

Chapter 11
Addition formulae

Exercise 11A

1 (a)

α	β	$\sin\alpha$	$\sin\beta$	$\sin\alpha + \sin\beta$	$\sin(\alpha + \beta)$
$30°$	$60°$	0.5	0.866	1.366	1
$90°$	$45°$	1	0.707	1.707	0.707
$\frac{\pi}{6}$	$\frac{\pi}{6}$	0.5	0.5	1	0.866

   (b) No

2 (a) $x\sin\alpha$ (b) $x\cos\beta$

3 $\frac{1}{2}x^2 \sin\alpha\cos\alpha, \ \frac{1}{2}x^2 \sin\beta\cos\beta$

Exercise 11B

1 (a) $\sin X \cos Y + \cos X \sin Y$

   (b) $\sin C \cos 45° + \cos C \sin 45°$

   (c) $\sin S \cos 2T + \cos S \sin 2T$

   (d) $\sin 3\beta \cos 2\alpha + \cos 3\beta \sin 2\alpha$

3 (a) $\dfrac{\sqrt{3}+1}{2\sqrt{2}}$ (b) $\dfrac{\sqrt{3}+1}{2\sqrt{2}}$

4 (a) $\sin(K + L)$ (b) $\sin 60° = \dfrac{\sqrt{3}}{2}$

   (c) $\sin\dfrac{3\pi}{4} = \dfrac{1}{\sqrt{2}}$ (d) $\sin\dfrac{\pi}{3} = \dfrac{\sqrt{3}}{2}$

5 (a) $\sin A = \frac{4}{5}, \cos A = \frac{3}{5}, \sin B = \frac{5}{13}, \cos B = \frac{12}{13}$ (b) $\frac{63}{65}$

7 $\frac{56}{65}$

Exercise 11C

1 (a) $\sin X \cos Y - \cos X \sin Y$

   (b) $\sin C \cos 30° - \cos C \sin 30°$

   (c) $\sin 2A \cos B - \cos 2A \sin B$

   (d) $\sin 3\beta \cos 4\alpha - \cos 3\beta \sin 4\alpha$

3 $\dfrac{\sqrt{3}-1}{2\sqrt{2}}$

4 (b) $\dfrac{\sqrt{3}-1}{2\sqrt{2}}$

5 (a) $\sin(S - T)$ (b) $\sin 30° = \frac{1}{2}$

(c) $\sin \dfrac{\pi}{2} = 1$ **(d)** $\sin(-15°) = -0.259$

6 (a) $\sin A = \frac{24}{25}, \cos A = \frac{7}{25}, \sin B = \frac{12}{15}, \cos B = \frac{9}{15}$

   (b) $\frac{44}{125}$

7 $\dfrac{\sqrt{3} - \sqrt{13}}{4\sqrt{2}}$

Exercise 11D

1 (a) $\cos X \cos Y + \sin X \sin Y$

   (b) $\cos C \cos 60° - \sin C \sin 60°$

   (c) $\cos 2A \cos B - \sin 2A \sin B$

   (d) $\cos 3\beta \cos 2\alpha + \sin 3\beta \sin 2\alpha$

4 $\dfrac{1 + \sqrt{3}}{2\sqrt{2}}$

5 (b) (i) $\dfrac{1 - \sqrt{3}}{2\sqrt{2}}$ (ii) $\dfrac{\sqrt{3} + 1}{2\sqrt{2}}$

6 (a) $\cos(P + Q)$ **(b)** $\cos 120° = -\frac{1}{2}$

   (c) $\cos(A - B)$ **(d)** $\cos \dfrac{\pi}{2} = 0$

   (e) $\sin(x - y)$ **(f)** $\sin 120° = \dfrac{\sqrt{3}}{2}$

7 (a) $\sin A = \frac{1}{2}, \cos A = \dfrac{\sqrt{3}}{2}, \sin B = \dfrac{1}{\sqrt{2}}, \cos B = \dfrac{1}{\sqrt{2}}$

   (b) (i) $\dfrac{\sqrt{3} + 1}{2\sqrt{2}}$ (ii) $\dfrac{\sqrt{3} - 1}{2\sqrt{2}}$ (iii) $\dfrac{\sqrt{3} + 1}{2\sqrt{2}}$

      (iv) $\dfrac{\sqrt{3} - 1}{2\sqrt{2}}$

8 (b) $90°$

Exercise 11E

8 (a) -1 **(b)** -1 **(c)** -1 **(d)** -1

Exercise 11F

2 (a) $y = (180 - 2x)°$ **4** $\dfrac{1}{\sqrt{442}}$

7 (a) $\beta - \alpha$ **8** $\dfrac{61}{5\sqrt{149}}$

Exercise 11G

2 (a) $2 \sin x° \cos x°$ **(b)** $\cos^2 y° - \sin^2 y°$

   (c) $2 \sin \beta \cos \beta$ **(d)** $\cos^2 \beta - \sin^2 \beta$

3 (a) $2 \sin 2\beta \cos 2\beta$ **(b)** $\cos^2 2\beta - \sin^2 2\beta$

4 (a) $2 \sin 3X \cos 3X$ **(b)** $\cos^2 3X - \sin^2 3X$

5 (a) $\cos^2 5x - \sin^2 5x$ **(b)** $2 \cos^2 5x - 1$

   (c) $1 - 2 \sin^2 5x$

6 (a) $2 \sin \dfrac{\alpha}{2} \cos \dfrac{\alpha}{2}$ **(b)** $\cos^2 \dfrac{\alpha}{2} - \sin^2 \dfrac{\alpha}{2}$

7 (b) $\frac{7}{25}$

8 (a) $\frac{120}{169}$ **(b)** $\frac{119}{169}$

9 (a) $\frac{4}{5}$ **(b)** $\frac{3}{5}$

10 (a) $\sin 2A$ **(b)** $\cos 2A$ **(c)** $\cos 2A$ **(d)** $-\cos 2A$

11 (a) $\dfrac{\sqrt{3}}{2}$ **(b)** $\frac{1}{2}$ **(c)** $\dfrac{1}{\sqrt{2}}$ **(d)** $-\dfrac{\sqrt{3}}{2}$ **(e)** $\dfrac{\sqrt{3}}{2}$ **(f)** $\frac{1}{2}$

12 (a) $\dfrac{3\sqrt{5}}{7}$ **(b)** $\frac{2}{7}$

Exercise 11H

1 (a) 0, 120, 180, 240, 360   **(b)** 90, 210, 270, 330

   (c) 30, 150, 270   **(d)** 0, 180, 360

   (e) 60, 180, 300   **(f)** 90, 120, 240, 270

   (g) 180   **(h)** 90

   (i) 60, 300   **(j)** 41.4, 180, 318.6

   (k) 60, 300   **(l)** 53.1, 120, 240, 306.9

2 (a) $0, \dfrac{2\pi}{3}, \pi, \dfrac{4\pi}{3}, 2\pi$ **(b)** $\dfrac{\pi}{6}, \dfrac{\pi}{2}, \dfrac{5\pi}{6}, \dfrac{3\pi}{2}$

   (c) $\dfrac{\pi}{3}, \pi, \dfrac{5\pi}{3}$ **(d)** $\dfrac{\pi}{3}, \dfrac{2\pi}{3}, \dfrac{4\pi}{3}, \dfrac{5\pi}{3}$

   (e) $0, \dfrac{2\pi}{3}, \dfrac{4\pi}{3}, 2\pi$ **(f)** $0, \pi, \dfrac{7\pi}{6}, \dfrac{11\pi}{6}, 2\pi$

3 (a) 0, 75.5, 180, 284.5, 360

   (b) A (75.5, 1.94), B (284.5, −1.94)

   (c) $0 \leqslant x \leqslant 75.5$ and $180 \leqslant x \leqslant 284.5$

4 (a) $\dfrac{\pi}{3}, \dfrac{5\pi}{3}$ **(b)** $A\left(\dfrac{\pi}{3}, -\dfrac{1}{2}\right) B\left(\dfrac{5\pi}{3}, -\dfrac{1}{2}\right)$

   (c) $\dfrac{\pi}{3} < x < \dfrac{5\pi}{3}$

5 (a) $a = 3, b = 2, c = 2$

   (b) 0, 70.5, 180, 289.5, 360

   (c) (0, 0), (70.5, 1.9), (180, 0), (289.5, −1.9), (360, 0)

6 (a) $y = \cos x, y = \cos 2x$ (0, 1), (120, −0.5), (240, −0.5), (360, 1)

   (b) $y = \cos 2x + 1, y = -\cos x$ (90, 0), (120, 0.5), (240, 0.5), (270, 0)

   (c) $y = \sin 2x, y = \sin x$ (0, 0), $\left(\dfrac{\pi}{3}, \dfrac{\sqrt{3}}{2}\right), (\pi, 0),$ $\left(\dfrac{5\pi}{3}, -\dfrac{\sqrt{3}}{2}\right), (2\pi, 0)$

   (d) $y = \cos 2x, y = 4\cos x + 5$ $(\pi, 1)$

   (e) $y = \cos 2x, y = 3\sin x - 1$ (30, 0.5), (150, 0.5)

   (f) $y = \sin 4x, y = \sin 2x$ (0, 0), $\left(30, \dfrac{\sqrt{3}}{2}\right), (90, 0),$ $\left(150, \dfrac{-\sqrt{3}}{2}\right), (180, 0)$

   (g) $y = 3\cos 2x, y = 7\cos x - 5$ (48.2, −0.33), (60, −1.5), (300, −1.5), (311.8, −0.33)

   (h) $y = 5\cos x, y = 3\sin 2x$ (56.4, 2.8), (90, 0), (123.6, −2.8), (270, 0)

Exercise 11I

1 (a) $\frac{1}{2}(1 + \cos 2\beta)$ **(b)** $\frac{1}{2}(1 - \cos 2\beta)$

   (c) $\frac{1}{2}(1 + \cos 2A)$ **(d)** $\frac{1}{2}(1 - \cos 2A)$

   (e) $\frac{1}{2}(1 + \cos 4x)$ **(f)** $\frac{1}{2}(1 - \cos 4p)$

   (g) $\frac{1}{2}(1 + \cos x)$ **(h)** $\frac{1}{2}(1 - \cos x)$

3 (a) $1 + \cos 2x$ **(b)** $1 - \cos 2x$

   (c) $2(1 + \cos 2x)$ **(d)** $\frac{1}{4}(1 - \cos 2x)$

   (e) $\frac{1}{4}(1 + \cos 2x)^2$ **(f)** $\frac{1}{4}(1 - \cos 2x)^2$

   (g) $2(1 + \cos 2x)$ **(h)** $4(1 - \cos 2x)$

Exercise 11J

1 (a) $\dfrac{3\sqrt{13}+4\sqrt{3}}{20}$ **(b)** $\dfrac{4\sqrt{13}-3\sqrt{3}}{20}$

2 $\cos C = \sqrt{\dfrac{2}{3}}$, $\sin 2C = \dfrac{2\sqrt{2}}{3}$

3 $\sin\theta = \frac{12}{13}$, $\cos 2\theta = -\frac{119}{169}$

4 (a) $\sin x° \cos 150° + \cos x° \sin 150°$
$\cos x° \cos 120° - \sin x° \sin 120°$
(b) 0

5 $-\dfrac{4}{\sqrt{41}}$

7 (a) $\dfrac{5}{\sqrt{34}}$ **(b)** $\dfrac{5}{\sqrt{34}}$ **(c)** 0 **(d)** 1

8 (a) 0, 60, 300, 360 **(b)** 90, 270
(c) 90 **(d)** 0, 90, 180, 360

9 (a) $\dfrac{\pi}{6}, \dfrac{\pi}{2}, \dfrac{5\pi}{6}$ **(b)** π

(c) $\dfrac{\pi}{3}, \dfrac{\pi}{2}, \dfrac{3\pi}{2}, \dfrac{5\pi}{3}$ **(d)** $0, \pi, 2\pi$

10 (a) (20.9, 2), (69.1, 2), (200.9, 2), (249.1, 2)
(b) $20.9 < x < 69.1$ and $200.9 < x < 249.1$

11 (a) 0, 30, 150, 180, 360
(b) A (30, 0.5) B (150, 0.5)
(c) $30 < x < 90$

12 $\dfrac{7\sqrt{3}}{26}$

15 (c) 8.9 miles
16 (a) $\phi - \theta$
18 (b) (i) 60°

Chapter 12   The circle

Exercise 12A

1 (a) AC = 6, BC = 8, AB = 10
(b) PN = 7, QN = 5, PQ = 8.6
(c) ST $= y_2 - y_1$, RS $= \sqrt{(x_2 - x_1)^2 + (y_2 - y_1)^2}$

Exercise 12B

1 (a) 5 **(b)** 10 **(c)** 13 **(d)** 15
2 PR = 15.8, PQ = 12.6, QR = 9.5, $PR^2 = PQ^2 + QR^2$
3 KL = MN = 10, LM = KN = 8.9
4 FG $= \sqrt{130}$, GH $= \sqrt{130}$, FH $= \sqrt{104}$
5 ST = 5, TU = 10, SU $= \sqrt{125}$; $SU^2 = ST^2 + TU^2$

Exercise 12C

1 (b) (0, 0), 5 **(c)** $x^2 + y^2 = 25$
2 (b) (0, 0), 13 **(c)** $x^2 + y^2 = 169$

Exercise 12D

1 (a) $x^2 + y^2 = 16$ **(b)** $x^2 + y^2 = 49$
(c) $x^2 + y^2 = 81$ **(d)** $x^2 + y^2 = 144$
(e) $x^2 + y^2 = t^2$

2 (a) $x^2 + y^2 = 100$ **(b)** $x^2 + y^2 = 9$
(c) $x^2 + y^2 = 34$ **(d)** $x^2 + y^2 = 5$

3 (a) 7 **(b)** $\sqrt{5}$ **(c)** 15
(d) $\sqrt{27}$ **(e)** $\frac{3}{2}$ **(f)** 0.5

4 $x^2 + y^2 = 49$
5 $x^2 + y^2 = 225$
6 $x^2 + y^2 = 256$
7 K(c), L(f), M(a), N(d), P(e), Q(b)

8 (a) ±5 **(b)** ±7 **(c)** ±10
(d) ±1 **(e)** −2, 1 **(f)** $\pm\sqrt{2}$

9 (a) A 13, B 61, C 50, D 32, E 29, F 52, G 29, H 50
(b) (i) $x^2 + y^2 < 36$ **(ii)** $x^2 + y^2 > 36$

10 (a) inside **(b)** outside **(c)** on
(d) inside **(e)** on **(f)** on

Exercise 12E

1 (b) (2, 3), 10 **(c)** $(x-2)^2 + (y-3)^2 = 10^2$
2 (b) (−1, −2), 13 **(c)** $(x+1)^2 + (y+2)^2 = 13^2$

Exercise 12F

1 (a) $(x-4)^2 + (y-1)^2 = 16$ **(b)** $x - 3)^2 + (y-3)^2 = 36$
(c) $x^2 + (y+9)^2 = 64$ **(d)** $(x+5)^2 + (y-2)^2 = 7$
(e) $(x+7)^2 + (y+1)^2 = 20$ **(f)** $(x-p)^2 + (y-q)^2 = s^2$

2 (a) (8, 3), 10 **(b)** (6, −6), 5
(c) (−1, 12), $2\sqrt{10}$ **(d)** (−7, 0), 13

3 15, $(x-7)^2 + (y+2)^2 = 225$
4 $(x-4)^2 + (y+1)^2 = 61$
5 $(x-3)^2 + (y+9)^2 = 16$
6 $(x+8)^2 + (y-5)^2 = 64$
7 $(x-4)^2 + (y+1)^2 = 49$
8 C (c), D (f), E (a), F (e), O (d), G (b)

9 (a) A, 5; B, 10; C, 25; D, 41; E, 10; F, 25; G, 9; H, 32
(b) (i) $(x-2)^2 + (y-1)^2 < 16$
(ii) $(x-2)^2 + (y-1)^2 > 16$

10 (a) outside **(b)** inside **(c)** outside
(d) on **(e)** outside **(f)** on

Exercise 12G

1 (a) $x^2 - 2x + y^2 - 4y - 11 = 0$
(b) $x^2 - 6x + y^2 - 8y - 11 = 0$
(c) $x^2 - 10x + y^2 + 2y + 17 = 0$
(d) $x^2 + 8x + y^2 - 4y + 16 = 0$
(e) $x^2 + 10x + y^2 + 10y + 49 = 0$
(f) $x^2 + y^2 + 14y - 15 = 0$

2 (a) (2, 3), 2 **(b)** (−1, −4), 4
(c) (−3, 1), 2 **(d)** (5, −5), 7
(e) (4, 3), 5 **(f)** (3, 0), 3
(g) (0, −6), 6 **(h)** (a, b), $\sqrt{a^2 + b^2}$

Exercise 12H

1 (a) $(-3, -1), 4$ **(b)** $(-3, -3), 4$ **(c)** $(-4, 2), 3$
(d) $(1, 6), 7$ **(e)** $(2, 4), 5$ **(f)** $(-5, 4), 7$
(g) $(9, -1), 10$ **(h)** $(-6, -8), 10$ **(i)** $(5, -12), 13$
(j) $(0, 2), 1$ **(k)** $(-\frac{1}{2}, 1), \frac{3}{2}$ **(l)** $(0, 0), 9$

2 (a) $x^2 - 8x + y^2 - 8y + 16 = 0$
(b) $x^2 + y^2 - 10y + 9 = 0$
(c) $x^2 + y^2 + 18x + 24y = 0$

3 A (c), B (f), C (a), D (e), E (d), F (b)

4 (a) -1 **(b)** -3 **(c)** 0 **(d)** -25
(ii) Radii are either negative or zero.

5 (a) 6 **(b)** not a circle **(c)** 9
(d) not a circle **(e)** 9 **(f)** 7
(g) 6 **(h)** not a circle

6 (a) $(-5, 3), 5$ **(b)** 13 **(c)** 12

7 A, C

8 -29

9 (a) (i) $x^2 - 16x + y^2 - 6y - 27 = 0$
(ii) $x^2 - 12x + y^2 + 12y + 47 = 0$
(iii) $x^2 + y^2 + 14y + 29 = 0$
(iv) $x^2 + 14x + y^2 - 120 = 0$
(b) $x^2 - 2ax + y^2 - 2by + a^2 + b^2 - r^2 = 0$

10 (a) $x^2 + y^2 - 16 = 0$, $(0, 0)$, 4
(b) $x^2 + 2x + y^2 + 8y + 1 = 0$, $(-1, -4)$, 4
(c) $x^2 + y^2 - 9 = 0$, $(0, 0)$, 3
(d) $x^2 + 4x + y^2 + 2y = 0$, $(-2, -1)$, $\sqrt{5}$

11 (a) $(0, 0), \frac{3}{2}$ **(b)** not a circle **(c)** $(0, 0), 2$
(d) not a circle **(e)** $(-1, 2), \sqrt{5}$ **(f)** $(0, 0), 6$
(g) not a circle **(h)** $(0, 3), 3$ **(i)** $(-2, -10), 12$
(j) not a circle

12 (a) $x^2 - 20x + y^2 - 20y + 100 = 0$
(b) (i) 234 cm **(ii)** 81 cm

13 25 m

14 (b) AC is the diameter; P, mid-point of AC, is the centre
(c) 5
(d) $x^2 + y^2 - 14x - 8y + 40 = 0$

15 (a) Circle A $(5, 6)$, 5; circle B $(-4, -6)$, 10
(b) $AB = 15$
(c) $(2, 2)$

16 $x^2 - 4x + y^2 + 16y - 157 = 0$

Exercise 12I

1 (a)

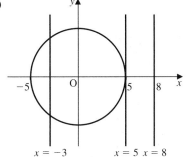

$x = -3$ $x = 5$ $x = 8$

(b) $x = -3, 2$; $x = 5, 1$; $x = 8, 0$
(c) $(-3, 4), (-3, -4), (5, 0)$

2 (a)

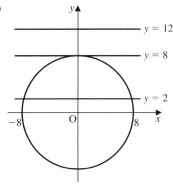

$y = 12$
$y = 8$
$y = 2$

(b) $y = 2, 2$; $y = 8, 1$; $y = 12, 0$
(c) $(2\sqrt{15}, 2), (-2\sqrt{15}, 2), (0, 8)$

Exercise 12J

1 (a) $(6, 6), (-6, -6)$ **(b)** $(5, 15), (-5, -15)$
(c) $(4, -4), (-4, 4)$ **(d)** $(10, 5), (-10, -5)$
(e) $(5, 1), (-5, -1)$ **(f)** $(-8, 2), (8, -2)$
(g) $(3, 3), (4, 4)$ **(h)** $(1, -3), (-2, 6)$

2 (a) $(-3, -4), (4, 3)$ **(b)** $(2, 9), (-6, -7)$
(c) $(0, 3), (3, 0)$ **(d)** $(-3, 1), (1, 3)$
(e) $(-1, 1)$ **(f)** $(-3, -2), (3, 4)$

3 (a) $(-2, 1), (1, 4)$ **(b)** $(1, 0), (-1, 2)$
(c) $(6, 0), (-2, -4)$ **(d)** $(8\frac{2}{5}, \frac{1}{5}), (2, -3)$
(e) $(0, 5), (0, -5)$ **(f)** $(9, 0), (-3, 0)$

4 6

5 $x^2 - 8x + y^2 + 7 = 0$

Exercise 12K

1 (a) $(8, 0)$ **(b)** $(0, 11)$ **(c)** $(-3, 6)$
(d) $(-1, 1)$ **(e)** $(-4, 0)$ **(f)** $(3, 2)$
(g) $(-4, 1)$

2 (a) $(-3, 3)$ **(b)** $(2, -8)$

3 $(-2, -4)$

4 (a) $(0, 9), (12, 9)$ **(b)** 12

5 (a) positive **(b)** zero **(c)** negative

6 (a) do not meet **(b)** two points
(c) one point **(d)** two points

7 (a) $4y + 3x - 20 = 0$ $4y - 3x - 20 = 0$
(b) $y - \dfrac{1}{\sqrt{3}}x - 2 = 0$ $y + \dfrac{1}{\sqrt{3}}x - 2 = 0$

Exercise 12L

1 $5x + 12y + 169 = 0$
2 $y = 8$
3 $7x - 3y - 11 = 0$
4 $6x - y = 17$ $6x - y = -57$
5 (a) $x = 10, x = -10$
(b) $4y - 3x + 50 = 0$ $3x + 4y - 50 = 0$
(c) $36.9°, 73.8°$
6 (a) $3x + 4y - 300 = 0$
(b) $x^2 + y^2 = 3600$
(c) B $(36, 48)$

Exercise 12M

1 $x^2 - 10x + y^2 - 26y + 185 = 0$

2 (a) $(10, 6)$
    (b) $x^2 - 20x + y^2 - 12y + 132 = 0$

3 $x + y - 2 = 0$

4 (a) $x^2 + y^2 - 2x - 2y + 1 = 0$
    (b) $2x + y - 5 = 0$
    (c) No. Girder would cut the tank in two places

5 $45\,\mathrm{m}$

6 $28.9\,\mathrm{cm}$

7 $x^2 + y^2 - 8x + 6y - 200 = 0$

8 Gap is exactly $5\,\mathrm{m}$

9 (a) $x + 3y = 72$
    (b) $(18, 18)$
    (c) $x^2 + y^2 - 36x - 36y + 448 = 0$
    (d) Yes, since $7x - y = 72$ intersects the circle

10 (a) $-1, 9$
    (b) $y + 2x + 1 = 0$, $(-1, 1)$
         $y + 2x - 9 = 0$, $(3, 3)$
    (c) $x - 2y + 3 = 0$

Revision exercise 2A

1 $(x + 3)(2x - 1)(x + 1)$

2 -7

3 $p = 3, \frac{5}{2}, -3$

4 1

5 $-2, -\frac{3}{2}, 1$

6 $-1, 1, 3$

7 $-4, \frac{1}{2}, 2$

8 (a) $x^2 + y^2 - 4x - 6y + 9 = 0$ **(b)** $y = 5$

9 $\frac{33}{65}$

10 $K \leqslant 2$

11 $16\frac{1}{3}$

12 (a) $k = 7$ **(b)** $(x - 1), (3x + 2)$

13 $x \geqslant 6$ or $x \leqslant -1$

14 $\dfrac{\pi}{6}, \dfrac{5\pi}{6}, \dfrac{7\pi}{6}, \dfrac{11\pi}{6}$

15 $\dfrac{4x^{\frac{3}{2}}}{3} + 4x - \dfrac{1}{4x^4} + C$

16 $y = 2x - 5$

17 96

18 $\dfrac{7\sqrt{15}}{32}$

19 (a) $(0, 0), (8, 24)$ **(b)** $85\frac{1}{3}$

20 $17.5°, 90°, 162.5°$

21 $70.5°, 180°, 289.5°$

22 $y = 33 + 7x - 2x^4$

23 $-8, 4$

24 (a) $\dfrac{1}{\sqrt{5}}$ **(b)** $-\frac{3}{5}$

25 (a) B $(-2, -2)$, A $(6, 6)$
    (b) $x^2 + y^2 - 4x - 4y - 120 = 0$

26 $(x + 1)^2 - 10$; max $= -\frac{1}{10}$

27 $p < -3$ **or** $p > 3$

28 $\dfrac{25\sqrt{3}}{2}$ units^2

Revision exercise 2B

1 (a) $(x - 1)^2(x + 2)$ **(b)** $(1, 0), (-2, 0), (0, 2)$
    (c) $(-1, 4), (1, 0)$

2 (b) $(4, -2)$

3 (b) 4 units^2

4 (a) $k = -5, 15$ **(b)** $x - 3y - 15 = 0$

5 (a) $(0, 0), (4, 0)$
    (b) Maximum $(0, 0)$; minimum $\left(\frac{8}{3}, -\frac{256}{27}\right)$
    (c)

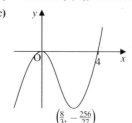

$\left(\frac{8}{3}, -\frac{256}{27}\right)$

    (d) $21\frac{1}{3}$ units^2

7 (a) $2p + q + 2 = 0$ **(b)** $p = -3$; $y = x^2 - 3x + 4$
    (c) Discriminant $= -7$. Graph does not cut x-axis
         therefore no real roots

9 $p = \pm 4$

11 $(1, 3)$

12 $\tan x$

13 $-\frac{63}{16}$

Chapter 13   Vectors

Exercise 13A

1 (i) Displacement, weight   **(ii)** Length, volume

2 $\mathbf{v} = \begin{pmatrix} 4 \\ 1 \end{pmatrix}$, $\overrightarrow{AB} = \begin{pmatrix} 2 \\ 3 \end{pmatrix}$, $\mathbf{u} = \begin{pmatrix} -3 \\ 3 \end{pmatrix}$, $\overrightarrow{ST} = \begin{pmatrix} -3 \\ -4 \end{pmatrix}$

    $\mathbf{x} = \begin{pmatrix} 5 \\ 0 \end{pmatrix}$, $\overrightarrow{LM} = \begin{pmatrix} 4 \\ -2 \end{pmatrix}$, $\mathbf{w} = \begin{pmatrix} 3 \\ 5 \end{pmatrix}$, $\overrightarrow{PQ} = \begin{pmatrix} -4 \\ 2 \end{pmatrix}$

    $\mathbf{h} = \begin{pmatrix} 2 \\ -4 \end{pmatrix}$, $\overrightarrow{CD} = \begin{pmatrix} 0 \\ -3 \end{pmatrix}$

3 $|\mathbf{v}| = 13$, $|\mathbf{w}| = 5$, $|\mathbf{p}| = 3\sqrt{5}$, $|\overrightarrow{AB}| = 4\sqrt{2}$, $|\overrightarrow{CD}| = 2\sqrt{5}$
    $|\overrightarrow{EF}| = 2\sqrt{17}$ $|\mathbf{s}| = 5$, $|\overrightarrow{ST}| = \sqrt{61}$, $|\mathbf{r}| = 2\sqrt{10}$
    $|\overrightarrow{XY}| = 2\sqrt{13}$

4 $3\sqrt{5}\,\mathrm{km/h}$

5 $10\,\mathrm{km}$

Exercise 13B

1 (a) $\mathbf{s} = \begin{pmatrix} 4 \\ 2 \end{pmatrix}$, $\mathbf{t} = \begin{pmatrix} 5 \\ 1 \end{pmatrix}$, $\mathbf{u} = \begin{pmatrix} -2 \\ -3 \end{pmatrix}$ $\mathbf{e} = \begin{pmatrix} -3 \\ -3 \end{pmatrix}$ $\mathbf{r} = \begin{pmatrix} 2 \\ 3 \end{pmatrix}$

    $\mathbf{f} = \begin{pmatrix} 5 \\ 1 \end{pmatrix}$, $\mathbf{a} = \begin{pmatrix} -2 \\ -3 \end{pmatrix}$ $\mathbf{d} = \begin{pmatrix} 2 \\ 2 \end{pmatrix}$ $\mathbf{b} = \begin{pmatrix} 4 \\ 2 \end{pmatrix}$

    (b) (i) $\mathbf{a}$ **(ii)** $\mathbf{b}$ **(iii)** $\mathbf{f}$

2 (a) and **(d)**

3 $x = 4$, $y = -8$

4 $p = 1$, $q = 3$

Exercise 13C

1 (a)
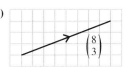
$\begin{pmatrix} 8 \\ 3 \end{pmatrix}$

(b)

$\begin{pmatrix} 1 \\ 5 \end{pmatrix}$

(c)

$\begin{pmatrix} 0 \\ -8 \end{pmatrix}$

(d)
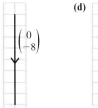
$\begin{pmatrix} -1 \\ 7 \end{pmatrix}$

2 (a) $\begin{pmatrix} 5 \\ -1 \end{pmatrix}$ **(b)** $\begin{pmatrix} -4 \\ 12 \end{pmatrix}$ **(c)** $\begin{pmatrix} 4 \\ 8 \end{pmatrix}$

(d) $\begin{pmatrix} -4 \\ -3 \end{pmatrix}$ **(e)** $\begin{pmatrix} -13 \\ 3 \end{pmatrix}$ **(f)** $\begin{pmatrix} 0 \\ 1 \end{pmatrix}$

3 (a) (i)

(ii) $\begin{pmatrix} 6 \\ 4 \end{pmatrix}$

(iii) $2\sqrt{13}$

(b) (i)

(ii) $\begin{pmatrix} 5 \\ 1 \end{pmatrix}$ (iii) $\sqrt{26}$

(c) (i)

(ii) $\begin{pmatrix} 1 \\ 3 \end{pmatrix}$ (iii) $\sqrt{10}$

(d) (i)
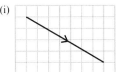
(ii) $\begin{pmatrix} 7 \\ -4 \end{pmatrix}$ (iii) $\sqrt{65}$

4 (a) (i) $\overrightarrow{AC}$ (ii) $\overrightarrow{AC}$ **(b)** $\mathbf{v} + \mathbf{u} = \mathbf{u} + \mathbf{v}$

5 (a)

(b)

(c), (d)
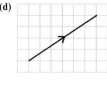

(e) $(\mathbf{u} + \mathbf{v}) + \mathbf{w} = \mathbf{u} + (\mathbf{v} + \mathbf{w})$

6 (a) $\overrightarrow{AC}$ **(b)** $\overrightarrow{AD}$ **(c)** $\overrightarrow{FD}$
(d) $\overrightarrow{FB}$ **(e)** $\overrightarrow{EB}$

7 (a) $p = 2, q = 4$
(b) $p = -2, q = -3$
(c) $p = 6, q = -13$

8 (a) $6.5\,\text{m/s}$ **(b)** $22.6°$

9 (a)

(b) $25\,\text{m/s}$ **(c)** $126.9°$

Scale: 1 square = 5 km/h

Exercise 13D

1 (a) $x = -2, y = -3$
(b) $x = -5, y = 1$
(c) $x = -4, y = 5$

2 (a) $\begin{pmatrix} -2 \\ -3 \end{pmatrix}$ **(b)** $\begin{pmatrix} 5 \\ 7 \end{pmatrix}$ **(c)** $\begin{pmatrix} 5 \\ -2 \end{pmatrix}$

(d) $\begin{pmatrix} -x \\ -y \end{pmatrix}$ **(e)** $\begin{pmatrix} -2x \\ -y \end{pmatrix}$ **(f)** $\begin{pmatrix} a \\ b \end{pmatrix}$

3 (a) $\begin{pmatrix} 1 \\ 1 \end{pmatrix}$ **(b)** $\begin{pmatrix} -3 \\ -13 \end{pmatrix}$ **(c)** $\begin{pmatrix} 9 \\ 11 \end{pmatrix}$

4 (a) (i)

(ii) $\begin{pmatrix} 0 \\ 3 \end{pmatrix}$ (iii) 3

(b) (i)

(ii) $\begin{pmatrix} 0 \\ 2 \end{pmatrix}$ (iii) 2

(c) (i)

(ii) $\begin{pmatrix} 7 \\ -5 \end{pmatrix}$ (iii) $\sqrt{74}$

(d) (i)

(ii) $\begin{pmatrix} -1 \\ 8 \end{pmatrix}$ (iii) $\sqrt{65}$

5 (a) $\overrightarrow{BD}$ **(b)** $\overrightarrow{DB}$ **(c)** $\mathbf{v} - \mathbf{u} = -(\mathbf{u} - \mathbf{v})$
6 (a) $\mathbf{t}$ **(b)** $-\mathbf{t}$ **(c)** $\mathbf{s}$ **(d)** $-\mathbf{q}$
(e) $\mathbf{s}$ **(f)** $\mathbf{0}$ **(g)** $-\mathbf{r}$
7 (a) $-\mathbf{t}$ **(b)** $\mathbf{t}$ **(c)** $\mathbf{t}$ **(d)** $-\mathbf{q}$

Exercise 13E

1 (a) (i) 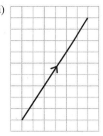 (ii)

(iii) (iv)

(b) (i) $\begin{pmatrix} 9 \\ 6 \end{pmatrix}$ (ii) $\begin{pmatrix} 4 \\ -4 \end{pmatrix}$ (iii) $\begin{pmatrix} 6 \\ -6 \end{pmatrix}$ (iv) $\begin{pmatrix} 1 \\ -1 \end{pmatrix}$

(c) (i) $\begin{pmatrix} 3k \\ 2k \end{pmatrix}$ (ii) $\begin{pmatrix} 2k \\ -2k \end{pmatrix}$

2 (a) (i) (ii)

(iii) (iv)

(v)

3 (a) $\begin{pmatrix} -24 \\ 18 \end{pmatrix}$ **(b)** $\begin{pmatrix} 48 \\ 40 \end{pmatrix}$ **(c)** $\begin{pmatrix} -4 \\ 3 \end{pmatrix}$

(d) $\begin{pmatrix} 9 \\ 7.5 \end{pmatrix}$ **(e)** $\begin{pmatrix} 24 \\ 58 \end{pmatrix}$ **(f)** $\begin{pmatrix} -72 \\ -22 \end{pmatrix}$

4 p, r, s

5 (b) $\overrightarrow{HD} = 2\overrightarrow{AB}$ **(c)** $\overrightarrow{GL} = \frac{1}{4}\overrightarrow{GC}$ **(d)** $\overrightarrow{LM} = \frac{1}{2}\overrightarrow{MC}$

(e) $\overrightarrow{FB} = 2\overrightarrow{FM}$ **(f)** $\overrightarrow{GJ} = \frac{3}{4}\overrightarrow{GC}$

(g) $2\overrightarrow{GL} + 2\overrightarrow{MI} = \overrightarrow{GA}$

(h) $3\overrightarrow{EK} + \overrightarrow{HI} = 2\overrightarrow{ED} + \frac{1}{2}\overrightarrow{CA}$

Exercise 13F

1 (a) $\begin{pmatrix} -\frac{3}{5} \\ \frac{4}{5} \end{pmatrix}$ **(b)** $\begin{pmatrix} \frac{12}{13} \\ \frac{5}{13} \end{pmatrix}$ **(c)** $\begin{pmatrix} -\frac{4}{5} \\ -\frac{3}{5} \end{pmatrix}$ **(d)** $\begin{pmatrix} -\frac{4}{5} \\ -\frac{3}{5} \end{pmatrix}$

2 (a) (i) $\begin{pmatrix} 3 \\ 4 \end{pmatrix}$ (ii) $\begin{pmatrix} 5 \\ 2 \end{pmatrix}$ (iii) $\begin{pmatrix} 2 \\ -2 \end{pmatrix}$ (iv) $\begin{pmatrix} 2 \\ -2 \end{pmatrix}$

(b) $\overrightarrow{AB} = \overrightarrow{OB} - \overrightarrow{OA}$

Exercise 13G

1 (a) $\mathbf{a} = \begin{pmatrix} -10 \\ 5 \end{pmatrix}, \mathbf{b} = \begin{pmatrix} 6 \\ -4 \end{pmatrix}$ **(b)** $\begin{pmatrix} 16 \\ -9 \end{pmatrix}$

2 (a) $\begin{pmatrix} 3 \\ 4 \end{pmatrix}, 5$ **(b)** $\begin{pmatrix} 12 \\ -5 \end{pmatrix}, 13$ **(c)** $\begin{pmatrix} -2 \\ 10 \end{pmatrix}, 2\sqrt{26}$

(d) $\begin{pmatrix} -5 \\ -10 \end{pmatrix}, 5\sqrt{5}$

Exercise 13H

1 (b) (i) $\begin{pmatrix} 1 \\ 2 \end{pmatrix}$ (ii) $\begin{pmatrix} 3 \\ 6 \end{pmatrix}$ **(c)** $\overrightarrow{BC} = 3\overrightarrow{AB}$

(d) They are parallel.
(e) They all lie on a straight line.

Exercise 13I

1 (c), (d), (e), (f)
2 Yes
3 Yes
4 No
5 No

Exercise 13J

1 (7, 12)
2 (a) $\frac{1}{2}\mathbf{a} + \frac{1}{2}\mathbf{b}$ **(b)** $\frac{2}{3}\mathbf{a} + \frac{1}{3}\mathbf{b}$ **(c)** $\frac{2}{5}\mathbf{a} + \frac{3}{5}\mathbf{b}$
3 (a) $\mathbf{p} = \frac{4}{9}\mathbf{a} + \frac{5}{9}\mathbf{b}$

(b) $\mathbf{p} = \frac{m}{m+n}\mathbf{b} + \frac{n}{m+n}\mathbf{a}$ or $\frac{n}{m+n}\mathbf{a} + \frac{m}{m+n}\mathbf{b}$

Exercise 13K

1 (a) (3, 4) **(b)** (−3, 2) **(c)** (2, 0) **(d)** (−1, 4)
2 (2, 8)
3 2 : 3
4 1 : 2
5 (a) (4.5, −1) **(b)** (2, 0)
6 (a) $x = -7.5$ **(b)** 2 : 3
7 Parallelogram

Exercise 13L

1 (a) (5, 3, 2)   **(b)** (4, 0, 11)   **(c)** (3, 5, −8)
2 B (12, 0, 0),   C (12, 3, 0),   D (0, 3, 0),   E (0, 0, 5),
F (12, 0, 5),   G (12, 3, 5),   H (0, 3, 5),   O (0, 0, 0)
3 Q (24, 0, 0),   R (24, 16, 0),   S (0, 16, 0),   T (4, 8, 6),
O (0, 0, 0)
4 M (8, 0, 0),   N (8, 8, 0),   P (0, 8, 0),   Q (4, 4, 9),
O (0, 0, 0)

Exercise 13M

1 (a) $3\mathbf{i} + 4\mathbf{j} + 5\mathbf{k}$ **(b)** $\begin{pmatrix} 3 \\ 4 \\ 5 \end{pmatrix}$

2 (a) $\begin{pmatrix} 2 \\ 5 \\ 7 \end{pmatrix}$ **(b)** $\begin{pmatrix} 6 \\ -4 \\ 3 \end{pmatrix}$ **(c)** $\begin{pmatrix} 5 \\ 0 \\ -2 \end{pmatrix}$ **(d)** $\begin{pmatrix} 0 \\ 0 \\ -7 \end{pmatrix}$

3 (a) $5\mathbf{i} + 3\mathbf{j} + 4\mathbf{k}$ **(b)** $6\mathbf{i} - 4\mathbf{j} - \mathbf{k}$
(c) $-3\mathbf{i} + 4\mathbf{k}$ **(d)** $\mathbf{j}$

4 (a) $\begin{pmatrix} 3 \\ 5 \\ -1 \end{pmatrix}$ **(b)** $\begin{pmatrix} -1 \\ -1 \\ -3 \end{pmatrix}$ **(c)** $\begin{pmatrix} 5 \\ 7 \\ 5 \end{pmatrix}$ **(d)** $\begin{pmatrix} 7 \\ 12 \\ -4 \end{pmatrix}$

Exercise 13N

1 (a) $\begin{pmatrix} 4 \\ 3 \\ 1 \end{pmatrix}$ **(b)** $\begin{pmatrix} 4 \\ 6 \\ -8 \end{pmatrix}$ **(c)** $\begin{pmatrix} 2 \\ -5 \\ 6 \end{pmatrix}$ **(d)** $\begin{pmatrix} -5 \\ -2 \\ 11 \end{pmatrix}$

2 (a) $\sqrt{38}$ **(b)** $\sqrt{27}$ **(c)** $\sqrt{38}$ **(d)** $\sqrt{29}$
(e) $\sqrt{73}$ **(f)** 4   **(g)** $\sqrt{53}$
3 $\pm\sqrt{3}$

4 (a) $\begin{pmatrix} -3 \\ 6 \\ -7 \end{pmatrix}$ **(b)** $\begin{pmatrix} -7 \\ 7 \\ 8 \end{pmatrix}$

(c) $-\mathbf{i} - 8\mathbf{j} + \mathbf{k}$ **(d)** $-\sqrt{2}\mathbf{i} + 2\sqrt{2}\mathbf{j} - \mathbf{k}$
5 (a) $6\mathbf{i} - 2\mathbf{j} - 2\mathbf{k}, -2\mathbf{i} + 8\mathbf{j} + 4\mathbf{k}$

(b) $\begin{pmatrix} -3 \\ 11 \\ 4 \end{pmatrix}, \begin{pmatrix} 7 \\ -1 \\ 2 \end{pmatrix}$

6 $\begin{pmatrix} 5 \\ 0 \\ 16 \end{pmatrix}$

7 (3, 2, 4)

8 (a) $\begin{pmatrix} 1 \\ 6 \\ 3 \end{pmatrix}$ **(b)** $\begin{pmatrix} 2 \\ 9 \\ 10 \end{pmatrix}$

9 $a = 7, b = 9$

10 (a) $\begin{pmatrix} 9 \\ 12 \\ -18 \end{pmatrix}$ **(b)** $\begin{pmatrix} -4 \\ 0 \\ 12 \end{pmatrix}$

11 (a) $\begin{pmatrix} 9 \\ 0 \\ 18 \end{pmatrix}$ **(b)** $\begin{pmatrix} 9 \\ -2 \\ -15 \end{pmatrix}$ **(c)** $\begin{pmatrix} -5 \\ 8 \\ 45 \end{pmatrix}$ **(d)** $\begin{pmatrix} -7 \\ 4 \\ -18 \end{pmatrix}$

12 (a) $\begin{pmatrix} 6 \\ 1 \\ -5 \end{pmatrix}$ **(b)** $\begin{pmatrix} 3 \\ 13 \\ 4 \end{pmatrix}$ **(c)** $\begin{pmatrix} 1.5 \\ 6.5 \\ 2 \end{pmatrix}$

13 $\begin{pmatrix} -5 \\ 7 \\ -12 \end{pmatrix}$ **14** $\begin{pmatrix} -4 \\ -6 \\ 10 \end{pmatrix}$ **15 (b)** 1 : 2

17 No   **18** $y = -2, z = -7$ **19** (2, 2, 7)
20 (a) (7, 7, 1)   **(b)** (5, 3, 3)   **(c)** (9, 11, −1)
(d) (10, 13, −2)   **(e)** (3, −1, 5)
21 (2, 7, 1)
22 (a) (i) (2, −2, 0)   **(ii)** (−1, −4, −1)
(iii) (−1, −2, −3)   **(iv)** $(0, -\frac{8}{3}, -\frac{4}{3})$
(c) Yes   **(d)** They meet at C (they are concurrent)
23 4 : 1
24 (a) A (3, 0, 7) B (7, 4, 7) C (7, 0, 3)   **(b)** 283.86 m²

Exercise 13O

1 (a) $10\sqrt{3}$ **(b)** 7   **(c)** −12   **(d)** $-20\sqrt{3}$
(e) $-28\sqrt{2}$ **(f)** 0
2 (a) Positive   **(b)** Zero   **(c)** Negative
3 (a) 0   **(b)** 0   **(c)** 0   **(d)** 1   **(e)** 1

Exercise 13P

1 (a) 49   **(b)** 22   **(c)** −18   **(d)** 32   **(e)** 11   **(f)** 1

2 (a) (i) $\begin{pmatrix} 1 \\ 2 \\ 3 \end{pmatrix}, \begin{pmatrix} 2 \\ -4 \\ -2 \end{pmatrix}$ **(ii)** −12

(b) (i) $\begin{pmatrix} 7 \\ 2 \\ 6 \end{pmatrix}, \begin{pmatrix} 6 \\ -5 \\ -2 \end{pmatrix}$ **(ii)** 20

(c) (i) $\begin{pmatrix} -3 \\ 2 \\ 6 \end{pmatrix}, \begin{pmatrix} -4 \\ 2 \\ -4 \end{pmatrix}$ **(ii)** −8

3 (a) 29   **(b)** 32   **(c)** 22

4 (a) (i) $\begin{pmatrix} 2 \\ 0 \\ -2 \end{pmatrix}$ **(ii)** $\begin{pmatrix} -2 \\ 2 \\ 0 \end{pmatrix}$ **(iii)** $\begin{pmatrix} 0 \\ 2 \\ -2 \end{pmatrix}$ **(b)** 4, 4

(c) $|\overrightarrow{AB}| = |\overrightarrow{BC}| = |\overrightarrow{CA}|$ and $\angle ABC = \angle BCA = \angle CAB$
$(= 60°)$

Exercise 13Q

1 (a) 37.2°   **(b)** 70.2°   **(c)** 129.5°
(d) 42.3°   **(e)** 78.7°   **(f)** 70.5°
2 168.3°
3 111°

4 (a) $\begin{pmatrix} 3 \\ -4 \\ 1 \end{pmatrix}, \begin{pmatrix} -1 \\ 2 \\ -9 \end{pmatrix}$ **(b)** 115.0°

5 40.4°
6 105.1°

Exercise 13R

1 **a.b** = 0
2 **n**, **p**
4 ∠PQR
6 −2
7 $a = 4$, $b = 4.5$
8 $a = 3$, $b = 2$

Exercise 13S

1 **(b)** $1:3$
2 **(a)** $(12, 2, 2)$ **(b)** $(8, 4, 4)$ **(c)** $1:2$
3 $53.1°$
4 **(a)** $\begin{pmatrix} 14 \\ 3 \\ 2 \end{pmatrix}$, $\begin{pmatrix} 2 \\ -5 \\ 4 \end{pmatrix}$ **(b)** $77.5°$
5 **(a)** $\begin{pmatrix} 3 \\ -2 \\ -5 \end{pmatrix}$ **(b)** 6.2 **(c)** $29.1°$
6 **(a)** $(5, 4, \frac{1}{2})$ **(b)** $22.2°$
7 **(a)** $137\,km$ **(b)** $60.5°$ **(c)** $\overrightarrow{T_1A}.\overrightarrow{T_2A} = 0$
   (d) $750\,km/h$

Exercise 13T

1 **(a)** $13, 13$ **(b)** **u.v** = **v.u**
2 **(a)** $\begin{pmatrix} 2 \\ 4 \\ 0 \end{pmatrix}$, 26 **(b)** $19, 7, 26$
   (c) **p.q** + **p.r** = **p.(q** + **r)**

Exercise 13U

1 **(a)** -8.5 **(b)** 18
2 **(a)** 23 **(b)** 41 **(c)** -18
3 They are perpendicular
4 17.5
5 27
6 2
7 25
8 0
9 0

Exercise 13V

1 **(b)** (i) $(3, 2, 0)$ (ii) $22.6°$
2 $(5, 0, -5)$
6 **(a)** $(13, 13, 8)$ **(b)** $38.5°$
7 **(a)** $60°$ **(b)** (i) $(\frac{7}{3}, \frac{10}{3}, \frac{4}{3})$ (ii) $PT = QT = RT$
   (c) (ii) T is the same plane as P, Q and R
8 $\frac{1}{2}(\mathbf{u} + 3\mathbf{v})$

9 **(a)** (i) $\mathbf{d} = \begin{pmatrix} -2 \\ 2 \\ 1 \end{pmatrix}$, $\mathbf{e} = \begin{pmatrix} 3 \\ 1 \\ 2 \end{pmatrix}$, $\mathbf{f} = \begin{pmatrix} 0 \\ 3 \\ 3 \end{pmatrix}$ (ii) $9, 45°$
   (b) $\overrightarrow{OF}.\overrightarrow{CE} = 0$ **(c)** $\begin{pmatrix} 0 \\ \frac{3}{2} \\ \frac{3}{2} \end{pmatrix}$,
   The midpoint of CE is $(0, \frac{3}{2}, \frac{3}{2})$.
12 **(a)** $\begin{pmatrix} 5 \\ 18 \\ 12 \end{pmatrix}$ **(b)** $\begin{pmatrix} -6 \\ 1 \\ -8 \end{pmatrix}$ **(c)** $26.9°$

Chapter 14
Further calculus

Exercise 14A

1 **(a)** $1, 0, 1, -1, 0, 1$
   (b)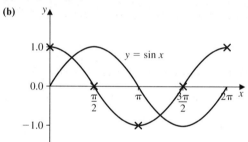
   (c) $\cos x$
2 **(a)** $0, -1, 0, 1, 0$
   (b)
   (c) $-\sin x$

Exercise 14B

1 **(a)** $-4\sin x$ **(b)** $-2\cos x$
   (c) $-8\sin x$ **(d)** $2\cos x - \sin x$
   (e) $-6\sin x + 5\cos x$ **(f)** $-7\sin x - \cos x$
   (g) $9\cos x + 4x^3$ **(h)** $-5\sin x - 6x$
   (i) $-3\sin x - 10\cos x + \dfrac{3}{2\sqrt{x}}$
   (j) $2\cos x + 6\sin x + \dfrac{2}{3\sqrt[3]{x}}$

2 (a) $6\cos r$ **(b)** $-3\cos t - 5\sin t$

(c) $-\sin\theta + 7\cos\theta - \dfrac{12}{\theta^5}$

3 (a) -1 **(b)** $\dfrac{-2}{\sqrt{2}}$ **(c)** -1 **(d)** 1

5 (a) $3x - 6y + 3\sqrt{3} - \pi = 0$ **(b)** $6x + 4y - 6\sqrt{3} - \pi = 0$

6 (a) -1 **(b)** $\dfrac{\pi}{4}, \dfrac{5\pi}{4}$

(c) Maximum at $\left(\dfrac{3\pi}{4}, \sqrt{2}\right)$, minimum at $\left(\dfrac{7\pi}{4}, -\sqrt{2}\right)$

(d)

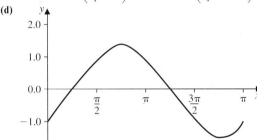

Exercise 14C

1 (a) $6\sin x + c$ **(b)** $-2\cos x + c$
(c) $3\cos x + c$ **(d)** $4\sin\theta - 9\cos\theta + c$
(e) $\sin z + 3\cos z + c$ **(f)** $-7\cos t - 12\sin t + c$

(g) $\dfrac{x^6}{6} + 2\sin x + c$ **(h)** $\dfrac{2t^{\frac{5}{2}}}{5} + \cos t + c$

(i) $-3\cos q - 10\sin q + \dfrac{5}{6q^6} + c$

2 (a) 6 **(b)** 2 **(c)** -3

(d) $\dfrac{\sqrt{2}+2}{2}$ **(e)** $\dfrac{5-4\sqrt{3}}{2}$ **(f)** 0

(g) $\sqrt{2} + \dfrac{\pi}{4}$ **(h)** $\dfrac{1}{1296}\left(\pi^3 + 18\pi^2 + 648\sqrt{3} - 1296\right)$

(i) $-3\sqrt{2}$
3 (a) (i) 2 (ii) -2 (iii) 0 **(b)** 4
4 2

5 (a) $3\sqrt{2} - 1$ **(b)** $\dfrac{9\sqrt{3}-4}{2}$

6 (a) 1 **(b)** 4
7 (a) (i) $0\,\text{m/s}$ (ii) $\pi\,\text{m/s}$ (iii) $2\pi\,\text{m/s}$

(b) (i) $1 + \sqrt{2}\cos t$ (ii) $\dfrac{3\pi}{4}\,\text{sec}, \dfrac{5\pi}{4}\,\text{sec}$
(iii)

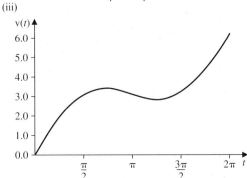

(c) (i) $\dfrac{t^2}{2} - \sqrt{2}\cos t$

(ii) $\dfrac{\pi^2}{8}\,\text{m}, \dfrac{\pi^2}{2} + \sqrt{2}\,\text{m}, 2\pi^2 - \sqrt{2}\,\text{m}$

Exercise 14D

1 (a) $2x + 4$ **(b)** $2x - 10$ **(c)** $3(x+1)^2$ **(d)** $3(x+2)^2$

Exercise 14E

1 (a) $9(x+4)^8$ **(b)** $3(x-3)^2$ **(c)** $-2(x+5)^{-3}$

(d) $\frac{1}{2}(x-3)^{-\frac{1}{4}}$ **(e)** $\dfrac{-1}{(x+4)^2}$ **(f)** $\frac{3}{4}(x+3)^{-\frac{1}{4}}$

2 (a) $2(x+1) + \cos x$ **(b)** $\frac{1}{2}(x-4)^{-\frac{1}{2}} + \sin x$

(c) $\cos t - \dfrac{1}{(t+8)^2}$

Exercise 14F

1 (a) $2(3x+5) \times 3$ **(b)** $2(7x+1) \times 7$
(c) $3(2x-1)^2 \times 2$ **(d)** $3(3x+5)^2 \times 3$

Exercise 14G

1 (a) $20(4x+3)^4$ **(b)** $48(6x-1)^7$
(c) $-3(x-9)^{-4}$ **(d)** $-\frac{9}{2}(4-6x)^{-\frac{1}{4}}$

(e) $\dfrac{1}{\sqrt{2x+5}}$ **(f)** $\dfrac{-5}{(5x-4)^2}$

(g) $30(5x-3)^5$ **(h)** $28(7x+1)^3$

(i) $5(0.5x+8)^9$ **(j)** $\dfrac{3}{\sqrt{6x+2}}$

(k) $\dfrac{-24}{(6x-1)^5}$ **(l)** $\dfrac{-8}{\sqrt[5]{(10x+1)^9}}$

Exercise 14H

1 (a) $3(9x^8+8)(x^9+8x)^2$ **(b)** $15x^2(x^3-1)^4$
(c) $3(2-2x)(3+2x-x^2)^2$
(d) $-21(2-3x)^6$ **(e)** $-5(2x+7)^{-\frac{7}{2}}$

(f) $\dfrac{14}{\sqrt{(4-7x)^3}}$

2 (a) $5\cos(5x+2)$ **(b)** $-3\sin(3x-1)$
(c) $6\sin(1-6x)$
3 (a) $-2\sin x\cos x$ **(b)** $5\sin^4 x\cos x$

(c) $\dfrac{2\sin x}{\cos^3 x}$

4 (a) $2\cos x$ **(b)** $2\cos 2x$
(c) $2\sin x\cos x$ **(d)** $2x\cos x^2$

(e) $\dfrac{-\sin\sqrt{x}}{2\sqrt{x}}$ **(f)** $\dfrac{-\sin x}{2\sqrt{\cos x}}$

5 (a) $12x(x^2 - 5)^5$ **(b)** $\frac{3}{2}(2x - 3)\sqrt{x^2 - 3x + 5}$

(c) $-6\sin(4 - 3\theta)\cos(4 - 3\theta)$ **(d)** $\dfrac{-9(6 - 4r^3)}{(6r - r^4)^4}$

(e) $\dfrac{2}{t^2}\sin\left(\dfrac{2}{t}\right)$ **(f)** $-\cos\phi\sin(\sin\phi)$

5 (a) $\frac{1}{8}$
(b) $\frac{2}{3}$

6 $\frac{1}{6}$

7 10

8 $7\frac{5}{16}$ unit^2

Exercise 14I

1 $y + 2x = 0$
2 $(-3, 2), (1, -2)$
3 (a) $(0, 0), (1.32, -1.125), (\pi, 2), (4.97, -1.125), (2\pi, 0)$

(b) $\left(\dfrac{\pi}{3}, \dfrac{3\sqrt{3}}{2}\right), (\pi, 0), \left(\dfrac{5\pi}{3}, \dfrac{-3\sqrt{3}}{2}\right)$

4 (b) $\left(\dfrac{3\pi}{2}, \dfrac{-3\pi}{2}\right)$

5 (a) (i) $2\cos\left(2t - \dfrac{\pi}{4}\right)$ **(ii)** $\sqrt{2}\,\text{m/s}$

     (iii) $\dfrac{3\pi}{8}, \dfrac{7\pi}{8}, \dfrac{11\pi}{8}, \dfrac{15\pi}{8}$

(b) (i) $-4\sin\left(2t - \dfrac{\pi}{4}\right)$ **(ii)** $\dfrac{7\pi}{8}\sec, \dfrac{15\pi}{8}\sec$

6 (b) $(1, 1), (-1, -1)$

7 (b) $\left(\dfrac{3\pi}{4}, \dfrac{3\pi}{4} + \dfrac{1}{2}\right), \left(\dfrac{7\pi}{4}, \dfrac{7\pi}{4} + \dfrac{1}{2}\right)$

(c)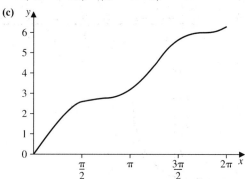

Exercise 14J

1 (a) $\frac{1}{4}(x + 3)^4 + c$ **(b)** $\frac{1}{3}(x - 3)^3 + c$

(c) $-\frac{1}{2}(x + 5)^{-2} + c$ **(d)** $\frac{2}{3}\sqrt{(x - 10)^3} + c$

(e) $\dfrac{-1}{t + 9} + c$ **(f)** $2\sqrt{q - 7} + c$

2 (a) (i) $\frac{1}{12}(2x + 5)^6 + c$ **(ii)** $\frac{1}{9}(3x - 8)^3 + c$

     (iii) $\frac{1}{40}(4x - 7)^{10} + c$

3 (a) $-(x + 3)^{-1} + c$ **(b)** $-\frac{1}{4}(2x + 3)^{-2} + c$

(c) $-\frac{1}{3}(1 - 2x)^{\frac{3}{2}} + c$ **(d)** $-\dfrac{1}{3(3x - 1)} + c$

(e) $\sqrt{2x + 1} + c$ **(f)** $\frac{3}{4}\sqrt[3]{(2x - 5)^2} + c$

4 (a) 13   **(b)** 74   **(c)** $4224\frac{1}{5}$

Exercise 14K

1 (a) $-\frac{1}{3}\cos(3x - 4) + c$ **(b)** $\frac{1}{6}\sin 6x + c$
(c) $\frac{1}{5}\sin(5x + 1) + c$ **(d)** $-\frac{1}{2}\cos 2x + c$

(e) $6\sin\frac{1}{2}x + c$ **(f)** $\dfrac{x^2}{2} + \dfrac{1}{3}\sin 3x + c$

(g) $\frac{1}{3}\cos(2 - 3t) + c$ **(h)** $-\frac{1}{2}\sin(1 - 4s) + c$
(i) $\frac{1}{25}(5z + 2)^5 + \frac{2}{3}\cos 3z + c$

2 (a) $\dfrac{\sqrt{3}}{4}$ **(b)** $\dfrac{2 - \sqrt{2}}{2}$ **(c)** 0

3 (a) 0   **(b)** 2
4 (a) $\frac{1}{3}$ **(b)** $1\frac{1}{2}$

5 $1 + \dfrac{\pi^2}{8}$

6 2

7 (a) $\dfrac{\pi}{4}$ **(b)** $\dfrac{\pi}{6} + \dfrac{\sqrt{3}}{8}$

8 (a) $\frac{1}{4}\sin 4x + c$
(b) $-\frac{1}{12}\cos 6x + c$
(c) $\frac{1}{2}x + \frac{1}{16}\sin 8x + c$

Exercise 14L

1 (a) $8\cos x$
(b) $3\sin t$
(c) $2\cos\theta - 6\sin\theta$
2 (a) $6\sin x + c$
(b) $-12\cos x + c$
(c) $-5\cos x - 3\sin x + c$
3 (a) $20(2x - 7)^9$
(b) $15\cos 3t$
(c) $-4\sin 4\phi - 360(2 - 9\phi)^7$

(d) $15\sqrt{(6t + 10)^3}$ **(e)** $\dfrac{-54}{(9z + 4)^3}$

(f) $-(2v - 2)\sin(v^2 - 2v)$ **(g)** $2\sin t\cos t$

(h) $20\sin^4 x\cos x + \dfrac{1}{x^2}$ **(i)** $\dfrac{-4s}{\sqrt{1 - 4s^2}} + 6\sin s\cos s$

4 (a) $\frac{1}{72}(6x + 1)^{12} + c$ **(b)** $\dfrac{-2}{15(5t - 7)^3} + c$

(c) $-\frac{1}{5}\cos 5t - \frac{1}{2}\sin(-2t) + c$

5 (a) 0   **(b)** $\frac{35}{72}$ **(c)** $\frac{3}{2}$

6 $(0, 0)$, $\left(\dfrac{\pi}{2}, 3\right)$, $(\pi, 0)$, $\left(\dfrac{3\pi}{2}, 3\right)$, $(2\pi, 0)$

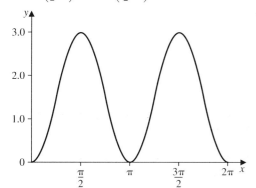

7 (a) $2x + 25y - 11 = 0$ **(b)** $y = 1$

8 $\dfrac{\pi}{8} - \dfrac{1}{4}$

10 $\dfrac{5\pi}{12}$

11 $\dfrac{6\sqrt{6} - 8}{3}$

12 (a) 0

(b)

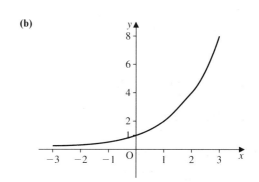

Total area
above x-axis
= area below it.

13 (b) $\frac{1}{12}\sin 3x + \frac{3}{4}\sin x + c$

14 (b) £127 million, 109 km

15 (b) 0.46 amps

16 (a) $\frac{4}{3}$ unit² **(b)** $\dfrac{4\sqrt{3}}{3}$ (2.3) **(c)** 2.3

Chapter 15
Exponential and logarithmic functions

1 (a) 1296 **(b)** 5 764 801 **(c)** 2
(d) 0.262 **(e)** 91.125 **(f)** 0.000 24
(g) 0.0019605 **(h)** 0.0024 **(i)** 0.016
(j) 1.01
2 (a) 5.20 **(b)** 0.008 **(c)** 6.56
(d) 0.000 000 030

3 (a) 3 **(b)** 4 **(c)** 5 **(d)** 3 **(e)** 4
4 (a) 2.3 **(b)** 3.6 **(c)** 3.0 **(d)** 2.1 **(e)** 3.1
5 (a) 5 **(b)** 11 **(c)** 18 **(d)** 4 **(e)** 5
6 (a) 11 **(b)** 5 **(c)** 3 **(d)** 4 **(e)** 6

1 (a)

x	-3	-2	-1	0	1	2	3
y	$\frac{1}{8}$	$\frac{1}{4}$	$\frac{1}{2}$	1	2	4	8

(b)

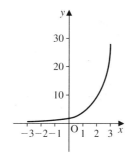

(c) $y = x^2$ has a minimum turning point, $y = 2^x$ does not.

2 (a)

x	-3	-2	-1	0	1	2	3
y	$\frac{1}{27}$	$\frac{1}{9}$	$\frac{1}{3}$	1	3	9	27

(b)

x	-3	-2	-1	0	1	2	3
y	$\frac{1}{64}$	$\frac{1}{16}$	$\frac{1}{4}$	1	4	16	64

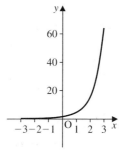

3 All pass through (0, 1); all above x-axis, all are increasing functions

4 (a) 2.5　　**(b)** 3.0　　**(c)** −1.0　　**(d)** 0.5　　**(e)** −1.5
　(f) 1.9　　**(g)** −0.08　**(h)** 1.4　　**(i)** 0.6　　**(j)** 0

5 (a) (i)

x	−3	−2	−1	0	1	2	3
y	8	4	2	1	$\frac{1}{2}$	$\frac{1}{4}$	$\frac{1}{8}$

(ii)

x	−3	−2	−1	0	1	2	3
y	27	9	3	1	$\frac{1}{3}$	$\frac{1}{9}$	$\frac{1}{27}$

(iii)

x	−3	−2	−1	0	1	2	3
y	64	16	4	1	$\frac{1}{4}$	$\frac{1}{16}$	$\frac{1}{64}$

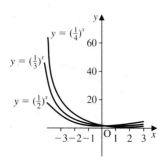

(b) They all pass through (0, 1); they are all above the x-axis; they are all decreasing functions.

6 (a) −2.3　**(b)** −0.3　**(c)** 0.7　　**(d)** −0.8　**(e)** 1.5
　(f) −1.9　**(g)** −1　　**(h)** −1.5　**(i)** 0.08　**(j)** 1

Exercise 15C

1 (a) $C_n = 1.2^n\,C_0$　　　　　**(b)** 4 days
2 (a) $V_n = 0.88^n\,V_0$　　　　**(b)** 6 weeks
3 (a) $P_n = 0.98^n\,P_0$　　　　**(b)** 6 years
4 (a) £811.20　　　　　　　　**(b)** 8 years
5 12 years
6 £2516.58
7 (a) 12 years　　　　　　　　**(b)** 25
8 (a) 40 years　　　　　　　　**(b)** 25 g
9 (a) No. Production should be at least 18 545
　(b) 7 years
10 (a) £9466.38
　(b) 9 years
　(c) 8 years

Exercise 15D

1 (a) 20.09　　**(b)** 29.96　　**(c)** 0.30　　**(d)** 1.95
　(e) 0.41
2 (a) 1096.63　**(b)** 4.48　　**(c)** 0.041　**(d)** 1808.04
3 (a) 2.71　**(b)** −1.05　**(c)** 0　**(d)** 1.39　**(e)** 1.04
4 403 428 793
5 39.33 g

Exercise 15E

1 (a) $\log_2 32 = 5$　　　　　　**(b)** $\log_4 64 = 3$
　(c) $\log_{10} 1\,000\,000 = 6$　**(d)** $\log_9\left(\frac{1}{3}\right) = -\frac{1}{2}$
　(e) $\log_7 y = 11$　　　　　**(f)** $\log_{12} x = y$
　(g) $\log_n m = 3$　　　　　**(h)** $\log_6 p = -5$
　(i) $\log_{25} 5 = \frac{1}{2}$　　　　**(j)** $\log_{16} 1 = 0$
　(k) $\log_8 4 = \frac{2}{3}$　　　　**(l)** $\log_{27}\left(\frac{1}{9}\right) = -\frac{2}{3}$
2 (a) 4　　　　　**(b)** 3　　　　　**(c)** 5
　(d) 4　　　　　**(e)** 2　　　　　**(f)** −2
　(g) −2　　　　**(h)** $-\frac{1}{2}$
3 (a) $y^x = 3$　　**(b)** $s^r = 5$　　**(c)** $4^p = q$
　(d) $2^t = g$　　**(e)** $x^w = y$　　**(f)** $a^{4m} = 6$
　(g) $b^{2a} = c$　　**(h)** $h^{2h+1} = 4$

Exercise 15F

1 (a) 3　　　　　**(b)** 2　　　　　**(c)** 3
　(d) 1　　　　　**(e)** 2　　　　　**(f)** 6
　(g) 2　　　　　**(h)** −3　　　　　**(i)** 0
　(j) 3　　　　　**(k)** 1　　　　　**(l)** $3\frac{1}{2}$
　(m) 1　　**(n)** 1
2 (a) 6　　**(b)** 9
3 (a) 4　　**(b)** 0　　**(c)** −2
4 (a) 9　　**(b)** −6　　**(c)** 15
5 $y = 2x^3$
6 $y = 7m^5$

7 $r = \dfrac{s}{t^2}$

Exercise 15G

1 (a) 3　　**(b)** 66　　**(c)** 4　　**(d)** 12　　**(e)** 9　　**(f)** 5
　(g) 25　**(h)** 2　　**(i)** 6
2 (a) 3　　**(b)** 3　　**(c)** 4　　**(d)** 48　　**(e)** 3　　**(f)** 10
3 (a) 3, 8　**(b)** 10　**(c)** 5　　**(d)** 4
4 100.48 phons

Exercise 15H

1 (a) 8103.08　　　　　　**(b)** 24 154 952.75
　(c) 6.05　　　　　　　**(d)** 3 269 017.37
　(e) 532 048 240 602
2 (a) 2.40　　　　**(b)** 3.04　　　　**(c)** 1.39
　(d) 0.86　　　　**(e)** 0.40
3 (a) 1.49　　　　**(b)** 2.68　　　　**(c)** 1.65
　(d) 0.86　　　　**(e)** 0.34
4 (a) 30　　　　**(b)** 27.7 min
5 (a) 369.24 g　**(b)** 69.3 years
6 (a) 0.075　　**(b)** Yes, pressure is 34.4
7 (a) 0.021　　**(b)** 33.0 min

Exercise 15I

1 In each question part (i) can be answered by drawing a graph of $\log_{10} y$ against $\log_{10} x$ and showing that it is a straight line.
   (a) $k = 2, n = 3$ (b) $k = 19.2, n = 2$
   (c) $k = 4, n = 0.7$ (d) $k = 2.5, n = 3$
   (e) $k = 3, n = 1.5$ (f) $k = 263, n = -1.06$
2 (a) $y = 100x^3$ (b) $y = 3.2x^2$
   (c) $y = 15.8x^4$ (d) $y = 79.4\sqrt{x}$
   (e) $y = \dfrac{10\,000}{x}$ (f) $y = \dfrac{3.2}{\sqrt[3]{x^5}}$

Exercise 15J

1 In each question part (i) can be answered by drawing a graph of $\log_{10} y$ against x and showing that it is a straight line.
   (a) $a = 3, b = 4$ (b) $a = 2, b = 0.8$
   (c) $a = 3.2, b = 2.4$ (d) $a = 1.2, b = 1.5$
   (e) $a = 0.5, b = 1.9$
2 (a) $y = 6.3 \times 3.2^x$ (b) $y = 10 \times 100^x$
   (c) $y = 3.2 \times 1.6^x$ (d) $y = 100 \times 316^x$
   (e) $y = 10^{18}(\frac{1}{10^9})x$ (f) $y = 1000\,(0.02)^x$

3 (a) (i)

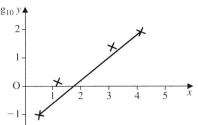

   (ii) $y = 0.04 \times 5.6^x$

   (b) (i)

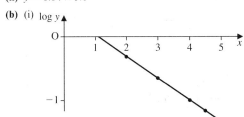

   (ii) $y = 2.1 \times 0.5^x$

Exercise 15K

1 (a) 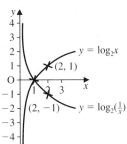   (b)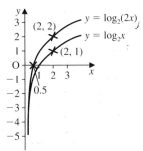

2 (a)

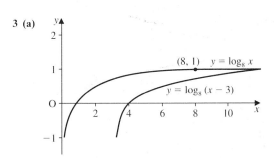

(b)

3 (a)

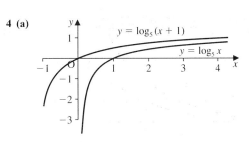

(b)

4 (a)

(b)

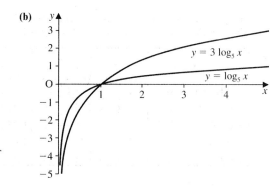

5 $a = 3$

6 $a = 2$

7 (a)

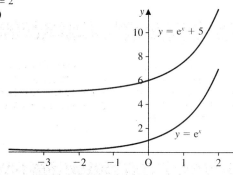

(b)

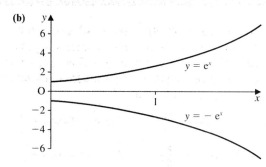

(c)

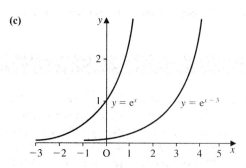

(d)

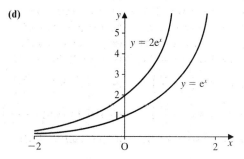

1 (a) 3.06   **(b)** 2.67
   (c) 0.67   **(d)** 10.52
2 (a) $P_n = P_0 \times (0.985)^n$ **(b)** 10.2 years
3 (a) 24.5   **(b)** 1.04
   (c) 13.28 years   **(d)** 221.1
4 (a) $8 = \log_3 6561$ **(b)** $9 = \log_x 19683$ **(c)** $5.2 = \log_8 m$
   (d) $6 = \log_a r$
5 (a) $4 = n^m$ **(b)** $r = s^q$ **(c)** $7 = p^{5n}$ **(d)** $8 = 4^{3h-1}$
6 (a) 4   **(b)** -4 **(c)** 0
8 (a) 9   **(b)** 1
9 $y = 10x^2$

10 (a)

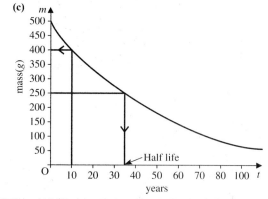

$x \approx 1.5$.

   (b) 1.76

11 (a) 409.4 g   **(b)** 34.7 years

   (c)

12 $P_2 = 134$ phons

Chapter 16
The wave function

1 (a) (i) $y = 3\sin x°$ **(ii)** max $= 3$, min $= -3$
   (b) (i) $y = 2\cos x°$ **(ii)** max $= 2$, min $= -2$
   (c) (i) $y = 6\sin x°$ **(ii)** max $= 6$, min $= -6$
   (d) (i) $y = 4\cos x°$ **(ii)** max $= 4$, min $= -4$
2 (a) (i) $y = \sin(x - 30)°$ **(ii)** max $= 1$, min $= -1$
   (b) (i) $y = \sin(x - 60)°$ **(ii)** max $= 1$, min $= -1$
3 (a) (i) $y = \cos(x - 60)°$ **(ii)** max $= 1$, min $= -1$
   (b) (i) $y = \cos(x - 30)°$ **(ii)** max $= 1$, min $= -1$
4 (a) (i) $y = 2\sin(x - 90)°$ **(ii)** max $= 2$, min $= -2$
   (b) (i) $y = 4\sin(x - 30)°$ **(ii)** max $= 4$, min $= -4$
5 (a) (i) $y = 5\cos(x - 30)°$ **(ii)** max $= 5$, min $= -5$
   (b) (i) $y = 10\cos(x - 60)°$ **(ii)** max $= 10$, min $= -10$

Exercise 16B

1 (a) (i)

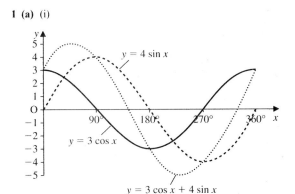

(ii)

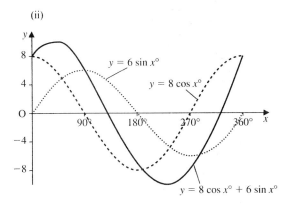

(iii)

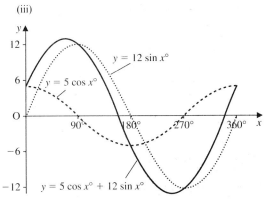

(iv)

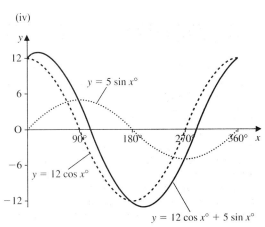

(b) (i) $y = 5\cos(x - 53)^\circ$ (ii) $y = 10\cos(x - 37)^\circ$
(iii) $y = 13\cos(x - 67)^\circ$ (iv) $y = 13\cos(x - 23)^\circ$

(c)

$y = k\cos(x - \alpha)^\circ$	a	b	k	α°	tan α°
$y = 1.4\cos(x - 45)^\circ$	1	1	1.4	45°	1
$y = 5\cos(x - 53)^\circ$	3	4	5	53°	1.33
$y = 10\cos(x - 37)^\circ$	4	3	5	37°	0.75
$y = 13\cos(x - 67)^\circ$	5	12	13	67°	2.4
$y = 13\cos(x - 23)^\circ$	12	5	13	23°	0.42

(d) $k = \sqrt{a^2 + b^2}, \tan\alpha^\circ = \dfrac{b}{a}$

Exercise 16C

1 $y = 10\cos(x - 53.1)^\circ$ **2** $y = 13\cos(x - 67.4)^\circ$
3 $y = 17\cos(x - 61.9)^\circ$ **4** $y = 2.82\cos(x - 45)^\circ$
5 $y = 2.24\cos(x - 63.4)^\circ$ **6** $y = 4.30\cos(x - 54.5)^\circ$
7 $y = 5\cos(x - 53.1)^\circ$ **8** $y = 5.83\cos(x - 31)^\circ$
9 $y = 5.70\cos(x - 15.3)^\circ$

Exercise 16D

1 (a) $y = 5\cos(x - 306.9)^\circ$ **(b)** $y = \sqrt{2}\cos(x - 315)^\circ$
(c) $y = 8.5\cos(x - 298.1)^\circ$ **(d)** $y = \sqrt{13}\cos(x - 303.7)^\circ$
(e) $y = \sqrt{61}\cos(x - 230.2)^\circ$ **(f)** $y = \sqrt{149}\cos(x - 215.0)^\circ$
(g) $y = 13\cos(x - 157.4)^\circ$ **(h)** $y = \sqrt{52}\cos(x - 146.3)^\circ$
(i) $y = \sqrt{8.5}\cos(x - 149.0)^\circ$

2 (a) $y = 2\cos\left(x - \dfrac{11\pi}{6}\right)$ **(b)** $y = 2\sqrt{2}\cos\left(x - \dfrac{3\pi}{4}\right)$

(c) $y = 2\cos\left(x - \dfrac{\pi}{6}\right)$ **(d)** $y = 3\sqrt{2}\cos\left(x - \dfrac{\pi}{4}\right)$

(e) $y = \sqrt{5}\cos(x - 4.25)$ **(f)** $y = 5\cos(x - 0.93)$

Exercise 16E

1 (a) $y = 2.5\cos(x + 306.9)^\circ$ **(b)** $y = 2.6\cos(x + 337.4)^\circ$
(c) $y = \sqrt{2}\cos(x + 315)^\circ$ **(d)** $y = 2\cos(x + 120)^\circ$
(e) $y = \sqrt{29}\cos(x + 338.2)^\circ$ **(f)** $y = 4.68\cos(x + 106.1)^\circ$
2 (a) $y = 5\sin(x - 233.1)^\circ$ **(b)** $y = \sqrt{2}\sin(x - 315)^\circ$
(c) $y = 17\sin(x - 208.1)^\circ$ **(d)** $y = 6.5\sin(x - 337.4)^\circ$
(e) $y = 3\sqrt{2}\sin(x - 225)^\circ$ **(f)** $y = 2\sin(x - 30)^\circ$
3 (a) $y = 5\sin(x + 126.9)^\circ$ **(b)** $y = \sqrt{2}\sin(x + 45)^\circ$
(c) $y = 17\sin(x + 151.9)^\circ$ **(d)** $y = 6.5\sin(x + 22.6)^\circ$
(e) $y = 3\sqrt{2}\sin(x + 225)^\circ$ **(f)** $y = 6.10\sin(x + 235.0)^\circ$

4 (a) $y = 2\sin\left(x - \dfrac{5\pi}{3}\right)$ **(b)** $y = \sqrt{2}\sin\left(x - \dfrac{5\pi}{4}\right)$

(c) $y = 2\sin\left(x - \dfrac{7\pi}{6}\right)$ **(d)** $y = 10\sqrt{2}\sin\left(x - \dfrac{3\pi}{4}\right)$

(e) $y = \sqrt{5}\sin(x - 5.82)$ **(f)** $y = 5\sin(x - 4.07)$

5 (a) $y = \sqrt{2}\sin\left(x + \dfrac{\pi}{4}\right)$ **(b)** $y = 2\sin\left(x + \dfrac{2\pi}{3}\right)$

(c) $y = 2\sin\left(x + \dfrac{\pi}{6}\right)$ **(d)** $y = 3\sqrt{2}\sin\left(x + \dfrac{\pi}{4}\right)$

(e) $y = \sqrt{11}\sin(x + 4.27)$ **(f)** $y = 6.5\sin(x + 2.75)$

Exercise 16F

1 (a) $\sqrt{2}\cos(2x - 45)°$ **(b)** $\sqrt{2}\cos(2x + 315)°$
(c) $\sqrt{2}\cos(2x - 315)°$
2 (a) $\sqrt{2}\cos(5x - 45)°$ **(b)** $\sqrt{2}\sin(5x - 315)°$
(c) $\sqrt{2}\sin(5x + 45)°$

3 (a) $\sqrt{2}\cos\left(8\theta - \dfrac{\pi}{4}\right)$ **(b)** $\sqrt{2}\cos\left(8\theta + \dfrac{7\pi}{4}\right)$

(c) $\sqrt{2}\sin\left(8\theta + \dfrac{\pi}{4}\right)$

Exercise 16G

1 (a) $10\cos(x - 53.1)°$, 10 when $x = 53.1°$
(b) $13\cos(x - 292.6)°$, 13 when $x = 292.6°$
(c) $17\cos(x - 241.9)°$, 17 when $x = 241.9°$
(d) $2\sqrt{2}\cos(x - 315)°$, $2\sqrt{2}$ when $x = 315°$
(e) $\sqrt{5}\cos(x - 63.4)°$, $\sqrt{5}$ when $x = 63.4°$
(f) $4.30\cos(x - 54.5)°$, 4.30 when $x = 54.3°$

2 (a) (i) $\sqrt{2}\cos\left(\theta - \dfrac{\pi}{4}\right)$ **(ii)** $\sqrt{2}$ when $\theta = \dfrac{\pi}{4}$

    (iii) $-\sqrt{2}$ when $\theta = \dfrac{5\pi}{4}$

(b) (i) $\sqrt{3}\cos(\theta - 0.62)$ **(ii)** $\sqrt{3}$ when $\theta = 0.62$
    (iii) $-\sqrt{3}$ when $\theta = 3.76$

(c) (i) $2\cos\left(\theta - \dfrac{7\pi}{6}\right)$ **(ii)** 2 when $\theta = \dfrac{7\pi}{6}$

    (iii) -2 when $\theta = \dfrac{\pi}{6}$

(d) (i) $2\cos\left(\theta - \dfrac{\pi}{3}\right)$ **(ii)** 2 when $\theta = \dfrac{\pi}{3}$

    (iii) -2 when $\theta = \dfrac{4\pi}{3}$

(e) (i) $27.50\cos(\theta - 1.8)$ **(ii)** 27.50 when $\theta = 1.8$
    (iii) -27.50 when $\theta = 4.9$
(f) (i) $2\sqrt{3}\cos(\theta - 5.7)$ **(ii)** $2\sqrt{3}$ when $\theta = 5.7$
    (iii) $-2\sqrt{3}$ when $\theta = -5.7$
3 (a) $29.2\cos(t - 31)°$ **(b)** 29.2 mm when $t = 31$ sec
4 (a) $125\sin(t - 306.9)°$ **(b)** -125 db when $t = 216.9$ sec
5 (a) max $= 2$ when $x = 60°$, min $= -2$ when $x = 240°$
   (b) 12
6 max $= 2 + \sqrt{2}$ when $x = 45°$, min $= \sqrt{2} - 2$ when $x = 225°$
7 max $= \pi + \sqrt{10}$ when $x = 1.3$, min $= \pi - \sqrt{10}$ when $x = 4.4$
8 $\sqrt{2}$ when $x = 15°$
9 -5 when $x = 6.0°$
10 $50\sqrt{2}$ when $\theta = \dfrac{\pi}{16}$ or $\dfrac{9\pi}{16}$
11 (a) $h = \sqrt{3}\sin(30t + 54.7)°$
   (b) max $= \sqrt{3}$ m, min $= -\sqrt{3}$ m
   (c) High at 1.11 am, low at 7.11 am

Exercise 16H

1 (a) 67.4°   **(b)** 53.1°   **(c)** 0°, 240°, 360°
(d) 23.1°, 263.1°   **(e)** 162.4°, 310.2°   **(f)** 114.3°, 335.7°

2 (a) $0, \dfrac{\pi}{2}, 2\pi$ **(b)** $\dfrac{\pi}{2}, \pi$ **(c)** $0, \dfrac{2\pi}{3}, 2\pi$

(d) $\dfrac{7\pi}{12}, \dfrac{23\pi}{12}$ **(e)** $0, \dfrac{5\pi}{3}, 2\pi$ **(f)** $0, \dfrac{4\pi}{3}, 2\pi$

3 (a) 90°, 135°, 270°, 315°
(b) 5.6°, 107.1°, 185.6°, 287.1°
(c) 77.7°, 107.7°, 197.7°, 227.7°, 317.7°, 347.7°
(d) 46.2°
(e) 170.2°
(f) 29.2°, 85.3°, 119.2°, 175.3°, 209.2°, 265.3°, 299.2°, 355.3°

4 (a) $0, \dfrac{\pi}{4}, \pi, \dfrac{5\pi}{4}, 2\pi$ **(b)** $\dfrac{\pi}{2}, \dfrac{3\pi}{4}, \dfrac{3\pi}{2}, \dfrac{7\pi}{4}$

(c) $0, \dfrac{4\pi}{3}$ **(d)** $\dfrac{5\pi}{6}$

(e) $0, \dfrac{5\pi}{9}, \dfrac{2\pi}{3}, \dfrac{11\pi}{9}, \dfrac{4\pi}{3}, \dfrac{17\pi}{9}, 2\pi$

(f) $0, \dfrac{\pi}{3}, \dfrac{\pi}{2}, \dfrac{5\pi}{6}, \pi, \dfrac{4\pi}{3}, \dfrac{3\pi}{2}, \dfrac{11\pi}{6}, 2\pi$

Exercise 16I

1 (a) $\sqrt{2}\cos(30t - 315)°$, $\alpha = 315°$, $k = \sqrt{2}$
(b)

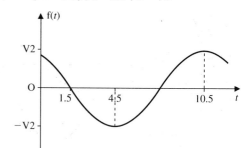

(d) 4.30 am
(e) Can always enter. Minimum depth $= 4.58$ m

2 (a) $f = 1000 + 200\sin(180t - 240)°$

(b)

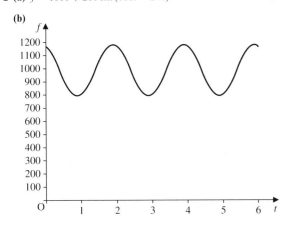

(c)

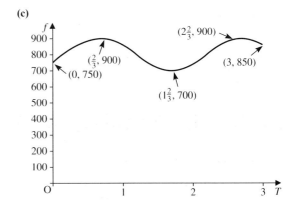

(c) 0.33 to 1.34 sec, 2.33 to 3.34 sec, 4.33 to 5.34 sec

3 Before 2.67 sec, between 18 and 20.67 sec etc.

4 Between $t = 0$ and $t = 1.5$

7 (b) $8\sqrt{5}\sin(\theta - 63.4)°$ **(c)** 114.9°

Revision exercise 3A

1 3 : 2

2 $\sqrt{70}$

3 $k = 6.31$, $n = -0.53$

4 $3\cos 3x + 32(2x - 3)^3$

5 $4x - \dfrac{x^2}{4} + \dfrac{1}{2}\sin 4x + c$

6 $1\frac{1}{8}$

7 $\sqrt{29}\cos(x - 111.8)°$

8 $\frac{1}{3}$

9 $p = 3$, $q = 7$

10 (a) $\sqrt{29}\sin(3x + 291.8)°$

(b) Max $= 2 + \sqrt{29}$ when $x = 52.73°$

11 $2\sin x\cos x - 120(2 - 5x)^7$

12 $k = 3$

13 (a) 0

Exercise 16J

1 (a) $k = 5\sqrt{5}$ **(b)** $5\sqrt{5}$

2 (a) $\sqrt{41}\cos(x - 51.3)$ **(b)** 123.1°, 339.5°

3 (a) $2\sin(2x - 60)°$ **(b)** 60°, 90°

(c) $0 \leqslant x \leqslant 60°$ and $90° \leqslant x \leqslant 180°$

4 (a) $\sqrt{2}\sin\left(\theta - \dfrac{\pi}{4}\right)$

(b) $\dfrac{\pi}{2}$, π

(c) $0 \leqslant \theta \leqslant \dfrac{\pi}{2}$

5 (a) $R = 20\sqrt{5}$, $\alpha = 63.4°$

(b) $20\sqrt{5}$

(c)

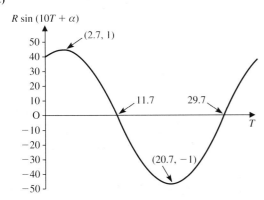

(b)

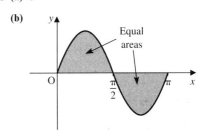

14 $f(x) = -\frac{1}{4}\cos 4x - 1\frac{1}{4}$

15 $17\frac{1}{2}$

16 (a) 40   **(b)** 27.7 min (28 min)

17 $66\frac{2}{15}$

18 $\frac{1}{6}(5\sqrt{2} + 10)$

6 (a) $R = 100$, $\alpha = \dfrac{\pi}{6}$

(b) 2

Revision exercise 3B

1 (a) K (1, 2, 0),   L (1, 4.5, −0.5),   M (2, 1.5, 0.5),
N (2, −1, 1)

(b) Parallelogram. The opposite sides are parallel.

2 (a) $30°, 150°$ **(b)** $\sqrt{3} + \dfrac{\sqrt{3}}{2}$

3 (a) T $(3, 4, 1)$ **(c)** $51.3°$

4 (a) $88.69\,\text{mg}$ **(b)** 2972 years **(c)** 5776 years

5 (a) $10\sin(4t + 53.1)°$ **(b)** 10
 (c) Max: $0.051\pi, 0.55\pi$; min: $0.30\pi, 0.80\pi$

6 (a)

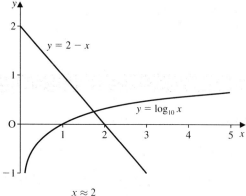

$x \approx 2$

 (b) 1.76

7 (a) $k = 0.067$ **(b)** Yes. $P_4 > 30$

8 (a) A $(1, 0, 0)$ B $(3, 2, 0)$ C $(3, 0, -2)$
 (b) $2\sqrt{3}\,\text{unit}^2$ **(c)** 4.7% decrease

9 (a) $\dfrac{3\pi - 4}{6}, \dfrac{5\pi - 4}{6}, \dfrac{7\pi - 4}{6}, \dfrac{9\pi - 4}{6}, \dfrac{11\pi - 4}{6}, \dfrac{13\pi - 4}{6}$
 (b) $-11.87\,\text{m/s}^2$ **(c)** $2.49\,\text{m}$

10 (a) $10\,\text{m}$ **(b)** $36\frac{1}{4}\,\text{m}^2$ **(c)** $2900\,\text{m}^3$

11 (a) $600\cos\left(\pi t + \dfrac{7\pi}{6}\right)$

 (b) Period $= 2$, amplitude $= 600$ **(c)** After 0.2 sec

12 (a) -9.9×10^{-10} **(b)** 2.56×10^7 years
 (c) 0.55%

13 (a) $4\cos\theta + 10\sin\theta$ **(b)** $\sqrt{116}\sin(\theta + 0.38)$
 (c) $10\cos\theta - 4\sin\theta$ **(d)** $\sqrt{116}$

14 (c) $x = 4, T = 10$

15 (b) 0.0132

Essential skills

Exercise 1

1 (a) $8pq$ **(b)** $7xy + 2zy$
 (c) $7\,km$ **(d)** $7cd^2$
 (e) $13rs^2 - 8r^2s$ **(f)** $7ax^2 + 3bx^2$
 (g) $7v^2w$ **(h)** $8p^2q^2$
 (i) $y^2 + 6y$ **(j)** $3r^3 - 3r$
 (k) $4b^2 - 3ab$ **(l)** $6x^2$
 (m) $6ab + 3xy$ **(n)** $8pq - kl$
 (o) $2xy^2 + xy$ **(p)** $8vw^2 - 7v^3w$
 (q) $-6cd$ **(r)** $a^3 + b^3 - a^3b^3$
 (s) $x^3 + 3x^2$ **(t)** $x^3 - 4x^2$

2 (a) 20 **(b)** $2p^2 + 3p$
 (c) $-m - 2$ **(d)** $-2b^2 + 8$

(e) $2a + b + 3c$ **(f)** $6p - 5q - 2r$
(g) $3x^2 - 7xy$ **(h)** $s^2 - 8r^2s^2 - 5r^2$
(i) $6k - 0.4j$ **(j)** $\frac{3}{4}t^2 - \frac{3}{2}s + \frac{3}{4}$
(k) $4x^2 + 2xy - 10y^2$ **(l)** $6a^2b - 8ab + b^2a$

Exercise 2

1 (a) $21a^3b$ **(b)** $-32x^2y^2$ **(c)** m^3n^3
 (d) $abpq$ **(e)** k^2m^2 **(f)** $-cd^3$

 (g) 1 **(h)** pr **(i)** $\dfrac{1}{w}$

 (j) $12b^3$ **(k)** $125ef^2$ **(l)** $7fg^3$

 (m) $49x^4$ **(n)** $-4p^3q^2g^2$ **(o)** $\dfrac{1}{a}$

 (p) $\dfrac{6r}{s}$ **(q)** y **(r)** $\dfrac{1}{ab}$

2 (a) $2b$ **(b)** $3x$ **(c)** 4
 (d) $7q$ **(e)** $5r$ **(f)** $6fg$

 (g) $3\dfrac{b}{a}$ **(h)** $\dfrac{2}{v}$ **(i)** $\dfrac{19}{b}$

 (j) $\dfrac{m}{6}$ **(k)** $\dfrac{g}{2h}$ **(l)** $4l$

 (m) $\dfrac{1}{13tu}$ **(n)** $3w^2$ **(o)** $\dfrac{7y}{x}$

3 (a) $15x^2 + 6x$ **(b)** $7y^3 - 7yz$ **(c)** $-6a^2 + 15a^4$
 (d) $-9p + q$ **(e)** $12rs^2 + 12r^2$ **(f)** $-vw^3 - w^2$
 (g) $39xy - 15y^2$ **(h)** $a^3bc + ab^3c$ **(i)** $-5d^3e - e^3$
 (j) $3f^2g^2 - 2f^3g$ **(k)** $km^3 + 5kmn$ **(l)** $-8t^3u + 8t^4u$

4 (a) $9x + 6$ **(b)** $7x^2 - y$ **(c)** $x - 5$

 (d) $3b + \dfrac{a}{4}$ **(e)** $6pq - 2q$ **(f)** $5rs + 7s$

 (g) $1 + pr$ **(h)** $2x^2y - 4 + x$

Exercise 3

1 (a) $x^2 + 7x + 12$ **(b)** $24 - 10y + y^2$
 (c) $p^2 - 15p + 26$ **(d)** $r^2 - r - 30$
 (e) $32 - 4s - s^2$ **(f)** $2t^2 - 9t - 35$
 (g) $21v^2 + 5v - 4$ **(h)** $8 - 42w + 27w^2$
 (i) $2x^2 + 24x + 70$ **(j)** $5a^2 - 35a - 90$
 (k) $28 - 35t + 7t^2$ **(l)** $-4m^2 + 32m + 80$

2 (a) $x^2 + 4x + 4$ **(b)** $9y^2 - 30y + 25$
 (c) $49 + 28a + 4a^2$ **(d)** $81 - 72q + 16q^2$
 (e) $x^2 - 4$ **(f)** $9k^2 - 1$
 (g) $400 - 49q^2$ **(h)** $3x^2 - 3$
 (i) $5a^2 - 20$ **(j)** $90 - 10p^2$
 (k) $6m^2 - 6n^2$ **(l)** $18k^2 - 32j^2$
 (m) $b^2 + 10b + 25$ **(n)** $d^2 - 12d + 36$
 (o) $64 - 16k + k^2$ **(p)** $100 + 20p + p^2$
 (q) $81 + 36z + 4z^2$ **(r)** $49 - 70v + 25v^2$
 (s) $9p^2 - 6pq + q^2$ **(t)** $25m^2 + 20mn + 4n^2$
 (u) $a^2 + 2ab + b^2$ **(v)** $g^2 - 14gh + 49h^2$
 (w) $25x^2 - 80xy + 64y^2$ **(x)** $36v^2 + 108vw + 81w^2$

3 (a) $-3x^2 + 7x + 30$ **(b)** $5x^3 + 4x^2 + 8x$
 (c) $37x^2 - 72x - 48$ **(d)** $y^3 + 4y^2 + 3y - 25$
 (e) $-4a^3 - 3a^2 - 117a + 324$

(f) $24p^2 + 20p - 25$ **(g)** $4f^3 - 58f^2 + 132f - 2$
(h) $9t^3 - 18t - 9$ **(i)** $36 - 318s - 80s^2 - 6s^3$
(j) $3w^2 - 14w - 12$
4 (a) $x^3 - x^2 + x + 3$ **(b)** $2y^3 + 14y^2 + 8y - 24$
(c) $15a^3 - 41a^2 + 34a - 8$ **(d)** $6b^3 + 29b^2 - 17b + 2$
(e) $21p^3 + 18p^2 - 75p - 54$ **(f)** $5 - 7q + 3q^2 - q^3$
(g) $64 - 16t + 21t^2 + 3t^3$ **(h)** $54 - 66s + 2s^2 + 10s^3$
(i) $3x^3 + 11x^2 + 11x + 2$ **(j)** $-7d^3 + 40d^2 + 20d - 48$
(k) $45 - 58f + 29f^2 + 4f^3$ **(l)** $18 - 24h - 51h^2 - 18h^3$
(m) $2w^3 + 4w^2 - 28w + 10$ **(n)** $6z^3 + 39z^2 - 33z + 6$
(o) $-15a^3 + 25a^2 + 20a - 20$
(p) $28 + 20b - 12b^2 - 4b^3$
5 (a) $k^3 + 12k^2 + 48k + 64$ **(b)** $27r^3 - 135r^2 + 225r - 125$
(c) $p^3 - 3p^2 + 3p - 1$ **(d)** $64 + 96q + 48q^2 + 8q^3$
(e) $a^3 + 6a^2 + 12a + 8$ **(f)** $b^3 - 3b^2 + 3b - 1$
(g) $8d^3 + 36d^2 + 54d + 27$ **(h)** $125e^3 - 150e^2 + 60e - 8$
(i) $1 + 12x + 48x^2 + 64x^3$

(i) $(t - \frac{3}{2})^2 - \frac{13}{4}$ **(j)** $(m + \frac{1}{4})^2 + \frac{3}{16}$
(k) $(n + 0.3)^2 - 1.09$ **(l)** $(w - 0.8)^2 + 1.36$
3 (a) $5 - (x - 1)^2$ **(b)** $9 - (x + 2)^2$
(c) $\frac{9}{4} - (x - \frac{1}{2})^2$ **(d)** $\frac{33}{4} - (x - \frac{3}{2})^2$
(e) $-5 - (x - 1)^2$ **(f)** $-2 - (x - 2)^2$
4 (a) $2(x + 1)^2 - 3$ **(b)** $3(y + 2)^2 - 7$
(c) $5(a - 3)^2 - 63$ **(d)** $2(n + \frac{1}{2})^2 + \frac{1}{2}$
(e) $4(b - \frac{3}{2})^2 - 14$ **(f)** $2(m - \frac{3}{4})^2 - \frac{57}{8}$

Exercise 4

1 (a) $5y(x + 3y)$ **(b)** $fg(7fg - 1)$
(c) $p(2q^2 + 14q - 7p)$ **(d)** $s(rs^2 - 3r + 6s)$
(e) $(t + 6)(t + 2)$ **(f)** $(r - 10)(r - 1)$
(g) $(y + 5)(y + 1)$ **(h)** $(p - 4)(p - 2)$
(i) $(8 - s)(3 - s)$ **(j)** $(w + 5)(w - 3)$
(k) $(v + 4)(v - 1)$ **(l)** $(w + 5)(w - 3)$
(m) $(z + 13)(z - 1)$ **(n)** $(1 - x)(x - 3)$
(o) $(5 - f)^2$ **(p)** $(a + 2)(a - 8)$
(q) $(x - 9)(x + 1)$ **(r)** $(7 + q)(5 - q)$
(s) $(b - 5)(b + 4)$ **(t)** $(h + 7)^2$
(u) $-(k - 1)^2$ **(v)** $(3y + 2)(y + 2)$
(w) $(2x + 1)(x + 4)$ **(x)** $(3m + 5)(2m + 1)$
(y) $(5d + 2)(2d - 3)$ **(z)** $(3p + 8)(3p - 2)$
2 (a) $(x + 5)(x - 5)$ **(b)** $(a + 1)(a - 1)$
(c) $(a + 10)(a - 10)$ **(d)** $(2p + 3)(2p - 3)$
(e) $(8p + 11)(8p - 11)$ **(f)** $(6 + 5u)(6 - 5u)$
(g) $(x + 4y)(x - 4y)$ **(h)** $(7t + 12s)(7t - 12s)$
(i) $(f + 30q)(f - 30g)$ **(j)** $5(x + 10)(x - 10)$
(k) $3(w + 9)(w - 9)$ **(l)** $10(v - 2)(v + 2)$
(m) $3(2p + 1)(2p - 1)$ **(n)** $5(2 + 3s)(2 - 3s)$
(o) $7(y + 2z)(y - 2z)$ **(p)** $3(3a + 4b)(3a - 4b)$
(q) $5(5d + 3e)(5d - 3e)$ **(r)** $2(7f + 10g)(7f - 10g)$
(s) $(v^2 + 4)(v + 2)(v - 2)$ **(t)** $(w^2 + 9)(w + 3)(w - 3)$
(u) $(x^2 + 100)(x + 10)(x - 10)$
(v) $7(y^2 + 1)(y + 1)(y - 1)$ **(w)** $(4a^2 + 1)(2a + 1)(2a - 1)$
(x) $2(9 + b^2)(3 + b)(3 - b)$

Exercise 5

1 (a) $x^2 + 2x + 1$ **(b)** $x^2 + 4x + 4$
(c) $y^2 + 12y + 36$ **(d)** $m^2 - 6m + 9$
(e) $t^2 - 14t + 49$ **(f)** $w^2 - 20w + 100$
(g) $x^2 + 3x + \frac{9}{4}$ **(h)** $a^2 + a + \frac{1}{4}$
(i) $n^2 + 7n + \frac{49}{4}$ **(j)** $r^2 - 9r + \frac{81}{4}$
(k) $v^2 - \frac{2}{3}v + \frac{1}{9}$ **(l)** $x^2 - \frac{1}{2}x + \frac{1}{16}$
2 (a) $(x + 3)^2 + 1$ **(b)** $(y - 1)^2 + 2$
(c) $(z + 4)^2 - 26$ **(d)** $(a - 5)^2 - 30$
(e) $(b + 9)^2 - 162$ **(f)** $(c - 20)^2 - 399$
(g) $(r + \frac{5}{2})^2 - \frac{45}{4}$ **(h)** $(s + \frac{1}{2})^2 + \frac{7}{4}$

Exercise 6

1 (a) $\dfrac{3e}{5}$ **(b)** $\dfrac{3m}{7}$ **(c)** $\dfrac{4r}{3}$

(d) $\dfrac{a + b}{3}$ **(e)** $\dfrac{3p - q}{7}$ **(f)** $\dfrac{11}{v}$

(g) $\dfrac{-1}{w}$ **(h)** $\dfrac{5a}{u}$ **(i)** $\dfrac{a - b}{x}$

2 (a) $\dfrac{x}{6}$ **(b)** $\dfrac{7n}{20}$ **(c)** $\dfrac{9u}{16}$

(d) $\dfrac{p - 2q}{4}$ **(e)** $\dfrac{3x - 5y}{25}$ **(f)** $\dfrac{3a + 33b}{22}$

(g) $\dfrac{5}{2a}$ **(h)** $\dfrac{2}{3b}$ **(i)** $\dfrac{4}{3g}$

(j) $\dfrac{-2}{39p}$ **(k)** $\dfrac{3 + x}{2x}$ **(l)** $\dfrac{3a - 2}{5a}$

(m) $\dfrac{7a}{18}$ **(n)** $\dfrac{19t}{24}$ **(o)** $\dfrac{11h}{35}$

(p) $\dfrac{2u + 3v}{6}$ **(q)** $\dfrac{45h - 28k}{63}$ **(r)** $\dfrac{20c + 9d}{30}$

(s) $\dfrac{3}{10m}$ **(t)** $\dfrac{19}{12r}$ **(u)** $\dfrac{-19}{36t}$

3 (a) $\dfrac{ab + 6}{2b}$ **(b)** $\dfrac{xy - 20}{5y}$ **(c)** $\dfrac{63 + rs}{9r}$

(d) $\dfrac{24 - tu}{3u}$ **(e)** $\dfrac{6mn - 35}{10n}$ **(f)** $\dfrac{18 - 14vw}{21v}$

(g) $\dfrac{cq + dp}{pq}$ **(h)** $\dfrac{9y + 5x}{xy}$ **(i)** $\dfrac{8d - 7b}{bd}$

(j) $\dfrac{fp - 3e}{ef}$ **(k)** $\dfrac{6ab + 63}{21b}$ **(l)** $\dfrac{10f - 9x}{18f}$

(m) $\dfrac{5x - 1}{6}$ **(n)** $\dfrac{a - 37}{20}$ **(o)** $\dfrac{10q + 10}{21}$

(p) $\dfrac{w - 55}{72}$ **(q)** $\dfrac{4t + 30}{15}$ **(r)** $\dfrac{13x + 62}{45}$

Exercise 7

1 (a) $\dfrac{5a + 3}{a(a + 1)}$ **(b)** $\dfrac{-3w - 21}{w(w + 3)}$

(c) $\dfrac{15e - 45}{e(e - 5)}$ **(d)** $\dfrac{10 - 3m}{m(m + 2)}$

(e) $\dfrac{10r - 7}{r(r - 7)}$ **(f)** $\dfrac{4v - 63}{v(v - 9)}$

(g) $\dfrac{5b + 11}{(b + 1)(b + 3)}$ **(h)** $\dfrac{10n - 22}{(n - 5)(n + 2)}$

(i) $\dfrac{3 - 3s}{(s + 4)(s + 7)}$ **(j)** $\dfrac{53 - 2t}{(t - 2)(t + 5)}$

(k) $\dfrac{6x - 36}{(x - 1)(x - 7)}$ **(l)** $\dfrac{3y + 3}{(y - 8)(y - 5)}$

2 (a) $\dfrac{1}{(a - 1)}$ **(b)** $\dfrac{-x}{(x + 1)(x - 1)}$

(c) $\dfrac{b + 4}{(b + 3)(b + 1)}$ **(d)** $\dfrac{3w - 1}{(w - 1)^2}$

(e) $\dfrac{p}{(p - 2)(p + 3)}$ **(f)** $\dfrac{2x - 15}{(x - 5)(x + 2)}$

(g) $\dfrac{2c}{(c + 1)(c - 1)(c - 1)}$ **(h)** $\dfrac{1}{(m + 3)(m - 3)}$

Exercise 8

1 (a) a^9 **(b)** n^{-3} **(c)** c^7 **(d)** $d^{\frac{7}{2}}$
(e) $15a^7$ **(f)** $8b^3$ **(g)** $56c^9$ **(h)** v^4
(i) y^{24} **(j)** k^7 **(k)** $2c^2$ **(l)** $8f^{14}$
(m) $30c^2$ **(n)** c^{30} **(o)** y^{-35} **(p)** $216h^{15}$
(q) $32x^{-10}$ **(r)** x^5y^5 **(s)** x^8y^{12} **(t)** $h^{-24}k^{-40}$
2 (a) 5 **(b)** 2 **(c)** 5 **(d)** 2
(e) 4 **(f)** 27 **(g)** 100 **(h)** 27
(i) $\frac{1}{5}$ **(j)** $\frac{1}{32}$
3 (a) $k^{\frac{3}{4}}$ **(b)** $t^{\frac{4}{3}}$ **(c)** $g^{\frac{1}{3}}$ **(d)** $y^{\frac{2}{3}}$
(e) $20d$ **(f)** $8e$ **(g)** $d^{\frac{1}{3}}$ **(h)** $d^{\frac{1}{2}}$
(i) 1 **(j)** $\frac{4}{5}d^{-1}$ **(k)** $2e^{-\frac{1}{3}}$ **(l)** $8d^{-\frac{3}{4}}$

(m) $\dfrac{1}{49t^2}$ **(n)** $c^9d^{\frac{1}{2}}$ **(o)** x^2y **(p)** $s^{\frac{1}{3}}t^{\frac{4}{9}}$

Exercise 9

1 (a) $x^3 + x^4$ **(b)** $x^5 - x^{15}$
(c) $\frac{1}{2} - \frac{1}{2}x$ **(d)** $2x^{-2} + 3x^{-4}$
(e) $x^2 - x^{-2}$ **(f)** $x^{-\frac{10}{3}} + x^{-\frac{13}{4}} + 2x^{-4}$
(g) $\frac{1}{2}x^2 + \frac{1}{2}x^3$ **(h)** $\frac{1}{3}x^3 + \frac{1}{3}x^{-2}$
(i) $\frac{1}{2}x^2 - \frac{1}{2}x^4$ **(j)** $x^{-\frac{2}{3}} + x$
(k) $2 + x^{\frac{3}{2}}$ **(l)** $6x^{-1} + 2x^{-\frac{1}{12}}$
2 (a) $x^{-1} + 4x^{-2} + 4x^{-3}$ **(b)** $2x + 5 - 3x^{-1}$
(c) $\frac{1}{2}x^{-1} - 1 + \frac{1}{2}x$ **(d)** $9x^{-2} - 24x^{-1} + 16$
(e) $x + 5 - 5x^{-1} - 25x^{-2}$ **(f)** $x^2 - \dfrac{1}{x^2}$
(g) $x^{\frac{3}{2}} - 2x^{\frac{1}{2}} + x^{-\frac{1}{2}}$ **(h)** $x^{\frac{1}{2}} + 4x^{-\frac{1}{2}} + 4x^{-\frac{3}{2}}$

(i) $\dfrac{1}{x} + 2 + x$

Exercise 10

1 $\sqrt{65}$, $\sqrt[3]{9}$, $\sqrt{50}$, $\sqrt[3]{33}$, $\sqrt{5}$, $\sqrt{1000}$,
2 (a) $x = \pm\sqrt{14}$ **(b)** $x = \pm\sqrt{30}$ **(c)** $x = 4$
(d) $x = \pm 1$ **(e)** $x = \sqrt[3]{39}$ **(f)** $x = -1$
3 $a = \sqrt{34}$, $b = \sqrt{61}$, $c = \sqrt{133}$, $d = \sqrt{98}$, $e = \sqrt{525}$, $f = \sqrt{7}$

4 $\sin a° = \dfrac{1}{\sqrt{2}}$, $\cos b° = \dfrac{1}{2}$, $\tan c° = 1$, $\sin d° = \dfrac{\sqrt{3}}{2}$,

$\cos e° = \dfrac{1}{\sqrt{2}}$, $\tan f° = \dfrac{1}{\sqrt{3}}$

Exercise 11

1 (a) $2\sqrt{3}$ **(b)** $2\sqrt{5}$ **(c)** $3\sqrt{3}$ **(d)** $4\sqrt{2}$
(e) $3\sqrt{5}$ **(f)** $4\sqrt{3}$ **(g)** $5\sqrt{2}$ **(h)** $3\sqrt{7}$
(i) $5\sqrt{3}$ **(j)** $2\sqrt{11}$ **(k)** $7\sqrt{2}$ **(l)** $10\sqrt{5}$
(m) $10\sqrt{2}$ **(n)** $9\sqrt{2}$ **(o)** $40\sqrt{2}$ **(p)** $30\sqrt{10}$
2 (a) $10\sqrt{2}$ **(b)** $4\sqrt{5}$ **(c)** $7\sqrt{3}$ **(d)** $3\sqrt{7}$
(e) 0 **(f)** $-7\sqrt{5}$ **(g)** $9\sqrt{2}$ **(h)** $3\sqrt{7} + \sqrt{5}$
(i) $2\sqrt{10} - 10\sqrt{2}$ **(j)** $2\sqrt{2}$
(k) $6\sqrt{10} - 6\sqrt{11}$
3 (a) $3\sqrt{5}$ **(b)** $5\sqrt{2}$ **(c)** $2\sqrt{11}$ **(d)** $4\sqrt{3}$
4 (a) $\pm 2\sqrt{7}$ **(b)** $\pm 5\sqrt{3}$ **(c)** $\pm 7\sqrt{2}$ **(d)** $\pm 7\sqrt{3}$
(e) -2 **(f)** $3\sqrt[3]{2}$

Exercise 12

1 (a) 3 **(b)** 7 **(c)** $2a$
(d) $2\sqrt{3}$ **(e)** $3\sqrt{2}$ **(f)** $5\sqrt{3}$
(g) $\sqrt{10}$ **(h)** $\sqrt{21}$ **(i)** $\sqrt{22}$
(j) 4 **(k)** 6 **(l)** 10
(m) $2\sqrt{5}$ **(n)** $3\sqrt{2}$ **(o)** $4\sqrt{6}$
(p) $10\sqrt{2}$ **(q)** 30 **(r)** $15\sqrt{15}$
2 (a) $\sqrt{2} + 2$ **(b)** $3 - \sqrt{3}$ **(c)** $\sqrt{5} + 5$
(d) $5\sqrt{7} + 7$ **(e)** $3\sqrt{2} - 4$ **(f)** $15 - 2\sqrt{5}$
(g) 2 **(h)** 1 **(i)** 2
(j) 3 **(k)** -6 **(l)** -6
(m) $4 + 2\sqrt{3}$ **(n)** $9 - 4\sqrt{5}$ **(o)** $9 + 2\sqrt{14}$
(p) $8 - 2\sqrt{15}$
3 (a) $6\,\text{cm}^2$ **(b)** $\sqrt{(10 + 4\sqrt{6})}\,\text{cm}$

Exercise 13

1 (a) $\dfrac{\sqrt{2}}{2}$ **(b)** $\dfrac{\sqrt{5}}{5}$ **(c)** $2\sqrt{3}$

(d) $4\sqrt{2}$ **(e)** $\dfrac{2\sqrt{3}}{3}$ **(f)** $2\sqrt{5}$

(g) $\dfrac{7\sqrt{3}}{3}$ **(h)** $\dfrac{3\sqrt{5}}{5}$ **(i)** $\dfrac{2\sqrt{2}}{5}$

(j) $\dfrac{7\sqrt{5}}{10}$

2 (a) $\dfrac{\sqrt{5}}{10}$ (b) $\dfrac{\sqrt{2}}{10}$ (c) $\dfrac{5\sqrt{3}}{3}$

(d) $\dfrac{7\sqrt{2}}{6}$ (e) $\dfrac{2\sqrt{3}}{15}$

3 (a) $\dfrac{3\sqrt{2}}{2}$ (b) $\dfrac{\sqrt{15}}{3}$ (c) $\dfrac{3\sqrt{10}}{10}$

(d) $\dfrac{\sqrt{3}}{3}$ (e) $\dfrac{\sqrt{15}}{5}$

4 (a) 22 (b) 47 (c) -11
(d) -1 (e) 2 (f) $a-b$
5 (a) $\sqrt{2}+1$ (b) $\sqrt{3}+1$ (c) $2\sqrt{5}-2$
(d) $9+3\sqrt{2}$ (e) $\sqrt{3}+\sqrt{2}$ (f) $\sqrt{7}-\sqrt{5}$
(g) $\sqrt{15}+2\sqrt{3}-\sqrt{5}-2$
(h) $8-4\sqrt{3}+2\sqrt{5}-\sqrt{15}$

Exercise 14

1 (a) 4 m (b) $12.8°$ (c) $x=8.66$ m
(d) $53°$ (e) $135°$ (f) $213.7°$
2 2.6 m
3 $43.9°$

Exercise 15

1 (a) 4.8 cm (b) 13.6 cm (c) $75.1°$
(d) 15.7 m (e) $83.3°$ (f) 7.6 m
2 (a) 10 m (b) 9.4 m
3 2.2 m

Exercise 16

1 $6.3°$
2 (a) $\sqrt{5}$ (b) $48.2°$
(c) both are the complement of angle CQR
(d) 4.5 units (e) 11.25 units^2
3 10.8 m
4 425 km, $041°$
5 19.8 miles
6 27.2 m
7 31.2 km
8 391 m

Specimen Unit assessment 1(H)

1 $4x-y-11=0$
2 0.7
3 (a) 3 (b) $-\frac{1}{3}$
4 (a) (i)

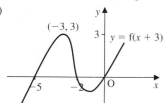

(ii)

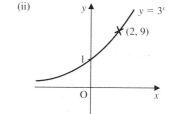

(b) (i) 2

(ii)

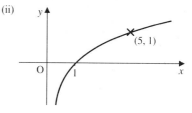

5 (a) (i) 2 (ii)

(b) (i) 10 (ii)

6 (a) $2(x-1)^2$ (b) $4\sin x$

7 (a) $2x+8$ (b) $\dfrac{3}{2}\sqrt{x}-\dfrac{1}{x^2}$

8 $7x-y-22=0$
9 max. $(-1, 16)$; min. $(2, -11)$
10 (a) $u_{n+1}=0.6u_n+100$
(b) Population settles at 250

Specimen Unit assessment 2(H)

1 (b) $(x-2)(x-1)(3x+2)$
3 $x^2+6\sqrt{x}+C$
4 $21\frac{3}{4}$
5 $\int_{-6}^{4} 24-x^3-2x \, dx$
6 10, 50, 130
7 (a) $\frac{4}{5}$ (b) 4
8 (a) $\cos\left(x+\dfrac{\pi}{6}\right)$ (b) $\dfrac{\pi}{6}, \dfrac{3\pi}{2}$
9 (a) $(x-3)^2+(y+4)^2=25$ (b) $(2, -3)$, 4
11 $x+2y=7$

Specimen Unit assessment 3(H)

2 B (2, 0, 6)

3 (a) -10,   **(b)** $106.9°$

4 (a) $5\cos x$ **(b)** $3\sin x$

5 (a) $-20(5-4x)^5$

6 (a) $\frac{1}{5}(x-1)^5 + c$ **(b)** $3\sin x + c$ **(c)** $-\frac{2}{3}\cos x + c$

7 (a) $4\log_a 2$ **(b)** 1

8 (a) 388 **(b)** $x = \log_2 10$
   (c) $k = 10^{2.3}$ **(d)** 0.903

9 (a) $k = 2,\ \alpha = 30°$

Specimen Course assessment

PAPER I

1 (a) $(\frac{1}{2}, -\frac{1}{2})$ **(c)** $x + 2y + 2 = 0$ **(d)** $(0, -1)$

2 $(x-7)^2 + (y-8)^2 = 9$

3 (a) $0 \leqslant 0.7 \leqslant 1$ **(b)** $\frac{100}{3}$

4 (b) $(-2, 0)\ (2, 0)\ (0, 8)$

   (c) max. turning point at $\left(-\frac{2}{3}, 9\frac{13}{27}\right)$

     min. turning point at $(2, 0)$

   (d)

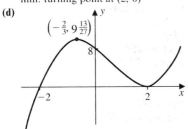

5 $-2;\ (x-3),\ (x-1)$

6 $\dfrac{x}{\sqrt{x^2 - 5}}$

7 $0,\ \frac{2}{3}\pi,\ \frac{4}{3}\pi,\ 2\pi$

8 (a) $\dfrac{5 - 2x}{2x - 4}$ **(b)** 2

9 (b) $x + \frac{1}{2}\cos 2x + c$

10 $0,\ -16$

11

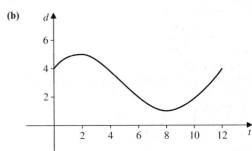

12 $a = 2,\ b = 3$

PAPER II

1 $3x + 2y - 21 = 0$

2 (a) 23.2 units   **(b)** level settles at 93.4 units

3 (a) $(5, 0)$ **(b)** $41\frac{2}{3}$ units^2

4 (b) $30°$

5 (a) $(x-2)^2 + (y+1)^2 = 5$ **(b)** $x - 2y + 1 = 0$
   (c) $(5, 3)$ **(d)** $2\sqrt{5}$ units

6 (a) $d = 2\cos(30t - 60)° + 3$

   (b)

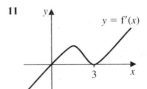

   (c) $02\,00$ hours   **(d)** between $04\,00$ and $12\,00$

7 (a) $h = \dfrac{32}{x^2}$ **(c)** $4\,\text{m}$ by $4\,\text{m}$ by $2\,\text{m}$

8 (a) 0.0446 **(b)** 15.5 days

9 $QP = r\sin\theta$

Index